THE DISNEY FILMS

FOURTH EDITION

BY THE SAME AUTHOR

*The Great American Broadcast: A Celebration of Radio's
    Golden Age*
Movie Comedy Teams
The Art of the Cinematographer (originally published
    as *Behind the Camera*)
Selected Short Subjects (originally published as The
    Great Movie Shorts)
The Great Movie Comedians
*Of Mice and Magic: A History of American Animated
    Cartoons*

AS COAUTHOR

The Little Rascals: The Life and Times of Our Gang
The Complete Guide to Home Video

AS EDITOR

Leonard Maltin's Movie & Video Guide
Leonard Maltin's Movie Encyclopedia
Leonard Maltin's Family Film Guide
The Real Stars
The Laurel and Hardy Book
Hollywood: The Movie Factory

© *1964 Walt Disney Productions*

THE DISNEY FILMS

FOURTH EDITION

LEONARD MALTIN

Disney
EDITIONS

New York

Dedicated to the memory of Walt Disney

Library of Congress Cataloging-in-Publication Data

Maltin, Leonard.
    The Disney films / Leonard Maltin.—4th ed.
        p.   cm.
    Includes index.
    ISBN 0-7868-8527-0 (pbk.)
    1. Walt Disney Company. 2. Motion pictures—United
States—Plots, themes, etc. I. Title

PN1999.W27 M36 2000
791.43'75'0973—dc21   00-030976

FOURTH EDITION
10   9   8   7   4   3   2   1

CONTENTS

PREFACE

I WROTE THIS BOOK OUT OF LOVE—A LIFELONG LOVE FOR ALL THINGS DISNEY. AT THE AGE of four I wore a coonskin cap, like most of young America, and even sang a line from "The Ballad of Davy Crockett" in a performance at my nursery school. I was also one of those kids who ran home every day in order to catch *The Mickey Mouse Club* . I loved to draw, and I wrote to the Art Corner at Disneyland for tips on how to draw my favorite characters. (I never did get very good at it.) Long before there were Disney stores, a Disney Channel, or a Web site available to me, I was hooked.

How strong was that influence on my childhood concepts? Let me put it this way: I still have a book of Grimm's fairy tales that my parents used to read to me when I was young. On the last page of one story, I drew a box in crayon around the words *The End* and added "A Walt Disney Production."

So, when Walt Disney died, in December of 1966, I took it hard. As the young editor-publisher of a film buff magazine (*Film Fan Monthly*), I determined on the spot to dedicate my next issue to Disney's memory, and do something no one had ever done before: prepare an annotated list of all his movies.

The magazine, with Mickey Mouse on the cover (in John Hench's famous pose of the star in his award-filled office), was especially well received within the Disney organization. To my great surprise, several people told me how useful it was, because they'd never had a ready list of all the studio's films! One executive asked if I had thought of expanding the issue into a full-length book . . . and that's exactly what I did.

Looking back on my original work from 1973, I am struck by several things: first and foremost, the change in the financial climate. There is something almost quaint about referring to then-impressive box-office figures of four, six, and eight million dollars—when today it costs upwards of 50 million simply to market and advertise a film!

Another change is the home-entertainment boom, which has brought previously unavailable Disney films (and TV shows) back to prominence via cable TV, videocassettes, laser discs, and DVDs. I'm especially happy to see some of the unsung (and financially unsuccessful) films being given this new lease on life.

Then there is the changing complexion of the American moviegoing audience in the post–*Star Wars* era. I tried to deal with this phenomenon, and how it affected the Disney studio, in my chapter "Without Walt," which was written for this book's first revision in 1984.

But I think the biggest change is also the subtlest. My image of Disney's world was not created with videocassettes, or by people in costumes parading through the streets of Disneyland. It came from a total immersion in Disneyana: addiction to the daily *Mickey Mouse Club*, subscription to *Uncle Scrooge* comic books, and the firm belief that the arrival of each new Disney film at my local theater was an event. (I also remember standing on line to see the Disney Christmas releases at Radio City Music Hall. It was usually worth the wait, even in freezing weather.) Most important, I watched Walt Disney himself on television every week, an affable man who might have been a favorite uncle, sharing wonderful stories and taking me behind the scenes at his Magic Factory.

I suspect that younger people who only know of Disney as a name, not a living person, might not understand the way so many of us feel about Walt *and* his work. I hope my book provides clues, and inspires some readers to dig even deeper into Disneyana.

Arlene Ludwig is my oldest friend at the Walt Disney Company; she has helped me in countless ways since I first started working on this book in the early 1970s, and earns my enduring thanks.

Two other young Disney veterans, my pal Howard Green and my colleague David R. Smith, have never turned me down for help, advice, or information.

Over the years, and this book's many incarnations, I've had valuable assistance from Zelda Wong, Robert Tieman, Greg Ehrbar, Fumiko Kitahara, Peter Adamakos, Brian Sibley, Luke Sader, the late Dennis Fine, Dennis Gaughan, Gary Grossman, Mark Evanier, Michael Scheinfeld, and Ben Herndon.

Jerry Beck has overseen the filmographies and been a much-needed sounding board for all the revised editions, including this one, for which I thank him three times over.

If it weren't for my editor, Wendy Lefkon, this 2000 edition of my "baby" wouldn't exist. Need I add how grateful I am to her?

Finally, it would be no fun working on a book like this if I couldn't share my Disneyphilia with my wife, Alice, and daughter, Jessie. I love them both more than words can say . . . almost as much as Spin and Marty.

Obviously, the Disney story isn't over—and never will be. Whatever new directions the company may take, there will always be links to its glorious past.

A press kit from the company recently touted the new generation of Disney True-Life Adventures made by Bruce Reitherman, son of longtime animation director Wolfgang Reitherman, and not so incidentally, the voice of Mowgli in *The Jungle Book.*

Recent revelations about the dark period of blacklisting in Hollywood have brought to light the fact that Tom and Helen August, who were credited with the scripts of *The Misadventures of Merlin Jones, The Monkey's Uncle,* and other Disney television projects, were in fact pseudonyms for Al and the late Helen Levitt.

Kira Obolensky's *Lobster Alice,* opened Off-Broadway in January 2000, deals with the fabled and fabulous artist Salvador Dali during the period of his life in the 1940s when he lived in Hollywood and worked briefly for Walt Disney. A brief existing snippet of his unfinished *Destino* even turns up in *Fantasia* 2000.

I once fooled myself into believing that my book was finite, since it dealt with the career of a man who had passed from this earth. Since then I've come to realize that Walt Disney's legacy was so vast, and so diverse, that it can never be fully documented, even in a dozen tomes.

Every time I talk to Richard and Robert Sherman, Frank Thomas, Ollie Johnston, Joe Grant, Peter Ellenshaw, or Ward Kimball, to name just a few, I feel a) lucky, and b) excited, because I'm listening to people who created the Disney history I care about so much . . . and, it seems, every time we talk, I learn something new.

I hope you learn something new from this book, and I hope it inspires you to see even more of the Disney films.

Leonard Maltin,
Los Angeles, California
February 2000

THE
DISNEY
FILMS

FOURTH
EDITION

1·Introduction

EVEN WALT DISNEY COULD NEVER EXPLAIN THE PHENOMENAL WORLDWIDE
acclaim that greeted him and his cartoon creations in the 1930s, and
which continued until his death in 1966. The answer, it seemed, was
self-evident: he made good films, both animated and live action, that
appealed to the young and young-at-heart around the world.

But why Walt Disney? There were cartoons being made before he
arrived in Hollywood, and good cartoons being produced all during his
reign as the King of Animation. Others made good family pictures with
wide appeal.

So why, and how, did Walt Disney get to the top of the heap and
stay there? Most of the answers are to be found in the man himself. He
was born in Chicago in 1901; his father, Elias Disney, moved his family
with him as he traveled throughout the Midwest seeking success at some
kind of work—first with a construction company, then a farm, later a
newspaper delivery service. One of five children, Walt was raised in an
atmosphere of hard work and tight purse strings. When his father bought
the newspaper route, Walt (then nine) and his older brother Roy had to
get up every morning at three thirty in order to begin the delivery. Late
in life, Disney recalled: "The papers had to be stuck behind the storm
doors. You couldn't just toss them on the porch. And in the winters
there'd be as much as three feet of snow. I was a little guy and I'd be up
to my nose in snow. I still have nightmares about it."

For relief from the drudgery of such work, Walt usually had to
amuse himself. Drawing caught his fancy at an early age, since he was not
athletically inclined. A gift he received of a pad of paper and some
pencils set him to work, and as years went by he became more serious
about drawing, and he enrolled in a class at the Kansas City Art Institute
when he was fourteen.

From his earliest years he was closely attached to his brother Roy, eight
years his senior, and when Roy decided to join the navy in 1918, Walt
thought it would be a good idea too. Being only sixteen, he enlisted in the
Red Cross Ambulance Corps, and served as a driver in France during the
last year of World War I. When he returned to America in 1919, he went to
Kansas City to seek employment as an artist, and got his first job with a
commercial art studio. It didn't last long, but it was there that Disney met
Ub Iwerks, another young artist who, when Disney was let go, went with
him to form their own commercial art company.

Disney abandoned the firm to take a job with the Kansas City Film
Ad Company, which made animated commercials for various concerns
and showed them in local theatres. Before long, Iwerks was working there
too, and the two men worked together at night making their own animated cartoons. They sold them to the Newman Theater, and named
them Newman Laugh-O-Grams. They were successful enough that Disney

2

A scene from Disney's early *Puss 'n Boots*. Note the full range of gray tones, something of a luxury for most silent-film cartoonists. *Courtesy Adam Reilly/Cinemaesthetics*

Disney poses with his staff in Hollywood in the 1920s: Rollin (Ham) Hamilton, Roy Disney, Hugh Harman, Walt, Margie Gay (one of the girls who portrayed Alice), Rudolph Ising, Ub Iwerks, and Walker Harman. Hugh Harman and Ising later had their own cartoon studio, as did Iwerks. *Courtesy British Film Institute*

was able to leave the Kansas City Film Ad Company and start an animation firm of his own, which he called Laugh-O-Gram.

Looking at one of these Kansas City-made cartoons today, *Puss 'n Boots,* one sees an undeniably primitive, but bright, imaginative, and funny little film—full of inventive touches, and some ambitious animated effects. (How much easier it would have been to have a motionless crowd than to animate movement as Disney did in a bullfight scene.) Though it would be foolish to read too much into one early cartoon, *Puss 'n Boots does* show that Disney was striving for quality, certainly a luxury in a business as small as his was at this time.

Indeed, Disney continually got himself into financial crises, never being able to make any profit from his films. Though the amounts involved were small, and he was already cutting corners, it is safe to conjecture that one reason for this was that Disney wanted a good product above all else. To come up with the results he wanted, he would impulsively spend more time on it than he should have, then later suffer the consequences. The consequences, in this case, meant leaving Kansas City, something of a failure—at least, monetarily. Disney decided to go to Los Angeles, hoping to find any sort of work. When none was waiting for him in Movieland, he decided to set up shop himself, again.

Just as he was about to go into the same kind of Laugh-O-Gram production he had done in Kansas City, word came from the East that a company that had taken one of his films—a combination cartoon and live-action reel called *Alice's Wonderland*—had sold an independent producer on the idea of making an *Alice* series. The distributor, M. J. Winkler, offered $1,500 per reel, and when Walt, joined as production partner by his brother Roy, turned out the first film for $750, the mood was nothing short of triumphant.

Like most loners who start in business for themselves, Walt wanted to do everything himself, but before long he sent to Kansas City for his friend and former partner Ub Iwerks to join him. He also sent for the little girl who had performed as Alice, and convinced her to come to California. Virginia Davis became Walt Disney's first live-action "star."

The *Alice* films were imaginative and often quite funny, though as with most silent cartoons there was little in the way of story construction; gags and movement were the order of the day. The amount of interaction between the live girl and her cartoon world varied from one episode to the next, which may have been a function of deadline pressures or budget, but some of these utterly simple "special effects" are still impressive today. The design of the animated characters was more than a bit reminiscent of such successful series as Paul Terry's *Aesop's Fables* and Pat Sullivan's *Felix the Cat*, a kind of outright imitation that Disney later admitted—just as he made no bones about the fact that the *Alice* series was simply Max Fleischer's *Out of the Inkwell* in reverse.

In 1927 Disney's distributor encouraged him to drop *Alice* and start a new series. The result was Oswald the Lucky Rabbit, a floppy-eared character who met with immediate success. Charles Mintz and his brother-in-law George Winkler were releasing the cartoons through Universal, and when Disney went to New York late that year to ask for a raise (he was getting $2,250 per short) they refused, told him that they intended to cut back that amount, threatened to hire away his staff (a process which had already begun), and reminded him that Oswald was copyrighted in *their* name. Disney refused to accept less money than he was already getting and went home empty-handed instead, without a staff or a starring character. (Winkler and Mintz did set up their own cartoon studio to make Oswald, but were soon up-ended by Universal, which, in fact, owned the rights to the character. The "lucky" rabbit wound up being animated by Walter Lantz.)

On the train returning to California, the story goes, Disney was inspired to create a new cartoon mouse, first named Mortimer, then rechristened Mickey. The truth of the matter is that Disney asked Ub Iwerks to design a new character—though "new" is hardly the best way to describe the early Mickey, who was sketched in the same manner as Oswald and most other simply-designed cartoon animals of that time. Still licking their wounds from the Oswald episode, Walt and Roy decided to make a couple of *Mickey Mouse* films with their own money and *then* seek distribution—in order to retain more control. Thus, in early 1928, the first *Mickey* cartoon was made: *Plane Crazy*, quickly followed by a second, *Gallopin' Gaucho*. Both of these were, of course, silent.

But just at this time *The Jazz Singer* was sweeping the country, unveiled by another struggling family of producers, the Warner Brothers. Its astounding success not only made the brothers Warner instant movie magnates, but it dealt the first deathblow to silent pictures. Most Hollywood showmen could not deny the impact of the talkie sequences in *The Jazz Singer,* but at the same time they expressed conservative views of sound's future. Indeed, it took two full years for silent films to cease production in Hollywood, by which time it was clear that talkies were here to stay.

Walt Disney was in the right place at the right time. And he had the nerve to try out the new medium when other more established film-makers were holding back. After all, not only did he have nothing to lose (except money), he had much to gain from the idea. Disney, and his chief aides, Ub Iwerks and Wilfred Jackson, decided to experiment with sound on their third Mickey Mouse cartoon, *Steamboat Willie.* They calculated that if film ran at ninety feet a minute (twenty-four frames a second), they could animate their silent cartoon to a musical beat by planning it out in advance. Their simple tunes could be played at two beats a second, so markings were made on the film every twelve frames, both as a guide to the animator, and, later, as an indicator for the orchestra, which would synchronize the musical track.

In September 1928 Walt took his completed film, and a written score, to New York. He had definite ideas about how the sound track should be made, and they did not coincide with those of RCA or Western Electric, which owned the sound-recording patents. Disney then allied himself with P. A. ("Pat") Powers, whose bootleg Cinephone Process was responsible for recording the first sound cartoon. After a calamitous initial recording session, with a twenty-piece band led by Carl Edwourds, a second session was held (at great expense) with only fifteen pieces, and everyone more willing to listen to Walt's original conception of how to do the track. Disney did the high-pitched voice of Mickey Mouse (the story goes that while auditioning actors, he tried to show one what he wanted, and it came out so well he decided to do it himself), and after no little aggravation, the finished product was ready.

Not long after completing *Steamboat Willie,* Disney embarked on another, entirely different kind of cartoon. The origin of the idea is not clear; veteran musical director Carl Stalling, then working for Disney, has said that he initiated the idea, which Walt liked immediately. Wilfred Jackson, then an animator and the harmonica player who originally worked out the score of *Steamboat Willie* with Disney, has recalled that Disney, in an effort to soft-pedal Stalling's desire to have music take precedence over action in the Mickey Mouse cartoons, promised him that they would do another series where action would be matched to music, instead of the other way around.

However the idea originated, Disney liked it, and before long he had produced the first "Silly Symphony," *The Skeleton Dance,* a cartoon with skeletons coming alive and dancing to music (always erroneously referred to as Saint-Saëns's "Danse Macabre"), written by Stalling, including a fragment of Edvard Grieg's "The March of the Dwarfs."

In both cases Disney had trouble getting distribution for his shorts, but in both cases the success of his films was gauged—as it has been ever since—by audiences. Individual producers and distributors who screened the shorts were not always impressed, but when the cartoons were shown in theatres, the reaction was always favorable, and usually overwhelmingly so.

Looking at the early Disney cartoons today, the word "primitive" instantly comes to mind. To understand the cartoons' success, one must try to put oneself back to 1928. There is no way to overstate the tumultuous effect of talking pictures. Indeed, in many cases, all previous criteria for judging films—both by critics as well as moviegoers—were completely forgotten. Sound became the principal factor in a film's evaluation, and if it talked, it hardly mattered if it moved, made sense, or did anything else. One need only look at two of 1929's biggest hits today—*The Cock-Eyed World* and *In Old Arizona*, both absolutely deadly—to see just how much critical taste suffered during this period.

This is not to disparage Disney's early animated efforts, but merely to place them in proper perspective. Though *Steamboat Willie* was pleasant enough, it is safe to say that had it come two years earlier, Disney never would have achieved the phenomenal success he did.

Here are samplings of the reviews *Willie* received, which were heavily publicized by Disney's distributor, Pat Powers, at the time: *The New York Times* wrote: "It is an ingenious piece of work with a good deal of fun. It growls, whines, squeaks and makes various other sounds that add to its mirthful quality." *Variety* said: ". . . a high order of cartoon ingenuity cleverly combined with sound effects. The union brought forth laughs galore." *Film Daily* noted: "This is what *Steamboat Willie* has: First, a clever and amusing treatment; secondly, music and sound effects added via the Cinephone method. The result is a real tidbit of diversion."

A corollary question must now be asked: Were those audiences laughing at Mickey, or at the sound effects and gags? The answer is clear. Mickey Mouse was not unlike many comedians of the silent-film era, who gained considerable, but transient, fame. Men like Billy Bevan and Snub Pollard made innumerable silent comedies, most of them quite funny, but the humor always arose from situations and sight gags—never from their characterizations. As long as the material was funny, *they* were considered funny. But when the material ran dry, as it did for Pollard in the late twenties, they stopped getting laughs.

Mickey Mouse, like his mentor, was in the right place at the right time. And when people left the theatres after seeing *Steamboat Willie* or one of the other cartoons that soon followed it, they were thinking of Mickey, not of Disney, or the gags, or anything else. He stayed in their minds most of all, and before long, he became a star . . . more by default than anything else.

It wasn't long before Mickey was surrounded by costars—Minnie, his ever-faithful girl friend, and Pegleg Pete, the villain, appeared with him in his first cartoon. Pluto, his dog, Horace Horsecollar, and Clarabelle Cow entered the scene not long thereafter. And, invariably, one's attention was focused on them, not the Mouse (Pluto even outranked Mickey as a cartoon star by the 1940s). Yet Mickey was the star, and that he remained through the late 1930s.

In 1935 L. H. Robbins, in the *New York Times Magazine,* wrote, quite accurately: "Mickey Mouse is the best known and most popular international figure of his day." He continued:

What is the secret of his appeal? How has an imaginary creature only 6 years old, going on 7, captured the interest of almost every tribe on this

Walt Disney with his special "Oscar" of 1932, and the
mouse that won it for him. *Courtesy British Film Institute*

terrestrial ball? Why is it that university presidents praise him, the League of Nations recommends him, Who's Who and the Encyclopaedia Britannica give him paragraphs, learned academies hang medals on him, art galleries turn from Picasso and Epstein to hold exhibitions of his monkey-shines, and the King of England won't go to the movies unless Mickey is on the bill?

. . . World-weary philosophers find in Mickey's antics "a release from the tyranny of things." He declares a nine-minute moratorium on the debt we owe to the iron facts of life. He suspends the rules of common sense and correct deportment and all the other carping, conventional laws, including the law of gravity, that hold us down and circumscribe and cramp our style.

These observers tell us there is in human nature a streak of rebellion, a yearning to cut loose, to be free to overlap the moon if we like, even at the cost of a headache and an unpleasant taste in the cold gray dawn of the morning after. This craving of ours, Mickey, with his absurdities, his defiance of reason and his accomplishment of the impossible, gratifies for us vicariously.

Some years later, on Mickey's twenty-fifth birthday, Walt Disney told the same magazine: "This is tough, trying to explain Mickey. It's been done by experts and the best any of us have been able to come up with is the fact that Mickey is so simple and uncomplicated, so easy to understand, that you can't help liking him."

The likability factor was all-important in Mickey's metamorphosis in the 1930s. At the outset, Mickey, like most other cartoon characters, was often rather crude. Would-be attackers of Walt Disney point with glee to scenes such as the famous one in *Steamboat Willie* where Mickey, in improvising various musical instruments, "plays" a cow's udder. Again, one cannot use today's standards to criticize a 1928 cartoon. Animated cartoons, which had existed since the first decade of the century, were still in their embryonic stage in the late 1920s. Disney, like most of his colleagues, was still feeling his way. The humor of the early Mickey Mouse cartoons was not his humor, but the humor of the day; and though it is easy to criticize Disney for the cow's udder gag, one must also remember that it drew one of the short's biggest laughs in the leading theaters of this country.

Once Mickey became a star—an almost overnight process—Disney and his staff had to be more conscious of what they did with the Mouse. He still had to get laughs, but, after all, there are some things a star just doesn't do. Surely this thought dictated much of what went into the Mickey Mouse cartoons of the early 1930s; it was certainly responsible for delegating many of the gags to subsidiary characters.

Evidence of the regard people had for Mickey can be found in an erudite article by playwright William Kozlenko that appeared in *The New Theatre* magazine, in which, at one point, he compared the Disney creations to Max Fleischer's Popeye.

> Popeye evinces no niceties of character. He is a tough, though apparently kind-hearted, pug. The salient features of his personality are illiteracy, stupidity, gruffness, and a pair of powerful muscles. (How versatile and refined, by comparison, is such a subject as Mickey Mouse, who can play the piano, ride a horse, conduct a band, fly an airplane, build a house, and do other constructive things with equal proficiency.)

As Mickey became more likable, he became more popular. It is staggering to try to conceive of the impact he had around the world;

before long he was the merchandising king of America, and it has been said, probably accurately, the the Disney studio couldn't have survived just making cartoons, that it was the supplementary income from the literally hundreds of licenses for everything from bookends to thermometers that kept the studio afloat.

Though Mickey remained a superstar in the eyes of the world, he became more of a problem to the Disney staff. Some years later, Disney explained: "Mickey's our problem child. He's so much of an institution that we're limited in what we can do with him. If we have Mickey kicking someone in the pants we get a million letters from mothers telling us we're giving their kids wrong ideas. [This was especially embarrassing because Mickey Mouse merchandising was being used to get kids to eat, wash, etc.] Mickey must always be sweet, always lovable. What can you do with such a leading man?"

The answer was in Mickey's supporting cast. Pluto rapidly became a major cartoon star in his own right; he was not only allowed to have a temper, but somehow, with his canine personality, the fits of anger seemed to suit him well, and frustration became a major trait in his appearances. But in 1934 the Disney people hit upon another character who not only was everything that Mickey wasn't, but who quickly surpassed him in popularity: Donald Duck.

Legend has it that Disney heard a fellow named Clarence Nash on a local radio show, doing his act, which was highlighted by his impression of a duck reciting "Mary Had a Little Lamb." Nash was hired to repeat the recitation for a Mickey Mouse cartoon, *The Orphans' Benefit*, at which a gangly sort of white duck tries to get through this speech despite the razzing of the youngsters in the audience. His peculiar voice, and inimitable way of expressing vociferous anger and frustration, caught on immediately, and the Disney people knew they had something special on their hands. (Donald's actual debut was in a cartoon called *The Wise Little Hen*.)

Donald reappeared the following year in what this writer considers to be the best Disney cartoon short—*The Band Concert*. In it, Mickey is conducting a Sunday afternoon concert in a park bandstand; the band is trying to play the *William Tell* Overture, but among other hazards, they are continually interrupted by Donald Duck, who's trying to sell ice cream to the spectators. When Donald hears the music, he produces (apparently out of his sleeve) a fife and begins to play "Turkey in the Straw" in exact counterpoint to the band's portion of *William Tell*. Before long, the whole band catches on with him and is playing "Turkey in the Straw," until maestro Mickey quiets them down and breaks Donald's flute in half. But the resourceful duck apparently has an endless supply of instruments, and he continues to confound Mickey throughout the piece. Further problems arise when a tornado approaches the town. The residents in the park scurry for shelter, but Mickey and his musicians are too wrapped up in the opening bars of "The Storm" section of the overture to notice. As the tornado hits them full force, they go into the appropriate part of the piece, their music matching the circumstances exactly as they are swept up into the air, along with the band shell and sundry other objects from the town.

Like the music, *The Band Concert* is perfectly orchestrated, a prime example of setting action to music, a formula later capitalized on by Walter Lantz in his many "cartunes" for Warner Brothers like *Rhapsody in Rivets,* MGM in *Cat Concerto,* and, of course, Disney himself in *Fantasia* and the later musical omnibus features.

Surprisingly enough, *Concert,* the first Mouse cartoon to be made in Technicolor, also gave Mickey one of his best "roles." He was never seen to better advantage than as the fiery conductor, whose brass-button uniform, several sizes too large, proved a major obstacle to his conducting efforts. As a vehicle for Mickey, the film was ideal, but once again it was Donald who stole the show. From that film on, he was a regular character in the Disney organization. The very next film, *Mickey's Service Station,* costarred the Mouse with both Donald and another character who was gaining in popularity, Goofy. Originally named Dippy Dawg, Goofy was a dumb but amiable fellow whose innocent ignorance and delightful voice (that of Disney staffer Pinto Colvig) made him another favorite character around the world.

During this time, the Silly Symphonies were also going full steam ahead, having made their conclusive mark in 1932 when Disney employed Technicolor for the first time for his short *Flowers and Trees.* From that time on, he made the series exclusively in color, waiting three years before giving Mickey a chance to do likewise. The Silly Symphonies dominated the cartoon category at the Academy Awards for many years, beginning with *Flowers and Trees* and continuing until 1940.

Though most of the Symphonies were quite enjoyable, color was as important to their success as sound was to *Steamboat Willie*'s. Disney's Christmas cartoons, *Santa's Workshop* (1932) and *The Night Before Christmas* (1933), were true holiday treats because the rich, vivid colors were so vital to the toyland theme. (In addition, color keeps them fresh. Times have changed quite a bit since 1932, but the magic of *Santa's Workshop* remains intact today—largely owing to the brilliant colors.)

Film historian Lewis Jacobs has written:

> Disney was the first to realize that color in motion pictures need not bear any resemblance to color in real life, that objects on the screen could be endowed with any pigmentation dictated by the imagination. Furthermore, he recognized that color on the screen need not be static, but could move, and that such mobility, affecting the emotions, produced new visual experiences. . . . When Pluto, lost and frozen blue in the Alps, was found by a St. Bernard who forced whiskey down Pluto's throat, a luminous warm color slowly seeped back into his body as he thawed out; when the wolf tried to blow down the house of the three pigs, he literally blew himself blue in the face; when the north wind swept through an autumn forest, the entire color scheme changed from golden red to icy blue . . .

Disney was equally meticulous about the technical aspects of color. Director H. C. Potter recalls:

> He discovered that with Technicolor film, no matter what color you photographed, a certain blue would come out a little bit deeper, or a little bit lighter. Invariably there would be an alteration in the color value. His technical people finally worked out a whole palette that his artists used religiously. They would take the original color, and a chart on the wall would show how

much change there was from what the artist had conceived into what the Technicolor would print. It ran six, seven feet high, and three or four columns. I always thought it was an example of how meticulous Walt was in trying to get something right.

The most famous Silly Symphony of all was *Three Little Pigs*, made in 1933. Disney had always known the importance of music to his cartoons, but here the impact of a song really made itself known. Frank Churchill composed a bright little song that went along with the classic story of the three pigs and their enemy, the wolf; several members of the staff contributed words, and the result, "Who's Afraid of the Big Bad Wolf?" not only had much to do with the film's success, but became one of the most popular songs of the 1930s, a symbol, many said, of the American people's spirit during the darkest days of the Depression.

Three Little Pigs was but one of many Silly Symphony cartoons that derived from longtime favorite fairy tales and Mother Goose stories, which lent themselves especially well to Disney treatment. Others included *Spider and the Fly, The Ugly Duckling, Old King Cole, Pied Piper, The Grasshopper and the Ants, The Tortoise and the Hare,* and *Who Killed Cock Robin?* The latter is well remembered for its use of a Mae West voice and personality for the character of Jenny Wren.

Most cartoon entrepreneurs used caricatures of movie stars in their films, but few of them with the scope of Disney. His first such attempt was in 1933 with *Mickey's Gala Premiere,* at which the premiere of a Mickey Mouse cartoon is attended by a bevy of movie celebrities, all delightfully caricatured: John, Ethel, and Lionel Barrymore, Wallace Beery, Marie Dressler, Laurel and Hardy, Joe E. Brown, Greta Garbo, Charlie Chaplin, Harold Lloyd, Wheeler and Woolsey, and numerous others. (P.S. It all turns out to be a dream.) Disney had similar success with *Mickey's Polo Team* in 1936 and *Mother Goose Goes Hollywood* in 1938, in which Katharine Hepburn was featured as Little Bo-Peep.

If Disney was free to "borrow" stars from other movie studios, he was equally generous with his own resources. He permitted Columbia's *Screen Snapshots* and Pathé's *Pathé Parade* to film sequences showing his studio at work, and when Hal Roach wrote him for permission to use the characters of the Three Little Pigs in his Laurel and Hardy feature, *Babes in Toyland,* Disney wrote a warm letter back not only granting permission, but offering his services in securing the women who did the pigs' voices, getting music clearance, and helping in any way possible. Thus, though Disney was not socially affiliated with most of his confreres in Hollywood, he earned their utmost respect and admiration, not only as a businessman, but as a gentleman.

Some of Disney's employees did not always hold him in such high regard, but this was not the usual employer-employee type of situation. Disney, as we have seen, would have loved nothing better than to do everything himself. It soon became obvious to him that he couldn't, and he began assembling a staff. At this time Disney's work was his life's blood—like most men burning with creative energy, he had no use for relaxation—and it meant everything to him. When others joined in his enterprise, he implicitly expected them to feel the same way. Most of them *were* dedicated men, but dedication does not always take the place of money, good working hours and conditions, and public recognition. It

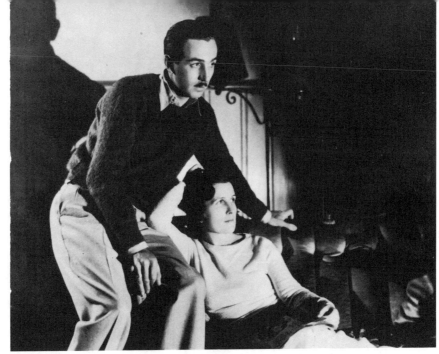

One mark of Hollywood success: a formal portrait with his wife by Clarence Sinclair Bull.   *Movie Star News*

took a bitter strike, in 1941, to settle most of these points of contention.

Despite the bitterness that sometimes came to the fore, Disney did engender remarkable loyalty from his associates, most of whom stayed with him for decades, and some of whom went on to run his studio. Some of these men did not stay because they loved Walt as a human being; most of them realized that they were working in a unique enterprise, one of the few places in Hollywood where the creative sparks did mean more than the bankbook. Disney became more and more aware of money matters, but it was his brother Roy who became the business head of the studio, who had to oversee financial problems; to Walt, nothing, but nothing, was more important than the quality of his product. Fortunately, in Roy he had not only a confidant with business sense, but someone who shared his enthusiasm and was willing to take risks that many more prudent advisers would have rejected.

Thus, it was not for monetary reasons that Disney first started thinking about an animated feature film. To be sure, the Disney studio was not as prosperous as it deserved to be in the 1930s. In 1934 the studio revealed that *Three Little Pigs* had cost $60,000 to make, and had grossed only $64,000, an outstanding income for any short subject, but for the fact that it had cost so much to produce. Therefore, one must not discount the fact that Disney stood to make considerably more money from an animated feature than he would from shorts; but it can be said with some assurance that it was not his principal motivation.

Throughout his career Disney always sought new worlds to conquer. By the mid-1930s he was the idol of millions around the world and the darling of America's intelligentsia. (It was only later, when he became more ambitious, that the critics first reared their heads.) He thought of the tremendous challenge of making a full-length animated feature. And he thought about the prestige.

Definite ideas took shape as early as 1934, as Disney started augmenting his staff, encouraging his animators to take art lessons, and signing on

The multiplane camera that did so much to broaden the horizons of the Disney cartoons. *Courtesy British Film Institute*

apprentices to learn the ropes at the studio. Meanwhile, some members of the Disney staff, principally Bill Garity, were developing a machine that was to revolutionize Disney animation, the multiplane camera.

It would not be quite accurate to say that Disney had gone as far as he could in technique by the mid to late 1930s. But there *had* been great advances, and certainly the animation style of the studio had progressed immeasurably since 1928. But a cartoon was still, after all, just a cartoon. Disney longed to top himself by doing something more than just an ordinary cartoon. One answer was length: doing a feature film. Another answer was artistic quality: hence the art lessons and additional staff. But the third answer, technical advancement, was provided by the multiplane camera.

This device made it possible, for the first time, to use camera movements which live-action films had been doing for years as a matter of course, but which the one-dimensional animated cartoon format had never been able to accomplish. The camera could now move backward and forward, filming the drawings as if they were live objects, and not having to worry about size distortion. Since this camera was capable of shooting through many separate layers of drawings, spaced according to perspective, there was a greater feeling of depth, and foregrounds and backgrounds could be made more elaborate. Best of all, the animators could now do special effects—a "blur" effect for underwater, the vague glow around a fire that could never be drawn on a conventional cell, etc.—by implementing these things on separate panels in the multiplane system.

In short, the multiplane camera enabled the Disney staff to make their cartoons look more realistic, a goal that has been criticized by many who find a nonartistry in merely duplicating live action in animated form. What these critics miss is the fact that Disney never favored *realism* in his cartoons at all; rather, it was an *idealization* of real life, which was made possible by this technical advance. Indeed, even Disney's live-action films seldom sought a realistic feeling.

Disney's animated features strove for the effect of a fantasy world set against realistic backgrounds: just true enough to be believable, just fanciful enough to be make-believe. One sees this formula in most of the classic films, most notably in *Pinocchio* and *Dumbo*.

The multiplane camera was not perfected soon enough to be used throughout *Snow White,* so the entire film, as impressive as it is, does not have the majestic scope of, say, *Pinocchio,* although the multiplane was responsible for several sequences—the witch sailing her boat through the swamp and bringing it ashore, for example—none of them, except the wishing-well scene, being particularly ostentatious.

Meanwhile, the Disney staff was experimenting, and finding out just how much they could do with the camera. Publicity for *Donald's Lucky Day,* a 1939 short, enthused: "Walt Disney is putting his magical multiplane camera to increasing good use, as is seen in *Donald's Lucky Day.* A waterfront at night forms most of the locale for Donald's newest funfest, which means that the backgrounds are not only unbelievably beautiful, but that they look almost real because of the illusion of depth brought to the screen by this new camera process."

This was not the first time that a cartoonmaker had tried to increase the illusion of depth. Ub Iwerks built a primitive, horizontally positioned version of the multiplane camera in 1934 and used it to good advantage in some of his cartoon shorts. Max Fleischer developed an even more interesting 3-D process in the mid-1930s that placed his characters (on cels) in the midst of miniature live-action sets.

For an even greater sense of realistic movement, the Disney staff decided to film live-action versions of their feature films, so the animators could study body movement in the various situations the plot presented. Marjorie Bell (Belcher), the wife of animator Art Babbitt, was recruited to pose as Snow White, and later as the Blue Fairy in *Pinocchio.* (She later became well known as Marge Champion.) In addition, a new department was established at the studio to provide scale models of every character, and, in some cases, every object (such as the toy clocks in Geppetto's workshop) in the cartoons. For Monstro, the whale, in *Pinocchio,* the staff even rigged up a rib cage and lungs in the scale model that could be pumped to simulate breathing action!

Furthermore, countless tests were shot of every scene before final animation was approved. Reporter Paul Harrison wrote in 1939:

> I have just seen some *Pinocchio* sequences, photographed in black and white from the original drawings, and several color tests. Both provide new evidence of the meticulous caution used in making such a feature.
>
> From the animators' pencil sketches the complete picture is shot—along with dialogue and sound effects—so that Disney and his editors can criticize it. When they have refined it as far as possible in that medium, the sketches are cleaned up so that the figures can be traced on the celluloid sheets, or "cells."
>
> Throughout the picture key scenes are completely painted with minute variations, then photographed and projected as color tests. For example, I saw seven slightly different treatments of the scene in which the woodcarver

Two of Disney's gagmen, Joe Grant and Dick Huemer, at work on *Dumbo*. Notice the detailed model of Dumbo in front of them; the studio made intricate models of every character who appeared in the feature films for the writers and animators to study.　*Movie Star News*

finishes painting the face of Pinocchio and then picks him up and walks away.

One test would be in rather bright colors, another paler; one would use dark shadows behind the figures, another light shadows, a third no shadows. Such tests have been made on hundreds of scenes. The labor involved is staggering even to think about.

It was most staggering to animators and directors working for other cartoon studios in Hollywood. They were often allowed to be more individually creative, and they certainly had a more freewheeling sense of humor and daring, but virtually every figure in this golden age of animation has admitted that he, at one time or another, longed to have the resources to turn out something as good-looking as Disney's cartoons. Even disenchanted ex-employees do not hesitate to admit what invaluable experience it was to work for Disney during this period.

As the animated features started coming out, entertaining millions and racking up impressive box-office figures, Disney became more of a target for certain highbrow critics. After all, there wasn't much one could say about a man making cartoon shorts, but once Disney showed more ambition, it was easier to throw stones. Even Walt himself found something lacking in calling a work such as *Snow White* a "cartoon."

It was mainly on artistic grounds that Disney was criticized. Famed caricaturist Al Hirschfeld wrote of *Snow White:*

. . . the characters Snow White, Prince Charming, and the Queen are badly drawn attempts at realism: they imitate pantographically the actions of their counterparts in factual photography. The illusion created by a well-directed pen line is an art not to be confused with the gingerbread realities of a Snow White. Disney's treatment of these characters belongs in the oopsy-woopsy school of art practiced mostly by etchers who portray dogs with cute sayings. Snow White with her full complement of fingers and fingernails, eyelashes, one-dimensional head, bare arms without solidity and uninventive neck is an anatomic automaton. These awkward symbols do not articulate, and the lovely voice with which she is endowed only heightens the effect of a ventriloquist's dummy. The staccato movements of Snow White and her cardboard lover, both wired for sound, are distinctly bad influences in this new art form. To imitate an animated photograph except as satire is in poor taste.

Thomas Burton, writing about *Pinocchio* in *Saturday Review,* said:

> His [Disney's] is the art of soft-focus caricature, of picturing animals and men as lovable and amusing people. His art is all good-natured curves. Disney has discarded the straight line as bad for animation and the pure joy he sees in life. Both his technical limitations and his background have kept him from being another Rowlandson, Daumier, Leech, Gavarini, or Hogarth. He cannot, like them, be casually cruel or see with their cold artistic lassitude.
>
> This gives him all his talents to be put into surface entertainment. There is no place for social bite, grand manner, art theory in his work. Walt Disney in *Pinocchio* lets nothing confuse his story. He sees it and tells it with a charm, a wit, a beautiful sense of pace and mounting. . . . It will keep you living in a wonderful world of form and color and excitement.

What many critics could not understand was that Disney had no desire to inject "social bite, grand manner, art theory" in his work. Like the man who says "I don't know anything about art, but I know what I like," Disney knew exactly what he liked, and as has been pointed out so many times, his audiences were Walt Disney multiplied many times over. His taste matched his audience's perfectly.

Throughout his career, when sniped at by critical attacks, Disney's answer was as logical as it was natural. He pointed to his films' overwhelming success around the world. And what better criterion for a man whose avowed purpose in making these films was to entertain people?

"This above all: to thine own self be true." Disney was true to himself every step of his career. When dissatisfied with *Pinocchio,* he completely scrapped five months of finished product. Why? It didn't look right to him. This kind of judgment was always based on integrity—personal integrity—and a dedication to the one goal Disney held above all others: entertainment.

It was wrong for critics to chide Disney for not living up to his potential, for it was his potential as *they* saw it. Disney was satisfied with his films because they lived up to his own visions of them, and when released to theatres, his judgment was echoed by countless millions who delighted in what he gave them.

Disney strove for something special with *Fantasia,* a *succès d'estime* if not a box-office smash (until recently), and then in the 1940s went into new areas of endeavor. He tackled live action, initially in *The Reluctant Dragon,* and to a greater extent as the decade wore on. Some of his staunchest supporters berated him for deserting the realm of animation, but Disney defended himself, saying:

> I'll keep on making pictures all-cartoon, mixed with human actors, or with an all-live cast. It's the story that appeals to me and the manner of

treatment is dictated from that. Yes, I've heard some people say I ought to stick to features like *Snow White* or *Pinocchio,* and it's true that the cartoon is my first love. I'll always go back to it. But I'm still experimenting and I've got to keep a busy schedule to make enough money to finance the big all-cartoon feature folks seem to expect of me.

During the war he went into a whole new sphere of filmmaking: the instructional film. In 1941 he produced a film called *Four Methods of Flush Riveting* for the Lockheed Aircraft Company; it was the beginning of four years of wartime morale, training, and instructional films, and the cornerstone of a new career for Disney in the nontheatrical film field.

Shortly after the Lockheed project, John Grierson, then head of the National Film Board of Canada, commissioned Disney to make four shorts promoting the Canadian War Savings plan and an army training film called *Stop That Tank.* The United States government ordered the first of many films when it assigned Disney the task of making a theatrical short that would explain to the public the importance of paying their taxes on time. The U.S. Senate debated the wisdom of spending wartime dollars on a Hollywood movie (remember, the government was just beginning to understand the power of film as a communications tool)—but *The New Spirit,* starring Donald Duck, reportedly inspired the most punctual tax payments in history, and a sequel *(The Spirit of '43)* was commissioned the following year.

Before long the Disney studio was busier than ever, churning out scores of films serving every conceivable purpose for members of the Armed Forces, Americans at home, and people of other countries as well. The Museum of Modern Art has saved a number of these films in its permanent collection, calling Disney's army-navy training films "[deserving of] study as among the most mature examples of the instructional film." Other notable wartime endeavors include *Out of the Frying Pan into the Firing Line* (1943), an Office of War Information short distributed to American theatres, with Minnie Mouse showing why it was important for housewives to save fat, and *Water, Friend or Enemy* (1943), one of a series of health films designed to be shown in South America and sponsored by the Coordinator of Inter-American Affairs. The museum's notes declare: "Here the lesson about the right and wrong place for a well, about the necessity of boiling water, is clarity itself."

Disney possessed an uncanny ability in the making of such films. He managed, with live action and animation, to take literally any subject (and his wartime shorts certainly ran the gamut) and make it interesting, while peerlessly getting across the point of the film. Some observers have labeled these films "nonhumorous" and made a distinction between them and Disney's theatrical product. This is not entirely true. These films were made with a keen awareness of the audience that would be watching them. Some of the training films are not only of a quality well up to contemporary animated films being shown in theatres, but contain an abundance of humor that appeals directly to the servicemen it was created for. There is even so-called barracks humor in many of the films.

In a 1944 speech Disney called the animated film "the most flexible, versatile, and stimulating of all teaching facilities." Indeed, schoolchildren (and a great many adults, too), who have been exposed to such Disney films as *Our Friend the Atom, Donald in Mathmagic Land,* and the informative *People and Places* series, sigh with annoyance that all their instruction cannot be as lively and intriguing as that of Disney.

Disney also, of course, got into commercial films in a big way after the war, and lent his touch to films for everyone from U.S. Steel to Kleenex. Many companies whose "sponsored films" either don't get shown, or are projected to lethargic audiences, have discovered the advantage of having Walt Disney prepare movies for them.

The war disrupted many of Disney's plans, but it kept his studio busy and also kept a money flow coming through the gates. Disney produced one propaganda film for theatrical release, *Victory through Air Power,* and two pet projects, combination live-action and cartoon salutes to the beauty of South America, *Saludos Amigos* and *The Three Caballeros.*

With the war over he was able to return to full production and revive some plans that had been dormant for the duration. A unique feature of the Disney studio throughout its history has been the length of time some ideas persisted in the studio before coming to fruition. The idea for *Peter Pan* existed as early as 1935. (It wasn't finished until 1952.) The rights to T. H. White's book *The Sword in the Stone* were bought in 1939 and the animated feature released twenty-four years later!

Often, projects were begun, then shelved temporarily; this was true of *Bambi,* which was planned to follow *Snow White,* and *Sleeping Beauty,* which first took shape in 1950. It was put aside in the middle of the decade when the studio concentrated its efforts on its TV shows and the new Disneyland park, only to be revived in 1956, when production began at full pace for a 1959 release.

Another discovery that Disney made in the 1940s was the value of his film backlog. Reissues are as old as the film industry itself, but Disney was uniquely equipped to take advantage of the system, since his films were basically timeless, unhampered by social change that rendered many other Hollywood films commercially impotent after several years. With the passage of time, reissues proved to be the backbone of the Disney company, an asset whose monetary value is infinite. Disney discovered this relatively early in his career, and to date no one (except MGM with *Gone With the Wind*) has had greater success with reissues. In 1948, in an unprecedented move, Radio City Music Hall booked the 1933 cartoon *The Three Little Pigs* for a very successful engagement, followed by two hundred other theaters across the country.

Disney also continued to make new one-reel cartoons over the years, a source of wonder to many in the industry who gave up on short subjects in the late 1940s. Ward Kimball, veteran Disney animator and director, has explained why Disney continued to produce short cartoons well into the 1950s:

> That was done as a buffer for animators. Schedules can't always be timed to accommodate your full working crew full time on features. Try as hard as we may, we can never seem to make one feature start right in step with the one we've just finished. There is always a period of animation doldrums while we are preparing the next feature. Back when we used the shorts as a filler, they would provide temporary work for animators between features. When we discontinued the shorts program, TV shows then provided this buffer.

In 1961 Disney told columnist Art Buchwald: "I saw the handwriting on the wall about ten years ago. I'll make an occasional short now to go with one of my features, just to keep the theatre owners from booking some horrible short subject with my own picture, but it costs $100,000 to make a seven-minute cartoon, and you can't get your money back."

Even so, the Disney cartoons continued to be amusing, ingenious, and full of verve right to the last (1957), after which Disney's only cartoon shorts were featurette-type "specials." In 1953 the studio briefly succumbed to the 3-D craze with two cartoon shorts, *Melody* and *Working for Peanuts.* A press-book for the latter—a Donald Duck/Chip 'n' Dale comedy—stated, "The gags with 3-D are plentiful as the chipmunks catch peanuts from the audience, and Donald almost sticks a foot in the aisle as he searches for the playful chips." Just to be sure, the studio made these films available in regular versions for theatres that weren't interested in handing out the special glasses.

The quality of the cartoons remained exceedingly high in the 1950s, although the animation staff did follow the trend of forgoing very detailed backgrounds for more impressionistic views of trees, buildings, and such. They did not go along with the swing to "limited animation," led by the much praised UPA studio, although the Disney people found it useful for deliberate comic effect in their Academy Award-winning *Toot, Whistle, Plunk, and Boom,* a lighthearted history of music, which was also the studio's first cartoon in CinemaScope. Adding further to the experimental nature of the short, the sound was conceived for stereophonic effects (used again in another short, *Grand Canyonscope*). The cartoon was enthusiastically received, and the Disney staff took special pride in being acclaimed for a short where limited animation was used in such a creative rather than economical way.

Disney's greatest, and most surprising, success in the late 1940s and 1950s, however, was with a series of nature films. For years, it was claimed that this came about by chance, when Walt was vacationing in Alaska and happened to meet camera store owners Alfred and Elma Milotte, who impressed him with their amateur wildlife movies. The truth is that Disney hatched the idea himself and then went looking for someone to bring it to life. Emery F. Tobin, publisher of *The Alaska Sportsman* magazine, recommended the Milottes, who were on tour in Los Angeles at the time, showing their wildlife films. Disney contracted for footage on Alaskan seals, and the results were edited down to a half-hour color short called *Seal Island.* Even Disney's brother Roy tried to discourage this project, as there was no interest from theatre owners at all. But Disney got it shown in one Los Angeles theatre in order to qualify for an Academy Award—and it won! It became a tremendous critical and financial success, and led to a long-running *True-Life Adventure* series that eventually expanded to feature length.

The shorts also raised considerable controversy, and even Richard Schickel, one of Disney's harshest critics, had to admit:

The nature films indeed present one of the most difficult problems of critical evaluation in the entire Disney history. On the one hand, no one can doubt that Disney's photographers did bring back the pearls and that they were displayed in a variety and profusion previously unknown on the theater

Disney accepts his Oscar for *Water Birds,* a nature short, in 1953 from Jane Wyman and Ray Milland. *UPI photo*

screens of the world. . . . In their sheer technical virtuosity, in their ability to put on the screen rarities and oddities from the natural world, the Disney films were so far above their competition as to deserve a category all to themselves. In them he satisfied the simplest, most basic demand of film making: he gave us a chance to see things we might not otherwise have ever seen. And yet he falsified this material in precisely the ways his critics suggested.

For all the wonder and delight and awesomeness of the films, one cannot help but bristle at some of the hoke Disney injected into them. Some of the ideas were good: a flight of birds set to Liszt's *Second Hungarian Rhapsody* provided a charming sequence that only served to emphasize the beauty of their ascent. But gimmicking up the film so that two Rocky Mountain sheep butted each other to the "Anvil Chorus," or making two deadly enemies seem like clowns, did not sit quite so easily.

This might have been somewhat easier to take, too, had not the Disney people assumed such a pretentious attitude toward the films. In a promotional booklet, writer-director James Algar stated:

> Factual honesty in essence as well as in detail is the distinguishing hallmark of the *True-Life Adventure* films. The theme of a Disney factual is usually elemental—often it is the fight for survival. The tempo of the telling must be leisurely. The tone must be respectful—no ridicule. No condescension, particularly when dealing with the wisdom of the ages and the tales of the master story-teller.

Factual honesty? No ridicule? No condescension? It was a bit hard to swallow.

Still, as Schickel pointed out, the scales were balanced to a large degree by the positive aspects of these films—and they were many, especially in the feature films *The Living Desert, The Vanishing Prairie, The African Lion,* etc. Here one must forgive Disney's misdirected showmanship; one *cannot* lambaste the man for making the films available in the first place, and though some people claim that the road to hell is paved with good intentions, Disney's route only led him slightly astray.

It is also worth noting that apparently the Disney staff took note of the films' criticism, for after the initial feature films in the series, such "gimmicky" treatment was generally abandoned in favor of a more sober approach. In the long run there is more good to say about the series than bad, and it remains a notable, if tarnished, achievement in Disney's career.

The 1950s were a decade of evolution for Walt Disney. He continued to make animated features that came out every year or two, but the period between them grew longer as the decade progressed. By the 1960s it had stretched to four years. Theatrically, the 1950s saw the change from an emphasis on animation to live action. Disney initially set up live-action filming in England with his memorable *Treasure Island,* followed during the next few years by three period swashbucklers.

His first ambitious undertaking on home ground was *20,000 Leagues under the Sea.* It was filmed in CinemaScope and color, with a prestigious cast (James Mason, Kirk Douglas, Paul Lukas, Peter Lorre) and impressive production values, directed, oddly enough, by Richard Fleischer, the son of Disney's onetime competitor Max Fleischer. It was also the first film, except for the nature feature *The Living Desert,* to be released by Disney's own distribution company, Buena Vista. The film was a tremendous box-office success, but instead of following it up with a string of other life features, Disney turned his attention to a new medium—television.

In 1950 Disney turned down an offer of $1 million—for the television rights to his 350 cartoon shorts. "The television people want to buy my films," he explained, "but I'm not selling. Why should I? They're still good for movie theatres. And, because they're timeless, they always will be." Disney did agree to mount a one-hour television special for Christmas viewing several years in a row. "But I insisted on one thing, and sponsors agreed with me. No commercials. All we do is tell you the name of the sponsor . . . and that's that."

But by 1954 Disney changed his tune slightly. He still wasn't going to sell out to any network or sponsor. He decided to produce his own *Disneyland* TV series, a weekly hour show that he would host; the series would be comprised of some material from the backlog, used sparingly, a lot of hours filmed especially for the show (most of this live action), and considerable coverage of his new amusement park, Disneyland.

Because Disney hated to cut corners, the cost of producing his hour-long films for TV most often exceeded the amount he earned on them. Asked about this procedure, Disney explained: "Television makes lots of friends. It's just good policy. When four million people see your television show, they carry away with them an image of what we're doing."

Of course, viewers carried away more than just an image. Many of the hour programs were really glorified advertisements for new Disney theatrical features or upcoming reissues. When during the show's first season Disney presented an hour called "Operation Undersea," about the difficulties of making *20,000 Leagues under the Sea,* industry pundits labeled it "The Long, Long Trailer," but the show won an Emmy Award as the Best Individual Program of the Year.

And although Disney's critics are quick to point out how he exploited the TV show to his own advantage in myriad ways, it should also be remembered that he couldn't have done any of it if the material he presented wasn't entertaining. Disney's plugs for feature films were often more enjoyable than hour-long installments of other series. And the original material shot for the series was bright, handsomely turned out programming, one of the most consistently good series on the air.

Disney decided to host the show himself; all reports of him being taciturn and/or shy were dispelled as he presented the various programs week after week with a natural and completely winning style that reminded one of a benign relative. Indeed, he was the best possible choice for a host, and in his twelve-year stint in that position he cemented forever the public image of Walt Disney that no amount of critical writing can eradicate from Americans' minds.

Disney soon learned that TV was also a useful proving ground for actors, writers, directors, and ideas in general. Often he would plan a segment for the TV show and it would turn out so well that he would release it as a feature instead—something that could never have been accomplished had Disney been using the same economical shooting methods as other TV producers.

But the biggest outgrowth of the TV series in the 1950s was a fellow named Davy Crockett. Disney produced a three-part program on the famous United States folk hero, and before he knew what was happening, the whole country was Davy Crockett-crazy. Disney reaped a fortune from merchandising rights as every red-blooded American boy (this writer included) donned coonskin caps and other Crockett regalia. The three TV hours were edited into a feature film, which then warranted a sequel. The shows also made a star of Fess Parker, who then appeared in four theatrical films for the Disney studio: *The Great Locomotive Chase, Westward Ho the Wagons, Old Yeller,* and *The Light in the Forest.*

Disney's hold on the children of the 1950s was completed with the emergence of *The Mickey Mouse Club,* which debuted on October 3, 1955. A daily filmed one-hour TV show that aired on ABC at five o'clock, the Club featured a group of likeable youngsters known as the Mouseketeers, led by singer-actor Jimmie Dodd, who entertained, presented various travel and educational segments, appeared in serialized stories ("The Hardy Boys," "Spin and Marty," "Corky and White Shadow"), and showed old Disney cartoons with Mickey, Donald, Goofy, and the other favorite characters.

The show was phenomenally successful; 260 hours and 130 half hours were filmed, and the series enjoyed a healthy run on the network, and later on local stations when additional material was filmed to bring the shows up to date. We needn't go into a comparison of the quality of this program to most of today's commercial kiddie fare.

The name of Disney's hour-long program was changed to *Walt Disney Presents,* as he continued to come up with quality material week after week. Eventually, several series within the series sprang up, including *Texas John Slaughter,* starring Tom Tryon, *The Swamp Fox, Elfego Baca, Moochie,* and *Zorro,* the latter proving so popular and so flexible that it was developed as a half-hour series starring Guy Williams, Henry Calvin, and Gene Sheldon, which ran on ABC and subsequently in endless reruns in syndication.

When Disney severed his relations with ABC and moved to NBC in the fall of 1961, the name of the show was changed once more, to *Walt Disney's Wonderful World of Color*, an indication that the show was to be aired in color, and a prestigious tie-in for NBC and RCA, the program's sponsor. In announcing the move Disney stated that all previously established characters would be abandoned and that the NBC program would present all new ideas. The most prominent of these was a new cartoon figure, Professor Ludwig von Drake, an erudite but absentminded duck whose delightful voice was provided by Paul Frees. The program, aired at seven-thirty (then seven o'clock) on Sunday night, was a solid ratings success, and remained a television staple for twenty years—a considerable feat in the fickle television world. When Walt died, the name of the show was changed to *The Wonderful World of Disney*.

The late 1950s saw the beginning of Disney's real plunge into live-action feature film production, which has continued ever since. A few standard formulas (slapstick comedy, action-adventure, animal films) served the studio well, and before long a kind of "house style" emerged, with the same proficient production team putting its stamp on every Disney picture. Even the TV segments had that Disney look and feel. Performers like Fred MacMurray, Hayley Mills, and Dean Jones became studio regulars—indeed, Disney revitalized MacMurray's career, and made young Mills an American star—while behind the camera, a handful of directors (Robert Stevenson, James Neilson, Norman Tokar) and producers (Bill Anderson, Bill Walsh, Winston Hibler) piloted virtually all of the company's product.

The great success of such fanciful comedies as *The Shaggy Dog* and *The Absent Minded Professor* led the studio to concentrate more and more on innocuous family comedies, predicating a feeling in some circles that the Disney magic was wearing thin. Then came *Mary Poppins*. The big-budgeted (nearly $5 million) live-action/animation musical grossed an estimated $40 million, and let it be known to all doubters that there was still only one Walt Disney and he was alive and well in Burbank.

Poppins was followed by another host of amiable comedies and a few adventure films, none of them outstanding, all of them adhering to certain patterns that had been set up over the years (clean-cut hero, wholesomely good-looking heroine, plenty of slapstick in the comedies, etc.) .

If these films weren't up to what one likes to consider "the Disney standard," it is probably because Walt himself wasn't involved with them to the extent he was in times gone by—or even in the case of a major production like *Mary Poppins*. Disney always had to have new worlds to conquer, and having set up his moviemaking machine at the Burbank studio, the excitement of it started to diminish. Certainly Disney took much more pride and interest in the development of his Audioanimatronics (automatically controlled robots, such as the famous one of Abraham Lincoln built for the New York World's Fair and later installed in Disneyland) than he did in *The Monkey's Uncle*. In Audioanimatronics he found something new and challenging—a way to re-create a likeness of Lincoln delivering a speech as if he were alive!

He took special pride in Disneyland and had great plans for his Florida complex, Walt Disney World. All this meant more to him than films or television toward the end of his life. For after all it would have been difficult for Disney to top himself filmwise at this stage of the game. There were few mountains left to climb in the field of animation. There

In 1961 Disney introduced a new character, Ludwig von Drake (officially Donald
Duck's uncle), on his NBC television
show. *NBC photo; © 1961 Walt Disney
Productions*

wasn't even the satisfaction of turning out a Mickey Mouse cartoon in a
few weeks anymore. In some ways sheer size defeated Walt Disney; there
could no longer be the simplicity and innocence of a *Dumbo* (or even the
brevity—*Dumbo* was sixty-four minutes, *Mary Poppins* 139!). It took a
fresh and beguiling subject—A. A. Milne's classic *Winnie the Pooh*—to
bring out the very best in Disney and his staff once more. *Winnie the
Pooh and the Honey Tree* and its sequel, *Winnie the Pooh and the
Blustery Day,* were undoubtedly the most charming cartoons, both
visually and otherwise, that the Disney studio had created in years. It is
worth noting that both films were less than a half hour in length.

One thing never changed at the studio, and that was the profes-
sionalism that Walt had instilled in every member of his staff. Even
Disney's color quality was better than most other studios, simply because
the studio insisted on the very best results from Technicolor labs.
(Technicolor was glad to comply, since Disney was largely responsible for
putting the company on the map in the 1930s.) The special effects in
Disney's live-action films far surpassed rival companies', with matte and
process-screen work that put many a Hollywood epic to shame. Disney
was even able to use animation to create undetected effects in his films—
the long shot of the mansion in *Blackbeard's Ghost,* scenes of fish swimming by Captain Nemo's observation window in *20,000 Leagues under
the Sea,* etc.

Roy Disney said that "it was Walt's wish that when the time came he
would have built an organization with the creative talent to carry on as

Walt Disney on the set of *Bon Voyage!* with his favorite star of the 1960s, Fred MacMurray. © *1964 Walt Disney Productions. Courtesy Doug McClelland*

he had established and directed it through the years." This came to pass on December 15, 1966, when Walt Disney died of acute circulatory collapse after surgery for the removal of a lung tumor one month earlier.

The world mourned the loss of its greatest fantasist, a man who entertained more people in more ways than any other figure of our time.

There were many who felt that the studio would never survive without him, but Roy Disney's words were more than an optimistic press statement. Disney *had* built a strong organization; his studio was filled with lifetime employees, some of whom had worked their way up from animator's assistants to major executive positions. These people understood the Disney tradition.

But there was still one thing missing: Walt.

He was no company figurehead. Even though his mind dwelt on other matters, he still involved himself in every studio project, right to the end, and there was no one who could match his judgment and keen story sense. (As late as *The Jungle Book,* he cut one entire sequence involving a rhinoceros because it followed the King Louie scene; he felt that two hyperactive segments in a row would cancel each other out.) He was sorely missed.

Ub Iwerks recalled the making of *Snow White and the Seven Dwarfs* on the occasion of its fifth reissue in 1967—just after Disney's death. "It would probably cost $20 million to make in today's market," he mused, "but there's more to it than that. I don't think we could find the necessary talent or the enthusiasm it took in those days.

"Walt," he concluded, "provided the enthusiasm."

And he provided the world with a cornucopia of entertainment unparalleled in the twentieth century. His work has already survived him, and stood the test of time. It's likely that people will continue to derive pleasure from Walt Disney's creations for many years to come.

He was a storyteller, a showman, a dreamer—a genius.

2·The Feature Films

SNOW WHITE AND THE SEVEN DWARFS

RELEASED BY RKO RADIO PICTURES; WORLD PREMIERE, December 21, 1937, released February 4, 1938. Multiplane Technicolor. Adapted from *Grimm's Fairy Tales*. Supervising director: David Hand. Sequence directors: Perce Pearce, Larry Morey, William Cottrell, Wilfred Jackson, Ben Sharpsteen. Supervising animators: Hamilton Luske, Vladimir Tytla, Fred Moore, Norman Ferguson. Story adaptation: Ted Sears, Otto Englander, Earl Hurd, Dorothy Ann Blank, Richard Creedon, Dick Richard, Merrill De Maris, Webb Smith. Art directors: Charles Philippi, Hugh Hennesy, Terrell Stapp, McLaren Stewart, Harold Miles, Tom Codrick, Gustaf Tenggren, Kenneth Anderson, Kendall O'Connor, Hazel Sewell. Character designers: Albert Hurter, Joe Grant. Animators: Frank Thomas, Dick Lundy, Arthur Babbitt, Eric Larson, Milton Kahl, Robert Stokes, James Algar, Al Eugster, Cy Young, Joshua Meador, Ugo D'Orsi, George Rowley, Les Clark, Fred Spencer, Bill Roberts, Bernard Garbutt, Grim Natwick, Jack Camp-bell, Marvin Woodward, James Culhane, Stan Quackenbush, Ward Kimball, Wolfgang Reitherman, Robert Martsch. Backgrounds: Samuel Armstrong, Mique Nelson, Merle Cox, Claude Coats, Phil Dike, Ray Lockrem, Maurice Noble. Music arrangers: Frank Churchill, Paul J. Smith, Leigh Harline. Running time: 83 minutes.

Songs by Frank Churchill, Larry Morey, Paul J. Smith, and Leigh Harline: "I'm Wishing," "One Song," "With a Smile and a Song," "Whistle While You Work," "Heigh Ho," "Bluddle-Uddle-Um-Dum," "The Dwarfs' Yodel Song," "Some Day My Prince Will Come."

Voices: Adriana Caselotti (Snow White), Harry Stockwell (The Prince), Lucille LaVerne (The Queen), Scotty Mattraw (Bashful), Roy Atwell (Doc), Pinto Colvig (Grumpy), Otis Harlan (Happy), Pinto Colvig (Sleepy), Billy Gilbert (Sneezy), Moroni

The Wicked Queen orders Snow White killed, and her
heart returned in this box. © *Walt Disney Productions;*
courtesy Al Kilgore

Olsen (The Magic Mirror), Stuart Buchanan (Humbert, The Queen's Huntsman), Marion Darlington (bird sounds and warbling), Jim Macdonald (yodeling).

How does one begin to talk about *Snow White*—the first full-length animated feature, the turning point in Walt Disney's career, a milestone in film history, and, as more and more people realize with each passing year, a great film?

Perhaps the way to start is with what exists on film—beginning, as most of Disney's subsequent animated features were to do, on a close-up of a storybook with "Some Day My Prince Will Come" being played on the sound track at a brisk tempo. The storybook opens and establishes in its first few pages the background of our story: the beautiful Snow White, orphaned at birth, growing up forced to do menial work in the Queen's household.

It is with a long shot of the Queen's castle that the action begins, as the majestic lady, proud and vain, approaches her Magic Mirror to ask, as she always does: "Who is the fairest of them all?" Today the Mirror replies that it is one within her very home . . . Snow White.

At this point the picture dissolves to our first scene of Snow White, doing her work with the garden birds fluttering happily about her. She does long for one thing (having long since accepted her tedious work) , and as she goes to the well to fill her wash pail, she sings "I'm Wishing," an echo duplicating her voice as she tells in song of her yearning for the man she loves to find her and take her away. As she finishes the song, a handsome prince who has heard her approaches, singing the last line of the song, much to Snow White's surprise. Although she is embarrassed and runs away, it is clear that here is the very man she has been wishing for.

Meanwhile, the Queen has sent for her huntsman, ordering him to take Snow White to the forest that afternoon and slay her. He must bring back her heart in order to prove that the deed has been done. That day the unsuspecting Snow White goes with the man into the forest, and while picking wild flowers,

Snow White flees through the forest, letting her imagination run away with her.   © *Walt Disney Productions; courtesy Al Kilgore*

Six of the dwarfs try to get the seventh, Grumpy, to wash his hands and face before dinner.   © *Walt Disney Productions*

turns to see him raising his gleaming hunting knife. But he cannot go through with it. He begs her forgiveness, and tells her to run—flee—escape from the power of the evil Queen.

She takes off into the forest, frightened not only by what has just happened, but by the specters her mind imagines around her. Finally she falls to the ground in tears, but then some of the haunting eyes that have peered at her from the brush emerge; they are merely the animals of the forest, as frightened of Snow White as she has been of them.

As they gingerly approach, however, she realizes her mistake, and brightens, making friends with the animals. Trying to forget her nightmarish experience, she sings "With a Smile and a Song," and the animals lead her out of the deep forest toward a house in the clearing. Finding the quaint little cottage caked with dust and its belongings in wild disarray, she decides to clean it up with the help of her animal friends, singing "Whistle While You Work."

Meanwhile, some distance away, the Seven Dwarfs are introduced in song as they "dig dig dig" in their mine. With the end of the workday approaching, they pack up their tools and head for home, singing "Heigh Ho" as they march back to their cottage.

Snow White, having finished her chores, explores the second floor of the house, and falls asleep draped over several of the curiously tiny beds in the room. When the animals hear the Dwarfs approaching the house, they scurry off in all directions, leaving Snow White alone.

When the Dwarfs arrive at the cottage, they find it has undergone an amazing transformation. It's spotlessly clean, with everything in its place. They decide that whoever is responsible must be upstairs, and they elect a patsy to go up and have a look around. This simpleminded Dwarf creeps into their bedroom, but with a vivid imagination, and with the shadows cast by his lantern, envisions the figure covered by a bedsheet to be a scary ghost!

When they all finally tiptoe into the room, Snow White wakes up and surprises them by identifying each one by name (having read the unusual names on each bedpost): Doc (the "leader"), Happy, Sleepy, Sneezy, Bashful, Grumpy, and Dopey. When she tells of her plight—and offers to cook and keep house for them if they will let her stay—they happily agree, except for Grumpy, who doesn't want any part of her or her problems.

She baffles them by insisting that they wash before sitting down to dinner, but before long she has won them over completely and the house sparkles as it never had before. When the Dwarfs go off to work the next morning, they beg Snow White to be careful while they're gone (even Grumpy showing interest in her well-being), and she kisses them good-bye, Dopey playfully coming back for seconds and thirds.

The night before, however, the Queen has discovered the trick played on her by the Huntsman, by asking the Magic Mirror who is the fairest and being told that Snow White is still alive. Determined to get rid of her for good, she hatches a diabolical scheme: she will disguise herself as an ugly old woman and offer Snow White a poisoned apple. She stalks down to her dungeon laboratory that night, where she mixes the ingredients for her transformation: a scream, to turn her hair white, etc. She drinks the potion, and detail by detail turns into a cackling old crone. Then she prepares the deadly apple, and during the foggy night sails her boat through the swamp to reach Snow White by morning.

After the Dwarfs have gone, the Queen appears and offers Snow White the luscious red apple to use in baking a pie, exhorting her to taste it. She does, and falls to the ground in a dead faint, which, according

to the Queen's curse, cannot be broken except by love's first kiss.

The animals see what has happened, and rush to get the Dwarfs, who race back to catch the Queen. Amidst thunder and lightning, they chase her up rocky terrain. She tries to shove a boulder down on the Dwarfs below, but lightning strikes the ledge where she is standing and she falls with the boulder to her death.

The Dwarfs are crushed by Snow White's death; even Grumpy dissolves into tears at the sight of her. A subtitle explains that she was "so beautiful, even in death, that the Dwarfs did not have the heart to bury her." Instead, they create a bier where she lies in state for all the forest animals, as well as the Dwarfs, to pay their respects.

But another comes to see Snow White; it is the Prince who approaches, and as a farewell gesture he kisses her. Miraculously, she awakens, and grief turns into joy as the Dwarfs and animals cheer for Snow White and the Prince who has finally come to take her off where they will live happily ever after.

The story of *Snow White and the Seven Dwarfs* is, of course, an old and fairly simple one. But here, for the first of many times, the Disney staff faced the challenge of taking a simple tale and stretching it out to the length of a feature film, achieving the proper balance between the plot motivation of the central character(s) and the comedy relief supplied, in this case, by the Dwarfs.

Just as Disney learned that his hero Mickey Mouse was downright dull in comparison with such colorful sidekicks as Pluto and Donald Duck, he quickly discovered that the heroes and heroines of fairy-tale stories were frequently the least interesting aspects of those tales. Yet one couldn't eliminate them or relegate them to supporting roles; the answer was to have their actions intertwined with those of the comedy characters so subtly that it would never seem as it did, for example, in the archetypal Broadway musical comedies of the 1920s and 1930s that two separate and distinct elements were at work.

One way of achieving this goal was seeing that the action never stayed with one character or setting too long. Practically every key scene in the film is interrupted by crosscutting to simultaneous action elsewhere. (The Dwarfs are introduced in the middle of Snow White's housecleaning sequence; the Queen's transformation takes place amid scenes of the after-dinner party at the Dwarfs' cottage.)

Mike Barrier has said it best: "The story is never just an excuse for the Dwarfs' comedy; instead, most of what they do has direct bearing on the plot. We care more about what happens to Snow White because the Dwarfs—far more vivid personalities than she—care so much for her, and much of the comedy arises from their concern."

Disney also realized that operetta-style villainy would never work in these films, so instead he went out for totally evil characterizations and sequences that were firmly rooted in horror elements. Snow White's peril is made distressingly real by the character and actions of the Queen. (For example, leaving her dungeon laboratory, down a winding staircase past prison cells, she spots the skeletal figure of what was once a man lying on the ground, his bony hand reaching through the bars for a pitcher of water that is *just* beyond his reach. She says mockingly: "Thirsty? Have a drink!" and kicks the cup and the skeleton into a dozen directions as she laughs wickedly. An ugly yellow and black spider scurries out of the overturned cup. This is just one of many truly terrifying vignettes throughout the film.)

With these factors—the sweetness of Snow White, the wickedness of the Queen, and the humor of the Dwarfs—firmly established, the film moves at a firm, steady pace, never seeming rushed or contracted (as some of the cartoon features did), or prolonged with dull stretches. The sequences lead one into another with perfect precision and harmony, seeming to flow as if this were the way the story had always been told.

Much of this fluidity, of course, was the result of judicial editing, a vital part of the four-year period spent making this film. Whole sequences were animated and fit into the film, and then taken out because they hindered the progress of the story.

The film originally showed Snow White's mother dying in childbirth; this was cut from the film at the very last minute. Indeed, stills from this sequence were printed in *Look* magazine's preview of the film, and the sequence itself was part of all the authorized book versions, comic strips, comic books, and related material that came out in advance of the film. (This, incidentally, was a practice Disney followed for years, having syndicated comic versions of his films appear before they were to be released to theatres, so that by the time youngsters went to see the film, they were fully versed in the background and plot of the film— an educated audience, as it were.)

Ward Kimball recalls:

I animated on *Snow White and the Seven Dwarfs,* and that was one of the early tragedies of my life. I was made a full-fledged animator, and they decided that Kimball would do a good job on the eating sequence, after Snow White makes the Dwarfs wash up. I would do the soup sequence, because I did funny stuff. I animated the whole sequence, and it got big laughs in the sweat box (Walt's projection room), but when Walt started seeing the whole picture, he thought that was one of the places that we ought to get on with the story, go right from making them wash to the next sequence. So as much as he hated to do it—he even called me up on the phone and apologized—he had to take it out of the picture. So then I went on a bed-building sequence; they had a big, ornate bed

that the Dwarfs were building as a present to Snow White. This also was taken out after I'd animated it, because it didn't help the story along.

The animated pencil test of the "soup sequence" was later shown on one of Disney's 1956 TV hours, "The Plausible Impossible."

But these personal setbacks were, as Kimball well realized, made for the good of the picture, and, indeed, when the last cut was made, Disney had a film with not one wasted minute, and a story that held the audience's attention from the first frame to the last.

There was not a detail of the film that had not been discussed, picked apart, tried, rejected, tried again, and perhaps again and again and again.

Thirty years later, Wolfgang Reitherman recalled:

I remember when I first came here as an animator and did the mirror sequence in *Snow White,* the atmosphere in the studio was alive with creativity, a marriage of many minds and talents. It was great to work under those conditions. We fabricated whole characters from thin air. We made life happen in cartoon form. There were no movie actors to fall back on to make the cartoon figures click. From our imagination we created frame by frame spontaneity.

The design of the human characters bothered Disney the most. Although, as in all later features, live models were used for the animators to achieve realism (Marjorie Belcher, the wife of animator Art Babbitt, posed for Snow White, and Louis Hightower for the Prince), it was for the drawing of the central human characters that Disney was most severely criticized.

Archer Winsten, in criticizing the film for the *New York Post,* wrote:

I am completely at a loss to understand how anyone can fail to sense the difference in the quality of draftsmanship between the animals and the dwarfs on the one hand and Snow White, Prince Charming, the Huntsman, and the Wicked Queen. Now to place it on an artistic plane, one can say that the former come to life completely whereas the latter remain drawings, not very pleasing ones, that move.

The Disney staff was more acutely aware of this problem than many may have guessed. They deliberately brought Prince Charming into the picture for only two brief scenes (at the beginning and the end), because they felt he looked unbearably stiff. (Today, ironically enough, with the soft, cuddly style of drawing on the outs and more realistic drawing popular, the Prince looks better than any of the other human characters in the film.)

The design of the Dwarfs provided a challenge of a different kind. Here the idea was to create seven distinct personalities who would be readily identifiable visually, not by their voices or actions. Once the characters' names were set, the artists went to work on their conceptions of the Dwarfs. These were revised and revised again before meeting with general approval. In general, the orders on these revisions was to make them look "more cute." Along these lines, someone came up with the idea of having Dopey's clothes and hat be far oversized, giving him a floppy, carefree look. The final version of the character was patterned after character comedian Eddie Collins.

According to one contemporary account:

Posture was also an important factor in defining the dwarfs' personalities. Doc always stands well back on his heels, his hands pressed behind whenever possible, which adds to his pompousness. Bashful's back is slightly arched and his stomach is out. Frequently he stands on one foot and twists the other around his ankle. . . . Grumpy has a slight hunch to his shoulders and a swagger to his walk which makes him look pugilistic.

Matching the voices to these characters was another important step. Disney auditioned dozens of young girls for the role of Snow White, staying in his office while their voices were piped through, so he wouldn't be affected by their appearance. Reportedly, he turned down Deanna Durbin for the job, saying she sounded too mature. He finally decided on a young girl named Adriana Caselotti, whose high-pitched voice still sounds disconcerting to this writer whenever he sees the film, although, it must be admitted, this discomfiture disappears after the first few scenes.

For the Dwarfs, various actors and veteran studio jack-of-all-trades Pinto Colvig (who was also the voice of Goofy) were pressed into service. In a few special cases distinctive voices were sought. Vaudeville comic Roy Atwell, famous for his spoonerisms (substituting the first syllables of consecutive words), was hired to play Doc, and he used his amusing malaprops as part of the character. When comedian Billy Gilbert read in *Variety* that one of the Dwarfs was to be called Sneezy, he telephoned Disney, who agreed to an impromptu audition. In Walt's office, Gilbert went into his famous sneezing routine; Disney smiled and said "You're my man."

Lucille LaVerne, a skilled actress most famous for her old hag characterizations in such films as *Orphans of the Storm* and *A Tale of Two Cities,* was the ideal choice for both the voice and model of the Queen-turned-Witch.

Of course, there was no voice problem when it came to Dopey, who was cast as a mute. At first, it was reported that he was going to be a chatterbox, but then someone came up with the marvelous idea of enhancing his endearing witlessness by having him remain silent (also provoking the comment that he was patterned after Harpo Marx). In the film his condition is explained by one of the Dwarfs, who, asked by Snow White if he can talk, replies: "He don't know—he never tried!"

Music played a more important role in the making of *Snow White* than in virtually any other Disney film, excepting, of course, *Fantasia,* for the songs in *Snow White* were designed from the very beginning to become integral parts of the story. (Reportedly, some twenty-five tunes were written before Disney settled on the eight used in the film.) What is more, however, the *entire film* was planned out to a musical beat. Some examples are obvious, such as the prolonged sequence that begins with Snow White and the animals in the forest, and ends with them going into the song "Whistle While You Work" in the Dwarfs' cottage. Between those two points, all movements, and all of Snow White's dialogue, are done in rhythm. The introduction of the Dwarfs in the mine, picking away in time to the "dig dig dig" verse they sing, is just a rhythmical lead-in to the marching theme of "Heigh Ho," which they sing as they walk back home.

Naturally, the most prominent and important aspect of *Snow White* was the visuals, and it was here that Disney did his most impressive work. The film is filled to overflowing with beautiful images, both spectacular and throwaway. Those in the former category owed much to the new multiplane camera, which, although it wasn't ready when animation began on *Snow White,* still was used in quite a few scenes.

In Snow White's run through the forest, there are many dark, winding, ominous trees in the foreground as well as in the background. As she scurries through, her mind visualizes various distortions: driftwood in the stream becomes alligators, hollows in the trees become elongated eyes staring at her, etc. What is important here is that Snow White is not running on a straight path, parallel to our eye view, but on a wildly twisting path that takes her back and forth at varying distances from the camera, with material passing in front of her as well as behind her. The feeling of *depth* is astounding.

The Queen's transformation scene is justifiably famous, a marvel of *directing* and *editing* as well as animation. After mixing the brew in her harshly candlelit laboratory, with her pet raven observing on the sidelines, she pulls the cup close to her, and we see her reflection on the side of the glass. She swallows it down, and starts to gag on the drink, as the entire room begins to spin around her! One by one in the maze we see the characteristics of the Witch overtake her—the scream turning her hair a ragged white, her hands growing into masses of wrinkles and bones, her voice changing into a cackle. When done, she has her back to us, and turns around in her black-hooded cape, keeping her face covered in best Dr. Jekyll fashion, until the camera moves in and she unveils her ugly countenance for the first time.

Much of the horror in this scene is conveyed not by the Witch, but by the reactions of her pet raven, who is truly frightened when the Queen completes her metamorphosis.

Cartoonist Al Kilgore feels that "the witch's trip from her castle to the forest, on her way to the Dwarfs' cottage, in the fog-shrouded dawn is the most under-rated scene in the entire film. It is the most subtle use of multiplane, color, and realistic animation."

Color is used with great care throughout the film. It was decided that to employ the bright, vivid colors of the one-reel cartoons throughout a feature would be a mistake. Instead, muted colors are used in most sequences (as in the forest, where there are no really rich greens) so that key color sequences would stand out all the more. A prominent example is the stunning silhouette of the Dwarfs marching home over a log, set against a dazzling sunset.

More than anything else, people were impressed with *Snow White*'s realistic touches in 1937; they are just as striking today. Few cartoons, before or since, depicted rain so vividly—not just having a torrent of drops superimposed over a setting, but actually showing the drops splashing on the ground! Seldom had there been such a concentration on shadows, from realistic ones such as that of the Huntsman as he towers over Snow White in the forest, to deliberately exaggerated ones cast by the Dwarfs' lanterns as they tiptoe into the darkened room where Snow White is asleep.

Few people will ever forget the menacing gleam of the Huntsman's knife just before he raises it to kill Snow White. And having the face in the mirror blur as wisps of smoke rise around it . . . well, it was just too much.

Other little things stand out in memory: Dopey's marvelous expressions, tongue protruding from the side of his mouth when he shows determination, eyes rolling in carefree abandon as he snaps his fingers and dances with Snow White . . . the haunting establishing shot of the Castle at twilight, seen from the forest below through a brace of branches as the Queen is about to make her potion . . . and the famous scene of Snow White's face reflected in the well when she sings "I'm Wishing."

There is also something more than mere animation in the final sequences of the film. The animals rushing to get the Dwarfs, the Griffithlike intercutting between the Dwarfs riding bareback and the Witch trying to escape, as lightning and thunder help set the mood, and then the absolute deadly silence after the Witch's fall over the cliff, with the Dwarfs timidly peering over the edge as two vultures silently swoop down into the mist to claim their prey.

Without seeing it, it's difficult to envision the emotional impact of *Snow White and the Seven Dwarfs*. There is terror (and that is the correct word) in the horrific scenes of the Queen/Witch, and there is heartrending sorrow in the apparent death of Snow White, with the Dwarfs' unspeakable sadness. (Mike

Barrier has commented on Grumpy's reaction in particular: "He's obviously crushed almost beyond endurance, his eyes wide with horror and disbelief. Grumpy's relationship with Snow White is handled very well; his attitude toward her changes subtly, so that his grief is more affecting.")

But most of all the film exudes a feeling of joy, a radiant glow of happiness that is so persuasive that, at the end of the film, you're ready to believe that somewhere in this world there must be happy endings such as this—they've just *got* to be real.

There is no way to overstate the effect of *Snow White and the Seven Dwarfs* on the film industry, the moviegoing public, and the world in general.

Howard Barnes of the *New York Herald Tribune* wrote:

> After seeing *Snow White and the Seven Dwarfs* for the third time, I am more certain than ever that it belongs with the few great masterpieces of the screen. It is one of those rare works of inspired artistry that weaves an irresistible spell around the beholder. Walt Disney has created worlds of sheer enchantment before with his animated cartoons, but never has he taken us so completely within their magic bounds. *Snow White and the Seven Dwarfs* is more than a completely satisfying entertainment, more than a perfect moving picture, in the full sense of that term. It offers one a memorable and deeply enriching experience.

His comments were echoed by critics around the world, but more importantly by the public. It ran for an unprecedented five weeks at New York's Radio City Music Hall, an amazing thirty-one weeks in Paris, and set new attendance records around the world.

It was dubbed into ten languages, with such titles as *Blanche Neige et les Sept Nains* (France) and *Schneewittchen und die Sieben Dwerge* (Germany). It was under a partial ban in several countries, such as England, where censors ruled that children under sixteen would not be allowed to see the film unless accompanied by adults, for fear of the tots having nightmares after seeing the film's horror sequences. Most of the other restrictions in countries ranging from South Africa to the Netherlands were lifted in response to public outcry (having been presold on the film by the same merchandising boom that took root in this country). At one point there was talk of Lily Pons recording the voice of Snow White for the French-language print, but apparently nothing came of it.

In Hollywood, rival movie studios gave serious consideration to full-length animated features, which a year before they wouldn't have touched. Paramount insisted that Max Fleischer, who supplied them with *Popeye* and *Betty Boop* cartoons, produce a cartoon feature; the result was *Gulliver's Travels*, which was released for Christmas 1939. (It's interesting to note that Fleischer had made his own version of *Snow White* in 1932—a wildly surreal interpretation of the fairy tale starring Betty Boop.) Universal announced that its resident cartoon producer, Walter Lantz, would make a feature called *Aladdin and His Wonderful Lamp,* on a budget of $750,000. (*Snow White,* which had originally been budgeted at $250,000, wound up costing $1,480,000.) Lantz even signed up Disney's music staffer Frank Churchill, but this feature never came to fruition.

Warner Brothers' cartoon department had no thoughts of doing a feature, but they did make one atypically "serious" short, *Tom Thumb in Trouble* (1940, directed by Chuck Jones), which was clearly patterned after the Disney style, and even had an original song. Several years later, *Snow White* was parodied more pointedly by Bob Clampett in *Coal Black and de Sebben Dwarfs,* a lightning-paced cartoon using deliberately outrageous black stereotypes. In recent years this has become a great favorite with animation buffs, not least of all because of its takeoffs on specific scenes and details from the Disney fairy-tale feature.

In 1938 it was estimated that *Snow White* had earned $4.2 million in the United States and Canada alone. After its eighth reissue in 1993* that total had swelled to more than $80 million. In 1989, *USA Today* computed that if one adjusted for inflation and changing box-office prices, *Snow White*'s theatrical earnings up to that time would exceed six *billion* dollars! When the film made its long-awaited video debut in 1994, it outsold *Jurassic Park* (its contemporary "rival" for release that fall) to become the biggest-selling video of all time.

As for Walt Disney, *Snow White* was little more than an experiment. "We've worked hard and spent a lot of money, and by this time we're all a little tired of it," he told reporter Paul Harrison just before the film's release. "I've seen so much of *Snow White* that I am conscious only of the places where it could be improved. You see, we've learned such a lot since we started this thing! I wish I could yank it back and do it all over again."

So for Walt Disney *Snow White and the Seven Dwarfs* was not a crowning achievement, as so many critics were to say. For him, it was only the beginning.

*for details on the 1993 restoration of *Snow White,* see page 298

PINOCCHIO

RELEASED BY RKO RADIO PICTURES; WORLD PREMIERE, February 7, 1940, released February 23, 1940. Technicolor. Based on the story by Collodi (Carlo Lorenzini). Supervising directors: Ben Sharpsteen, Hamilton Luske. Sequence directors: Bill Roberts, Norman Ferguson, Jack Kinney, Wilfred Jackson, T. Hee. Animation directors: Fred Moore, Franklin Thomas, Milton Kahl, Vladimir Tytla, Ward Kimball, Arthur Babbitt, Eric Larson, Wolfgang Reitherman. Story adaptation: Ted Sears, Otto Englander, Webb Smith, William Cottrell, Joseph Sabo, Erdman Penner, Aurelius Battaglia. Music and lyrics: Leigh Harline, Ned Washington, Paul J. Smith. Art directors: Charles Philippi, Hugh Hennesy, Kenneth Anderson, Dick Kelsey, A. Kendall O'Connor, Terrell Stapp, Thor Putnam, John Hubley, McLaren Stewart, Al Zinnen. Character designers: Albert Hurter, Joe Grant, John P. Miller, Campbell Grant, Martin Provensen, John Walbridge. Animators: Jack Campbell, Berny Wolf, Don Towsley, Oliver M. Johnston, Jr., Don Lusk, John Lounsbery, Norman Tate, John Bradbury, Lynn Karp, Charles Nichols, Art Palmer, Joshua Meador, Don Tobin, Robert Martsch, George Rowley, John McManus, Don Patterson, Preston Blair, Les Clark, Marvin Woodward, Hugh Fraser, John Elliotte. Backgrounds: Claude Coats, Merle Cox, Ed Starr, Ray Huffine. Running time: 88 minutes.

Songs: "When You Wish Upon a Star," "Little Woodenhead," "Hi Diddle Dee Dee (An Actor's Life for Me)," "I've Got No Strings," "Give a Little Whistle."

Voices: Dickie Jones (Pinocchio), Christian Rub (Geppetto), Cliff Edwards (Jiminy Cricket), Evelyn Venable (The Blue Fairy), Walter Catlett (J. Worthington Foulfellow), Frankie Darro (Lampwick),

Geppetto puts the finishing touches on his wooden doll as
Figaro, the cat, and Cleo, the goldfish, look on admiringly.
© *Walt Disney Productions*

Charles Judels (Stromboli and The Coachman), Don
Brodie (Barker).

Pinocchio is one of Disney's most visually innovative films and also his "meatiest" animated feature. If
parents worried about their young ones having bad
dreams after watching *Snow White*, they would have
done well to spare them the trauma of seeing *Pinocchio,* which has some of the most terrifying scenes of
any of Disney's films—although, oddly enough, much
of the terror, and some of the nuances of the allegory,
are too subtle for very young minds to understand.

Although *Pinocchio* has a definite direction, the
story is very episodic. Indeed, five months' worth of
animation was scrapped at one point during production in order to start from scratch.

But the film does not seem to ramble, and its
sequences tie together quite naturally. The emotional

high points are cleverly spaced throughout the film so
that one will not dissipate the impact of the other.

Jiminy Cricket sings "When You Wish Upon a
Star" over the main titles; we see him finish the song
as he rests on a shelf above a storybook entitled *Pinocchio.* He says hello to the audience and, referring to
the song's message (that when you wish upon a star
your dream will come true), says, "I bet some of you
don't believe that." He tells us that he didn't believe
it either until a startling experience changed his
mind. He opens the storybook and starts to narrate
the tale of Pinocchio.

One night, the only lighted window in town was
that of the wood-carver, Geppetto. "So," says Jiminy,
"I hopped over," and the camera literally hops into
town, toward the shop, where Jiminy creeps in and
makes himself at home.

Geppetto comes in and finishes painting the smile

Jiminy and Pinocchio (partially converted into a jackass) wonder how to save Geppetto. © *Walt Disney Productions*

Cecil B. De Mille poses with Pinocchio and Jiminy Cricket in this publicity still for the *Lux Radio Theatre,* which broadcast the story on Christmas Day, 1939. *CBS photo; courtesy David Chierichetti*

on his latest marionette, that of a little boy he names Pinocchio. Before he goes to sleep, Geppetto looks up and sees the Wishing Star; he wishes that somehow Pinocchio could be a real live boy. As he sleeps, the Blue Fairy descends from the sky into his shop and transforms Pinocchio into a living being—albeit still a wooden one. She tells him that if he can prove himself brave, unselfish, and able to tell right from wrong, he will become a real live boy. When Jiminy interrupts to explain what a conscience is, the Blue Fairy decides to appoint him Pinocchio's official conscience—which Jiminy hopes will earn him a gold badge.

At this point Geppetto wakes up and, with his cat Figaro and goldfish Cleo, celebrates Pinocchio's miraculous transformation. The next morning he sends Pinocchio off to school, but on his way he encounters a sly fox named J. Worthington Foulfellow ("Honest John") and his feline sidekick Gideon. When they realize what Pinocchio really is, they sense a way to make a small fortune. The Fox dissuades Pinocchio from going to school by telling him the wonders of the stage, singing "An Actor's Life for Me," and succeeding in getting Pinocchio stagestruck. Jiminy's admonitions go unheeded.

That night Jiminy goes to see Pinocchio's premiere as part of Stromboli's puppet show. He comes out and sings "I've Got No Strings," and does a dance with a group of other marionettes. Although he is unsure of himself, his fumbling only makes him more popular with the audience. From this Jiminy concludes that perhaps that *is* the life for Pinocchio.

He goes to bid his wooden friend good-bye aboard his wagon in the troupe's caravan, only to discover that Pinocchio is locked in a cage! Stromboli is a wicked slave driver who has threatened to chop Pinocchio into firewood if he does not obey. Jiminy tries to undo the lock on the cage, but to no avail. Just then who should appear but the Blue Fairy, who asks Pinocchio how he got into this predicament. He invents a tall tale about the situation, and as he spins the yarn, his nose grows longer and longer—even sprouting branches! The Fairy explains that "a lie grows and grows until it's as plain as the nose on your face." He promises never to do it again, and she decides to give him (and Jiminy) a second chance. She unlocks the cage, enabling them to escape and start anew.

But it isn't long before they run into Foulfellow and Gideon once more. This time, the Fox convinces Pinocchio to join a band of young boys who are headed for Pleasure Island. Jiminy goes along to keep an eye on his ward. Little do they dream that the Fox has been hired by an unscrupulous coachman who sends them to the island from which they "never come back . . . as boys." When they arrive, he exhorts them to have all the fun they want. "Give a bad boy enough rope and he'll soon make a jackass of himself."

Late that night all is dark and deserted on the island, except in the pool hall (shaped like an eight ball), where Pinocchio and his newfound friend, Lampwick, are playing pool, smoking cigars, and drinking beer. Jiminy tries to talk Pinocchio out of such behavior, but he refuses to listen, so Jiminy stalks out. Lampwick makes fun of Jiminy's warnings.

"You'd think something was going to happen," he says mockingly, at which moment he sprouts donkey's ears! While Pinocchio is gawking at him, Lampwick grows a tail. Pinocchio laughs—in a donkey's voice—and Lampwick finds this funny, until his own laugh becomes a hee-haw. Then Pinocchio's ears turn mulelike. Lampwick looks in a mirror and grows frantic, crying out in fear. Within an instant he has become a donkey!

Meanwhile, Jiminy has seen what is happening on the other side of the island—boys-turned-asses are being shipped overseas by the mercenary scoundrel who brought them there. He hurries back to grab Pinocchio just in time to stop him from the same fate. They run to the edge of the island and jump off a high cliff into the ocean below. They swim to shore and return to Geppetto's workshop, only to find it deserted. A dove brings them a message from the Blue Fairy explaining that Geppetto went to sea and was swallowed by Monstro, the Whale, but he is still alive inside Monstro's giant stomach.

Pinocchio announces that he must save his father . . . and Jiminy reluctantly goes along. They dive into the water, weighted down, and ask the fish about Monstro's whereabouts, causing them to scatter in all directions. When they do find the Whale, it's just as Monstro is about to have lunch; when he opens his gigantic mouth, Pinocchio is caught in the avalanche of water and fish that go inside. Once there, however, he is fished up by Geppetto, who is still aboard his little, wrecked boat with Figaro and Cleo.

There is a happy reunion, but then Geppetto tells the boy that it is hopeless. Pinocchio disagrees and says that if they light a fire, Monstro will sneeze, and they can get out on the raft Geppetto has built. They manage to do so, but once outside, they see that Monstro is angry about the trick they've played, and is coming after them. There is a frantic chase, with Pinocchio and Geppetto paddling for their lives; they try to reach a rocky cove where Monstro cannot follow, but they are forced to abandon their raft when the Whale's tail lashes down on it.

Floating in the water, Geppetto tells Pinocchio to save himself, but the boy will hear none of it. He drags Geppetto toward the cove and freedom. But when the wood-carver wakes up onshore, joined by Jiminy, he sees Pinocchio's body lying in a pool of water—dead.

Back in Geppetto's workshop, there is great sorrow as Pinocchio lies on the bed, his friends grieving his noble death. But then the Blue Fairy's voice is heard, echoing her promise that if Pinocchio were to prove himself worthy, he would become a real live boy—and he does. It is, indeed, a miracle, and joy becomes elation. During the celebration Jiminy says, "This is practically where I came in," and steps outside. He looks up, sees the Blue Fairy's twinkling star, and thanks her for all she's done. Just then a shiny gold medal appears on his chest, reading, "Official Conscience/18 Kt." Jiminy loves it and uses it to twinkle back at the star. As the camera pulls back over the peaceful village—with the star shining above—we hear Jiminy and chorus reprise "When You Wish Upon a Star."

Pinocchio is a film of amazing detail and brilliant conception. Sheer technical virtuosity would mean nothing, if it were not employed so beautifully. Like all of Disney's best work, it has tremendous emotional impact as well, although as a whole the film is characterized by action, excitement, and terror more than humor.

Indeed, one can see where the Disney staff was hard pressed to maintain a humorous element throughout the film. Pinocchio himself is not a funny character, although he is more interesting and appealing than many other Disney "heroes." Jiminy could hardly be called comedy relief, since he serves such an important function in the film, but he *is* one of the characters who provides humorous sidelights on otherwise straightforward scenes. (When Pinocchio is swallowed by Monstro, Jiminy is left outside; he bangs on the Whale's locked teeth, shouting, "Hey, Blubbermouth, open up!" In fact, most of Jiminy's humor is in the form of contemporary wisecracks.)

Geppetto's absentmindedness is good for several laughs and serves to relieve tension in a number of scenes . . . as when he's reunited with Pinocchio in Monstro's belly, but somehow finds himself embracing a fish! At the end of the film, when Pinocchio comes to life, he asks, "Father, whatcha crying for?" and Geppetto replies, "Because you're dead, Pinocchio . . . now lie down"—before doing a whopping double-take.

Similarly, Figaro offsets much of the sentimentality in the film with his puckish sense of humor. For instance, while Geppetto is wondering why Pinocchio hasn't come home from school, Figaro's only thought is eating the celebration dinner that's been prepared. While Geppetto is wishing at night for a real boy of his own, Figaro is tossing and turning in frustration, unable to get to sleep.

Foulfellow's cohort Gideon is one of the few purely comic characters in the film, offsetting his partner's treachery with constant bungling.

The elements of terror are much more vivid and widespread in the film. While traveling with Stromboli, Pinocchio has his first taste of the seamy side of life. "When you grow too old," says the puppeteer, "you will make good firewood," as he tosses his

hatchet into the remnants of another ragged marionette, now a pile of splinters and sawdust, a meekly
smiling face the only reminder of its former "life."

The Pleasure Island segment of the film builds
masterfully to its exciting climax. At the outset, the
neon lights, rides, and general atmosphere of the
place have a decidedly creepy tone. (With one throwaway gag: the pool hall is in the shape of an eight ball,
with a cue standing alongside, a neat takeoff on the
Trylon and Perisphere of the 1939 New York World's
Fair.) But the first shock comes when we see the
coachman preparing the donkeys for shipment.
When he finds one who hasn't yet lost his ability to
talk, he shoves him against the wall with others like
him, and (in a menacing shot, showing his hulking
shadow covering the frightened young "boys") he
cracks his whip.

Back in the pool room, the transformation of
Lampwick starts almost as a joke, with his ears. But
the direction of the scene and the music create a growing sense of fear and fright. He begs for Pinocchio
to help him, and we see Pinocchio's reaction over
Lampwick's shoulder as his hands turn into hoofs. As
he becomes more frantic, the music grows louder and
more discordant. Finally, with the metamorphosis
almost complete, he screams "Mama!!" his cry turning into a long, loud bray as we see the finishing
touches of his shadow on the wall. William K. Everson
has called this scene "surely one of the screen's
supreme moments of horror," and that it is, as downright terrifying as any fright sequences devised by
others for live-action movies.

The Monstro sequence is the film's other highlight, a matchless exercise in *excitement*, made all the
more fascinating because of the very concept of being
inside a whale, much less being chased by one. The
shot of Monstro's mouth opening, as seen from the
inside, as a cascade of water, fish, and Pinocchio pour
in is unforgettable. The chase is beautifully staged,
draining audience emotion as Pinocchio and Geppetto do their best to outdistance the seagoing monster. The tension reaches its apex when Monstro tries
to plow into them, misses, but in turning around
lashes his tail behind him. Geppetto looks up and a
broad shadow starts to cover the raft. We look up with
him and get a first-person view of the tail about to
crash down. "JUMP!" shouts the wood-carver, as the
tail strikes the raft and smashes it into a thousand
pieces.

The underwater scenes with Pinocchio and
Jiminy are much more easygoing and a lot of fun. As
they drop to the ocean floor, Pinocchio says, "Gee,
what a big place," his words gurgling from the sound
track. (How this effect was accomplished was a source
of great wonderment at the time of the film's release—
proof that the full potentials of sound had hardly
been scratched in the dozen-odd years since its development.)

There are other delightful, lighthearted scenes:

Geppetto's workshop coming alive with his dozens of
music boxes, each an intricate contraption with a myriad of moving parts (and for each of which, incidentally, a model was built for animators to work from);
Pinocchio's stage debut, singing "I've Got No Strings"
as backdrops and wooden co-stars are changed all
around him; Foulfellow and Gideon marching along
with Pinocchio through the city streets as they sing
"Hi Diddle Dee Dee (An Actor's Life for Me)" (this
scene "shot" from the city rooftops); and the sidelight
glimpses of Figaro and Cleo, who became very popular Disney characters, Figaro appearing in a number
of subsequent short cartoons.

In addition to well-executed action sequences and
delightful characterizations, *Pinocchio* has some fantastic detail work made possible by the multiplane
camera, most notably a breathtaking shot of the village on the morning after Pinocchio's coming to life.
The shot shows the church bell tower in the foreground, and the city below, stretching off as far as the
eye can see, toward the distant hills. This is not a
painting, but an amazingly lifelike panorama, each
house having depth and dimension of its own. Reportedly, some twelve separate planes were employed
in the filming of this one shot, which pans down into
the town and Geppetto's workshop for the next scene.

When Jiminy first comes into Geppetto's house,
he warms up by the fireplace; the flames not only look
real, but there is actual heat distortion above them!
Shadows on both characters and objects in this opening segment are also quite lifelike, and on the other
end of the spectrum we get an amusing view of
Pinocchio, as Cleo the fish sees him blurred and
elongated through her fishbowl.

When Jiminy attempts to stop Pinocchio from
going with Honest John and Gideon, he chases after
them, and we see the villains from Jiminy's point of
view. When he jumps up, the camera cuts to a bird's-
eye view with Jiminy landing atop Honest John's hat.
The use of perspective and cutting are most impressive here.

One of the film's most amazing pieces of animation, from a technical standpoint, occurs when Pinocchio is trapped in a cage inside Stromboli's wagon.
The wagon is moving, and Pinocchio is inside the
swinging cage, while lightning flashes outside cause
changes in color and shadows!

Once again the sound track is as important to the
film's success as the picture on the screen. Disney chose
twelve-year-old child actor Dickie Jones for his lead
character because he had "a typical nice boy's voice."
The role of Jiminy Cricket gave a new lease on life to
Cliff Edwards, who had scored a hit in the 1920s as
"Ukulele Ike," and added his ebullience to many films
of the 1930s. Unlike most other characters originating
in Disney features, Jiminy became a staple of Disney
films, appearing in one other feature (*Fun and Fancy
Free*), numerous shorts (most notably the *I'm No
Fool* series) , and on the *Mickey Mouse Club* television

show. Edwards later did the voice for one of the Black Crows in *Dumbo* as well.

Christian Rub *was* Geppetto, having essayed essentially the same characterization in most of his other films; indeed, he served not only as the voice, but as the model for the character. Evelyn Venable's pure, sweet voice was ideal for the Blue Fairy, an ethereally lovely blonde, blue-eyed woman. (Walt insisted that "although she must give the appearance of loveliness, she can't look like a glamour girl." Marjorie Belcher, who had posed for Snow White, was the model for the Fairy.) Walter Catlett, like Christian Rub, was used to playing characters much like the one he voiced in *Pinocchio*, J. Worthington Foulfellow, and Frankie Darro, the voice of Lampwick, was fairly well established as one of the screen's leading tough kids. Charles Judels's voice as Stromboli was readily recognizable from the whinnying sound of frustration that was the comic actor's trademark.

Miss Venable recalls that she recorded all her lines separately, and they were later intercut with those of the other characters. "I recorded it line by line, each line several times with different inflections, emphasizing different words each time (I kept the pacing about the same each time, though). Then they chose whichever recording captured the dramatic feeling they wanted."

The musical score was one of the finest Paul J. Smith ever wrote for Disney, not only supplementing the action but playing a major role in creating the desired moods. Smith explained to Rose Heylbut of the *Etude Music Magazine* how he prepared the score for the animated film:

The songs are the first basis of the complete score. We like to use them as leitmotifs, to suggest both characters and situations throughout the picture. Take, for instance, the little theme with the hoppity-hop rhythm that symbolizes Jiminy Cricket. It is stated as the Cricket's tune, and appears as the inner voice of a more important theme, or merely as a rhythmic suggestion, in every scene in which Jiminy is about to assume the center of the stage. The star song is sung but twice in the picture, but it appears (in free variation, parallel chords, and so on) in every sequence where Jiminy and the Fairy combine their powers in working out Pinocchio's destiny. The development of these variations of the theme requires the most detailed care. The spectator must be aware of the theme and of its slightly altered form, but neither theme nor

variation may at any time rise to the point of occupying his conscious attention.

In *Pinocchio*, Disney reached not only the height of his powers, but the apex of what many of his (later) critics considered to be the *realm* of the animated cartoon. The wonder, the brilliance of *Pinocchio*, is in depicting the wondrous fantasy of the story—a boy turning into a donkey, a man living on a boat inside the stomach of a whale—things that could not be shown with equal effectiveness by a live-action movie. It was when Disney tried to make his films more and more lifelike that the criticism mounted.

But most critics had only complimentary things to say about *Pinocchio*. Archer Winsten, who had criticized Disney's first feature film, wrote: "The faults that were in *Snow White and the Seven Dwarfs* no longer exist. In writing of *Pinocchio*, you are limited only by your own power of expressing enthusiasm. To put it in the simplest possible terms, this film is fantastically delightful, absolutely perfect, and a work of pure, unadulterated genius."

There were some complaints that Disney had changed the original story and altered its characterizations, but none so strong as that of Paolo Lorenzini, nephew of the fable's author, who asked the Italian Ministry of Popular Culture to sue Walt Disney for libel in portraying Pinocchio "so he easily could be mistaken for an American," when, indeed, he was Italian. Apparently nothing came of the protest.

The film cost an estimated $2.5 million. It was dubbed into seven languages at a reported additional cost of $65,000. Unfortunately, at the time of *Pinocchio*'s release, the European market was cut off, due to the war, and Disney lost one of his major sources of revenue for the film. This problem continued through the mid-1940s, and was partially responsible for Disney's involvement with South America at that time. Nevertheless, the film was successful in the United States, both critically and at the box office, and has since performed admirably in reissue.

With *Pinocchio*, Disney found that his originally stated goal of turning out two feature-length animated films a year was a mere pipe dream, in spite of a staff of approximately eleven hundred, and a new studio facility in Burbank. But in spite of the time factor involved in producing animated features, Disney set to work on a number of projects at once, buying and negotiating for several properties at the same time and seeing to it that his studio would be busier than ever. He then tackled the most ambitious film of his career.

FANTASIA

RELEASED BY RKO RADIO PICTURES; WORLD PREMIERE, November 13, 1940, no general release date. Technicolor, Fantasound. With Leopold Stokowski and the Philadelphia Orchestra. Narrative introductions by Deems Taylor. Production supervisor: Ben Sharpsteen. Story direction: Joe Grant, Dick Huemer. Musical director: Edward H. Plumb. Musical film editor: Stephen Csillag. Recording: William E. Garity, C. O. Slyfield, J. N. A. Hawkins. Running time: 120 minutes.

"Toccata and Fugue in D Minor" by Johann Sebastian Bach. Director: Samuel Armstrong. Story development: Lee Blair, Elmer Plummer, Phil Dike. Art director: Robert Cormack. Animators: Cy Young, Art Palmer, Daniel MacManus, George Rowley, Edwin Aardal, Joshua Meador, Cornett Wood. Background paintings: Joe Stanley, John Hench, Nino Carbe.

"The Nutcracker Suite" by Peter Ilich Tchaikovsky. Director: Samuel Armstrong. Story development: Sylvia Moberly-Holland, Norman Wright, Albert Heath, Bianca Majolie, Graham Heid. Character designers: John Walbridge, Elmer Plummer, Ethel Kulsar. Art directors: Robert Cormack, Al Zinnen, Curtiss D. Perkins, Arthur Byram, Bruce Bushman. Animators: Arthur Babbitt, Les Clark, Don Lusk, Cy Young, Robert Stokes. Background paintings: John Hench, Ethel Kulsar, Nino Carbe.

"The Sorcerer's Apprentice" by Paul Dukas. Director: James Algar. Story development: Perce Pearce, Carl Fallberg. Art directors: Tom Codrick, Charles Philippi, Zack Schwartz. Animation supervision: Fred Moore, Vladimir Tytla. Animators: Les Clark, Riley Thompson, Marvin Woodward, Preston Blair, Edward Love, Ugo D'Orsi, George Rowley, Cornett Wood. Background paintings: Claude Coats, Stan Spohn, Albert Dempster, Eric Hansen.

"The Rite of Spring" by Igor Stravinsky. Directors: Bill Roberts, Paul Satterfield. Story development and research: William Martin, Leo Thiele, Robert Sterner, John Fraser McLeish. Art directors: McLaren Stewart, Dick Kelsey, John Hubley. Animation supervision: Wolfgang Reitherman, Joshua Meador. Animators: Philip Duncan, John McManus, Paul Busch, Art Palmer, Don Tobin, Edwin Aardal, Paul B. Kossoff. Background paintings: Ed Starr, Brice Mack, Edward Levitt. Special camera effects: Gail Papineau, Leonard Pickley.

"Pastoral Symphony" by Ludwig van Beethoven. Directors: Hamilton Luske, Jim Handley, Ford Beebe. Story development: Otto Englander, Webb Smith, Erdman Penner, Joseph Sabo, Bill Peet, George Stallings. Character designer: James Bodrero, John P. Miller, Lorna S. Soderstrom. Art directors: Hugh Hennesy, Kenneth Anderson, J. Gordon Legg, Herbert Ryman, Yale Gracey, Lance Nolley. Animation supervision: Fred Moore, Ward Kimball, Eric Larson, Arthur Babbitt, Oliver M. Johnston, Jr., Don Towsley. Animators: Berny Wolf, Jack Campbell, John Bradbury, James Moore, Milt Neil, Bill Justice, John Elliotte, Walt Kelly, Don Lusk, Lynn Karp, Murray McLennan, Robert W. Youngquist, Harry Hamsel. Background paintings: Claude Coats, Ray Huffine, W. Richard Anthony, Arthur Riley, Gerald Nevius, Roy Forkum.

"Dance of the Hours" by Amilcare Ponchielli. Directors: T. Hee, Norman Ferguson. Character designers: Martin Provensen, James Bodrero, Duke Russell, Earl Hurd. Art directors: Kendall O'Connor, Harold Doughty, Ernest Nordli. Animation supervision: Norman Ferguson, Animators: John Lounsbery, Howard Swift, Preston Blair, Hugh Fraser, Harvey Toombs, Norman Tate, Hicks Lokey, Art Elliott, Grant Simmons, Ray Patterson, Franklin Grundeen. Background paintings: Albert Dempster, Charles Conner.

"Night on Bald Mountain" by Modest Mussorgsky, and "Ave Maria" by Franz Schubert. Director: Wilfred Jackson. Story development: Campbell Grant, Arthur Heinemann, Phil Dike. Art directors: Kay Nielsen, Terrell Stapp, Charles Payzant, Thor Putnam. Animation supervision: Vladimir Tytla.

Animators: John McManus, William N. Shull, Robert W. Carlson, Jr., Lester Novros, Don Patterson. Background paintings: Merle Cox, Ray Lockrem, Robert Storms, W. Richard Anthony. Special animation effects: Joshua Meador, Miles E. Pike, John F. Reed, Daniel MacManus. Special camera effects: Gail Papineau, Leonard Pickley. Special lyrics for "Ave Maria" by Rachel Field; "Ave Maria" chorus directed by Charles Henderson; Julietta Novis, soloist.

Fantasia was Disney's most ambitious undertaking and in all respects his most controversial endeavor. Not much of a money-maker in its initial release, it has, in the past few years, become a phenomenal favorite of the younger generation, who have no concern with Disney's tampering with the musical pieces, and no deep thoughts about possible sacrilege in pictorializing these compositions. They are simply bowled over by the film's imagination.

The idea grew out of plans to make a Mickey Mouse short of "The Sorcerer's Apprentice" in 1938. Reportedly, Disney met the great conductor Leopold Stokowski at a party around this time (Stokowski had been working in several Hollywood features in the late 1930s), and mentioned the idea. Stokowski was enthusiastic and agreed to conduct the score for the cartoon, which he did in Los Angeles with a group of local musicians.

But Stokowski, always an innovator, prodded Disney about expanding his idea and doing a whole series of visualizations of musical themes. Disney was intrigued, and embarked on a series of discussions with the conductor and members of his staff. Disney also brought in Deems Taylor, the popular musicologist whose reputation for making music meaningful to American audiences (notably on New York Philharmonic radio broadcasts) made him a logical candidate for inclusion in this project.

The result, even the film's critics (and they were many) had to admit, was completely different from anything that had ever been done before.

The opening title card appears on a silent screen; as it fades, a curtain opens to reveal a blue cyclorama, as silhouetted musicians, talking among themselves, walk onto the orchestral platform. As they sit down and begin to tune up, yellow light emanates from each of the instruments playing.

Then Deems Taylor walks onto the podium to introduce the film. Although wearing white tie and tails, he puts his hand in his pocket when he begins to speak (a rather too-obvious attempt to show that this is not going to be a highbrow occasion). He tells us that there are three kinds of music: music that tells a story, music that paints a picture, and "absolute music," or music for music's sake. The first piece of music, the "Toccata and Fugue in D Minor," fits into this latter category, so the Disney artists have illustrated it in abstract fashion.

The silhouette of Leopold Stokowski walks to the

Poetry in motion, from the "Dance of the Hours" sequence. © *Walt Disney Productions*

Chinese mushrooms strike a pose from "The Nutcracker Suite." © *Walt Disney Productions*

podium. As the first strains of the piece are played, bright yellow light is cast upon his face from below, indicating the sound coming from the orchestra slightly below him.

The first images we see are colored silhouettes of the various musicians, some superimposed on each other. Then Stokowski's face dissolves into a vision of clouds. We see a partial picture of bows playing on

Mickey Mouse, as the Sorcerer's Apprentice, teaches the
brooms to do his work.   © *Walt Disney Productions*

floating strings, and then a series of impressions of
waves, concentric circles, beams of light, and other
patterns in time with the music on the sound track.
The beams of light finally consolidate into a huge
orange sun, as at sunrise, and as the final strains of the
composition are heard, Stokowski's figure is superimposed over the brilliant orange sky. During the final
notes the camera moves in to end the piece on a tight
shot of the conductor.

We return to Deems Taylor, who introduces the
next piece on the program, "The Nutcracker Suite."
A close-up of Stokowski fades into a screenful of fireflies, which evolve into luminescent ballerinas, who
perform "The Dance of the Sugar Plum Fairies." The
dew droplets these creatures spread throughout the
forest wake up other little fairies who cascade around
the forest for a most ethereal celebration of nature.

The second section of the suite, "Chinese Dance,"
is performed by mushrooms, who assume an Oriental
appearance with their crowns becoming hats for their
wide, round heads.

"The Dance of the Reed Flutes" is enacted by

petals cascading in the breeze and mingling with the
lily pads floating on the water. This segues into an
underwater setting for "Arabian Dance," highlighting
a group of fish with magnificent, flowing tails. A flurry
of bubbles, which introduced the scene, also provides
the transition aboveground for the next sequence, the
"Russian Dance," energetically performed by thistles,
whose long, lean shape resembles that of a cossack,
and orchids, whose petals are made to appear like
peasant dresses.

This dance ends with the flower-dancers in close-
up, filling the screen. As they form a still life, the
picture dissolves into a vision of the forest. Butterflies
fly through and bring with them the colors of autumn,
causing the leaves to drop from their branches and
create the setting for the final segment of the composition, "The Waltz of the Flowers." The swirling leaves
form a ballet troupe, followed by milkweeds, all of
whom are laid to rest by the Frost Fairies who come
and spread the setting of yet another season. Snowflakes complete the change, and end the ballet with a
lovely snowy pattern.

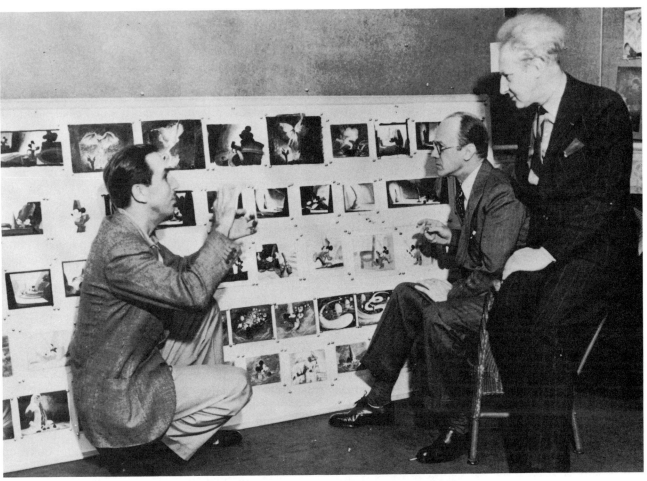

Walt Disney goes over the storyboards for *Fantasia* with
Deems Taylor and Leopold Stokowski. *UPI photo*

The next segment is "The Sorcerer's Apprentice," which opens with the mystical Sorcerer practicing his craft, conjuring up smoky spirits that create the misty form of a butterfly above him. But it's late, and he's ready to go to sleep. He leaves behind his tall, cone-like hat, which glows as an indication of the powers it holds within. His hardworking apprentice (none other than Mickey Mouse), who is tired out from carrying buckets of water back and forth to do his cleaning chores, spies the hat and can't resist trying it out himself. He points his now powerful hands at a broom leaning against the wall, lures it to an upright position, and makes it grow arms and hands that take the bucket for him and do the bulk of his work while he just sits back.

His laziness overcomes him, however, and as the broom's shadow passes over him, going back and forth for water, he falls asleep and dreams of reaching greater heights—controlling cascades of stars in the sky with the flick of a wrist and even having oceans perform as he commands. But he suddenly awakens to find himself waist-deep in water, and an ocean already created before his very eyes by the persistent broom, which walks right over Mickey when he tries to stop it. Frantically, he grabs an ax and (shown in shadow on the wall) splits the broom into dozens of pieces. Then, in unison, each splinter rises up and becomes a broom, complete with arms, hands, and a bucket! They stubbornly march toward the well, pouring the water again and again. Mickey's attempts to bail out the room are doomed to failure. He floats along on his master's book of magic, looking for an antidote to the problem, and is suddenly caught in the swirl of a whirlpool.

By now the brooms are totally submerged, but continue to march underwater, and go through the motions of pouring still more water. Just then, at the head of the stairs, the Sorcerer himself appears, surveys the situation, and, with a majestic sweep of his hands, causes the water to disappear. He summons Mickey forward to reclaim his belongings. His eyes are glowing candles, his expression absolutely piercing. There is perhaps just the faintest hint of amusement. Mickey coyly smiles at him, hands him the broom, and starts to walk away. The Sorcerer takes the broom and whacks Mickey in the rear, sending him out of the room as the music whirls to a close.

The next shot is of Stokowski, again in silhouette on his podium. Suddenly, the silhouette of Mickey Mouse, also dressed in tails, runs up to the platform and tugs on the conductor's coat. He just wants to congratulate Mr. Stokowski for his work. Says the conductor, "Congratulations to you, Mickey." Mickey runs off excitedly, and Stokowski waves after him.

Stravinsky's once revolutionary composition "Rite of Spring" becomes a depiction of the creation of the world, beginning with a cosmos in space and evolving through the universe until a planet is created (first as a sphere that flies right into the camera's eye). Then we first see clouds, hills, volcanoes—giant eruptions that send mountains jutting out of the surface, and lava that carves out patterns in the earth.

Microscopic particles are shown. They form and split and gradually metamorphose into undersea life —first as floating particles, then as fish. From the beginning the earliest living creatures have natural enemies, as these fish discover. Above water, on land, are other beings—dinosaurs, roaming the earth and learning the fight of survival. Pterodactyls fly above land, but one who comes too close to water level is snatched by a sea creature, which pulls the prehistoric bird underneath.

There are enemies on land as well, and the brontosaurus, stalking his domain, confronts and does battle with a stegosaurus, as Nature provides a dramatic setting with rain, thunder, and lightning.

Time passes, and the sun grows brighter, drying everything it touches. The animals migrate, in hope of finding some relief from the blazing heat. One by one they drop to the ground, others managing to carry on into the misty horizon. Soon only skeletons remain.

An eclipse of the sun brings the dawn of a new era. The planet trembles and the land crumbles under the pressure of tremors. Mountains spring up from the ground, other chunks of rock fall off and create caverns and valleys. Finally a new element is added as the ocean roars its presence on the planet. As the eclipse reaches its apex, the planet lies still. Earth has been created.

It is now intermission, and for relief the musician on string bass starts plucking out a jazz tempo. Other musicians join in for a brief, informal jam session. Then Deems Taylor introduces one of the major, unsung stars of this concert: the sound track. Timid at first, it finally comes on camera and shows us how it reproduces various sounds from the orchestra (harp, violin, flute, trumpet, bassoon), concluding with a jazzy solo from the drummer and a final chime from the triangle, which creates, amusingly enough, a triangular shape on the track.

Next on the program is Beethoven's "Pastoral Symphony," interpreted with freedom by the Disney people as a paean to the characters of Greek mythology. By a beautiful countryside, unicorns, centaurs, and nymphs cavort in a gay celebration of life. Female centaurs bathe in the stream, and then spruce up with the help of some enthusiastic cupids, in anticipation of a call by their male friends, who go off with them for an idyllic afternoon. When one female centaur and a male counterpart are left stranded, the cupids go to work and strike up a match between them.

A feast is planned, and wine is pressed for the occasion. Cherubic Bacchus is soon happily soused, blissfully riding about on his donkey, enjoying the party with the others.

But soon clouds cast a grim shadow over the festivities, and a storm brews. It's Zeus, happily tossing bolts of lightning to earth as they are handed to him by Vulcan, who fashions them on his anvil in the clouds. A bolt strikes the wine vat, creating a river of wine, a not unhappy turn of events for Bacchus below. But soon enough Zeus grows tired and goes to sleep, rolling the clouds over him like a blanket. They roll away, and Iris, goddess of the rainbow, signals that all is calm once more. The creatures below come out to admire the sun—symbolized by Apollo, riding a fiery chariot in the sky.

Then, as sunset approaches, Morpheus flies over the land bringing a cloak of darkness. It is time for sleep, and below all is quiet. While above, the crescent moon reveals the goddess Diana, who shoots her arrow into the air and creates the stars that shine down on our peaceful springtime setting.

Now we turn to ballet and "The Dance of the Hours." This charming set piece is beautifully executed by an ostrich, backed by a chorus of her peers, a hippopotamus who emerges from a lily pool in the midst of the Great Hall where all this takes place, a group of elephants who surround the sleeping Hippo, and a male chorus of crocodiles who playfully duet with the lead Hippo and her cronies. For the finale there is a mad chase, with the leering crocodiles leaping after the hippos (the principal figures having done a pas de deux), which climaxes in a grand finale featuring all the hippos, elephants, ostriches, and crocodiles who have appeared in the piece. The camera dollies back through the Great Hall's procession of columns to its entrance, where the iron doors slam shut and crumble off their hinges.

For the finale of the program there is a medley of "Night on Bald Mountain" and "Ave Maria," which, as Taylor explains, provides a picture of the struggle between the profane and the sacred. As night falls, near Bald Mountain, spirits rise in the local graveyard and travel, amid a flurry of devil bats, to the mountain for a celebration of Evil—a ritualistic bow to Tchernobog, the Black God. The flames become dancers, then animals, then lizards, at the whim of the fire monster. The Black God revels in this passionate exhibition; the ghostly figures swirl before the camera as in a whirlpool, with the smoke, flames, and fiery flashes covering the mountainside throughout the night.

Then, with morning approaching, church bells are rung. The Black Monster recoils in horror; with each tolling of the bell he is driven farther back until he hovers on the ground vanquished. As the sky lightens, the specters return to their graves. Monks carrying torches stand out in the morning mist, as they proceed over a bridge and into the forest on their mission. We travel through the dark forest into a beautiful pasture, its canvas painted by the first rays of daylight. The sunlit trees, the clear sky, the clouds create a heavenly vision on earth, as the strains of "Ave Maria" bless God's presence. The camera travels upward as the hymn comes to a close, remaining fixed on the brilliant rays of the sun.

Fantasia is a tribute to the brilliance of Walt Disney's staff of artists and animators. Throughout the 1930s he had urged them to improve their work, sent them to art classes, insisted on greater and still greater quality. Toward what end? Many feared it was moving toward a goal of total realism in animation, which they felt would be disastrous.

Fantasia answered their questions and showed them what the skill of these artists, combined with the imagination of the Disney people, and the progress being made by studio technicians, could accomplish. For here was a whole new concept in animation—not only in appearance, but in content. Here was an opportunity to showcase visual fantasy that would never present itself again.

As much as some of the pictorial ideas bothered music critics, none of the sequences seems to have disturbed Leopold Stokowski, who was in on every phase of preparation for the film. He realized the potential impact of the film, not for his regular followers, or a handful of music aficionados, but for a much wider audience than would ever be seen in a concert hall or listen to a radio concert. He knew that here was a way to create a new medium of presenting this music, not to reduce it to the lowest common denominator, but to enhance the music's inherent qualities with the addition of visuals, and thus intrigue a segment of the public that had kept a closed mind with regard to classical music.

Thus, it was not "sacrilege," as some critics said, to portray the "Rite of Spring" as the creation of the world, or the "Pastoral Symphony" as a mythical celebration.

As Pare Lorentz commented in *McCall's:*

I advise you to disregard the howls from the music critics; *Fantasia* is a Disney and not a classical conception of a concert, and even though the music is broader and more powerful than any you've ever heard from the screen, it is the imagery, and not the scores you will follow during the show. Thus, you can dismiss the complaints of the little

hierarchy of music men who try to make music a sacrosanct, mysterious, and obscure art. Disney has brought it out of the temple, put it in carpet slippers, and an old sweater, and made it work to surround, and support, and synchronize a brilliantly-drawn series of animated color sketches.

Stokowski, said music critic Virgil Thomson at the time, was the only symphonic conductor who "has given himself the trouble to find out something about musical reproduction techniques and to adapt these to the problems of orchestral execution. Alone among the famous musicians who have worked in the films, he has forced the spending of money and serious thought by film producers and engineers."

Thus, it was undoubtedly he who convinced Disney that *Fantasia* warranted something more than the usual sound system. Disney agreed and had his staff, led by chief engineer Bill Garity, look into the concept of a broader recording and playback method for the film. The result was dubbed "Fantasound," and it predated many of the stereophonic "innovations" of the 1950s and 1960s.

The film's score was recorded over a two-month period in 1938 at the Philadelphia Academy of Music. Nine "sound cameras" were at work, one recording the entire orchestra and each of the other eight focusing on one specific section. There were thirty-three microphones in all. Some 420,000 feet of film were used during the marathon recording sessions, of which 18,000 ended up in the final print.

The impact did not come from the method of recording alone, of course. The effect of Fantasound was determined by the playback system, and the first working model was built by RCA at a cost of $100,000. Each additional unit cost $30,000.

Of the process Sam Robin wrote in the *New York Times Magazine:*

When the waters hurl Mickey Mouse down a flight of stairs in Dukas' "The Sorcerer's Apprentice," the music pours out of one corner of the theatre and floods the auditorium . . . [but it] has not been used to play little jokes on the music of the composers represented on the program. It has been used to obtain greater depth and roundness for the works themselves . . .

Great care was taken in producing the ballet sequences of the film as well. Members of the Ballet Russe, notably Roman Jasinsky, Tatiana Riabouchinska, and Irina Baranova, modeled for the elephants, hippos, and ostriches (respectively) in the "Dance of the Hours" sequence. They wholeheartedly approved of the ballet spoof and agreed to pose for the animal caricatures. Indeed, the sequence was one of the least criticized in the entire film, except, ironically, by Pare Lorentz, who praised the feature but noted:

I feel Disney should have had an old-fashioned

low comedy selection in his second section, and I presume he felt that was what he was doing in "The Dance of the Hours," but either the high company of the Messrs. Taylor and Stokowski subdued him, or he felt low comedy out of place in such an austere presentation; whatever his reason, "The Dance of the Hours" isn't as earthy and violent as a number in this place in the concert should have been.

Dance critic Walter Terry wrote that "in *Fantasia* Walt Disney has assembled the richest qualities of his choreography: humans, animals, and flowers dance in ballets which poke fun at dancing and in ballets which exalt it. . . . Dance lovers will find much of *Fantasia* rewarding in its choreographic scope, stimulating in its brilliant use of a great art . . . bringing great dance and simple dance to everyone."

Music critics were less enthusiastic, for nearly every work used in the film had been "adapted" in one way or another to meet animation demands or time restrictions. Stravinsky was reportedly very upset that his "Rite of Spring" had been altered, although the Disney studio has always reported that the composer, after seeing the film, was moved to comment, "Ah yes, I suppose that is just what I meant."

Each critic had different thoughts on various sequences in the film. One of the most frequently criticized was the "Pastoral Symphony," which was one piece of music that had been created with a specific image in mind, and which Disney had matched to an entirely different pictorialization. Furthermore, in the opinion of such critics as John Rosenfield, "Stokowski's conducting of the 'Pastoral' . . . was so distorted as to be objectionable."

Dorothy Thompson, in the *New York Herald Tribune,* wrote:

I left the theater in a condition bordering on nervous breakdown. I felt as though I had been subjected to an attentat, to an assault, but I had no desire to throw myself in adoration before the two masters who were responsible for the brutalization of sensibility in this remarkable nightmare. . . . Since the chief characteristic of this decade of the twentieth century is the collapse of the civilized world, the impetus to the collapse everywhere given by the very persons and groups most certain to be destroyed with it, the *Fantasia* is a social symptom worth this column's recording.

What Miss Thompson and many other critics objected to was not just the specifics of *Fantasia,* but the idea. Disney was attacked on the grounds that the music was not meant to be visualized, and that in doing so he had removed one of music's basic qualities, letting the listener create his own concept of its meaning.

But many other critics, even those with reservations about the film's success, praised Disney for his boldness in undertaking such an experiment in the first place. *Look* magazine called it a "masterpiece" and proclaimed: "Disney revolutionizes movies again . . ." Bosley Crowther in the *Times* deemed it "simply terrific," and Howard Barnes in the *Tribune,* while voicing some qualms about the film's format, still called it "a courageous and distinguished production."

Disney had special plans for *Fantasia*'s release. He wanted to treat it as a concert, instead of a film (there was even talk, for a time, of opening it in concert halls instead of conventional theatres). Because of the expense of installing Fantasound equipment, he planned to have the film playing in a limited number of theatres at any one time, each one having exclusivity in its location. Gradually, the film would move around to other theatres, perpetually playing as a reserved-seat attraction, and perhaps never going into neighborhood theatres at all. He even visualized filming new numbers and inserting them into the print at various times, making *Fantasia* a permanent fixture in movie theatres around the country.

(Debussy's "Clair de Lune" had been part of the film as late as July 1939, when it was still being referred to as "Concert Feature." *Fantasia*, a working title, was kept when no one could think of a better name for the film. When it opened in New York, the souvenir program announced that "from time to time the order and selection of compositions on this program may be changed." They never were. However, the "Clair de Lune" sequence did turn up, incognito, six years later in *Make Mine Music.* Disney had new music written to accompany the completed sequence, which, under the title "Blue Bayou," gave no indication that it had been sitting on the shelf so long.)

From the start there was trouble with Fantasound. Preparing the Broadway Theater in New York (formerly the Colony, where, ironically, *Steamboat Willie* had premiered) with the special sound equipment, a labor dispute arose between the International Alliance of Theatrical Stage Employees and the International Brotherhood of Electrical Workers, as to who had jurisdiction over installation of the new machinery. Fortunately, a compromise was reached, and both unions set to work on twenty-four-hour shifts to get the theatre ready in time for the November 13 opening.

Then, with twelve Fantasound units ready, the government stepped in and declared that national defense priorities would prevent RCA and Disney from completing any further sets for the time being. Plans to open *Fantasia* in seventy-six theatres across the country were scotched.

Although Disney was willing to wait, his backers weren't. These were financially precarious times for

Disney, who had spent the profits he made from *Snow White* on future films like this, and a large new studio in Burbank. To make matters worse, a labor strike was in the offing.

Disney was forced to submit to pressure and put *Fantasia* into general release, with a standard sound track. For this release the film was cut to eighty-eight minutes (most of the cuts involving Deems Taylor and orchestral interludes).

The film did not do well, despite Disney's proclamation that "it isn't highbrow to like good music." Apparently, the public that had flocked to see *Snow White* and *Pinocchio* was simply put off by the high-toned aura of *Fantasia*. The film, which cost $2¼ million, was many years in recouping its investment. Another attempt to reach the masses in 1946 was heralded by the catch line "*Fantasia* will amaze-ya," a source of subsequent embarrassment for all involved.

The proposed additions to the film were never made. Among the properties in the talking stage were Weber's "Invitation to the Waltz," featuring Peter Pegasus from the "Patoral Symphony" segment, "Humoresque," featuring the mushrooms from the "Nutcracker Suite," a reinsertion of "Clair de Lune," Sibelius's "Swan of Tuonela," Wagner's "Ride of the Valkyries," and "Peter and the Wolf," which *did* find its way into a later feature, *Make Mine Music*.

Among the boosters of *Fantasia*, there was comment that Disney should turn his hand to an illustrated film of popular music, an idea he did pick up after the war.

Fantasia was reissued in 1944, 1946, 1953, 1956, 1963, and 1969 (since which time it has remained in almost perpetual release). In the 1950s, to beef up business, it was decided to show the animated portions of the film in SuperScope, a wide-screen process that sent the film's devotees running from the theaters in horror. (It should be noted that Disney originally wanted to do the film in a wide-screen format, but this idea never came to fruition.) Portions of the feature were shown on the Disney TV hour, and the "Rite of Spring" sequence was distributed on 16mm to schools as a geology film.

Walt Disney did not live to see his film be taken up by the younger generation of the 1970s, who finally made it a financial success. He might have been dismayed by its new reputation as a psychedelic experience—an adjunct to pot smoking—but he certainly would have been pleased that these young people appreciated the picture's overpowering display of visual imagination. (Some kids were so staggered by this creative explosion that they felt certain it must have been drug induced. Asked about this, animator Art Babbit, who brought the dancing mushrooms to life, remarked, "Yes, it is true. I myself was addicted to Ex-Lax and Feenamint.")

In 1977 a rechanneled stereophonic print of the film was put into release, but some studio executives decided that with the ongoing advances in motion-picture sound and growing audience awareness of such process as digital stereo and Dolby noise reduction it was imperative that *Fantasia* be completely rerecorded with state-of-the-art technology. Oscar-winner Irwin Kostal, who had supervised the music for *Mary Poppins* and other Disney productions, was given the task of re-creating, and reconducting, Stokowski's score, trying to match his timing, often on a frame-by-frame basis. (Musically astute listeners will note that Kostal used different arrangements for the Toccata and Fugue and "Night on Bald Mountain", the latter especially noticeable for its enhanced power and sheer volume. Kostal also arranged a suitable musical bridge for the brief sequence involving a black centaurette that had been cut from the racially sensitive 1950s.)

Musical purists quarreled with this revision of Stokowski, but Disney purists were even more upset. Deems Taylor was no longer in the film. If one accepted the premise that *Fantasia* needed modernizing, this might have made sense—after all, Taylor is virtually unknown today—but his *narration*, in some ways the most dated aspect of *Fantasia*, remained intact, spoken by an unidentified voice (actor Tim Matheson). Surely some tasteful rewriting would have been as welcome as any musical recording.

Those issues were put to rest when, in 1990, the film's picture negative and soundtrack were meticulously restored for its fiftieth anniversary reissue—by far the most successful in its long and checkered history. This in turn was followed by an extraordinarily successful video release. (At the same time, archivists found the original recording of "Clair de Lune"—a sequence designed for, but dropped from, the finished film—and matched it, as best they could, to its intended footage, which was later used for the "Blue Bayou" sequence in *Make Mine Music*.) Later, the studio's Scott MacQueen won approval to spend a little more money and prepare a more finished version of the previously unreleased sequence.

The subject of a new *Fantasia* was active at the studio for many years. Andre Previn tells in his memoir, *No Minor Chords,* of a meeting in the 1980s at which Jeffrey Katzenberg tried to persuade him to serve as musical director for a new *Fantasia* to be based solely on the music of the Beatles! Ultimately, Roy E. Disney took it upon himself to supervise an ambitious new *Fantasia*, which took the better part of a decade to produce, and emerged at the turn of a new century as *Fantasia/2000*. Only one segment was retained from the original, the enduringly popular "The Sorcerer's Apprentice."

Disney himself always hoped that *Fantasia* would last. "*Fantasia* is timeless," he said at the time of its release. "It may run ten, twenty, thirty years. *Fantasia* is an idea in itself. I can never build another *Fantasia*. I can improve. I can elaborate. That's all."

THE RELUCTANT DRAGON

Robert Benchley is his usual bumbling self when he joins Walt Disney in a screening room during a scene from *The Reluctant Dragon*.   © *Walt Disney Productions*

The remarkable Baby Weems is presented with a college diploma in a scene from *The Reluctant Dragon*.   © *Walt Disney Productions*

RELEASED BY RKO RADIO PICTURES ON JUNE 20, 1941. Technicolor. Live-action director: Alfred L. Werker. Cartoon directors: Hamilton Luske, Jim Handley, Ford Beebe, Erwin Verity, Jasper Blystone. Screenplay: Ted Sears, Al Perkins, Larry Clemmons, Bill Cottrell. Live-action cameramen: Bert Glennon, Winton Hoch. Art director: Gordon Wiles. Technicolor color director: Natalie Kalmus. Cartoon art directors: Ken Anderson, Hugh Hennesy, Charles Philippi. Special effects: Ub Iwerks, Joshua Meador. Animators: Ward Kimball, Fred Moore, Milt Neil, Wolfgang Reitherman, Bud Swift, Walt Kelly, Jack Campbell, Claude Smith, Harvey Toombs. Film editors: Paul Weatherwax, Earl Rettig. Running time: 72 minutes.

Songs: "Oh Fleecy Cloud," "To an Upside Down Cake," "Radish So Red," " 'Tis Evening," by Frank Churchill and Larry Morey. "I'm a Reluctant Dragon" by Charles Wolcott and Larry Morey.

With Robert Benchley (himself), Frances Gifford (studio artist), Nana Bryant (Mrs. Benchley), Buddy Pepper (studio guide), Florence Gill and Clarence Nash (themselves), Alan Ladd, John Dehner, Truman Woodworth, Hamilton McFadden, Maurice Murphy, Jeff Corey, Henry Hall (studio cop), Frank Faylen (orchestra leader), Lester Dorr (Slim), Gerald Mohr (guard), and members of the staff, including Walt Disney, Ward Kimball, and Norman Ferguson. With the voices of Barnett Parker (The Dragon), Claud Allister (Sir Giles), Billy Lee (The Boy), The Rhythmaires, Clarence Nash (Donald Duck), Pinto Colvig (Goofy), Gerald Mohr (*Baby Weems* narrator).

The Reluctant Dragon served two purposes for Walt Disney. The first was to capitalize on his worldwide popularity and do what many people had asked him to do—show how cartoons are made. The other purpose was to produce some working capital for future projects by making a relatively inexpensive feature (it was budgeted at $600,000) that would bring in a substantial return.

The film was only a partial success in meeting both goals.

It was decided to use Robert Benchley to provide the admittedly thin thread that held the picture together. The film opens at the Benchley home, where

Mrs. B. (Nana Bryant) urges Benchley to take a charming children's book she has just read, *The Reluctant Dragon,* to Walt Disney and suggest that he film it. Benchley doesn't like the idea, and has to be pushed into going to the Disney studio. His wife drops him off at the studio gate.

A distressingly eager young boy arrives to give Benchley a tour of the studio and bring him directly to Walt. But Benchley has other ideas, and repeatedly sneaks away from his tour guide, inadvertently getting a better look at studio life than he would have otherwise. He stumbles into a story conference, where a group of animators (one portrayed by Alan Ladd) asks for his reaction to a prospective project now in the storyboard stage called *Baby Weems*.

He walks into a recording session and meets a young girl (Frances Gifford) doing special voice effects; she explains how the sound track for a cartoon is created, with an orchestra following special timing, and sound-effects men coming up with the appropriate noises. Then she takes him into a room where the cartoons are shot (as he walks into the room the film

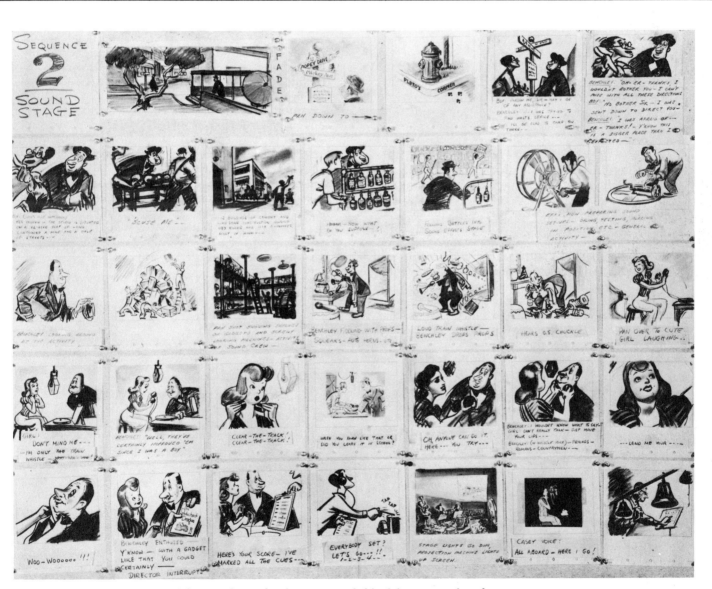

Disney artists and writers prepared this elaborate storyboard to help director Alfred Werker visualize the live-action sequences in *The Reluctant Dragon.* Even camera instructions are included. *From the private collection of Alfred L. Werker*

switches from black and white to color, and Benchley, noticing the change in his clothing, remarks upon the transformation).

He meets an animator (Ward Kimball) who shows him his latest work, a Goofy cartoon called *How to Ride a Horse;* a cameraman, who is photographing a Donald Duck cartoon (*MacDonald's Farm*), during which process Donald himself explains to Benchley how his movements are made; the paint department, a studio art class, the model department, and yet another recording session where he witnesses a historic duet between Clarence Nash and Florence Gill as Donald Duck and Clara Cluck.

Finally, he can avoid it no longer, and the energetic tour guide gets Benchley into a projection room where he meets Walt Disney and some of his staff, about to watch their latest product, an animated version of *The Reluctant Dragon*.

Driving home from the studio that day, Mrs. Benchley starts nagging her husband about his procrastination, and finally Benchley displays one of the tricks he's learned at the studio, squawking back at his wife à la Donald Duck.

The Reluctant Dragon is an extremely pleasant film, but little more. In its attempt to tell a mass audience how cartoons are made, it whitewashes much of the technique and omits most of the detail. It gives the erroneous impression that the sound track is matched to the cartoon, instead of vice versa. It uses actors in the roles of animators, musicians, cameramen, and never lets us in on the real creative process that produces Disney's cartoons. It's certainly a far cry from the cinema-verité technique that has more recently been used to show filmmakers at work!

There is little of Benchley's humor in the film; he too is relegated to the position of actor, and though he is an engaging one, it is a far cry from the humorist who achieved such popularity in his series of how-to short subjects.

The film *does,* however, have its moments. Best of all is the *Baby Weems* sequence, which is a classic that deserves wider exposure. It is shown as a series of still frames, as one would see them on a storyboard, with occasional animation within each frame—a unique method for Disney.

The delightful story deals with a baby born to two happy young parents. When he is two days old, the baby opens his mouth and begins to talk! Not just baby talk, but fantastically intelligent conversation. What is more, the youngster is a genius.

Overnight Baby Weems becomes a celebrity. Albert Einstein and George Bernard Shaw come to learn from him. Newspapers feature him on the front page. He endorses various products. He composes symphonies on his toy piano. His poor parents can't even get to see him; they must be content to watch him in the newsreels and hear him on the radio.

One evening Baby Weems is set to broadcast to the world his theory on "How to Find Happiness."

Everyone is listening; his parents rock their little radio in Baby Weems's cradle. Suddenly, the baby takes ill. His fever rises, and the world holds its breath. (A giant thermometer is erected on the Eiffel Tower to keep track.)

He recovers and goes before a multitude of microphones to speak. When he opens his mouth, however, only "goo-goo" and gurgling sounds come out.

The fickle public denounce him as an impostor; he is dropped like a cold potato and forgotten by everyone. Everyone, that is, except his parents, who are happy to have him back for themselves, and happier still that he is just a normal, happy baby.

Baby Weems is a charming cartoon that seems as fresh, both in its style and content, as the day it was made. Though seemingly it is an innocuous tale, its satiric thrust is quite sharp, and there are some marvelous throwaway gags throughout the sequence, poking fun at the world's penchant for exploitation and commercialization.

Subtlety is the hallmark of *The Reluctant Dragon* sequence, which, like *Ferdinand the Bull*, depicts a supposedly ferocious animal who turns out to be quite peaceful; its spoof of veddy-British stereotypes anticipates the even more successful *The Wind in the Willows*. But this twelve-minute sequence works quite well on its own terms—with delightfully whimsical humor and superb personality animation.

The live-action portion of the film is quite well made, having been directed by veteran 20th Century Fox contractee Alfred Werker. He recalls:

The Reluctant Dragon was the first live-action film that the studio made. They had a soundproof building which had been used to record the orchestra for *Fantasia*. This we converted into a small sound stage. I brought a young art director from Fox to do the sets, and we were in business. We rented lighting equipment, etc., and there were no difficulties in setting up the facilities.

Technicolor sent a color consultant, and as Walt had worked a lot in color cartoons, the color was beautiful. It was, of course, Walt's idea to go from black and white to color when Benchley entered the color department. Walt was deeply involved in the production of the film, but never intruded. As I remember, we had a six weeks' shooting schedule.

An interesting aspect of the project was how the script was prepared. The entire story was drawn in a series of sketches which were placed on what they called a story board, and when we had a story conference, the story board took the place of a script. Although I followed the sketches in general, Walt gave me a completely free hand in making the picture.

One of these storyboards is reproduced here. This technique was so successful that Disney used it from that point on for his live-action films. It enabled him to visualize a live scene with almost as much thoroughness as he could an animated sequence—a great boon in preparing to shoot a film. Other filmmakers adopted this technique over the years, to the point where it has become common practice in Hollywood.

Werker calls Disney "one of the nicest people I ever worked with, and the studio [was] the happiest one I ever saw. Walt had a delightful sense of humor and a fine understanding of what people wanted to see."

And, in this case, Disney was correct in assuming that people wanted to get a look at his studio. The trouble was that most moviegoers were unprepared for such an unspectacular, casual kind of film. Having enjoyed the richness of his previous features (*Snow White, Pinocchio, Fantasia*), they thought they were being somehow cheated with this film.

Oddly enough, looking at the film today, it seems almost lavish. The color is stunning, and the sets have a bright yet natural look about them. The cast is appealing and fairly believable.

But critics complained that customers should not be expected to pay good money to see an advertisement for Walt Disney Studios. (The same complaint was lodged against Disney's subsequent TV series, which often devoted segments to promotion of the studio and its theme parks—but the public never

seemed to mind. Of course, no admission was being charged to watch.) Most of the reviewers singled out such sequences as *Baby Weems*, but thought on the whole that the film was a cheater and a disappointment.

Reception to the film was not improved by the unfortunate timing of its release—just weeks after five hundred Disney workers went on strike. To protesting employees, the depiction of the studio as one big happy family was bitterly ironic.

The Reluctant Dragon was never reissued, though portions of it were reused and shown on TV. For years, it could only be seen in excerpt form (including a twenty-minute condensation of the Benchley material, which was distributed on 16mm as *Behind the Scenes of Walt Disney Studio*). Finally, the entire feature was released to the nontheatrical market in 1981.

The Reluctant Dragon does not deserve its long-standing obscurity. For general audiences it's an entertaining piece of fluff; for Disney buffs it's a fascinating look at the Burbank studio and some of its most illustrious residents. (There's even a bonus in the main titles—caricatures of all the people listed in the credits by famed story man T. Hee!) Most important, it's the film that showcases *Baby Weems*, which by any standards is one of the all-time best Disney cartoons.

DUMBO

RELEASED BY RKO RADIO PICTURES ON OCTOBER 23, 1941. Technicolor. From a story by Helen Aberson and Harold Pearl. Supervising director: Ben Sharpsteen. Screen story: Joe Grant, Dick Huemer. Story director: Otto Englander. Sequence directors: Norman Ferguson, Wilfred Jackson, Bill Roberts, Jack Kinney, Sam Armstrong. Animation directors: Vladimir Tytla, Fred Moore, Ward Kimball, John Lounsbery, Arthur Babbitt, Wolfgang Reitherman. Story development: Bill Peet, Aurelius Battaglia, Joe Rinaldi, George Stallings, Webb Smith. Character designers: John P. Miller, Martin Provensen, John Walbridge, James Bodrero, Maurice Noble, Elmer Plummer. Art directors: Herb Ryman, A. Kendall O'Connor, Terrell Stapp, Donald Da Gradi, Al Zinnen, Ernest Nordli, Dick Kelsey, Charles Payzant. Animators: Hugh Fraser, Howard Swift, Harvey Toombs, Don Towsley, Milt Neil, Les Clark, Hicks Lokey, Claude Smith, Berny Wolf, Ray Patterson, Jack Campbell, Grant Simmons, Walt Kelly, Joshua Meador, Don Patterson, Bill Shull, Cy Young, Art Palmer. Backgrounds: Claude Coats, Albert Dempster, John Hench, Gerald Neivus, Ray Lochrem, Joe Stahley. Music: Oliver Wallace, Frank Churchill. Lyrics: Ned Washington. Orchestrations: Edward H. Plumb. Running time: 64 minutes.

Songs: "Look Out for Mr. Stork," "Baby Mine," "Pink Elephants on Parade," "Casey Junior," "Song of the Roustabouts," "When I See an Elephant Fly."

Voices: Edward Brophy (Timothy Mouse), Herman Bing (ringmaster), Verna Felton (elephant), Sterling Holloway (stork), Cliff Edwards (Jim Crow).

Dumbo is one of the shortest animated features Disney ever made. It is one of the least pretentious. It is also one of the finest.

Ward Kimball, who has worked on virtually every animated feature at the studio, says:

Sure, we've done things that have had a lot more finish, frosting, and tricky footwork, but basically, I think the Disney cartoon reached its zenith with *Dumbo*. To me, it is the one feature cartoon that has a foolproof plot. Every story element meshes into place, held together with the great fantasy of a flying elephant. The first time I heard Walt outline the plot I knew that the picture had great simplicity and cartoon heart.

Dumbo was also one of the cheapest films we

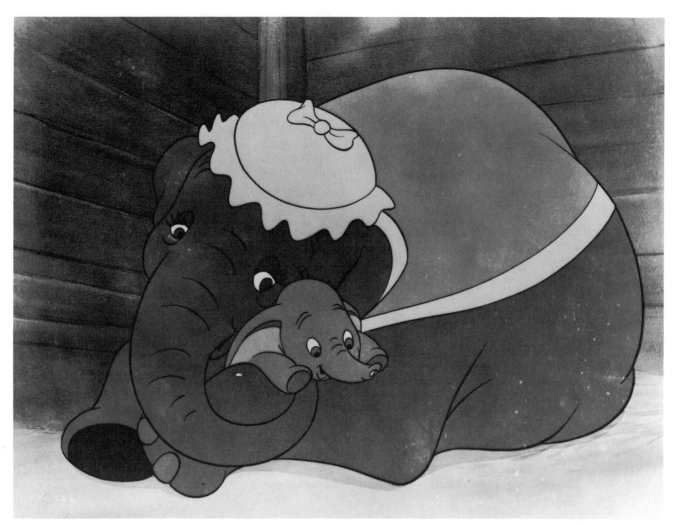

Mrs. Jumbo loves her little Dumbo, even if none of the
other elephants do. © *1940 Walt Disney Productions*

ever made. It came in for around $950,000 which
was damn reasonable, even for 1940, when our
cartoon features like *Bambi* climbed into the $2
million or $3 million bracket. The reason we
brought it in for a low price was that it was done
quickly and with a minimum amount of mistakes.
The story was clear and air-tight to everyone involved in the project. We didn't do a lot of stuff
over due to story-point goofs. There were no sequences started and then shelved, like in *Pinocchio.*
Walt was sure of what he wanted and this confidence was shared by the entire crew. *Dumbo,* from
the opening drawing, went straight through to the
finish with very few things changed or altered.

The story *is* quite simple. The stork pays a visit to
the circus, blessing most of the animals with new
arrivals, including Mrs. Jumbo, the elephant. The
other elephants come to admire the youngster, who
suddenly sneezes, and as he does his ears enlarge to
huge proportions. The other female elephants express
horror, sarcasm, and disdain, saying he ought to be
called Dumbo instead of Jumbo.

When some thoughtless children mistreat
Dumbo, and the circus people take him away, Mrs.
Jumbo becomes frantic and causes a commotion. The
ringmaster orders her locked up as a "mad elephant."
Left alone and brokenhearted, Dumbo finds an unlikely friend and champion in a saucy little mouse
named Timothy. They become inseparable pals.

Dumbo is made part of the clown act, a great
humiliation for him, but a great success for the
clowns. During their celebration they accidentally
knock a bottle of champagne into a bucket of water.
When Dumbo gets the hiccoughs, he drinks from the
bucket, and gets very, very drunk. After a nightmarish
hallucination, he and Timothy awaken the next
morning perched high in a tree!

Some local crows can't get over the sight, but in
trying to figure it out Timothy discovers that Dumbo

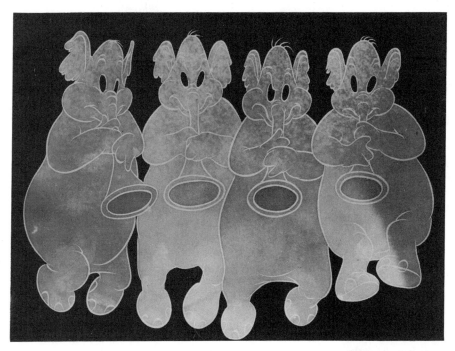

It's "Pink Elephants on Parade" all right. © *1940 Walt Disney Productions*

Disney artists Norman Ferguson and John Lounsbery work on the design for Timothy the Mouse, as Timothy's voice and inspiration, character actor Ed Brophy, looks on. *Movie Star News*

flew up into the tree. With the help of the crows, he gets Dumbo to fly again. That night at the circus, during the clown act, he surprises everyone by exhibiting his newfound talent. Overnight he becomes a sensation, the star of the circus. Now, when the circus travels, Mrs. Jumbo has her own streamlined car on the circus train, with Dumbo flying alongside.

Because the story was so simple, the Disney staff had plenty of elbow room to come up with ingenious ideas to add sparkle to the narrative. The result is a film overflowing with delightful touches and memorable sequences.

For instance, Dumbo doesn't speak, and his mother never speaks directly to him, except in the song "Baby Mine." The story is told *visually*, and as delightful as the sound track is, especially with Timothy's dialogue, one could turn it off and still follow every scene.

There are innumerable details that contribute to

the whole. When the circus arrives at its new destination, and the arrival is heralded with a circus parade, the animals, still tired at this early morning hour, are shown yawning, just barely awake. When the circus train tries to climb a steep hill, the locomotive (Casey Jones, Jr.) chugs "I think I can, I think I can . . ." all the way up the hill; just making it over the crest, it chugs "I thought I could, I thought I could," as it goes downhill.

When Mrs. Jumbo sings a lullaby, "Baby Mine," to her young one, we see similar scenes of mothers and offspring throughout the circus, including Mrs. Hippopotamus and her baby, resting underwater, and sending bubbles to the surface as they snore away.

The fantasy of a flying elephant and talking animals is played out against the stylized reality of a circus backdrop. There are some beautiful shots in the film, including the impressive master shot of the circus winter headquarters as the train pulls in to take them away. When they arrive, it's nighttime and rain is falling; men jump off the cars and start to pitch the tent, with the elephants' help. (The men are kept in shadow, since this is basically an animal film and the humans are only incidental. Later, when the clowns celebrate their success, we see them in silhouette from outside their tent; when one of them voices a hesitation to making Dumbo leap from a high platform in their act, another says, "Ahh, elephants ain't got no feelings.")

One critic said that *Dumbo* had "more camera angles than *Citizen Kane*," and, indeed, its highlight sequences are brilliantly conceived. When Dumbo makes his initial appearance as part of the elephant act, he stumbles over his own ears and causes a "wall" of elephants to tumble. There is tremendous intercutting as the toppling pachyderms systematically wreck the entire circus, knocking over poles, hitting one another, propelling further destruction, and climaxing with the entire tent collapsing. Now all is quiet, as the camera moves in from a long shot to show Dumbo's trunk emerging from under a flap in the tent, waving the little flag he was to use in the act. As he does, the banner falls off the wooden flagpole for a quiet finale to a raucous scene.

There is no way to overpraise the "Pink Elephants" scene. It is one of the best things ever done at the Disney studio, and, to use a much overworked but appropriate phrase, years ahead of its time. It begins when Dumbo takes a trunkful of the spiked water, gulps it down, and starts to feel woozy. He hiccoughs champagne bubbles. Timothy tests out the "water" and likes it so much he falls in to get the most of it. Then he starts challenging Dumbo to blow various kinds of bubbles through his trunk; one of these turns into the shape of a pink elephant.

That elephant blows another elephant out of *his* trunk, and soon there are four elephants using their trunks as trumpets to herald the song "Pink Elephants on Parade." This begins the surreal fantasy of design, space, color, light, and gags, all to the tune of this minor-key march. For example, two elephants are marching along, one big one stepping on the small one in front of him, causing the little one to inflate as he does. Finally the little one kicks the big one in the rear, causing the big one to split into three giant elephants. Then the little one inflates, takes a pair of gold cymbals and crashes them on the three elephants, who are squished into a dozen or more tiny ones, who march out of the picture and start climbing up the side of the frame, over a close-up of Dumbo's face, as he watches the march with dreamy-eyed amusement.

For a finish, the elephants start to "melt," as the predominantly black background lightens and turns into the morning sky, with the elephants evolving into clouds. The sequence ends as the camera pans over to one prominent tree on the horizon, whose leaf formations give the vaguely rounded impression of being elephants. Fade-out.

The characterizations in *Dumbo* are, of course, a major part of the film's success. The idea of having a mouse as Dumbo's pal is marvelous; in the film Dumbo follows Timothy around, holding his tiny tail in his trunk. Ed Brophy is ideal as the voice of Timothy, who takes pleasure in scaring off the other "catty" elephants who have been picking on Dumbo, and then prodding his pal to have more confidence in himself.

Sterling Holloway, who has probably done voices for more Disney cartoons than anyone else, is charming as the one stork who arrives late at the circus, having lost his map of Florida. When he finally delivers Dumbo to Mrs. J. on the circus train, he takes out a pitch pipe and dutifully sings "Happy Birthday" to the baby elephant.

The other voices are all first-rate, with Cliff Edwards as the Black Crow who sings the jaunty song "When I see an Elephant Fly," full of delightful puns ("I've seen a peanut stand, an' heard a rubber band . . .").

There has been considerable controversy over the Black Crow sequence in recent years, most of it unjustified. The crows are undeniably black, but they are black *characters*, not black *stereotypes*. There is no denigrating dialogue, or Uncle Tomism in the scene, and if offense is to be taken in hearing blacks call each other "brother," then the viewer is merely being sensitive to accuracy.

There is another interesting aspect to the crow sequence, as Ward Kimball tells it. "I was in charge of the crows, [and] I wanted to try something different; I wanted to make each crow a separate character. One example was the little crow with the big horn-rimmed glasses. When he rolled his eyes, the eyes went out beyond the head mass, they rolled around inside the big glasses."

The last sequence in the picture, a montage showing Dumbo's success, has many of the "little" throwaway gags that popped up so much in Disney cartoons. A series of headlines show the worldwide attention given Dumbo—he sets atmospheric records, his ears are insured for a million dollars, and, lastly, his manager, Timothy Mouse, signs a Hollywood contract for the famed elephant.

Dumbo was not only cheaper than other Disney feature cartoons, but only a year and a half in production, from inception, when Walt read the galleys of a story by Helen Aberson and Harold Pearl, to story construction and design (which took six months), and completion (another year).

The critics welcomed it as a breath of fresh air, *Newsweek* commenting that *Fantasia* wasn't the "real" Disney, and *The Reluctant Dragon* was a "disappointment."

Cecilia Ager summed everything up in her review of the film in *PM:*

Dumbo is the nicest, kindest Disney yet. It has the most heart, taste, beauty, compassion, skill, restraint. It marks a return to Disney first principles, the animal kingdom—that happy land

where Disney workers turn into artists; where their imagination, playfulness, ingenuity, daring flourish freest; where, in short, they're home.

Dumbo's the most enchanting and endearing of their output, maybe because it's the least pretentious of their works, the least self-conscious. It tries only to be a wonderful example of a form they themselves created—the fable expressing universal human truths in animal guise.

Indeed, the viewer feels a warmth and empathy for Dumbo and his friends that is rare in any kind of film, animated or live action. (For decades, people have been crying during the "Baby Mine" lullaby—where Mrs. Jumbo reaches out from her cage to soothe her frightened child with her trunk. This moment and its inevitable reaction was even chronicled, with some affectionate humor, in Steven Spielberg's movie *1941*, in which General Joseph Stilwell, played by Robert Stack, sheds tears as he watches the famous scene.) It is this depth of feeling, more than anything else, that makes *Dumbo* such a special film.

BAMBI

Released by RKO radio pictures on August 13, 1942. Technicolor. Based on the book by Felix Salten. Supervising director: David Hand. Story director: Perce Pearce. Story adapter: Larry Morey. Story development: George Stallings, Melvin Shaw, Carl Fallberg, Chuck Couch, Ralph Wright. Sequence directors: James Algar, Bill Roberts, Norman Wright, Sam Armstrong, Paul Satterfield, Graham Heid. Art directors: Tom Codrick, Robert Cormack, Al Zinnen, McLaren Stewart, Lloyd Harting, David Hilberman, John Hubley, Dick Kelsey. Supervising animators: Franklin Thomas, Milt Kahl, Eric Larson, Oliver M. Johnston, Jr. Animators: Fraser Davis, Bill Justice, Bernard Garbutt, Don Lusk, Retta Scott, Kenneth O'Brien, Louis Schmidt, John Bradbury, Joshua Meador, Phil Duncan, George Rowley, Art Palmer, Art Elliott. Backgrounds: Merle Cox, Tyrus Wong, Art Riley, Robert McIntosh, Travis Johnson, W. Richard Anthony, Stan Spohn, Ray Huffine, Ed Levitt, Joe Stahley. Music: Frank Churchill, Edward H. Plumb. Orchestrations: Charles Wolcott, Paul J. Smith. Conductor: Alexander Steinert. Choral arrangements: Charles Henderson. Running time: 69 minutes.

Songs: "Love Is a Song," "Let's Sing a Gay Little Spring Song," "Little April Shower," "Looking for Romance (I Bring You a Song)."

Note: Although no voice credits were issued, it is known that Peter Behn did the voice of Thumper.

Bambi is the gentlest of Disney's animated features, a delicate rendering of Felix Salten's classic story. It stands unique among the Disney cartoons in its style and atmosphere, and indeed, it would be quite some time before the studio would again go to such lengths to achieve the realistic detail found in this film.

Its theme and format, however, became the basis for many of Disney's later True-Life features, and *Perri* in particular owes much to *Bambi* for its basic framework.

The opening music, "Love Is a Song," and script titles set the initial mood for *Bambi*. The film opens on a slow pan through the dim forest, somewhat hazy in outline. A flying owl is the first sign of life in this idyllic setting, as dawn slowly breaks. The owl has been up all night and is about to go to sleep, when one by one the other animals awaken and come to tell him the exciting news: the Prince has been born. He goes with them to see the Little Prince, a newborn fawn, open his eyes for the first time. His father stands majestically on a cliff overlooking the forest.

Mother starts to teach the young one such things as walking, but much of his education is taken over by a young rabbit friend named Thumper; they are soon joined by a third friend, a skunk named Flower. Bit by bit Bambi learns about life, picking up words from

Thumper gives Bambi a hand as he falters on the ice.
© *Walt Disney Productions*

Bambi first meets Flower, the skunk, in this scene. Courtesy of Al
Kilgore. © *Walt Disney Productions*

Thumper, learning about the forest, being exposed to lightning and thunder for the first time during an April shower.

The next day Mother takes him for the first time to the meadow, which she tells him is a wonderful place. But before they can go out in the field, he must wait. Mother explains that "out there, we're unprotected." She goes out first to see if it is safe, then she calls for Bambi, and they romp together throughout the meadow. He also meets another deer for the first time—a female deer named Faline, who teases him and engages in a chase around the meadow.

Bambi thus strays away from his mother and encounters many of the older deer, who stand silently as the Great Prince of the Forest walks by—a noble animal indeed, who stops to look at Bambi before continuing on. His mother later explains who he is, telling Bambi: "He is very brave, and very wise." Then suddenly there is noise. The Great Prince leads the others in scurrying for shelter. Bambi is lost and confused; his mother calls for him but he cannot hear her. The Great Prince comes by and urges him to run, eventually leading him back to Mother. After much commotion, with all the deer back in the forest, there is quiet once more, and Mother says simply: "Man was in the forest."

Time passes and autumn arrives, followed quickly by winter and Bambi's first snowfall. Thumper coaxes him out onto the ice, where Bambi discovers that he isn't very graceful as a skater. Winter is very long, and Bambi soon gets bored. Then one day Mother calls him to show him the first patch of new grass growing out from the melting snow. They are in the meadow now, and suddenly Mother senses something wrong. She tells Bambi to move, to run as fast as he can and don't look back. The two of them scurry for the forest, and, as Bambi presses on, there is a shot, and soon he is running alone. He gets back home, but doesn't see his mother. He goes back to look for her as it starts to snow again, and he finds the Great Prince waiting for him. He tells Bambi: "Your mother can't be with you any more."

Soon it is spring again and much has changed. Bambi, Thumper, and Flower are now grown, Bambi having grown antlers. Their old friend the owl tells them about love, but they scoff at the idea; as they walk along, however, each one meets an attractive female and is drawn away from the group. Bambi gets his turn as well, when he meets Faline once more. She kisses him, and he is soon on Cloud Nine, in a dream sequence of Bambi and Faline romping through a forest of clouds.

He is brought back to reality by the presence of another deer who is vying for Faline's attention. Bambi is forced to do battle against his will with the other deer. Locking horns, ramming each other, they move into the darkness of the forest; Bambi wins the fight, only to discover that yet another peril is present: man. The animals hide as the sound of man gets closer and closer. One quail can't stand the suspense and tries to fly away, only to be shot down.

Panic grows, and the Great Prince tells Bambi to run, but Bambi's only thought is of Faline. He runs to find her, and discovers her being trailed by a pack of vicious hunting dogs who have her trapped on a ledge several feet up in the air. He takes on the whole pack and urges her to run. She escapes, and he follows behind, leaping over a precipice to safety, but being shot in midair. He lands wounded on the edge of the forest.

Meanwhile, the humans' campfire spreads, and sets the entire forest ablaze. Fire is everywhere, and the Great Prince comes to find Bambi to tell him to flee. The weakened Bambi follows instructions, and, with the Prince's help, runs from the quickly attacking flames in and out of paths and through streams, finally over a waterfall to safety along the river's shore with most of the other animals, including his waiting Faline. They are together once more, safe from both man and the fire.

The cycle now becomes complete; it's spring again, the owl is trying to sleep, and the children wake him to tell him that a young Prince has been born. Indeed, it is Flower's child (named Bambi) who spreads the news. Faline has given birth to twins, and, as they are admired by the forest animals, high on a cliff overlooking the forest is Bambi, now a majestic prince himself. The camera pulls back into the forest, and the film ends as it began.

Bambi is a beautiful film, and the extraordinary effort that went into making it shows in the finished product. The project was initiated in 1937 when Disney read Felix Salten's book and decided it would be a good project for the studio. He discovered that the rights had already been bought by director Sidney Franklin, and negotiated with him to acquire the story. Franklin capitulated, and served as a sort of artistic consultant on the project. A title card on the film reads: "To Sidney A. Franklin, sincere appreciation for his inspiring collaboration."

When Disney announced that he was going to make *Bambi*, the Maine Development Commission sent two live fawns to serve as models for Bambi and Faline. The artists were able to follow the young fawns' growth over the years they worked on the film, and soon augmented their little zoo to include other animals appearing in the film.

Maurice ("Jake") Day was sent to Maine to take hundreds of photographs in the forests there. He had specific instructions to get shots of trees after snowstorms, light coming into the forest at various times during the day, spider webs covered with dew, etc. It is precisely this kind of detail that makes *Bambi* so striking, most notably during the "April Shower" sequence, with drops landing on various plants and trees in the forest and lightning casting harsh shadows on the flora and fauna.

Human models were used as well, principally for the ice-skating sequence; actress Jane Randolph and *Ice Capades* star Donna Atwood skated, and fell, for animator Frank Thomas.

The nature of the story, and the detail it required, made it clear that *Bambi* was not going to be a quick production, and before long Disney pushed it aside to take care of other matters, such as *Pinocchio, Fantasia,* and *Dumbo.* But he assigned Frank Thomas, Milt Kahl, Oliver Johnston, and Eric Larson to stay with *Bambi* all during this time, and, except for occasional breaks to work on other projects, notably training films during the war, they kept *Bambi* in production from 1937 to 1942.

It was decided to use nonprofessional children to do the leading voices; two animators discovered the ideal voice for Thumper while visiting the home of a professor friend. His young son, Peter Behn, did a delightful job as the playful rabbit. There was one anxious moment, however, when some three years after the recording had been made, it was necessary to do some new scenes. They worried that Peter's voice might have changed, but luckily he was able to duplicate the pitch and quality exactly. A lady named Marion Darlington, who specialized in birdcalls, was also used on the sound track.

Thumper, as the most humorous character in the film, became a new Disney favorite, as had so many other supporting characters before him, but, like most of the others, he never appeared in another animated cartoon, although the character was adopted for Disney's popular comic books.

As real as Disney tried to be in the details of *Bambi,* the film also had a marvelous stylization, particularly in the use of color. The *New York Herald Tribune* noted: ". . . in *Bambi,* Disney does arbitrary and daring things with color to heighten the dramatic effects. There is a scene where Bambi and his mother venture out into an open field and then, alarmed by the approach of hunters, flee back to the forest. When they wheel and flee they are shown in a yellowish-white silhouette, a symbol of livid fear . . ." An even more notable example occurs when Bambi does battle with another deer in the forest. The entire scene is played in harsh, darkened colors, with reddish-black silhouettes prevailing (and appropriately discordant, pounding music on the sound track). The coming of autumn is shown in a swirl of brightly colored leaves before the camera.

The only effect in the film that doesn't come off is the forest fire, which is *too* stylized. (The effect was achieved by painting directly onto cels, without any inked outlines.) The idea of giving the flames a sort of animated life goes against the grain of the film, and clashes with the meticulously drawn forest and the animals that the flames pursue. The only really impressive shot of the fire is the last one, as seen from the river's edge by the animals, the distant forest mountain ablaze.

The drama in *Bambi* is one of understatement, and its effectiveness is great. Dialogue, which is kept to a minimum, is used in a quiet way to contrast the vociferous nature of the film's climaxes. Man is never shown in the film, yet the simple statement by Bambi's mother, after a frenzied chase with dozens of deer running for shelter, that "man [pause] was in the forest" creates an impact no literal device could accomplish.

Similarly, the death of Bambi's mother, the introduction of the Great Prince of the Forest, Bambi's first meeting with Faline, are all done with a refreshing simplicity.

For some, this style was *too* understated. Indeed, *New York Post* critic Archer Winsten, who loved the film, pointed out:

> This picture is less occupied with the humors and slapstick of the ordinary Disney opus. It is a much more serious and elemental showing of nature. As such there is some question about its appeal to the very young. . . . This reviewer is of the opinion that, like many another work of art dealing with activities of the young, its greatest appeal will be for thoroughly adult minds.

Other adults, like the *Times*'s Bosley Crowther, found the film to have "a shade too much cuddly charm."

But for the most part people went to see *Bambi* knowing what to expect, for its spirit was that of the famous Salten book (even though there had been one omission, the character of Gobo, and several additions, namely the forest fire and the character of Flower), and the ads billed *Bambi* as "a Great Love Story."

Few were disappointed. *Bambi* did well in its initial release, both critically and monetarily (although the European market was still absent), and it has continued to delight audiences through several reissues.

It remains one of the Disney studio's loveliest works, dealing in qualities of nature and life that will keep it young and fresh forever.

SALUDOS AMIGOS

RELEASED BY RKO RADIO PICTURES ON FEBRUARY 6, 1943. Technicolor (with live-action sequences from a 16mm original). Production supervisor: Norman Ferguson. Story: Homer Brightman, Ralph Wright, Roy Williams, Harry Reeves, Dick Huemer, Joe Grant. Story research: Ted Sears, William Cottrell, Webb Smith. Musical director: Charles Wolcott. Art supervisors: Mary Blair, Herb Ryman, Lee Blair, James Bodrero, Jack Miller. Backgrounds for *El Gaucho Goofy* inspired by F. Molina Campos. Sequence directors: Bill Roberts, Jack Kinney, Hamilton Luske, Wilfred Jackson. Animators: Fred Moore, Ward Kimball, Milt Kahl, Milt Neil, Wolfgang Reitherman, Les Clark, Bill Justice, Vladimir Tytla, John Sibley, Hugh Fraser, Paul Allen, John McManus, John Engman, Dan MacManus, Joshua Meador. Backgrounds: Hugh Hennesy, Albert Dempster, Claude Coats, Ken Anderson, Yale Gracey, Al Zinnen, McLaren Stewart, Art Riley, Dick Anthony, Merle Cox. Music: Edward H. Plumb, Paul J. Smith. Foreign supervisor: Jack Cutting. Associates: Gilberto Souto, Alberto Soria, Edmundo Santos. Narrators: Fred Shields, Aloysio Oliveira. Running time: 43 minutes.

Songs: "Saludos Amigos" by Charles Wolcott and Ned Washington; other songs incorporated into film, although not written especially for the film: "Brazil" by Ary Barroso, English lyrics by S. K. Russell, "Tico Tico" by Zequinta Abreu, Aloysio Oliveira, Ervin Drake.

Voices: Clarence Nash (Donald Duck), Jose Oliveira (Joe Carioca), Pinto Colvig (Goofy).

Saludos Amigos is a combination travelogue, chamber-of-commerce goodwill film, and cartoon, and, considering the diversity, it comes off rather well. Along with *The Three Caballeros,* it is truly a film of its time, although it is eminently enjoyable today. But one must remember the context in which it was made in order to appreciate the film.

With Europe one large battleground, America in the 1940s turned to its southern counterpart and established a Good Neighbor Policy that took the country by storm. The Latin-American influence on the United States during the war was best personified by Carmen Miranda and her infectious songs, the meanings of which were obscure to most listeners, but the rhythms of which were delightful.

For Hollywood, the Good Neighbor Policy had yet another meaning: a way to beef up the distribution market and try to offset the loss of the European curcuit for the duration of the war.

Disney, like many others, was charmed by South America, and, under the auspices of the State Department, chartered a plane to visit several countries on the continent with some of his staff and produce a series of cartoons inspired by the colorful nations. Having done this, the government complained that each cartoon would only be valid in the country at hand, so Disney strung his four shorts together, with the aid of 16mm color footage that had been taken of himself and his staff during their trip. The result was a hybrid, too long to be called a short and too short to be called a feature. It received feature-film release and bookings, and was tremendously popular both here and in South America; its name was *Saludos Amigos.*

The film opens with the Disney staff boarding their plane in Los Angeles (the narrator coyly avoids the name of Disney or anyone else, referring to them as "a group of artists and musicians") for a trip to South America. Then there is some travelogue footage, with frequent shots of Disney artists sketching picturesque scenes. We then join another typical American tourist at Lake Titicaca—Donald Duck.

This is the first of the animated sequences, with Donald acting as the typical tourist, dressing in a native costume, and having a native take his snapshot, etc. He rents a llama to travel along the mountainside, but while crossing a treacherous rope bridge over a deep valley, the llama gets stubborn. Donald gets excited, and soon the planks start to fall from the bridge. There is some frantic byplay with the llama, and, as Donald hangs onto the rope for dear life, the narrator says: "Above all, one should never lose one's temper." "Ahhh, shut up!" Donald shouts at the camera.

The Disney troupe travels on to Chile, where the artists are quite taken with the local airport that flies the mail over the perilous mountains to Mendoza. They create the character of Pedro, a little airplane, and we go into the second animated sequence. Pedro is the offspring of a proud mama and papa plane. (He

Walt Disney joins a band of musicians in Santiago while
scouting material for *Saludos Amigos*. *Movie Star News*

Little Pedro wants to be an airmail plane just like his dad.
© *Walt Disney Productions*

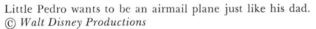

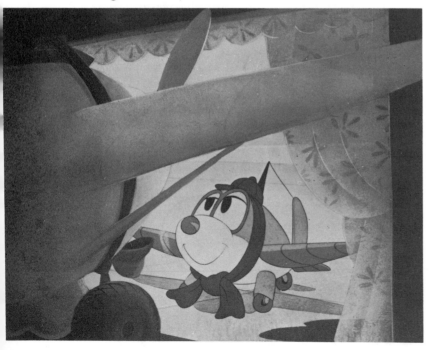

is first seen drinking gasoline out of a nipple at the
end of a gas pump.) He goes to school to learn various
things, but, most importantly, the flying route over
the mountains from Santiago to Mendoza. One day,
when his father has a terrible cold, it's up to Pedro to
fly the mail.

He is very nervous, but, after a shaky takeoff, gets
up in the air and does pretty well, managing to avoid
a famous mountain, whose face is in the shape of a
scowl, and which has always signified bad luck. He
gets the mail in Mendoza, and is confidently flying
home when he encounters a buzzard that leads him on
a chase. Straying from his route, he has come far too
close to the treacherous mountain, and runs into
problems with frost and altitude. He is scared—the oil
freezes in his cylinders. Just as he is about to cross the
final hurdle, he sputters, apparently out of gas. Meanwhile, at the airport, his worried parents search
through the fog for their baby, and, finally, hearing a
sputter, realize he is on his way. Pedro lands, upside
down, but he lands. "Don't ask me how he did it,"
says the narrator, who goes on to praise Pedro's performance in this most important service—making

Donald Duck is a typical American tourist at Lake Titicaca.
© *Walt Disney Productions*

sure the mail goes through. Then a look in the pouch reveals its contents to be one postcard, which reads, "Dear Pancho, Having wonderful time, wish you were here" (all in Spanish) . "Well," says the narrator, "it *might* have been important."

In the Pampas region Disney and his staff meet the gauchos, and are inspired to see what happens when an American cowboy is transplanted into this new setting. The result is the third segment, *El Gaucho Goofy.* This cartoon is done in the style of the Goofy *How To* series, the narrator citing the various clothing and equipment of the gaucho as poor Goofy tries to accustom himself, without much success. At one point, after Goofy has captured a wild animal with the deadly bolas, the sequence is played again in slow motion (the narrator's voice also slowed down) to capture the beauty and grace of the action. Unfortunately, the slow motion reveals nothing but clumsiness as Goofy gets himself tangled up in the bolas, along with his horse.

Finally, we visit the Carnaval in Rio; the narrator explains the annual songwriting competition for the Carnaval theme. The winner this year is "Aquarela do

Brasil" ("Watercolor of Brazil"), sung by Jose Oliveira. The Disney artists sketch a tropical bird and create the character of Joe Carioca, who takes Donald Duck on a tour of South America with the aid of a paintbrush that fills in the backgrounds as they go along. Joe teaches Donald the samba (to two of the composition's main themes, "Brazil" and "Tico Tico"), and the two of them go out and paint the town red for the finale of the film.

Saludos Amigos is a very disjointed film, but each of the four sequences is so enjoyable that it seems pointless to carp about construction, especially noting the way the film was put together "on order." Oddly enough, it is the cartoons that seem like interruptions to the live-action footage, instead of the other way around.

With hindsight, one can view *Saludos Amigos* as a dry run for Disney's full-length feature *The Three Caballeros,* which expanded on many elements first found in *Saludos,* particularly in the last two cartoons. *El Gaucho Goofy,* though typically fast and funny, like most of the 1940s Goofy outings, also has some hints of the slightly surreal kind of gag that fully blossomed in *Caballeros*. Here it is a running gag involved "wipe" dissolves that cut across the screen to bridge two scenes. Twice, with a horizontal and diagonal wipe, the background dissolves, but Goofy and his horse get squashed by the moving line!

The final sequence was, of course, the real blueprint for *The Three Caballeros*, with the invention of Joe Carioca, and the interpolation of the wonderful Latin songs into the film. But here, too, is a hint of the crazy kind of gag that permeated the later film, for although the animated paintbrush fills in the backgrounds for Joe and Donald as they samba along, at one point Donald walks right into the brush and is covered with blue paint.

Saludos Amigos opened in South America in late 1942 to tremendous acclaim and tremendous crowds. It wasn't released in the United States until February, at which time it was enthusiastically greeted. Howard Barnes called it "at once a potent piece of propaganda and a brilliant job of picture-making."

But John T. McManus in *PM* had a different outlook on the film.

. . . watching *Saludos,* I think most of us will experience the same general set of emotions, a mingled pride and sadness over the growing up of a beloved something we all foolishly hoped could stay young forever. For *Saludos,* as a whole is not the fable-minded Disney child of before, stalking wild fantasy in its own wonderland; it is a fairly sophisticated young man of the Western world, exchanging bright and pointed pleasantries with our Latin-American friends, bringing our viewpoints into accord like a witty ambassador, and generally doing a job in hemisphere relations that no one before has managed to achieve. The great redeeming hope is that the child is not grown up for good, but only for the duration.

The war was, of course, a turning point for Disney in many ways, and McManus was one of the first critics to sense a definite change in the Disney style and outlook. The biggest change, however, was in the critical reception to his work, which was never to be the same again. Though critics kept hoping for another *Pinocchio*, Disney moved in new directions and lost some of the support he had enjoyed up to that time, particularly among highbrow critics.

But Disney's measure of success, as always, was in public reaction, and the best way to gauge that reaction was at the box office, which evidence led him to ignore the critics and continue to follow his own instincts.

Although *Saludos Amigos* has never been reissued, its material has been used on the Disney TV show, and all four cartoon segments were released separately as short subjects in 1955.

VICTORY THROUGH AIR POWER

RELEASED BY UNITED ARTISTS ON JULY 17, 1943. Technicolor. From the book by Major Alexander de Seversky. Scenes with Major de Seversky directed by H. C. Potter. Director of photography: Ray Rennahan, A.S.C. Art director: Richard Irvine. Technicolor color director: Natalie Kalmus. Associate: Morgan Padleford. Interior decorations: William Kiernan. Narrator: Art Baker. Animation supervisor: David Hand. Story director: Perce Pearce. Story adapters: T. Hee, Erdman Penner, William Cottrell, James Bodrero, George Stallings, Jose Rodriguez. Sequence directors: Clyde Geronimi, Jack Kinney, James Algar. Art directors: Herbert Ryman, Donald Da Gradi, Tom Codrick, Charles Philippi, Elmer Plummer, Don Griffith, Cliff Devirian, Glen Scott, Karl Karpe, Bill Herwig. Animators: Ward Kimball, John Lounsbery, Hugh Fraser, George Rowley, John Sibley, Norm Tate, Vladimir Tytla, Joshua Meador, Carleton Boyd, Bill Justice, Ed Aardal, John McManus, Oliver M. Johnston, Jr., Marvin Woodward, Harvey Toombs. Backgrounds: Albert Dempster, Dick Anthony, Claude Coats, Ray Huffine, Robert Blanchard, Joe Stahley, Nino Carbe. Music: Edward H. Plumb, Paul J. Smith, Oliver Wallace. Production manager: Dan Keefe. Film editor: Jack Dennis. Sound recording: C. O. Slyfield. Lodge Cunningham. Running time: 65 minutes.

Victory through Air Power is a fascinating footnote to Disney's career. By 1942 he was busy making training films for the army, navy, and every conceivable division of the government; at the end of the war Disney estimated he had turned out some 300,000 feet of film for Uncle Sam.

But *Victory* was not another training film. Indeed, if anything, it went against the predominant thinking among the military hierarchy. Major Alexander de Seversky, a major figure in the history of

Major Alexander de Seversky poses with one of the maps and models used in *Victory through Air Power*. © *Walt Disney Productions*

aviation and a colleague of General Billy Mitchell, had written a book called *Victory through Air Power,* outlining his ideas about strategic long-range bombing and how it could help win the war. It was cause for a great deal of comment, but the highest echelon among the military planners did not agree with the Major's philosophy.

Disney was fascinated by Seversky's ideas, however, and felt so strongly about their importance to the war effort that he decided to illustrate them in a film that he would produce himself and release to theatres to win public support for the program. For a man whose financial standing was rather shaky, and whose studio was thriving on military assignments, it was a bold move.

The film opens with an introductory passage: "Our country in the past has struggled through many storms of anguish, difficulty, and doubt. But we have always been saved by men of vision and courage who

opened our minds and showed us the way out of confusion." It goes on to show how one of these men, General Billy Mitchell, was "ignored and ridiculed," and it inserts a newsreel clip of Mitchell from 1934 defending his ideas. A title card concludes: "To the memory of Billy Mitchell and . . . other gallant airmen, this film is dedicated."

A book called *History of Aviation* is opened, and we follow the story of flight in this country—from the Wright brothers' historic moment at Kitty Hawk, through the first transcontinental flight, into World War I and the first use of aircraft for warfare, through the 1920s and a series of new aviation "firsts," up until the present day and our modern airships.

We then see a scrapbook of the achievements of Major de Seversky, his many contributions to the progress of aviation over the years. We join him in his office (in live action) as he recounts the background of World War II and the military strategy first used in

A German pilot in World War I soon discovered that using an ordinary machine gun cut off his own propellers!   © *Walt Disney Productions*

A visual symbol of the progress aviation has made since the turn of the century.   © *Walt Disney Productions*

Europe in 1939. Back into animation, we see how the Maginot Line and other so-called fortresses on land and sea were easily neutralized by Hitler, simply by flying over them; the analogy is made that Hitler created a "shield of air power," and this thought is visualized on a map of Europe.

The Battle of Britain was the turning point in Europe, for here at last Britain learned that in order to ward off attack it would have to gain control of its skies. Then, of course, came Pearl Harbor and our entry into the war.

Seversky then explains the difference between our supply lines and the enemy's: ours depend on various shipping routes that take us within range of enemy fire in many instances—this means we have to go to great lengths to avoid such zones and waste that much more time in delivery; Hitler's supply lines are all concentrated within the interior of his domain—his stronghold can be compared to a wheel, with the factories at the hub, sending supplies out through the various spokes.

The only way to weaken his strength, Seversky explains, is to attack the hub from above and stop his supply lines at their source.

The other problem we face is attacking Japan, and the only way to overcome it is by designing long-range bombers, which can take off from existing Allied air bases (such as those in Alaska) and fly toward their destination. New bombs are needed, and strategy must be employed to make optimum use of this power—hitting dams, for instance, the source of power for most of the munitions factories.

Finally, Seversky says, there must be one single air command to coordinate such actions around the world and ensure victory.

The final animated sequence shows Seversky's idealized air force in action, taking off for Japan, bombing the cities and factories and crippling their power. Then a giant eagle soars through the air, aiming for an octopus on the ground below; the eagle jabs at the head of the octopus, again and again, until it retreats and loses its grip on the map under it. The eagle triumphantly perches on top of the globe, and a zoom backward shows it to be the top of a flagpole flying the American flag in victory.

When Disney started making training and morale films for the government, he learned the real power of the motion-picture medium. But unlike so many producers of factual and educational films, Disney understood that an enthusiastic, *interested* audience would grasp and retain much more than an audience that felt it was watching an illustrated lecture.

The same technique was applied to *Victory through Air Power*: not a matter of sugarcoating the information, but merely presenting it in a simple, graphic manner, using the tools of an entertainment medium to instruct at the same time.

Victory through Air Power is phenomenally powerful propaganda because it makes its points so crystal clear. When Seversky refers to a shield of air power, we see an actual shield atop a relief map of Europe and see just how it works. When he talks about Hitler's wheel-like stronghold, the wheel is shown and the metaphor made real. The film is perfect propaganda because it leaves no room for argument; it *shows* you that what it says is true.

There is, of course, *some* sugarcoating to the film, and that is contained in its introductory sequence on the history of aviation. Much of this segment is treated in a lighthearted manner, and, although the gags are undeniably funny, one feels uneasy laughing in the midst of what is essentially a serious matter. (Fortunately, plans to include Donald Duck in the film were later scrapped.) Only here does the film go off target, by making the origin of airborne warfare during World War I a joke. (A German and a Frenchman, Fritz and Pierre, coexist peacefully in the sky, until one day one of them throws a brick at the other, and retaliation builds into full-scale war.)

Even with its jokes, this section of the film does provide a helpful background to the main topic at hand, and once Seversky enters the scene, jokes are

forsaken, although there are still some very inventive animated touches.

Indeed, much of the film is done in a sort of limited animation style; backgrounds are sparse, and there are corner-cutting devices such as not bothering to animate the whirring propellers on some of the planes. Many of the points are illustrated with relief maps and abstract figures.

But, paradoxically, there are other points where the animation is unusually elaborate, such as the final sequence of our "dream Air Force" in action. At the airfield it is raining heavily, as the crewmen prepare the long-range bombers to go off on their missions. The rain does produce a satisfying dramatic effect, but it also would have been much simpler to animate the scene without it. Conclusion: Disney was willing to cut corners for the film, but not at the sacrifice of an important effect.

The live-action scenes are also well done, and though it might seem that these could have been shot by anyone, it is precisely that kind of thinking that sets most factual filmmakers apart from Disney. Disney hired successful stage and film director H. C. ("Hank") Potter to do the sequences with Seversky, largely because Potter was a flyer himself (then working for the Air Transport Command), and he already knew Seversky.

Potter knew that simply shooting Seversky at his desk, straight on, would be deadly, so instead he kept him moving constantly and broke up the action with a number of different angles, "luxuries" another less inspired director might have eschewed. In addition, says Potter:

We didn't want . . . to suddenly stop the animation and all of a sudden have Sasha [Seversky's nickname] standing there lecturing. What I did was to tie it in as much as possible by starting with an insert, of a map or a globe, or something, which would look like animation at first, and then you'd hear Sasha's voice and we'd pull the camera back, and he'd be standing in his office, talking. We made the transitions smoother that way.

Of the filming, Potter recalls:

Sasha had no experience as an actor, but essentially, he's a wonderful character. He has this very thick White Russian accent, and of course part of the problem was to try and smooth out the Russian accent so that everybody would understand him. We got as much casual movement, wandering around the office set, as possible, which always bothered him, because he had to keep remembering all these moves.

We had to shoot the whole thing at night, at the Disney studio, because there was little or no soundproofing, and Lockheed Airport was right next door, where they were making all the P-38s and Hudson bombers, so there were airplanes taking off all day long there, roaring over the studio. It was absolutely impossible to shoot during the day, so we started shooting at 10 at night, and worked until dawn. I remember one night Sasha couldn't hit the damn marks, and he stopped and said, "Hank, how can I remember the words, the expression, the meaning, the walking without limping [he had one wooden leg], and hit these marks, and think of what I am saying at the same time?" I said, "When you're flying airplanes, you're flying a plane, you're navigating, you're looking down at the ground to see if you're going where you're supposed to be going, you're listening to the radio, you're watching for other planes, and you're checking the instruments, all at the same time." I said, "Your motto should be 'Diwide the attention.'" He roared at that. He didn't have any marks from that point on, and every time we would start, the whole crew would holler at him, "Diwide the attention!"

Critical reaction to the film was mixed. Thomas M. Pryor in the *New York Times* enthused: "If *Victory through Air Power* is propaganda, it is at least the most encouraging and inspiring propaganda that the screen has afforded us in a long time. Mr. Disney and staff can be proud of their accomplishment." Howard Barnes in the *Tribune* was more guarded, saying: "From a technical standpoint, it is difficult to quarrel with the production. . . . It is the ideological content of the offering which is likely to give one pause." Other critics, like James Agee, were completely turned off by what they considered the film's hard-sell approach.

Advertised as "Walt Disney's Full-Length Sensation," and touted in one comic-book handout as "The Newest, The Greatest Triumph in Screen History," *Victory through Air Power* was not in the same league as *Pinocchio* or *Snow White* at the box office.

But it did have another kind of audience. Says H. C. Potter:

The British Air Force thought this was the greatest thing that ever came down the pike, and the picture was much better known in England than it was here, in official circles, and early in the game. Walt told me this story, and swore this was what happened. When Churchill came over to the Quebec conference, they were trying to get Roosevelt interested in this long-range bombing idea, and Roosevelt didn't know what the hell they were talking about. Churchill said, "Well, of course, you've seen *Victory through Air Power . . .*" and Roosevelt said, "No, what's that?" Air Marshal Tedder and Churchill worked on Roosevelt until Roosevelt put out an order to the Air Corps to fly a print of *Victory through Air Power* up to Quebec. Churchill ran it for him, and that was the beginning of the U.S. Air Corps Long Range Bombing.

Which, of course, was Disney's real reason for making the film in the first place.

The Disney studio has never reissued this film or (as of this writing) permitted it to be shown in Disney retrospectives, but the "History of Aviation" sequence has long been available for rent as a 16mm short subject.

THE THREE CABALLEROS

RELEASED BY RKO RADIO PICTURES ON FEBRUARY 3, 1945. Technicolor. Production supervisor/director: Norman Ferguson. Sequence directors: Clyde Geronimi, Jack Kinney, Bill Roberts. Director (Pátzcuaro, Veracruz, Acapulco): Harold Young. Story: Homer Brightman, Ernest Terrazzas, Ted Sears, Bill Peet, Ralph Wright, Elmer Plummer, Roy Williams, William Cottrell, Del Connell, James Bodrero. Brazilian and Spanish supervisor: John Cutting. Associates: Gilberto Souto, Aloysio Oliveira, Sidney Field, Edmundo Santos. Assistant production supervisor: Larry Lansburgh. Animators: Ward Kimball, Eric Larson, Fred Moore, John Lounsbery, Les Clark, Milt Kahl, Hal King, Franklin Thomas, Harvey Toombs, Bob Carlson, John Sibley, Bill Justice, Oliver M. Johnston, Jr., Milt Neil, Marvin Woodward, John Patterson. Special effects animation: Joshua Meador, George Rowley, Edwin Aardal, John McManus. Backgrounds: Albert Dempster, Art Riley. Ray Huffine, Don Douglass, Claude Coats. Layout: Donald Da Gradi, Hugh Hennesy, McLaren Stewart, Yale Gracey, Herbert Ryman, John Hench, Charles Philippi. Art supervisors: Mary Blair. Kenneth Anderson, Robert Cormack. Live-action sequences photographed by Ray Rennahan, A.S.C. Art director: Richard F. Irvine. Choreography: Billy Daniels, Aloysio Oliveira, Carmelita Maracci. Technicolor director: Natalie Kalmus. Associate: Morgan Padleford. Color consultant: Phil Dike. Process effects: Ub Iwerks. Process technician: Richard Jones. Music directors: Charles Wolcott, Paul J. Smith, Edward H. Plumb. Technical adviser: Gail Papineau. Film editor: John Haliday. Sound recording: C. O. Slyfield. Production manager: Dan Keefe. Running time: 70 minutes.

Original songs: "The Three Caballeros" by Manuel Esperon, Ray Gilbert, Ernesto Cortezar. "Baia" by

Ary Barroso, Ray Gilbert. "Os Quindins De Yaya" by Ary Barroso. "You Belong to My Heart" by Agustin Lara, Ray Gilbert. "Mexico" by Charles Wolcott, Ray Gilbert, E. Santos. "Have You Ever Been to Baia?" by Dorival Cayymi. "Pandeiro & Flute" by Benedicto Lacerda. "Pregoes Carioca" by Joao de Barro, Carlo Braga. "Lilongo" by Charro Gil.

Cast: Aurora Miranda, Carmen Molina, Dora Luz, Nestor Amarale, Almirante, Trio Calaveras, Ascencio Del Rio Trio, Padua Hill Players, and the voices of Sterling Holloway, Clarence Nash (Donald Duck), Jose Oliveira (Joe Carioca), Joaquin Garay (Panchito), Fred Shields, Frank Graham. "Mexico" sung by Carlos Ramirez.

Joe Carioca, Panchito, and Donald Duck, *The Three Caballeros.* © *Walt Disney Productions*

The Three Caballeros followed *Saludos Amigos* by two years (it would have been sooner, but war priorities made it difficult to get color prints), expanded on its themes and ideas, and resulted in a bright, fast-moving, and often brilliant mélange of sights and sounds. Somewhat like *Fantasia,* it was the cause of considerable controversy among critics in 1945, and only recently has become one of the most admired Disney features among film buffs.

The film opens with a spotlight on a giant gift-wrapped package; it's a birthday gift for Donald Duck, who excitedly opens it up and discovers, first, a movie projector. "Oh, boy," says Donald, "home movies!" as he snaps a reel of film into threading position and throws it onto the machine. The first film on the screen is *Aves Raras (Strange Birds),* which tells principally of Pablo the Penguin, who never could get used to his Antarctic home and sailed for the South Seas. Another strange bird is the aracuan, a crazy bird with a raucous song who walks out of the movie screen to shake hands with Donald and walks off *our* screen as well. (He and Donald would meet again in *Melody Time* and *Clown of the Jungle.*)

The next story is about Little Gauchito, who goes hunting and finds a flying burrito (a donkey), whom he enters in a local race, winning with ease, but having his scheme backfire when the crowd sees the donkey's wings.

Movies are over, and Donald opens his next gift, a book on Brazil. He flips open the cover only to find his old pal Joe Carioca inside. The volume is a giant pop-up book, and Joe paints a beautiful picture of his country for Donald by singing "Baia," as we see a beautiful panorama of Brazil, with its homes, soft skyline, mountains, jungle, a boat on the calm water, beautiful ancient churches, etc. Joe asks Donald if he's ever been to Brazil; when Donald says no, Joe goes into a whole song and dance about it, splitting himself into a quartet, and eventually taking out a sledgehammer and crowning Donald, which shrinks the duck to Joe's miniature size (after all, he came out of a book) so he can go with him. They hop on a train, which appears on the next leaf of the pop-up book,

Donald shows off for the lovely bathing beauties south of the border. © *Walt Disney Productions*

and go to Brazil, where they meet Aurora Miranda, with whom Donald promptly falls in love. He joins Aurora and her musical friends in a long production number that combines live action and animation. She finally kisses Donald, which sends him into a whirlpool of fantasy—drums, tambourines, a montage of unreal colors, tinted footage of live dancers, a phantasmagoria of images. When he comes back down to earth, the whole background setting sways in time to the music, the lamppost and houses moving back and forth rhythmically. Finally the entire scene comes to a finale, and the book, still swaying, closes. Donald and Joe squeeze out of the binding and return to their normal size.

The last present is Mexico, represented at first by a sound track, whose variations are shown in the shapes of the instruments playing (illustrated as symmetrical forms emanating from the sound track's vertical line). At one point Donald gets caught in the sound track, and *his* image comes out of the track. But the music gets so wild that it finally explodes, sending a new visitor bursting forth—Panchito, a Mexican charro rooster.

He, Joe, and Donald sing "The Three Caballeros," full of wild, incredibly fast-moving gags. Then Panchito tells his friends about his country: of Mexican traditions, like the children's celebration of Christmas and the origin of the piñata. He encourages Donald to try to hit the piñata, and when he does a cascade of surprises are showered on him. A storybook provides the history of Mexico and live-action pictures of Mexico today. A magic sarape becomes the trio's flying carpet, taking them into the scenes of the storybook. They visit a fiesta where, in the midst of traditional dances, Donald starts to jitterbug with a lovely señorita. Then Panchito lassos Acapulco Beach and they travel there. Donald immediately goes after a bevy of bathing beauties, who play with him.

Dora Luz sings "You Belong to My Heart," sending Donald into another flight of fantasy. The girl appears in his eyes . . . he dances among the stars . . . everything he sees becomes a neon sign, then flowers, and wildly colored geometric figures . . . then silhouettes, gradually turning into shadows of his dream girl, who evolves back into a flower. After a burst of chorus girls, photographed from above, complete the number, there is quiet, and slowly a figure appears on a distant horizon. It is Carmen Molina, who marches forward to dance the famous "Jesusita," joined by a group of surrounding cactus plants, and playful Donald, who does his best to keep in step.

Finally, Donald plays a mock bullfight with his two friends, and they load the mock bull with fireworks. When Donald hits the bull head on, there is a tremendous explosion, as they sing a final chorus of "The Three Caballeros" and the fireworks in the sky spell out The End.

It is impossible to describe *The Three Caballeros* adequately on paper. First, there is simply so much

going on, and second, there are no words to pinpoint many of the startling visual effects employed in the film. It is one long barrage of dazzling sights, accompanied on the sound track by some sixteen delectable songs, including several that became standards.

The film is full of visual puns, even in the "mildest" of its episodes, the story of Pablo the Penguin, in which the narrator (Sterling Holloway) tells us that "a blanket of fog rolled in," and we see literally that, or Pablo's little iceboat reaching the equator and bouncing off the hemisphere line. In the story of Little Gauchito, when the first-person narrator, telling of the race, says, "We passed them as if they were standing still," that's just what happens.

This is only a lethargic warm-up to what follows, particularly in the "Three Caballeros" number, where things happen so fast it is difficult to keep track of them. When a line of the song goes, "Through fair and stormy weather . . ." on the word "stormy," a sudden downpour erupts and flows over the brims of the singers' sombreros. When Panchito hits a high note and decides to hold it, Donald and Joe scurry around to find devices to shut him up, planting bushes that instantly grow around him, burning them down, putting out the fire with an avalanche of water, etc., all to no avail.

Donald's dream sequences are reminiscent of *Dumbo*'s "Pink Elephants" sequence in their imagination and constant evolution from one far-out concept to another, with perfectly logical transitions linking the bizarre visuals.

Much of this was too offbeat for some viewers, including at least some of the Disney staff, according to Ward Kimball, who refers to this film as "the only animation I can look back on with pride." Kimball told Mike Barrier of *Funnyworld:*

It's fun to look at today. Everything else I've done, I criticize, I say I should have done this or I should have done that, but on *Three Caballeros*, I had a lot of fun. When you see it now, it's kind of old hat, characters going out on the left and coming in from the right, with no hookups, sort of a magic animation.

There is a variety of styles within *The Three Caballeros;* not only Kimball's frantic, no-holds-barred animation, but the soft, almost pastel quality of the Pablo and Gauchito segments, and the loveliness of Panchito's story of Mexican children at Christmas, which is shown as a series of tableaux.

The combination of live action and animation (the first time the studio had tried it to any great extent since the old *Alice in Cartoonland* efforts of the 1920s) was perfect. The synchronization of movement between the actors and the cartoon characters is right on target, and the illusion is such that you are willing to believe that Donald and the bathing beauties are really frolicking together, or that Donald is actually dancing with Aurora Miranda and her musicians. These processes were developed by Walt's long-time colleague Ub Iwerks, who continued to refine them right through the 1960s and *Mary Poppins*.

Despite the episodic nature of the film and frequent shifts of locale, mood, and style, *The Three Caballeros* maintains its breezy pacing beautifully, allowing no lulls or feeling of superfluous material. The stream of music on the sound track is constant, and the whole film seems to have been laid out to one continuous rocking beat. It is difficult to leave a screening of the film without carrying this lilting music in your head.

Although the film was capitalizing again on the strong Latin-American bonds of the 1940s, it has little of the propaganda feeling of *Saludos Amigos,* although one is constantly fed a series of definitions, explanations of customs, and picture-postcard footage (both literal, as in Panchito's live-action storybook, and animated, as in the vision of Baia, which was obviously animated from detailed photographs).

The Three Caballeros was well under way in the midwar years, but its production was constantly delayed by breaks during which the staff had to turn out government material; once completed, there was another long delay to get enough Technicolor prints to open the film. Said Disney in late 1944: "You have to stand in line now." Although the film was completed by October 1944, it did not open in New York until February 1945.

As with *Saludos,* Disney went right to the source for most of his material, hiring such prominent South American composers as Ary Barroso, Agustin Lara, and Manuel Esperon, and three leading female stars, Aurora Miranda of Brazil, and Dora Luz and Carmen Molina of Mexico. The musical aspect of the film paid off handsomely, for "You Belong to My Heart" and "Baia" became top song hits.

Building up the combination of live action and animation, *The Three Caballeros* was immodestly advertised as "the most startling advancement in motion picture technique since the advent of sound." Whereas it was warmly greeted by most mass-audience critics (although many professed to be confused by it all) and deemed a "socko feature production" by *Variety,* some of the more sophisticated reviewers were aghast at the animated mélange.

Under the headline WHAT HATH WALT WROUGHT?,

The New Yorker called the film:

> . . . a mixture of atrocious taste, bogus mysticism, and authentic fantasy, guaranteed to baffle any critic not hopelessly enchanted with the word "Disney." . . . In the first place, a somewhat physical romance between a two-foot duck and a full-sized woman, though one happens to be a cartoon and the other pleasantly rounded and certainly mortal, is one of those things that might disconcert less squeamish authorities than the Hays office. . . . It might even be said that a sequence involving the duck, the young lady, and a long alley of animated cactus plants would probably be considered suggestive in a less innocent medium.

It was, however, a box-office success . . . though it never received a theatrical reissue because studio executives apparently decided that, like *The Reluctant Dragon* and *Saludos Amigos,* it was too firmly moored to the 1940s. Frequent exposure on the Disney TV show kept its memory—and its characters Joe Carioca and Panchito—alive, and its availability for rental on 16mm, especially at a time when the major Disney animated features were *unavailable,* helped it foster a new reputation among cartoon buffs in the 1960s and 70s. It took on particular luster in the wake of *Yellow Submarine* and the Peter Max graphic explosion; its dynamic, often surreal (even "psychedelic") animation and design put it years ahead of its time in conception and execution. But the Disney studio was slow to recognize its renewed potential. (The film was conspicuously absent from a fiftieth anniversary studio retrospective held at New York's Lincoln Center in 1973.)

Then, in 1976, *The Three Caballeros* was given its first theatrical release in thirty-one years—in a severely truncated, and poorly edited, "featurette" version. There was no sense to the editing, and much of the film's charm was lost. Fortunately, the complete print has been shown on The Disney Channel and made available on home video. Whatever stigma may have been attached to it at one time—for being dated, or not in the classic Disney tradition—seems to have disappeared, and *The Three Caballeros* has finally taken its place among the studio's proud achievements.

MAKE MINE MUSIC

RELEASED BY RKO RADIO PICTURES ON AUGUST 15, 1946. Technicolor. Production supervisor: Joe Grant. Directors: Jack Kinney, Clyde Geronimi, Hamilton Luske, Robert Cormack, Joshua Meador. Story: Homer Brightman, Dick Huemer, Dick Kinney, John Walbridge, Tom Oreb, Dick Shaw, Eric Gurney, Sylvia Holland, T. Hee, Dick Kelsey, Jesse Marsh, Roy Williams, Ed Penner, James Bodrero, Cap Palmer, Erwin Graham. Art supervisors: Mary Blair, Elmer Plummer, John Hench. Animators: Les Clark, Ward Kimball, Milt Kahl, John Sibley, Hal King, Eric Larson, John Lounsbery, Oliver M. Johnston, Jr., Fred Moore, Hugh Fraser, Judge Whitaker, Harvey Toombs, Tom Massey, Phil Duncan, Hal Ambro, Jack Campbell, Cliff Nordberg, Bill Justice, Al Bertino, John McManus, Ken O'Brien. Backgrounds: Claude Coats, Art Riley, Ralph Hulett, Merle Cox, Ray Huffine, Albert Dempster, Thelma Witmer, Jim Trout. Layout: A. Kendall O'Connor, Hugh Hennesy, Al Zinnen, Ed Benedict, Charles Philippi, Donald Da Gradi, Lance Nolley, Charles Payzant, John Niendorf. Effects animation: George Rowley, Jack Boyd, Andy Engman, Brad Case, Don Patterson. Musical director: Charles Wolcott. Associates: Ken Darby, Oliver Wallace, Edward H. Plumb. Process effects: Ub Iwerks. Color consultant: Mique Nelson. Sound: C. O. Slyfield, Robert O. Cook. Running time: 74 minutes.

Songs: "Johnny Fedora and Alice Blue Bonnet" by Allie Wrubel and Ray Gilbert; "All the Cats Join In" by Alec Wilder, Ray Gilbert, and Eddie Sauter; "Without You" by Osvaldo Farres, English lyrics by Ray Gilbert; "Two Silhouettes" by Charles Wolcott and Ray Gilbert; "Casey, the Pride of Them All" by Ray Gilbert, Ken Darby, and Eliot Daniel; "The Martins and the Coys" by Al Cameron and Ted Weems; "Blue Bayou" by Bobby Worth and Ray Gilbert; "After You've Gone" by Henry Creamer and Turner Leighton; "Make Mine Music" by Ken Darby and Eliot Daniel.

Voices: Nelson Eddy, Dinah Shore, Benny Goodman and Orchestra, The Andrews Sisters, Jerry Colonna, Andy Russell, Sterling Holloway, The Pied Pipers, The King's Men, The Ken Darby Chorus, and featuring Tatiana Riabouchinska and David Lichine.

After the release of *Fantasia*, Walt Disney was urged to adapt the same format to popular music. Disney did not commit himself to the idea, but in 1944 started formulating plans for just such a film. Initially, the feature was to run the full gamut of musical styles, and Leopold Stokowski was again to be involved. Plans changed, however, and though some classical pieces remained in the finished film, the accent was clearly on popular music. For "marquee value," he hired an array of popular singers and musicians.

The titles are done in a theatre-marquee and poster format, each poster bringing us closer to the theatre entrance. When the titles are completed, we go in the doors and our eyes fall upon a program, which reads, "A Music Fantasy in Ten Parts." Then the curtain opens and the first sequence begins.

A Rustic Ballad is "The Martins and the Coys," sung by the King's Men, a fast and straightforward cartoon of the hillbilly hit about an age-old mountain feud. A monumental shoot-out sends most of the two families up to heaven, where on neighboring clouds, they watch the precedent-breaking love match between young Henry Martin and Grace McCoy. They get married, but after a hoedown wedding ceremony, it turns out that the feud hasn't ended after all: Grace is a battle-ax supreme, who showers her husband with a flurry of rolling pins, crockery, etc. The angels above all have a good laugh.

Next is *A Tone Poem*, sung by the Ken Darby chorus, "Blue Bayou." This is one of the deliberately "arty" segments in the film, opening on a beautiful shot of the moon, with clouds passing across its face; this dissolves into a view of the bayou, with an egret stopping to rest. He looks at his reflection in the water, dips into it, and the ripple is carried across the lake. When it stills, we see, not the egret, but the moon again, in reflection. Then as the camera looks up, the egret and a companion fly off toward the moon as the song concludes.

For a change of pace, there is *A Jazz Interlude*

These four instruments go on a surreal trip to the music of the Benny Goodman quartet in "After You've Gone." ©
Walt Disney Productions

Willie the Whale treats his seagoing friends to an impromptu concert. © *Walt Disney Productions*

Walt Disney shows one of his singing stars, Dinah Shore, around the Burbank studio. © *Walt Disney Productions*

Walt Disney goes over the score for "Casey at the Bat" with hammy Jerry Colonna. *Courtesy British Film Institute*

with Benny Goodman and his orchestra, "All the Cats Join In," subtitled "A Cari*cat*ure." A pencil draws the sequence's characters in a sketchbook, flipping the page for each new character or new scene. There are no backgrounds, except sparse details to indicate immediate backdrops like a sidewalk or a house. The pace is very fast as the song is illustrated in a vignette of a 1940s bobby-soxer going down to the malt shop with her boyfriend for a jitterbug session.

Next is *A Ballad in Blue,* "Without You," sung by Andy Russell. This segment tries to capture a mood with colors and images that relate to the atmosphere the song describes. As the scene opens we are in a long, dark room, with just a hint of detail at the far end, lit by the natural light coming in from a tall window, revealing a handwritten note left on a chair nearby. As we move in closer, the rain outside crawls down the windowpane, and, taking on various colors, forms the backgrounds outside of roads, hills, trees, etc., then moving up to a starry blue sky, which in turn dissolves into a vision of trees against a far blue horizon. As the song comes to a close, we pull back into the room once more and the sequence ends as it began.

Jerry Colonna is featured in *A Musical Recitation* of "Casey at the Bat." It opens with a chorus singing the theme song, visualized by a series of old-fashioned lithographs reflecting the Gay '90s. Then we move into the ball park itself for the story of Casey, as sung and told by Colonna. The famous poem is injected with visual hyperbole in the form of endless sight gags (the ball sliding up the first baseman's foot right into his hand, the bat getting caught in one player's long waxed moustache, etc.). At the climax of the story, on the third strike, the line "the force of Casey's blow" is illustrated by a tremendous gust of wind, shown over a scene of the spectators in the stands. The gust turns the picture into a blur, and it dissolves into a picture of birds singing in the trees (as the poem continues), bands playing in the park, etc. But back in Mudville, we see Casey, alone in the stadium as it begins to rain, going berserk, chasing the ball all around the field with his bat.

Ballade Ballet features Tatiana Riabouchinska and David Lichine, of the Ballet Russe, performing as Dinah Shore sings "Two Silhouettes." A heart melts into two cupids against a lacy background, which they open as a curtain to reveal the silhouettes of the two dancers against a pink background. They begin to dance, and the backgrounds behind them change randomly. Soon the silhouettes are lifted out of conventional time and space and become part of the animation; during one of the ballerina's pirouettes, a cupid lifts her by the arms onto an animated ledge high above, where the dance continues. The sequence closes with the silhouettes in repose, and the two cupids closing the curtain and returning into the shape of a heart.

"Peter and the Wolf" is *A Fairy Tale with Music,* told by Sterling Holloway. It is the classic story that accompanied Prokofiev's music, with numerous additions and embellishments, such as specific names and identities for each of the animals (Sasha the bird, Sonja the duck, Ivan the cat) who accompany Peter on his premature hunting trip in the Russian forest.

Benny Goodman returns with his quartet (Cozy Cole, Teddy Wilson, Sid Weiss), this time for "After You've Gone," a surreal vision of the four instruments (clarinet, drums, piano, bass) engaging in a wild, chaselike battle. The clarinet and bass go at it in a boxing ring, engage in a chase over an endless, winding keyboard . . . the clarinet gets "hot," catches fire, and a river of music (notes, keys, clefs, etc.) puts it out, as the four instruments run off into infinity as the swinging improvisation draws to a close.

A Love Story is sung by the Andrews Sisters: "Johnny Fedora and Alice Blue Bonnet," the tale of two hats who fall in love in the window of a department store. They are separated when each is sold, and Johnny spends every moment on his buyer's head searching for Alice to no avail. He jumps around so much that he eventually is blown away and brought down to the point of being discarded. Just as he is about to be washed down a sewer, a man picks him up, cuts holes in his brim, and puts him on his horse. (The new owner is an iceman.) And lo and behold, who should be next to him on the companion horse but Alice.

The finale is *Opera Pathetique,* featuring Nelson Eddy, who does all the voices for "The Whale Who Wanted to Sing at the Met." The story is told musically at first, then Eddy lapses into straight narration. Headlines tell of "Mystery Voice at Sea," and it is revealed that the voice belongs to a whale! Professors scoff, people don't believe it, but famed opera impresario Professor Tetti Tatti surmises that the whale must have swallowed an opera singer. He goes out to sea to harpoon the whale and rescue his latest discovery. A sea gull tells Willie the whale that Tetti Tatti is on his way, and, after much consideration, Willie decides to sing "Figaro" for his audition, doing tenor, baritone, and bass roles all at once. "He's swallowed *three* opera singers!" cries Tetti Tatti, determined to shoot him. But the three crewmen on board the ship are enjoying the music too much, and stand in his way. Willie serenades them, singing the entire sextet from *Lucia* himself.

At this point he dreams of his debut at the Met, standing on the stage, filling the entire house, the spotlight focused on his three tonsils. When he bows, he towers over the audience. The sailors, seals, and sea gulls are in attendance (the audience directly below the gulls wearing protection on their heads). This is followed by triumph after triumph. As Pagliacci he wears a huge clown's nose, and, instead of crying, spouts water, causing the orchestra members to wear raincoats, and the conductor to carry an umbrella. He plays in *Tristan und Isolde, Mephistopheles,* but his dream is curtailed when Tetti Tatti gets to the gun and harpoons poor Willie in the midst of a stormy sea.

The narrator urges us not to be too harsh on Tetti Tatti. "People aren't used to miracles," he explains, adding that "miracles never really die." And, sure enough, as we make a tremendous ascent to Heaven through towering cloud formations, Willie is singing again—in a hundred golden voices—and on the Pearly Gates hangs a sign reading "Sold Out."

It is pleasing that *Make Mine Music* ends on such a delightful note, for "The Whale Who Wanted to Sing at the Met" (later known as "Willie the Operatic Whale") is surely one of the film's highlights, and tends to overshadow the film's very definite weaknesses.

Make Mine Music is a film of ups and downs, the ups being most of the popular material and the downs being the attempts to work with classical music, and/or become "artistic."

The Martins and the Coys is hardly a Disney classic, but it is certainly innocuous, whereas *Blue Bayou* and *Two Silhouettes* are embarrassing attempts at "culture." *Blue Bayou* is quite lovely, and actually a showcase for Disney's corps of effects animators, who really did raise their craft to a fine art. It might have worked better in its original context, when it was set to Debussy's beautiful "Clair de Lune" and intended for inclusion in *Fantasia*. But here its "illustrated music" stylings seem pretentious and out of place.

Two Silhouettes was unanimously chosen as the nadir of the film by its many critics, including some who thought the film as a whole had its moments. Brushing aside for the moment the (valid) criticism that the combination of live-action ballet and animation techniques negated both art forms, the sequence again seems to have no purpose, no direction, unlike, for instance, Norman McLaren's acclaimed short *Duo*, which presents a pas de deux in stroboscopic fashion. The very format of cupids and doilies spelled disaster for most viewers before the sequence was even under way.

One finds this artiness invading even some of the more pleasant sequences, such as *A Ballad in Blue*, which rests on the borderline between the two styles to be found in the film. Even when some of its abstracts start to "work," the effect is spoiled when the lyric "I pray . . ." cues the transformation of a tree into a cross.

Most disappointing of all is *Peter and the Wolf*, which at first glance would seem a most likely subject for Disney treatment. But there is an inherent problem with the piece; it was designed to be heard, not seen. The famous narration, keyed to special orchestration of the music, was intended to fascinate children by making them use their imaginations to visualize the story. Hence, *any* visual treatment destroys the essential meaning of the piece.

However, one must concede that it might be possible to do justice to Prokofiev's work. The problem here was that the Disney people went overboard. The charm of *Peter and the Wolf* is its simplicity, which is pummeled to death by naming every single solitary character in the story—Sonja the Duck, Micha, Yasoha, and Vladimir the hunters, Ivan the Cat, etc., etc., etc. The narration is no longer the classic one, but a more up-to-date and pointed kind, with sportscaster overtones ("Look out, Sacha!"). Here, for a change, the animation is quite pleasing, and it is the *concept* that fails.

What, then, are *Make Mine Music*'s moments? First, the two Benny Goodman pieces, which seem, unlike most of the other musical compositions, to have actually *inspired* the Disney crew to match the music with something original and appropriate on the screen. "All the Cats Join In" is a delightful evocation of the bobby-sox generation, done in a striking format that even pokes fun at itself. The pencil that is drawing the characters can't keep up with the rapid pace of the action; it starts to draw a jalopy for the teen-agers, but they ride off with it before the pencil is through! It races ahead and draws a stoplight that forces the car to stand still while the finishing touches are added. The sequence ends as the jukebox explodes, sending records, musical notes, and other musical symbols flying in a million directions.

"After You've Gone" is among the best surreal animation Disney ever did, buoyed by the sparkling sounds of the Goodman quartet. It moves very fast, its imagination unflagging in presenting the four humanized instruments on the lam in their nightmarish world. The same critics who condemned *Two Silhouettes* praised this segment as the highlight of the feature.

"Casey at the Bat" is also quite satisfying, in a more standard way, with all the accouterments of a typical 1940s Disney short subject—clever direction (one shot shows a close-up of a mitt as the ball is thrown into it), rapid-paced sight gags (a player on first base "leads" so energetically that it appears there are two of him running back and forth from the base to the midway point), and, in this case, a perfect choice for narrator-singer, Jerry Colonna.

"Johnny Fedora and Alice Blue Bonnet" is also very pleasing, with the smooth harmonies of the Andrews Sisters. The idea of telling the story from a hat's eye view, and minimizing the display of human faces, is a difficult one to maintain, and one can see definite stumbling blocks in the sequence, but, generally, it's quite well done.

Best of all is "The Whale Who Wanted to Sing at the Met." This is Disney doing what he does best, a combination of fantasy and gentle satire—getting in spoofs not only of opera, but of human nature, and even a little joke at Nelson Eddy's expense. (When we first join Willie, he is singing "Shortnin' Bread," one of Eddy's popular hits.) The visions of Willie at the

Met are simply priceless, topping each other with inventive gags (simply the *sight* of Willie made up as Pagliacci is hilarious), and including a generous helping of the most popular classical arias.

Appropriately enough, "Willie" has had the most exposure outside of the feature, playing independently as a short and being run many times on the Disney TV show.

When the film was released, in mid-1946, it met with widely mixed reaction. As Disney's first feature release since the war, it was highly anticipated (*The Three Caballeros* having been considered part of the general wartime atmosphere), and many critics became apologists for the film, feeling that even if it weren't top Disney, it would just be a short while before he was back in form.

Otis L. Guernsey, in the *Herald Tribune,* wrote: "*Make Mine Music* merely boils the pot without mixing in the ingredients of a masterpiece . . . [but] those who do not insist on the rare experience of a Disney masterpiece will have the delightful experience of a Disney potboiler, whose comedy, artistry, and fantasy make most of the live actor entertainments look drab and pedestrian by comparison."

The film provided the final break between Disney and the intellectuals who had made him their darling in the 1930s. Most expressive of this feeling is a review written by Hermine Rich Isaacs for *Theatre Arts* magazine:

Suppose you go to visit a friend. You know that he has a warm heart and is kind to animals, that his sense of humor is infectious, his professional skill beyond compare. But when you enter his house you find to your dismay that his walls are festooned with second-rate art; romantic scenes of white doves against lush blue backgrounds; vapid landscapes; valentine motifs, complete with lace cutouts, tinsel stars and hearts of assorted sizes. You discover that his furniture is carelessly assembled with little regard for harmony or any other concern except to fill space. You would not therefore cease to love the man, to laugh at his jokes or admire his skill; but you would have to admit with regret that his taste is deplorable. On similar internal evidence, this is the reluctant conclusion of a visitor to *Make Mine Music* . . .

After its initial release, *Make Mine Music* was never reissued intact. Instead, as with the other Disney omnibus features to follow, its segments were reissued separately as short subjects. (Four pieces were combined with five more from *Melody Time* to form a "new" feature called *Music Land* in 1955.) And most of this material was used in a variety of ways on the Disney TV program over the years.

Make Mine Music was a sharp disappointment to the millions who had eagerly awaited another Disney classic. They did not give up on him, however, and hoped that soon he would make another feature film to rate alongside his prewar achievements. For some, that film never came; others learned that Disney was simply changing and moving on to new areas where he hoped he could succeed as completely as he had with the animated feature.

SONG OF THE SOUTH

RELEASED BY RKO RADIO PICTURES ON NOVEMBER 1, 1946. Technicolor. Associate producer: Perce Pearce. Cartoon director: Wilfred Jackson. Photoplay director: Harve Foster. Screenplay: Dalton Raymond, Morton Grant, Maurice Rapf. Original story: Dalton Raymond, based on the *Tales of Uncle Remus* by Joel Chandler Harris. Photography: Gregg Toland. Film editor: William M. Morgan. Art director: Perry Ferguson. Costumes: Mary Wills. Special processes: Ub Iwerks. Sound director: C. O. Slyfield. Sound recording: Fred Lau, Harold Steck. Art treatment: Elmer Plummer. Technicolor color director: Natalie Kalmus. Associate: Mitchell Kovaleski. Music director: Charles Wolcott. Photoplay score: Daniele Amfitheatrof. Cartoon score: Paul J. Smith. Vocal director: Ken Darby. Orchestrations: Edward H. Plumb. Cartoon story: William Peet, Ralph Wright, George Stallings. Cartoon art directors: Kenneth Anderson, Charles Philippi, Hugh Hennesy, Harold Doughty, Philip Barber. Directing animators: Milt Kahl, Eric Larson, Oliver M. Johnston, Jr., Les Clark, Marc Davis, John Lounsbery. Animators: Don Lusk, Tom Massey, Murray McClellan, Jack Campbell, Hal King, Harvey Toombs, Ken O'Brien, Al Coe, Hal Ambro, Cliff Nordberg, Rudy Larriva. Background and color stylists: Claude Coats, Mary Blair. Background artists: Ralph Hulett, Brice Mack, Ray Huffine, Edgar Starr, Albert Dempster. Effects animation: Joshua Meador, George Rowley, Blaine Gibson, Brad Case. Running time: 94 minutes.

Songs: "How Do You Do?" by Robert MacGimsey.

Glenn Leedy and Bobby Driscoll listen to James Baskett as
Uncle Remus in *Song of the South*. © *Walt Disney Productions*

"Song of the South" by Sam Coslow, Arthur Johnston. "That's What Uncle Remus Said" by Eliot
Daniel, Hy Heath, Johnny Lange. "Sooner or Later"
by Charles Wolcott, Ray Gilbert. "Everybody's Got
a Laughing Place," "Zip-a-dee Doo-Dah" by Allie
Wrubel, Ray Gilbert. "Let the Rain Pour Down,"
"Who Wants to Live Like That?" by Foster Carling.

Cast: Ruth Warrick (Sally), James Baskett (Uncle
Remus), Bobby Driscoll (Johnny), Luana Patten
(Ginny), Lucile Watson (grandmother), Hattie Mc-
Daniel (Aunt Tempy), Glenn Leedy (Toby), George
Nokes, Gene Holland (The Favers Boys), Erik Rolf
(John), Mary Field (Mrs. Favers), Anita Brown
(maid), and the voices of James Baskett (Brer Fox),
Nicodemus Stewart (Brer Bear), and Johnny Lee
(Brer Rabbit).

Song of the South was advertised as "an epochal
event in screen history." This would seem to be
stretching things too far, but it was indeed an important film in the chronology of Disney's career, for it
relied more on live-action dramatic footage than any
previous film (*The Reluctant Dragon* having been
mutually forgotten by both Disney and the press),
and perfected the combination of animation and live
action to a height of perfection, outdoing even *The
Three Caballeros* in this respect.

The opening titles of the film are set against
rustic engravings of the Old South. An introductory
title states: "Out of the humble cabin, out of the
singing heart of the Old South have come the tales of
Uncle Remus, rich in simple truths, forever fresh and
new."

The film's action begins with little Johnny being
brought to live with his mother and grandmother at
the latter's plantation. He doesn't understand that his
parents are separating, and when his father says good-
bye, Johnny is distraught. That evening, he decides to
run away from home, but along the way he encounters
Uncle Remus telling stories to some black children.
When Remus hears that Johnny is running away from
home, he decides to use psychology to lure him back.
He tells Johnny he was thinking of running away too,

Brer Fox has the last laugh on Brer Rabbit . . .
© *Walt Disney Productions*

. . . and shares the laugh with Brer Bear at the dinner
table.   © *Walt Disney Productions*

With cartoon storyboards for a background, Disney shares
some Uncle Remus with his two discoveries, Luana Patten
and Bobby Driscoll.   *Courtesy British Film Institute*

and would like to go with him, but first they must
stop at his cabin for some provisions. While there, he
tells Johnny a story. As he starts to describe what kind
of day it was when the story took place, the camera
dollies in, and as he begins to sing "Zip-a-dee Doo-
Dah," the background around his head (now in close-
up) bursts away to reveal a brilliantly blue sky, with
Uncle Remus walking through an animated countryside, singing. As he ambles along, the birds flutter
around him, and all the local animals get into the
spirit of things.

Then he encounters Brer Rabbit, who is boarding up the entrance to his home in the Briar Patch
and "never comin' back." As he goes off, he is spotted
by Brer Fox, who has left a trap for him. The trap
catches Brer Rabbit by the foot and has him dangling
upside down from a tree limb. The Fox comes running after his prey from his hilltop hideout, but
meanwhile Brer Bear walks by. Brer Rabbit uses Tom

Sawyer-like psychology to convince Brer Bear that he's
earning a dollar a minute for hanging there acting as
scarecrow. Since he has plenty of money by now, he
offers to let Brer Bear take his place, which the oafish
Bear is happy to do. By the time Brer Fox reaches the
trap, the Rabbit is on his way down the road; Brer
Fox convinces Brer Bear that he's been made a fool of,
and the two of them start fighting, as Brer Rabbit goes
on his way, laughing uproariously.

The moral, Uncle Remus tells Johnny, is "You
can't run away from trouble—there ain't no place
that far." Johnny takes the hint and returns home to
his worried mother, who has the impression that
Uncle Remus led him astray in the first place.

Without many friends, without a father, and
under the thumb of his overprotective mother,
Johnny soon comes to rely on Uncle Remus more and
more as a companion. One day he meets up with two
rowdy brothers who bully their little sister and her pet

dog. To save the dog from being drowned, Johnny adopts it himself, and becomes friendly with Ginny, the little girl. But he doesn't know how to handle the two brothers.

Uncle Remus tells him the story of Brer Rabbit and the Tar Baby, which picks up where the last tale left off. The Fox and Bear fashion a human figure out of tar, and leave it sitting by the side of the road. Brer Rabbit comes by, sings "How Do You Do?" to the fellow, and becomes annoyed that he doesn't answer back. After several attempts, he punches the Tar Baby in the nose, and becomes entangled in the gooey mess, a sitting duck for Brer Fox and Brer Bear; the Fox wants to roast him, while the Bear wants to "knock his head clean off."

Again, Brer Rabbit uses psychology. He says he'll welcome roasting, hanging, or whatever, but "please don't fling me in dat briar patch." He makes them believe that there would be no worse fate than that, so the Fox falls for it, and hurls him into the midst of the thorny field. Brer Rabbit makes sounds of pain from underneath, but then springs up laughing hysterically. "I was born and bred in the briar patch," he sings mockingly. The lesson: you see what happens when you get mixed up in somethin' you got no business getting mixed up in.

Johnny uses the same idea when the two nasty brothers threaten to tell his mother that he's taken their dog. Johnny tells them to go ahead, but whatever they do, not to tell their *own* mother. They fall for it, and get a whipping from their mother for having treated the dog so badly in the first place. After that, they do tell Johnny's mother, who once again blames Uncle Remus for encouraging the boy.

Johnny's mother decides to give him a birthday party, to enliven his spirits. He insists on inviting Ginny, even though she comes from a poor family, duly noted by Mother. When she is late, Johnny goes to get her, and on the way her brothers taunt her and push her into a mud puddle, spoiling her new dress. Ginny cries uncontrollably, upset not only about the dress, but too ashamed to go to Johnny's party. Uncle Remus comes upon the scene, and, instead of sharing her sorrow, starts laughing. The youngsters ask him why, and he says he's thinking about his Laughing Place.

This leads to the next story, as Brer Rabbit has been captured once again by the Fox and Bear. He starts singing, "Everybody's Got a Laughing Place," as he is about to be cooked. Brer Bear asks him what he's talking about, and Brer Rabbit explains that it's a secret place he knows about. Not wanting to be fooled again, the Fox and Bear make the Rabbit lead them to this laughing place, which turns out to be a giant beehive. As Brer Bear is chased about by the angry insects, he hollers to the Rabbit, asking what's the big idea. "I didn't say this was *your* laughing place,'" Brer Rabbit replies, "I said it was *my* laughing place, Brer Bear!" And indeed, he can't stop laughing at the sight of his adversaries running about in a frenzy.

The story succeeds in cheering up Johnny and Ginny, but then Johnny's mother arrives and blames Uncle Remus for keeping the children from their party. She demands that he never speak to Johnny again.

Heartbroken and convinced that he's a good-for-nothing, Uncle Remus decides to go away. When Johnny sees him riding away in his carriage, he runs after him, across a field where a bull is grazing. The bull runs after Johnny and knocks him unconscious. That night, Johnny's father is sent for, but even his presence can't bring Johnny out of his delirium. They plead with Uncle Remus to come to see the boy, and he does, soothing the youngster's anxieties and helping him back to normal. Johnny's father and mother now realize how important it is that they stay together.

Soon all is right with the world. Johnny is no longer dependent upon Uncle Remus and can appreciate him as a friend. He romps along with Ginny and his black friend, singing "Zip-a-dee Doo-Dah," conjuring up the cartoon animals that previously only Uncle Remus had been able to bring to life. Seeing them prancing along, Remus can't believe his eyes, and calls for them to wait, running to join them at the crest of the hill as they all join hands and walk into the sunset on what is *truly* a beautiful day.

The critics were virtually unanimous in their appraisal of *Song of the South*. Bosley Crowther wrote that "the ratio of 'live' to cartoon action is approximately two to one, and that is approximately the ratio of its mediocrity to its charm." *Time* thought that "it could have used a much heavier helping of cartooning," claiming that except for the two youngsters, "the live actors are bores."

Even *Variety* concurred. "Story of misunderstood Johnny gets away to an ambling start, and only picks up . . . when the live Uncle Remus segues into the first cartoon sequence . . . the rest of the story, including the confused and insufficiently explained estrangement of the parents, overbalances the three cartoon sequences, and could be cut . . . these cartoon sequences are great stuff."

There is no denying that it is the cartoon segments that make this film. They have a joy, a cheerfulness about them that is absolutely irresistible, and, of course, they are populated with delightful songs, such as the Academy Award winner "Zip-a-dee Doo-Dah," and "Everybody's Got a Laughing Place." The color in these sequences is probably the most bright and vivid ever seen in motion pictures, a quality characteristic of most of Disney's 1940s cartoon output.

The combination of live action and animation is startling, and the transitions used to link them are ingenious, from the first, with a literal burst of blue introducing the live Uncle Remus walking down an animated path, to later, more intricate dissolves. In the first such sequence Brer Rabbit dances about

Uncle Remus's feet, casting a shadow as he does! It is virtually impossible to tell where the live film ends and the animation begins, with such later highlights as Uncle Remus lighting the pipe of an old bullfrog who is sitting by the stream fishing.

The cartoon sequences also stand out because they are from the pen of Uncle Remus (Joel Chandler Harris), and rate among the most memorable in American folklore. Their little morals, in showing how brains can always outwit brawn, are cunning, and a treat to watch as Brer Rabbit tries them out on his adversaries.

More than one critic wondered why Disney didn't simply call his film *Uncle Remus* and make total use of these marvelous tales. Of course, this was not Disney's idea at all; he was looking for a new kind of entertainment form, and he believed *Song of the South* was it. In interviews given at the time of the film's release, he indicated that he planned to make most of his films a blend of live action and animation from that time on, including *Alice in Wonderland*.

Song of the South also, being Disney's deepest plunge into live filming, presented him with his first "contract players." Disney was justifiably proud of Bobby Driscoll and Luana Patten, two extremely winning and talented young children, and, just like every other studio in town, signed them to contracts and built them up as his own personal stars over the next few years with considerable success.

Not that they are the only good things about the live sequences. James Baskett, who was then a regular character on the Amos 'n' Andy radio show, is ideal as Uncle Remus, eliciting just the right kind of warmth and humor, and later poignancy, from the character (in fact, he was voted a special Academy Award for his performance). He and Hattie McDaniel contribute one of the film's most delightful moments, when she sings "Sooner or Later" as she feeds him some of her apple pie.

But not everyone found this kind of setting "charming," particularly some liberal reviewers and Negro organizations. *Time* commented that Uncle Remus was "bound to enrage all educated Negroes, and a number of damnyankees." They were correct. The NAACP, though noting the "remarkable artistic merit" of the film, deplored "the impression it gives of an idyllic master-slave relationship which is a distortion of the facts." The National Urban League called the film "another repetition of the perpetuation of the stereotype casting of the Negro in the servant role, depicting him as indolent, one who handles the truth lightly."

A Disney spokesman, quoted in *PM,* noted that the film did not depict slavery, since it took place after the Civil War, and that Disney "was not trying to put across any message, but was making a sincere effort to depict American folklore, to put the Uncle Remus stories into pictures."

The Disney spokesman also pointed to a review written by Herman Hill in a black newspaper, the *Pittsburgh Courier,* reading in part: "The truly sympathetic handling of the entire production from a racial standpoint is calculated . . . to prove of inestimable good in the furthering of interracial relations."

Indeed, protest was not widespread among the American public (certainly not in the South, where the *Atlanta Journal*'s film critic rated the film alongside *Gone With the Wind*), who flocked to see the film and made it a major Disney money-maker, both in its initial release and on reissue in 1956.

It was only in the 1960s, when civil rights became a major concern of the entire United States, that it became clear that *Song of the South* and films of that kind would be touching sensitive spots if shown again. Even the reissue of *Gone With the Wind* in 1967 sparked some (relatively minor) protest among certain Negro groups who objected to the depiction of slavery and southern plantation life.

In February 1970, prompted by one exhibitor's request to make the film available, the Disney company announced, in the pages of *Variety,* that the film was "permanently" withdrawn and would not be shown again.

But by late 1971 Disney executives had second thoughts, probably noting a change in black attitudes, with more tolerance toward the inescapable facts of history, and a more objective acceptance of formerly taboo Hollywood products of the 1930s and 1940s. In January 1972 *Song of the South* was reissued to overwhelming nationwide reaction; reportedly it was one of the most successful reissues in the company's history.

Its subsequent reissue, in 1986, was modestly successful, and yielded only a handful of critical comments in the press. But heightened sensitivity has kept the studio from releasing the film on home video in the U.S. (Laserdisc owners have been able to purchase a copy imported from Japan.)

The worst complaints against *Song of the South* seem mild compared to the reception given Ralph Bakshi's live-action/animated *Coonskin* in 1975—a protest so fiery that the film was disowned by its distributor (and later released, on a limited basis, under the misleading title *Street Fight*). Ironically, *Coonskin* was a modern-day satire based in part on *Song of the South*.

As for the original, *Song of the South* can speak for itself. Accusations of Uncle Tomisms and quibbles over its syrupy storyline are ultimately defeated by the film's sheer entertainment value. It has some of the most delightful moments Disney ever captured on film. . . . and that's what really counts.

FUN & FANCY FREE

RELEASED BY RKO RADIO PICTURES ON SEPTEMBER 27, 1947. Production supervisor: Ben Sharpsteen. Live-action director: William Morgan. Cartoon directors: Jack Kinney, Bill Roberts, Hamilton Luske. Authors: Homer Brightman, Harry Reeves, Ted Sears, Lance Nolley, Eldon Dedini, Tom Oreb. *Bongo* based on an original story by Sinclair Lewis. Directing animators: Ward Kimball, Les Clark, John Lounsbery, Fred Moore, Wolfgang Reitherman. Character animators: Hugh Fraser, Phil Duncan, Judge Whitaker, Arthur Babbitt, John Sibley, Marc Davis, Harvey Toombs, Hal King, Ken O'Brien, Jack Campbell. Backgrounds: Ed Starr, Claude Coats, Art Riley, Brice Mack, Ray Huffine, Ralph Hulett. Layout: Donald Da Gradi, Al Zinnen, Ken O'Connor, Hugh Hennesy, John Hench, Glen Scott. Effects animation: George Rowley, Jack Boyd. Musical director: Charles Wolcott. Musical score: Paul J. Smith, Oliver Wallace, Eliot Daniel. Live-action cameraman: Charles P. Boyle. Film editor: Jack Bachom. Process effects: Ub Iwerks. Sound supervision: C. O. Slyfield. Sound recording: Harold J. Steck, Robert Cook. Technicolor color director: Natalie Kalmus. Associate: Morgan Padleford. Running time: 73 minutes.

Songs: "Fun and Fancy Free" By Bennie Benjamin, George Weiss. "Lazy Countryside" by Bobby Worth. "Too Good to Be True," "Say It With a Slap" by Eliot Daniel, Buddy Kaye. "Fee Fi Fo Fum" by Paul J. Smith, Arthur Quenzer. "My Favorite Dream" by William Walsh, Ray Noble. "I'm a Happy-Go-Lucky Fellow" by Eliot Daniel, Ned Washington. "Beanero" by Oliver Wallace. "My, What a Happy Day" by Bill Walsh and Ray Noble.

Cast: Edgar Bergen, Luana Patten, Charlie McCarthy, Mortimer Snerd, and the voices of Dinah Shore, Anita Gordon (The Singing Harp), Cliff Edwards (Jiminy Cricket), Billy Gilbert (The Giant), Clarence Nash (Donald Duck), The Kings Men, The Dinning Sisters, The Starlighters.

Fun & Fancy Free was one of the bread-and-butter movies Disney made after the war to get material into release as quickly as possible, and regain his studio's lost momentum. As such, it is a pleasant enough film, but hardly outstanding. Its greatest notoriety derives from the fact that it is one of the few Disney feature films to include his short-subject stars Mickey Mouse, Donald Duck, and Goofy.

The film opens with Jiminy Cricket floating on a leaf in a lily pond, singing "I'm a Happy-Go-Lucky Fellow." The pond turns out to be a planter in a house, and in his wanderings Jiminy comes upon a doll and teddy bear seated together, looking rather glum. To cheer them up, he puts on a record, *Bongo*, "A Musical Story Sung by Dinah Shore."

Bongo, the Wonder Bear, is a circus star who rides a unicycle, even on a tightrope, juggles, and dives three hundred feet into a wet sponge. Offstage, however, he is "tossed around like an old shoe" by his trainers. During a train ride to the next town, Bongo works up the courage to hop off on his unicycle and flee into the woods. Being a circus animal he isn't used to the forest and revels in nature's beauty—as indicated by the song "I Love to Hang Around Lazy Countryside."

Bit by bit he tries to accustom himself to nature's ways, and while hunting for food he comes upon a lovely female bear. He absolutely flips, and a dream sequence illustrates his reverie in the form of a heart-themed sequence. All seems idyllic until a ferocious bear, Lumpjaw, arrives on the scene to compete with Bongo for his mate. She turns around and slaps Bongo. He is bewildered. She slaps him again, and he walks away heartbroken. She tries once more, but this time she accidentally slaps Lumpjaw, turning him from a devil into an angel. This leads to an explanation, via song, "[A Bear Likes to] Say It with a Slap," which tells that this is how bears express their love. When Bongo finally figures this out, he runs back to his girl to save her from the clutches of Lumpjaw. This isn't so easy, and he is forced to do battle with the bear; the fight takes them over the river, through a canyon, down a waterfall, into the mountains. After a logrolling climax, Lumpjaw goes sailing down the river and Bongo claims his mate for a happy ending.

Having thus cheered up the dolls, Jiminy notices on the bureau an invitation sent to the dolls' owner, Luana Patten, inviting her to a party being given that evening by Edgar Bergen, Charlie McCarthy, and Mortimer Snerd at the house across the way. He hops over to see what's going on, and joins Edgar and friends, being careful to stay in the background.

Willie the Giant helps concoct a posed still with the principals of *Fun & Fancy Free:* Mickey, Goofy, Donald, Charlie McCarthy, Luana Patten, Edgar Bergen, and Mortimer Snerd. © *Walt Disney Productions*

Lumpjaw antagonizes happy-go-lucky Bongo in the first half of *Fun & Fancy Free.* © *Walt Disney Productions*

The party is charming, and Edgar decides to add to the fun by telling a story. "I think I'll run out and wind the sundial," Charlie says, trying to escape. But he is held back, and Edgar spins the tale of Happy Valley, which is called that because a Singing Harp spreads joy across the land with her songs. One day a great shadow is cast over the valley, and the Harp disappears. Happy Valley deteriorates into a woeful state. "All was misery," says Bergen. "Just like the eighth grade," adds Charlie.

An example of the local destitution is shown in the plight of three starving farmers, Mickey, Donald, and Goofy. Mickey slices bread for them from their remaining loaf . . . slices so thin they are transparent! Narrator Bergen pays tribute to the fact that Donald doesn't complain, doesn't crack under the pressure. "Shut up!" Donald shouts hysterically, "I can't stand it!" He becomes desperate and suggests killing their pet cow for dinner, but Mickey convinces him it would be much better to sell it. He does, and receives in payment some magic beans. At this point the story becomes "Jack and the Beanstalk," with Mickey, Donald, and Goofy as our collective hero.

The beanstalk grows up into the sky, and the trio set out for the beautiful castle that rests on a cloud in front of them. They encounter Willie the Giant, try to avoid him, and then outsmart him, and make him so angry he locks them up in a treasure chest with the Singing Harp, whom he kidnapped some time ago. He accidentally drops Mickey during this procedure, so while the Harp sings Willie to sleep, Mickey tries to secure the key to the chest and free his friends. He succeeds, but wakes the Giant in the process, and there is a mad chase down the beanstalk; when they get to the bottom, they chop it down and send Willie to an untimely end.

That's the end of the story, but Mortimer is unhappy because they killed the Giant. Bergen tries to explain that he needn't be sad, that the Giant is only a figment of his imagination. Just then, the house shakes as the behemoth Willie lifts up the roof and pokes his face inside. Bergen faints, Mortimer wishes Willie goodnight, and the giant continues on his way, lumbering into Hollywood, and picking up the Brown Derby restaurant to wear as a hat.

Fun & Fancy Free is a sometimes uneven blend of elements, but it does have its moments. Jiminy Cricket (drawn with much bolder face lines than when he appeared in *Pinocchio*) has a bright opening tune, and adds some wry comments throughout the film. In the final segment, with Edgar Bergen and company in live-action footage, the camera periodically cuts to the animated Jiminy helping himself to some of the party food.

Bongo, based on a story by Sinclair Lewis, is an innocuous but unaccountably weak featurette. Its story could have been told in five minutes, so the additional footage used is comprised of aimless action and "mood" songs. It is animated much in the style of the Disney shorts, with occasional exceptions when Bongo strolls through the countryside and we see impressive views of a picture-postcard mountain and lake, with a shimmering reflection, lush green countryside, etc. (Incidentally, two of the forest animals who become friendly with Bongo are early incarnations of Chip 'n' Dale, who made their short-subject debut just around this time.)

The countryside idyll, and the dream sequence with a heart motif (one giant heart explodes into a thousand smaller cupids, hearts, etc. . . . . Bongo and his girl nestle under a heart-shaped sun in the cotton-candy clouds, when they are swept away by a waterfall that takes them down through a heart-shaped hatch in the bottom of a cloud, etc.), is very nice, but it is impossible to become involved with the characters or the story, because they are *so* rambling and easygoing. This was apparently a general reaction, for several times, both at the time of the feature's release and in subsequent reissues of the short alone, the Disney company tried to build up the character of Bongo, to no avail.

The live-action footage with Edgar Bergen, Luana Patten, and Bergen's famous dummies is quite amusing, and provides a good framework for the forthcoming cartoon, with Charlie McCarthy's wisecracks bringing Bergen down to earth several times when he becomes a bit too sanctimonious in narrating the story.

The Happy Valley segment, which had originally been planned as an extended Mickey Mouse cartoon called *Mickey and the Beanstalk,* is a nice variation on the classic fairy tale, with some particularly bright touches. As usual, most of the big laughs come from Donald Duck's doings, as in the climax when Mickey is trying to get the key into the treasure-chest keyhole. Inside, Donald pushes Goofy aside and walks toward the hole declaring, "Let me have it, Mickey," at which instant the key plunges in and knocks him flat with a funny "honk" sound effect.

The voice of Willie the Giant is amusingly essayed by Billy Gilbert, whose presence is especially noted when Mickey tries to engineer the escape, and succeeds, but accidentally opens the Giant's package of snuff, causing him to "erupt" in a mad sneezing fit—Gilbert's famed specialty.

But again, this sequence is hardly of feature-film caliber, looking more like just what it is: an elongated short subject.

The final live-action sequence, and punch-line gag of the Giant coming to Bergen's house (and donning the Brown Derby afterward), adds a nice offbeat touch to the otherwise standard finish of the story.

With *Fun & Fancy Free*'s theatrical release, most critics welcomed Disney back to his home territory, but noted that he seemed to be "coasting" with such halfhearted fare. It was true, and it was not until the "Wind in the Willows" sequence of *Ichabod and Mr. Toad* that Disney impressed his admirers with the kind of inventiveness they expected of him.

In the 1960s Disney prepared a new framework for TV showings of the Happy Valley sequence, with the animated Ludwig von Drake (and his bootle beetle Herman) replacing Edgar Bergen and friends, but the original version has been released on 16mm and home video (under the title *Mickey and the Beanstalk*).

MELODY TIME

RELEASED BY RKO RADIO PICTURES ON MAY 27, 1948. Technicolor. Production supervisor: Ben Sharpsteen. Cartoon directors: Clyde Geronimi, Wilfred Jackson, Hamilton Luske, Jack Kinney. Story: Winston Hibler, Harry Reeves, Ken Anderson, Erdman Penner, Homer Brightman, Ted Sears, Joe Rinaldi, Art Scott, Bob Moore, Bill Cottrell, Jesse Marsh, John Walbridge. "Little Toot" by Hardie Gramatky. Folklore consultant: Carl Carmer. Directing animators: Eric Larson, Ward Kimball, Milt Kahl, Oliver Johnston, Jr., John Lounsbery, Les Clark. Character animators: Harvey Toombs, Ed Aardal, Cliff Nordberg, John Sibley, Ken O'Brien, Judge Whitaker, Marvin Woodward, Hal King, Don Lusk, Rudy Larriva, Bob Cannon, Hal Ambro. Backgrounds: Art Riley, Brice Mack, Ralph Hulett, Ray Huffine, Merle Cox, Dick Anthony. Layout: Hugh Hennesy, A. Kendall O'Connor, Al Zinnen, Don Griffith, McLaren Stewart, Lance Nolley, Robert Cormack, Thor Putnam, Donald Da Gradi. Effects animation: George Rowley, Jack Boyd, Joshua Meador, Hal McManus. Color and styling: Mary Blair, Claude Coats, Dick Kelsey. Musical directors: Eliot Daniel, Ken Darby. Associate: Paul J. Smith. Special arrangements: Vic Schoen, Al Sack. Technicolor color director: Natalie Kalmus. Associate: Morgan Padleford. Live-action photography: Winton Hoch, A.S.C. Special processes: Ub Iwerks. Film editors: Donald Halliday, Thomas Scott. Sound director: C. O. Slyfield. Sound recording: Robert O. Cook, Harold J. Steck. Running time: 75 minutes.

Songs: "Melody Time" by George Weiss and Bennie Benjamin. "Little Toot" by Allie Wrubel. "The Lord Is Good to Me," "The Apple Song," "The Pioneer Song" by Kim Gannon and Walter Kent. "Once Upon a Wintertime" by Bobby Worth, Ray Gilbert. "Blame It on the Samba" by Ernesto Nazareth, Ray Gilbert. "Blue Shadows on the Trail," "Pecos Bill" by Eliot Daniel, Johnny Lange. Also featuring "Trees," poem by Joyce Kilmer, music by Oscar Rasbach, and "The Flight of the Bumble Bee" by Rimsky-Korsakov.

Cast: Roy Rogers, Luana Patten, Bobby Driscoll, Ethel Smith, Bob Nolan, Sons of the Pioneers, and the voices of Buddy Clark, The Andrews Sisters, Fred Waring and his Pennsylvanians, Frances Langford, Dennis Day, with Freddy Martin and his Orchestra featuring Jack Fina.

Melody Time was the last of Disney's musical mélanges, and certainly the best. In its choice of material, presentation, and artistic style it managed to avoid most of the pitfalls of its predecessors and emerge as a solidly enjoyable outing.

The opening titles are shown as sheet music. At the conclusion of the titles, a brush and palette appear, and the brush paints a comic masque (voiced by Buddy Clark) who introduces the first number. Thereafter, he is not seen, but heard, introducing each sequence as the brush paints a title logo and voice credit.

Frances Langford sings "Once Upon a Wintertime," which is done as a greeting-card-come-to-life, with deliberately exaggerated characters and backgrounds, as the song is illustrated with a boy and girl going skating, having a quarrel, and ending as he saves her from drowning, for a happy reconciliation. The actions of the boy and girl are duplicated by a pair of young rabbits who go through the same cycle. The whole sequence is shown as a flashback, as we see a double-hinged picture frame of the couple, much older and married, in a Victorian living room.

Bumble Boogie is a jazz interpretation of "The Flight of the Bumble Bee" with Freddy Martin and his Orchestra, featuring Jack Fina at the piano. Our host describes it as an "instrumental nightmare," and that it is, with a bumblebee caught in a surreal musical world, chased by piano hammers across an endlessly winding musical staff, repeatedly encountering blockades and such, all with musical motifs.

Next is the story of *Johnny Appleseed*, with Dennis Day doing the voices of Johnny, the Old Settler, and Johnny's Angel, in telling the story of this famous folklore hero who follows his guardian angel's advice to "get on the wagon rollin' west," and finds his purpose in life as he travels around the land planting apple trees, which bring so much pleasure to people in so many ways. When it comes time to die, the Angel awakens him from a nap, and he leaves his "mortal husk" behind as the two of them march off to

Luana Patten and Bobby Driscoll listen as Roy Rogers and the Sons of the Pioneers spin the tale of Pecos Bill in *Melody Time*. *Movie Star News*

Johnny Appleseed tests out a prime specimen. © *Walt Disney Productions*

Heaven, where, Johnny is told, there aren't yet any apple trees. That's why, the narrator explains, when he sees a majestic group of clouds in the sky, they aren't clouds at all, but apple blossoms.

The Andrews Sisters sing the story of *Little Toot*, a young tugboat who wants to be as successful as his Dad, but keeps getting into mischief and disgracing his poor father. As punishment, Little Toot is sent out beyond the twelve-mile limit, but while out there one night, a ship becomes lost in a storm, and Little Toot brings it in, against all odds, safely to port, making himself a hero and reinstating his Dad for a happy ending.

"Trees," sung by Fred Waring and his Pennsylvanians, is the film's only nod to "art," in a sweeping mosaic of images illustrating Kilmer's famous poem, showing trees in light, shadow, night, rain, sunshine, sunset, etc., with a provocative punch line as the tree, atop a mountain at the end of the storm, is shown, in

backlighting courtesy of the sun, to be a cross!

Blame It on the Samba, with Ethel Smith and the Dinning Sisters, reunites Donald Duck and Joe Carioca, who are (literally) blue, until the crazy aracuan bird (also from *The Three Caballeros*) cooks up a dose of the samba that gradually restores their color and perks them up. He mixes a giant cocktail in a huge glass, which reveals inside Ethel Smith at the organ. Donald and Joe dive in and join her, dancing on and around her and the organ. Then the backgrounds begin to change behind them with increasing rapidity until they return to the Cafe de Samba for a bright finale.

The last segment in the film is *Pecos Bill,* which opens with lovely views of the desert at night, as Bob Nolan and the Sons of the Pioneers sing "Blue Shadows." After this haunting panorama, we see, in long shot, Roy Rogers, the Sons, and young Bobby Driscoll and Luana Patten gathered around a campfire in the midst of this animated desert. When Bobby asks Roy why coyotes howl at the moon, Roy answers by telling the tale of Pecos Bill, a famous tall tale about a boy who was raised by coyotes until he could outdo every animal in the land at their own game. He finds his match in a wonder horse, Widowmaker, and the two are inseparable pals, until Bill meets the beautiful Slue Foot Sue, a heck of a cowgirl, and falls madly in love with her. They decide to get married, and on her wedding day Sue determines to ride the stubborn Widowmaker, who hasn't liked her from the start. He gives her a hard time, and finally throws her; she lands on her bustle, which bounces her into the air. Every time she lands, she bounces higher, and no one, not even Bill, can catch her. Pretty soon she's bouncing up into outer space, toward the moon, from which she never returns. Heartbroken, Bill returns to the coyotes, and every night howls at the moon for his poor Slue Foot Sue.

Melody Time is an extremely winning film, and if it hasn't the brilliance of Disney's more coherent animated features, it does have a number of points to recommend it. For one thing, there is a very noticeable move away from literalism in all the segments of the film, encompassing various styles of drawing. *Once Upon a Wintertime* strives for a greeting-card effect, and, in keeping with that style, uses unreal colors, using what would look interesting or attractive, not necessarily what would look natural. There is a good ice-floe sequence, but even here there is only the impression of a rushing river, whereas a few years earlier in a Disney feature it would have been detailed down to the last bubble.

This is also true of *Johnny Appleseed,* where the trees have no detail, no leaves (in the style adopted by most cartoon producers during the 1950s); Johnny's cabin is *blue,* and the rolling hills in the background are done in an impressionistic, rather than realistic, style.

Bumble Boogie is a successful attempt to duplicate the feel of the surreal "After You've Gone," which was the best-received segment of *Make Mine Music,* and, again, it is short, sweet, and full of marvelous surreal cartoon images that make it a unique Disney work, not a literal transformation of live action into animated form.

Trees is done in Disney's consciously arty method of animation, although unlike such former endeavors as "Blue Bayou," it at least has a theme to work with and some sense of direction. Many of the images *are* beautiful, and some of the visual ideas are quite striking: the reflection of the sun breaking through a rainstorm turns out to be a drop of water from which the camera pulls *way* back to move into the next scene. Similarly, a close-up of the colorful sky becomes a multicolored leaf when the camera pulls back and reveals a flurry of leaves swirling about.

Blame It on the Samba revives the style and feel of *The Three Caballeros,* and rather well, although not going to some of the extremes of that feature. Still, there are many complex ideas in the brisk-moving sequence, starting when Donald and Joe dance with Ethel Smith as she and the organ float around a full 360 degrees, then joining her in the jungle where she plays conga drums that illuminate on every beat, and continuing to samba as the backgrounds change behind them in a window-shade format of dissolves.

Pecos Bill marks the first encounter between Disney and the famous American tall tales, and it is a felicitous collaboration. The best moments in *Pecos Bill* are those that bring to life the marvelous exaggerations: Bill roping a cyclone, igniting his cigarette with a bolt of lightning, digging the Rio Grande as an irrigation ditch, etc. In fact, one wishes there were even more of such material in the segment, for this, one feels, is what cartoons are all about—to present precisely this kind of visual hyperbole that captures the viewer's imagination with its very impossibility. (Disney knew when he had a good thing, and went on to animate Paul Bunyan and other famous folklore heroes.)

The feature is filled with good songs, notably the score for *Johnny Appleseed,* well sung by Dennis Day, "The Lord Is Good to Me," "The Apple Song," sung by Johnny's angel and amusingly illustrated as he comes to each new apple invention, and "The Pioneer Song." The "Blue Shadows" segment of *Pecos Bill* is also quite lovely, the Western harmonies perfectly matching the beautiful views of nighttime on the prairie.

What *Melody Time* lacks is unity. The paintbrush format and Buddy Clark's introductions are a poor substitute for cohesion, and, though one can enjoy the various segments, there is a feeling, when *Pecos Bill* brings the film to an abrupt conclusion, that something is missing. *Fantasia* was episodic, too, but one felt that it was cut from a whole cloth, as it were. There was never a feeling of fragmentation.

But Disney was counting on the appeal of his seven cartoon segments carrying the film without undue stress on format, and he was right in this respect. Bosley Crowther echoed most of the critical faction when he dubbed the film "a gaudy grab-bag show in which a couple of items are delightful, and the rest are just adequate fillers-in." Once more, there was that cry for the genius that Disney had shown once upon a time.

As with the other omnibus features, *Melody Time* did not receive reissue as a complete feature; instead, the segments were cut up and rereleased separately. Two of them, *Trees* and *Bumble Boogie,* became a "new" short called *Contrasts in Rhythm,* while five of the sequences were paired with four others from *Make Mine Music* to create a feature film called *Music Land,* which was released in 1955.

SO DEAR TO MY HEART

RELEASED BY RKO RADIO PICTURES ON JANUARY 19, 1949. Technicolor. Director: Harold Schuster. Screenplay: John Tucker Battle, based on the book *Midnight and Jeremiah* by Sterling North. Photoplay art director: John Ewing. Director of photography: Winton C. Hoch, A.S.C. Editors: Thomas Scott, Lloyd L. Richardson. Musical score: Paul J. Smith. Vocal director: Ken Darby. Orchestrations: Edward H. Plumb. Music editor: Al Teeter. Photoplay set director: Mac Alper. Special process shots: Ub Iwerks. Sound director: C. O. Slyfield. Sound recording: Max Hutchinson, Robert O. Cook. Technical director: Larry Lansburgh. Technicolor color director: Natalie Kalmus. Associate: Morgan Padleford. Associate producer: Perce Pearce. Cartoon director: Hamilton Luske. Cartoon story treatment: Marc Davis, Ken Anderson, William Peet. Cartoon art treatment: John Hench, Mary Blair. Dick Kelsey. Cartoon layout: A. Kendall O'Connor, Hugh Hennesy, Don Griffith, Thor Putnam. Cartoon backgrounds: Art Riley, Ralph Hulett, Jim Trout, Dick Anthony, Brice Mack, Ray Huffine. Animators: Eric Larson, John Lounsbery, Hal King, Milt Kahl, Les Clark, Don Lusk, Marvin Woodward. Effects animation: George Rowley, Joshua Meador, Dan McManus. Running time: 84 minutes.

Songs: "So Dear to My Heart" by Ticker Freeman and Irving Taylor. "Ol' Dan Patch," "Lavender Blue (Dilly Dilly)," "Stick-to-it-ivity" by Eliot Daniel and Larry Morey. "It's Whatcha Do with Whatcha Got" by Don Raye and Gene DePaul. "County Fair" by Robert Wells and Mel Torme.

Cast: Burl Ives (Uncle Hiram), Beulah Bondi (Granny Kincaid), Harry Carey (judge), Luana Patten (Tildy), Bobby Driscoll (Jeremiah Kincaid), Raymond Bond (storekeeper), Walter Soderling (villager), Mat Willis (horse trainer), Spelman B. Collins, and the voices of John Beal, Ken Carson, Bob Stanton, and The Rhythmaires.

There has been a lot of talk about nostalgia, but if a working definition were needed, one could point to *So Dear to My Heart* as a personification of the word. It is one of Disney's finest live-action films, brimming with period (1903) atmosphere and detail, rich characterizations, and moving performances. Although cast in the same mold as *Song of the South,* it is a much better film, and, unlike its predecessor, is essentially live action, with a few brief animated sequences. Indeed, if anything, it is the cartoon material that seems intrusive, not the live action.

The film opens in an attic, as the camera moves in on an old scrapbook. The pages turn, showing drawings of the country locale of the story, with mementos of the period: cutouts, a Christmas card, an old calendar, an old-fashioned valentine, each one leading into a short animated vignette, as a chorus sings the theme song of the picture. The final picture dissolves into a live-action establishing shot of the farm where our first-person narrator lived as a small boy, the Kincaid homestead, with Granny plowing the field outside.

The off-screen voice reminisces about what it was like, as we go down the main street, visit the general store, and witness the arrival of the famed trotting horse Dan Patch, who is taken for a short trot to stretch his legs during a break in a long railroad trip. The chorus sings "So Dear to My Heart," as this introductory sequence concludes with a shot of the Kincaid house at night, where the story begins.

The family sheep is about to give birth, and Jeremiah goes out to the barn with Granny to witness the event. There are twins, one white and one black. The mother shuns the black sheep, and, seeing this, Jeremiah decides to adopt it himself. Granny doesn't like the idea, but when she sees how sincere the boy is, she gives in.

In the next scene Jeremiah pastes a picture of the lamb (named Danny, after Dan Patch) in his scrapbook. The scrapbook is full of wise sayings, and an owl who accompanies most of them comes to life and sings to Jeremiah that "it's what you do with what you got that counts," explaining that there's nothing wrong with being a black sheep.

Except, of course, that over the next few months Danny grows up and becomes quite mischievous. Jeremiah's strongest ally in defending the sheep to Granny is Uncle Hiram, the town blacksmith and handyman. He puts the idea in the boy's head that he

Beulah Bondi and Burl Ives worry about Bobby Driscoll's latest mischief in *So Dear to My Heart*. © *Walt Disney Productions*

The wise owl in Jeremiah's scrapbook helps illustrate a valuable lesson to Danny: It's what you do with what you got that counts.   © *Walt Disney Productions*

might train Danny and take him to the county fair to compete. Granny is dead set against the idea, but that night the owl in Jeremiah's scrapbook comes to life again to sing to him of "Stick-to-it-ivity," illustrating his point with the stories of Columbus, who crossed the sea in spite of a brutal storm, and Robert Bruce, who was inspired to go into battle in Scotland after several defeats when he saw the doggedness of a spider trying to spin his web.

Jeremiah is inspired to earn his own money to go to the fair, and is told by the local storekeeper that honey is scarce, and he would gladly pay ten cents a pound for it. Jeremiah and his young girl friend Tildy spot a honeybee in the nearby field and follow it "home" into the swamp, where they discover a busy hive that yields (with Hiram's assistance) some seventeen dollars' worth of honey.

All looks well for the county fair trip, until one night when Danny runs away. Despite a severe thunderstorm, Jeremiah goes out into the night to look for Danny, and Granny has to drag him home. She gives him a stern lecture, telling him that he no longer loves the lamb as he once did, that his only reason for now wanting to go to the fair is self-gratification. She is particularly shocked when she warns him that the Lord may not spare Danny during the night, and he refuses to accept it. She tells him how ashamed she is of his attitude.

The next morning Jeremiah is up at the crack of dawn, and soon returns with the lamb, safe and sound. But he announces that he isn't going to the fair, because last night he promised God that if He spared the lamb, he wouldn't go. Granny, fighting back tears, tells the boy that she too made a promise to God, that if He spared the lamb they *would* go, and since she has known Him longer than Jeremiah, He won't mind him overlooking his favor in deference to hers.

A souvenir program from the fair in Jeremiah's scrapbook comes to life, and introduces the wondrous event. Before the competition Granny tells the boy that no matter what happens, he must come out of that arena proud, in the tradition of the Kincaids. When the judge comes around to Jeremiah and his lamb, the boy is forced to admit that his pet has no pedigree, unlike his competitors. To make matters worse, as the judge is leaving, Danny butts him in the rear. Sure enough, another sheep wins the Blue Ribbon. But as Jeremiah is leaving the arena, the judge makes another announcement. He declares that Danny is something special: a lamb with no special background, who has been made a prize animal by love and care. "It's what you do with what you got that counts," he explains, in presenting Danny and his owner with the Award of Special Merit, being given for the first time in forty years.

When the ecstatic group returns home, Hiram emerges from the train and "clears the way" for Danny in the same way that Dan Patch's owner had

Bobby Driscoll and "Danny" receive a special award from Judge Harry Carey. © *1964 Walt Disney Productions*

Beulah Bondi, Walt Disney, and director Harold Schuster discuss a scene on location. *From the private collection of Harold Schuster*

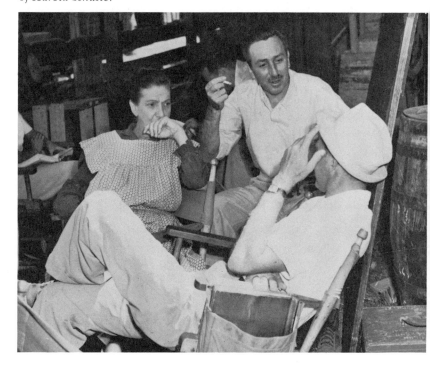

done for the famous horse. The whole town is out to greet their famous son, and his return is cause for celebration. We dissolve back to the scrapbook in the attic, and the film ends as it began.

So Dear to My Heart is a truly lovely film; its characters and their emotions are real and vivid, and this is what makes the film a special experience.

Although one seldom thinks of directors exerting their own style and influence on a Disney film, this was an instance of selecting the ideal man for the job.

Says Harold Schuster today:

At my first meeting with Walt Disney he told me that he had run *My Friend Flicka* at his home, and that Mrs. Disney and his two daughters had liked it so much that they had run it many times. He said that he felt I was the right director for *So Dear to My Heart* and that he would like me to read the book. After reading the book and the first draft screenplay I was very enthusiastic over the project; also, the idea of working with Walt Disney appealed to me greatly. I told him so and how I felt, which seemed to please him. I was under contract at 20th Century Fox at the time, so things were arranged with my home studio, and I was on my way.

During the preparatory period I worked with the writer, John Battle, on the screenplay, had meetings with Walt and Perce Pearce, the producer, on a wide variety of subjects including story, sets, music, casting, etc. Also during this period I made trips to the location, which was in the San Joaquin valley, near the town of Visalia. Also in Sequoia National Park where some of the sets were built. This whole area is very lush with olive, grape, and cotton farming, one of the loveliest valleys in the world. At Walt's suggestion I brought my first assistant, Jasper Blystone, over from 20th. He wanted to have as many pros with me as possible, as from what I gathered, they had lost production time on *Song of the South*.

Casting was simplified by the fact that Bobby Driscoll and Luana Patten were already under contract, and ideal for the two juvenile roles. Of the former, *Time* wrote: "Bobby Driscoll is a rarity among child actors; when relaxed, he is an attractive kid, and when called upon to act, he is not at all repellent." Schuster suggested using Beulah Bondi, having worked with her before. A test was made of Burl Ives, as this was his first film, and, like Bondi, he proved to be ideal. Choosing Harry Carey to play the judge was a sentimental decision for Schuster, who had worked with John Ford and shared with the director a warm affection for this marvelous character actor. Alas, Carey did not live to see the film's release; he died in late 1947 at the age of sixty-nine.

As was now standard practice, elaborate storyboards were drawn for each scene, and careful thought was given to the transitions from live action to animation and back again. These are extremely well handled in the film, most memorably in the first animated segment, where Danny the lamb is shown romping through various pages of the scrapbook. He reaches a fence and starts to leap over it, when the camera cuts to live action and the live animal bursts through Granny's screen door.

The animated sequences themselves are quite charming, although, with hindsight, one wonders just how necessary they were. In the film they serve the function of instilling certain attitudes in the young hero, but these points probably could have been settled in another manner if Disney had so desired. But just at this point he wasn't ready to abandon cartoons entirely. (Indeed, one might speculate that the success of this predominantly live-action film might have given Disney enough confidence to proceed with his first *all* live-action endeavor.) And Disney explained: "I saw the cartoon characters as figments of a small boy's imagination, and I think they were justified." The cartoon segments are done in a stylized method not seen before; the earliest scenes try to maintain the idea of an old-fashioned scrapbook come to life, with great success. The longest animated sequence is tied to the song "Stick-to-it-ivity." When the owl talks about Columbus facing a bitter storm, the visual style is that of a children's storybook, with the howling wind given a human face. In the tale of Robert Bruce there is a different kind of stylization, the major battle scene depicted in abstract figures, harshly shown with contrasty shadows and directional lighting, concluding with Bruce standing triumphant atop the castle he has taken, holding his gleaming sword against the bright blue sky.

The songs, considering their direct function to the story, are quite pleasant in conveying their message. But the film's true musical highlight is an extended scene where Burl Ives comes calling on Beulah Bondi and sings "Lavender Blue," duetting with her on "Billy Boy."

More than anything else, however, the film oozes with atmosphere, this the result of having chosen such a perfect location, and making optimum use of it (although one establishing shot of the Kincaid home at night employs an animated sky). One hazard was carefully avoided; shooting started much later in summer than had been planned, and the countryside had begun to dry up. So every night twenty-seven "greens men" worked diligently watering the soil and plants that they might look fresh and green for the camera in the morning.

Says Schuster:

Some of the interior sets were built on the location in conjunction with the exteriors, mostly because there was only the one small stage at the studio. The Grundy store was one of these. They found an old, and I mean old, hardware store near the town of Porterville. It was closed, and the various wares inside were bought lock, stock, and barrel, and moved into the Grundy store. Both the barn and Granny's house were built on the location. The railroad station was already there as were the railroad tracks. We rented the old engine and cars from Paramount, who had used them for *Union Pacific.*

Walt would come up sometimes on weekends, we would have Sunday breakfast, and talk over the rushes. He was a very enthusiastic gentleman, and a joy to be around. His suggestions were always presented as suggestions only. He left the reins firmly in my hands.

This was a method that may have come as a surprise to Disney's staff of animators and cartoon directors, who were well accustomed to Disney's involvement with every phase of production. But Disney realized, early on, that the only way live-action filming would get done would be if he stayed out of the director's way and confined his ideas to the preparation stages or post-production. This made him extremely popular with visiting directors, who without exception found assignments on the Disney lot to be rewarding experiences, especially after having dealt with the production heads of other Hollywood studios.

Asked if he felt there was a conscious effort to duplicate the feel of *Song of the South,* Schuster replies:

As far as I know there was no conscious effort to form *So Dear to My Heart* into any previous mold. Any resemblance to *Song of the South* would only reflect the Disney studio's general attitudes about what constituted entertainment. In the sense

that Walt's selection of screen subjects remained consistent with his beliefs, one might agree that *Song* and *So Dear* were generically members of the same family.

The reviews of *So Dear to My Heart* were among the most favorable Disney had received in several years. *Variety* called it "a first-rate job of sentimental storytelling," and Howard Barnes in the *New York Herald Tribune* declared that "Walt Disney has finally found a gracious and engaging formula for blending real drama with the pictorial imagination of an animated cartoon."

One of the film's songs, "Lavender Blue," which Larry Morey and Eliot Daniel adapted from an English folksong, even earned an Academy Award nomination.

The film's only problem was one of timing, coming as it did at the tail end of a cycle of Hollywood films based on turn-of-the-century nostalgia: *Meet Me in St. Louis, State Fair, Centennial Summer,* etc., a fact that was noted by most of the reviewers.

So Dear to My Heart held another drawback for the Disney company, in that it wasn't as easy a film to "sell" as most previous efforts; there were no characters to build up, or sources to boast of (even though it had been adapted from Sterling North's *Midnight and Jeremiah,* which had been a popular book). Its simple story, simply told, made it less marketable than, say, *Song of the South,* and, as a result, it never made as much money in its initial release or in reissue as other Disney features.

But it was a source of personal satisfaction for Disney. He told one reporter: *"So Dear* was especially close to me. Why, that's the life my brother and I grew up with as kids out in Missouri. The great racehorse, Dan Patch, was a hero to us. We had Dan Patch's grandson on my father's farm."

It remains today one of his loveliest films.

THE ADVENTURES OF ICHABOD AND MR. TOAD

RELEASED BY RKO RADIO PICTURES ON OCTOBER 5, 1949. Technicolor. Production supervisor: Ben Sharpsteen. Directors: Jack Kinney, Clyde Geronimi, James Algar. Directing animators: Franklin Thomas, Oliver Johnston, Jr., Wolfgang Reitherman, Milt Kahl, John Lounsbery, Ward Kimball. Story: Erdman Penner, Winston Hibler, Joe Rinaldi, Ted Sears, Homer Brightman, Harry Reeves. Character animators: Fred Moore, John Sibley, Marc Davis, Hal Ambro, Harvey Toombs, Hal King, Hugh Fraser, Don Lusk. Backgrounds: Ray Huffine, Merle Cox, Art Riley, Brice Mack. Layout: Charles Philippi, Tom Codrick, Thor Putnam, Al Zinnen, Hugh Hennesy, Lance Nolley. Effects animation: George Rowley, Jack Boyd. Music director: Oliver Wallace. Vocal arrangements: Ken Darby. Orchestrations: Joseph Dubin.

Cyril and Mr. Toad express wide-eyed wonderment at one point of *The Wind in the Willows.*   © *Walt Disney Productions*

Ichabod Crane runs head on into the Headless Horseman in *The Legend of Sleepy Hollow.*   © *Walt Disney Productions*

Film editor: John O. Young. Color and styling: Claude Coats, Mary Blair, Donald Da Gradi, John Hench. Special processes: Ub Iwerks. Sound director: C. O. Slyfield. Sound recording: Robert O. Cook. Music editor: Al Teeter. Based on "The Legend of Sleepy Hollow" by Washington Irving and "The Wind in the Willows" by Kenneth Grahame. Running time: 68 minutes.

Songs: "Ichabod," "Katrina," "The Headless Horseman" by Don Raye, Gene DePaul. "Merrily on Our Way," music by Frank Churchill and Charles Wolcott, lyrics by Larry Morey and Ray Gilbert.

"Ichabod" narrated by Bing Crosby. "Willows" narrated by Basil Rathbone, with the voices of Eric Blore (Mr. Toad), Pat O'Malley (Cyril), Claud Allister (Water Rat), John Ployardt (prosecutor), Collin Campbell (Mole), Campbell Grant (Angus Mac-Badger), Ollie Wallace (Winky).

In the late 1940s Disney admirers were seriously worried that the filmmaker was slipping into a pattern of mass-audience mediocrity. The first film to really reassert Disney's staff as the leading exponents of animated film was *The Adventures of Ichabod and Mr. Toad*, the awkwardly named feature film (originally titled *Two Fabulous Characters*) comprised of two half-hour sequences: Kenneth Grahame's *The Wind in the Willows* and Washington Irving's *The Legend of Sleepy Hollow*.

The film opens on a stained-glass window and moves inside to a colorful library, dollying closer and closer to the bookshelf, where we see one volume with Mr. Toad stamped in gold on the red spine. The book comes off the shelf and opens to the title page; we flip through the first few pages, in storyboard style, as narrator Basil Rathbone sets the scene for the story.

It seems that Toad Hall has been in uproar ever since J. Thaddeus Toad has adopted a horse (named Cyril) and carriage. The two go prancing along singing "We're merrily on our way to nowhere in particular," when the fun-loving Toad spies an automobile for the first time. "A motorcar!" he exults, "what have I been missing!" His eyes become a whirlpool as he drifts off into flights of fancy, imagining himself to *be* a motorcar. His friends, Rat and Mole, lock him up for the night, for his own good, but he escapes, and the next morning is arrested for having stolen a car.

In court all seems hopeless until the bartender, Winky, is called on to testify. Only he can tell the truth, knowing that Toad did not steal the car, but traded Toad Hall for it to a bunch of crafty weasels. But when Winky gets on the stand, he says that Toad *did* steal the car! Toad is convicted and sentenced to prison.

That Christmas, Cyril helps Toad escape from jail, and sets about, with his friends, to prove himself innocent. They discover that he was framed, since Winky and the weasels have taken the deed of Toad

Hall for their own. Toad and his comrades go to the Hall to recapture the deed, and engage in a slam-bang fight for the valuable scroll, eventually emerging victorious. Toad is cleared, and his friends relax, now that Toad has "reformed" his ways. Then they look out the window and see Toad and Cyril riding Toad's lastest discovery, an airplane.

The camera then moves into an adjoining library and Bing Crosby assumes the narration as *The Legend of Sleepy Hollow* comes off the shelf and opens to a map that sets up the locale of our story. Ichabod Crane is the new schoolmaster in town; he likes his job, because he can depend on free dinners from the mothers of his students. He also wins over the young ladies of the town by giving them singing lessons.

When he first spies a beautiful young lass named Katrina Van Tassel, Ichabod falls hopelessly in love, and she returns the favor. But the town's self-styled Don Juan, a burly fellow named Brom Bones, isn't giving up Katrina so easily. He can't make any headway over the effortlessly charming Mr. Crane, until he discovers Ichabod's Achilles' heel: he is wildly superstitious.

At a Halloween party given by Katrina, Brom tells the story of the Headless Horseman, and frightens the wits out of poor Ichabod, who has to ride home late that night, alone, through Sleepy Hollow. His imaginagion runs wild, and before long he sees the Horseman, laughing satanically as he holds a jack-o'-lantern in one hand. Ichabod runs for his life, toward the wooden bridge that means safety, but before he can get across, the Headless Horseman throws the jack-o'-lantern straight for Ichabod's head.

There is a dissolve to the following morning; all that's left at the scene of the incident is a smashed pumpkin, and Ichabod's hat lying on the ground. It was rumored that Ichabod merely moved away and started life anew in a nearby town, married to a local widow, but the residents of Sleepy Hollow know better, as they reprise Brom Bones's song: "Don't try to figure out a plan; You can't reason with a Headless Man!"

The Adventures of Ichabod and Mr. Toad is one of Disney's most beguiling animated features: *The Wind in the Willows* in particular has some of the finest work the studio ever did.

This opening sequence is a marvel of perfection, first in the casting of the voices. Basil Rathbone's crisp narration provides a nice contrast to the veddy-British tinge of the others. Eric Blore simply *is* Mr. Toad, the wild-eyed, whimsical hero of the tale. (Indeed, the choice was so natural that Disney thought of it back in 1941, when the project was first announced.) Pat O'Malley and the others provide first-rate support.

The fanciful air of Kenneth Grahame's story, written in 1908, is perfectly captured by Disney with a multitude of subtle touches and skillful direction. When Rat lectures Toad on his foolishness, Toad holds his hands over his ears, and the sound track becomes muffled. Intrigued with the effect, Toad tries it out continually during his friend's tirade.

The trial is perhaps the highlight of the film. One's lingering impression of the prosecuting attorney is that of a flowing cape, as the prosecutor turns on his heels after questioning a witness. Toad acts as his own counsel, striking hilarious poses as a British barrister, complete with wig and monocle (which he nonchalantly polishes during his speech). When Winky gets on the witness stand, he absent-mindedly begins to polish the rail, as he would his bar.

The jail and subsequent breakout segments are masterfully done. Full of remorse, Toad cries, creating a puddle on the floor of his cell. Each teardrop landing in the puddle conjures up a picture of one of his friends. Then Cyril gets in to see him, disguised as his mother; he whispers his scheme to Toad as the camera moves in to watch Toad's eyes widen and start turning into whirlpools, growing larger and larger. Suddenly there is a cut to clouds of smoke, which clear to reveal escape whistles blowing in the night. A succession of images follows: a bobby on the telephone, searchlights on the prison walls, bobbies riding into the streets on bicycle, in the nighttime fog, etc., before we see Toad running ahead of them, excited and confused. He jumps onto a train about to pull out of the station, and dives off when it goes over a river trestle.

The battle for the repossession of the deed is cunningly choreographed, with Toad, Rat, and Mole doing their best to outwit the band of weasels—people running back and forth, over and under each other, etc.

Key points in the story are told via newspaper headlines. When Toad escapes in search of an automobile, narrator Rathbone says: "He was determined to get a motorcar, even if he had to beg, borrow or—" and the sentence is finished with the flash of a morning headline: TOAD ARRESTED. After the fracas with the weasels, Toad emerges holding the deed, and another newspaper flashes before the camera reading: TOAD EXONERATED/GOOD NAME CLEARED.

The Legend of Sleepy Hollow lacks this kind of invention, for it has a totally different feel, exemplified by the choice of Bing Crosby as narrator. Easygoing Bing wastes no time in making his mark on the film, referring to its hero as "old Icky" and telling the story in both words and music (nicely kidding himself when, as Ichabod giving voice lessons, he warbles "boo-boo-boo-boo").

The gags come fast and funny throughout the film, with dozens of throwaways, in depicting Ichabod's lack of dedication to the teaching profession (either daydreaming about food, or later, daydreaming about Katrina), and more broadly in his competition with Brom Bones for Katrina's attention.

Naturally, the showiest part of the film is Ichabod's ride home at night, which is masterfully done. Clouds close in on the moon above; trees seem to close in on him as he passes them upon entering the forest. His whistle is eerily echoed . . . the wind blows the leaves about . . . there are strange cries in the night . . . fireflies form "eyes" inside a tree hollow . . . crickets seem to be chirping his name, and the frogs seem to be saying "headless horseman, headless horseman."

Ichabod tries to convince himself that all of this is innocent, and is relieved when his eyes betray most of these incidents for what they really are. Then, suddenly, he sees it: a black figure in a scarlet cape, perched upon a formidable black stallion pawing the air in defiance, backlit against the sky—the Horseman laughing wickedly, sparks flying from his horse's hooves, brandishing a sword in one hand and a jack-o'-lantern in the other. It really is a frightening vision and gives the impetus to the frightening chase scene that follows, with Ichabod scrambling for the wooden bridge.

Together, these sequences form a most engaging feature, with, as the saying goes, something for everyone. The half-hour length seems ideal for each of the stories, with neither a feeling of abruptness, nor a hint of padding to reach that length. And somehow the two tales seem to complement each other quite well, providing an interesting contrast, notable in style and execution, and more obviously in the change of narrator.

Although there was some mild carping about toying with Kenneth Grahame's original (with the addition of Cyril and Winky to the plot), the reaction to *The Adventures of Ichabod and Mr. Toad* was generally favorable. *Time* magazine particularly praised the first half, saying, "This lighthearted, fast-moving romp has inspired some of Disney's most inventive draftsmanship and satire." (No one pointed out one mild economy measure, in the artists' using the model of Grace Martin from the *Martins and Coys* sequence of *Make Mine Music* for Katrina in *Sleepy Hollow*. Both bore a close resemblance, as well, to Slue Foot Sue in *Pecos Bill*.)

In 1998, the studio's home-video division released an imaginative new live-action version of the story written and directed by Monty Python's Terry Jones, who also costarred. It had received a brief U.S. theatrical release by another company as *The Wind in the Willows*, but the Disney company decided to rename it *Mr. Toad's Wild Ride*, after the enduring popular Disneyland attraction that was inspired by Walt's 1949 film.

Both sequences have proved to be hardy Disney perennials, in single reissue and television exposure.

CINDERELLA

RELEASED BY RKO RADIO PICTURES ON FEBRUARY 15, 1950. Production supervisor: Ben Sharpsteen. From the original story by Charles Perrault. Directors: Wilfred Jackson. Hamilton Luske, Clyde Geronimi. Directing animators: Eric Larson, Ward Kimball, Norman Ferguson, Marc Davis, John Lounsbery, Milt Kahl, Wolfgang Reitherman, Les Clark, Oliver Johnston, Jr., Franklin Thomas. Story: Kenneth Anderson, Ted Sears, Homer Brightman, Joe Rinaldi, William Peet, Harry Reeves, Winston Hibler, Erdman Penner. Character animators: Marvin Woodward, Hal Ambro, George Nicholas, Hal King, Judge Whitaker, Fred Moore, Hugh Fraser, Phil Duncan, Cliff Nordberg, Ken O'Brien, Harvey Toombs, Don Lusk. Backgrounds: Dick Anthony, Merle Cox, Ralph Hulett, Brice Mack, Ray Huffine, Art Riley, Thelma Witmer. Layout: A. Kendall O'Connor, Thor Putnam, Charles Philippi, Tom Codrick. Don Griffith, McLaren Stewart, Lance Nolley, Hugh Hennesy. Effects animation: George Rowley, Joshua Meador, Jack Boyd. Music directors: Oliver Wallace, Paul J. Smith. Orchestrations: Joseph Dubin. Film editor: Donald Halliday. Color and styling: Claude Coats, Mary Blair, Donald Da Gradi, John Hench. Special processes: Ub Iwerks. Sound director: C. O. Slyfield. Sound recording: Harold J. Steck, Robert O. Cook. Music editor: Al Teeter. Running time: 74 minutes.

Songs: "Bibbidi Bobbidi Boo," "So This Is Love," "A Dream Is a Wish Your Heart Makes," "Cinderella," "The Work Song," "Oh Sing, Sweet Nightingale" by Mack David, Jerry Livingston, Al Hoffman.

Voices: Ilene Woods (Cinderella), William Phipps (Prince Charming), Elenor Audley (stepmother), Rhoda Williams, Lucille Bliss (stepsisters), Verna Felton (Fairy Godmother), Luis Van Rooten (King, Grand Duke), James Macdonald (Jaq, Gus), Don Barclay, Claire DuBrey, Mike Douglas (singing voice of Prince).

Disney had not made a full-length animated feature since *Bambi*. His pastiche films were often well received, but they lacked the warmth, the sustained artistry, and the impact of his earlier features.
For his return to this field, Disney chose *Cinderella;* it was hoped that the obvious family relationship to *Snow White* would create audience excitement that

The birds and the mice get together to make Cinderella's ball gown. © *Walt Disney Productions*

Cinderella's ugly stepsisters have their own way of keeping Cinderella from going to the ball. © *Walt Disney Productions*

The Fairy Godmother steps in to make things right.
© *Walt Disney Productions*

had been lacking from the multiepisode cartoons of late.

This return to the fairy-tale genre also provided a challenge to the Disney staff to come up with fresh angles to a timeworn tale. They succeeded remarkably well.

Every child knows the story of Cinderella, who is abused by her cruel stepmother and ugly stepsisters, whose fairy godmother transforms her into a ravishing beauty so she can attend a royal ball, where she completely captivates the Prince. At the stroke of midnight she must flee from the ball or be seen as a scullery maid once more. Running off, she drops one glass slipper. The Prince is determined to find the girl he loves, and tests the slipper on each maiden in the kingdom, until he is reunited with Cinderella for a happy ending.

The task facing the Disney staff was similar to that of *Snow White:* to provide enough secondary characters and diversionary sequences to surround this simple and familiar tale. The major inventions along this line were Cinderella's animal friends: Jaq and Gus the mice; the bluebirds; Bruno the dog; and their collective enemy, Lucifer the cat.

The animals figure importantly throughout the film, beginning with the very first scene (after the traditional storybook opening): the little birds awaken Cinderella and help her get up and get dressed, as she sings "A Dream Is a Wish Your Heart Makes." In the midst of this cheery scene, we see the mice waking up too. Jaq is awakened by the singing; he stretches a yawn, licks his hair, brushes it back (it falls back into disarray immediately), and finds, to his annoyance, that his tail has become knotted during the night.

Jaq then solicits Cinderella's help in rescuing a mouse who's been caught in one of the traps downstairs. She and her little friends investigate and find the victim to be a chubby, frightened rodent. Cinderella assures him that he is welcome in the household, and names him Octavius—Gus for short.

The mice's principal enemy is Lucifer, a cagey cat, who also makes things difficult for Bruno, an extremely easygoing dog. Cinderella chides Lucifer and tells him to live and let live, as she goes upstairs to serve breakfast to her stepmother and stepsisters.

To get *their* morning meal the mice must distract Lucifer long enough to sneak out into the yard and bring back provisions. It works, but on the way back Gus takes too much at once, and spills his food, catching Lucifer's eye and leading to a mad chase. When Gus rests for a moment against a teacup, Lucifer traps him inside; then an unknowing Cinderella brings this very cup to one of her stepsisters, with disastrous results. Her stepmother accuses her of deliberately playing a wicked joke on the girl.

Throughout the rest of the film, the actions of the humans and the animals are perfectly integrated this way, with one scene leading into another naturally. One can imagine the endless work by story men to achieve this perfectly rounded result.

Other new characters to the tale are the King and Grand Duke. The King is upset because his son is still single, and apparently has no interest in women. So he and the Grand Duke plan to hold a ball, inviting every eligible female in the kingdom in the hope that the Prince will find one to his liking.

When Cinderella sadly realizes that she has no time to make a dress for the ball, her animal friends decide to make one for her. This is easily the highlight of the film, an absolutely enchanting sequence that begins with the birds singing "Cinderella" (or, as they pronounce it, "Cinderelly"), bemoaning her fate in this household. This is followed by a parody, as Suzy the mouse sings, "We can do it, we can do it," urging her comrades to help in fashioning a ball gown. Then, as the birds and mice go to work gathering remnants from the sisters' rooms and putting them together, they sing the tune of "A Dream Is a Wish Your Heart Makes."

That night, as the stepmother and two stepsisters are about to leave the house, Cinderella descends the stairway, looking radiant in a beautiful gown. The sisters, ugly and garishly dressed, pounce on Cinderella, recognizing the origin of the various materials, and rip the dress to shreds!

She runs out into the backyard, crying, and there is met by her fairy godmother, who cheers her up as she sings "Bibbidi Bobbidi Boo." A pumpkin turns into a glowing coach with a wave of the fairy's wand; the mice become noble horses; a horse becomes a

stylish coachman; and the dog a footman. A new gown materializes, complete with glass slippers, and Cinderella is off to the ball—warned that the spell will last only until midnight.

At the ball the Prince has been stifling yawns all evening, but he suddenly perks up when he first catches sight of Cinderella. He asks her to dance, and they become the center of attraction; the Prince then takes her out into the courtyard. The King is beside himself with joy at his son's sudden awakening. Just then the clock strikes twelve, and Cinderella breaks away. The Prince, distraught, runs after her, followed by the Grand Duke, who scoops up the slipper that Cinderella drops on the palace staircase. The King's horsemen chase after Cinderella's carriage, but by the time they get close, the twelfth chime has struck, and the coach is again a pumpkin, the horses mice.

The King is fast asleep, dreaming happily about his future grandchildren, when the Grand Duke awakes him with the bad news. The King orders the Duke to search every house in the land until he finds the slipper's rightful owner.

When Cinderella hears this news, her stepmother senses from her reaction exactly what has happened—and locks Cinderella in her room in the attic of the house, before the Duke arrives. The mice vow to get the key back, and actually succeed in sneaking the key out of the stepmother's pocket. . . . But they then face a long journey up a flight of stairs, pushing an object that is twice their size! When they finally reach the top, all seems well until Lucifer arrives, blocking their way and trapping Gus. The others go to get the lazy dog Bruno, who, for once, asserts himself and does battle with Lucifer, allowing the mice to open the door and free Cinderella.

By now the Duke has tried the slipper on the two stepsisters and is about to leave when Cinderella appears for her turn. The Duke walks toward her with the slipper, and the quick-thinking stepmother trips him, sending the slipper shattering on the floor. All seems lost, but Cinderella calmly announces that it's all right—she has the matching slipper!

The picture dissolves to a royal wedding scene, with Cinderella's pet horse leading the others driving the royal coach, with the mice, dressed in their finery, throwing rice at the happy couple. "And they lived happily ever after," as the storybook closes for The End.

It is easy to dismiss *Cinderella* as an unremarkable Disney product, but those who do so obviously haven't seen it recently.

It is a work of genuine charm, thanks to skillful characterizations and storywork, and, most importantly, an especially winning score. Songs can literally make or break a film like this, and, in this case, as with most other Disney animated features, the songs enhance the qualities already present and help to establish others that might not be clear otherwise.

Cinderella is a likable enough character, especially in her dealings with the animals who share her household. But our fondness for her is crystallized in scenes such as the one where she sings "Sing, Sweet Nightingale." In the parlor the stepmother is giving vocal lessons to her two tin-eared daughters; their screechy bursts of song are unbearably bad. Inside Cinderella is washing the floor. As she begins to sing her tune, soap bubbles rise in the air echoing her voice. Each bubble reflects her face in a different color scheme, until a group of bubbles creates a chorus to bring the song to life. It's a lovely and imaginative scene.

The sequence of the birds and mice making Cinderella's dress simply would not work without the key musical numbers that give it direction and tempo. The high-pitched voices of the various animals bring to the rendition an endearing quality that makes it especially memorable.

Similarly, the jovial nature of the Fairy Godmother is perfectly expressed as she sings the bouncy "Bibbidy Bobbidi Boo." Every song in the score makes a definite contribution to the film—none seems arbitrarily inserted into the narrative.

Visually, Cinderella is not a flamboyant film, but it does have a full quota of inventive ideas. The stepmother's face is always seen in the shadows, particularly striking when her beady eyes are highlighted. The Fairy Godmother materializes out of twinkling stars in the sky, in a very pleasing special effect. And the romantic aura of Cinderella and Prince Charming dancing at the ball is evoked by creative use of color and backlighting, particularly when they walk out into the garden.

Admittedly, these are mild innovations when compared to the startling discoveries of Pinocchio or other earlier films, but the facile style of Cinderella makes it no less entertaining.

The film's strongest point is its ability to elicit emotional response from its audience. There are more scenes calculated to traumatize a viewer in Cinderella than in practically any other feature, a surprising statement when one considers the horrific elements of other Disney films, but still true. The most sophisticated audience would have difficulty not reacting audibly when the stepmother trips the Grand Duke, and the glass slipper—Cinderella's only hope, it seems—smashes to bits on the floor. By the same token the scene where the stepsisters rip Cinderella's dress to shreds is a terrifyingly real display of wickedness, on a level more likely to strike a responsive chord with children than many a more elaborate "horror" scene.

The sequence of the mice trying to bring the key upstairs is another example of involving an audience. We see the staircase from the mice's point of view,

each step a tremendous hurdle to overcome. We suffer and strain with them as they push the key up the steps, one by one, and we feel the satisfaction they enjoy at reaching the top—when suddenly Lucifer's evil face appears to spoil the whole thing.

The greatest part of Cinderella's success lies in its ability to get hold of its audience this way and make them feel they are experiencing the entire film. It is a quality many other filmmakers have tried to achieve without success.

In following this idea through to its logical conclusion, however, there is one thing missing from Cinderella, and that is retribution for the evil stepmother and stepsisters. It would not have had to be major (as it was in the Grimm version of this tale, wherein their eyes were pecked out by angry birds!)— it could have been as simple as a shot of their humiliation at seeing Cinderella marrying the Prince. But the lack of any such sequence does seem curious, and must send a lot of toddlers out of movie theatres asking their beleaguered parents what ever happened to the wicked ladies.

With Cinderella Disney hoped to return to the full-length animated feature story on a yearly basis, a schedule he found he could maintain for but a very brief time. Indeed, the film was advertised as being "six years in the making," although much of that time was taken up by preliminary ideas and discussions.

Comparisons to Snow White were inevitable, and the Disney people decided that it was a healthy association. The key advertising copy began: "Not since Snow White and the Seven Dwarfs a picture like this . . ."

Bosley Crowther in the New York Times reported that "although [Cinderella is] no chef d'oeuvre, it is well worth the love and labor spent," which seems as good a description as any.

The public, however, responded as it hadn't for any Disney feature since Bambi, going to see Cinderella in such numbers that the animated film became one of the year's top-grossing films, and Disney's biggest money-maker in many a year, grossing over $4 million in its initial release (and more than holding its own in subsequent reissues; the 1981 Christmas release left many other major-studio blockbusters at the starting gate, earning $17 million domestically) proving that what the Disney name alone could not do, the pairing of the Disney name with a story of universal appeal could. He took the hint and chose similarly famous tales for his next two cartoon endeavors, Alice in Wonderland and Peter Pan.

As before, Disney knew that his best measuring stick was the box office, the only real reflection of what his audience wanted to see.

TREASURE ISLAND

RELEASED BY RKO RADIO PICTURES ON JULY 19, 1950. Technicolor. Producer: Perce Pearce. Director: Byron Haskin. Screenplay: Lawrence E. Watkin, from the novel by Robert Louis Stevenson. Photography: F. A. Young, B.S.C. Editor: Alan L. Jaggs. Music: Clifton Parker, played by the Royal Philharmonic Orchestra. Conductor: Muir Mathieson. Production executive: Fred Leahy. Production manager: Douglas Peirce. Assistant director: Mark Evans. Matte artist: Peter Ellenshaw. Production designer: Thomas Morahan. Location directors: Russell Lloyd, Alex Bryce. Location cameramen: L. Cave Chinn, Stanley Sayre. Camera operator: Skeets Kelly. Continuity: Joan Davis. Technicolor color consultant: Joan Bridge. Makeup: Tony Sforzini. Hairstyling: Vivienne Walker. Sound engineer: Jack Locke. Sound editor: Kenneth Healey Ray. Running time: 96 minutes.

Cast: Bobby Driscoll (Jim Hawkins), Robert Newton (Long John Silver), Basil Sydney (Captain Smollett), Walter Fitzgerald (Squire Trelawney), Denis O'Dea (Doctor Livesey), Ralph Truman (George Merry), Finlay Currie (Captain Bones), John Laurie (Pew), Francis de Wolff (Black Dog), Geoffrey Wilkinson (Ben Gunn), David Davies (Arrow), Andrew Blackett (Gray), Paddy Brannigan (Hunter), Ken Buckle (Joyce), John Gregson (Redruth), Howard Douglas (Williams), and, as Silver's pirates, Geoffrey Keen (Israel Hand), William Devlin (Tom Morgan), Diarmuid Kelly (Bolen), Sam Kydd (Cady), Eddie Moran (Jack Bart), Harry Locke (Haggott), Harold Jamieson (Scully), Stephen Jack (Job Anderson), Jack Arrow (Norton), Jim O'Brady (Wolfe), Chris Adcock (Pike), Reginald Drummond (Vane), Gordon Mulholland (Durgin), Patrick Troughton (Roach), Leo Phillips (Spotts), Fred Clark (Bray), Tom Lucas (Upson), Bob Head (Tardy).

There are few adventure tales greater than Robert Louis Stevenson's *Treasure Island;* what is more, it's a story overflowing with cinematic possibilities. These were realized most vividly in Walt Disney's live-action version of the classic tale, filmed in England in 1949.

There could hardly have been a more perfect choice for Disney at this stage of his producing career.

Both he and RKO, his distributing company, had "frozen" pounds in England from film revenues there; they could not be spent except *in* England. Solution: make a film there. But Disney, despite his international popularity, had always been considered as American as Uncle Sam. Solution: take advantage of the British location and resources to make a British-based film that would still have universal appeal (like Stevenson's book) and retain some American identity factor by casting Bobby Driscoll as Jim Hawkins.

Everything meshed perfectly. Disney appointed veteran Perce Pearce as his producer, a job he was to maintain on most subsequent overseas ventures, and hired cameraman-turned-director Byron Haskin to pilot the film.

The resulting film is less Disneyesque than any other up to this point, largely because of the subject itself, but also because Disney had less to do with the actual making of the film than any other before. He visited the English location several times during filming, but only briefly, and took a hands-off attitude toward director Haskin and screenwriter/adaptor Lawrence Watkin.

Where the Disney touch is most evident, aside from certain changes in the Stevenson plot, is in the actual appearance of the film. It was budgeted at $1,800,000, a considerable sum for a film with no stars. The settings, interior, exterior, and artificial, are all on a lavish scale befitting the atmosphere of the story. The film was photographed by subsequent Academy Award-winner Freddie Young, who brought out all the rich possibilities in every shot. And Tom Morahan, the film's production designer, injected as much color into the production as possible without becoming garish; the opening sequences, on the seacoast and at the inn where Jim lives and works, are properly stark, but never devoid of color.

The first shot of the film shows waves crashing against a rocky shore on a gray and windy day. The camera travels up a craggy coastal road to the Admiral Benbow Inn, where Black Dog enters the deserted establishment and leaves his message for Captain Billy Bones with young Jim Hawkins. Then the dying captain gives Jim a treasure map, and the adventure is on.

The script is faithful to Stevenson's book for the most part; introductory material about Jim's parents

Long John Silver (Robert Newton) befriends Jim Hawkins (Bobby Driscoll) when they first meet at the tavern.
© *Walt Disney Productions*

Long John's eyes widen when he sees the treasure stashed away by wily old Ben Gunn; Squire Trelawney is interested too. © *Walt Disney Productions*

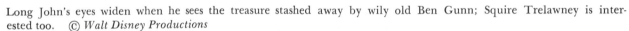

is eliminated, and other matters condensed from time to time. But basically the story is the same one young boys have thrived on for years, with Jim accompanying Doctor Livesey and Squire Trelawney on a treasure hunt abroad the schooner *Hispaniola,* where they discover that their one-legged cook, Long John Silver, is actually the head conspirator in a devilish scheme to mutiny and claim ownership of the map. Battles between the two factions, mysterious characters coming in and out of the narrative, bargains and doublecrosses fill out the rest of the story in the scramble for buried riches on Treasure Island.

But central to the book, and emphasized in the film, is the relationship between young Jim and Long John Silver. Jim is rather mature for his age, and is beyond the fairy-tale stage of hero-worshiping pirates. But he is still a boy, and he relishes the opportunity to go to sea on a great adventure. He *does* get taken in by Long John's facade of good humor and courtliness, but this is not due so much to Jim's naïveté as to Silver's convincingness.

Long John is a very magnetic character; a completely unscrupulous man who remains in his most wicked moments totally beguiling, to Jim as well as to us. His sense of humor and irony almost never desert him, and it is the knowledge that his facade is not entirely phony that makes him so irresistible.

For his part Silver develops a genuine admiration for Jim as well. Even when he holds the boy prisoner in his makeshift fortress on Treasure Island, he shows concern for his welfare, and tells his motley crew that Jim is "more of a fighter than any two of you."

Their mutual regard is put to several difficult tests during the course of the story: Jim has given his word to Silver, while his prisoner, that he will not try to escape, and given the chance, refuses to renege on Long John. Similarly, when Long John and his men finally arrive at the treasure site and find it barren, Silver hands Jim a gun so that the two of them can escape the wrath of the crew.

But screenwriter Watkin builds on Stevenson's foundation for an original finale to the scenario. The last reel of the film has more twists and turns than one can keep track of, especially in the hot-and-cold relationship between the boy and the pirate. After Jim and his friends, with the repentant Silver in tow, discover the treasure in Ben Gunn's cave and prepare to leave, Long John commandeers the rowboat, kicks two crewmen and Squire Trelawney overboard, and orders Jim to steer him to safety. Instead, Jim runs the boat aground. Long John threatens to shoot him if he doesn't help shove the boat back out to sea, but Jim stands motionless—and Silver realizes he can't shoot the boy. Then, as the others start to catch up, Jim decides to help Long John escape after all, freeing the boat and heading it in the right direction. Silver thanks him and calls, "Goodbye, matey!" as he rows past the range of gunfire. . . . And the two friends wave to each other for the last time.

Disney and Robert Newton toast a visitor to the set of *Treasure Island,* Lady Tedder, wife of the British chief of the Air Staff. *Courtesy British Film Institute*

Although this changes Stevenson's finale (in which Silver escapes, without Jim's help or knowledge, with only a small sack of coins), it is most assuredly in keeping with the spirit of the author's work, and enhances the already fascinating relationship between these two characters.

This effect is also brought about by the actors playing the lead roles. There was anticipatory criticism of Bobby Driscoll, an American, playing the British Jim Hawkins, but he carried it off masterfully, certainly much better than the affected and stiffened Jackie Cooper in MGM's 1934 version of the story.

The film, however, belongs to Robert Newton, as Long John Silver. Rereading Stevenson, one finds that Newton *is* Long John, and the "hamminess" that many found overbearing in the performance is really as much Stevenson as it is Newton.

Director Byron Haskin explains:

In orchestrating the cast of thirty-six speaking parts, Long John was very near the top in flamboyant playing. I would rate the performances as beginning with the least offensive, the doctor. He was the measuring stick by which the others were to be judged. On up the scale came the squire, etc. Handling such an unwieldy number was one of the greatest tasks of making the film. By the time Newton's manners were to be considered I could do little more than let him "rip," in the language of the period. I cast Ralph Truman in the role of George Merry, however, giving him full scope to out-ham Newton whenever he could. At times, Newton, by contrast, looked downright under-played!

"Anyhow," he concludes, "the film was a children's story, told by Stevenson to children. Kids don't go in much for subtleties."

Indeed, Newton was so powerful as Long John that he found himself locked into the characterization, repeating it for Haskin in an Australian-filmed feature, *Long John Silver,* a TV series of the same name, and similar roles such as the title part in *Blackbeard the Pirate.* Newton's trouping may have been ham, but his performance remains in the memory long after everything else about the film has been forgotten.

Not that there aren't other outstanding qualities to the movie; the entire cast is filled with skilled British actors giving life to the fictional characters created by Stevenson. Walter Fitzgerald as the bumbling, loose-tongued Squire Trelawney, Finlay Currie (who appeared in virtually every film Disney made in England) as the dying Billy Bones, Geoffrey Wilkinson as the slightly lunatic Ben Gunn, all add color to the fast-paced proceedings.

The film also has the look of authenticity, thanks not only to skillful art direction, but ample use of "glass shots," whereby artificial backgrounds and extensions are painted onto glass in front of the camera lens, yielding an amazingly lifelike result. When Jim Hawkins arrives in the port town of Bristol, the sky is filled with the masts and riggings of dozens of ships in the harbor—all paintings giving the illusion of reality. This intricate work was done by a man named Peter Ellenshaw, who had worked on such famous British fantasies as *The Thief of Bagdad,* and who later joined the Disney staff.

An actual sailing ship was chartered for the duration of the filming, as well, for matching with studio-built interiors and establishing shots at sea. There were three camera units at work on the film, one shooting out on the ocean (under the direction of Russell Lloyd), one shooting exteriors, and another shooting interiors at Denham Studios.

Director Haskin had served as cinematographer on other seagoing films, notably *Captain Blood* and *The Sea Wolf* at Warner Brothers. He was to go on to make some of the most memorable science-fiction films of the 1950s for George Pal. Haskin brought a good sense of pacing and, to use his word, orchestration, to the film, and made the most of a first-rate script: (His one regret was that, because Bobby Driscoll did not have an extended work permit, he had to shoot all the young actor's scenes first and complete the rest of the film without him. Haskin always felt he could have done a better job if the youngster had been available to him throughout production.) Adapter/scenarist

Lawrence E. Watkin, best known as the author of *On Borrowed Time,* subsequently did the scripts for Disney's three British-made swashbucklers in the 1950s.

Perhaps the film's most famous scene occurs when young Jim tries to recapture the ship from Long John's two motley crewmen on board. One is knifed in the back, but the other comes stalking Jim, causing the youngster to climb into the crow's nest as a place of refuge. The mutineer, Mr. Hand, climbs the rigging, to be greeted at the top by Jim aiming a pistol (given him by Silver!) at the pirate. Hand is sure Jim is bluffing, and suddenly tosses a knife into the boy's shoulder, inciting Jim to pull the trigger and send his adversary plummeting to a watery death.

This is not the only example of full-blooded violence in the film; another sequence uses jump-cutting to make a sailor's death (by gunshot in the forehead) doubly dramatic. Credit goes to Haskin for bringing out the full potential of each situation. (Ironically, these exciting scenes created a thorny dilemma for the studio twenty-five years later when *Treasure Island* was slated for reissue. Buena Vista routinely submitted the feature to the Motion Picture Association of America's Ratings Board—and received a PG rating! The Board was adamant in its ruling that the violence in *Treasure Island* warranted this parental guidance tag. Buena Vista was equally determined that a Disney classic not carry a PG rating. So the offending scenes were trimmed for this 1975 release, and young viewers were cheated out of some vital—and memorable—moments. These alterations were made only in theatrical prints, and the complete version is still shown on television and in 16mm distribution. Unfortunately, the cut theatrical print was used as the source of Disney's home video release.)

Reaction to the film was the same in England and in America; intellectual critics chastised Disney for what they felt was diluting the original. (A British headline read: "Yo Ho Ho and a Coca-Cola.") John Mason Brown wrote in *Saturday Review:* "Mr. Disney's movie . . . is meant for those who have never read *Treasure Island* or who have forgotten it long ago."

But *Time* magazine captured the essence of the film perfectly. "It is played so broadly by British actors in stock company style that even the youngest fan can follow the adventures of the cast's only U.S. actor, Bobby Driscoll, as cabin boy Jim Hawkins."

The film did not perform as well as had been hoped at the box office, and eventually was shown on the Disney television show instead of being reissued. It finally made its way back to theatre screens—in its somewhat adulterated form—in 1975. But there is no reason why this feature should be treated as a second-class citizen. It's one of Disney's all-time best live-action films, and a truly outstanding adventure tale that puts most of its more contemporary imitations to shame.

ALICE IN WONDERLAND

RELEASED BY RKO RADIO PICTURES ON JULY 28, 1951. Technicolor. Production supervisor: Ben Sharpsteen. Directors: Clyde Geronimi, Hamilton Luske, Wilfred Jackson. Animating directors: Milt Kahl, Ward Kimball, Franklin Thomas, Eric Larson, John Lounsbery, Oliver Johnston, Jr., Wolfgang Reitherman, Marc Davis, Les Clark, Norman Ferguson. Story: Winston Hibler, Bill Peet, Joe Rinaldi, Bill Cottrell, Joe Grant, Del Connell, Ted Sears, Erdman Penner, Milt Banta, Dick Kelsey, Dick Huemer, Tom Oreb, John Walbridge. Character animators: Hal King, Judge Whitaker, Hal Ambro, Bill Justice, Phil Duncan, Bob Carlson, Don Lusk, Cliff Nordberg, Harvey Toombs, Fred Moore, Marvin Woodward, Hugh Fraser, Charles Nichols. Effects animation: Joshua Meador, Dan MacManus, George Rowley, Blaine Gibson. Color and styling: John Hench, Mary Blair, Claude Coats, Ken Anderson, Don Da Gradi. Layout: Mac Stewart, Hugh Hennesy, Tom Codrick, Don Griffith, Charles Phillipi, Thor Putnam, A. Kendall O'Connor, Lance Nolley. Backgrounds: Ray Huffine, Ralph Hulett, Art Riley, Brice Mack, Dick Anthony, Thelma Witmer. Musical score: Oliver Wallace. Orchestrations: Joseph Dubin. Vocal arrangements: Jud Conlon. Running time: 75 minutes.

Songs: "Very Good Advice," "In a World of My Own," "All in a Golden Afternoon," "Alice in Wonderland," "The Walrus and the Carpenter," "The Caucus Race," "I'm Late," "Painting the Roses Red," "March of the Cards" by Bob Hilliard and Sammy Fain. "'Twas Brillig" by Don Raye and Gene DePaul. "The Unbirthday Song" by Mack David, Al Hoffman, and Jerry Livingston. "We'll Smoke the Blighter Out," "Old Father William," "A E I O U" by Oliver Wallace and Ted Sears.

Voices: Kathryn Beaumont (Alice), Ed Wynn (Mad Hatter), Richard Haydn (Caterpillar), Sterling Holloway (Cheshire Cat), Jerry Colonna (March Hare), Verna Felton (Queen of Hearts), Pat O'Malley (Walrush, Carpenter, Tweedledee and Tweedledum), Bill Thompson (White Rabbit, Dodo), Heather Angel (Alice's Sister), Joseph Kearns (Doorknob), Larry Grey (Bill), Queenie Leonard (Bird in the Tree), Dink Trout (King of Hearts), Doris Lloyd (The Rose), James Macdonald (Dormouse), The Mello Men (Card Painters), Pinto Colvig (Flamingoes), Ken Beaumont

Alice, suddenly enlarged, scolds the egotistical Queen in Wonderland. © *Walt Disney Productions*

(Card Painter), Ed Penner (Baglet), Larry Grey (Card Painter), Queenie Leonard (Flower), Don Barclay.

One could say that Disney's first contact with Lewis Carroll's fable came in the 1920s, with the *Alice in Cartoonland* series, featuring a live girl playing in a cartoon world. In 1937 Mickey Mouse starred in an ambitious short inspired by Carroll's classic called *Thru the Mirror*. But the idea of a bona fide feature-length adaptation of this literary classic occurred to Disney many times. In 1933 there was serious talk of Mary Pickford starring in such a film, combining live action and animation. In 1945 the studio announced that Ginger Rogers was going to star. Then, after *Song of the South*, Disney planned to build the film around his new juvenile star, Luana Patten. (He formally registered the title with the MPAA in 1938.)

Finally, in 1946, he decided to go ahead with the film as an all-cartoon feature. Initially, the studio declared that it would be drawn in the style of the famous Sir John Tenniel illustrations. Disney ex-

The Mad Hatter pours, after a fashion, at his un-birthday party © *Walt Disney Productions*

Disney shows some sketches to Kathryn Beaumont, the voice of Alice. *Courtesy British Film Institute*

plained: "When you deal with such a popular classic you're laying yourself wide open to the critics."

But before long, as the feature took shape, it became clear that simply bringing the Tenniel drawings to life was both impractical, and not what Disney-lovers would expect. So the artists and animators consulted Tenniel's work and came up with free translations of his characters, close enough to the originals to be identifiable, distinctive enough to be recognized as Disney creations.

And for the first time since the classic animated features of the early 1940s, a full-length live-action film was shot for the animators to consult (featuring most of the actors who supplied the film's voices). The resulting cartoon feature took five years to complete at an estimated cost of $3 million.

Unlike the other Disney features derived from classic books, *Alice* does not open on a storybook. Rather, it begins with a view of Big Ben, pulling back to reveal Alice and her older sister sitting under a shady tree by a stream. As her sister reads, Alice daydreams, lying in the grass, and suddenly discovers before her a quaint White Rabbit singing "I'm Late," as he runs into a nearby hole.

Alice follows, and falls down the rabbit hole, floating through space, passing all kinds of distorted objects and settings, and unreal color patterns. When she finally lands, it is on her head, and she turns rightside up to follow the rabbit, who has gone through a doorway.

From this point on, it is Lewis Carroll's story, with all the familiar elements: Alice trying to get herself the right size to pass through the keyhole of the door, encountering Tweedledee and Tweedledum, who tell the story of the Walrus and the Carpenter, and meeting such unusual characters as an opium-smoking caterpillar and the Cheshire Cat.

She attends a Mad Tea Party with the Mad Hatter and March Hare, and wanders off to meet the Queen, who invites Alice to participate in a most unscrupulous game of croquet, after which Alice is put on trial, and forced to escape this insane world back through the keyhole . . . at which time she wakes up and finds the whole episode has been a dream.

Alice is the most episodic of Disney's full-length story features, and as such has more trouble maintaining pace and continuity than most. The Walrus and Carpenter story, for instance, although faithful to Carroll, seems extraneous and bothersome in that it keeps Alice from moving on and proceeding with her adventures. Of course, most of her encounters are essentially obstacles to Alice, but they are taken care of with more dispatch than this.

The caterpillar, for instance, asks Alice "Who-O R U?" blowing those letters into the air as he puffs away. She valiantly attempts to hold a conversation with him, though his non sequiturs make it almost impossible. At the brink of exasperation, she tries to continue, but he disappears in a cloud of smoke;

when it clears, he's floating overhead, a butterfly who's content to flutter off and leave her behind in a daze.

Directing animator Ward Kimball feels that the film

degenerated into a loud-mouthed vaudeville show. There's no denying that there are many charming bits in our *Alice,* but it lacks warmth and an overall story glue. *Alice* suffered from too many cooks—directors. Here was a case of five directors each trying to top the other guy and make his sequences the biggest and craziest in the show. This had a self-cancelling effect on the final product.

For example, I was in charge of the animation for the Mad Tea Party, Tweedledee and Tweedledum, and the Cheshire Cat, but because all of the other sequences in the show tried to be "mad," the result was that the only real "mad" thing in the whole picture, in my opinion, turned out to be the Cheshire Cat! Why? Because compared to the constant, all-out, wild gyrations of the other characters, he played it real cool. His quiet, underplayed subtleties consequently stole the show!

The Cheshire Cat is, unquestionably, one of the most memorable things about the film. He first appears as a toothy smile, the rest of his body gradually materializing around it, as he sings an offhand rendition of "Jabberwocky." He playfully asks Alice, "Can you stand on your head?" as his body swings aside and hops on top of his head, perched atop a tree.

As great as the Cat is visually, however, it and all of *Alice*'s other characters benefit tremendously from their voices, and for this film Disney chose very formidable actors to supply them. It is one of the first times in Disney animated features where the viewer is thinking about the actor while watching the character on screen, an unhealthy trend that resurfaced in the 1960s.

For the most part the idea worked to *Alice*'s advantage, however. Sterling Holloway is delightfully coy as the Cheshire Cat, Richard Haydn is ideal as the Caterpillar, and in the Mad Tea Party sequence, Ed Wynn and Jerry Colonna are hilarious as the Mad Hatter and the March Hare, respectively.

What one remembers specifically about the Tea Party are those two delightful voices, and "The Unbirthday Song," more than the visuals, although there are some very funny gags, as when the White Rabbit stumbles in and makes the mistake of mentioning that his watch is broken. The Hatter takes it in hand, opens it up, and, with the Hare, gives the watch a lightning-paced going-over that involves pouring every conceivable item on the table into the tiny timepiece. Finally, when the Hare hands him some mustard, the Mad Hatter stops dead in his tracks, looks at the mustard and comments, "Don't let's be silly!"

One of the best visual scenes in the film involves the march of the cards, heralding the Queen's arrival. Here colors flash on the screen and the cards form a succession of geometric figures as they march along, with various imaginative camera angles heightening the effect. The scene concludes with a ready-made card game; the cards shuffle themselves and deal out to nonexistent players.

The climactic sequence with the Queen is quite funny, also benefiting from a particularly strong voice characterization by Verna Felton.

The film's other visual highlight is the flower sequence, where Alice finds herself wandering among oversized and strongly individualistic flowers, which take on various personality traits (a snooty society woman with a laced bodice, two drunken buttercups, etc.) in an especially colorful and beautifully designed scene.

In all, *Alice in Wonderland* is a very flashy and generally entertaining film, but it lacks that essential thread that made Disney's best features hang together, and, moreover, it lacks *warmth*. Of course, *Alice* is not *Snow White* or *Cinderella,* and one shouldn't demand the same things of it. Yet Disney's best animated features have always communicated something to their audience that would leave the viewer with an afterglow, feeling he had just undergone an experience, as opposed to watching a cartoon. *Alice* has no such aftereffects. Once over, it can be dismissed, and though one wouldn't have wanted Disney to turn the story into a Grimm's fairy tale, there should have been some way to give the audience more empathy with its heroine.

The critics, as Disney had anticipated, had their knives sharpened in readiness for *Alice.* The *New Yorker* wrote:

In Mr. Disney's *Alice* there is a blind incapacity to understand that a literary masterwork cannot be improved by the introduction of shiny little tunes, and touches more suited to a flea circus than to a major imaginative effort. . . . Possibly nobody is going to create a visualization of *Alice* that won't do violence to the nostalgic imagery of the piece that remains in the mind's eye of those who grew up on Tenniel's illustrations. But even granting a certain latitude for variations in approach, [the film is] a dreadful mockery of the classic.

Even *Life* magazine, one of Disney's staunchest supporters, noted that "the leering loony faces he has concocted will be a shock to oldsters brought up on the famous John Tenniel illustrations."

For the most part critical reaction has played a small role in shaping the popularity of Disney's films, but somehow, either because of the bad reviews or simply because *Alice* did not have the appeal of the more universal Grimm's fairy tales and such, *Alice in Wonderland* did not perform as well at the box office as Disney had expected. Accordingly, it was one of the few cartoon features he allowed to be shown on his

TV program, and consequently it was not reissued theatrically for many, many years. It was made available for 16mm rental, however, and in the late 1960s became a great success on the college circuit, with its "mind-blowing" surrealism and natural links to the drug culture. Although the studio did not discourage such identification with *Fantasia* around this time, there seems to have been some reluctance to have *another* movie "high" associated with Disney, and *Alice* was withdrawn from 16mm release. Then, in 1974, *Alice in Wonderland* was given its first theatrical reissue—with a psychedelic poster!

Another sidenote concerns the fact that when *Alice* was about to be released, a small New York distribution company cleverly acquired the rights to a French puppet film of *Alice in Wonderland* made by Louis Bunin, and scheduled it to open at the same time as the Disney cartoon. The Disney company tried to obtain an injunction to withhold the rival film for eighteen months, claiming that the public would be misled by competitive advertising, but the motion was denied and the Bunin film opened, to generally bad reviews. There *was* some confusion in cities where both films were playing, but the Bunin film did not affect the overall outcome of the Disney feature at the box office.

The enduring success of the music score to *Alice in Wonderland*—particularly "I'm Late" and "The Unbirthday Song"—helped to keep the memory of the film alive during its long absence from general public view. But now the film itself is back, and sharing the spotlight with Disney's other "golden age" animated features.

THE STORY OF ROBIN HOOD

RELEASED BY RKO RADIO PICTURES ON JUNE 26, 1952. Technicolor. Producer: Perce Pearce. Director: Ken Annakin. Screenplay: Lawrence E. Watkin. Director of photography: Guy Green, B.S.C. Editor: Gordon Pilkington. Art directors: Carmen Dillon, Arthur Lawson. Music: Clifton Parker, played by the Royal Philharmonic Orchestra. Conductor: Muir Mathieson. Production manager: Douglas Peirce. Unit manager: Anthony Nelson-Keys. Assistant director: Peter Bolton. Matte artist: Peter Ellenshaw. Camera operator: Dave Harcourt. Technicolor color consultant: Joan Bridge. Location directors: Alex Bryce, Basil Keys. Location cameramen: Geoffrey Unsworth, Bob Walker. Makeup: Geoffrey Rodway. Hairstyling: Vivienne Walker. Sound director: C. C. Stevens. Sound editor: Wyn Ryder. Running time: 83 minutes.

Cast: Richard Todd (Robin Hood), Joan Rice (Maid Marian), Peter Finch (Sheriff of Nottingham), James Hayter (Friar Tuck), James Robertson Justice (Little John), Martita Hunt (Queen Elea- nor), Hubert Gregg (Prince John), Bill Owen (Stutely), Reginald Tate (Hugh Fitzooth), Elton Haytes (Allan-a-Dale), Antony Eustrel (Archbishop of Canterbury), Patrick Barr (King Richard), Anthony Forwood (Will Scarlet), Hal Osmond (Midge the Miller), Michael Hordern (Scathelock), Clement McCallin (Earl of Huntingdon), Louise Hampton (Tyb), Archie Duncan (Red Gill), Julian Somers (posse leader), Bill Travers (posse man), David Davies (forester), and, as the Merrie Men, Ivan Craig, Ewen Solon, John Stamp, John Brooking, John Martin, Geoffrey Lumsden, Larry Mooney, John French, Nigel Neilson, Charles Perry, Richard Graydon, Jack Taylor.

Having formed RKO–Walt Disney British Productions Ltd., and succeeded in filming a most creditable live-action feature, Walt Disney decided to continue making films in England, with Perce Pearce as his producer. They decided to continue in the

Robin (Richard Todd) and Maid Marian (Joan Rice) realize that they still love each other. © *Walt Disney Productions*

At one point Robin is forced to hold Maid Marian captive in Sherwood Forest. James Hayter is Friar Tuck; Michael Hordern is at extreme left. © *Walt Disney Productions*

action-adventure genre, and chose as their next project Robin Hood.

This time out, in addition to using an all-British crew, Disney hired a British director as well, a young man who had made an impressive start at Rank studios with such films as *Trio* and *Quartet,* Ken Annakin. At the time he joined the production, some preparatory work had already been done by Disney and Pearce with their cameraman, Guy Green, and art director, Carmen Dillon. As on *Treasure Island,* three separate shooting units were established, one doing

action work on exterior location, and two doing interiors at Denham Studios.

Disney spent part of the summer in England, working closely with Annakin. The director recalls:

I remember talking about the original Errol Flynn *Robin Hood,* and I looked at it, just to get an idea what had been done before, because I never like to do anything twice. Walt didn't seem very worried about seeing the original, and in fact, I doubt if he ever did. His approach is always that the film is a Disney picture, and therefore, because of his attitudes and his approach, the picture is bound to be different from anything else made on that subject before.

That was exactly what happened, of course; the Disney film adheres to the Robin Hood legend, yet it is a work unto itself. One is hard pressed to make comparisons between the Disney *Robin Hood* and earlier versions, not because one is better than another, but simply because each one is different.

The film opens on a storybook, which dissolves into a city scene, where a strolling minstrel sings a ballad of Robin Hood. He reappears throughout the film, as a narrative device, and adds a unique flavor to the period piece.

The story is as everyone remembers it. King Richard leaves his domain to go on a crusade, appointing his brother Prince John to reign during his absence. The Prince, in turn, appoints a new sheriff of Nottingham to carry out the new laws he has in mind. Before long, the happy kingdom becomes a dictatorship, where the people are driven mercilessly and taxed beyond endurance.

At a public archery tournament young Robin Hood and his father show up the Sheriff's bowmen; the angered Sheriff has Robin's father killed. To avenge this death Robin takes to the woods with others who have been wronged by the new rulers, and forms his band of Merrie Men. They are soon joined by John Little, redubbed Little John, and jovial Friar Tuck.

Robin and his Men soon become public heroes, much to the consternation of the Prince and Sheriff, who are unable to capture these "bandits." The "bandits" then prove their loyalty to the King when it is discovered that the good Richard is being held hostage in Austria for a ransom of 100,000 marks.

The Queen is to deliver the ransom money, but the Prince has his men dress as Robin Hood's cohorts and steal the money, to turn the Queen against Robin. Robin manages to foil this plot, but he then learns that the Prince has locked Maid Marian in his castle to keep her from exposing this scheme. Robin returns to the castle for a fight to the death with the Sheriff of Nottingham, and rescues Maid Marian. Soon afterward Robin's forest hideout is visited by a mysterious stranger, who reveals himself to be King Richard! He expresses his thanks to Robin and the Men, and then dubs the bandit leader the Earl of Locksley, and orders Maid Marian to marry the newly created nobleman for a resoundingly happy ending.

The Story of Robin Hood is an eminently satisfying film. It takes all the familiar elements of the story—the confrontation between Robin and Little John on a wooden bridge over a stream, the archery tournament, the climactic duel—and plays them out with such gusto that one forgets ever having seen them before.

There are delightful variations as well. Robin and his men communicate with each other by shooting whistling arrows throughout the forest—different arrows producing different pitches, and thus signifying different things.

Robin's relationship with Maid Marian is newly expanded. They are shown at the beginning of the film as youthful sweethearts; then they are separated for a long time, before they meet again, with Marian in the charge of the Queen, and Robin as the bandit/hero who tries to rekindle their romance.

A particularly delightful scene invented for this scenario has Robin and his Men sneaking into town during a public meeting to raise funds for the King's ransom. The Sheriff has made a magnanimous gift, claiming that he has donated every cent he has. Meanwhile, the Merrie Men discover a strongbox in the Sheriff's quarters filled to the brim with gold coins and precious trinkets. They open the box, bring it into the town square, and dump its contents into the public kitty. As the Sheriff turns pale, Robin, disguised in the crowd, shouts, "Three cheers for the Sheriff!"

The performances are uniformly fine, with an impressive roster of talented players; James Robertson Justice as Little John and Peter Finch as the wicked Sheriff stand out. Richard Todd, in the first of his three assignments for Disney, is ingratiating as Robin Hood, and plays his scenes with Joan Rice quite nicely for an attractive and believable romance.

This is an extremely good-*looking* film as well. The locations are beautiful, with lush green countrysides; the sets are truly formidable and realistic.

The seemingly effortless pacing and knowing use of camera angles and cutting is doubly impressive when one considers certain background facts. For instance, Annakin has vivid memories of the difficulties in shooting Technicolor at that time.

It was the very elaborate three-strip system, with a very immobile camera. When you wanted to reload the camera in its very heavy blimp, you had to have it lifted on chains, and it took the first-class technicolor crew a minimum of eleven minutes to reload the camera. After every single shot the camera had to be opened and the gate had to be examined; the prism was the great thing because this was the light splitter which gave the registrations on the three strips.

For this reason, if you were making a big picture like *Robin Hood,* you had to be very certain that you were not wasting setups or wasting shots, because it was a big industrial process every time to set up your camera.

Annakin's prescreening of the Errol Flynn *Robin Hood* was probably responsible for the decision to find a new approach to the inevitable climactic battle between Robin and the Sheriff. In the earlier version there is the justly famous duel between Flynn and Basil Rathbone on the castle steps. In this film the duel takes the two adversaries all around the castle, climaxing in a chillingly exciting encounter with the drawbridge. As Robin tries to escape, the Sheriff starts to pull the bridge upright. Robin climbs to the top, hoping to squeeze out before it closes shut. The Sheriff, trying to stop him, gets caught and is crushed by the closing platform, a grisly but satisfying end for this most nefarious of villains.

The use of storyboards was new to Annakin, "but it appealed to my logical brain very, very much," and prompted ingenious scenes such as the first meeting between Prince John and the Sheriff of Nottingham after King Richard has left, played on the balcony of the castle against a brilliant but ominous orange sky at sundown.

At the time of its release *The Story of Robin Hood* was greeted with muted enthusiasm. One British critic opined: "The most that can be said for it is that it is unmemorable," whereas the *New York Times*'s A. H. Weiler found it "an expert rendition of an ancient legend that is as pretty as its Technicolor hues, and as lively as a sturdy Western."

Time has been kind to the film, as so many inferior films in this genre have followed it; today it seems better than ever. As for comparisons with other versions, it holds its own quite well. Douglas Fairbanks's 1922 *Robin Hood* is an excellent film, but the enormity of the settings and the scope of the production tend to dwarf the characters somewhat. The 1938 Warner Brothers epic, filmed in color, is strongly personality-oriented, with the brilliant playing of Errol Flynn, Basil Rathbone, Claude Rains, and a first-rate cast dominating the action.

Disney's *The Story of Robin Hood* strikes a happy medium, leaning heavily on strong characterizations, but placing them against a colorful and sumptuous tableau that gives the film a fine period flavor. It's far superior to Disney's own animated feature of 1973, which placed a greater emphasis on comedy, but the prominence—and success—of that film seems to have obliterated the memory of this earlier endeavor. That's an unfortunate fate for such an entertaining picture.

PETER PAN

Released by RKO Radio Pictures on February 5, 1953. Adapted from the play by Sir James M. Barrie. Directors: Hamilton Luske, Clyde Geronimi, Wilfred Jackson. Directing animators: Milt Kahl, Franklin Thomas, Wolfgang Reitherman, Ward Kimball, Eric Larson, Oliver Johnston, Jr., Marc Davis, John Lounsbery, Les Clark, Norman Ferguson. Story: Ted Sears, Bill Peet, Joe Rinaldi, Erdman Penner, Winston Hibler, Milt Banta, Ralph Wright. Color and styling: Mary Blair, Claude Coats, John Hench, Donald Da Gradi. Backgrounds: Ray Huffine, Art Riley, Albert Dempster, Eyvind Earle, Ralph Hulett, Thelma Witmer, Dick Anthony, Brice Mack. Layout: Mac Stewart, Tom Codrick, A. Kendall O'Connor, Charles Philippi, Hugh Hennesy, Ken Anderson, Al Zinnen, Lance Nolley, Thor Putnam, Don Griffith. Character animators: Hal King, Cliff Nordberg, Hal Ambro, Don Lusk, Ken O'Brien, Marvin Woodward, Art Stevens, Eric Cleworth, Fred Moore, Bob Carlson, Harvey Toombs, Judge Whitaker, Bill Justice, Hugh Fraser, Jerry Hathcock, Clair Weeks. Effects animation: George Rowley, Blaine Gibson, Joshua Meador, Dan MacManus. Musical score: Oliver Wallace. Orchestrations: Edward H. Plumb. Vocal arrangements: Jud Conlon. Running time: 76½ minutes.

Songs: "The Elegant Captain Hook," "The Second Star to the Right," "What Makes the Red Man Red?," "You Can Fly, You Can Fly, You Can Fly," "Your Mother and Mine" by Sammy Cahn and Sammy Fain. "A Pirate's Life" by Oliver Wallace and Erdman Penner. "March of the Lost Boys (Tee Dum Tee Dee)" by Oliver Wallace, Ted Sears, and Winston Hibler. "Never Smile at a Crocodile" by Frank Churchill and Jack Lawrence.

Voices: Bobby Driscoll (Peter Pan), Kathryn Beaumont (Wendy), Hans Conried (Captain Hook, Mr. Darling), Bill Thompson (Mr. Smee), Heather Angel (Mrs. Darling), Paul Collins (Michael Darling), Tommy Luske (John), Candy Candido (Indian chief), Tom Conway (narrator), Don Barclay, Roland Dupree.

James Barrie's *Peter Pan* seemed like an ideal subject for Walt Disney—and Disney knew it as early as 1935. In 1939 he arranged with the Great Ormond Street Hospital in London (to whom Barrie bequeathed ownership of the play) to produce an animated film of the classic show, which had been filmed once before in 1925.

Although random thoughts were given to the project throughout the 1940s, it wasn't until the last year of that decade that production finally began,

Tinker Bell interferes with Peter as he is about to open a deadly package from Captain Hook.   © *Walt Disney Productions*

Peter fights it out with Captain Hook as Wendy and Mr. Smee look on.   © *Walt Disney Productions*

with another live-action film being made for the animators' benefit. The film, which was released in early 1953, cost some $4 million.

The film opens on a shining star in the sky, panning down to a view of London at twilight, then gradually into the neighborhood of the Darling residence. The narrator introduces the family, whom we first see as silhouettes against the window shades.

Mr. Darling, upset by his children's harping on Peter Pan, the hero of older sister Wendy's bedtime stories, decides that it is Wendy's last night in the nursery, and the last night for Nana, the nurse-dog, as well. He ties Nana outside as he and Mrs. Darling go out for the evening.

But as they leave, Mr. Darling making sarcastic remarks about the existence of this character, the camera swings up to the roof and there, silhouetted in the moonlight, is Peter himself. He and Tinker Bell creep into the nursery to reclaim Peter's shadow, which Wendy has captured and locked up. In the ensuing commotion the children wake up, and Peter, hearing that Wendy is going to leave them, offers to take her to Neverland, where she won't have to grow up, and where she can continue to tell stories about him. Tinker Bell, jealous of the attention Peter is paying to Wendy, doesn't like the whole idea.

Nevertheless, Peter, Wendy, and her younger brothers Michael and John all think wonderful thoughts, get sprinkled with pixie dust, and fly off into the night, "the second star to the right and straight on till morning."

The rest of the film takes place in Neverland, where Captain Hook does his best to capture the elusive Peter, Tinker Bell tries very hard to sabotage any plans that involve Wendy, and Michael and John frolic with Peter's Lost Boys, who get homesick when Wendy sings of "Your Mother and Mine."

Hook kidnaps Princess Tiger Lily in the hope of luring Peter, and does so, but Peter manages to rescue the Indian maiden and foil Hook at the same time. Undaunted, Hook captures Tinker Bell and plays on her jealousy to get her to reveal Peter's hideout, where he plants a time bomb. Tinker escapes just in time to save Peter from the blast, but not before Hook's crew have captured Wendy, Michael, John, and the Lost Boys and taken them captive aboard their ship.

Peter meets Hook on his own territory, and after a battle in the ship's rigging, the unfortunate Captain falls overboard into the jaws of a crocodile who acquired one of his hands long ago and has been waiting for the rest of him ever since. The determined crocodile chases the frantic Hook off to the horizon.

Tinker Bell covers the entire ship with pixie dust, so it can sail back to London. When Mr. and Mrs. Darling come home that night, and Wendy and the boys try to tell them of their adventures, they go to the window and point to Peter's ship, which can be seen in the form of a cloud sailing in front of the moon. Mr. Darling looks at it and says gently that he

seems to remember having seen it himself, long, long ago.

It is difficult to find fault with *Peter Pan;* it is one of Disney's brightest, most straightforward animated features, a film in which everything clicks. One is tempted to say that it lacks the innovative brilliance of a *Pinocchio* (which is perfectly true), but it seems unfair to criticize the film for what it isn't, when it *is* such an unpretentious, delightful endeavor.

In some ways the Disney version of *Peter Pan* was revolutionary. It was the first enactment of the Barrie play where Peter was not played by a girl . . . to show Tinker Bell and the Crocodile . . . to be able to have Nana be a real dog (onstage it was always an actor) . . . and not to ask the audience to revive Tinker Bell after the explosion by clapping hands.

The latter decision was the most momentous for the Disney staff, the others having been taken care of rather simply. Even in the silent film with Betty Bronson, this timeworn but effective technique, with Peter beseeching the audience to prove it believes in fairies by applauding, was included. Yet Disney seemed to sense that this was, after all, a stage-play innovation, and not really appropriate for his film. The fact that the film works well without it, and remains faithful to its source, proves him to have been correct.

The actual design of Tinker Bell was another problem, since the sprite had always been shown as merely a beam of light (even in the silent film). Existing character sketches trace Tinker Bell's development from inception in 1938 to the design finally used; in the 1940s the Disney artists considered modeling her after the current conception of female attractiveness, an idea that would have proved disastrous, if employed. Disney claimed in a magazine article that the final decision on Tinker Bell's looks was cemented by the popularity of Marilyn Monroe, which made good copy, but was later denied by animator Marc Davis, since Monroe hadn't become a sensation when Peter Pan was in production. Still, the character's shapeliness caused criticism in some circles.

As with *Alice in Wonderland,* much publicity was generated by the unique Disney procedure of filming a live-action movie for animators to study. Explaining its use, director Hamilton Luske told Aline Mosby of UPI:

Cartoonists, just like artists, must have living models to draw from. Otherwise, they'd be drawing what they think certain characters would do in a situation, not what they really would do. We could, of course, have the live models act out a scene on a stage. But then the animators would have to trust their memories when they go back to their drawing boards. A film is easier, as it can be run over and over for the artists. And they can correct any mistakes in a scene before the drawing is made.

Hans Conried, who did the voice of Captain

Hook, was also hired to portray him in this film. He recalls:

> Usually they had pantomimists and/or dancers, but they felt that I could play the part. Now when I say I worked two and a half years, I don't say that I worked constantly, but over that period they would say "Have you got two weeks?", "Have you got four days?", "Have you got a week?" I was in costume, and they had an elemental set, and I would go through the business making my physical action coincide with the sound track, which was already finished. Usually, in dubbing, which I've done a lot of for foreign actors, you have to make your sound coincident with his latent action, but here you make your physical action coincident with the sound track. That was lots of fun; it was a very friendly, familial surroundings at Disney, particularly in those days.

Dancer Roland Dupree appeared as Peter in the live-action film, with June Foray, Margaret Kerry, and Connie Hilton as mermaids.

Students of the musical film would do well to study *Peter Pan*, not only to hear the beautiful choral arrangements by Jud Conlon, but to observe how masterfully the musical element of the film was integrated into the story. When the children ask Peter how they get to Neverland, he tells them it's easy, and begins to talk the lyrics of "You Can Fly." The kids join him, speaking rhythmically, but naturally, and almost, but never quite, bursting into song; the actual singing is taken up by the chorus, as the children fly out of the nursery window and into the night. Throughout the rest of the film, songs are introduced, and sometimes sung, in fragments, or so naturally that one is hardly aware they have begun. Even in the midst of Wendy's tender song "Your Mother and Mine," action is continuing, as Captain Hook's crew gathers outside the hideout to capture the Lost Boys.

Hook's crew gathers outside the hideout to capture the Lost Children.

Visually, the film is also rather straightforward, with bright splashes of color and sharply defined drawings, except in the scenes of London, which are the lushest in the film. When the children fly out the nursery window and sail over London, there is an absolutely stunning view of the city below—virtually a full-scale relief map, tinted in dark blue, seen through the clouds! The opening and closing scenes of the film also boast beautiful views of the city, with the memorable shot of the stardust ship sailing in front of the moon.

There is as much adventure as anything else in *Peter Pan*, with most of the humor deriving from the broadly funny activities of Captain Hook and his crew, but the film does have many small touches as well: Michael sprinkling pixie dust on Nana so she too can fly to Neverland (and fly she does, except that she is tied to the doghouse and cannot break away, so as she floats in the air, she waves goodbye to Michael) . . . Captain Hook, preparing to meet Tinker Bell, sprucing up, and screwing in a special golden hook . . . Michael's teddy bear confounding a live bear about to pounce on the children in the forest . . . and the Crocodile himself, a sly, smiling creature whose presence is made known by a constant tick-tock caused by an alarm clock he swallowed long ago.

In all, *Peter Pan* is a brisk and entirely winning adaptation of the Barrie play. Inevitably, comparisons were made with the 1950s Broadway musical version which starred Mary Martin (and which became a frequently broadcast TV special), but these were simply two different interpretations, and assessing which was "better" served no purpose. The melodic stage version (which was successfully revived in the late 1970s with Sandy Duncan) was ideally suited to its medium, just as Disney's was a perfect animated cartoon feature. The Disney film has proved to be one of the studio's biggest hits, in reissue after reissue—a tribute to both the timelessness of James Barrie's story and Walt Disney's wonderfully entertaining cartoon treatment.

THE SWORD AND THE ROSE

RELEASED BY RKO RADIO PICTURES ON JULY 23, 1953. Technicolor. Producer: Perce Pearce. Director: Ken Annakin. Screenplay: Lawrence E. Watkin. Photography: David Harcourt. Editor: Gerald Thomas. Art director: Carmen Dillon. Costumes: F. Arlington Valles. Music: Clifton Parker, played by the Royal Philharmonic Orchestra. Conductor: Muir Mathieson. Production manager: Douglas Peirce. Assistant director: Peter Bolton. Unit manager: George Mills. Matte artist: Peter Ellenshaw. Dance director: David Paltenghi. Technicolor color consultant: Joan Bridge. Makeup: Geoff Rodway. Hairstyling: B. Chrystal. Running time: 93 minutes.

Cast: Richard Todd (Charles Brandon), Glynis Johns (Mary Tudor), James Robertson Justice (Henry VIII), Michael Gough (Duke of Buckingham), Jane Barrett (Lady Margaret), Peter Copley (Sir Edwin Caskoden), Rosalie Crutchley (Queen Catherine of Aragon), D. A. Clarke-Smith (Cardinal Wolsey),

Ernest Jay (Lord Chamberlain), John Vere (lawyer-clerk), Phillip Lennard (chaplain), Bryan Coleman (Earl of Surrey), Philip Glasier (royal falconer), Jean Mercure (Louis XII of France), Gerard Oury (Dauphin of France), Fernand Fabre (De Longueville), Robert LeBeal (royal physician), Gaston Richer (Antoine Duprat), Helen Goss (Princess Claude).

Having succeeded with *Robin Hood,* Disney was anxious to keep the same production team together for a second venture, *The Sword and the Rose,* based on *When Knighthood Was in Flower* by Charles Major. Director Annakin, producer Pearce, scenarist Lawrence Watkin, art director Carmen Dillon, and leading actor Richard Todd were all summoned to duplicate the success of their previous film.

Annakin and Dillon were flown to the Burbank studio for a three-month period of preparation, along with the writer and producer. Annakin recalls:

As the script developed, it was always fed to Walt, who made his comments, and one began to see how important and helpful the thumbnail sketches were. After one had gotten a few pages done, Walt would come and look at them, and from his experience in cartoons would quickly put his finger on where the action looked as if it might be slacking, and where it was perhaps too long. By addition and elimination, we were all (but Walt especially) able to make sure we had very good action sequences at the right times in the picture.

For me as a director, the fact that we did our creative work in Walt's office and on the drawing-board so far as action scenes were concerned meant that I was completely free to develop the dialogue scenes and the scenes between people in my own way. Walt obviously wanted to know if the dialogue was as sparse as possible, but he was very happy that one made one's own interpretation with the actors. There was no question of being tied down by a diagram with the actors, which of course would have been a very serious handicap to this system. But I was getting to know Walt better and he was getting to know me better; he was starting up a relationship which gave me every advantage, and complete freedom.

The story takes place in the court of King Henry VIII. His sister, Mary Tudor, falls in love with a young man who is only passing through on his way to America. To detain him, she has him appointed Captain of the Guards, blind to the fact that the Duke of Buckingham is in love with her, and is consequently madly jealous of the new Captain.

The Captain decides to move on to America rather than involve himself in a potentially dangerous romance, but Mary follows him and, disguised as a boy, persuades him to take her along. They are found

Glynis Johns as Mary Tudor and Richard Todd as the man she loves, Charles Brandon, in *The Sword and the Rose.* © *Walt Disney Productions*

Mary uses her charms on her brother, Henry VIII (James Robertson Justice), unaware that she's also charming the Duke of Buckingham (Michael Gough). © *Walt Disney Productions*

out, however, and the Captain is sent to the Tower of London. Meanwhile, Mary is sent to marry the aging King of France, part of Henry's scheme to woo that ruler. She goes under protest, and decides to wear out the King as quickly as possible; her scheme works, and the King dies. Unfortunately, his successor, a former Dauphin, is a slimy, lecherous man.

The Duke comes to rescue Mary, and tells her on the way home that the Captain died in an escape attempt; actually, the escape was framed by the Duke, as was a murder attempt. What he doesn't know is that the Captain is still alive, which he discovers en route back to England when the Captain finds him and engages him in combat. Mary and her lover make a quick escape, followed in hot pursuit by the Duke; as they are about to sail for England, the Duke catches up to them, and he and the Captain fight a duel that ends in the Duke's death.

Back in court, Mary uses her wiles to get Henry to call off his attempt to buy France's favor through her. She wins her Captain a title and an estate—and he, in turn, suggests that Henry keep her dowry gift from France, a crooked scheme that delights the roguish King.

The Sword and the Rose has about as much to do with history as *Pinocchio,* but accuracy aside, it is a hugely entertaining, lavishly mounted costume drama. Once again, director Annakin manages to keep the film consistently arresting on a personal level, while maximizing the grandeur of the settings and costumes.

The extensive research into period detail that occupied the production staff for many months pays off beautifully in the finished product. It is overflowing with atmosphere, a myriad of details that combine to create a convincing portrait of Tudor England. Much of this atmosphere was created by Peter Ellenshaw's remarkable matte work.

Says Annakin:

Walt specifically had the picture designed in such a way as to use the maximum number of painted mattes; in fact we used sixty-two mattes in all, and it allowed us to give the picture a much broader sweep visually than it ever could have had. It resulted in Peter being given a life contract by Walt Disney. I got very taken up with this technique and continued to use it on later pictures, but I almost had to train new artists myself, and pass on to them the sort of tricks I thought Peter Ellenshaw relied on. But Peter just knew how to modify reality to make it look even realer than real.

This is absolutely true; many of his shots in *The*

Sword and the Rose are simply breathtaking, and as in all of Ellenshaw's work, it is impossible to tell where the real picture ends and the painting begins.

The narrative of the picture is such that one questions a child's ability to follow and understand it all. Obviously, such a viewer is compensated by the action scenes of escape from prison, the swordplay, etc., but the dialogue is quite literate and, at times, witty (especially in the instance of Henry VIII) beyond the comprehension of the typical Disney fan.

This is all to the film's credit as a costume drama, of course, for it stands as thoroughly engaging entertainment, thanks to a deliciously serpentine plot, winning performances by Richard Todd as the hero, Glynis Johns as the capricious Mary Tudor, James Robertson Justice as the rousing Henry VIII, and steely-eyed Michael Gough as the black-hearted Duke of Buckingham, and the eye-filling production itself.

The film never stands still, even in the final confrontation between Todd and Gough, which begins in a chapel where Gough is trying to force Glynis Johns to marry him. Suddenly, Todd appears, silhouetted in the doorway against a brilliant blue sky. He leaps inside and locks Gough in a closet so he and his lady can make a getaway. This provides for an exciting chase scene, which in turn leads to the inevitable duel, played along the French coast, in and out of the water, and on the shoreline rocks, until the villain finally gets his just deserts.

In fact, when the film *does* stand still, it finds new ways to entertain; in one elaborate sequence showing a staid palace ball, where the guests are dancing a slow, formal processional, the camera cuts to the host, King Henry, who is dozing off in boredom.

Unfortunately, critical reception to the film was cold. In England most of the attacks were based on the glaring lack of fidelity to facts, although the London *Times* critic had to admit that "there are moments when Mary, the sister of Henry VIII . . . comes remarkably to life, and Mr. James Robertson Justice gives to Henry the gleam of mingled cunning and good nature which may well have peered out of those shrewd Welsh eyes."

In America there was less concern about accuracy, but no more enthusiasm for the film itself. Weiler in the *New York Times* called it "a genteel and sometimes plodding period imbroglio."

For the filmmakers, however, it was a moral victory; they had worked hard to make the film something special, and they took pride in their achievement. Disney joined in this sentiment, and looked forward to the production team coming up with an even greater success for their third endeavor, *Rob Roy, The Highland Rogue.*

THE LIVING DESERT

RELEASED BY BUENA VISTA ON NOVEMBER 10, 1953. Print by Technicolor (from 16mm). Associate producer: Ben Sharpsteen. Director: James Algar. Screenplay: James Algar, Winston Hibler, Ted Sears. Photography: N. Paul Kenworthy, Jr., Robert H. Crandall. Additional photography: Stuart V. Jewell, Jack C. Couffer, Don Arlen, Tad Nichols. Narrator: Winston Hibler. Animation effects: Joshua Meador, John Hench, Art Riley. Musical director: Paul J. Smith. Orchestrations: Edward H. Plumb. Film editor: Norman Palmer. Special processes: Ub Iwerks. Sound director: C. O. Slyfield. Sound recording: Harold J. Steck. Running time: 73 minutes.

A hawk and a rattlesnake engage in a fierce battle in *The Living Desert.* © *Walt Disney Productions*

With the success of the True-Life nature short subjects, Disney became the recipient of endless wildlife film submitted by naturalist-photographers around the country. Some particularly fascinating footage was shot by N. Paul Kenworthy, Jr. He had studied insect life on the great American desert as part of a doctoral thesis for UCLA, and this film was the result. Its highlight was a breathtaking sequence of a wasp battling it out with a tarantula, attempting to paralyze its enemy by stinging it in exactly the right spot.

Disney was intrigued enough to hire Kenworthy and assign him to return to the desert for more footage. He accepted other free-lance material, and had his staff assemble it into the first feature-length subject in the nature series, *The Living Desert.*

He saw no reason why the same material that had received audience enthusiasm in his short subjects couldn't be adapted to a feature format, using real-life footage but presenting it in an entertaining manner.

The format of *The Living Desert* is one that became the standard for all successive True-Life features. It opens with the impressive True-Life logo, a gleaming globe turning within a frame, set against a sky-blue background. After the title credits, the film is introduced by a series of background pictures painted by an animated paintbrush on camera.

In *The Living Desert* the brush paints the North American continent, and illustrates the presence of trade winds in the Pacific and their effect. The brush then goes back over the continent, turning it into a relief map to illustrate how the winds are blocked

The little kangaroo rat is fascinated by the movements of the sidewinder, but not so intrigued that he doesn't know enough to get out of the way. © *Walt Disney Productions*

from moving further east by the Rocky Mountains. This phenomenon creates the desert that we are about to explore.

The narrator for the films is Winston Hibler, a veteran on the Disney staff. The decision to have him narrate the series was not accidental, to be sure. He has a pleasant midwestern kind of speech that imbues the films with a reassuring air of homeyness; when his voice is first heard, it is clear that this won't be a college lecture, but, instead, an interesting talk.

Hibler co-wrote the script for *Desert* with director James Algar and Ted Sears. They like to indulge in flowery dramatics (the introduction tells us that this is "a drama as old as time itself," etc.), but somehow these phrases *work* as spoken by the unpretentious Hibler.

The scenarists display a reverence for the ways of God, as personified by Nature, with a capital N. Near the beginning of the film's animal footage, Hibler explains that "nature knows neither villain nor hero," so the ensuing battle between rattlesnake and tarantula is a question of might versus might, cunning versus cunning, not a good-guy bad-guy confrontation.

But this reverence does not carry over to specifics in the rest of the film, for much of the material in *The Living Desert* is played for laughs. One of the film's first shots is of the bubbling vats found near desert geysers. Hibler calls the scene "a symphony of the mud puddles," a well-edited series of gurglings with appropriate music and sound effects. The outstanding use of sound effects in the films should be particularly mentioned, for though most of the footage was shot silent, it is sometimes hard to tell, so beautifully are the actual sounds of nature dubbed in.

From that point on there are numerous "gag" sequences throughout the film. Hibler even refers to a roadrunner seen early in the proceedings as "comedy relief" in the animal world of the desert. The narration is full of cute references; the chuckwalla is called a "second-story man" as he scrounges through other animals' homes. A skunk is dubbed "Sweet William."

Worst of all is the musical humor. A millipede moves along to railroad music on the sound track. A burrowing snake inspires a ballet. And in two sequences stop and reverse motion are added so that the courtship of two tarantulas is set to a tango, and the mating of two scorpions is done in the form of a square dance (with Hibler doing the calls, using special material: "Stingers up for the stingaree, but watch out gal, you don't sting me . . ."). An owl observing the scene seemingly cocks his head in time to the music.

It was this Disneyesque touch that gave the series a bad name with many critics. It wasn't that these sequences weren't funny or clever; it was just that they didn't belong in what was being touted as a factual film. Bosley Crowther commented: ". . . Mr. Disney and his writers and editors are inclined to do with nature pictures pretty much what they have always done with cartoons." This was a far cry from the

predictions of Richard Dyer McCann, who, during the film's preparation, had said that the film "may well be the biggest single step toward a new kind of maturity in American motion pictures," referring to widespread acceptance of documentary films. The real shame is that this kind of treatment was unnecessary, as later films in the series proved. Viewing the films with youngsters in the audience demonstrates that this audience does not get restless during the film's "straight" moments. The sheer majesty and excitement of the actual footage is enough to rivet their attention to the screen.

In *The Living Desert* this is largely due to the close-up camera work. There are, to be sure, panoramic views of the desert, but these are used mostly as establishing shots before getting into the actual meat of the sequences, which are played with the camera at ground level so that we can become involved in the action of the animals, and not remain aloof observers.

Desert also has some of the best footage ever shot for the series. One segment concerning bats opens inside a cave just as the sun is setting. As if on cue, hundreds upon hundreds of the winged animals suddenly swarm out of the cave, literally blackening the sky as they go out for their nightly prowl.

The battle of the rattlesnake and the tarantula, and the later fight between a rattlesnake and a hawk, are both tremendously exciting, the effect of the latter augmented by the fact that the scene was intercut with several different camera angles. A less violent, but no less fascinating, scene has a little kangaroo-rat burrowing into the ground when a vicious sidewinder slithers along. The rat isn't afraid of the snake, only annoyed, and tries to shoo him away by kicking sand in his face, repeatedly hopping forward to see if the job is done, then leaping backward on the chance that the snake might strike. He is so persistent that the venomous snake actually gives up and goes away!

The final portion of the film has a series of impressive scenes. A dry spell is broken by a sudden cloudburst, at first a welcome relief for the desert, but then too much of a good thing. As the camera shows an apparently peaceful spot set between some craggy rocks and hills, there is a thunderous sound in the distance, and suddenly a "wall of water" rumbling toward the lens—it's a flash flood caused by the downpour. This instant river swallows everything in its path, but eventually it leaves its canyonlike place of origin to spread out over the vast desert, where the combination of expanse and the heat of the sun dries it up rather quickly.

It leaves behind one aftereffect, however, a new life for the flora of the desert. That evening the desert comes alive with night-blooming flowers (filmed in time-lapse photography) that blossom into desert beauty, only to close up with the first rays of the sun.

As the sun sets at the end of that day, narrator Hibler tells us that on the desert "there are no endings, only new beginnings."

The Living Desert's popularity and box-office

success (it was released as a package with *Stormy,* a live-action short, and the animated *Ben and Me*), capped by the Academy Award for the year's best documentary feature, was a source of special satisfaction for Disney. He had been discouraged from doing the initial True-Life shorts, even by people within his organization, and when he embarked on a feature enterprise, he met with resistance from RKO, his distributor. It was this dispute that led to the formation of Disney's own distribution company, Buena Vista, an idea that had been in the back of brother Roy Disney's mind for some time.

What Disney was *not* prepared for was the anger of critics around the country for tampering with what was supposedly factual film; the scorpion dance in particular was the target of considerable attack. Though Disney had long since learned to ignore most criticism, he and his staff apparently did take heed in this case, for after the next feature, such gimmicky and "cute" material was virtually eliminated from the True-Life series.

In a 1967 filmed interview with the BBC's Philip Jenkinson, series director James Algar said that "there wasn't much of that material in the films," which "were done as outright straight reports of how an animal's life is led." But he also gave an indication of the naïveté of many viewers when he reported that "I have had people ask how we possibly get animals to move in time to music. The answer is evident to anyone who works with such films . . . we put the music to the action." It was precisely the fear that children would grow up thinking that scorpions moved in time to square-dance music that caused many critics to lambaste Disney for imposing his "touch" on the material in the film.

The real crime is that such critics, who still mention the series in a derogatory light, never bothered to recheck the series later on, when the viewpoint started to change. Nor did they stop long enough to weigh the relative merits and liabilities of the film. For with all its faults, *The Living Desert* is still a magnificent film, with some of the most remarkable action ever caught on film. Its success opened the door for acceptance of such material with an audience that otherwise might have forever shunned documentary films.

And today, decades after its release, with all the changes the years have brought in documentary film technique and attitudes, *The Living Desert* retains its power and magnitude. The reasons are simple: the raw material is undated, and the photography is magnificent. Those qualities will surely keep *The Living Desert* fresh for many years to come.

ROB ROY, THE HIGHLAND ROGUE

RELEASED BY RKO RADIO PICTURES ON FEBRUARY 4, 1954. Technicolor. Producer: Perce Pearce. Director: Harold French, Screenplay: Lawrence E. Watkin. Editor: Geoffrey Foot. Director of photography: Guy Green, B.S.C. Costumes: Phyllis Dalton. Music: Cedric Thorpe Davie. Music director: Muir Mathieson. Production manager: Douglas Peirce. Assistant director: Gordon Scott. Matte artist: Peter Ellenshaw. Technicolor color consultant: Joan Bridge. Production designer: Carmen Dillon, Location director: Alex Bryce. Running time: 85 minutes.

Cast: Richard Todd (Rob Roy MacGregor), Glynis Johns (Helen Mary MacGregor), James Robertson Justice (Duke of Argyll), Michael Gough (Duke of Montrose), Finlay Currie (Hamish MacPherson), Jean Taylor-Smith (Lady Glengyll), Geoffrey Keen (Killearn), Archie Duncan (Dougal MacGregor), Russell Waters (Hugh MacGregor), Marjorie Fielding (Maggie MacPherson), Eric Pohlmann (King George I), Ina de la Haye (Countess von Pahlen), Michael Goodliffe (Robert Walpole), Martin Boddey (General Cadogan), Ewen Solon (Major General Wightman), James Sutherland (Torcal), Malcolm Keen (Duke of Marlborough).

Walt Disney's winning team of British filmmakers was all set to embark upon their third joint project, *Rob Roy,* when Ken Annakin's home studio, J. Arthur Rank, refused to let him work again for the Disney company. Rather than break his contract, Annakin reluctantly had to go along with the Rank decision, and a new director was summoned to pick up where Annakin had left off in the preparatory stages.

It is always difficult to speculate about what might have been, but it seems unlikely that the same team that had scored so resoundingly with *Robin Hood* and *Sword and the Rose* would have missed the mark with similar material. Yet with a new director, Harold French, that is exactly what happened.

Rob Roy, The Highland Rogue is an uncommonly heavy-handed production. What is more, the central issues that figure in the plot would surely go

Rob Roy leads an attack.   © *Walt Disney Productions*

In one of Rob Roy's (Richard Todd) lighter moments, he dances with his wife (Glynis Johns).   © *Walt Disney Productions*

over the head of any child—they seem confusing even to some adult viewers! There is precious little action to offset the ponderous goings-on, and an abrupt and unsatisfying conclusion.

The film is set in Scotland during the eighteenth century. The Scotsmen are opposed to the new English King, George, who is by birth a German. The MacGregor clan, led by rowdy Rob Roy, decide that violent confrontation is the only course of action. This leaves the Scottish Secretary of State in an awkward position; he too wants freedom, but he still represents the King and thinks things should be done in an orderly manner.

He is soon deposed and replaced by an unscrupulous aide, who hates Rob Roy and stoops to new lows in trying to capture him. Rob's wife and the deposed secretary try to convince Rob Roy that he should give the new king a chance to make peace, but the stubborn Scot refuses to listen.

When he finally realizes that he has been doing battle not with the King, however, but with the crooked new secretary of state, he gives in, sees King George, and, on behalf of his clansmen, makes peace once and for all.

It is difficult to know where to place the blame for this endeavor, for not only is the direction staid and unremarkable, but the story itself does little to inspire an audience. The fun of the earlier films was in painting characters of good and evil in the extreme, and pitting them against each other in actionful climaxes. *The Sword and the Rose* tampered with history, but in doing so made a lively, colorful story. *Rob Roy*'s conflicts are ideological, and a bit too real to be taken in the same light as the fanciful conflicts in *Robin Hood.*

Rob Roy leaves no room for imagination or idealization, and in mooring its story and characters to reality takes all the fun out of the film.

That this flaw was not evident to the film's director can be noted in a quote reportedly picked up at a royal performance of the film in London. When introduced to the Queen, director French explained: "It's a Western in kilts, Your Majesty."

Would that it had been!

Oddly enough, *Rob Roy* received many glowing reviews, particularly in England, but Dilys Powell in the Sunday *Times* gave it a backhanded compliment by writing: "To say that this is the best of what

Disney calls his all-live action films is, I fear, not saying much, but one must do what small kindnesses one can."

All publicity for the film was careful to explain that the scenario was not based on the famous novel by Sir Walter Scott, but on original source material.

Perhaps it would have been a better idea to use the more engaging fiction of Scott.

More significant than anything else is the fact that with this film Disney suspended operations in England and decided to make his live-action films at home.

THE VANISHING PRAIRIE

RELEASED BY BUENA VISTA ON AUGUST 17, 1954. Print by Technicolor (from a 16mm original). Associate producer: Ben Sharpsteen. Director: James Algar. Screenplay: James Algar, Winston Hibler, Ted Sears. Photography: Tom McHugh, James R. Simon, N. Paul Kenworthy, Jr., Cleveland P. Grant, Lloyd Beebe, Herb Crisler, Dick Borden, Warren Garst, Murl Deusing, Olin Sewall Pettingill, Jr., Stuart V. Jewell. Narrator: Winston Hibler. Musical director: Paul J. Smith. Orchestrations: Edward H. Plumb, Joseph Dubin. Production manager: Erwin Verity. Animation effects: Joshua Meador, Art Riley. Film editor: Lloyd Richardson. Special process: Ub Iwerks. Sound director: C. O. Slyfield. Sound recording: Harold J. Steck. Music editor: Al Teeter. Running time: 75 minutes.

As soon as the footage for *The Living Desert* was completed, Disney sent his photographers out again to tackle a new topic, the American prairie. Once again this material was supplemented by footage purchased from freelance cameramen who shot film on their own and submitted it to Disney. Another two years was needed to complete the second True-Life feature, but since work had begun while the first film was in the editing stages, Disney was able to release *The Vanishing Prairie* in 1954, less than a year after his initial success.

The magic paintbrush this time paints a picture of the United States to show how it is divided into three regions by the Rocky Mountains on the West and the Mississippi River toward the east, creating a natural boundary for the great American prairie, a region that, we are told, is dying a slow death.

The brush paints examples of cave drawings made by Indians that depict animals that once existed on the prairie, but that are now extinct.

As the spring thaw comes to the prairie today, life begins its new yearly cycle. Birds return to the region

Two buffalo meet head on in this scene from *The Vanishing Prairie*. ©*Walt Disney Productions*

This prairie dog can't figure out where all the buffalo have come from. © *Walt Disney Productions*

and alight on the streams and ponds—except that some are still partially frozen, causing the winged creatures to make some very slippery landings. Grebes, whooping cranes, and grouse all appear during the first days of spring.

A buffalo gives birth to a calf, removing the membranous sac and eating it, then massaging the newborn to build its circulation. The mother then helps its child as it tries to stand and walk. Finally on its own, the calf takes its place among the other buffalo in the herd.

Prong-horn antelope and big-horn sheep (who are amazingly surefooted along mountain paths) roam freely. But the deer is victimized by the mountain lion, which kills the weaker animal for one reason only: food for its young.

Prairie dogs build underground homes, with levees around the entranceways to protect them from enemies and from the elements. A coyote, the prairie dog's greatest enemy, tries to invade his underground home, but the little animal is too fast, leading the coyote on an underground chase that results only in frustration.

Another enemy of the prairie dog is the falcon, who swoops down from above to catch its prey.

Even kindred animals fight each other, and one vicious buffalo battle incites a massive stampede. But fighting is forsaken when disaster strikes. A lightning bolt sets the prairie ablaze, the fire spreading with amazing rapidity until flames cover everything in sight. Nature provides relief in the form of a cloudburst, but soon there is too much of a good thing as a flash flood results, routing the prairie dogs from their homes.

Before long, however, the prairie returns to normal, the elements under control and life continuing in its everyday pattern. The narrator explains that we have seen examples of a life that is quickly going out of existence—actually a "look into the past."

Like *The Living Desert, The Vanishing Prairie* is a dazzling collection of sequences, brilliantly photographed and edited for maximum results. And like its predecessor, *The Vanishing Prairie* won the Academy Award for the year's best documentary feature film.

It also brought Disney into conflict with the state censorship board in New York—a confrontation no one dreamed would ever happen. That Walt Disney, the purveyor of the screen's finest family entertainment, should ever have censorship problems was the target of many a snicker in 1954—and a cause of considerable embarrassment for the New York board of censors.

The board decided to ban *The Vanishing Prairie* from New York State because of the sequence showing a buffalo giving birth. Disney was stunned by the decision. "The birth scene would never have appeared on the screen if I believed it might offend an audi-

ence," he said, adding, "it would be a shame if New York children had to believe the stork brings buffaloes, too."

After considerable comment, and a complaint lodged by the American Civil Liberties Union, the board reversed its decision and the film was allowed to be shown intact. The *New Yorker*'s critic wrote: ". . . Mr. Disney shows us the birth of a buffalo calf—an episode that, I understand, caused the state censors (who themselves must at one time have been born) a bit of uneasiness. I lived through the scene, and I suspect you will, too."

Generally speaking, the film was well received by most critics, although there were still complaints about such sequences as two bighorn sheep locking horns to the tune of "The Anvil Chorus." But there was less of this material in *Prairie* than there had been in *Desert,* and criticism was proportionately milder.

The film espouses the same themes as earlier True-Life films: the endless cycle of life, the inevitability of nature (one animal must be killed so that another may survive, etc.). The life-styles of the various animals are well presented, giving each species a feeling of individuality in the viewer's mind.

The miracles of life are presented in a straightforward manner, most notably the birth scene, which in its utter simplicity is absolutely fascinating. There is no attempt to doctor the sequence or impose human viewpoints on the animals' actions.

Though the Disney company usually tried to keep their photographers' techniques a secret, Hollywood correspondent Joe Hyams presented a revealing article on how a great deal of the film was made. Tom McHugh shot most of the buffalo footage over a long period of time. Patience was the key ingredient in getting the footage he wanted. In order to get close to the animals, he covered himself and his camera with an old buffalo hide and wandered into the midst of the herd. When he found a buffalo who was carrying a calf, he simply stayed by its side until the birth took place.

For the stampede he set up a series of cameras along the path the buffalo were sure to follow, stringing trip wires across the road. When the animals ran through, they set off the cameras and provided one of the film's most impressive sequences. Indeed, the film is full of ingenious photography, such as the scene of the hawk attacking the prairie dog; the camera is at ground level, with the dog in tight close-up, as the hawk swoops down right into the lens, missing its target by a hair. For some scenes three to five cameramen shot the same action, providing a variety of angles for the editor to assemble.

The sequences of the prairie dogs' homes were artificially prepared by creating a controlled situation, a replica of the prairie earth "sliced in half," bordered on one side by a dark plate glass, much like ant farms. After giving the animals plenty of time to get accustomed to the new surroundings, the photographers were able to shoot their footage through the glass and simulate what must actually happen on the prairie.

An estimated 120,000 feet of 16mm film was shot and edited down to the 30,000 used in the release print of the film. Only in this fashion could the Disney staff present such truly outstanding material—

by giving its photographers the opportunity to *wait* and get exactly what they were after.

Reissues of *The Vanishing Prairie* showed that, like the other films in this series, it retains its full dramatic impact for audiences of all ages to marvel at an existence they otherwise might never have a chance to observe.

20,000 LEAGUES UNDER THE SEA

RELEASED BY BUENA VISTA ON DECEMBER 23, 1954. Technicolor, CinemaScope. Director: Richard Fleischer. Screenplay: Earl Felton, based on the novel by Jules Verne. Photography: Franz Planer, A.S.C. Special effects photography: Ralph Hammeras, A.S.C. Underwater photography: Till Gabbani. Editor: Elmo Williams, A.C.E. Art director: John Meehan. Set decorations: Emile Kuri. Costumes: Norman Martien. Music: Paul J. Smith. Orchestrations: Joseph S. Dubin. Production manager: Fred Leahy. Second unit director: James Havens. Assistant directors: Tom Connors, Jr., Russ Haverick. Matte artist: Peter Ellenshaw. Special processes: Ub Iwerks. Special effects: John Hench, Joshua Meador. Diving master: Fred Zendar. Production development: Harper Goff. Sketch artist: Bruce Bushman. Technicolor consultant: Morgan Padleford. Makeup, hairstyling: Lou Hippe. Sound director: C. O. Slyfield. Sound recording: Robert O. Cook. Running time: 127 minutes.

Song: "A Whale of a Tale" by Al Hoffman and Norman Gimbel.

Cast: Kirk Douglas (Ned Land), James Mason (Captain Nemo), Paul Lukas (Professor Aronnax), Peter Lorre (Conseil), Robert J. Wilke (first mate of *Nautilus*), Carleton Young (John Howard), Ted de Corsia (Captain Farragut), Percy Helton (diver), Ted Cooper (mate of *Lincoln*), Edward Marr (shipping agent), Fred Graham (Casey Moore), J. M. Kerrigan (Billy), Harry Harvey (shipping clerk), Herb Vigran (reporter).

20,000 Leagues under the Sea was Disney's most ambitious live-action film to date, and it remains one of the most successful he ever made.

Disney knew that no amount of money, technical wizardry, or inventiveness could take the place of a good story. And he was certain that Jules Verne's futuristic tale of a despotic sea captain and his fan-

A view of the fantastic, futuristic submarine *Nautilus*.
© *Walt Disney Productions*

tastic submarine was a story worthy of a major production. Consequently, no expense was spared in putting this story on the screen. Since Disney had no full-time live-action crew on the payroll, the personnel were handpicked from the Hollywood hopper.

Ironically, the man chosen to direct the film was Richard Fleischer, the son of Disney's onetime rival Max Fleischer, who had started in short subjects and shown tremendous promise with modest low-budget films like *Narrow Margin* and *So This Is New York*.

The inside of the *Nautilus* is also something to see. Here Captain Nemo treats his captives to a sumptuous dinner. James Mason, Kirk Douglas, Peter Lorre, and Paul Lukas.   © *Walt Disney Productions*

A highlight of the film has Captain Nemo battling a giant squid atop his submarine.   © *Walt Disney Productions*

Planning *20,000 Leagues* entailed more complex work than any live film Disney had yet tackled. Compared to the logistics of shooting, the screenplay must have been relatively simple, although director Fleischer recalls that "it was a very difficult book to translate to the screen, because there wasn't really any story."

Characters and their interplay were developed, with appropriate thought given to limited comedy relief from the tense dramatics of the story line. For the first time Disney decided to hire well-known names to head his cast, and he made an ideal selection with Kirk Douglas as the swaggering sailor Ned Land, James Mason as the Machiavellian Captain Nemo, Paul Lukas as the distinguished professor, and Peter Lorre as his aide-de-camp.

Art director John Meehan was imported from Paramount studios, where he had won Academy Awards for his work on *The Heiress* and *Sunset Boulevard*. His creations, particularly the main lounge of the submarine, replete with velvet chairs, divans, rococo ornaments, and a pipe organ, are largely responsible for the film's success.

Veteran cameraman Franz Planer had the double challenge of working in the newly developed Cinema-Scope process, and trying to create believable and sufficient lighting in sets that were built with viewable ceilings (in order to emphasize the submarine's interior settings).

The submarine itself, the *Nautilus,* was built to scale, two hundred feet long, shaped as Verne had described it, as an undersea monster, its headlights appearing as "eyes" in the dark waters.

Although most underwater filming was done on location, a special sound stage was built at the studio to house a giant tank for more intimate and complex shots. Most of the seagoing material was shot off the coast of Nassau in the Bahamas, where the fifty-four-man crew spent eight weeks filming. Aware that the story of how the film was made could be in some ways as interesting as the film itself, Disney assigned a second unit to make a documentary about the filming of *20,000 Leagues*. The resulting hour-long film, shown on the Disney TV show as *Operation Undersea,* won an Emmy award as the year's best television documentary.

The plot of the film has to do with the strange reports of a sea monster attacking ships in the Pacific in 1868. The armed frigate *Abraham Lincoln* is sent out to sea to find and destroy this monster; aboard the ship are harpooner Ned Land, Professor Pierre Aronnax, a specialist on sea creatures, and his assistant Conseil. The *Lincoln* does indeed find the monster, but is attacked and sunk; Land, Aronnax, and Conseil withstand the crash and are rescued by the "monster," which turns out to be a submarine.

Its commander, Captain Nemo, is a misfit genius who has harnessed some of the world's greatest discoveries, but is bound to use them to destroy mankind. The Professor welcomes the opportunity to learn from the *Nautilus*'s expeditions, but Ned Land's only thought is of escape, and gradually he wins Conseil to his way of thinking. When the sub makes a stop at a tropic island, Ned sends a flurry of bottles with notes in them out to sea on the chance that one might be spotted.

The *Nautilus* is heading for Vulcania, the island headquarters of Nemo and his men. Along the way the submarine is attacked by a giant squid; Ned rescues Nemo from the clutches of the sea beast and earns his gratitude.

Prodded by the Professor, Nemo decides to make peace with the world and share the fantastic secrets he has learned—of atomic energy, electricity, and other wonders. But when they reach Vulcania, warships are waiting in ambush, having received Ned's message. Infuriated, Nemo determines that no one shall learn his secrets; he plants a deadly explosive on the island, returns to the submarine, and holding Ned, the Professor, and Conseil captive, orders the *Nautilus* to make a final trip to the ocean floor. He has been shot while planting his bomb, and this will be his last voyage.

Ned manages to break loose, and rescues his comrades just in time to flee the submerging vessel. As they float to safety, they see the results of the bomb, which completely destroys the island, the warships, and everything in sight, as the *Nautilus* goes down for the last time.

20,000 Leagues under the Sea is fantasy at its best, with the Disney production team making the unbelievable come to life, in order to project a convincing tale against real-life backgrounds. The sumptuous mounting and careful attention to detail contribute immeasurably to the overall effect.

James Mason is compelling as Captain Nemo, wavering on that fine line between genius and madman, playing Bach's "Toccata in D Minor" on his pipe organ one moment, and planning a murderous attack the next. The balance of the cast fills the various roles to perfection, Douglas's byplay with Nemo's pet seal and Lorre's unique personality providing gentle but welcome comedy relief.

In fact, everything about the film seems unmistakably *right*. It was obviously the result of tremendous effort, and director Richard Fleischer recalls one instance of Disney's insistence upon perfection, no matter the cost.

The fight with the octopus was very difficult, more a mechanical problem than anything else. The first time we tried it, the monster just didn't work; it got waterlogged, and started to sink. It wasn't engineered properly, and it couldn't do all the things we needed it to do. It looked very phony anyway. After we spent a lot of money on it, and a lot of time, Walt and I finally decided to stop this sequence, go on to something else, and give us a chance to redo this animal.

I was talking to the writer, and we realized

that the concept was wrong. When we first did the sequence it was done on a flat, calm sea at sunset, and everything was very clear; you could see the mechanics of this thing too clearly. We came up with the idea that this should be done at night, during a storm at sea, so we had spray, and waves, and great excitement and obscuring action so that you don't see all the flaws. It made it a hundred times more expensive to do that way, but when we presented the idea to Walt, he said, "You're absolutely right, do it that way."

Another frequent problem was getting fish to

swim by the camera; most of them carefully avoided the production areas. In more than one instance this problem was solved by having animated fish "swim" in front of the lens (particularly noticeable in the first scene of Paul Lukas standing with Mason in the picture-window nose of the submarine).

Such perfectionism, made possible by the resources of the Disney studio, was responsible for *20,000 Leagues under the Sea* becoming one of the great films of its kind, as well as one of Disney's biggest grossing films. It would be some time before Disney would top this achievement in the field of live-action films.

DAVY CROCKETT, KING OF THE WILD FRONTIER

RELEASED BY BUENA VISTA ON MAY 25, 1955. TECH-nicolor. Producer: Bill Walsh. Director: Norman Foster. Screenplay: Tom Blackburn. Photography: Charles P. Boyle. Editor; Chester Schaeffer. Art director: Marvin Aubrey Davis. Set decorations: Emile Kuri, Pat Delaney. Costumes: Norman Martien. Music: George Bruns. Orchestrations: Edward H. Plumb. Unit production manager: Henry Spitz. Assistant director: James Judson Cox. Matte artist: Peter Ellenshaw. Special artwork: Joshua Meador, Art Riley, Ken Anderson. Special processes: Ub Iwerks. Makeup: Lon Philippi. Sound: C. O. Slyfield, Robert O. Cook. Running time: 93 minutes.

Songs: "The Ballad of Davy Crockett" by Tom Blackburn, George Bruns. "Farewell" by Davy Crockett, George Bruns.

Cast: Fess Parker (Davy Crockett), Buddy Ebsen (George Russel), Basil Ruysdael (Andrew Jackson), Hans Conried (Thimblerig), William Bakewell (Tobias Norton), Kenneth Tobey (Colonel Jim Bowie), Pat Hogan (Chief Red Stick), Helene Stanley (Polly Crockett), Nick Cravat (Bustedluck), Don Megowan (Colonel Billy Travis), Mike Mazurki (Bigfoot Mason), Jeff Thompson (Charlie Two Shirts), Henry Joyner (Swaney), Benjamin Hornbuckle (Henderson), Hal Youngblood (opponent political speaker), Jim Maddux (first congressman), Robert Booth (second congressman), Eugene Brindel (Billy), Ray Whitetree (Johnny), Campbell Brown (Bruno).

The phenomenal success of Davy Crockett caught everyone by surprise, including Walt Disney. The character was developed as a subject for some "Frontierland" episodes on the Disneyland TV show, and as Disney later told it: "We had no idea what was going to happen to 'Crockett.' Why, by the time the first show finally got on the air, we were already shooting the third one and calmly killing Davy off at the Alamo. It became one of the biggest overnight hits in TV history, and there we were with just three films and a dead hero."

Where there's a will, there's a way, however, and Disney did his best to keep Davy alive. First of all there was that song, an innocuous little tune called "The Ballad of Davy Crockett," which before long was on the lips of every young boy in America. Then came the merchandising boom, headed by coonskin caps and followed by a wide assortment of unrelated products.

Finally it was decided to take advantage of the Crockett boom and splice the three one-hour programs into a feature film for theatrical release, just in time for summer vacation. Here is where Disney's policy of turning out quality TV programming paid off, for the finished product, trimmed to ninety minutes, hardly betrays its television origin—a neat trick that few other producers could have pulled off. Disney also had the foresight to film his series in color.

The resulting feature film is an episodic but well-paced entertainment. Special animation involving Davy Crockett's *Journal,* and a colorful relief map of the country, provide transitions between segments,

Davy Crockett engages in hand-to-hand combat with Chief Red Stick (Pat Hogan). © *Walt Disney Productions*

Davy (Fess Parker), Georgie (Buddy Ebsen), and Thimblerig (Hans Conried) survey the territory ahead of them. © *Walt Disney Productions*

accompanied by special lyrics to the Davy Crockett theme song.

The opening segment deals with Davy the Indian Fighter, an unorthodox civilian volunteer scout whom the British grow to find invaluable. Assigned to track down the savage Chief Red Stick, he does, but instead of killing him, wins his admiration and respect.

He and his sidekick Georgie Russel then help a small town get rid of a thieving troublemaker called Bigfoot Mason. Davy becomes a local hero, and is encouraged to run for office. When he receives word that his young wife has died suddenly, he decides that he has nothing tying him down anymore, and agrees.

Once in the Nashville legislature, he is approached by his former General, Andrew Jackson, who is running for President and wants Davy to run for Congress on the same ticket. When elected, Davy goes around the country on speaking tours, bolstering the legend created by his friend Georgie's pulp fiction about their exploits. Then he discovers that Jackson has used his absence to try to put through a bill taking land away from the Indians. He returns to Congress just in time to head off a vote, register his disgust, and resign.

He and his sidekick then take off for new adventure in Texas, encountering a sly dandy named Thimblerig along the way. They arrive at the Alamo and find a rapidly deteriorating situation. Leader Jim Bowie is injured and cannot leave his bed; he tells Crockett in confidence that they are running out of food and ammunition. Later, when Davy tells the men that things look bleak and they are free to go, everyone stays to finish the fight. The Mexicans break into the fort and fight hand to hand. The men put up a valiant fight, knowing it is their last. Our final view of Davy Crockett shows him swinging his rifle to ward off attackers, as the ballad tells us he did not die, because his spirit lives on.

There are several indications in this film that the Disney people did not expect Davy to become a national hero all over again. Though he is an admirable man, he is violent when he has to be, as in the hand-to-hand fights, as well as the initial Indian battle, where he is seen bayoneting various red men, hollering "Give it to 'em, boys!" and such. He is also shown to have a not inconsiderable ego ("We'll give 'em the old Crockett charge," he announces at one point), perfectly willing to play on his fame during the speaking tour.

After Davy became the idol of millions, writers Tom Blackburn and Norman Foster (the latter also directed) were more careful to make him a pious and fault-free character.

It is also interesting to note that a film made under the aegis of Walt Disney shows Davy Crockett being "used" by the President of the United States! Those who find nothing but pablum in Disney's product ought to look again.

The film itself is fairly well made, although occasional economies are apparent. Throughout the film Georgie will say to Davy, "Hey, look at that," and there will be an insert of a bear, alligator, or other animal obviously snipped from a Disney nature reel. There is a glass shot of the Capitol building in Washington, but on the other end of the scale authentic locations are used for the legislature and Jackson's colonial home, which adds a nice feeling of reality to the otherwise fictitious doings.

It is easy to see where the three segments begin and end, but basically the editing job is smooth. One jarring note is the character played by Hans Conried, Thimblerig, whose appearance is insufficiently explained in the feature-film version of the story.

It has been reported that Buddy Ebsen was originally being considered for the role of Davy. Then one day some Disney people were screening a science-fiction film called *Them!*, and took a fancy to a young actor who had a brief but prominent scene. They tested him and decided that here was their Davy Crockett. Overnight Fess Parker became a star.

There is something about Parker that projects sincerity to an audience, and obviously he was a perfect choice to play Davy. Subsequent roles for Disney showed him to be a competent and likable actor, but one of limited range. Director Norman Foster later recalled: "I found if I didn't do something to get adrenaline in his system, he would get slower and slower. He seemed to lack vitality. I told him to take vitamin pills."

Buddy Ebsen provided a perfect counterpart for Parker's dry, understated manner with his affable and often boisterous performance as Georgie Russel. It is his exuberance, not Parker's, that puts over a scene, such as the one where the two scouts save some British soldiers from an Indian ambush by giving the appearance of having the redskins "surrounded," purely by verbal tricks.

Obviously, Davy Crockett was too good a thing to let go with just a one-shot TV exposure and feature-film follow-up. He would be heard from again the following year.

LADY AND THE TRAMP

RELEASED BY BUENA VISTA ON JUNE 16, 1955. TECHnicolor, CinemaScope. Associate producer: Erdman Penner. Directors: Hamilton Luske, Clyde Geronimi, Wilfred Jackson. Directing animators: Milt Kahl, Franklin Thomas, Oliver Johnston, Jr., John Lounsbery, Wolfgang Reitherman, Eric Larson, Hal King, Les Clark. Story: Erdman Penner, Joe Rinaldi, Ralph Wright, Donald Da Gradi, based on an original story by Ward Greene. Animators: George Nicholas, Hal Ambro, Ken O'Brien, Jerry Hathcock, Erick Cleworth, Marvin Woodward, Ed Aardal, John Sibley, Harvey Toombs, Cliff Nordberg. Don Lusk, George Kreisl, Hugh Fraser, John Freeman, Jack Campbell, Bob Carson. Backgrounds: Claude Coats, Dick Anthony, Ralph Hulett, Albert Dempster, Thelma Witmer, Eyvind Earle, Jimi Trout, Ray Huffine, Brice Mack. Layout: Ken Anderson, Tom Codrick, Al Zinnen, A. Kendall O'Connor, Hugh Hennesy, Lance Nolley, Jacques Rupp, McLaren Stewart, Don Griffith, Thor Putnam, Collin Campbell, Victor Haboush, Bill Bosche. Effects animation: George Rowley, Dan McManus. Music score: Oliver Wallace. Orchestrations: Edward H. Plumb, Sidney Fine. Vocal arrangements: John Rarig. Film editor: Donald Halliday.

Lady and Tramp meet in a kiss when they both nibble on the same strand of spaghetti at Tony's. © *Walt Disney Productions*

Trusty and Jock try to divert the driver of the paddy wagon carrying Tramp away. © *Walt Disney Productions*

Sound director: C. O. Slyfield. Sound recording: Harold J. Steck, Robert O. Cook. Music editor: Evelyn Kennedy. Special processes: Ub Iwerks. Running time: 75 minutes.

Songs: "He's a Tramp," "La La Lu," "Siamese Cat Song," "Peace on Earth," "Bella Notte" by Sonny Burke and Peggy Lee.

Voices: Peggy Lee (Darling, Peg, Si, and Am), Barbara Luddy (Lady), Larry Roberts (Tramp), Bill Thompson (Jock, Bull, Dachsie), Bill Baucon (Trusty), Stan Freberg (Beaver), Verna Felton (Aunt

Sarah), Alan Reed (Boris), George Givot (Tony), Dallas McKennon (Toughy, Professor), Lee Millar (Jim Dear, Dog Catcher, Man in Pet Shop), The Mello Men.

For his first animated feature since *Peter Pan,* Disney chose a story by Ward Greene called *Lady and the Tramp.* He later explained: "We were free to develop the story as we saw fit, which is not the case when you work on a classic. Then you must adhere rigidly to the sequences conceived by the author, which are familiar to your audience. Here, as the characters came to life and the scenes took shape, we were able to alter, embellish, eliminate and change to improve the material." Although the statement was made as a publicity release, it does make clear the advantage the Disney staff enjoyed with this film.

The result is a well-thought-out, enjoyable cartoon feature, not as compelling as many earlier works, but certainly more handsome than some, due in large part to Disney's decision to make the film in Cinema-Scope. Thus, an added emphasis was given to the layout and design departments to create a succession of picturesque backgrounds against which the story could be played.

The film opens on a panoramic view of a quaint New England town in the early part of the century during a snowfall. Darling (the human heroine) opens her Christmas package to find a female puppy inside, a gift from her husband Jim Dear. They name her Lady, and in a filmic transition we see her grow up.

She lives in an exclusive section of town with her canine friends Jock (a Scottish terrier) and Trusty (a bloodhound devoid of the sense of smell) on the same block. When they chance to encounter a dog from the wrong side of the tracks (Tramp), they treat him with disdain.

Darling gives birth to a baby; at first Lady is apprehensive, because she has been ignored in all the excitement, but when the baby arrives, Jim Dear and Darling apologize and introduce her to the new member of the family. Unfortunately, they must go away for a few days, and Darling's Aunt Sarah comes to mind the baby. She takes an instant dislike to Lady, heightened when her scheming Siamese cats make a shambles of the living room and foist the blame on Lady. Aunt Sarah buys a muzzle for the perplexed dog.

At this, Lady breaks loose, but she soon finds herself in unfamiliar territory, being chased by some tough street dogs. Luckily, Tramp is nearby, and he rescues her, taking her to the zoo where he persuades an industrious beaver that the muzzle would be of value to him in hauling logs. The beaver obligingly cuts through the muzzle and sets Lady free.

Then Tramp takes Lady around town, showing the sheltered pet his freewheeling view of life and romancing her over spaghetti dinner at the back entrance to Tony's restaurant.

The next morning Lady awakens to her responsibility, to return home and look after the baby; Tramp is unable to persuade her to stay footloose and fancy free. On their way home he goads her into joining him for a quick spree through a chicken coop, and she is trapped by a dogcatcher. In the dog pound she meets some other canines who tell her that Tramp is a bit of a rogue and a ladies' man; Lady is totally disillusioned.

Aunt Sarah comes to claim Lady and chains her to the doghouse in the backyard. When Tramp comes to apologize, Lady refuses to listen to him. Then she sees a slimy neighborhood rat coming up the side of the house and into the baby's room. She calls to Tramp for help and breaks her chain as he goes upstairs to save the child. Tramp engages in a vicious scrap with the rodent, emerging triumphant but knocking over the baby's crib in the process. Sarah comes in, doesn't see the rat, and thinks that Tramp has attacked the child!

She has the dogcatcher come to take him away. Just then, Jim Dear and Darling arrive home and discover what has happened. Jock and Trusty decide not to waste any time in going after the dogcatcher to stop him; using Trusty's nonexistent sense of smell, they try to track down the wagon, and miraculously they do, racing after it with Jim Dear and Darling not far behind in a cab. They succeed in stopping the wagon and saving Tramp, but in the excitement the wagon overturns, crushing poor Trusty.

The next scene, however, shows that Trusty has only suffered a broken leg, as he and Jock come to pay a Christmas visit to Lady, Tramp, and their growing brood of children—three little ladies, and one little tramp. The film ends on the same snowy panorama with which it began.

Though *Lady and the Tramp*'s story may not be much, its varied assets—highlight sequences, the songs, some of the visuals—are strong enough to make the film a most congenial piece of fluff.

The story is told from a dog's-eye view, the humans never really shown in much detail, although they figure prominently in key sequences. Animation buff Mike Barrier has pointed out that there is a conflict, however, between two approaches in the film: part of the time the situations stress the fact that these are dogs, and at other times an attempt is made to give them human characteristics. It is as if the Disney staff considered both angles, saw that both could work, and then didn't have the heart to reject one set of gags in favor of the other, resulting in a combination of both.

Most of the film's best sequences are built around songs, and the film's score is particularly delightful, as written by Peggy Lee and Sonny Burke, and in several cases, sung by Miss Lee, who does the voices for Darling, the Siamese cats, and Peg. When Tramp takes Lady to dinner at the back door of the Italian restaurant, the owner, Tony, and his cook, Joe, do their best to make it a special occasion. (They admire Lady, and the restaurateur tells Tramp: "You take-a Tony's advice and settle down with this-a one, eh?") After serving a meal of spaghetti and meat balls, they serenade the canine couple with a love song, "Bella Notte," accompanying themselves on accordion and violin. During the song Lady and Tramp nibble at the same strand of spaghetti, bringing their lips together in a kiss.

When the song speaks of "stars in her eyes," we see stars in Lady's eyes, and the camera pans up between two tenement buildings toward the moon, partially obscured by laundry strung between the two buildings. Then an off-screen chorus picks up the song for another verse as we see a series of romantic vignettes with Lady and Tramp throughout the evening (admiring the moon from a lover's lane where humans are doing the same thing).

Later, when Lady is thrown into the dog pound, she meets a colorful assortment of dogs, including a cockney bulldog, an aristocratic Russian wolfhound, and the saucy Peg, who fills Lady in on her boyfriend by singing "He's a Tramp."

This sequence also has a curious but very engaging spoof of prison films, with one dog working on a tunnel and another being taken off to the gas chamber. ("Poor Nutzy is taking the long walk," another dog comments sadly.) Though such humor is momentarily jarred amidst the general straightforwardness of the rest of the film, it does add a nice touch to the now jaunty proceedings.

There is also humor inherent in the felines' song, which begins, "We are Siamese if you please/We are Siamese if you don't please . . ." Though their subsequent actions are a bit hard to take, the coyness of the two slithery cats in this song makes the scene a delight.

Another comic highlight is the attempt to convince the beaver of the muzzle's value to him, thanks in large part to Stan Freberg's amusing voice characterization for the animal. When he does bite the muzzle off, and tries to use its teeth to pull a log downhill for him, he gets tangled up and soon finds himself tumbling down the hill in a state of utter disarray. When the log miraculously lands right in place at his dam, however, and he looks up, unharmed, he smiles the smile of a satisfied customer.

There are other, smaller, visual ideas in the film, such as the scene near the beginning where Lady, her first night in the house, insists on sleeping on the bed with Jim Dear and Darling. Jim finally gives in, warning, "But tonight only." The pictures dissolves to show Lady's growth while she continues sleeping, an ingenious way to show considerable passage of time and establish an important point (Jim and Darling's pampering of Lady) with an absolute minimum of effort.

There is an amusing dreamlike sequence where Tramp tells Lady what life will be like for her when the baby arrives and her masters' attention will be drawn away from her, and another nice transitional scene of months passing until the baby's birth (with Lady walking through the transparent pages of a calendar to show passage of time).

The climactic sequences have considerably more atmosphere than the rest of the film, with its pastel colors and meticulous backgrounds. The fight with the rat takes place during a rainfall, with flashes of lightning outside, and especially dramatic cutting to heighten the emotional impact (in addition to which, the rat itself is designed to be especially disgusting).

The subsequent chase through the streets for the dogcatcher's wagon takes place after the rainfall, on muddy streets lit only by the moon and occasional streetlamps casting reflections in the puddles scattered about. It is one of the most visually impressive sequences in the film.

The use of CinemaScope is especially skillful, without being ostentatious, as it was in many live-action films at this time. Ward Kimball wrote about the experience of first using 'Scope in an article for *Films in Review:*

> Our layout men, whose work is analogous to that of set designers, had to re-scheme the staging of all action to suit backgrounds twice as long as those we had been using. In doing so they soon made a discovery: in CinemaScope, *cartoon characters* move, not the backgrounds. Because there is more space, the characters can move about without getting outside the visual angle. They can also move about more in relation to each other. In CinemaScope cartoon characters no longer perform in one spot against a moving background, *but are moved through the scenes.*
>
> Fewer separate scenes and fewer cuts [are] needed, since the action takes place in continuous, unbroken movement across one wide vista, where formerly numerous cuts back and forth had to be employed. Also, panoramic backgrounds are fewer and more figures can be shown simultaneously.

If there is a criticism to be made about the animation in the film, it is that this film represents the height of literalism in Disney's work. *Sleeping Beauty* was more elaborate than *Lady and the Tramp*, but, because it was a fairy tale, offered more opportunity for visual invention.

Though *Lady* does have its share of pictorial ideas, the film as a whole seems to be striving for a goal of realism in its setting, backgrounds, movements, and detail work. From one point of view this is something to marvel at, an achievement Disney was able to carry out better than any other animation studio. From another standpoint, it takes a lot of the fun out of animation. Where is the wonderful visual hyperbole of *Dumbo*, the boundless imagination of *Fantasia*, the surrealism of *The Three Caballeros*, or even the stylistic vision of reality of *Bambi*?

One of *Lady and the Tramp*'s biggest laughs with a small-fry audience comes at the beginning of the dog-pound sequence, where four scruffy mongrels howl out a pitiful version of "Home, Sweet Home." The incongruity of the situation, plus the amusing rendition, make it one of the solid gag points in the film. But there is little of such material in *Lady;* it tries to compensate with a full quota of charm, more likely to appeal to older audiences.

Much of the "charm" was lost on critics, however, who gave the film a surprisingly negative reaction. The *New Yorker* thought the story was handled "with a sentimentality that Albert Payson Terhune might have found excessive," and found the leading characters singularly unappealing. The critic also seemed bent on attacking CinemaScope, which, he said, "gives them [the dogs] the dimensions of hippos." The same quixotic streak ran through Bosley Crowther's review in the *New York Times,* in which he noted that Cinema-Scope made the film's "flaws" more apparent, adding that "the artists' work is below par." (One begins to wonder if these critics saw the same film everybody else did—"dimensions of hippos"? "flaws"?) Meanwhile *Variety,* in a generally favorable review, commented: "Curiously, in making a hero out of the Jaunty Tramp, the writers worked in a fight with a rat that recalls to mind the terror of the bat episode in *Lost Weekend.* This is for kids?"

So once more Disney's accolades were to come not in the form of reviews, but from the public, which made the film a substantial hit. It was accompanied in general release by the first "People and Places" subject in CinemaScope, *Switzerland.*

The film received a major shot in the arm on Disney's own TV show, where Peggy Lee explained how the score came about, and demonstrated some of the songs from the movie with Sonny Burke and the Mello Men. Miss Lee expressed her warm memories of the film by saying: "Walt Disney was such a wonderful man to work with—so enthusiastic and full of ideas, just brimming."*

In its theatrical reissues, *Lady and the Tramp* has continued to please audiences, and though it has been the subject of some debate among animation buffs, there is no question of its utter likability—and considerable charm. When one is caught up in the film, these qualities make it difficult to nit-pick.

Lady and the Tramp cost an estimated $4 million and took over three years to produce. Disney wanted to go one step further for his next animated endeavor, and he envisioned *Sleeping Beauty* as the screen's ultimate cartoon feature.

*In 1988 Lee filed suit against Disney for releasing the film on home video, which she claimed was not covered in her contract; the court awarded her $3.83 million.

THE AFRICAN LION

RELEASED BY BUENA VISTA ON SEPTEMBER 14, 1955. Technicolor (from 16mm). Associate producer: Ben Sharpsteen. Director: James Algar. Photography: Alfred G. Milotte, Elma Milotte. Writers: James Algar, Winston Hibler, Ted Sears, Jack Moffitt. Narrator: Winston Hibler. Music: Paul J. Smith. Orchestrations: Joseph Dubin. Production manager: Erwin Verity. Special processes: Ub Iwerks. Film editor: Norman Palmer, A.C.E. Animation effects: Joshua Meador, Art Riley. Sound director: Robert O. Cook. Music editor: Evelyn Kennedy. Running time: 75 minutes.

The African Lion is a stunning film. Every time it produces an obvious highlight sequence, one settles back to relax, but before long there is another equally exciting piece of film to top the one before it.

Alfred and Elma Milotte, who had filmed the first True-Life short subject, *Seal Island,* and launched the entire series, spent three years in Africa and exposed 100,000 feet of film for this feature, a far cry geographically from their initial venture.

The time was well spent, for *African Lion* abounds with thrilling and beautiful scenes. What is more, it conforms to the True-Life formula without resorting to the much criticized gimmickry of earlier True-Life features. This not only doesn't diminish the interest in its subject matter, but it actually enables the audience to become *more* involved. This is not to say that there isn't room for lighter moments in these documentaries; there is some very amusing footage of playful baboons in *African Lion,* and narration that brings the animals' lives and characteristics into focus for a young audience, explaining, for instance, that a giraffe is "three times as tall as a tall man" or observing that "the king of beasts is a helpless male compared to his mate."

A foreword declares that "the story is nature's own, the actions of her creatures, completely spontaneous."

The film opens with the paintbrush filling in a picture of the African continent, then filling in the various sections as narrator Winston Hibler points out the various regions and their characteristics. The lion's life-style is considered in the cyclical format used throughout these films; with each season we not only examine the lion, but his compatriots in the jungle, and the physical characteristics of the region.

The film's high points stand out in one's memory: an antelope leaping through the air in a mad chase . . . a beautiful shot of a pride of lions sleeping under a picturesque tree whose branches bend over them . . . a cheetah racing after a gazelle at eighty

The African lioness with her cubs. © *Walt Disney Pro-ductions*

Disney toasts Elma and Alfred Milotte as they embark on their journey to Africa. (Note the beverage used—Donald Duck orange juice.) *Courtesy British Film Institute*

miles per hour before making his kill (the camera following laterally, catching the excitement of the chase perfectly) . . . a lioness stalking her prey, and trying to ward off the scavengers (a jackal, a vulture, and a hyena) who want to distract her long enough to get at the meat and tear it apart . . . elephants digging impromptu wells during the dry season . . . a rhino inexorably stuck in the mud, struggling to get out (which he can't do) . . . terrible dust storms . . . fantastic shots of a locust invasion, showing how their wings filter sunlight to produce incredible visual effects.

The lion family is shown under various conditions, with the female providing for the male and her cubs, killing other animals only to supply food for the family.

The film ends with the coming of tropical rains that begin the new yearly life cycle.

The Milottes considered this their favorite film, and expressed unending gratitude to Walt Disney for enabling them to pursue such a lengthy project without economic pressure or interference.

Appropriately, *The African Lion* received accolades. Bosley Crowther called it "the purest of the Disney nature films," and in retrospect, Pauline Kael, while condemning the series as a whole, singled out *African Lion* as a choice item for children's viewing.

Ironically, though the earlier features, which had earned the series wide disfavor, won two Academy Awards, this one was bypassed in favor of *Helen Keller in Her Story,* an independent production.

An interesting sidenote to the film is an incident that occurred during filming in Africa. (The Milottes traveled through Kenya, Uganda, Tanganyika, South Africa, and Zululand to collect their footage.) The Milottes are documentarians in the truest sense of the word, and they attempted to remain passive observers as much as possible in filming their wildlife studies. But after shooting the sequence of a rhinoceros stuck in a deep mudhole, they decided that it was more important to be compassionate human beings than merely zoological filmmakers, and, with considerable effort, dislodged the animal from the mud. The rhino showed its appreciation by charging after Alfred Milotte, who scrambled into his trailer, which soon shook with a resounding thud from the crash of the animal's horn against the side. So much for humanity.

THE LITTLEST OUTLAW

RELEASED BY BUENA VISTA ON DECEMBER 22, 1955. Technicolor. Producer: Larry Lansburgh. Director: Roberto Gavaldon. Screenplay: Bill Walsh. Original story: Larry Lansburgh. Photography: Alex Phillips. Second unit camera: J. Carlos Carbajal. Set decorations: Rafael Suarez. Music: William Lava. Orchestrations: Charles Maxwell. Film editor: Carlos Savage. Production manager: Luis Sanchez Tello. Assistant director: Jesus Marin. Sound: Manuel Topete. Filmed with the facilities of Churubusco Studio. Running time: 75 minutes.

Cast: Pedro Armendariz (General Torres), Joseph Calleia (padre), Rodolfo Acosta (Chato), Andres Velásquez (Pablito), Pepe Ortiz, matador (himself), Laila Maley (Celita), Gilberto Gonzales (tiger), José Torvay (vulture), Ferrusquilla (Señor García), Enriqueta Zazueta (Señora Garcia), Señor Lee (gypsy), Carlos Ortigoza (doctor), Margarito Luna (Silvestre), Ricardo Gonzales (Marcos), Maria Eugenia (bride), Pedrito Vargas (groom).

The 1950s showed people that Walt Disney was not going to be tied down to animated features exclusively, as he ventured into the realm of live-action films, and to encourage diversity he allowed various members of his staff to work out independent production ideas. Larry Lansburgh, who had been with the studio since the mid-1940s, had been working on live-action short subjects and featurettes like *Stormy* during recent years—unpretentious animal stories, usually shot on real locations with nonactors and a decidedly nonstudio look.

When he submitted the story of *The Littlest Outlaw,* it was developed into a feature-length script by Bill Walsh, and Lansburgh was given the reins as producer to shoot the film in Mexico, using the same techniques he had put to work in his short subjects with a few key differences. First, he was able to hire some first-rate actors, namely Pedro Armendariz, Rodolfo Acosta, and Joseph Calleia (the only non-Mexican in the cast), and secondly, he was required to shoot the film twice, once in English and once in Spanish, for simultaneous release south of the border.

For his hero Lansburgh found a completely winning yet unaffected youngster named Andres Velásquez.

The story is that of a ten-year-old boy whose cruel stepfather is a Mexican general's horse trainer. The trainer "coaches" a prize horse to jump for the grand race by torturing him—putting spindles atop one of the jumps, so if he doesn't clear it, he will feel the pain. From that time on the horse becomes deathly afraid of jumps, and at the race he humiliates the general by refusing to try. The general's daughter doesn't understand, and takes the horse out riding herself; she forces him to make a jump, and the frightened animal falters badly, throwing the girl and injuring her seriously. The general angrily orders his trainer to shoot the horse.

Little Pablito cannot bear to see this happen, so he runs away with the horse. He becomes a fugitive, traveling throughout Mexico, encountering two bandits, a railroad worker who tries to turn him in, and, finally, a friendly priest who shelters the boy and his horse, and tries to convince him to turn himself in. The boy refuses, and in the ensuing events the horse runs away, is found by a gypsy caravan, and then sold for use in the bullfight arena as a lure.

The boy and the priest go to the gala bullfight, and Pablito, recognizing his horse about to be gored by the bull, runs into the ring, hops onto the horse and rides him out of the arena, making a fantastic leap over the fence as he does so. Some time later, the boy and the horse show up at the general's home. Pablito turns himself in, very humbly, but the general, who has come to his senses, presents the horse to his daughter, who had always wanted it. The finale shows Pablito and the girl riding together around the general's ranch, happy and carefree once more.

The secret of this charming film is in the way it was shot. The story is so slight that it would have been pointless unless it had seemed *real*. By filming it entirely on location, using interior and exterior sites alike, and getting natural, winning performances from the cast, producer Lansburgh and director Roberto Gavaldon succeeded in their goal.

The characterizations are good because they do not stretch credibility. The general is not an evil man; his temper simply gets the best of him at a weak moment, when he orders the horse destroyed. The stepfather *is* played as a complete villain, yet even this is nicely handled, especially in the scene where he comes into Joseph Calleia's church looking for the boy. The padre welcomes him and shows him around to prove there is no one hiding there. The horse trainer is very ill at ease, however, put off by the beauty and ornamentation of the church (nicely felt through clever cutting of shots), and the sly priest saying: "It has been some time since you were inside a church, eh?"

The padre is, of course, one of the most enjoyable characters in the film, especially as played by veteran Calleia, more noted for his gangster portrayals in Hollywood films. Even this kindly priest is painted as a three-dimensional character. After hiding the boy *and* his horse inside the church, he prays, and asks God: "Did I do wrong?" Contemplating the thought for a moment, he concludes: "I don't think so."

Little Pablito (Andres Velásquez) and his adopted horse. © *Walt Disney Productions*

Pablito begs the Padre (Joseph Calleia) to let him stay in the church. © *Walt Disney Productions*

Calleia even gets to sing a little ditty about his ramshackle car called "Doroteo," which he uses to pass the time as he drives Pablito to the bullfight.

The sequences in the bullring are quite exciting and reveal more of what actually happens at a bullfight than most Hollywood features—including the sight of a matador being gored by the bull! (More Disney pablum?)

The dialogue is a bit more Americanized in syntax and expression than one might like, for authenticity's sake, but the overall effect is tremendous, the film literally overflowing with atmosphere, as the situations take the boy from an ancient church to a horse-breeding ranch to a street carnival. The ranch was the real life Xajay ranch, while most of the rest of the film was shot in and around San Miguel Allende.

Variety said of the young Velásquez that his performance "has seldom been equaled by a child thespian in point of appeal. His scenes never descend to maudlin sentimentality as he limns his narrative . . ."

Other critics were not so kind, finding the film routine at best. One gets the idea that they still expected a blockbuster from Disney every time around, and couldn't readjust to his release of a programmer such as this (which was distributed in tandem with *Johnny Appleseed*). But Disney was pleased, and Larry Lansburgh has continued to make realistic and entertaining featurettes for the company over the years.

THE GREAT LOCOMOTIVE CHASE

RELEASED BY BUENA VISTA ON JUNE 8, 1956. TECHnicolor, CinemaScope. Producer, screenplay: Lawrence E. Watkin. Director: Francis D. Lyon. Photography: Charles Boyle, A.S.C. Editor: Ellsworth Hoagland, A.C.E. Art director: Carroll Clark. Set decorations: Emile Kuri, Pat Delaney. Costumes: Chuck Keehne, Joseph Dimmitt. Music: Paul J. Smith. Orchestrations: Franklyn Marks. Unit manager: Russ Haverick. Assistant director: Robert Shannon. Matte artist: Peter Ellenshaw. First assistant: Albert Whitlock. Special processes: Ub Iwerks, A.S.C. Technical adviser: Wilbur G. Kurtz. Production research: Harper Goff. Makeup, hairstyling: David Newell, Louis Haszillo. Sound supervision: Robert O. Cook. Sound recording: Virgil Smith. Running time: 85 minutes.

Song: "Sons of Old Aunt Dinah" by Stan Jones and Lawrence E. Watkin.

Cast: Fess Parker (James J. Andrews), Jeffrey Hunter (William A. Fuller), Jeff York (William Campbell), John Lupton (William Pittenger), Eddie Firestone (Robert Buffum), Kenneth Tobey (Anthony Murphy), Don Megowan (Marion A. Ross), Claude Jarman, Jr. (Jacob Parrott), Harry Carey, Jr. (William Bensinger), Lennie Geer (J. A. Wilson), George Robotham (William Knight), Stan Jones (Wilson Brown), Marc Hamilton (John Wollam), John Wiley (John M. Scott), Slim Pickens (Pete Bracken), Morgan Woodward (Alex), W. S. Bearden (a switchman), Harvey Hester (Jess McIntyre), Douglas Bleckley (Henry Haney).

The story of Andrews's Raiders and their Civil War adventures had already been filmed by Buster Keaton as a background for his comedy in *The General* (1927). But there was still room for a more serious, straightforward account of this fascinating and true story, and Disney decided to film it with his new star Fess Parker as James J. Andrews.

Andrews is a Union spy who asks for volunteers from various regiments to accompany him on a dangerous and intricate mission. They must penetrate the South, pretending to be Kentuckians on their way to join the Confederate army, board a passenger train, and at the first opportunity abscond with it!

They actually manage to carry this off, but they do not reckon with the persistence of a young conductor on the train, William A. Fuller (Jeffrey Hunter), who immediately takes after them in hot pursuit of "his" train. He runs, uses a handcar, enlists help, and eventually procures a train himself in order to catch up with Andrews, who has his runaway attempt timed precisely in order to get through towns and stations without arousing suspicion.

Fuller follows close behind, however, at one point running his train backwards in order to follow Andrews's course. The raiders let one car loose to run back and smash their pursuers, but they see it in time, back up, and let the car ease into their train. Andrews's men leave another car in the middle of a wooden bridge and set it on fire, but even this is foiled by the wily Fuller. "Won't anything stop that train?" Andrews says angrily. And nothing does.

Finally, Andrews's men are forced to abandon the train and run for cover. They split up, but one by one they are captured and thrown in jail together at a Confederate stockade. Rather than languish in prison, they plan an escape. Getting out of the cell is easy, but when they hit the prison yard, they expose themselves to enemy fire; Andrews stays behind to divert attention while the others scale the wall, and is taken into custody again, tried, and sentenced to death.

The day before his execution he calls for Fuller to tell him that he was only doing his job for a cause he believed in—that some day there will be an end to hostilities between the North and South, but he won't live to see it. He asks if they can shake hands now, and Fuller agrees.

The story, having been told in flashback, returns to a ceremony where the surviving members of Andrews's Raiders are decorated, and James J. Andrews himself is awarded a posthumous medal for bravery.

The Great Locomotive Chase is a good, solid, well-made film. Its only real flaw is that after the lengthy and arresting chase scenes on the train, the balance of the story seems anticlimactic. One character, a member of the Raiders portrayed by Jeff York, does not ring true; a hothead who doesn't understand the need for the southern guise during the opening phase of the operation or the meticulousness of the rest of the scheme, he redeems himself at the end by staying in the prison yard with Andrews to fight it out with their captors. But it is difficult to understand why such a man would have been accepted for the mission in the first place.

Otherwise, the film is a winner all the way. The decision to make it in CinemaScope offered possibilities for exciting shots during the chase scene, and lovely expanses of scenery, that otherwise would have been impossible—or certainly less effective. Director Francis D. ("Pete") Lyon says: "I found it much more facile in staging and more economical by reducing setups than the normal lens, especially in a primarily outdoor subject. It worked particularly well in filming *The Great Locomotive Chase*." The elaborate storyboards prepared for this film were drawn in CinemaScope scale to enable the staff to envision precisely how each shot would look on the screen. Two of the most striking shots in the film are enhanced by the anamorphic lens: Jeffrey Hunter sitting on the tail (now the head) of a coal car, writing a message for a young telegraph messenger to send ahead, the camera slightly overhead as the train rumbles along. The wide screen is also impressive when a train passes along the entire length of the picture (as in a night scene near the end of the film).

Lyon recalls: "We found a railroad that ran through Clayton, in northern Georgia, that paralleled the actual road (now modernized) about fifty miles west. It worked very well for our purposes, and of course was beautiful country." Disney went to great lengths to acquire special railroad cars to use in the film, and the film included an acknowledgment to

James J. Andrews (Fess Parker) introduces himself to William A. Fuller (Jeffrey Hunter); little does Fuller realize what Andrews is up to.   © *Walt Disney Productions*

Fuller runs his train backward in order to chase after Andrews' Raiders; his aide-de-camp is played by Kenneth Tobey.   © *Walt Disney Productions*

"the generous cooperation of the Baltimore and Ohio Railroad Museum."

Of his relationship with Disney, Lyon says:

When we were preparing the picture Walt was very attentive to the Park, as he called the then-under-construction Disneyland, so we didn't see much of him. I know, however, that he often came in on weekends when few were around in the studio to review the many subjects in work. He could do this efficiently by scanning the storyboards posted about the offices. When one didn't hear from Walt one could assume that he approved progress to date. I don't believe any of his employees successfully concealed their efforts from him, regardless of his many time-consuming interests.

At the start of principal photography on location in Georgia, Walt spent a few days there watching us get started. He seemed to enjoy being away from his problems in Hollywood for a bit and especially the train activities. He was a train enthusiast, which is evidenced by the fact that he once had a miniature narrow-gauge in his huge garden at home.

At the studio, when we returned home for interior shooting, Walt came on the set a few times but said little about my work. When I found time to speak to him he was always pleasant and liked to kid a lot. When asked about the Park he beamed and jumped at the chance to talk about the new ideas he was going to develop there. In other words, he did not interfere in any way during the shooting. His attitude created a relaxed confidence in my approach to the job at hand. He found time to sit in on a few editing sessions and was most helpful and considerate of one's suggestions to that end.

Actual supervision of the project was left to screenwriter Lawrence Watkin, whom Disney also appointed to the position of producer for the first time with this film. Most directors found the casual, team-effort approach to live-action films a very congenial way of working, and many did their best work on Disney products.

The Great Locomotive Chase was well received by both critics and the public. Bosley Crowther called it "great entertainment for youngsters and for anybody who ever had a yen for trains."

DAVY CROCKETT AND THE RIVER PIRATES

RELEASED BY BUENA VISTA ON JULY 18, 1956. TECHnicolor. Producer: Bill Walsh. Director: Norman Foster. Screenplay: Tom Blackburn, Norman Foster. Photography: Bert Glennon. Editor: Stanley Johnson, A.C.E. Art director: Feild Grey. Set decorations: Emile Kuri, Bertram Granger. Costumes: Carl Walker. Music: George Bruns. Orchestrations: Edward H. Plumb. Unit manager: John Grubbs. Assistant director: Ivan Volkman. Matte artist: Peter Ellenshaw. Special processes: Ub Iwerks. Makeup: David Newell, Phil Sheer. Sound recording: Robert O. Cook. Running time: 81 minutes.

Songs: "Ballad of Davy Crockett," "King of the River," "Yaller, Yaller Gold" by George Bruns and Tom Blackburn.

Cast: Fess Parker (Davy Crockett), Buddy Ebsen (George Russel), Jeff York (Mike Fink), Kenneth Tobey (Jocko), Clem Bevans (Cap'n Cobb), Irvin Ashkenazy (Moose), Mort Mills (Sam Mason), Paul Newlan (Big Harpe), Frank Richards (Little Harpe), Walter Catlett (Colonel Plug), Douglass Dumbrille (saloon owner).

It goes without saying that Disney couldn't let his most popular hero go up in smoke just because he died at the Alamo. So the next season of the Disney TV show brought the coonskin-capped legend back to life under the title "The Legends of Davy Crockett." Two key episodes were strung together to make another feature film that again was released just in time for summer vacation.

The background of the film is nicely established by an off-screen chorus with new lyrics to the Davy Crockett theme, telling about the King of the River, Mike Fink. This story takes place along the Ohio River in 1810, where Davy and Georgie meet this self-styled river ruler. "What a small world," says Fink to Davy. "You're about a foot shorter than you ought to be." "He's still growing," Georgie explains.

Mike Fink (Jeff York) laughs at the prospect of Davy ever beating him to New Orleans. Kenneth Tobey and Irvin Ashkenazy join in the jeering. © *Walt Disney Productions*

Just one of many interruptions along the way to New Orleans. © *Walt Disney Productions*

Their meeting turns into a challenge when Mike learns that Davy is hiring an old river salt to take him and Georgie down to New Orleans with their furs instead of paying Mike's outrageous fees. That night, while he's suppose to be out signing up a crew, Georgie falls prey to Mike, who gets him roaring drunk, at which point he accepts Mike's challenge of a race to New Orleans, the prize being the shipment of furs. Davy refuses to let Georgie go back on his word, so the next day the race is on.

Mike and his men cheat like crazy, while Davy and his men are continually beset by problems; but in the end Davy beats Fink to New Orleans. Yet he and Georgie refuse to accept any bounty from him; after all, they explain, Mike is the only King of the River—they're just frontiersmen, new to this game. Mike is really touched by this, and strikes up a lasting friendship with Davy, but he insists on making good one part of the bet, by resignedly eating his hat.

The second segment begins with Davy and Georgie returning upriver when they are suddenly captured by Indians. Davy, who is known to the Indian chief, learns that war is imminent because of Indian-white battles along the river. Davy tells him that they must have peace at all costs, and also tells the chief that he believes these Indian attacks are phony. He swears that if they will let him and Georgie go free, they will get to the bottom of things.

They soon discover that a conniving white man is having his men dress as Indians and raid various ships sailing downstream. They enlist Mike Fink's help to set up a decoy, spreading the word along the river ports that they are carrying a cargo of gold down to New Orleans. The bandits' stoolie, a banjo-playing old-timer named Colonel Plug, asks for a lift, and once on board sends the signal ashore by singing "Yaller, Yaller Gold."

When the "Indians" attack, however, Davy and Mike are ready for them and succeed in licking them soundly. Then they go ashore to track down the brains of the outfit. They follow him to his cave hideout, where he and Davy engage in a fierce battle, climaxing in the fellow dynamiting his own storehouse. With peace restored anew, Davy and Georgie thank Mike Fink for his help and bid him good-bye as he returns to the river and they return to the frontier.

While the division between the two segments is abundantly clear, they tie together fairly well to make a compact, enjoyable feature. Each story has a definite sense of direction, with no wasted time in developing the problem and solution.

The first segment is essentially a comedy, centered around Jeff York's broad characterization of Mike Fink. The fights between the two crews are basically slapstick in nature, with a lot of falling into the water, unexpected grapplings, sliding on molasses on the deck, ducking so someone else gets hit, etc. At the other extreme, the finale of the second segment, in the cave, is pretty potent stuff, Davy and his adversary using torches, chains, and other such weapons to fight each other.

Davy's righteousness is played up in the first segment as well, beginning when he refuses to wriggle out of the race, because Georgie gave his word. Later, Mike secretly loosens Davy's rudder so it will fall off at an inopportune moment. Georgie suggests that it would be easy to swap rudders that night. "Nope," says Davy, "we gotta win this race fair and square." But they do need time to repair their rudder, so Davy and Georgie go to the local saloon where they overawe Mike with an exaggerated demonstration of Davy's prowess at shooting.

The next day Davy's boat is holding a comfortable lead, when they spot a castaway flagging them down from a nearby island. Davy insists on stopping to help him, and they offer to take him aboard. The man accepts gratefully, but adds that he must bring his livestock along! Georgie tells Davy that this will surely lose them the race, and Davy replies, "Maybe the good Lord didn't mean for us to win." But Davy is repaid for his good deed. When they drop off the passenger, he clues them in to a secret shortcut, which they take, and which brings them out into the main channel right alongside Mike Fink.

Thus, the theme of doing good is put across quite nicely, making Davy Crockett even more of an upstanding individual than he was in the original outings.

This film also has a richer look than its predecessor in many ways. A rapids sequence features some excellent process work that makes it utterly believable, and the final trek into New Orleans is shown via a beautiful and elaborate glass shot. The enthusiastic cast is peppered with veteran performers who contribute some nice moments to the action: Clem Bevans as the old-timer who captains Davy's boat, Walter Catlett as the garrulous, banjo-playing stool pigeon, and (unbilled) Douglass Dumbrille as the saloon proprietor.

As for the leads, they are their usual ingratiating selves, so much so that Disney, while discontinuing the Crockett series (which died out as most fads do within a year), retained both Fess Parker and Jeff York for a number of subsequent feature films, trading on their familiarity and acceptance in creating "new" characterizations that weren't really so new at all.

SECRETS OF LIFE

RELEASED BY BUENA VISTA ON NOVEMBER 6, 1956. Technicolor (from 16mm original). Producer: Ben Sharpsteen. Director, screenplay: James Algar. Photography: Stuart V. Jewell, Robert H. Crandall, Murl Deusing, George and Nettie MacGinitie, Tilden W. Roberts, William A. Anderson, Claude Jendrusch, Arthur Carter, Fran William Hall, Jack C. Couffer, Roman Vishniac, Donald L. Sykes. Time-Lapse photography: John Nash Ott, Jr., Stuart V. Jewell, William M. Harlow, Rex R. Elliott, Vincent J. Schaefer. Narrator: Winston Hibler. Music: Paul J. Smith. Orchestrations: Franklyn Marks, Edward H. Plumb. Consulting biologists: Rutherford Platt, Tilden W. Roberts. Production manager: Erwin L. Verity. Special processes: Ub Iwerks, A.S.C. Animation effects: Joshua Meador, Art Riley. Film editor: Anthony Gerard. Sound: Robert O. Cook. Music editor: Evelyn Kennedy. Running time: 75 minutes.

Secrets of Life details the existence of honeybees. © *Walt Disney Productions*

Secrets of Life is the most diverse of all the True-Life feature films; it covers plant life, insect life, sea creatures, and even volcanoes, all under the general umbrella of Nature's miracles in shaping this earth.

Because such a wide range of topics is covered, the animated paintbrush does double duty in this film, creating transitions between subjects. The film opens on a red screen; this is shaped into a red dot, which evolves into the earth. The paintbrush fills in the various regions of the globe as the narrator tells of the earth's evolution, and the effect of such things as the Ice Age on the earth's history.

Then we first discover plant life: how various seeds actually "walk" themselves to proper positions to grow, how buds burst open to develop and grow, etc. Then begins a fantastic sequence that might be called a symphony of plant life—a series of time-lapse images of things growing, set to a rousing bolero. The eye is treated to amazing sights: a cherry growing from a bud, to a tiny yellow ball, turning red and ripening, tomatoes and strawberries reddening and swelling, flowers, plants bursting into full blossom.

From here it is a natural transition to a study of bees, first seen collecting pollen from flowers, and then in their colonies, where a strange and regimented existence is seen. The Queen lays her eggs, while the other bees produce honey and fashion the elaborate honeycomb. The new Queen is chosen from several eggs; the

The film also goes underwater for a look at an unusual fish like this. ©*Walt Disney Productions*

first one to hatch becomes the Queen, who must then kill her rivals as they hatch from the other eggs. A forest fire threatens to destroy the hive; the bees beat their wings frantically to keep the area cool, but when this fails, they desperately try to suck up as much honey as possible to store for the future.

Ants lead a totally different life. Honey-husk ants have such a voracious appetite for honey, sugar, and sweets that their abdomens grow to enormous proportions, until they become the community depository for such goods, hanging from the ceiling underground.

Red and black ants are constantly waging war, trying to eat each other's larvae; when one group catches the other in the act, they go into combat, trying to cut off each other's limbs.

From here we look at microscopic views of protozoa, the smallest pieces of living matter. This segues into an examination of undersea life. We see fish that eat other fish, including those who affect ingenious camouflages, and unique beings like the archer fish, which shoots down insects from above water level with a built-in water gun. Grunion lay their eggs ashore during low tide; the timing must be perfect so that the sea does not wash them away, but will still be able to carry the adults back when the process is over and later activate the eggs.

The crashing of waves dissolves into the crashing of lava in the final segment on volcanoes and volcanic action. The narrator explains that while this might seem mindlessly destructive, even this lava serves a purpose, that of remaking the earth's crust, perpetuating the earth itself, in a way. This, he says, is nature's "ultimate secret of life," as the film ends on beautiful color shots of lava intercut together.

Secrets of Life seems to ramble at times, not having any fixed focus, but what it does present is truly astounding.

Though Paul Smith's scores for Disney films and the other True-Life features (where, one must re-member, there must be music for a solid seventy-five minutes without a break) are always impressive, the bolero accompanying the time-lapse sequence in this film is surely one of the highlights of his career. The effect is that of adding exciting, rousing music to already breathtaking photography, a high point of the entire True-Life series.

The film is full of amazing sights, so diverse that more photographers than ever were involved in gathering material. As always, it is not only the subject matter, but the inventive presentation, that makes the effect so unusual. The sequence of the archer fish, for instance, is shot with the lens half submerged so that we see the fish aiming his jet underwater, shooting above the surface and hitting an insect on the nose (figuratively speaking) obviously the ideal way to get across this fish's unique prowess to an audience. The segment of bees begins with a first-person camera shot of a bee flying over a field of flowers toward one particular daisy.

Each of the eighteen photographers working on the film contributed his own specialty. Robert H. Crandall shot the ant footage (similar to that which had inspired Disney to make *The Living Desert* several years back), some of it in a sixteen-foot-deep excavation. Stuart V. Jewell, another True-Life veteran, worked on both the time-lapse sequence and the bee segment. Other contributors ranged from Murl Deusing, curator of the Milwaukee Museum (who filmed the stickleback fish), to Dr. William M. Harlow, an official with the New York State Division of Forestry.

James Algar tied up the package with his customarily well-organized script as read by Winston Hibler, with a more generous than usual helping of animation effects by Joshua Meador and Art Riley, the frosting on the cake that always set Disney's documentaries apart from those of his rivals.

This, the fourth True-Life feature, was again well received, with welcome sighs of relief from those who applauded the films' more serious approach of late.

WESTWARD HO THE WAGONS!

RELEASED BY BUENA VISTA ON DECEMBER 20, 1956. Technicolor, CinemaScope. Producer: Bill Walsh. Director: William Beaudine. Screenplay: Tom Blackburn, based on a novel by Mary Jane Carr. Photography: Charles Boyle, A.S.C. Editor: Cotton Warburton, A.C.E. Art director: Marvin Aubrey Davis. Set decorations: Emile Kuri, Bertram Granger. Costumes: Chuck Keehne, Gertrude Casey. Music: George Bruns. Orchestrations: Edwin H. Plumb. Sec-ond unit director: Yakima Canutt. Assistant director: William Beaudine, Jr. Matte artist: Peter Ellenshaw. First assistant: Albert Whitlock. Special processes: Ub Iwerks, A.S.C. Unit manager: Ben Chapman. Makeup: David Newell. Hairstyling: Lois Murray. Sound supervision: Robert O. Cook. Sound recording: Dean Thomas. Running time: 90 minutes.

Songs: "John Colter," "Westward Ho the Wagons!"

by George Bruns and Tom Blackburn. "Pioneer's Prayer" by Paul J. Smith and Gil George. "Wringle Wrangle" by Stan Jones. "I'm Lonely My Darlin'" by George Bruns and Fess Parker.

Cast: Fess Parker (John "Doc" Grayson), Kathleen Crowley (Laura Thompson), Jeff York (Hank Breckinridge), David Stollery (Dan Thompson), Sebastian Cabot (Bissonette), George Reeves (James Stephen), Doreen Tracey (Bobo Stephen), Barbara Woodell (Mrs. Stephen), John War Eagle (Wolf's brother), Cubby O'Brien (Jerry Stephen), Tommy Cole (Jim Stephen), Leslie Bradley (Spencer Armitage), Morgan Woodward ("Obie" Foster), Iron Eyes Cody (Many Stars), Anthony Numkena (Little Thunder), Karen Pendleton (Myra Thompson), Jane Liddell (Ruth Benjamin), Jon Locke (Ed Benjamin).

Westward Ho the Wagons! is a very good-looking film, and in the long run this becomes its greatest asset as it ambles through ninety minutes (rather long for a Disney film) of halfhearted action. There is no plot to the film, just a series of interrelated episodes broken up by frontier-type songs, and that gorgeous scenery, beautifully filmed in color and Cinema-Scope.

Basically, the film details a series of incidents that occur to a wagon train of settlers moving west; their head scout is level-headed, amiable "Doc" Grayson (Fess Parker), who between crises has his eye on pretty Laura Thompson (Kathleen Crowley), who is traveling west with her younger brother and sister.

During one stopover, some of the children wander off and attract the attention of a band of Indians. To protect the others, the eldest boy (David Stollery) allows himself to be captured; that night he escapes from the Indian camp, precipitating an attack the next morning. The settlers move up onto a hill, hoping to ward off the redskins, but nothing seems to work until Doc contrives a scheme to set all their horses loose against the Indians. It means a great sacrifice, but it seems the only hope for saving their lives—and it works.

Later, while camped outside a fort, the settlers are visited by local "peaceful" Indians. The chief believes that a young blonde child (Karen Pendleton) is a goddess of some sort, a good-luck charm, as it were, and he offers various goods in trade for her. When the girl's father, who also happens to be the wagon leader (George Reeves) refuses, the chief is upset, and the settlers worry about the effect of this rebuff.

The next day an Indian boy injures himself as he is practicing riding tricks. The tribe's medicine man does all he can for the boy, but his condition does not improve. "Doc," who hasn't actually practiced medicine but has devoted himself to its study, decides to offer his services, and after some tense moments saves the youngster's life, sharing credit with the medicine man for diplomatic purposes. Harmony is restored between the Indians and the settlers, and the wagon

Two scouts (Morgan Woodward, Fess Parker) from the wagon train try to make peace with Chief Many Stars (Iron Eyes Cody). © *Walt Disney Productions*

Doreen Tracey, Cubby O'Brien, and Tommy Cole, all loyal Mouseketeers, play children in the wagon train party. © *Walt Disney Productions*

train moves on once more.

None of these incidents is particularly arresting, and those that seem to have some potential aren't carried out especially well. The Indian attack, a major portion of the film, has some good intricate close-up action, thanks to veteran second-unit director Yakima Canutt, but the overall sequence falls flat. Part of this may be due to the fact that there are no long shots of the entire battle to give the viewer some sense of perspective; by fragmenting the incidents there is no opportunity to appreciate exactly what is going on.

One of the film's main attractions at the time of its release was the inclusion of several Mouseketeers from the "Mickey Mouse Club" TV show in the cast: Doreen Tracey, Cubby O'Brien, Tommy Cole, and Karen Pendleton, as well as David Stollery, who starred in the "Spin and Marty" segments of the program. Their minor but nicely showcased roles in the film proved anew that they were genuinely appealing, personable kids.

There was also an attempt to duplicate the success of the "Davy Crockett" theme by promoting the film's five songs, particularly "Wringle Wrangle," which enjoyed some measure of success. Another echo of Davy Crockett was the presence of Jeff York, providing comic relief as Fess Parker's sidekick. (The film, incidentally, was scripted by Tom Blackburn, who also wrote the Crockett series for Disney.)

But viewing the film today, through all its lackluster story points, the major asset remains the scenery. William Beaudine, Jr., who worked on the film as assistant director, recalls:

The panoramic shots were all done on the Janss property called Conejo Ranch at Thousand Oaks, California. A good deal of the property now has been converted into housing units, but at the time we shot, it looked like the rolling hills of Wyoming, very virgin territory. Because of that, one of our primary problems was access to the loca-

tion. The picture was shot in the winter months, and because of the adobe dirt roads, any rain would make it impossible for our heavy equipment to get in or out. We had planned, in the event of bad weather, to do a lot of the wagon train camp scenes on the stage at Disney studios, but we were in luck, because that January was the driest California ever experienced, and we were able to do most of it on location. The wagons traveling up the notch were also shot there, but for long shots we used a painting or matte shot, and these were beautifully done by Peter Ellenshaw.

It is difficult to understand how Disney at this point in his career could pursue a film without a strong story line, yet this is *Westward Ho*'s one major fault. The scenario repeatedly milks an incident, builds it to an exciting climax, and then concludes, going on to an entirely new subplot that repeats the cycle. Thus, instead of a denouement at the end of the film, it merely stops, having resolved the latest of these episodes, cueing a long shot of the wagon train rolling into the sunset.

The grandeur of the film, the presence of Fess Parker, and the casting of the Mouseketeers were enough to keep most young audiences happy with the film. But *Westward Ho the Wagons!*, in the general scheme of things, is one of Disney's more forgettable-live-action films.

JOHNNY TREMAIN

RELEASED BY BUENA VISTA ON JUNE 19, 1957. TECHnicolor. Director: Robert Stevenson. Screenplay: Tom Blackburn, based on the novel by Esther Forbes. Photography: Charles P. Boyle. Editor: Stanley Johnson. Art director: Carroll Clark. Set decorations: Emile Kuri, Fred MacLean. Costumes: Chuck Keehne, Gertrude Casey. Music: George Bruns. Orchestrations: Franklyn Marks, Edward H. Plumb. Assistant director: William Beaudine, Jr. Production design: Peter Ellenshaw. Special processes: Ub Iwerks. Technical adviser: D. R. O. Hatswell. Makeup: David Newell. Hairstyling: Lois Murray. Sound supervision: Robert O. Cook. Sound recording: Frank McWhorter. Running time: 80 minutes.

Songs: "Johnny Tremain," "The Liberty Tree" by George Bruns, Tom Blackburn.

Cast: Hal Stalmaster (Johnny Tremain), Luana Pat-

ten (Cilla Lapham), Jeff York (James Otis), Sebastian Cabot (Jonathan Lyte), Dick Beymer (Rab Silsbee), Walter Sande (Paul Revere), Rusty Lane (Samuel Adams), Whit Bissell (Josiah Quincy), Will Wright (Ephraim Lapham), Virginia Christine (Mrs. Lapham), Walter Coy (Dr. Joseph Warren), Geoffrey Toone (Major Pitcairn), Ralph Clanton (General Gage), Gavin Gordon (Colonel Smith), Lumsden Hare (Admiral Montagu), Anthony Ghazlo, Jr. (Jehu), Charles Smith (horse tender).

Johnny Tremain is a first-rate adaptation of Esther Forbes's novel about a young boy who gets caught up in the revolutionary war. It takes some dramatic liberty with facts, but, what is more important, it makes real and three-dimensional what most history books put down in flat, hackneyed prose. It is an ideal film for young people.

It was originally filmed as a two-part program for the Disney TV show, and is structured as such. The first segment takes place in 1773. Johnny Tremain has great ambitions as a silversmith, apprenticed to one of the leading craftsmen in Boston. When an aristocrat brings a teapot to be repaired, and the smith says he cannot do it, Johnny takes it upon himself to fix it, disobeying orders by working on the Sabbath. In his haste to cover up his work when a constable approaches, he burns his hand in molten silver, rendering it curled and useless. He cannot find a job.

Always having been apathetic to the cause of revolution, he now finds that their headquarters is the only place he is welcome and useful. It takes another incident to really win him over, however. He goes to nobleman Jonathan Lyte and tells him of his true birthright as a Lyte, presenting a silver cup with the family crest as proof, given him by his late mother. Lyte accuses him of having stolen the cup, and sends him to jail. One of Boston's finest lawyers represents Johnny as part of the patriotic cause. Another patriot, Paul Revere, explains to Johnny that they care about people who are abused by men like Lyte.

When he is exonerated at the trial, Johnny joins the Sons of Liberty and works with them in executing the Boston Tea Party, which is carried out in a workmanlike and orderly manner. From an overhead balcony, merchant Jonathan Lyte is aghast, but the British admiral in charge of the harbor comments wryly that "those 'Indians' seem to prefer principle to profit," a concept the mercenary Lyte cannot grasp. The tea party a fait accompli, the patriots march into the middle of town, lighting the liberty tree with their torches as they sing "The Liberty Tree."

The second segment takes place in 1775. General Gage, in charge of the colonies, calls in the leader of the patriots to tell him that he can no longer, under orders, ignore what is right under his nose: the training of militia, storing of weapons, etc. He promises that if they call off such activities, they will be treated fairly by the British, but he is rejected.

Suspense is in the air as each side awaits the other's first move. As sentiment of war grows within the Sons of Liberty, a final meeting is held, and James Otis, one of the founders, now mentally unbalanced, delivers a beautifully eloquent speech on war, telling his comrades that if they are to undergo this painful ordeal, they must know *why* they are fighting, and have some goal to reach by winning.

One of General Gage's officers, a Colonel Smith, assures the general that he can overpower the colonials without bloodshed, and is given permission to do so. The British and the colonials meet head on at Lexington Green. The colonel tells his men that they are not to fire unless so ordered; the colonials refuse to fire until the British fire first. Suddenly there is a shot and the battle abruptly begins. An aide asks the colonel who fired the shot. "One of our men, one of theirs, perhaps," he says ruefully. "What does it matter now?"

Johnny Tremain (Hal Stalmaster) and his friends (Luana Patten, Dick Beymer) lead the Sons of Liberty into Boston. © *Walt Disney Productions*

Johnny Tremain goes on trial, accused of theft by Jonathan Lyte. © *Walt Disney Productions*

The British conduct themselves like wooden soldiers, while the colonials use guerrilla tactics to overcome them. Within a day General Gage is forced to admit that his men are surrounded—trapped—by the enemy. At the colonial camps bonfires burn as a symbol of the growing flame of liberty spreading throughout the land.

Johnny Tremain is a vivid fictionalization of the events leading up to the revolutionary war. It is good because it doesn't attempt to boil issues down to simple blacks and whites; the British are not cardboard villains, but real people with mixed emotions about the colonies. Even the Sons of Liberty are shown to be uncertain at times about what course of action to take. Most realistically of all, the film depicts the apathy on the part of people like Johnny, who don't want to get involved—until they have to.

The performances are convincing, with such veteran supporting players as Walter Sande (as Paul Revere) and Whit Bissell (as Josiah Quincy) in key roles. Particularly notable is Jeff York as James Otis in a rare noncomic role for Disney. Hal Stalmaster as Johnny was "introduced" in this film as a Disney discovery, and carried out the role quite nicely, but his career never progressed any further. Also featured in the film was a former Disney protégée, Luana Patten, in her first grown-up role for the studio as Johnny's love interest.

The film marked a more important debut, however. It was the first Disney film directed by British-born Robert Stevenson, who went on to make most of the studio's major live-action successes of the 1960s.

The quality of the film belies its TV origin. Assistant director William Beaudine, Jr., recalls that "it was intended originally for the Disney TV show and it was because of the expense that it was decided to release it as a regular theatrical feature. We did shorten the schedule, but it was very difficult to economize to the point of making it practical just for television release, because Walt Disney expected top quality."

To that end, matte artist Peter Ellenshaw was given the assignment of production design for this film, and provided it with endless mattes showing Boston harbor, the city at night, Lexington Green, and the final long shot of campfires blazing all around the city at nightfall. These impeccable optical effects, all rich in color, give the film a lush, expensive look beyond its actual cost. The only shots that occasionally show signs of economy are those daytime street scenes in Boston that have interior sound-stage lighting so indigenous to TV productions.

Finally, it is worth noting that as in so many Disney films, a song plays an important part in establishing a mood; here it is "The Liberty Tree," sung by the Sons of Liberty as a rousing march proclaiming their unity in devotion to their noble cause.

PERRI

RELEASED BY BUENA VISTA ON AUGUST 28, 1957. Technicolor. Producer, narrator: Winston Hibler. Directors: N. Paul Kenworthy, Jr., Ralph Wright. Screenplay: Ralph Wright, Winston Hibler, based on a novel by Felix Salten. Photography: N. Paul Kenworthy, Jr., Joel Colman, Walter Perkins, William Ratcliffe, James R. Simon, John P. Hermann, David Meyer, Warren E. Garst, Roy Edward Disney. Music: Paul J. Smith. Song arrangements: Carl Brandt. Orchestrations: Carl Brandt, Franklyn Marks. Production manager: Louis Debney. Special processes: Ub Iwerks, A.S.C. Film editor: Jack L. Atwood. Special art effects: Peter Ellenshaw, Joshua Meador. Sound: Robert O. Cook. Music editor: Evelyn Kennedy. Running time: 75 minutes.

Songs: "Break of Day" by George Bruns, Winston Hibler. "And Now to Sleep (Lullaby of the Wildwood)" by George Bruns, Winston Hibler, Ralph Wright. "Together Time" by Paul J. Smith, Gil George, Ralph Wright, Winston Hibler.

Perri was Walt Disney's first "True-Life Fantasy,"

a genre that he hoped would provide his staff with the best of all possible worlds. By making no bones about the "fantasy" angle of the film, it was felt that the Disney nature-film staff could now do what they had tried to hold in check in the bona fide True-Life films—manipulate the documentary footage to their hearts' content and fashion it into a story.

The perfect subject for such treatment was found in Felix Salten's book *Perri*, and the Disney staff had the advantage of what they had learned from their previous experience with Salten, in *Bambi*. Indeed, the format and overall atmosphere of *Perri* owes a great deal to the earlier animated feature.

The film opens with a biblical quotation ("To everything there is a season . . ."). First we see a beautiful starlit sky, with the sun gradually rising and brightening the landscape (this done with animation), then a slow dissolve to live action with beautiful scenes of the sky, greenery, and morning life in the forest, as an off-screen chorus sings "Break of Day." The theme of the film, we are told, is the endless stream of life, season by season.

The seasons are identified by such names as Time

of Beauty, Time of Beginnings, Time of Hunting, Time of Peace, etc. Throughout this progression, we follow the life of Perri, a young female squirrel, from birth, when she is first exposed to the laws of survival (a marten killing her father as her mother tries to move her offspring away to a safe place), to maturity, and the continuing fight for life against the squirrels' forest enemies: the winter of hibernation, the spring and mating season when she meets Porro, a climactic forest fire, and the inevitable happy ending, when she and Porro settle down as a new yearly life cycle begins.

With each seasonal change, after we catch up with Perri and watch her development, we see other animals as well, and their various life styles in the forest. Most of the key sequences involve animals trying to ward off predators, often without success. As the narrator explains, "Death is a necessary evil; some die that others may survive."

When Perri hibernates for the winter, the film presents a winter fantasy, a surrealistic dream sequence with Perri and other animals frolicking in the snow against a beautiful deep-blue sky. Glimmering snowflakes converge in the form of rabbits; Perri and the other animals leave glittering trails as they fly through the air. Then the enemy weasel appears and tries to stalk his prey, to no avail, for this is, after all, a fantasy. When he catches a rabbit, it disintegrates into a flurry of snowflakes once more. Finally, an owl is angered at all the commotion and takes off after the

Perri herself.   © *Walt Disney Productions*

A scene from the winter fantasy.
© *Walt Disney Productions*

weasel (flying directly into the camera). The entire scene is played against an ethereally lovely setting of snow and sky, each unreal in the beauty of its colors.

Aside from this flashy sequence, the major difference between this film's technique and that of a True-Life film is the actual use of film. There are numerous first-person shots, of a hawk swooping down to catch Perri, perched atop a tree, of Perri herself as she edges out onto a very unsteady branch to escape a marten, and at the top of a tree as it is cut down and falls to the ground.

Some scenes, like the one near the beginning where a marten chases the mother squirrel, are tremendously exciting, because there is a variety of angles intercut to give the sequence a genuine feeling of movement. There are, throughout the film, superbly edited pieces of action made possible by the kind of preplanning impossible in the factual nature films. There are also subtle optical effects that would be considered cheating in a nonfiction film, such as using slow motion to make a too brief close-up of Perri linger on screen a few seconds longer.

All this was made possible by the same kind of patience and skill that went into the True-Life films. Nine cameramen, led by True-Life veterans N. Paul Kenworthy, Jr., and Ralph Wright, spent two complete life cycles in the Uintah National Forest of Utah to get appropriate footage for all four seasons, as well as winter material from Jackson Hole, Wyoming. Some shots were spontaneous, but most of the film's impressive camera work was the result of hard work and careful planning. Many camera platforms were constructed as high as fifty feet in the air to get tree-top footage.

Some 200,000 feet of 16mm film were exposed, and then edited down to 8,000 feet for the finished film, an incredible ratio of 25 to 1. The result, however, is a truly dazzling accomplishment. With that much material to choose from, Winston Hibler and his staff were able to pick precisely the actions they wanted to express. There is not a wasted second on screen, and the diversity of the footage is put to work, especially in such lovely sequences as the lullaby scene, strongly reminiscent of *Dumbo*'s "Baby of Mine," with assorted families clinging to their mothers as they prepare for sleep.

Although the film is carefully scripted, and film-making tricks were imposed on the actuality in the forest, *Perri* does not really invent much that does not exist. If the plot points are fictitious, the actions of the animals are not, and in depicting the mating season and the fight for survival against natural enemies, *Perri* paints an exciting and accurate picture of animal life in the forest. Though the word "sex" is never uttered, and the mating season is referred to as "Together Time," the film still takes a healthier and more open view of the mating ritual than any other contemporary film aimed at children, as well as a good many supposedly made for adults in this preliberated screen era.

As always, the music is an essential part of the film's success, and Paul Smith's score is, as might be expected, first-rate. The lovely choral arrangements of the film's three songs are also outstanding in creating a mood of beauty and happiness.

Generally speaking, *Perri* was well received, although most critics had moments of uncertainty about the integrity of combining fictional ideas with factual footage; most were more critical, however, of the sentimental nature of the film.

John Beaufort wrote:

Mr. Disney's effort to combine pictorial record with narrative fiction is not, unfortunately, an unqualified success. The producer's assertion that "fantasy never impairs reality" will certainly not get by the naturalists unchallenged. There is, furthermore, a cloying and cheapening coyness to some of the basic concepts. Such arch phrases as "time of beginning . . . time of alone . . . together time, etc." are decidedly hard to take.

Archer Winsten in the *New York Post* thought the film fine for children but warned that "there is an element of baby-food mush that could be considered a hindrance to some adults."

On the whole Disney's experiment was warmly greeted, more so by the public than by the critical community. For future endeavors, the producer decided to eschew all classifications, and in later fictional animal films Disney decided to simply let the material speak for itself.

OLD YELLER

RELEASED BY BUENA VISTA ON DECEMBER 25, 1957. Technicolor. Director: Robert Stevenson. Screenplay: Fred Gipson, William Tunberg, from a novel by Gipson. Photography: Charles P. Boyle. Editor: Stanley Johnson. Art director: Carroll Clark. Set decorations: Emile Kuri, Fred MacLean. Costumes: Chuck Keehne, Gertrude Casey. Music: Oliver Wallace. Orchestrations: Clifford Vaughan. Second unit director: Yakima Canutt. Assistant director: Robert G. Shannon. Matte artist: Peter Ellenshaw. Makeup: Pat McNalley. Hairstyling: Elaine Stone. Sound supervision: Robert O. Cook. Sound recording: Frank McWhorter. Music editor: Evelyn Kennedy. Running time: 83 minutes.

Song: "Old Yeller" by Oliver Wallace, Gil George, sung by Jerome Courtland.

Cast: Dorothy McGuire (Katie Coates), Fess Parker (Jim Coates), Tommy Kirk (Travis Coates), Kevin Corcoran (Arliss Coates), Jeff York (Bud Searcy), Beverly Washburn (Lisbeth Searcy), Chuck Connors (Burn Sanderson), and Spike (Old Yeller).

Tommy Kirk and Kevin Corcoran with Old Yeller.
© *Walt Disney Productions*

Pa (Fess Parker) tries to explain to Travis (Tommy Kirk) that we have to face up to some things we don't like—such as Yeller's death.   © *Walt Disney Productions*

Having enjoyed major success with nature films involving animals, and equal success on television with the "Mickey Mouse Club," where the emphasis was on children, Walt Disney reasoned that combining these two sure-fire elements would result in widely popular film fare. *Old Yeller* was to be the first of innumerable Disney projects about a boy and his dog. With the many spin-offs that have followed, this film is still one of the best of its kind.

The setting is Texas in 1869. Jim Coates is forced to leave his family for three months to go on a cattle drive, hoping to earn enough money so that he can settle down for good. Fifteen-year-old Travis becomes the head of the household during his absence, dedicating himself to the regimentation of farm life. When his playful younger brother falls in love with a stray dog who wanders onto the farm and causes temporary havoc, he is irritated, but his mother reminds him that little Arliss is lonely, and craves the friendship of the dog.

Before long, the yellow dog wins over the whole family, proving to be a brilliant watchdog and protector as well as a friend. A cowboy comes to the farm one day and explains that the dog is his; he's been tracking it for a long time. But when he sees how attached young Arliss is to the canine, he softens and "trades" with the youngster for it, acquiring a horned toad in the deal.

Travis takes Yeller with him on an expedition to trap some wild pigs; he follows the advice of a shiftless neighbor, Bud Searcy, and sits in a tree, trying to rope the pigs from above. When he falls into the midst of the pack, Yeller fights off the vicious animals as best he can. Travis's leg is badly hurt and bleeding at the end of the fracas, but Yeller is even worse off. The pigs may have rabies. Later, a wolf attacks Yeller at a bonfire, and Mother fears it, too, was rabid. Yeller is kept in confinement for several weeks to be safe.

One evening when it seems that the danger has passed, Travis notices Yeller acting strangely, becoming insanely vicious for no good reason. He suddenly realizes what has happened, and with cold determination shoots the dog.

From that time on he is disconsolate. Bud Searcy's daughter Lisbeth gives Travis one of Yeller's little pups (the mother is the dog owned by Lisbeth in the story), but Travis rejects it cruelly. Just then, Father comes home; his wife explains what has happened, and he has a talk with his son, telling him that we can't control life, as much as we'd like to, that we should always try to look for a brighter side to things. Travis tells him he's trying, but it's very difficult. When he returns to the farm from Yeller's grave, however, he meets the puppy again, and sees in it for the first time a glimmer of Yeller himself. He brightens and adopts the dog as his own, for a happy ending.

Old Yeller is a lovely film, under the able guidance of Robert Stevenson, who treats his subject with the dignity and understatement that brings out all the emotion inherent in the story. In less skilled hands the same material could have been cloying and phony;

this film never sinks to that level.

The rigors of farm life and interfamily relationships in such an environment are beautifully portrayed. The performances are first-rate. Fess Parker has relatively little to do in the film, but he communicates the warmth and sincerity that had become his hallmark by now (many observers noting the similarities between his personality and that of Gary Cooper). Dorothy McGuire is fine as the mother, and little Kevin Corcoran is his usual self, having established the character of Moochie on TV, which overlapped into most of his subsequent screen roles for Disney. In many ways the outstanding performance of the film is that of Tommy Kirk, complete with Texas accent. His subsequent comedy roles in Disney films never gave him the scope of this characterization, and he carries off the full range of intense emotions with uncanny skill. Knowing that he was capable of this makes it all the more sad to watch him in the bumbling comedy parts he played later on.

The film's vignettes are told in a compact, straightforward manner, with Yakima Canutt's second-unit direction lending excitement to the few action scenes in the narrative. One nice touch of Stevenson's occurs when little Arliss has to face the cowboy stranger to bargain with him for ownership of Yeller. The shot of the boy walking up to the cowboy is shown from the youngster's point of view, looking up at the very tall man—a charming idea that works perfectly.

Old Yeller was well received by the critics, and, released at Christmastime, grossed an incredible $8 million in domestic showings alone. It was the phenomenal success of this film and a few follow-ups that convinced Disney for good that if his studio was to prosper, it had to concentrate its energies on modest live-action endeavors and relegate animation to a sideline activity.

THE LIGHT IN THE FOREST

RELEASED BY BUENA VISTA ON JULY 9, 1958. TECHnicolor. Director: Herschel Daugherty. Screenplay: Lawrence E. Watkin, based on the novel by Conrad Richter. Photography: Ellsworth Fredericks. Editor: Stanley Johnson. Art director: Carroll Clark. Set decorations: Emile Kuri, Fred MacLean. Costumes: Chuck Keehne, Gertrude Casey. Music: Paul J. Smith. Orchestrations: Franklyn Marks. Assistant director: Robert G. Shannon. Matte artist: Peter Ellenshaw. Technical adviser: Iron Eyes Cody. Makeup: Pat McNalley. Hairstyling: Ruth Sandifer. Sound supervision: Robert O. Cook. Sound recording: Dean Thomas. Running time: 93 minutes.

Songs: "The Light in the Forest" by Paul J. Smith, Gil George. "I Asked My Love a Favor" by Paul J. Smith, Lawrence E. Watkin.

Cast: James MacArthur (Johnny Butler/True Son), Carol Lynley (Shenandoe), Fess Parker (Del Hardy), Wendell Corey (Wilse Owens), Joanne Dru (Milly Elder), Jessica Tandy (Myra Butler), Joseph Calleia (Chief Cuyloga), John McIntire (John Elder), Rafael Campos (Half Arrow), Frank Ferguson (Harry Butler), Norman Fredric (Niskitoon), Marian Seldes (Kate Owens), Stephen Bekassy (Colonel Henry Bouquet), Sam Buffington (George Owens).

Like so many Disney films, *The Light in the Forest* centers around a young boy, in this case a white boy who has lived most of his life with Indians. In 1764 a peace treaty between the Delaware Indians and the British requires that all white prisoners be returned to their people; this includes Johnny Butler, who is now more Indian than white. In fact, he is bitterly antiwhite, and rebels when his real parents try to reacquaint him with their way of life. Army Indian scout Del Hardy has been assigned to stay with Johnny through this period and see that he gets readjusted.

Conflict arises when Johnny encounters his uncle Wilse, leader of a pack of men who engage in raids in which they senselessly murder Indians. He also meets Wilse's indentured servant, a girl named Shenandoe who at first resists Johnny, harboring nightmarish memories of her parents' death at the hands of an Indian party. But soon the two fall in love, and Johnny starts to behave more and more like a white man, even while deploring many of his brethren's habits and attitudes.

Then one night Wilse kills an Indian friend of Johnny who was coming to speak to him. This sends Johnny back to his tribe, more embittered than ever. But when the Indians want to use him as a decoy to lure an innocent party of whites into an ambush, he finds he cannot do it. He returns to his home and decides to meet Wilse and fight him "like a white man" with his fists. He outducks, outdodges, and outlasts Wilse, beats him to a pulp, and Wilse is forced to admit, as he crawls away, that "he's white, all right."

He and Shenandoe find an idyllic spot in the forest where they will live with nature; in town, Del Hardy is also settling down with Milly, the local clergyman's daughter.

The Light in the Forest is an absorbing and fairly intelligent film with an enlightening moral for young viewers, showing that there are good and bad men in every part of life, and that before one can be at peace with others, one must be at peace with oneself. The only glaring weakness of the story is the finale, with Wilse, played with relish by Wendell Corey as a slimy, despicable villain (who even lusts after Carol Lynley in a drunken binge), suddenly mending his ways after a fistfight with the "Indian" boy.

In all other respects the tale is well told. This was television director Herschel Daugherty's feature-film debut, and a most creditable one, although the balance of his career has continued to be devoted to TV. The film was also Carol Lynley's debut (she received "and introducing" credit in the main titles), and James MacArthur's second film, his first for Disney. Walt had first seen Broadway and TV actress Lynley on the cover of *Life* magazine, and MacArthur in some television dramas. He signed both to contracts, although Miss Lynley never did any further work for the studio, while MacArthur was built into a Disney

Shenandoe (Carol Lynley) and Johnny Butler (James MacArthur) fall deeply in love. © *Walt Disney Productions*

Wendell Corey taunts the "Indian" boy (off camera), as John McIntire and Fess Parker watch disapprovingly. © *Walt Disney Productions*

star over the next few years. Despite their lack of experience in films, they both did extremely well in their highly individualized roles, winning kudos for their sensitive and wholly convincing love scenes. The film marked another milestone at the opposite end of the spectrum. It was Fess Parker's last for Walt Disney; the actor grew tired of playing the same role in every film, although he didn't fare much better on his own. His secondary romantic scenes with Joanne Dru did add a nice touch to this film, however.

The film boasts a strong supporting cast, with each role handled by a well-seasoned veteran, from Frank Ferguson as MacArthur's white father to Joseph Calleia as his Indian chief guardian.

Most of the footage was shot on location in Tennessee, some twenty miles outside Chattanooga, but the Indian camp was built back in California on the Rowland V. Lee ranch, supervised by technical adviser Iron Eyes Cody, also known for his many Indian roles in films over the years. The period atmosphere throughout the film is rich in flavor and detail, adding to the believability of the story.

Critical reaction was mixed, with by now polarized pro- and anti-Disney factions becoming clear. The *New York Herald Tribune* called it "another of Walt Disney's impeccable little pioneer stories." *Variety* thought the film gave "depth to a story that would otherwise seem too placid," while *Time* magazine called it "another strong-legged, soft-headed pioneer epic, in which each character, action, and motive is painted in shrieking monotone . . ."

It was a suitable summer release, however, if not a smash hit in the tradition of *Old Yeller*. It has subsequently turned up on the Disney TV show, where it remains above-average entertainment for young people, with more brains behind it than most such fodder.

WHITE WILDERNESS

RELEASED BY BUENA VISTA ON AUGUST 12, 1958. Technicolor (from 16mm original). Producer: Ben Sharpsteen. Director, screenplay: James Algar. Photography: James R. Simon, Hugh A. Wilmar, Lloyd Beebe, Herb and Lois Crisler. Additional photography: William Carrick, Tom McHugh, Carl Thomsen, Cecil Rhode, Dick Bird, Richard Tegstrom. Narrator: Winston Hibler. Music: Oliver Wallace. Orchestrations: Clifford Vaughan. Production manager: Erwin L. Verity. Special process photography: Ub Iwerks. Animation effects: Joshua Meador, Art Riley. Film editor: Norman Palmer. Sound: Robert O. Cook. Music editor: Evelyn Kennedy. Running time: 73 minutes.

Although *White Wilderness* covers a region quite remote from those of previous True-Life features, it follows the same format as its predecessors. The traditional paintbrush paints a view of the globe from the Arctic position, and shows cave drawings revealing early animal life of this region.

We get our first view of the Arctic as the spring thaw arrives, manifesting itself in various spectacular ways: a series of avalanches, a frozen river breaking up and flowing once again, gnawing at glaciers along the way.

The film depicts most of the famous residents of this area, including the walrus and the polar bear; it seems that the former are scared to death of the latter, even (in one case) when two playful bear cubs come to frighten a group of walruses who are lounging on an ice floe. "This," says the narrator, "is what's known as trading on your father's reputation."

An extended sequence deals with the lemmings, and the legend of their mass suicide. This occurs at irregular intervals, probably in response to overpopulation. They emerge from their underground homes, and the sprightly little creatures start to move away; as a few start, others follow, and soon there is a mass migration. Such predators as the ermine (a member of the weasel family) and the raven pick off many of them as they travel along, but nothing stops them from moving on. When they reach a cliff beyond which there is only the Arctic Ocean, they dive over and keep swimming, apparently thinking that there is only a small body of water before they will reach another stretch of land. This is not the case, however, and they eventually perish at sea. This is the truth behind the legend of their mass suicide.

On the outskirts of the Arctic, we see other animals: the musk ox, the wolf, and his prey, the caribou, who are shown in mass migration—hundreds of these deerlike animals moving together, easy targets for the wolves.

A prolonged segment deals with a member of the weasel family called the wolverine, a vicious and very determined killer who engages in a long chase with a rabbit, and then climbs a tree to devour a nestful of young birds, while the mother bird watches, helpless.

Finally, "summer" is over. Winter arrives. The caribou and reindeer make the trek south again. A blizzard erupts. The shadow of the fading sun falls over the Arctic mountains as the great seasonal change comes over the white wilderness.

White Wilderness maintains the standard of excellence set by this series, with a formidable array of sights rarely, if ever, captured on film. The grandeur and excitement of the settings themselves (with spectacular views of glaciers falling apart with the spring thaw) are matched by the exciting lives of the animals that inhabit this region. The extended sequences on the lemming, wolf, walrus, and wolverine are all

Two inhabitants of the *White Wilderness.*
© *Walt Disney Productions*

Some of the magnificent ice and glacial formations seen in the film. © *Walt Disney Productions*

simply fascinating, with equally intriguing views of the snowshoe rabbit, arctic gull, the loon (who is seen escaping from the clutches of a polar bear by sheer stamina), and the white whale (dolphin), among others.

As always, there is a seasonal theme to the film, and the usual outlook on the laws of survival, with just enough sidelight material (the playful polar bear cubs, the dolphin swimming in formation with his peers, etc.) to provide a full spectrum of emotions in the study of arctic life.

Nine photographers spent nearly three years gathering the material for this film, and again various "specialists" were engaged to do what they knew best. Hugh A. Wilmar shot the polar bear footage, at considerable risk to life and limb, while Herb and Lois Crisler set up a makeshift camp on the spot where caribou and wolf were most likely to converge. James R. Simon was responsible for the fascinating segment on the lemmings—a matter of finding a group of the animals before embarking on their journey and following them on the entire trek. Another True-Life veteran, Lloyd Beebe, followed the migration of the caribou and then located a herd of musk-oxen for another sequence.

The patience and know-how of these photographers was well rewarded, of course, in the final product, a completely absorbing and unique film that met with the expected success of this ongoing series, despite carping by various critics. The *New York Times* found it "a bit redundant" and "stimulating rather than thrilling," and *Time* criticized its "cloying narration and a soundtrack that often seems loudly superfluous." However, they admitted that on the whole the film was truly spectacular and eminently worthwhile.

TONKA

RELEASED BY BUENA VISTA ON DECEMBER 25, 1958.
Technicolor. Producer: James Pratt. Director: Lewis
R. Foster. Screenplay: Lewis R. Foster, Lillie Hay-
ward, based on the novel *Comanche* by David Appel.
Photography: Loyal Griggs. Editor: H. Ellsworth
Hoagland. Art director: Robert E. Smith. Set decora-
tions: Emile Kuri, Oliver Emert. Costumes: Chuck
Keehne, Gertrude Casey. Music: Oliver Wallace. Or-
chestrations: Clifford Vaughan. Assistant director:
Horace Hough. Matte artist: Peter Ellenshaw.
Makeup: Pat McNalley. Hairstyling: Ruth Sandifer.
Sound: Robert O. Cook, Harry M. Lindgren. Run-
ning time: 97 minutes.

Song: "Tonka" by Gil George, George Bruns.

Cast: Sal Mineo (White Bull), Philip Carey (Captain
Miles Keogh), Jerome Courtland (Lieutenant Henry
Nowlan), Rafael Campos (Strong Bear), H. M.
Wynant (Yellow Bull), Joy Page (Prairie Flower),
Britt Lomond (General Custer), Herbert Rudley
(Captain Benteen), Sydney Smith (General Terry),
John War Eagle (Chief Sitting Bull), Gregg Martell
(Corporal Korn), Slim Pickens (Ace), Robert
"Buzz" Henry (Lieutenant Crittenden).

Long before the cultural explosion of the 1970s
that saw Indian injustice replace black injustice as the
prime civil rights issue of the day, Walt Disney's films
were teaching respect for the red man, and showing
history through his eyes. In that respect alone, *Tonka*
is an honorable and worthwhile endeavor. Although
modestly produced, it is a well-crafted film, helmed by
veteran director/writer Lewis R. Foster (who also did
many of the Disney *Zorro* TV shows).

Sal Mineo plays White Bull, a young Indian
brave in the Sioux tribe who is trying hard to prove
himself a man. When he manages to capture and tame
a magnificent wild horse, he feels a great sense of
accomplishment, but his cruel cousin Yellow Bull
takes advantage of his seniority and claims the horse
as his own, beating and torturing it. Rather than see
this happen, White Bull sets the horse, which he has
named Tonka, free.

Tonka is captured along with other wild horses
and sold to the cavalry. A genteel captain named

Miles Keogh takes the horse for his own, recognizing
its worth, and recalling having seen it on an earlier
chase. He renames the horse Comanche.

White Bull learns of Tonka's whereabouts, and,
while on a scouting party, sneaks into the fort to see
his beloved horse. He is seen by Keogh, but they both
discover their common bond in the noble animal and
become friends. After routine questioning, White Bull
is set free.

Battle plans take shape within the Indian camps
as well as the cavalry lines. Many of the soldiers are
wary of the zealous General Custer, who seems intent
on slaughtering every Indian he sees. On his way to a
preplanned checkpoint, Custer cannot resist what
seems like a surefire opportunity at Little Big Horn,
unaware that he is walking into a trap. The massacre
takes place, but it is Custer's men who are slaugh-
tered, not the Indians. They suffer total defeat. Indeed, the only cavalry survivor of the massacre is the
horse! A friend of the dead Keogh recognizes the
animal, and remembers White Bull, who has also survived the holocaust.

At the fort Tonka/Comanche is honored by the
7th Cavalry for bravery, and put in the special charge
of honorary trooper White Bull.

Though this story line seems solid, the film has
definite lulls in its none too short ninety-seven minutes. The problem arises when the focus is taken off
White Bull and the Indian tribe and put on the horse
itself, as it is taken up by the cavalry captain. The
character of White Bull has been so compelling that
this sudden change of scenery and characters is somewhat unwelcome.

The credibility factor is also stretched to the limit
in the series of incidents that fill the second half of the
film. Custer is depicted here as a maniac (when he
announces that he wants war on Indians, Keogh asks,
"Even the friendly ones?" and Custer snarls "They're
all bad!"), and the men under him are extremely dis-
trustful. The fact that the horse was the only survivor
of Little Big Horn has been billboarded as an introduction to the film, yet the finale shows that he was
the only *cavalry* survivor, because young White Bull
has miraculously come through the attack as well.

Worst of all is the final scene, where the Indian

White Bull (Sal Mineo) sets Tonka free. © *1958 Walt Disney Productions*

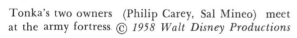

Tonka's two owners (Philip Carey, Sal Mineo) meet at the army fortress. © *1958 Walt Disney Productions*

brave, who has repeatedly shown his allegiance to his tribe and his hatred for the white man, is now an honorary member of the 7th Cavalry! Horse or no horse, it doesn't ring entirely true.

Custer's Last Stand is depicted in a series of fragmented close-ups, giving a good idea of what the battle was like on a man-to-man basis, but providing no scope or sweep to the battle. Some panoramic shots of the massacre might have been in order.

The most salient aspect of the film, which despite its flaws is rather good, is Mineo's performance as White Bull. He is totally convincing, and in his solo scenes at the beginning, trying to tame the wild horse, he captures the fancy of every boy in the audience with his combination of cockiness and inexperience in achieving this formidable task.

Philip Carey is also good as the civilized captain,

and the balance of the supporting cast is uniformly first-rate. But it is really Mineo's film, his arresting performance making the scenes where he is off screen seem that much duller.

The scenery is superbly captured by cameraman Loyal Griggs, who is best known for his lovely outdoor work on such films as *Shane*. The film was shot at the Warm Springs Indian Reservation in Oregon, with many local Indians recruited to appear in the film and aid in the reconstruction of settings and events.

The film was well received, the *Times* calling it "another nice serving of Disney Americana" and *Variety* adding that "from the juvenile delinquents which he has essayed in the past, Mineo makes quite a leap to portray this clean-limbed young Indian, but he does it with ease and conviction." The film has subsequently been aired on the Disney television show.

SLEEPING BEAUTY

RELEASED BY BUENA VISTA ON JANUARY 29, 1959. Technicolor, Technirama. Production supervisor: Ken Peterson. Supervising director: Clyde Geronimi. Sequence directors: Eric Larson, Wolfgang Reitherman, Les Clark. Directing animators: Milt Kahl, Franklin Thomas, Marc Davis, Oliver Johnston, Jr., John Lounsbery. Story adaptation: Erdman Penner, from the Charles Perrault version of "Sleeping Beauty." Additional story: Joe Rinaldi, Winston Hibler, Bill Peet, Ted Sears, Ralph Wright, Milt Banta. Production design: Donald Da Gradi, Ken Anderson. Backgrounds: Frank Armitage, Thelma Witmer, Albert Dempster, Walt Peregoy, Bill Layne, Ralph Hulett, Dick Anthony, Fil Mottola, Richard H. Thomas, Anthony Rizzo. Layout: McLaren Stewart, Tom Codrick, Don Griffith, Erni Nordli, Basil Davidovich, Victor Haboush, Joe Hale, Homer Jonas, Jack Huber, Ray Aragon. Color styling: Eyvind Earle. Character styling: Tom Oreb. Character animation: Hal King, Hal Ambro, Don Lusk, Blaine Gibson, John Sibley, Bob Carson, Ken Hultgren, Harvey Toombs, Fred Kopietz, George Nicholas, Bob Youngquist, Eric Cleworth, Henry Tanous, John Kennedy, Ken O'Brien. Effects animation: Dan MacManus, Joshua Meador, Jack Boyd, Jack Buckley. Music adaptation: George Bruns, adapted from Tchaikovsky's "Sleeping Beauty Ballet."

Choral arrangements: John Rarig. Film editors: Roy M. Brewer, Jr., Donald Halliday. Sound supervision: Robert O. Cook. Music editor: Evelyn Kennedy. Special processes: Ub Iwerks, Eustace Lycett. Running time: 75 minutes.

Songs: "Once Upon a Dream" by Sammy Fain, Jack Lawrence. "Hail the Princess Aurora" by Tom Adair, George Bruns. "I Wonder" by Winston Hibler, Ted Sears, George Bruns. "The Skumps" by Tom Adair, Erdman Penner, George Bruns. "Sleeping Beauty Song" by Tom Adair, George Bruns.

Voices: Mary Costa (Princess Aurora), Bill Shirley (Prince Phillip), Eleanor Audley (Maleficent), Verna Felton (Flora), Barbara Jo Allen (Fauna), Barbara Luddy (Merryweather), Taylor Holmes (King Stefan), Bill Thompson (King Hubert), Candy Candido (Goons), Marvin Miller (Narrator).

Walt Disney envisioned *Sleeping Beauty* as his masterpiece, the ultimate in animated filmmaking. The project was first considered in 1950, when preliminary work was begun on a small scale. The next few years saw the story take shape. In 1954 the project was laid aside for two years, while the Disney staff concentrated on the Disneyland park and the studio's

Sleeping Beauty (Briar Rose) sings, as her forest friends listen attentively.   © *1970 Walt Disney Productions*

Maleficent kidnaps Prince Phillip so he won't be able to rescue Sleeping Beauty.   © *Walt Disney Productions*

Flora, Fauna and Merryweather help Phillip escape; here they
are confronted by Maleficent's pet raven. © *Walt Disney
Productions*

two television series. Work resumed in earnest in
1956, and consumed the next three years. By the end
of that time the cost of the seventy-five-minute film
had mounted to $6 million, making it the most expen-
sive animated cartoon of all time.

The fantastic effort and phenomenal expense do
show up on the screen; it is unquestionably Disney's
most elaborate cartoon film, the visuals on screen enhanced by the wide-screen Technirama process and
the aural stereophonic sound system. The critical
question, beyond that of choice of subject matter, was
the wisdom of allowing an animated film to become so
elaborate, many feeling that this concerted effort to
reproduce reality on a grand scale was the height of
nonart. It was a question even Disney had to face,
much as he disdained the opinions of critics, once the
film was released and digested by the public.

Curiously, just as critical lambasting of many of
Disney's earlier feature films seems hollow and unim-

portant today, when the films stand on their own and
provide consummate entertainment, so the criticisms
of *Sleeping Beauty* seem slightly irrelevant so many
years after its initial release. One can imagine reviewers going to see the film in 1959, ears abuzz with
the scandalous news that $6 million had been spent,
minds agog with thoughts on other recent Disney features to use for comparison, all subjected to the promotional assault prepared by the Disney company to
ensure the film's success.

Times have changed since 1959, more so than one
might imagine at first glance. When *Sleeping Beauty*
was reissued in 1971, it came at a time when children's
and so-called family entertainment had sunk to a new
low on television and in theatres. Viewed in this context, it is difficult to dismiss it as second-rate Disney,
or overproduced, or any of the other descriptions
leveled at the film. Its imagination and its florid animation style are a welcome breath of fresh air after a

brief perusal of Saturday-morning kiddie fare on the tube.

Not that *Sleeping Beauty* looks good only in comparison to the current competition. But seen today, it seems much better than anyone gave it credit for in 1959. The so-called heavy-handedness just isn't there, and, at seventy-five minutes, it makes its point and provides more entertainment than most other, lengthier, films of this kind.

Disney knew the risk he was taking in producing another well-known fable like *Sleeping Beauty*. "[It] was tough," he told Bob Thomas, "because it had many of the elements we had already used in *Snow White* and *Cinderella*. You've got to give the creators new things to work with so they'll be able to keep their enthusiasm up. You're in trouble if they start saying, 'Haven't we done this before?' "

Indeed, they *had* done this before, and entirely new approaches to the story had to be conceived. The basic story is elementary. Celebrating the birth of a daughter (their first), the King and Queen hold a royal celebration, but neglect to invite a bad fairy, who, offended at the rebuff, casts a curse on the child that will cause her to prick her finger on a spindle when she turns sixteen and die. A good fairy is able to alter the curse so that death becomes sleep. Despite all precautions, the prophecy is fulfilled on the Princess's sixteenth birthday, and she falls into a deep sleep, awakened (in the story) one hundred years later by an adventuresome Prince who kisses her and breaks the spell.

As in *Cinderella* and *Snow White,* the Disney staff's challenge was to provide enough diversions and additions to stretch the story to feature film length without letting the seams show.

In the Disney script three good fairies named Flora, Fauna, and Merryweather take the royal child with them into the forest where they raise her in seclusion as a normal child, keeping her out of sight of the evil witch named Maleficent. She has been promised since birth to Prince Phillip, but she does not know her own identity; thus, when the two accidentally meet in the forest and fall in love, they are unaware that they are already engaged to be married. When, on Princess Aurora's sixteenth birthday, she is discovered by Maleficent and put to sleep, the Good Fairies place the entire kingdom under a spell so as to rescue Aurora without anyone knowing what has happened. The Fairies discover that Maleficent has already kidnapped the Prince, but they help him escape, and do battle with the fiery witch. After a spectacular battle, in which Maleficent takes the form of a dragon, the Prince emerges victorious, finds Aurora, and awakens her with a kiss. The kingdom is brought to life once more in the midst of its celebration for Aurora's sixteenth birthday and her impending marriage to the Prince.

The embroidery is neat and effective. The three fairies provide gentle comedy relief, trying to live in the forest as normal women, without the aid of their magical powers. They finally summon up their magic on Aurora's birthday in order to create a dress for her, leading to a running gag of whether it should be pink or blue; the two fairies in disagreement continue to change the color back and forth right through the last scene of the film.

Further comedy is provided by Aurora's father, King Stefan, and Prince Phillip's father, King Hubert, who eagerly anticipate the joining of their families in marriage. A prolonged comedy scene involving them is built around "The Skump Song," as they toast each other's happiness and engage in a teasing sort of rivalry.

Horror and suspense is provided by Maleficent, her pet raven, and her "goons," comic/evil characters who waddle around her castle as protectors (their amusing mumbles having been recorded by Candy Candido). Maleficent is evil personified, not only in the design of her face and costume, but in the black magic she conjures up, from a nightmarish vision of her prophecy, at Aurora's birth, to the flaming reality of her countenance as a dragon battling the Prince in the climactic scenes.

Aurora herself, called Briar Rose during her stay with the Fairies, is, as might be expected, pleasant, attractive, and largely nondescript, which just about sums up the Prince as well. Conscious of this, the film's creators find ways of providing additional points of interest in all their scenes. Virtually every scene of the Prince (until the final battle) is stolen by his horse, Samson, who is far more amusing than his stoic master.

The romantic scenes between Briar Rose and Phillip are abetted by an attractive song ("Once Upon a Dream"), a sequence of them dancing, their bodies reflected in a stream among picturesque forest settings, and a whole flock of cute animals who are Briar Rose's friends. One has no time to get involved with either Briar Rose or Phillip, which is as it should be.

The visual aspect of the film is quite staggering. After the traditional storybook opening, we join the royal celebration of the Princess's birth, heralded by the song "Hail the Princess Aurora." The pageant is shown from a lateral point of view, with five or six rows of people marching through the street—guards, jesters, spectators, banners flying, flags waving. This dissolves into the interior of the palace, seen from afar. From high up in the great hall, the camera slowly pans forward and downward to the center of activity. As it does, the camera passes through innumerable layers of columns, banners, arches, and such, a fantastic conglomeration of detail for what is essentially an establishing shot. (Its closest ancestor is the equally stunning shot of the village at morning in *Pinocchio*.)

Throughout *Sleeping Beauty*, detail is piled upon detail, with never-ending backgrounds, and a brilliant panorama of layout for each setting. Effects animation is brought into play in the opening sequence, when Flora and Fauna bestow their good wishes on the Princess, and these graces are envisioned in dreamlike visions. Then, when Maleficent describes her curse, we view it as a whirlpool of nightmarish scenes, swirling through the air as a montage shows us the fate that is to befall her.

Many critics found such details "oppressive," but it is difficult to pin this word on the film. There is no denying that *Sleeping Beauty* is much ado about nothing, while a film like *Dumbo* took its simple story and, through a general brightness and unpretentiousness, made every inch count without seeming "heavy." Yet *Sleeping Beauty* is only "heavy" in terms of the amount of effort put into the construction of the visuals. As entertainment, it moves very briskly, with an abundance of humor, romance, song, and suspense, skillfully intertwined so none of these elements seem out of proportion with the whole.

This time around, Disney was determined to have his human characters as realistic as possible. Once again, a live-action film was shot for the animators' use (with Helene Stanley, who had posed for Cinderella, repeating in the role of Sleeping Beauty, Ed Kemmer as the Prince, and Jane Fowler as the witch), and Disney insisted on perfection. "I had only one general suggestion for our animators [regarding the characters]," he explained. "Make them as real as possible, near flesh-and-blood . . . That is why we used living models more carefully than ever before, in order to give the artists inspiration, to help them shape the anatomy of movement and expression of the cartoon figures."

This, like Disney's other goals, was fully achieved in *Sleeping Beauty,* for unlike the two former princes in *Snow White* and *Cinderella,* Prince Phillip seemed to come to life, his climactic battle with Maleficent seeming chillingly real—too real for some observers, in fact. Bosley Crowther in the *New York Times* called the fight "the noisiest and scariest go-round he has ever put into one of his films . . . the question is whether he has fouled [the film] as a safe entertainment for little kids." The sight of a fire-breathing dragon filling the Technirama screen with searing flames aimed at Our Hero was indeed a considerable jolt for many small fry—and adults as well. The mood of the scene is heightened by George Bruns's electrifying music, adapted from Tchaikovsky. Though the score for the film is generally pleasant, it is this extended piece of music, accompanying the Prince's battle to reach Briar Rose, that really dazzles.

The flaw in *Sleeping Beauty* is the limit of its appeal. The problem is not that the dragon sequence is too scary for youngsters, but that it comes so late in the film. There is little else of an exciting nature in the narrative, and very little outright comedy for a red-blooded child to sink his teeth into. There are no patently comic creations in the film (like the dwarfs in *Snow White,* or the mice in *Cinderella;* the three fairies are a shallow substitute) to relieve the "ickiness" of the story for young boys who like to think they are beyond the stage of fairy tales but are still too young for the nuances of characterization that dot this film's comedy-relief personalities.

In short, *Sleeping Beauty* is a very good film, but more so for older audiences than for young children. The visual grandeur and the intricacy of the animation are lost on the tiny tots, who only want to see lots of color and movement, and be provided with some fun. The songs are lovely, based on Tchaikovsky themes that are certain to appeal to adults; but there is no "Heigh Ho" or "Cinderelly" to capture the fancy of eager kids. Girls might enjoy the situations of the three fairies trying to fashion a ball gown, but for young boys, it's hardly the thing.

To Disney's credit, he was aware of a possible barrier against this sector of his audience. "We had to find out what we had and whether it would please the public," he said. "I'm never sure myself what they're going to buy."

With *Sleeping Beauty*'s astronomical cost, the Disney organization decided to take no chances on losing their collective shirt, so in addition to a massive promotional campaign for the film, *Sleeping Beauty* was premiered at road-show prices around the country, even though there was no reserved-seat policy. To ward off criticism that $2.40 (the admission price in New York) was a lot to pay for a seventy-five-minute movie, a wide-screen short, *Grand Canyon,* was paired with the feature to round out the program.

The elaborate screen and sound processes were amply touted. This particular wide-screen process, Technirama 70, was based on a special system of film running through the camera horizontally, exposing two 35mm frames simultaneously. This unusual film is then printed normally on standard 35mm film and shown with an anamorphic lens for the wide-screen, extra-dimension effect. The promotion campaign had to combat some rather unenthusiastic reviews that, even in praising the film, compared it unfavorably with earlier Disney products.

In London, C. A. LeJeune wrote in the *Observer:*

Once upon a time, a couple of generations ago, Walt Disney, still a simple barnyard artist and the happy contriver of the Silly Symphonies, astonished the world and delighted most of it with his first full-length cartoon in color, *Snow White and the Seven Dwarfs.* Even where we criticized, we felt that Disney had the root of the matter in him. Here was a splendid new way of telling fairy stories, which should grow even better as the years went on.

Twenty-one years have passed since *Snow White,* and now Walt Disney Inc., master of many enterprises, presents us with Snow White's sister *Sleeping Beauty.* The two films have a great deal in common, apart from the marked family resemblance between the heroines, and the question naturally arises, has Disney's work developed from that time to this time? So far as techniques are concerned, yes, undoubtedly. In all that affects the imagination, regrettably but definitely no.

Still, *Sleeping Beauty* managed to gross $5.3 million in its initial release—helpful money for the depleted Disney coffers, but not enough to make it a success, official or otherwise. (It must be remembered that much of that money was accumulated from admission fees double those of most other Disney films.) The same year a modest comedy called *The Shaggy Dog*, produced for less than $1 million, earned back an astounding $9 million—and that without reserved-seat prices.

an astounding $8 million—and that without reserved-seat prices.

It proved to Disney that times indeed had changed since *Snow White,* that the fairy tale was no longer a viable format (except in the case of reissues, where he was bringing back films with established reputations), especially at his studio, where the well had apparently run dry for new variations on old themes. Animated cartoons were still feasible, but, obviously, they would have to rely on the same formulas that were making his live-action movies so successful—stories involving boys, dogs, and other animals.

As always, Disney took his cue from public response. *Sleeping Beauty* marked the end of an era at the Walt Disney studio.

THE SHAGGY DOG

RELEASED BY BUENA VISTA ON MARCH 19, 1959, Director: Charles Barton. Screenplay: Bill Walsh, Lillie Hayward, suggested by the novel *The Hound of Florence* by Felix Salten. Associate producer: Bill Walsh. Photography: Edward Colman. Editor: James D. Ballas. Art director: Carrol Clark. Set decorations: Emile Kuri, Fred MacLean. Costumes: Chuck Keehne, Gertrude Casey. Music: Paul J. Smith. Orchestrations: Joseph Mullendore. Assistant director: Arthur J. Vitarelli. Special titles: T. Hee, Bill Justice, Xavier Atencio. Animal supervision: William R. Koehler. Sound: Robert O. Cook, Harry M. Lindgren. Music editor: Evelyn Kennedy. Title song by Gil George and Paul Smith. Running time: 104 minutes.

Cast: Fred MacMurray (Wilson Daniels), Jean Hagen (Frieda Daniels), Tommy Kirk (Wilby Daniels), Annette Funicello (Allison D'Allessio), Tim Considine (Buzz Miller), Kevin Corcoran (Moochie Daniels), Cecil Kellaway (Professor Plumcutt), Alexander Scourby (Dr. Mikhail Andrassy), Roberta Shore (Franceska Andrassy), James Westerfield (Officer Hanson), Jacques Aubuchon (Stefano), Strother Martin (Thurm), Forrest Lewis (Officer Kelly), Ned Wever (E. P. Hackett), Gordon Jones (Captain Scanlon), John Hart (police broadcaster), Jack Albertson (reporter), Mack Williams (Betz), Paul Frees (psychiatrist), and Shaggy. Opening narration by Paul Frees.

Though essentially just a low-budget comedy,

shot in black and white, *The Shaggy Dog* is an important film in the chronology of Walt Disney's output. It was the first live-action comedy he ever made, and it was the first of his films to star Fred MacMurray. Its astounding success (grossing over $8 million in its first release) led to important changes in Disney's production outlook in the years that followed.

The story has a misfit teen-ager (Tommy Kirk) visiting a nearby museum and inadvertently taking with him (in his pants cuff) a ring which through an ancient spell transforms him into a large shaggy dog, identical to the one owned by neighbor Franceska Andrassy. Since the boy's father is allergic to dogs, he spends most of his time as a canine in the neighboring house, causing considerable confusion as he changes back and forth from boy to dog. While in the house, however, he overhears Franceska's father talking with an associate, and realizes that they are spies, planning to steal government missile plans. As the boy/dog convinces his father of his identity and is then discovered by the spies, a mad chase ensues, with Franceska being kidnapped by her own father, who hops aboard a motorboat to escape. The dog goes after it and saves Franceska when she is thrown overboard. When the police arrive and the enemies are caught, however, the dog is now a boy again, and the *real* dog gets the credit for everything.

On this slim story line the film is built, with various twists and turns and isolated gag sequences that have little to do with the story at hand.

The Shaggy Dog is a curious film. By rights, it

Tommy Kirk, as the shaggy dog, drives to the heroine's rescue.   © *Walt Disney Productions*

Now a hero, Fred MacMurray poses with the shaggy dog, along with Forrest Lewis, James Westerfield, Kevin Corcoran, Tommy Kirk, Tim Considine, and Jean Hagen.   © *Walt Disney Productions*

should be fast paced, broad entertainment, but, instead, it takes its own sweet time, never pushing for laughs, and ambling through 104 minutes of running time. There isn't even a final punch line, just a fade-out. In some ways this relaxed attitude is preferable to that of later Disney films where things are driven home so hard as to be obnoxious. Yet on the other hand, there is an almost lethargic manner to much of the film that kills many obvious opportunities.

Disney later revealed that the story was being originally considered as a TV series, and the film most definitely has its genesis in TV situation comedy. Father, as played by Fred MacMurray, is a total idiot,

and, although he is said to be a postman, he is never once shown working. Any hope of believability is tossed away in the scene where bumbling MacMurray goes to the police and tells them that his son is a dog, prompting a scene with a psychiatrist that Bosley Crowther pointed out "comes straight from *Harvey*."

The characters are purposely treated that way by director Charles Barton, a veteran of innumerable movies and, of course, TV situation comedies. He gets some nice moments out of this formula (such as husband and wife kissing each other good morning, blithely unaware that they have missed each other by a foot or two), but the film's most solid laughs involve simple sight gags of the sheep dog performing human tasks like brushing his teeth, gargling, wearing pajamas, and driving a car. It is this material that formed the foundation of the film's premise, and one wonders why it wasn't put to more extensive use.

Most critics were agreed that the premise of the comedy was a good one, but, in *Time*'s words, "Disney tells his shaggy-dog story so doggedly that he soon runs it into the pound." The premise alone was enough to draw millions of kids and adults into theatres around the country, and Disney realized that this combination of situation comedy and fantasy was one well worth pursuing (along with another idea, that of designing imaginative main titles, in order to capture the audience right away).

Of the film's star, *Variety* noted: "It's a pleasure to see such a master of timing and emphasis as Fred MacMurray back in comedy again, even though he is somewhat limited in his material. Where he has a good line, he shows that he has few peers in this special field of comedy." The romantic comedies that had made MacMurray a star in the 1930s were no longer being done in Hollywood, and of late he had drifted into routine Westerns. His expertise in *The Shaggy Dog* not only reaffirmed his comic prowess, but

convinced Disney that here was someone he should hold onto for future projects. The Disney-MacMurray relationship became a most fruitful one in years to come.

The final thing that the Disney people learned from this film was that repetition, and the obvious, were the surest laugh-getters of all. Running gags involving Forrest Lewis as a perplexed policeman paid off so well in this film that it was decided to use the actor again in *The Absent Minded Professor*. And from that film, elements were borrowed and repeated in the next comedy. It got to the point where audiences, particularly youthful ones, anticipated with glee the same faces and reactions they had enjoyed in earlier Disney comedies every time they went to the theatre. This preconditioning became a staple of Disney's product throughout the 1960s.

The film was successfully reissued in 1967 on a double bill with *The Absent-Minded Professor*. Then in 1976 the studio produced a popular sequel, *The Shaggy D.A.* Harry Anderson starred in a pair of TV movie remakes in 1988 and 1989; Ed Begley, Jr. toplined a 1995 TV remake in which the boy "morphed" into his shaggy alter ego, while Animatronics served as the dog's double in other scenes.

DARBY O'GILL AND THE LITTLE PEOPLE

RELEASED BY BUENA VISTA ON JUNE 26, 1959. TECHnicolor. Director: Robert Stevenson. Screenplay: Lawrence E. Watkin, suggested by the Darby O'Gill stories by H. T. Kavanagh. Photography: Winton C. Hoch. Editor: Stanley Johnson. Art director: Carroll Clark. Set decorations: Emile Kuri, Fred MacLean. Costumes: Chuck Keehne, Gertrude Casey. Music: Oliver Wallace. Orchestrations: Clifford Vaughan. Assistant director: Robert G. Shannon. Special photographic effects: Peter Ellenshaw, Eustace Lycett. Animation effects: Joshua Meador. Technical adviser: Michael O'Herlihy. Makeup: Pat McNalley. Hairstyling: Ruth Sandifer. Sound: Dean Thomas, Robert O. Cook. Running time: 93 minutes.

Songs: "The Wishing Song," "Pretty Irish Girl" by Oliver Wallace, Lawrence E. Watkin.

Cast: Albert Sharpe (Darby O'Gill), Janet Munro (Katie O'Gill), Sean Connery (Michael McBride), Jimmy O'Dea (King Brian), Kieron Moore (Pony Sugrue), Estelle Winwood (Sheelah), Walter Fitzgerald (Lord Fitzpatrick), Denis O'Dea (Father Murphy), J. G. Devlin (Tom Kerrigan), Jack Mac-

Gowran (Phadrig Oge), Farrell Pelly (Paddy Scanlon), Nora O'Mahony (Molly Malloy).

Darby O'Gill and the Little People is not only one of Disney's best films, but is certainly one of the best fantasies ever put on film. The key to its success is its convincingness; Disney knew this, and decided to carry out the theme of credibility to the last degree. Publicity stills of the producer "conferring" with King Brian of the Leprechauns were issued, stories of lengthy negotiations before permission was secured from the Little People were planted. And, as a finishing touch, a title on the film itself reads, "My thanks to King Brian of Knocknasheega and his leprechauns, whose gracious cooperation made this picture possible—Walt Disney."

Darby O'Gill is a roguish old storyteller who works as a caretaker on the governor's estate. When a younger man comes to take his place, and move into his house, Darby asks for time to break the news to his daughter Katie. That night Darby chases a runaway horse to the top of a haunted hill, where the horse suddenly rears, turns flaming colors and backs the

Find the special effects: that's Darby O'Gill playing for the leprechauns.   © *Walt Disney Productions*

Michael McBride (Sean Connery) and Katie O'Gill (Janet Munro) are off in Darby's horse cart to be married. © *Walt Disney Productions*

frightened man into a well. Darby tumbles down into the land of leprechauns, where King Brian explains that he has brought him there as a favor, so Darby won't have to make embarrassing explanations to his daughter.

The King asks Darby to play his violin, and the resulting celebration climaxes with the leprechauns opening the wall of their mountain home to ride outside and paint the town red. Darby manages to escape through the opening, and when Brian tracks him to his home, he gets the leprechaun into an all-night drinking session, until it is morning and the King's powers to return home are gone. Darby says he won't let the King go until he is granted three wishes.

Brian agrees, but tricks Darby into wasting two of his wishes. The third, Darby tells him, will be when he sees Katie and the new caretaker Michael McBride united in marriage. Brian tries to fix things in that direction, but the courtship is disrupted when Katie learns from meddlesome Pony Sugrue that Michael is taking her father's job away. That evening she goes after a runaway horse to the top of the same haunted hill, and, when the horse acts up, she falls and hits her head against the rocks.

Katie lies near death, and Darby hears the cry of the banshee, a sure sign that the worst is near. Then, from the sky, comes the dreaded Costa Bower, the Death Coach. Darby, in anguish, tells Brian that his third wish is to be taken away in Katie's place, and Brian reluctantly agrees. The coach lands and its headless driver asks for Darby, who gets inside. Then Brian tricks Darby into making a fourth wish—and everyone knows that a fourth wish always cancels out the previous three. Brian kicks Darby out of the coach, and he lands in front of his own house, where inside, Katie has undergone a miraculous recovery.

Michael challenges his rival, Pony Sugrue, to a fight, in return for the trouble he has caused between himself and Katie, and, having licked him, wins Katie's hand in marriage. Darby drives them off in his carriage for the finale.

Darby O'Gill and the Little People was more than twenty years in the making. Disney had his eye on the original stories in the mid-1940s, and in the summer of 1946 sent several artists to Ireland for background material. In 1947 he hired Lawrence Watkin to work on a script for the film. In December 1948 Disney himself visited Ireland, and announced that the film, then called *The Little People,* would be made soon. When he saw the Broadway hit *Finian's Rainbow,* with Albert Sharpe as the canny Irishman, he knew he had his star player.

Yet the project was constantly being set aside in favor of more immediate tasks. The twenty years were not wasted, however, for it is likely that the detail and meticulous handling the film received could not have resulted from a standard one to two year preparation period. Here was a case of Disney knowing exactly what he wanted, and having the patience to wait for the best results.

The special effects are breathtaking, and in the instance of the Death Coach, absolutely terrifying. The coach travels down from the skies in a winding route, becoming more horrifying as it gets closer and we see the color-negative image of the coach and four being driven by a headless man.

Yet the most impressive effects in the film are the ones that inspire the least immediate reaction, namely the scenes with the leprechauns. Disney's idea was to make these sequences *so* realistic that they would seem absolutely natural, and, indeed, after a while, one finds oneself believing completely that Darby is really talking to a twenty-one-inch king! The scene of Darby standing in the great hall of Knocknasheega, playing the violin as the little people dance gaily around him, is an example of this movie magic. There cannot possibly be any trickery here—he's really standing there surrounded by leprechauns!

There are many other subtle effects throughout the film, such as the delightful scene where King Brian talks to Michael and then Katie in their sleep, trying to bring the couple together. He climbs up Katie's bedpost and talks to her; when she involuntarily answers him, she wakes herself up, and he instantly disappears. Then when she goes back to sleep, he materializes once more and continues his conversation.

The film is also full of Peter Ellenshaw's exquisite matte shots, showing the village, the local scenery, and the haunted hill—all responsible for making it seem as if the film were really shot in Ireland, when the entire picture was made in California on the Albertson and Rowland Lee ranches and on two large sound stages at the Disney studio.

Color control is also magnificent in this film, dictated down to the smallest detail. In the opening scene, for instance, when a magistrate drives up in a horse-drawn carriage, the high wheels of the coach are painted bright yellow—a minor point, to be sure, yet just one of hundreds of factors that combine to make *Darby* such a visual delight.

The performances are also a joy, with a hand-picked cast largely imported from the Dublin stage, and such troupes as the Abbey and Ulster theatres. *Variety* wrote: "Sharpe's performance is a gem. He benefits from the combination of being lovable, yet humanly frail and prone to greed and pride . . . but embellishes the role with a refreshingly individual manner of expression that should endear him." Jimmie O'Dea is every bit his match as King Brian, striking the perfect blend of charm and deviousness that characterizes the leprechauns in general.

With this film Disney signed Janet Munro to a contract, and her fresh beauty and ingratiating charm became a solid asset for several Disney films over the next few years. Her screen partner, Sean Connery, impressed no one at this time, and it was several years before he became a superstar with the James Bond series.

Lawrence Watkin's screenplay is little short of brilliant, deriving humor, horror, romance, and *humanity* from the basic situations, giving voice to breezy Irish wit but also leaving room for sentimentality. The question of whether the leprechauns are real or just a figment of Darby's imagination is nicely handled throughout the film, with a satisfying conclusion implying that if someone believes in something, that's all that really counts—*not* what others may think.

This was Robert Stevenson's first major film for Disney, and on the strength of it earned the director many plum assignments from the studio in years to follow. Though most Disney features are a team effort, there can be no denying that without a good director at the helm, seemingly surefire elements can fizzle out. Stevenson brought to his films a skill and taste that always got the most out of every given situation, instead of merely recording the action on film. It is no coincidence that many of Disney's best live-action films bear his name.

As with many of Disney's best films, this production, with its visual beauty, great performances, lilting music (which propels so much of the film's action),

and genuine wit, has more appeal to older audiences than it has for children, especially very young children. The *New York Time*'s A. H. Weiler reported that "a large, restless contingent of small fry at yesterday's initial showing of the picture . . . seemed more entranced by the cavortings of Donald Duck and Pluto in an old short called *Beach Picnic* than in the adventures of Darby and his ilk." There was also concern that many, especially younger, viewers would have difficulty cutting through the heavy Irish accents. There was so much concern, in fact, that when *Darby* didn't do as well as anticipated at the box office, Disney had the film dubbed for reissue!

Critical reaction to the film was mild at best, the *New York Herald Tribune* echoing the lukewarm response by calling it "an innocent diversion." This kind of assessment, coupled with the film's disappointing box-office take, must have been a bitter pill for Disney to swallow, having lavished so much love and care (not to mention money) on the production. It is certainly a sad comment on mass taste to note that a beautiful film like this should fail to attract half the audience that rushed to see *The Shaggy Dog*. It also answers the question of why the following years saw so few Disney films the caliber of *Darby* and so many in the spirit of *The Shaggy Dog*.

THIRD MAN ON THE MOUNTAIN

Released by buena vista on november 10, 1959. Technicolor. Producer: William H. Anderson. Director: Ken Annakin. Screenplay: Eleanore Griffin, based on the book, *Banner in the Sky*, by James Ramsey Ullman. Photography: Harry Waxman. Mountain unit photography: Georges Tairraz. Editor: Peter Boita. Music: William Alwyn. Conductor: Muir Mathieson. Choreography: Mme. Derivaz. Associate producer: Alan L. Jaggs. Production manager: Basil Keys. Assistant director: Gerald O'Hara. Matte artist: Peter Ellenshaw. Mountain unit director: Gaston Rebuffat. Production design: John Howell. Zermatt liaison: Bernhardt Biner. Sound: Chris Greenham. Running time: 105 minutes.

Songs: "Climb the Mountain" by Franklyn Marks, By Dunham. "Good Night Valais" by G. Haenni, Tom Adair.

Cast: Michael Rennie (Captain John Winter), James MacArthur (Rudi Matt), Janet Munro (Lizbeth Hempel), James Donald (Franz Lerner), Herbert

Lom (Emil Saxo), Laurence Naismith (Teo Zurbriggen), Lee Patterson (Klaus Wesselhoft), Walter Fitzgerald (Herr Hempel), Nora Swinburne (Frau Mott), Ferdy Mayne (Andreas), James Ramsey Ullman, and in a cameo role as a tourist, Helen Hayes.

"At this time," director Ken Annakin recalls, "Walt had taken a shine to Switzerland and everything Swiss. He used to go there on his summer holidays every year, and adored it, and this story he felt would be the thing for all young people. No effort was spared to make it as entertaining as the holiday which Walt was taking in Switzerland proved to be for him."

But expansive Swiss scenery is not what makes this an exceptional film; rather, it is the excellent script, based on a true story of a famous mountain climber and the determined Swiss boy who vowed to climb the impregnable Matterhorn (here called the Citadel). The boy has a special incentive in that his father was killed making the same attempt. After

James MacArthur, Michael Rennie, and Herbert Lom on their way to the top of the Citadel. © *Walt Disney Productions*

Director Ken Annakin supervises the setups on location in Zermatt.   *Courtesy Ken Annakin*

Janet Munro stands by MacArthur and encourages him to climb the mountain.   © *Walt Disney Productions*

saving the life of Captain Winter, the mountaineer, he is invited to join the expedition, but his youthful inexperience and foolish daring cause trouble during the first climb, and he is humiliated. His mother and uncle, still shaken from the death of his father, forbid him to do any more climbing.

Young Rudi will not be discouraged, however, and with the help of his friend Lizbeth and employer, Herr Zurbriggen, he practices climbing until he is expert; more important, he learns some fundamental principles: that one must never put another man's life in jeopardy, and that one must always think of one's fellow climbers first.

None of the local climbers or guides will accompany Winter on his trip up the Citadel, so he hires a surly but expert guide named Emil Saxo from a rival village. Their pride wounded, the local guides decide to go after Winter and join him. Young Rudi makes the same decision, but before joining the others, he searches for the secret passageway his father was seeking when he died, and miraculously finds it, all on his own. He returns to the cabin where the others are staying and tells of his discovery. It is then decided that four men will make the final climb: Rudi, Winter, Emil, and Rudi's uncle. But Winter hits his head and lies in pain during the night. Saxo tries to sneak off alone, but Rudi sees him and goes along. The next day, as both groups of two are nearing the top, Saxo falls. He tells Rudi to go on and get to the peak, but Rudi remembers his teachings, and works instead to help the injured man and return him safely to the village. Winter and Rudi's uncle are proclaimed the heroes, for conquering the Citadel, but Winter explains to the cheering townspeople that Rudi is the *real* hero—truly his father's son.

What may read as being corny is carried off beautifully on film, for *Third Man on the Mountain* is youthful adventure at its best, breathtakingly exciting, and at the same time a valuable story at the human level. Throughout there is the theme of the young boy doing what he was born to do; in the climax there is the lesson of unselfishness that figures crucially in Rudi's decision between seeking personal glory or doing what he knows is right.

Time magazine captured the film's essence perfectly when it predicted that it "may well become a children's classic of the screen, a sort of 'Tom Sawyer in the Alps.'" The comparison is not inapt, for like Twain's best works, which never sacrifice entertainment value while making observations about people and life, *Third Man on the Mountain* strikes the same happy medium.

The performances are excellent in the first-rate cast, from James MacArthur as the young hero, and delightful Janet Munro as his girl friend who spurs him on to success, to supporting players such as Laurence Naismith, who runs the inn where the day-dreaming MacArthur works.

But the script and performances would be meaningless without the epic scope of this production, which makes every moment vividly *real*—largely because most of it *was*.

Says director Annakin:

Walt found one of the great Alpine climbers, Gaston Rebuffat, a Frenchman whose home was in Chamonix. Before we ever started we had to go to Chamonix and go up Mont Blanc with him, and watch him climbing a rock face. It became obvious that neither I nor the actors nor any unit could do the sort of climbs that Rebuffat did. His whole life seemed to be hanging on ledges literally by his fingernails. He had no nerves at all, and to our point of view was quite mad. But he was also a very good photographer, and it was arranged that after we had laid out the action for the film, the climbing action, he would come study it and then go out and shoot doubles.

I went to Burbank and worked there for three months with Walt on the story and drawings. Then Rebuffat came over for a week. We sent him back fully briefed to Chamonix, where he produced all the astounding stuff that's in the film. I was then able to match, not in the studio, but on real rock faces, much of the action he had done with doubles, but of course in this picture it was impossible to tackle it at all unless the actors became climbers too, unless they knew how to react as climbers, and be in some position where one really did have falls below them.

So I got the cast together and for two weeks they each had a guide allocated to them and learned to climb. Jimmy MacArthur took to it like a duck to water, and actually on his first rest day sneaked off, to the horror of the insurance people when they learned about it afterwards, and climbed the Matterhorn.

Even with this general enthusiasm on the part of the cast and crew, there were still tremendous problems in getting certain shots, because of inaccessibility to locations. Mule packs had to be used to reach certain spots, and when that was impossible helicopters were recruited. On at least one occasion, however, the entire company had to walk back to camp at day's end along a treacherous glacier, because it was too foggy for the helicopters!

Some apparently simple shots also required considerable ingenuity, such as one lovely sequence where James MacArthur and Janet Munro walk through a field of bright yellow flowers. Says Annakin:

There was only one week when we were able to shoot this, because of the flowers coming out. We had to take great care to have sufficient area to work on so when we tramped down the flowers we could still move on to another patch. This is something that one was able to do in films at that time. A producer like Walt was prepared to let you take any reasonable amount of time to achieve beauty, or the effect that he agreed was good. Today, when they're having to make pictures on a million or two million dollars with the accountants watching every single move, that sort of shooting would be quite impossible.

In spite of all the outstanding real-life locations, some trickery was still necessary. It was felt that one of Peter Ellenshaw's painted mattes could show the depth of fall in many cases more convincingly than the real view, obscured by clouds, shadows, intervening ledges, etc.

The overall effect of the film is staggering. As in Disney's best films, the audience becomes truly involved with the characters, and, in this case, MacArthur's characterization is designed to capture the hearts of every red-blooded viewer in the theatre. From the opening shot of the film, where he climbs a mountain peak and contentedly surveys the beautiful surroundings, the audience is with him all the way. The combination of this empathy with the people on screen and the grandeur of the scenery makes the film an exciting and memorable experience.

Variety said of *Third Man on the Mountain:* "It has the sort of high altitude thrills to send the viewer cowering deep in his seat and the sort of moving drama to put him on the edge of it." Some critics, like Crowther of the *Times,* were a bit more aloof, but most agreed it was rousing adventure, and no one could fault the magnificent scenery.

Very few viewers would have noticed the author of the book, James Ramsey Ullman, doing a walk-on in the film, but some astute people in the audience got an unexpected treat spotting James MacArthur's mother, Helen Hayes, in an amusing cameo as a tourist asking directions.

Unfortunately, *Third Man on the Mountain* was another example of a meticulously crafted, expensive Disney film that did not perform especially well at the box office. It has since been shown on the Disney TV show, retitled *Banner in the Sky.*

TOBY TYLER, OR TEN WEEKS WITH A CIRCUS

RELEASED BY BUENA VISTA ON JANUARY 21, 1960. Technicolor. Director: Charles Barton. Screenplay: Bill Walsh, Lillie Hayward, based on the novel by James Otis Kaler. Photography: William Snyder. Editor: Stanley Johnson. Associate producer: Bill Walsh. Art director: Carroll Clark, I. Stanford Jolley. Set decorations: Emile Kuri, Fred MacLean. Costumes: Chuck Keehne, Gertrude Casey. Music: Buddy Baker. Orchestrations: Walter Sheets. Assistant director: Arthur J. Vitarelli. Matte artist: Peter Ellenshaw. Special effects: Ub Iwerks. Makeup: Pat McNalley. Hairstyling: Ruth Sandifer. Sound: Robert O. Cook, Dean Thomas. Music editor: Evelyn Kennedy. Running time: 96 minutes.

Song: "Biddle-dee-dee" by Diane Lampert, Richard Loring.

Cast: Kevin Corcoran (Toby Tyler), Henry Calvin (Ben Cotter), Gene Sheldon (Sam Treat), Bob Sweeney (Harry Tupper), Richard Eastham (Colonel Sam Castle), James Drury (Jim Weaver), Barbara Beaird (Mademoiselle Jeanette), Dennis Joel (Monsieur Ajax), Edith Evanson (Aunt Olive), Tom Fadden (Uncle Daniel), Ollie Wallace (bandleader),

and Mr. Stubbs (himself). With The Flying Viennas, The Jungleland Elephants, The Marquis Family, and the Ringling Brothers Clowns ("Eddie Spaghetti" Emerson, Abe "Korky" Goldstein, Duke Johnson, Harry Johnson).

Before the main titles of this film, young Toby Tyler (played by Kevin "Moochie" Corcoran) scampers out of his farmhouse to read the circus posters and see the big parade. The film takes place at the turn of the century, when "the day the circus came to town was the biggest day of the year."

In that spirit the film paints a colorful, nostalgic picture of circus life as orphan Toby runs away from home after being abusively scolded by his "Uncle" Daniel. He is offered a job by sharpie concessionaire Harry Tupper, and immediately falls in love with circus life. He is befriended by the circus strong man, Ben Cotter, whose gruff exterior covers a warm heart, and whose no-nonsense attitude holds Harry Tupper in check when Cotter catches him mistreating the boy. Toby also gets friendly with a wildly mischievous monkey named Mr. Stubbs.

He is most intrigued with the young bareback rider, Mademoiselle Jeanette, much to the chagrin of her partner, Monsieur Ajax. Trying to show off for

Harry Tupper (Bob Sweeney) takes Toby (Kevin Corcoran) under his wing. © *Walt Disney Productions*

Gene Sheldon feeds castor oil to an ailing Mr. Stubbs, as
Corcoran watches apprehensively. © *Walt Disney Productions*

Jeanette, Ajax attempts a practice run without his safety harness, and falls, injuring himself. Colonel Castle, the circus owner, is distraught, until Jeanette suggests that Toby could take Ajax's place. It takes a lot of training, but he finally gets in shape to perform the difficult routine. What he doesn't know is that Tupper is collecting a weekly finder's fee for Toby, and hiding from him letters from his aunt that tell of his uncle's illness. (After all, if Toby goes home, Tupper will lose his weekly commission.)

Toby finds the letters, however, and runs off; Mr. Stubbs follows close behind. A hunter inadvertently shoots the monkey, just as Tupper finds Toby to bring him back. When he returns, however, his aunt and uncle are there; he has recovered, and is apologetic for the unkind things he said to Toby. What's more, Mr. Stubbs is recuperating nicely. Toby's aunt and uncle stay for the performance, proudly watching their boy, as does another youngster—Tupper's *new* assistant.

Toby Tyler has little plot to speak of; instead, it presents a series of vignettes against the magnetic background of a turn of the century traveling circus, making the central character as identifiable to a young audience as possible in the best Disney tradition. The resulting film is quite pleasant, and, since it lacks pretentious goals, seems to fulfill its obligations very nicely.

The depiction of circus life is neatly delineated, leaving room for oily con men as well as kindly clowns (as in the character played by Gene Sheldon, the friendliest person in the film), with others falling in between the two extremes.

The hardest thing to take in the narrative is the monkey, Mr. Stubbs, whose supposedly hilarious antics cause nothing but trouble and hardship for Toby and everyone else in the circus. The ever-growing penchant for finding destructive animals "cute" in Disney films was already beginning to pall on adult audiences at this time, though provoking absolutely surefire laughter from the small fry.

Toby Tyler was directed by Charles Barton, following his successful *Shaggy Dog,* and, as with most free-lancers who worked at the studio, Barton found the working atmosphere ideal; he refers to Disney as "a wonderful man." The cast was made up largely from Disney contractees. Kevin Corcoran was at this time a star with the younger set, known as Moochie from his character in the serialized adventures on the Disney TV show. Both Henry Calvin and Gene Sheldon were equally well known for their major roles on the *Zorro* series. Bob Sweeney was a familiar face to most adult TV fans from his prolific appearances on the tube; it was later that he eschewed acting for a career as producer/director.

The final card title in the credits for this film reads, "and introducing Ollie Wallace." This was really an inside joke at the studio, for veteran Disney composer/conductor Wallace was cast in the film as the circus bandleader, a colorful if minor role.

Oddly enough, *Toby Tyler* won Disney some of his best reviews in years, most critics singling out the simplicity of the production as its major asset. Howard Thompson wrote in the *New York Times:* "The very smallness of the setting pulls the gallery of circus people into cozy focus . . . this little picture . . . shines from within, mildly but sweetly." And the *Herald Tribune*'s Paul V. Beckley called it "a minor classic among children's movies."

But with its modest intentions and modest backing, *Toby Tyler* was only a modest success; fortunately, its period setting and flavor will keep it fresh for reissue and television showing for many years to come, giving more people an opportunity to enjoy the warmhearted nostalgia it has to offer children of all ages.

KIDNAPPED

RELEASED BY BUENA VISTA ON MARCH 25, 1960 (PRE-release engagements, February 24, 1960). Technicolor. Director, screenplay: Robert Stevenson, based on the novel by Robert Louis Stevenson. Photography: Paul Beeson. Editor: Gordon Stone. Associate producer: Hugh Attwooll. Art director: Carmen Dillon. Set decorations: Vernon Dixon. Costumes: Margaret Furse. Music: Cedric Thorpe Davie. Conductor: Muir Mathieson. Production manager: Frank Ernst. Assistant director: Peter Manley. Special photographic effects: Peter Ellenshaw. Story sketches: Donald Da Gradi. Camera operator: Alan Hume. Continuity: Pamela Carlton. Casting: Maude Spencer. Dialect adviser: John Breslin. Makeup: Stewart Freeborn. Hairstyling: Florrie Hyde. Sound: Lionel Selwyn, Leo Wilkins, Bill Daniels. Running time: 97 minutes.

Cast: Peter Finch (Alan Breck Stewart), James MacArthur (David Balfour), Bernard Lee (Captain Hoseason), Niall MacGinnis (Shaun), John Laurie (Uncle Ebenezer), Finlay Currie (Cluny MacPherson), Peter O'Toole (Robin Oig MacGregor), Miles Malleson (Mr. Rankeillor), Oliver Johnston (Mr. Campbell), Duncan MacRae (The Highlander), John Pike (cabin boy), Andrew Cruickshank (Colin Roy Campbell), Abe Barker (Donald Dhu Mac-

Laren), Eileen Way (Jennet Clouston), Alex Mac-Kenzie (the ferryman).

Kidnapped was Walt Disney's first stab at Robert Louis Stevenson since *Treasure Island* a decade before, and his first British-based production since *The Sword and the Rose*. This time, curiously enough, the film was directed by a transplanted Briton who had established himself with Disney in California! Although innumerable press releases claimed that Robert Stevenson was a distant relative of the author, Stevenson later denied any such puffery.

True to his namesake, Stevenson's script is a faithful retelling of the famous novel. It opens as young David Balfour sees his father buried. A letter written before his death tells David that he should go to see his Uncle Ebenezer and stay with him. Uncle, it turns out, is a crabby and crafty old gent who tries to do David in as soon as he arrives. The boy then starts investigating the mystery of the relationship between his father and his uncle, and discovers that the estate rightfully belonged to his father, not to Ebenezer. When Ebenezer senses that the boy knows too much, he has him shanghaied aboard a strange vessel.

When the cabin boy is murdered by a drunken ship's mate, David is pressed into service. One night the ship collides with a smaller boat in the fog, and the lone survivor is taken aboard. He is Alan Breck Stewart, a Scottish loyalist who opposes British rule. He bargains with the captain to take him to Scotland, but David learns that the captain really plans to kill Stewart. He tells this to Stewart and sides with him; together, they miraculously manage to defeat the rest of the crew and take the ship. Near shore, they run aground, and David is washed overboard.

When he arrives safely on shore, he tries to find Stewart, and, as he is walking along, encounters Colin Roy Campbell and his militia; they stop to question David, and as they do, Colin Roy is assassinated. David runs, and finds Stewart lurking in the hills; he swears to David that he didn't fire the shot, and persuades him to join him in fleeing to free land outside British rule. It takes a lot of doing, but after a number of dangerous incidents, they make it.

Returning home, David sees his family lawyer, who confirms what he had suspected, that the Balfour estate is now rightfully his, but he must have evidence of Ebenezer's chicanery, so he enlists the aid of Stewart for a return favor. With David and the lawyer hiding outside where they can hear everything, Stewart goes to the estate and wrings the truth out of him. When the words come out of Ebenezer's mouth, the lawyer moves in to claim the estate for David.

Now a young man with responsibilities, David stays behind as Stewart sails off for new adventure; but they part as friends, who have helped each other before and may do so again.

Kidnapped is a carefully made, properly atmospheric rendering of Stevenson's story, with excellent performances by all concerned. Unfortunately, many of the film's key plot points, and motivations, are foggy, especially to younger viewers, and *Kidnapped* never arouses much excitement. American critics who had found *Treasure Island* a bit too flamboyant now found themselves longing for that quality in the new film.

Variety wrote: "It is never clear what the aim of the principals is, so there is not much for the spectator to pull for. Individual scenes play, but there is no mounting or cumulative effect." And *Time* added: "Stevenson's casual classic was written, he confessed, with 'no more desperate purpose than to steal some young gentleman's attention from his Ovid.' Disney's movie version may persuade the young gentleman that Latin homework is a comparative pleasure . . ."

This is really a shame, because director/scenarist Stevenson obviously put so much into the film. There is no shortage of atmosphere, as in an opening scene where, amid darkened skies and gusty winds, David approaches his uncle's estate and meets two strange passersby who warn him against going there. Life on the ship is equally vivid; in one memorable scene where David and Stewart are holding off the crew's attack from inside their cabin, one pirate gets inside, forcing David to shoot him at close range. Afterward he is distraught at his own brutality, and Stewart sympathizes with him. (Critic Arthur Knight, in a favorable review of the film, noted that "not the least of its virtues is the fact that the film takes a forthright stand against killing, drinking and gambling without ever being mealy-mouthed or self-conscious about it.")

There is vigor in the character performances as well. Old reliable Finlay Currie is good as a friendly laird who gives the two refugees shelter for a night, and other venerable British actors such as Niall MacGinnis and Miles Malleson contribute assured performances. One of the film's key points of interest, in retrospect, is the casting of then unknown Peter O'Toole (with his original nose) as the son of Rob Roy MacGregor, who contemplates turning in Stewart, but, after challenging him to a battle of bagpipes, acknowledges that they are of equal mettle.

But alas, the film seems more intent on reproducing Stevenson's tale than providing genuine full-blooded entertainment. There is the famous scene of David running to the top of Ebenezer's winding stairway, which ends in a precipice, many feet up in the air, but such exciting scenes are few and far between.

British critics praised the film for its "remarkable fidelity" to the book, but American critics were less impressed (and somewhat put off by the Scottish accents), and, consequently, the film was not very successful. It played on the Disney TV show just a few years after its theatrical release.

Alan Breck Stewart (Peter Finch) and David Balfour (James MacArthur) do their best to hold off the savage crew. © *Walt Disney Productions*

Finlay Currie toasts Finch and MacArthur during a stop-over on their way back to England and safety. © *Walt Disney Productions*

POLLYANNA

RELEASED BY BUENA VISTA ON MAY 19, 1960. TECH-
nicolor. Director, screenplay: David Swift, based on
the novel by Eleanor H. Porter. Associate producer:
George Golitzen. Photography: Russell Harlan. Edi-
tor: Frank Gross. Art directors: Carroll Clark, Robert
Clatworthy. Set decorations: Emile Kuri, Fred Mac-
Lean. Costumes: Walter Plunkett. Assistants: Chuck
Keehne, Gertrude Casey. Music: Paul J. Smith. Or-
chestrations: Franklyn Marks. Assistant director:
Joseph Behm. Matte artist: Peter Ellenshaw. Special
effects: Ub Iwerks. Sequence consultant: Donald Da
Gradi. Dialogue coach: Leon Charles. Makeup: Pat
McNalley, Hairstyling: Ruth Sandifer. Sound: Robert
O. Cook, Dean Thomas. Music editor: Evelyn Ken-
nedy. Running time: 134 minutes.

Cast: Hayley Mills (Pollyanna), Jane Wyman (Aunt
Polly), Richard Egan (Dr. Edmund Chilton), Karl
Malden (Reverend Paul Ford), Nancy Olson (Nancy
Furman), Adolphe Menjou (Mr. Pendergast), Don-
ald Crisp (Mayor Karl Warren), Agnes Moorehead
(Mrs. Snow), Kevin Corcoran (Jimmy Bean), James
Drury (George Dodds), Reta Shaw (Tillie Lagerlof),
Leora Dana (Mrs. Paul Ford), Anne Seymour (Mrs.
Amelia Tarbell), Edward Platt (Ben Tarbell), Mary
Grace Canfield (Angelica), Jenny Egan (Mildred
Snow), Gage Clarke (Mr. Murg), Ian Wolfe (Mr.
Neely), Nolan Leary (Mr. Thomas), Edgar Dearing
(Mr. Gorman), Harry Harvey (editor), William
Newell (Mr. Hooper).

Critics who went to see *Pollyanna* expecting a
sloppily sentimental, tear-jerking film were astonished
to discover a beautifully acted, intelligently scripted
film of genuine warmth, one of the best live-action
films Disney ever made. It marked the American
debut of the remarkable young Hayley Mills, daughter of actor John Mills, and, more surprisingly, the
feature-film debut of director/scenarist David Swift. It
also boasted a star cast unusual for a Disney film, and
many behind-the-scenes technicians imported from
other studios especially for this picture. Obviously,
Pollyanna was earmarked as something special, and
that's exactly what it turned out to be.

The story is basically the familiar one written by
Eleanor H. Porter. Orphaned Pollyanna comes to live
with her wealthy Aunt Polly in Harrington, circa
1912. She immediately starts upsetting things in the
very proper household and throughout the town, with

her uncanny knack for seeing the bright side of things
(in what she calls "the glad game," always finding
something to be glad about), with which she overpowers some of the town's leading malcontents.

Her first friend in town is Jimmy Bean, a carefree
youngster from the town orphanage. Together they
engage in various adventures.

Pollyanna first goes to visit crotchety old Mrs.
Snow, a hypochondriac invalid who feels sorry for
herself. Pollyanna is the first person who doesn't sym-
pathize with the old woman, and eventually wins her
over with her honesty and friendliness.

Then she and Jimmy meet the hermitlike Mr.
Pendergast, who catches them trespassing on his property, but instead of scolding them, becomes another
friend, interesting the youngsters in glass prisms, and
the colorful light they spread around his home.

Pollyanna then works her magic on the town
preacher, Reverend Ford. Every Sunday his hellfire-
and-brimstone sermons (usually recommended by
Aunt Polly, who for all intents and purposes runs the
entire town) give everyone indigestion. The young
girl finds him rehearsing a sermon one afternoon, and
he confesses to her that he feels he isn't reaching his
congregation. She tells him that her father, a missionary, taught her a valuable lesson, which he inscribed
on a charm: When you look for the bad in mankind,
you will surely find it. He is dumbfounded with the
shock of discovery, and that Sunday he comes to
church a new man, telling the congregation that he
intends to spend future sermons exploring the *joy* in
the Bible—and he also vows to get to know his people
much better.

Finally, Pollyanna plays matchmaker for Aunt
Polly and young Dr. Chilton, who had once been
sweethearts several years ago. Since then, Aunt Polly
has become more and more spinsterish, and her niece
is determined to do something about it.

One thing that comes between Polly and Dr.
Chilton is the subject of the town orphanage, which
Aunt Polly sponsors. A new one is needed, and Chilton organizes a bazaar to raise money for it. At first,
most of the townspeople are afraid to oppose Polly
Harrington openly, but bit by bit enthusiasm grows,
especially when meek Reverend Ford decides to take a
stand and support the event.

Pollyanna is forbidden to go, but Jimmy Bean
helps her climb through her window, down a tree, in
order to attend. She has the time of her life, and even
wins a doll—her very first. Going home that night, she

climbs the tree and is almost inside when she drops her doll; reaching for it, she falls to the ground with a scream.

The next day it becomes clear that her legs are paralyzed. Dr. Chilton arranges to take her to Baltimore for immediate surgery, but he tells Aunt Polly that surgery cannot do anything for Pollyanna's state of mind. For the first time she is sullen, and she rejects the glad game as being stupid. But then an amazing thing happens. People, hundreds of them, gather on the front lawn and knock on Aunt Polly's door. They say that they are friends of Pollyanna, and they want to wish her well. Dr. Chilton brings her downstairs, and she sees just how much she has meant to so many people in town. Mrs. Snow is no longer an invalid, Reverend Ford is now part of the community, and Mr. Pendergast is even going to adopt Jimmy Bean. And Aunt Polly realizes that all this time she has given everything to Pollyanna, and to the town, but love, and that's more important than anything. As Pollyanna is taken to the train, the whole town comes to see her off, and as the train pulls out of the station, a sign is hung from the station platform: Harrington—The Glad Town.

Pollyanna is a lovely film in every respect. Its sentiment is derived from natural situations, and it never descends into bathos. The characters are all three-dimensional in situations where they might have been played as stereotypes. Aunt Polly, for instance, is not wicked, but a woman with a flaw—she has become cold and unloving. None of the other transformations are miraculous, because the people had goodness in them all along—even Mr. Pendergast, who clearly has a gleam in his eye even while bawling out little Jimmy Bean. It just took Pollyanna to bring out the goodness inside these people. Contrast this with the earlier version of the film made in 1920 with Mary Pickford. It too is most enjoyable, but it's largely played for comedy, and the characters surrounding Mary, especially Aunt Polly, *are* caricatures. This doesn't take away from the comic aspect of the film; it just makes it less real.

The settings of the film are appropriately realistic. Most of the exteriors were filmed in Santa Rosa, California, and in the Napa Valley, doubling quite nicely for early century New England. Actual settings such as the train station, with a period locomotive, add to the flavor. The interiors, from the church (apparently real) to the sumptuous home of Aunt Polly, are ideal in carrying out the goal of realism.

Scenes like the opening one, in which the main titles are superimposed over shots of Jimmy Bean rolling a hoop through the picturesque town, are delightful in capturing the nostalgic feeling for such lovely period settings.

Both the art director, Robert Clatworthy, and the costume designer, Walter Plunkett, were hired for the picture from other studios, bringing with them a skill for creating exactly the kind of colorful stylishness required for the film. *Pollyanna* has a rich, quality look unique among Disney films of this period.

Publicity releases declared that *Pollyanna* boasted "the most important star cast in the history of the Disney studios," and this was not exaggeration. The large cast was obviously handpicked, resulting in

Hayley Mills, Jane Wyman, and Anne Seymour in *Pollyanna.* © *Walt Disney Productions*

Pollyanna plays with one of the prisms in the home of Mr. Pendergast (Adolphe Menjou). © *Walt Disney Productions*

a fantastic array of first-rate character portrayals, with Karl Malden, Adolphe Menjou (whose last film this was), and Agnes Moorehead standing out. Even the character bits were filled by such reassuringly familiar faces as Ian Wolfe, Edgar Dearing, and Harry Harvey, screen veterans all.

Variety called the film "a personal triumph for Hayley Mills," echoing the sentiments of most reviewers. Walt Disney happened to be watching a British film called *Tiger Bay* to see John Mills, whom he was considering for the leading role in *The Swiss Family Robinson*. At the same time he was amazed at the performance of Mills's daughter in this, her first film, and he immediately signed her to a contract. Wrote the London *Observer:* "It is sheer joy to watch and listen to her, and since she seems to have the gift of touching off the talents in her fellow actors, *Pollyanna* turns out to be a very charming and amusing film, with a spring freshness that is never mawkish."

The film also marked another equally impressive debut; it was the first feature film for director/writer David Swift, who had worked for Disney in the late 1930s, starting as office boy and working up to becoming assistant animator to Ward Kimball. He left in the 1940s, and made his mark the following decade when he created the successful TV series "Mr. Peepers." After considerable work in television, Disney gave him his first chance at doing a feature, and he did a remarkable job.

Someone once asked Samuel Goldwyn how long a movie should be. "How long is it good?" Goldwyn replied. *Pollyanna* is one of the longest films Disney ever released, yet its length is justified by the carefully crafted script that constantly provides new angles to the story, maintaining a high level of interest at all times. Swift's scenario is full of marvelous touches, both humorous and poignant. When preacher Karl Malden is shown delivering one of his typical sermons, he walks quietly to the pulpit, looks heavenward, then downward meditatively, and suddenly shouts at the top of his lungs, "Death comes unexpectedly!" He goes on to deliver what is, in essence, a hilarious double-talk lecture keyed to this phrase.

Swift, as director, lingers over the bazaar, including as many details as possible to create a complete aura of what a small-town fair might have been like in 1912. A highlight comes when a group of girls dressed as the American flag sing "America" from the bandstand, with Pollyanna taking a solo.

There are other little moments—items that go by rather quickly on the screen, yet contribute to the film's overall flavor. For instance, when Jimmy Bean takes Pollyanna fishing for the first time, he sticks his face underwater to watch the fish, a shot viewed by the audience from below the surface! The whole plot device of the kids' fascination with prisms is a lovely visual idea, as well as a means of providing a bond between the children and Mr. Pendergast.

In every respect *Pollyanna* is an excellent film, and it received generally outstanding notices. Arthur Knight wrote in the *Saturday Review:* "Pollyanna has the feeling for Americana, the nostalgic glow of a simpler, gentler way of life that has characterized most of the Disney live-action features. . . . There is warmth here. . . . More fundamental, there seems to be a genuine belief that the art of positive thinking, as practiced by Eleanor H. Porter's little heroine, is every bit as applicable today as when the 'glad game' was first invented."

Time magazine, in a curiously backhanded yet favorable review, called the film "the best live-actor movie Disney has ever made," qualifying that remark by calling it "a Niagara of drivel and a masterpiece of smarm."

Yet again, for the third time in a year, a high quality, high cost Disney film did not do especially well at the box office. *Pollyanna*'s gross of $3,750,000 fell far short of the $6 million goal, and Walt Disney thought he knew why. "I think the picture would have done better with a different title," he explained. "Girls and women went to it, but men tended to stay away because it sounded sweet and sticky." He may have been correct.

In any event the film has been shown on the Disney television show, the mark of failure in theatrical release. Again, it seems a shame.

JUNGLE CAT

RELEASED BY BUENA VISTA ON AUGUST 10, 1960. Technicolor (from a 16mm original). Director, screenplay: James Algar. Photography: James R. Simon, Hugh A. Wilmar, Lloyd Beebe. Editor: Norman Palmer. Narrator: Winston Hibler. Music: Oliver Wallace. Orchestrations: Clifford Vaughan. Production manager: Erwin L. Verity. Special processes: Ub Iwerks. Animation effects: Joshua Meador, Art Riley. Sound: Robert O. Cook. Running time: 70 minutes.

The True-Life paintbrush opens this film with a picture of a cat on a pedestal; this dissolves into film of a live domestic cat, as the narrator tells of similarities among all cats. Cave drawings and primitive paintings show various species of felines through the ages. Then we see the "cats" that inhabit the various continents around the world. Finally, we are introduced to the jaguar, the jungle cat—"the greatest hunter of them all."

The rest of the film focuses on the jaguar, his environment, and his companions in the forests of South America. Most other animals in the region fall under the category of fair game for the jaguar, however, and he pursues them all. One of the toughest contenders is the peccary (wild pig) because he is a fast and violent fighter. In this case Mr. and Mrs. Jaguar team up to catch him, one distracting the pig's attention while the other one does the dirty work.

The jaguar's worst enemy is the alligator, and the jaguar is clever in pursuing this animal as well. The jungle cat knows no fear and teases the alligator mercilessly, even though this places him in a dangerous position. Then he hops around so much that when the alligator is ready to attack, he is too, and the jaguar grabs the 'gator by the head and shoves it underwater, where the animal soon drowns.

Monkeys are the happiest jungle creatures, since living high up in the trees, they are virtually the only ones not threatened by the jaguar. Living with them are the sloths, who also live a tree existence, upside down, but they are too slow and helpless to take care of themselves. The jaguars go after them, but in the instance we see, the sloths win out, not by cunning, but by virtue of the fact that they *do* know their habitat. The jaguar gets one sloth up a tree and tries to climb after it, but the sloth goes all the way out on a thin limb and manages to transfer to another tree nearby, while the jaguar can't take the chance of following, for fear of breaking the limb and falling to the ground.

Another tough party the jaguar faces is the boa constrictor, but again it is simply a matter of teamwork. The trick is to grab the boa by the neck before it can lash out and bite, so one jaguar gets the boa's attention as the other sneaks up from behind. It works.

In a lighter moment we see the mother jaguar training her youngster how to swim and get used to water, how to taunt an enemy without leaving himself open to attack, and other laws of the jungle. We get to see other jungle inhabitants, such as the giant anteater, which boasts a long, sticky tongue that doesn't give ants a chance to escape, and underwater, the pirarucu, a fish that gulps air at the surface, returns below, and belches through its gills, making a most unusual sound that can be heard far and wide.

The film's finale gives us a quick reprise of these various animals before bidding good-bye to the picturesque jungle with a beautiful sunset over the Amazon River.

Jungle Cat is a beautifully photographed and well-made film in all departments. Unfortunately, for all its natural wonders, it lacks a certain basic excitement to keep audience interest at a high pitch throughout its seventy minutes. *Variety* seemed to capture its essence when it wrote: "Somewhat less astonishing, considerably less amusing, but equally as meticulous and painstakingly filmed as Walt Disney's previous True-Life Adventure pieces."

The jaguar—the jungle cat.   © *Walt Disney Productions*

The jaguar tangles with a panther.   © *Walt Disney Productions*

The general press was very enthusiastic, however. Howard Thompson in *The New York Times* called it "one of Mr. Disney's best—intimate, tasteful, strong, and matter-of-fact." He also praised the soft-pedaling of extreme violence in this entry. *Time* found another aspect worthy of singling out: "Unlike some of Disney's early wildlife films, it lets the animals provide their own humor."

The Sunday *London Times* called it simply "a fascinating film."

But audience reaction, and his own showman's sense of the public pulse, told Disney that the True-Life format was wearing thin. Indeed, much of *Jungle Cat* seems unexciting only because one has seen similar material in earlier features.

Jungle Cat was the last True-Life Adventure feature. Disney opted instead for hybrid productions that utilized factual footage in a fictional modus operandi—and, as always, his timing and decision proved to be right.

TEN WHO DARED

RELEASED BY BUENA VISTA ON OCTOBER 18, 1960. Technicolor. Associate producer: James Algar. Director: William Beaudine. Screenplay: Lawrence E. Watkin, based on the journal of Major John Wesley Powell. Photography: Gordon Avil. Editors: Norman Palmer, Cotton Warburton. Art directors: Carroll Clark, Hilyard Brown. Set decorations: Emile Kuri. Costumes: Chuck Keehne. Music: Oliver Wallace. Orchestrations: Joseph S. Dubin. Matte artist: Albert Whitlock. Special effects: Ub Iwerks. Makeup: Pat McNalley. Sound: Robert O. Cook, Harry M. Lindgren. Running time: 92 minutes.

Songs: "Ten Who Dared," "Roll Along," "Jolly Rovers" by Lawrence E. Watkin, Stan Jones.

Cast: Brian Keith (William "Bill" Dunn), John Beal (Major John Wesley Powell), James Drury (Walter Powell), R. G. Armstrong (Oramel Howland), Ben Johnson (George Bradley), L. Q. Jones (Billy "Missouri" Hawkins), Dan Sheridan (Jack Sumner), David Stollery (Andrew "Andy" Hall), Stan Jones (Seneca Howland), David Frankham (Frank Goodman), Pat Hogan (Indian chief), Ray Walker (McSpadden), Jack Bighead (Ashtishkel), Roy Barcroft (Jim Baker), Dawn Little Sky (Indian woman).

Ten Who Dared is rock-bottom Disney. In fact, it's hard to think of another Disney film so totally bad. The curious part is that the project itself sounds interesting, and was placed in the hands of extremely competent men. Scenarist Lawrence Watkin had turned out many of Disney's best films over the past decade; director William Beaudine, though never considered inspired, was always workmanlike; and the cast is filled with seasoned veterans. But they all goofed on this one. Even the usually unimpeachable technical aspects of the film are second-rate.

The story is the true one of Major John Wesley Powell, who in 1869 set out to explore the Colorado River. The one-armed man recruits nine others to join him on this serious scientific expedition, which is doomed from the start. A drinking Britisher is put in a boat with another man about whom the Britisher knows too much. Powell's surly brother, Walter, bitter since being held a prisoner by the South during the war, is teamed in a boat with Bradley, a former Confederate. The film is doomed from the start as well, with as tedious a piece of exposition as you're likely to find; as the boats pull out, a reporter on the shore calls to the crew and asks for their names and backgrounds; each man replies in turn, in a recitation that drones on far too long.

Unsurprisingly, before the crew has gone very far, the drunk and the man-with-a-past start a fight, and become so preoccupied that they drift into the rapids and smash their boat in two.

Then Powell's brother Walter starts getting really obnoxious with his teammate, which leads to an elaborate knockdown, drag-out fight. Powell comments sagely: "I could see that Bradley and Walter weren't hitting it off too well." Then, Bradley goes off hunting, and Walter goes gunning after him (no one trying to stop Walter, incidentally). Bradley helps his adversary when he slips and dangles on a rock ledge. When he has the chance to kill him, he doesn't. Walter asks why, and Bradley replies quietly, "the war's over, Walter." They return to camp that night, friends, and when the repentant Walter starts to sing around the campfire, Bradley joins in, in close harmony!

There are incidental geological pointers thrown in along the journey. ("Fantastic erosion!" says Powell of one site.) But soon the men start to mutiny. Several leave when a scout and his Indian squaw tell the legend about a waterfall ahead. Others remain, but rebel when they run low on food and realize that they might have a better chance of survival walking

James Drury discovers that David Stollery has smuggled a dog along on the trip; John Beal is at right. © *Walt Disney Productions*

Brian Keith is fed up with the long trip. R. G. Armstrong is at left, L. Q. Jones at right. © *Walt Disney Productions*

on land. Several more are apparently killed or lost as they go off in search of civilization, while the major and his few remaining crewmen get through one last series of rapids and complete their triumphant journey. The film ends with a shot of the plaque honoring Powell that stands at the Grand Canyon today.

"Clumsy" is the word for *Ten Who Dared,* in every department. The characters are patently unbelievable from the very start, and the resolution of the conflict between Walter and Bradley is unintentionally hilarious. Powell himself is a dull and dimensionless character, with apparent dedication to his task, but no sense of pioneer spirit is conveyed to the audience, and he becomes as cardboard as the rest of his crew. Brian Keith, as the most rambunctious mem-

ber of the expedition, is a bit overbearing in his rowdy performance, but at least he's lively.

Though a great deal of location work was done for this film, most of it is for naught, because important scenes are played in obvious studio interiors, and many important action scenes are done with mattes, such as the initial rapids action. The photography relies far too much on a zoom lens, totally inappropriate for this kind of subject, and badly used to boot.

Even a winning team (and this certainly was) is entitled to a few losses. But it's still difficult to understand how they could miss the mark so completely. *Variety* called the film "an easy, appealing way to learn some fifth grade American history, but dramatically second-grade." To put it mildly.

SWISS FAMILY ROBINSON

Mother (Dorothy McGuire) and Father (John Mills) relax as Francis (Kevin Corcoran) enjoys the local recreation in *The Swiss Family Robinson*. © *Walt Disney Productions*

James MacArthur and Tommy Kirk, set ashore at a cove on the island, discover pirates up to no good. © *Walt Disney Productions*

RELEASED BY BUENA VISTA ON DECEMBER 10, 1960. Technicolor, Panavision. Producer: Bill Anderson. Director: Ken Annakin. Screenplay: Lowell S. Hawley, based on the novel by Johann Wyss. Photography: Harry Waxman. Additional photography: Paul Beeson. Editor: Peter Boita. Art director: John Howell. Assistant art directors: John Hoestli, Peter Murton. Set decorations: Jack Stephens. Costumes: Julie Harris. Music: William Alwyn. Conductor: Muir Mathieson. Second unit director: Yakima Canutt. Associate producer: Basil Keys. Production manager: Bill Hill. Assistant director: Rene Dupont. Matte artist: Peter Ellenshaw. Special effects: Dan Lee, Walter Stones. Production designer: John Howell. Sketch artist: John L. Jensen. Makeup: Bill Lodge, Charles Nash. Hairstyling: Eileen Bates. Sound: Leslie Wiggins, John S. Dennis, Gordon K. McCallum. Running time: 128 minutes.

Song: "My Heart Is an Island" by Terry Gilkyson.

Cast: John Mills (father), Dorothy McGuire (mother), James MacArthur (Fritz), Janet Munro (Roberta), Sessue Hayakawa (pirate chief), Tommy Kirk (Ernst), Kevin Corcoran (Francis), Cecil Parker (Captain Moreland), Andy Ho (pirate), Milton Reid (pirate), Larry Taylor (pirate).

Ken Annakin recalls:

While we were in the mountains near Zermatt shooting *Third Man on the Mountain*, I remember Bill Anderson saying to me that *Swiss Family Robinson* was the subject Walt was toying with as our next picture. I read the book. It was very old-fashioned, and I wondered what Walt's approach was going to be. Bill Anderson and I returned to Burbank and we sat down with Walt. He said "Well now, let's throw the whole book out the window. Let's just keep the idea of a Swiss family emigrating, trying to emigrate to America. They get shipwrecked, but they are able to save all the things in the ship. They then make a life on an idyllic island, I think you ought to think of all the things you might like to do, all the animals you could use in an entertaining way. Let's make it a wonderful show for the whole family, with all ideas possible."

And that's exactly what they did. Filmed on a grand scale, the resulting film was thought a bit overpowering by some critics, but audiences flocked to see it, loved it, and made it one of the biggest hits in Disney history.

The main titles appear over sequences of a storm at sea. Stranded alone on the ship, when the storm dies down, the Robinson family decides to build a raft and flee for shore, taking with them as many supplies and animals as they can.

Mother is the most upset about being stranded, but when her husband and three sons complete their tree house and present it to her, she is delighted. They find life a dream on the island. "Everything we need," says Father blissfully, "right at your fingertips." Mother corrects him, however; there are no girls, and she questions the idea of her two grown sons not knowing any more of life than this island. So the two boys, Fritz (the eldest) and Ernst, take off to sail around the coast and make sure that this really *is* an island.

They wreck their boat on the rocks, but, coming ashore, discover a band of pirates holding two prisoners, a sea captain and his grandson. They manage to rescue the boy and set off into the forest in an effort to find their way back to the family overland. The boys can't understand why their companion can't keep up with them—until they discover that "he" is really a girl, at which point they fall over themselves trying to help her. Their journey home is long and tortuous, and back at the tree house Mother, Father, and young Francis don't know if they will ever see the boys again. Happily, they do make it back, just in time for Christmas, and the girl, Roberta, is welcomed as if she were one of the family.

Some friction develops, however, as the two boys begin to rival for her attention, the younger Ernst growing explosive at his older brother's cool self-assurance.

But they all realize that the pirates will be coming after them, and they prepare a fantastically elaborate series of traps, as well as a hilltop fortress. Then they sit back and wait for the pirates to come. Fritz tells Roberta of his dream, to go on to New Zealand and help shape the new world there. Ernst wants to return to England and continue his schooling, and Roberta tells him that her grandfather can get him into one of the finest universities. They forget about the impending attack, and the whole family participates in a wild animal race. Just as they get going, however, the pirates are spotted coming in to shore; the family retreats to the fortress.

As the pirates come ashore, the booby traps are set off one by one: a bridge collapses under the pirates' feet, a barrage of arrows is launched by automatically operated crossbows, they are pelted with coconut bombs, and, when they climb up the hill, are

John Mills and friends on location for *Swiss Family Robinson*. Note that although this is outdoor shooting, on a beautiful day, lights and reflectors are still necessary. © *Walt Disney Productions*

greeted by an avalanche of logs and rocks, not to mention some concealed tiger pits. The pirates continue on, however, and things start to look bleak, when Roberta's grandfather comes into the cove with his ship. At this, the pirates flee, and all is safe once more.

The captain offers to take the whole family back to England with him, but now there are second thoughts. Ernst goes to attend the university, but Roberta decides to stay with Fritz. He declares that he doesn't want to go to New Zealand; he'd rather stay on the island, and, as it turns out, so would Mother, Father, and Francis. They *do* have everything they could ever want, after all.

Swiss Family Robinson is a hugely entertaining film, and a beautiful one as well, with eye-filling scenery everywhere the camera turns. It was filmed on the island of Tobago, which turned out to be a perfect choice.

Disney and his collaborators sensed the key ingredient for this film's success right from the start: create a paradiselike situation, and have the family give the audience the vicarious pleasure of doing exciting, amusing things everyone would love to be able to do. This is the film's great appeal.

For instance, the tree house, a fantastically elaborate affair, was built in a giant tree just as it is seen on screen. It has an elevator, a stove, running water, a skylight, all the comforts of home. The swimming hole, complete with Tarzanlike vines to swing on, ready-made sliding ponds, and the cool water itself, is another dream spot (although not so dreamy for the crew; this location, because it was surrounded by foliage, got only three hours of sunlight a day, and took an inordinate amount of time to film).

The friendly animals also provide a lot of fun. Who wouldn't love to ride an ostrich in a race, or sit atop an elephant in the crashing surf. Most of all, who wouldn't love to live in such an absolutely *beautiful* place?

Of course, all this beauty, and diversity, and ingenuity on screen required a tremendous amount of effort off screen. The entire film took twenty-two weeks to shoot at a cost of $4.5 million.

The first thing was to find a good location: Jamaica, Puerto Rico, Trinidad, and the Galapagos islands were scouted before Tobago was discovered. It was ideal for filming purposes, with one hitch: there were no animals to be found. Thus, a menagerie was assembled—colorful tropical birds, gulls, ostriches, snakes, tigers, zebras, baby elephants, monkeys—and flown to the island, along with appropriate trainers.

The director recalls:

There were fourteen trainers in all, and about 4:00 each day, they would come to me and say, "Mr. Annakin, can you tell me what attitude you want from my animal tomorrow," and then they would discuss it and put in last-minute work each night trying to get the desired results. One afternoon at 3:30 our flamingos took off from Tobago and headed south to British Guiana! We couldn't do anything about this, but fortunately the animal handler was right, and they returned the next day at feeding time.

It took five months to build the necessary sets and incidental objects on the island, including the wreckage, which was built on scaffolding at sea, with divers participating. "It was absolutely real shooting," says Annakin, "something which appealed to me very much because of my documentary beginnings. I liked shooting exteriors. I think it gives much more satisfaction to the audience in the end, and in this case I wanted to keep very much away from the original version that was made by RKO (in 1940), which we ran at Disney. It was a good picture, but you could feel the restrictions of them having to work in a tank."

But Annakin and the crew had to pay the price for realism; it took ten days to shoot the sequence of floating the animals and supplies ashore. "The lines were always getting crossed. You'd find a pig or a cow was tied with a barrel underneath, he'd suddenly turn upside down, and the continuity girl on the camera raft would suddenly shriek, and someone would have to dive in to put the animal right so it wasn't hurt."

Every move, every shot was calculated in advance; Annakin, Bill Anderson, Disney, a sketch artist named John Jensen, and stuntman-turned-second-unit-director Yakima Canutt worked together on storyboards, first deciding what they would like to do and then deciding if it *could* be done. Disney was concerned that there should be something happening every minute, particularly in the climactic pirate attack. He would examine the storyboards and comment: "That works, that works, yeah, that works, although there is a little hole here; we need a bit of action here. Devise some action here." And they would.

The performers almost seem to take a back seat to this spectacular action in considering such a film, but in reality they can be taken for granted only because they are all so smoothly professional. John Mills strikes just the right note of adventurism, tempered with humor and a genuine feeling of enjoying the whole escapade. Dorothy McGuire is warm and real as the mother who worries every step of the way. Equally realistic are the two battling brothers, played by James MacArthur and Tommy Kirk, and the girl they fight over, Janet Munro. The only sour chord is struck by Kevin ("Moochie") Corcoran, whose cuteness and sense of mischief did him well in earlier endeavors, but here seem merely obnoxious. What is more, though his actions are supposed to be funny, it is he who causes many of the worst crises the family faces. One is yearning for John Mills to give the kid a good whipping.

Sessue Hayakawa as the pirate chief has the film's single most memorable shot. As he leads his clan up the hill to the family's fortress, a coconut bomb rolls down into his hand. He picks it up, examines it, can't figure out what it is, and, shrugging, tosses it over his shoulder, where it explodes!

This is part of the massive pirate attack for which many critics took Disney to task, saying that he had soft-soaped the menacing angle by making it a slapstick travesty. This, however, was the intention of Disney and the entire staff, in keeping with the fun of the rest of the film, and at least one critic took it in the proper spirit. Wrote Arthur Knight in the *Saturday Review:*

Although Lowell Hawley's screenplay takes considerable liberty with the original classic . . . everything is at once so genial and so generous that it would take a stern soul indeed to mourn the absence of Johann Wyss' incessant preachments and homilies. . . . By casting it with seasoned and attractive players . . . Disney has avoided the one-dimensionality that afflicts most children's films. And by playing it tongue-in-cheek—including a pirate attack in which everyone is blown up but nobody dies—director Ken Annakin has dodged both the cloying sweetness and the bloody horror of earlier Disney efforts in this field.

Other reviewers generally found the film to be first-rate family entertainment, the *New York Times* calling it a "grand adventure yarn," and *Time* declaring it "good Disney and bad culture," although that magazine shared some others' reservations about the finale, calling it "a regular Donald Duck comedy in live action."

Yet no complaints were heard from youthful audiences, who adored the film and went to see it in droves. Any apprehensions the Disney higher echelon had about the film's rather high budget were dispelled by its tremendous box-office returns—$7.5 million on its first U.S. release, and almost as much in its first reissue in 1969. Its worldwide total and continuing potency in rerelease has made it one of the studio's all-time biggest moneymakers.

Even so, it would be some time before the Disney company would invest this much time, effort, and money in a live-action film. (This was one of the studio's few recent wide-screen endeavors, a definite asset to the eye-popping action and scenery.) Still, it was nice to see that kind of all-out effort by so many people pay off so nicely.

THE SIGN OF ZORRO

RELEASED BY BUENA VISTA ON JUNE 11, 1960. PRODUCER: William H. Anderson. Directors: Norman Foster, Lewis R. Foster. Screenplay: Norman Foster, Lowell S. Hawley, Bob Wehling, John Meredyth Lucas, based on the "Zorro" stories by Johnston McCulley. Director of photography: Gordon Avil. Art director: Marvin Aubrey Davis. Set decorations: Emile Kuri, Hal Gausman. Costumes: Chuck Keehne. Music: William Lava. Film editors: Roy Livingston, Stanley Johnson, Cotton Warburton, Hugh Chaloupka. Unit manager: Roy Wade. Assistant directors: Vincent McEveety, Russ Haverick. Matte artist: Peter Ellenshaw. Production coordinator: Louis Debney. Fencing manager: Fred Cavens. Makeup: Pat McNalley. Sound: Robert O. Cook. Running time: 91 minutes.

Title song by Norman Foster and George Bruns.

Cast: Guy Williams (Zorro/Don Diego), Henry Calvin (Sergeant Garcia), Gene Sheldon (Bernardo), Britt Lomond (Monastario), George J. Lewis (Don Alejandro), Tony Russo (Martinez), John Dehner (viceroy), Lisa Gaye (viceroy's daughter), and Romney Brent, Than Wyenn, Elvira Corona, Eugenia Paul.

When Davy Crockett became a hit on TV, Disney spliced some TV episodes together and released them to theatres. There seemed no reason not to follow through with Disney's newest TV hit, Zorro, and in May 1960 *The Sign of Zorro* appeared in theatres.

The film takes place in 1820, and opens with Don Diego and his servant Bernardo sailing for America at his father's request. It seems that the local commandant in California is a despot, making life difficult for men of courage and justice like Diego's father, Don Alejandro. Diego tells Bernardo that he will play the role of a foppish man of letters, that no one will see through his disguise as Zorro, an avenger of the people. He tells his mute servant to pretend to be deaf as well as dumb, so he can act as a spy. The scheme works, except that Diego's father is heartbroken at having such a cowardly son.

It is the father who leads his comrades in an attack on the fort where innocent men are being held prisoner; the commandant is waiting for them, prepared to ambush. But Zorro finds out and arrives on the scene in time to warn all the men but one, his father, who is wounded and caught. A rigged trial seems certain, until Zorro sneaks up behind the "judge" with his sword, causing the phony magistrate to pronounce Don Alejandro innocent.

Then the commandant tries to discredit Zorro by hiring a man to wear the avenger's costume and rob a dinner party he is giving that night. Diego, who is at the party, sneaks out, returns as Zorro, and unmasks the charlatan. When the commandant asks where Don Diego was during the fracas, he replies that he was hiding under a table.

But other incidents lead the commandant to believe that Diego is really Zorro. Everyone he tells this to, including his own Sergeant Garcia, thinks the suggestion ludicrous, yet he has Diego arrested. Just then, word comes that the viceroy is going to visit the town that day. The commandant has all the prisoners released on orders that they should line the street and

Guy Williams, Lisa Gaye, and John Dehner in *The Sign of Zorro.* © *Walt Disney Productions*

The commandant (Britt Lomond) and Zorro (Guy Williams) are in the midst of a duel when a distraction captures their attention. © *Walt Disney Productions*

cheer, to make it seem that everyone is content. When the commandant presents his prisoner to the viceroy and his daughter, they are aghast; they know Don Diego well, and refuse to believe that he could be Zorro. Then the wily officer forces Diego to duel with him to prove that he is handy with a sword.

Just in the nick of time Zorro rides up outside and hurls a note onto the door impaled on a knife. It convinces everyone for good that Don Diego could not be Zorro, since they all knew he was inside at the time. (Actually, it was Bernardo who disguised himself as Zorro.) The viceroy has the commandant arrested, and appoints Sergeant Garcia in his place. Garcia declares a holiday in honor of his promotion.

While the *Zorro* TV series seemed enjoyable, this patchwork feature film is rather clumsy and not terribly exciting. It begins with introductory material, to set up the situation: what passes for exposition is Don Diego explaining all his plans to Bernardo for an interminable amount of time. Because the film is strung together from more than one episode, there are several climaxes and resolutions, which create a problem of unevenness in continuity. What's more, the plot

material becomes repetitious, and, inevitably, dull.

Worst of all, the series was shot in typical cut-and-dried television style—in black and white. The results look particularly bad on a movie screen, and make *The Sign of Zorro* seem distinctively lackluster.

The most redeeming factor in the film (as in the series) is the supporting work by Gene Sheldon as Bernardo and Henry Calvin as Sergeant Garcia. Their comic expertise makes up for a lot of *Zorro*'s weaknesses.

It is worth noting that George Lewis, who plays Diego's father in this film, was the star of the Republic serial *Zorro's Black Whip* in 1944. And William Lava, who composed the music for the Disney TV show, had scored most of Republic's *Zorro* serials as well.

Indeed, both Republic, with feature versions of *Ghost of Zorro* and *Zorro Rides Again,* and 20th Century Fox, with the 1940 version of *The Mark of Zorro,* tried to cash in on the Zorro market created by Disney with theatre reissues. Apparently none of them, Disney included, did spectacularly well with the idea.

ONE HUNDRED AND ONE DALMATIANS

RELEASED BY BUENA VISTA ON JANUARY 25, 1961. Technicolor. Production supervisor: Ken Peterson. Directors: Wolfgang Reitherman, Hamilton Luske, Clyde Geronimi. Art director, production designer: Ken Anderson. Directing animators: Milt Kahl, Marc Davis, Oliver Johnston, Jr., Franklin Thomas, John Lounsbery, Eric Larson. Story: Bill Peet, based on the book *The Hundred and One Dalmatians* by Dodie Smith. Backgrounds: Albert Dempster, Ralph Hulett, Anthony Rizzo, Bill Layne. Layout: Basil Davidovich, McLaren Stewart, Vance Gerry, Joe Hale, Dale Barnhart, Ray Aragon, Dick Ung, Homer Jonas, Al Zinnen, Sammy June Lanham, Victour Haboush. Layout styling: Don Griffith, Erni Nordli, Collin Campbell. Color styling: Walt Peregoy. Character styling: Bill Peet, Tom Oreb. Character animation: Hal King, Cliff Nordberg, Eric Cleworth, Art Stevens, Hal Ambro, Bill Keil, Dick Lucas, Les Clark, Blaine Gibson, John Sibley, Julius Svendsen, Ted Berman, Don Lusk, Amby Paliwoda. Effects animation: Jack Boyd, Ed Parks, Dan MacManus, Jack Buckley. Music: George Bruns. Orchestrations: Franklyn Marks. Film editors: Donald Halliday, Roy M. Brewer, Jr. Sound supervision: Robert O. Cook. Music editor: Evelyn Kennedy. Special processes: Ub Iwerks, Eustace Lycett. Running time: 79 minutes.

Songs: "Cruella De Vil," "Dalmatian Plantation," "Kanine Krunchies Commercial," words and music by Mel Leven.

Voices: Rod Taylor (Pongo), Lisa Davis (Anita), Cate Bauer (Perdita), Ben Wright (Roger Radcliff), Fred Warlock (Horace), J. Pat O'Malley (Jasper, miscellaneous dogs), Betty Lou Gerson (Cruella De Vil; Miss Birdwell), Martha Wentworth (Nani, goose; cow), Tom Conway (collie), George Pelling (Great Dane), Micky Maga (Patch, a puppy), Barbara Beaird (Rolly, a puppy), Queenie Leonard (cow), Marjorie Bennett (cow).

Like most of Disney's films at this time, *One Hundred and One Dalmatians* opens with a brightly inventive title sequence. A series of dots spread before the camera and evolve into 101 dogs who all start barking at once! This leads into the main title, and each successive card or credit brings with it a unique concept. The

Pongo arranges for Roger and Anita to meet; it isn't subtle, but it works. © *1964 Walt Disney Productions*

One of Disney's most colorful villainesses of all time. Cruella De Vil. © *1961 Walt Disney Productions*

Pongo, Perdita, and the puppies watch their favorite TV star, Thunderbolt.   © *1961 Walt Disney Productions*

Dalmatian spots become musical notes when composer George Bruns's name appears. The layout is splashed onto the screen when that department is credited, and gradually colored in as color credits appear. A typewriter clicks out the original story credit, etc.

Many live-action films have suffered from overly imaginative title sequences, when the rest of the film was unable to maintain the same level of ingenuity. *One Hundred and One Dalmatians,* on the other hand, is merely off to a flying start.

The opening shot is of London from the air. A jaunty British voice narrates in the first person, and, as we come into the hero's apartment, we see that it's the dog who is talking, not the man, as one would presume. In fact, Pongo refers to songwriter Roger as "my pet." He decides that Roger is spending too much time with his work and needs a mate—and so, incidentally, does he. When he gazes out the window and sees a beautiful female Dalmatian, being walked by an equally lovely girl, he instantly gets Roger to take him out for a walk, and Pongo tries to arrange a meeting of the two duos in the park. It works out badly, with the humans getting tangled up in the dog leashes and falling in a brook. Despite this mishap, it's love at first sight, for both humans and canines, and the picture dissolves to a wedding ceremony, with Roger and Anita inside the church, and Pongo and Perdita taking the same silent vows outside.

Married life is hectic but most pleasant, with a housekeeper who loves the dogs as much as Roger and Anita. Just as Perdita is about to give birth, a schooldays chum of Anita's named Cruella De Vil shows up, insisting that she must have the puppies when they arrive. Cruella is a flighty and impossible character, but Roger senses evil in her as well, and even writes a song about her expressing his feelings.

When the puppies—fifteen of them—arrive, and Cruella comes to claim them, Roger stands firm and refuses, upsetting the wealthy woman, who is used to having things her own way. A short time later, while Roger and Anita are out walking their dogs, two cockney crooks force their way into the house and steal all fifteen puppies.

The police are unable to find any clues, although Roger and Pongo are convinced Cruella is behind the evil deed. That evening Pongo tells his mate that "the humans have tried everything; now it's up to us dogs." He makes use of The Twilight Bark to send a relay of signals out of London into the countryside, where the Colonel, an aging dog of military bearing, takes on the search with his aides, a horse called The Captain and a cat named Tibbs. They find the puppies locked up in the long-deserted De Vil mansion, along with a passel of other young Dalmatians. There are ninety-nine in all; it seems that Cruella has been storing them up to make herself some magnificent fur coats—one for herself, and others to sell!

Tibbs decides to effect an escape plan, while Jasper and Horace (the crooks) are engrossed in a TV show. By now Pongo and Perdita have arrived on the scene, and Pongo goes inside to ward off the thugs while the Colonel and Tibbs take the puppies back to their barn headquarters. Jasper and Horace track them there, however, necessitating a sudden retreat; Pongo and Perdita must now keep track of ninety-nine cold, tired little pups in a blinding snowstorm, as they make their way back to London.

A collie comes to their aid with a place to stay overnight, and a tip that a truck is going to London in the morning. That morning, however, Cruella joins in the chase, discovers the dogs in the back of the truck, and embarks on a wild run over icy, mountainous roads, trying to knock the truck off the road. In the end, Cruella's car is driven off the road by her own henchmen! They all end up on a snowy hill, their cars in a hundred pieces, with Cruella calling them idiots for bungling the job.

Back in London, Roger and Anita are in deep sorrow until the dogs arrive; there is a joyous reunion, and the realization that there are one hundred and one dalmatians in all. They decide to keep them all, and perhaps move to the country. Roger suggests: "We'll have a Dalmatian plantation," and turns the rhyme into a song. They all join in singing, as the camera moves back into the London night, the music waking up the entire city.

One Hundred and One Dalmatians is Disney in his element, a thoroughly delightful film that many considered to be his best animated feature in years. Unlike some of his 1950s endeavors, this cartoon is not weighed down by attempts to duplicate reality. In fact, it revels in the stylistic exaggeration of reality, best exemplified by the character of Cruella De Vil. Her design is a caricature; her body is a thin line, encased in a huge, billowing white fur coat. Her face is bony and angular, suggesting the canineness of her personality, and her hair is a shock of black and white moplike strands. She carries at all times a mile-long cigarette holder and leaves behind her a trail of smoke wherever she goes. Even her car is an exaggeration—a long, long luxury limousine that careens down the city streets and screeches to a halt in front of the Radcliffs' home. Cruella is doubly striking, of course, in contrast to Anita, who is drawn much in the classic style of Disney heroines.

But this is the joy of *One Hundred and One Dalmatians:* it is real enough to be believable and engrossing, but at all times retains its identity as an animated cartoon, to be enjoyed and laughed at.

The film is full of ingenious visual ideas, a prime one being the similarities between dog and owner. The human Roger is drawn with an oversized nose and angular chin to accentuate the parallel between his face and Pongo's. When Pongo scours the sidewalk outside his window for likely prospects to meet, he sees a parade of dog-walkers who match their pets' looks to a tee: a droopy female artist-type walking her droopy dog, whose floppy ears match her mistress's hairdo, a pampered French poodle whose owner's furs match her natural fur, etc.

The settings are also on the borderline between reality and invention. The opening view of London is much more stylized and caricatured than the similar opening in *Peter Pan*, for instance. This formula meshes nicely with the attitude toward the characters themselves.

The personality of virtually every supporting character is conveyed visually as much as through dialogue: the Colonel has a proud but absentminded look about him that helps to solidify his C. Aubrey Smith–like character. The collie that helps the Dalmatians during their long wintry trek not only sounds reliable and authoritative (thanks to Tom Conway's voice), but looks that way. Jasper and Horace are hilariously speedy; one look at them is to know that they'll bungle the job.

One of the key plot points in the climax is visual. In order to pass by Cruella unnoticed, and climb aboard the truck to London, the puppies cover themselves with soot, so that they no longer look like Dalmatians. The scheme is foiled when a drop of water from a rooftop splashes on one of the dogs and reveals his identity.

The delightful visual aspect of the film is matched by a witty script. The songs, which are really incidental and not large-scale production numbers, are fun, especially "Cruella De Vil," in which Roger takes out his venom in a set of saucy lyrics.

There are some amusing jibes at television throughout the film. At home the puppies are captivated by the canine TV star Thunderbolt, who invariably foils his human adversaries. The show is sponsored by Kanine Krunchies, represented by a hilariously silly commercial. Later, Jasper and Horace pass the time at the lonely mansion by watching "What's My Crime." The guest crook signs in, and a panel, aided by a loquacious moderator, tries to identify him. When the show is over, the host asks the crook if he can come back next week, but the firm hand of a jailer seems to indicate that it won't be possible. (Incidentally, in one scene, the puppies watch a clip from Disney's *Flowers and Trees* on the TV set.)

There are warm, realistic touches to the film that give depth to the characters and heighten the audience involvement in their lives. When the puppies arrive, several at a time, the fifteenth appears not to survive. But Roger takes the infant pup and massages its heart, stirring it back to life. He and Pongo happily dance a jig in celebration of this event. Later, when the housekeeper discover the puppies gone, she screams in horror and runs out into the London streets crying in anguish.

In short, everything works in *101 Dalmatians*, bringing the picture together into a briskly paced, cohesive whole with nary a dull spot in sight. *Time* magazine called it "the wittiest, most charming, least pretentious cartoon feature Walt Disney has ever made . . . one of the nicest things that have happened so far this year to dog's best friend." Joseph Morgenstern in the *New York Herald Tribune* noted that "it is in the province of sophisticated humor that Mr. Disney is a late arrival, and a welcome one. *101 Dalmatians* comes up with some engaging spoofs of the British spy thriller genre, and does it without for a moment compromising its appeal for the young . . . In their flight the pups are aided by a shaggy dog who sounds like Colonel Blimp, a Ronald Colman collie, a sturdy village Labrador whose accent slips occasionally, and a whole animal underground stationed strategically throughout the countryside."

Howard Thompson in the *Times* declared that Cruella "makes the *Snow White* witch seem like *Pollyanna* . . . Imagine a sadistic Auntie Mame, drawn by Charles Addams and with a Tallulah Bankhead bass . . . Even with a lady Lucifer hell-bent for their hides, the Dalmatians are a friendly lot worth knowing."

101 Dalmatians was made possible (or perhaps "more feasible") because of a then-revolutionary development called Xerography. Put simply, the Xerox system made it possible for Disney animators to copy initial drawings many times over, eliminating the necessity to draw 101 separate dogs for those mass scenes. ("Of course," commented cartoon director Chuck Jones, "only the Disney studio would think of doing a hundred and one spotted dogs. We have trouble doing *one* spotted dog.") Even so, the animation staff of approximately three hundred worked on the film for three years, bringing the cost of the feature to $4 million.

Coupled with the Xerox process, however, was a new drawing style that seemed appropriate to this film, less so to later ones. For the first time Disney animators used a rough-line technique that most closely resembled their rough sketches before undergoing the finishing process. It was, of course, that smooth, polished style that had won Disney the reputation for slickness in his work of recent years; this was apparently a backlash reaction that, in some observers' eyes, went too far in the opposite direction.

This naturally had no bearing on the film's entertainment value, and certainly had nothing to do with blocking its success, which was considerable. Indeed, the film was a bigger hit than Disney's more ambitious *Sleeping Beauty*, and has stood the test of time through several reissues, taking its place alongside the other Disney cartoon classics. In fact, some aficionados believe that it was the studio's *last* great cartoon feature.

A 1996 live-action remake was successful enough to spawn a sequel, *102 Dalmatians*, in 2000. In the fall of 1998, the characters returned to animation on television in *101 Dalmatians: The Series*.

THE ABSENT MINDED PROFESSOR

RELEASED BY BUENA VISTA ON MARCH 16, 1961. As-
sociate producer: Bill Walsh. Director: Robert Ste-
venson. Screenplay: Bill Walsh, based on a story by
Samuel W. Taylor. Director of photography: Edward
Colman, A.S.C. Editor: Cotton Warburton, A.C.E.
Art director: Carroll Clark. Set decorations: Emile
Kuri, Hal Gausman. Costumes: Chuck Keehne,
Gertrude Casey. Music: George Bruns. Orchestra-
tions: Franklyn Marks. Second unit director: Arthur
J. Vitarelli. Assistant director: Robert G. Shannon.
Special effects: Peter Ellenshaw, Eustace Lycett, Rob-
ert A. Malley, Joshua Meador. Sequence consultant:
Donald Da Gradi. Makeup: Pat McNalley. Hairstyl-
ing: Ruth Sandifer. Sound supervision: Robert O.
Cook. Sound mixer: Dean Thomas. Music editor:
Evelyn Kennedy. Running time: 97 minutes.

Songs: "Medfield Fight Song," special lyrics to "Sweet
Betsy of Pike" by Richard M. Sherman and Robert B.
Sherman.

Cast: Fred MacMurray (Ned Brainard), Nancy Olson
(Betsy Carlisle), Keenan Wynn (Alonzo Hawk),
Tommy Kirk (Bill Hawk), Ed Wynn (fire chief),
Leon Ames (President Rufus Daggett), Wally Brown
(Coach Elkins), Alan Carney (first referee), Elliott
Reid (Shelby Ashton), Edward Andrews (defense
secretary), David Lewis (General Singer), Jack Mul-
laney (air force captain), Belle Montrose (Mrs.
Chatsworth), Forrest Lewis (Officer Kelly), James
Westerfield (Officer Hanson), Ned Wynn (youth),
Gage Clarke (Reverend Bosworth), Alan Hewitt
(General Hotchkiss), Raymond Bailey (Admiral
Olmstead), Wendell Holmes (General Poynter), Don
Ross (Lenny), Charlie Briggs (Sig), Wally Boag (TV
newsman), Leon Tyler (basketball player #18),
Gordon Jones (rival basketball coach), Paul Frees
(voice of army alert, pilot on radio, radio announcer).

The film opens with Professor Ned Brainard
working an experiment, as he lectures his class. He
mixes a potion and sets off an explosion, at which
time the main titles appear.

The Prof is to be married that night; he's missed
his own wedding twice before, but he can't resist playing around in his lab for a while before the big event.

Nancy Olson and Fred MacMurray go for a high-flying spin in his
Model T (over an aerial shot of the Walt Disney Studios in Burbank) in this publicity still. © *Walt Disney Productions*

The Medfield basketball team springs into action, thanks to Flubber. © *Walt Disney Productions*

This time there's a big explosion that knocks him out cold. Next morning, when he wakes up, he notices that a metal container is sailing up into the air. It contains a gooey substance that floats, and he calls it Flubber (flying rubber). He hopes his fiancée Betsy will forgive him for missing the wedding when she hears about this great discovery, but she's too angry to listen, and he's too bumbling to make a coherent explanation.

That night he rigs up his old model T with flubber and gets the thing to fly! He tries to show Betsy, but she refuses, going to the Medfield basketball game with his rival, Shelby Ashton. At the game Medfield is being pummeled by a team twice its size. The star player, Bill Hawk, can't play because Brainard flunked him, and Bill's father, Alonzo Hawk, shifty president of the Auld Lang Syne Finance Company, has bet heavily against Medfield, certain that they will lose. During half time, Brainard irons flubber onto the soles of the team's sneakers, and during the second half they spring into action—literally. They hop all over the court, making basket after basket, and blocking every shot by the opposing team for a tremendous victory. The Prof tries to explain to Betsy that this was his doing, but she thinks he's try-

ing to take credit for the team, and belittles him. She just doesn't understand.

After he drops Betsy off, Shelby drives home, and is suddenly pursued by a strange otherworldly force. It's Brainard, flying his car above Shelby's, bouncing on the roof, honking his horn, and eventually causing him to crash into a police car, leaving him with a thoroughly outlandish alibi.

Unfortunately, Alonzo Hawk has been up late that night, and has seen Brainard's car flying. He catches on immediately, and tries to make a deal, but Brainard says no. The Prof then calls Washington, but gets only a runaround. Representatives of the three armed forces are intrigued, however, and they come to Medfield to see a demonstration. Meanwhile, Hawk switches cars on Brainard, leaving him with a duplicate Model T. When the Professor tries to get his car to fly, it won't budge, and he is made to look like a fool. Betsy pities him, and at last believes what he says.

She and Ned determine to get the car back from Hawk, but first they must take care of Hawk himself. They get him to try on some flubberized shoes, and, on the sidewalk outside his home, he starts to bounce up in the air. He's crazy about it, as he bounces higher and higher; when he asks how they get it to stop, they tell him they don't know, and leave him there in a most unusual predicament. Then they go off to his warehouse, and foil his henchmen in order to retrieve the flubberized car.

He and Betsy then fly to Washington, but instead of a warm greeting, they are treated as an Unidentified Flying Object. Then the army, navy, and air force men hear of it and come to his rescue. Brainard is received as a hero at the White House. And he actually gets married to Betsy; as they fly off in his car, the "Just Married" sign on the back has been changed to read "Finally Married."

Disney staffer Ward Kimball has recalled that Walt's greatest pleasure in making live-action movies was when he could produce some cartoonlike effect on the screen. Thus, the fantasy of a flying car and bouncing basketball players must have appealed to his imagination—as he knew it would to millions of others.

The Absent Minded Professor cannot really be called one of Disney's *best* films, but it surely is one of his biggest audience-pleasers. Everything is tailored toward getting laughs on the broadest possible basis, and one cannot argue with success.

The key effects sequences are quite well done. The car footage is done with a combination of live action wires (such as shots of the car taking off, and bouncing on other cars), miniatures (which are the least convincing), matte and process work. By intercutting these various types of shots, the overall effect is rather good. There are nice individual touches, too, such as Brainard driving the car into a cloud to avoid an army bomber during the Washington finale.

The filmmakers decided that such trickery could only be carried off in a black-and-white film,* a decision repeated for *Son of Flubber.* A few short years later, the Disney technicians surpassed even these effects for *Mary Poppins,* in color. The basketball game goes on at some length, and, although the shots of the kids bouncing high in the air really are amazing, they start to wear thin. There are some good variations, though, such as one play shown entirely in the eyes of the referee, whose openmouthed face follows the team bounce by bounce across the court. Undercranking (to make the movement faster) and even frame-cutting are ingredients in this sequence.

The scene of Keenan Wynn, as Alonzo Hawk, bouncing on the flubberized shoes is one of the most impressive in the film, because it is shot outdoors, where you realize trickery is at a minimum; there is also a marvelous shot from his point of view of Brainard and Betsy standing on the ground, with the camera bouncing high in the air.

There are other striking moments: while the professor is bouncing atop Shelby's car, the victim's eyes widen into a look of unspeakable horror, accentuated by the fact that he is wearing dark makeup that offsets the whites of his eyes. Later, when Brainard is being chased by Alonzo Hawk, he gets through the alleyway by driving his car on the side of a building!

The script itself is really rather obvious, with few surprises; indeed, the film's major laughs come from the anticipation of what is about to happen. This is based largely on typecasting, including the police officer from *The Shaggy Dog,* Forest Lewis, and a partner, played by James Westerfield; snooty Alan Hewitt (who has been in countless Disney films ever since) as an army officer; Elliott Reid as the sniffy intellectual; Edward Andrews as the hypocritical soft-soaping Government official, etc.

Keenan Wynn is, of course, thoroughly despicable as Alonzo Hawk, but there is a nice piece of irony in one sequence where he's bouncing up and down uncontrollably. Fire engines come to his rescue, and who should be playing the fire chief but Ed Wynn—Keenan's father, as well as the venerable Fire Chief of radio fame.

The most important casting of all, however, was that of Fred MacMurray, and he is inspired in the lead role. He plays his part with such utter conviction that you believe him completely—his naïveté, his absent-mindedness, his determination, and even his occasional stupidity.

This was not the last Disney film to poke fun at the government, which also came in for a ribbing in the sequel to this picture. Some have found a parallel between Professor Brainard's rejection and running around from the government and Disney's own

career, in which he repeatedly had to do things on his own, without the support of others. In any event, the satire is healthy, and yet another example of nonsugary content, however innocuous, in Disney films.

The Absent-Minded Professor won rousing reviews from critics. *Time* called it "the season's kookiest science-fiction farce . . . *Flubber* provides fuel for a very funny piece of hyperbolic humor in the grand American tradition of Paul Bunyan . . ." The *New York Times* called it "remarkably bouncy entertainment."

Variety went a bit deeper:

On the surface, *The Absent-Minded Professor* is a comedy-fantasy of infectious absurdity, a natural follow-up to Walt Disney's *The Shaggy Dog.* But its mass appeal goes deeper than that. For beneath the preposterous veneer lurks a comment on our time, a reflection of the plight of the average man haplessly confronted with the complexities of a jet age civilization burdened with fear, red tape, official mumbo jumbo and ambitious anxiety, Deeply rooted within the screenplay is a subtle protest against the detached, impersonal machinery of modern progress. It is an underlying theme with which an audience can identify. It is the basic reason why the film is going to be an enormously popular attraction . . .

The wordage may have been a bit erudite for Disney, but the sentiment was definitely true, resoundingly reaffirmed by the studio's other comedies of the 1960s.

The Absent-Minded Professor was launched by a special hour program on the Disney TV show featuring MacMurray explaining "Serendipity," defined as "the art of happy accidents." The film took off at the box office for astronomical results, so much so that Disney decided that a sequel was warranted. The original showed its staying power in 1967 when it did big business all over again on a double bill with *The Shaggy Dog.*

Incidentally, *Time* magazine supplied, for interested readers, the special effects department's recipe for Flubber: "To one pound of salt water taffy add one heaping tablespoon polyurethane foam, one cake crumbled yeast. Mix till smooth, allow to rise. Then pour into saucepan over one cup cracked rice mixed with one cup water. Add topping of molasses. Boil till it lifts and says 'Qurlp.'"

In 1997, Robin Williams inherited the role of Professor Brainard in a remake titled *Flubber.* He drove a Thunderbird convertible rather than a Model T, and Fred MacMurray's leading lady, Nancy Olson, made a brief appearance as a Ford executive secretary. It wasn't nearly as well received as the original had been in its day.

*The film was later computer-colorized for TV and home video.

THE PARENT TRAP

RELEASED BY BUENA VISTA ON JUNE 12, 1961. TECH-nicolor. Director, screenplay: David Swift, based on the book *Das Doppelte Lottchen (Lisa and Lottie)* by Erich Kastner, Director of photography: Lucien Ballard. Editor: Philip W. Anderson. Art directors: Carroll Clark, Robert Clatworthy. Set decorations: Emile Kuri, Hal Gausman. Costume designer: Bill Thomas. Costumers: Chuck Keehne, Gertrude Casey. Music: Paul J. Smith. Orchestrations: Franklyn Marks. Associate producer: George Golitzen. Assistant director: Ivan Volkman. Special photographic effects: Ub Iwerks. Sequence consultant: Donald Da Gradi. Dialogue coach: Leon Charles. Sound supervision: Robert O. Cook. Sound mixer: Dean Thomas. Music editor: Evelyn Kennedy. Running time: 124 minutes.

Songs: "The Parent Trap," "For Now, For Always," "Let's Get Together" by Richard M. Sherman and Robert B. Sherman.

Cast: Hayley Mills (Sharon McKendrick; Susan Evers), Maureen O'Hara (Maggie McKendrick), Brian Keith (Mitch Evans), Charlie Ruggles (Charles McKendrick), Una Merkel (Verbena), Leo G. Carroll (Reverend Mosby), Joanna Barnes (Vicky Robinson), Cathleen Nesbitt (Louise McKendrick), Ruth Mc-Devitt (Miss Inch), Crahan Denton (Hecky), Linda Watkins (Edna Robinson), Nancy Kulp (Miss Grunecker), Frank DeVol (Mr. Eaglewood). Title song sung by Tommy Sands and Annette Funicello.

After the rave reviews she received for *Pollyanna,* it was clear that the only thing better than one Hayley Mills would be *two* Hayley Millses. That is the premise of *The Parent Trap,* written and directed by David Swift, who also was responsible for *Pollyanna.* Basically, it deals with thirteen-year-old identical twins who meet for the first time at summer camp. At first they feud with each other, but then it gradually dawns on them that they are sisters, one having lived in Boston most of her life with her mother, the other having stayed with her father in California. Sharon is eager to see her father, while Susan would love to see her mother again, so they spend the summer coaching each other on their respective lives. At summer's end, they switch places, hoping in the bargain to be able to bring their parents together again.

Things get rough in California, since Father is about to remarry; what's more, the girl is a catty, shrewd little gold digger only after his money. Sharon phones Susan and tells her that if she doesn't show up soon, it may be too late. So Susan tells her mother the whole story, forcing her to bring her back to California. Mother arrives at a most inopportune time, necessitating explanations to the fiancée and her mother.

The girls try to play matchmaker for their parents, but an argument spoils the whole setting. The next morning, when Mother is ready to go home to Boston, the girls refuse to identify themselves, insisting that they won't do so until after a camping trip Father is preparing to take. The fiancée is persuaded to go along on the trip, and the girls do everything they can to make the journey living hell for her, to such an extent that she walks out on her husband-to-be.

He returns home to find his ex-wife still there, and he slowly realizes that this is all for the best; it's what he really wanted all along. They reunite for a happy ending.

The Parent Trap is no great shakes, but it provides a good vehicle for some extremely winning players, most notably Hayley Mills, but also the adult leads, and character actors Charlie Ruggles, Leo G. Carroll, and Frank DeVol, to name a few.

The film wavers uneasily between very broad slapstick and more subtle humor, obviously trying to bridge the gap between younger and more mature viewers in the audience. At summer camp, before they know they are sisters, the twins play a series of practical jokes on each other, culminating in a melee at a Saturday night dance, in which the directress of the girls' camp gets a creamy chocolate cake in the face and the director of the boys' camp is doused with punch. Later, when the fiancée goes on the camping trip with Father and the girls, they pour honey on her feet while she's sleeping, and she is wakened by bear cubs licking her toes!

This is contrasted with some very amusing repartee involving the minister who is to marry Father to the girl. Instead of being shocked or angry at the appearance of Father's ex-wife in a bathrobe, he revels in the whole thing, actually sorry to have to leave when the fiancée's mother drags him away. There are also some delicious moments involving the twins' Bostonian grandfather, played by Charlie Ruggles, the only one with a twinkle in his eye in the staid household.

The elements do not always mix. The film shows its overlength in the final portion, for though the camping trip is amusing, it's merely a delay tactic before getting to the inevitable conclusion. By now the audience *knows* that Brian Keith and Maureen O'Hara are going to get together again; it's just a matter of *when*. Even after arriving home, there is a lot of unnecessary business before the final clinch.

Best of all is the business of the twins. Hayley Mills truly *is* remarkable, giving credibility to both characterizations, and she is the film's principal raison d'être. Dilys Powell in the Sunday *London Times* saw a definite parallel between Miss Mills and an earlier child star, Mary Pickford. Pickford, it was pointed out, also projected an image of sweetness tempered with mischief, and often had roles where she played matchmaker for adults, or tried to reform a drunken father, etc.

Of course, acting ability in the dual roles would have been negated if the illusion were not effective. Cameraman Lucien Ballard recalls:

They'd worked out this whole film using an English process, much like the old blue-backing process, to get the twins into various scenes. It involved double-exposure with the backgrounds and it was very complicated. Plus, when you were shooting, you could never tell the girl which light to look into or anything. I told them it was too complex, and asked instead for a double. Usually they sent relatives out for assignments like that, but I told them this time I wanted a *real* double who really looked like Hayley. Finally I found a girl who was the same height, had the same features—everything was the same except her eyes were a different color, but I was able to compensate for that. And at several figures away, you couldn't tell the difference between the girl and Hayley. So I did a lot of over-the-shoulder shots, and threw out most of the vapor shots. . . . But Walt made me put some of the trick shots back, because he . . . liked technical things.

The actual double-exposure and split-screen shots are remarkable, and after a while one is hardly conscious of the fact that it *is* trickery. Oddly enough, it is the fairly rudimentary material that looks phony in the film; when Maureen O'Hara and Hayley have a picnic in a Boston park, it's done with a very obvious process screen, and afterward they walk away on a treadmill. It is certainly strange that such elementary tricks as these should look artificial while the really complicated scenes look fine.

One of the film's brightest assets is another of Disney's delightful animated main-title sequences. This one involves two cupids, and variations on a sampler that reads "Bless Our (Broken) Home." There are many clever ideas, as the title song is sung

Hayley Mills meets . . . Hayley Mills for the first time, in this scene from *The Parent Trap*. © *1961 Walt Disney Productions*

Hayley confounds her parents, Maureen O'Hara and Brian Keith. © *1961 Walt Disney Productions*

on the track; the "O" in Maureen O'Hara's name turns into a teardrop, for instance. In fact, Disney devoted an entire hour of his TV show to a behind-the-scenes look at the preparation of this title sequence, including the recording of the title song.

Writer-director David Swift was apparently so taken with the possibilities of a comic summer camp that he used the first segment of this movie for the basis for a TV series several years later called *Camp Runamuck,* and even rehired Frank DeVol (better known as a musical director) to play a camp leader. It was rather broad slapstick and did not last long.

This was Swift's last film for Disney, but just the beginning of a durable relationship with the star, Brian Keith, who later expressed his gratitude to Disney for taking him out of the action mold and casting him into a romantic role. The film also continued the Disney tradition of hiring well-known character actors to round out his casts, including two, Charlie Ruggles and Una Merkel, who appeared in several later productions. Unfortunately, it was the lovely Maureen O'Hara's only film for the studio.

The Parent Trap received generally excellent reviews. *The New York Times* said that it "should be most appealing to parents, as well as children, because of the cheerfully persuasive dual performances of Hayley Mills." *Time* called it "delightful . . .

The important thing about a children's picture is that children like it. If they are old enough to enjoy some mild mush and young enough to know childhood's most prized secret—that all adults are boobs—they should like this one."

And *Variety*'s reviewer, like most others, singled out Hayley Mills for making the film work. "When Miss Mills is not on the screen, the film labors, not because of any lack of comic savvy on the part of other members of the cast, but because the yarn is absolutely predictable from the outset and stretches itself interminably in the romantic passages . . ."

It was also apparent that Hayley Mills was the one bringing people into the theaters to see the film—enough people, in fact, to make *The Parent Trap* a whopping box-office success, both in its initial run and in a reissue later in the decade. She was, obviously, one of the prime assets of the Walt Disney studio at this time.

A grown-up Hayley returned to the studio in 1986 to star—as a parent with twins of her own—in the Disney Channel movie *The Parent Trap II.* It was followed by *The Parent Trap III* (1989) and *Parent Trap Hawaiian Honeymoon* (1989).

The original film was faithfully remade by Disney in 1998.

NIKKI, WILD DOG OF THE NORTH

RELEASED BY BUENA VISTA ON JULY 12, 1961. TECHnicolor. Producer: Winston Hibler. Screenplay: Ralph Wright, Winston Hibler, based on a novel by James Oliver Curwood. Narrator: Jacques Fauteux. Additional narration: Dwight Hauser. *For Walt Disney Productions:* Associate producer: Erwin L. Verity. Continuity sketches: Sam McKim, Dale Hennesy. Film editor: Grant K. Smith. Music: Oliver Wallace. Orchestrations: Clifford Vaughan. Sound: Robert O. Cook. Music editor: Evelyn Kennedy. *For Calgary Ltd.:* Director: Jack Couffer. Photography: Lloyd Beebe, Jack Couffer, Ray Jewell, William V. Bacon. *For Westminster Films Ltd.:* Director: Don Haldane. Photography: Donald Wilder. Unit manager: Leo Ewashun. Assistant directors: Phil Hirsch, Jerry Stoll. Set decorations: Jack McCullagh. Costumes: Jan Kemp. Makeup: Ken Brooke, Barry Nye. Sound recording: George Mulholland, Andre de Tonnancourt. Running time: 74 minutes.

Cast: Jean Coutu (Andre Dupas), Emile Genest (Jacques LeBeau), Uriel Luft (Makoki), Robert Rivard (Durante), Nikki and Neewa.

Nikki, like *Perri* before it, uses the skill and technique of the True-Life film to tell a fictional tale. The result is first-rate entertainment, with many astounding sights filmed on location in Canada.

The film opens with Andre Dupas, a trapper, and his wolf dog Nikki, pulling their canoe ashore during a trip down the river. Nikki runs off and encounters a bear cub whose mother is murdered by a killer-bear. Nikki brings the cub back to his master and insists that he go along with them. Dupas ties the two together as he takes off downstream, but when they come to a section of rapids, the boat overturns and the animals are washed ashore far from Dupas.

The two animals, still tied together, try to fend for themselves. They don't get along (one sleeps in a tree, the other on the ground, the rope preventing much movement), and finally break loose. When they find they can't get along very well without each other, they reteam, but when winter comes, Neewa, the bear, hibernates, leaving Nikki on his own.

He is captured by a wicked trapper in retaliation for Nikki raiding his traps of meat. When the trapper, LeBeau, sees what a powerful dog Nikki is, he decides

Trapper Dupas brings his boat ashore, and Nikki wastes no time in running off. © *Walt Disney Productions*

Nikki and Neewa, tied together, for better and for worse (mostly the latter). © *Walt Disney Productions*

to make a fighter out of him, and starts the training by treating him as cruelly as possible. He explains to his Indian guide that Nikki must hate *everything* in order to be a good fighter. He takes the dog to a local trading post, where the new factor has outlawed the so-called pit fights. LeBeau and another man with a fighter-wolf ignore the rule and stage a vicious fight in the ditch dug out of the ice. The factor arrives and tells LeBeau to stop, but LeBeau shoves him into the pit and jumps in after him to fight him. After a dirty fight, LeBeau sets Nikki loose to attack the factor, but Nikki recognizes the man as his old master, Dupas! Instead, he turns on LeBeau just as he is about to plunge a knife into Dupas, and the evil trapper falls on his own knife.

Dupas takes Nikki with him, and the Indian guide too; when they stop at the same place where the dog and master were parted, Nikki runs off to find Neewa after his hibernation. But Neewa is grown now, and has no desire to play any more with Nikki. At Dupas's call, Nikki returns to his master for good, and they sail off for new adventure.

Nikki is a fast-paced, exciting film, combining a solid story with great animal footage and beautiful scenery. Disney engaged two Canadian film units (one headed by Jack Couffer, who had worked on earlier True-Life films) to shoot footage to match the script his staff had prepared, based on James Oliver Curwood's *Nomads of the North.*

It is beyond this writer's understanding how many of the shots for the film were obtained, but there are many startling ones: Nikki and Neewa trying to sleep in their respective positions on the ground and in the tree; Nikki trying to lure a muskrat out of its underground home in the middle of an iced lake; the dog and bear, now friends, rollicking together. There are many interestingly staged shots as well, such as the climactic pit fight, filmed with a hand-held camera to excellent effect, and first-person shots such as one from inside Nikki's cage as he is brought into the trading post by LeBeau.

The film's final shot is especially impressive, showing the boat containing Dupas, Nikki, and the Indian sailing down the river, as seen by Neewa, at the top of a hill—with the entire panorama a spectacular array of springtime color.

One would think that the combination of dialogue scenes, with actors, and true-life scenes, with music and narration, might not mix, but they are perfectly blended, and the performances are all quite good. Emile Genest makes the character of LeBeau a thoroughly despicable one, so that his death at the end of the film is a satisfying moment for the entire audience. (Incidentally, that lengthy fight between Dupas and LeBeau is very brutal, Disney or no Disney.)

The film was greeted by largely favorable reviews. The *New York Times*'s Bosley Crowther said: "It is not what you would call superior drama, and the humans do not perform with anything like the natural instinct and charm of the puppy and the cub. But then, human actors are seldom the peers of animals in Disney films." *Variety* called the film "pleasant diversion," while *Time* said the film would "delight every ten-year-old who ever wrestled with his pillow and pretended it was a grizzly bear."

Disney retained the factual/fictional format that worked here in several future projects.

GREYFRIARS BOBBY

RELEASED BY BUENA VISTA ON SEPTEMBER 28, 1961. Technicolor. Director: Don Chaffey. Screenplay: Robert Westerby, based on the book by Eleanor Atkinson. Photography: Paul Beeson. Additional photography: Ray Sturgess. Editor: Peter Tanner. Art director: Michael Stringer. Set decorations: Vernon Dixon. Costumes: Margaret Furse. Music conductor: Francis Chagrin. Associate producer: Hugh Attwooll. Production manager: Peter Manley. Assistant director: Dennis Bertera. Special photographic effects: Albert Whitlock. Continuity: Phyllis Crocker. Casting: Maude Spector. Dialect adviser: John Breslin. Makeup: Harry Frampton. Hairstyling: Barbara Ritchie. "Bobby" trained by John Darlys. Sound editor: Terry Poulton. Sound recordists: Norman Boiland, Red Law. Running time: 91 minutes.

Cast: Donald Crisp (James Brown), Laurence Naismith (Mr. Traill), Alex MacKenzie (Old Jock), Kay Walsh (Mrs. Brown), Duncan MacRae (constable MacLean), Andrew Cruickshank (lord provost), Gordon Jackson (farmer), Rosalie Crutchley (farmer's wife), Freda Jackson (old woman caretaker), Moultrie Kelsall (magistrate), Joyce Carey (first lady), Vincent Winter (Tammy), Jameson Clarke (constable), Jack Lambert (doctor), Joan Buck (Ailie), Jennifer Nevinson (farmer's daughter), Bruce Seton, Hamish Wilson, Sean Keir.

Greyfriars Bobby is a sentimental tale, based on a true story, which takes place in Edinburgh, Scotland, in 1865. The opening scenes are of a farm in the Scottish countryside. A farmer is forced to let his elderly caretaker, Old Jock, go, and is driving him into town. The farmer's daughter's pet dog, Bobby, is very attached to the old man, and runs into town after him. He finds Old Jock, who is ill, and is by his side when the old man dies that night while sleeping in a flophouse. When he is buried the next day, the dog refuses to leave the grave site. Caretaker James Brown tries to chase him away, and local restaurant owner Mr.

Traill decides to take care of Bobby. He wants to adopt the dog, but every night Bobby sneaks back into the graveyard and sleeps on Old Jock's grave. This is strictly against the rules, and caretaker Brown is angry, but bit by bit both he and Traill grow very fond of the dog and welcome his visits. The dog is also taken in by the poor urchins who live near the graveyard, who play with him during the day.

One day a stuffy constable on the beat sees the dog in Traill's eating house and threatens to turn him in for not having a collar, which costs seven shillings. Traill refuses to pay the money on principle; since the dog doesn't sleep in his home, he says he doesn't own him. Brown volunteers to pay the fee, but Traill says he has no right to do so either.

The case is argued in court, at which time the children of the town appear with seven shillings, which they have raised penny by penny from all the local youngsters, who feel they have a stake in Bobby. The lord provost is so impressed by this action that he gives the dog the Freedom of the City, making him city property, so to speak, with a special collar declaring this fact.

Now Bobby runs free, spending time with all his friends, and still returning to the grave site every night to sleep with his oldest friend and master. As he lies there, cries of "Good night, Bobby" fill the air from the people of the town who now know that he belongs to all of them.

Greyfriars Bobby is a film of considerable charm and beautiful atmosphere (especially the studio-built set of Edinburgh village), but, unfortunately, it moves very slowly and takes an interminable length of time to get to the point of the film. Up until that time, well into the picture, there is an aimlessness to the story that frequently produces boredom, as well as impatience, on the part of the viewer. It isn't until the final third of the film that one has any indication of where the plot (such as it is) is leading.

This, along with the general low-key nature of the presentation, works against the film. At least one critic, Eugene Archer in the *New York Times,* pointed out the perennial problem of Disney's imports, which adds to the difficulty of enjoying *Bobby:* "A good British cast trill their r's to such an extent that the children in yesterday's audience scarcely understood a word they said."

Still, most reviews of the film were enthusiastic. *Variety* called it "warm and refreshing. . . . Only the toughest, most snide cynic, or maybe a real dedicated dog-hater, will fail to be beguiled . . ." Paul V. Beckley in the *New York Herald Tribune* deemed it "one of the tidiest, nicest, and prettiest movies of the year." And Archer in the *Times,* the least impressed, still called it "prettily colored, pleasantly paced and generally inoffensive."

As always in the Disney British productions, a prime reason for remembering the film at all is the outstanding cast, in particular the two "stars," a joy to watch in their slowly building feud, Donald Crisp and

Donald Crisp and Laurence Naismith fight a continuing battle over little Bobby.   © *Walt Disney Productions*

At last, Bobby shows some affection for Naismith in court. © *Walt Disney Productions*

Laurence Naismith. The cast is rounded out by an impeccable array of supporting players, who give the film what substance it has.

Director Don Chaffey fared somewhat better when he made *The Three Lives of Thomasina* for Disney several years later.

BABES IN TOYLAND

RELEASED BY BUENA VISTA ON DECEMBER 14, 1961. Technicolor. Director: Jack Donohue. Screenplay: Joe Rinaldi, Ward Kimball, Lowell S. Hawley, based on the operetta by Victor Herbert and Glenn McDonough. Photography: Edward Colman. Editor: Robert Stafford. Art directors: Carroll Clark, Marvin Aubrey Davis. Set decorations: Emile Kuri. Costumes: Bill Thomas, Chuck Keehne, Gertrude Casey. Music: George Bruns, based on Herbert's musical score. Orchestrations: Franklyn Marks. Libretto: Mel Leven. Choral arrangements: Jud Conlon. Choreography: Tommy Mahoney. Special effects: Robert Mattey. Animation sequences: Eustace Lycett, Joshua Meador, Bill Justice, Xavier Atencio. Makeup: Pat McNalley. Hairstyling: Ruth Sandifer. Sound: Robert O. Cook, Dean Thomas. Music editor: Evelyn Kennedy. Running time: 105 minutes.

Songs: "I Can't Do the Sum," "Just a Toy," "Floretta," "Castle in Spain," "We Won't Be Happy Till We Get It," "Lemonade," "Just a Whisper Away," "March of the Toys," "Toyland" by Victor Herbert. "The Workshop Song," "The Forest of No Return," "Slowly He Sank into the Sea" by George Bruns, Mel Leven.

Cast: Ray Bolger (Barnaby), Tommy Sands (Tom Piper), Ed Wynn (The Toymaker), Annette Funicello (Mary Contrary), Henry Calvin (Gonzorgo), Gene Sheldon (Roderigo), Tommy Kirk (Grumio), Mary McCarty (Mother Goose), Kevin Corcoran (Boy Blue), Brian Corcoran (Willie Winkie), Ann Jilliann (Bo Peep), Marilee and Melanie Arnold (The Twins), Jerry Glenn (Simple Simon), John Perri (Jack-Be-Nimble), David Pinson (Bobby Shaftoe), Bryan Russell (The Little Boy), James Martin (Jack), Ilana Dowding (Jill), Bess Flowers (villager).

This lavish, colorful, Disneyized version of the Victor Herbert classic opens with a puppet named Sylvester J. Goose talking to the audience through the part in a stage curtain. He is followed by Mother Goose, who invites us all to join her in Mother Goose Village. The curtain opens, and the camera moves into an unbelievably bright and colorful setting, where the storybook characters are celebrating the impending marriage of Tom Piper to Mary Contrary.

The villainous Barnaby is jealous, however, and has his two henchmen, Gonzorgo and Roderigo, kidnap Tom and do away with him. Instead of killing the boy, they sell him to a gypsy camp to make extra money on the deal. The next day, when Mary learns of Tom's demise, Barnaby plays on her sorrow to ask her hand in marriage. She refuses, but that night realizes that she is in dire financial straits, and next day agrees to marry the leering rogue. At a prewedding celebration that night a gypsy troupe comes to entertain, and a gypsy hag sings a song—at the end of which "she" removes her wig to reveal none other than Tom! He and Mary are reunited, and the marriage with Barnaby is called off.

When Mary's younger brothers and sisters wander off into the Forest of No Return, Mary and Tom go after them and end up in Toyland, where they offer to help the harried Toymaker meet his Christmas deadline. The Toymaker's inventor helper Grumio concocts a ray gun that can shrink anything to miniature size. Barnaby invades the toy factory, uses the ray gun to put Tom out of the way and have the Toymaker marry him to Mary. Tom takes advantage of his new size to activate the toy soldiers and lead them into battle against Barnaby. They emerge victorious, Grumio's new ray gun returning Tom to normal size. Back in the village it's celebration time once more as Tom and Mary are finally wed.

Babes in Toyland is filled to the brim with gimmicks, ranging from minor (animated stars bursting out of Tom's head when he is bopped with a sledgehammer by the two henchmen) to major (talking/singing/dancing trees in the Forest of No Return), an endless procession of songs, staged in a variety of fashions to avoid repetition from one to the next, and a large cast performing in the most colorful settings ever devised for a live-action Disney film.

Unfortunately, all these elements combined cannot overcome some basic and serious flaws that hamper the picture.

First, there is no heart to the film. The viewer feels no emotion for any character on the screen, and when there is no empathy with a hero or heroine, a film is off to a bad start. Besides a lack of charisma on the part of the main characters, there is no menace to the villains. The whole film is played in an *opera comique* style that keeps everything at the most super-

Ray Bolger, Mary McCarty (with Sylvester the Goose), Marilee and Melanie Arnold, Kevin and Brian Corcoran, and Annette Funicello listen to Henry Calvin and Gene Sheldon tell the story of Tommy Sands's demise. © *1961 Walt Disney Productions*

Tommy Sands, Kevin Corcoran, Annette Funicello, and toymaker Ed Wynn examine the rubble after an explosion in the toy factory. © *1961 Walt Disney Productions*

ficial level. Barnaby is simply not a villain; there is never any feeling of danger in any of his schemes, and the tone of the picture is such that even the supposedly scary sequence, with the living trees, is sugarcoated to keep it from ever getting *too* frightening.

In trying to keep the film at the level of fluffy entertainment, the filmmakers forgot to breathe life into the whole production.

For older viewers there is an air of contrivance about the film. Every movement, every gag, every gimmick has a preplanned, mechanical look about it that in its very calculatedness leaves the viewer cold.

That the film has these shortcomings is a shame, because it also has the kind of imagination and potentiality that indicates what it *could* have been. Some of the musical numbers are excellent. When Ray Bolger sings "Castle in Spain" to Annette Funicello, he goes into an elaborate dance number involving a fountain of dancing waters that, at one point, match his movements precisely. "I Can't Do the Sum" has Annette sitting down at a table trying to balance her books. As she sings of her problem, four other Annettes hop out of her skin to join her in the song, each one tinted a different color. Later, she looks in a full-length mirror while singing, and as she walks away the four Annettes walk out of the mirror to join her. As she sings of the confusion of figures, assorted numbers fly in the air around her head. The gypsy hag number provides Tommy Sands with his best moment in the film, in an amusing and effective performance of the song.

One of the film's true highlights involves its two best performers, Henry Calvin and Gene Sheldon, performing a quasi-Laurel and Hardy act as Barnaby's thick-witted henchmen. They are easily the funniest thing in the film, and their number "Slowly He Sank into the Sea" is a comic gem, with Calvin singing the (fictitious) saga of Tom's death at sea as Sheldon dances about him; with every chorus the puddle at their feet, from Sheldon's crocodile tears, grows deeper and deeper.

Would that the same could be said for the rest of the cast. Ray Bolger has no business playing a villain, even though he does a creditable job; his broad rendition of the role renders the part thoroughly unbelievable. Annette Funicello and Tommy Sands may well be the dullest romantic team ever depicted on the screen, and the overemphasis on them, and their uninspired renditions of the Victor Herbert songs really bog down the film and kill its interest for the adolescent audience that rejects such "mush." As for Ed Wynn, a little of him goes a long way, although he does contribute some of the film's more humorous moments. Tommy Kirk is saddled with another idiotic role as Wynn's assistant.

The Toyland finale, with the wooden soldiers attacking Barnaby, is good, although curiously not as exceptional as one would expect from Disney. The sequence is fairly short, and the animated trickery rather routine, considering the special effects that have preceded it (Bolger's piggy bank, which projects alluring dollar signs in the air, sending his henchmen falling after them; night "falling" at Toyland, literally; the living trees). The material in this sequence is not on par with, say, George Pal's Puppetoons, which were used to such good effect in *tom thumb* a few years earlier.

The reviews of *Babes in Toyland* reflected these failures in the film's conception. *Variety* deemed it "great for the moppets . . . but some of the more mature patrons may be distressed to discover that quaint, charming *Toyland* has been transformed into a rather gaudy and mechanical 'Fantasyland.' What actually emerges is *Babes in Disneyland.*" *Time* commented: "*Babes in Toyland*, Walt Disney's first live-action musical, is a wonderful piece of entertainment for children under five, but children over five who plan to see it will be well advised to take some Berlitz brushup lessons in baby talk." Paul V. Beckley summed up his review in the *New York Herald Tribune* by saying that "the whole film has the character of frosting without any cake underneath."

Oddly enough, even though this was Disney's Christmas release, and was well promoted with an hour-long special on the Disney TV show giving behind-the-scenes glimpses of the making of the film, it did not do all that well at the box office. Considering its cost and potential, it grossed just $4,600,000 in domestic release, or a little more than half what the *Shaggy Dog* pulled in.

Babes in Toyland was filmed only once before, by Hal Roach in 1934, with Laurel and Hardy as the stars, and Charlotte Henry and Felix Knight as the romantic leads. It hasn't the color or special effects of the new version, but it is everything the Disney film should have been: charming, funny, frightening, and truly memorable.

The film was just a case of Disney trying to outdo himself, and channeling his energy in the wrong direction. It was his first live-action musical, and he profited by the experience. A few years later he turned out a little something called *Mary Poppins*. Remember?

MOON PILOT

RELEASED BY BUENA VISTA ON FEBRUARY 9, 1962. Technicolor. Coproducer: Bill Anderson. Director: James Neilson. Screenplay: Maurice Tombragel, based on a story by Robert Buckner. Photography: William Snyder. Editor: Cotton Warburton. Art directors: Carroll Clark, Marvin Aubrey Davis. Set decorations: Emile Kuri, William L. Stevens. Costumes: Chuck Keehne, Gertrude Casey. Associate producer: Ron Miller. Assistant director: Joseph L. McEveety. Special effects: Eustace Lycett. Makeup: Pat McNalley. Hairstyling: Ruth Sandifer. Sound: Robert O. Cook, Harry M. Lindgren. Music editor: Evelyn Kennedy. Running time: 98 minutes.

Songs: "Seven Moons of Beta Lyrae," "True Love's an Apricot," "The Void" by Richard M. Sherman and Robert B. Sherman.

Cast: Tom Tryon (Captain Richmond Talbot), Brian Keith (Major General John Vanneman), Edmond O'Brien (McClosky), Dany Saval (Lyrae), Tommy Kirk (Walter Talbot), Bob Sweeney (Senator McGuire), Kent Smith (secretary of the air force), Simon Scott (medical officer), Bert Remsen (Agent Brown), Sarah Selby (Mrs. Celia Talbot), Dick Whittinghill (Colonel Briggs), Cheeta (Charlie the Chimp), Nancy Kulp (nutritionist), Bob Hastings (air force officer), Muriel Landers (fat woman in lineup), William Hudson, Robert Brubaker.

Moon Pilot, a sophisticated, satirical, and wholly disarming comedy, took everyone by surprise at the time of its release. Said *Time:*

> Sacred cows, if skillfully milked, produce tons of fun; but Hollywood usually avoids them because they often kick back. The more reason to be pleasantly surprised that Walt Disney, not specifically known for sociopolitical daring, should have herded three of these pampered critters—the FBI, the Air Force, and the astronaut program—into the same plot. Under the deft manipulation of Director James Neilson and Scenarist Maurice Tombragel, they produce a fairly steady stream of healthy nonsense.

The nonsense involves the United States space program. Having successfully orbited a chimp around the moon, a man is next in line, but no one in the inner circle volunteers. The chimp, however, sticks a fork into Captain Richmond Talbot when he isn't looking, and his reaction is taken as a gesture of willingness. He is given permission to take a short leave to see his mother at home, but the mission is to remain top secret. On the plane, flying home, he encounters a lovely, unusual girl who seems to know who he is and what he is scheduled to do. She tells him she has something important he should know, concerning the composition of the rocket. He tries to elude her, but even in his hometown, she mysteriously appears.

When he reports her presence to his commanding general, the FBI is assigned to the case, and Talbot is put under lock and key in a hotel room. Even there, the girl materializes, and finally persuades Talbot to listen to her. He is won over by her charm, and apparent sincerity, as she tells him that she is from the planet Beta Lyrae, and she only wants to help him by suggesting a special formula to coat the rocket's surface.

Talbot sneaks out of the hotel to spend some time with the girl, named Lyrae, causing a major holocaust when it's discovered that he is gone. The FBI and the air force clash head on, with endless confusion about what should be kept secret from whom, and who is in charge of what. Talbot is finally located, and the blast-off takes place as scheduled, with the formula applied to the rocket ship. Once he is up in the air, however, who should appear in his cabin but Lyrae, whom Talbot has come to love. She teaches him a song about the Seven Moons of Beta Lyrae, and they sing it together, to the consternation of the commanding general on earth, listening in on the communications radio. "What's going on up there?" he shouts, as Talbot and Lyrae, who plan to get married, continue singing. "What's going on up there?" he continues to shout in frustration.

Much of the humor in *Moon Pilot* is far from

Tom Tryon, with the chimp that starts all his troubles. © *1961 Walt Disney Productions*

Tryon and Dany Saval, as Lyrae. © *1961 Walt Disney Productions*

subtle, but most of it works. Some amusing and potent swipes are taken at meddlesome but ignorant senators (when one asks too many questions at space head-quarters, he is asked why he hasn't read their booklet, "Simple Science for Senators"), San Francisco beat-niks (one of whom repeatedly mumbles, "Nobody can avoid the void"), and Secret Service men who can see everything except the nose in front of their faces.

Tom Tryon is ideal as the hapless astronaut who has greatness thrust upon him, so to speak, and lovely Dany Saval (who was "introduced" in this film and then promptly forgotten) is delightful as the pixieish girl from Beta Lyrae. Most of the humor revolves around cigar-chomping General Brian Keith and for-ever-flustered FBI man Edmond O'Brien, but their constant hollering becomes a bit overbearing several times during the film. The supporting cast is well chosen, with Tommy Kirk rating a "guest star" billing for his small role as Tryon's younger brother.

The monkey, it goes without saying, contributes many of the film's biggest laughs, and, like all Disney animals, is hopelessly mischievous.

The reviewers, caught off guard, were delighted by the Disney spoof. The *New York Times*'s Crowther wrote: "Of all people, Mr. Disney is making good-natured fun of the high-minded scientific project of firing a man around the moon," although he qualified his enthusiasm by noting that "it's wacky, but not as witty as it might be—not by a lot. . . . Mr. O'Brien rants and mugs something awful. So does Brian Keith. And Mr. Tryon does a lot of mugging too. But Charlie is natural and amusing (isn't every chimpan-zee?) and the rocket stuff is fascinating. This should be a fun film for the kids."

Variety wrote: "It's a healthy country that can take time out to laugh at its most sacred, troublesome issues, and a healthy industry that supplies the tonic to ease such excess anxiety." Paul V. Beckley in the *New York Herald Tribune* called it a "flippant fantasy."

Moon Pilot, not an especially costly or ambitious picture, was only a modest success at the box office. But it kept the movie mills running at the Disney studio, which now hoped to turn out at least five or six films a year, and provided a movie vehicle for Tom Tryon, who had achieved stardom of sorts as Texas John Slaughter on the Disney television show. It also marked the Disney debut of director James Neilson, who stayed with the studio for several years, directing a variety of films before branching out on his own.

BON VOYAGE!

RELEASED BY BUENA VISTA ON MAY 17, 1962. TECH-nicolor. Director: James Neilson. Screenplay: Bill Walsh, based on the book by Marrijane and Joseph Hayes. Photography: William Snyder. Editor: Cotton Warburton. Art directors: Carroll Clark, Marvin Aubrey Davis. Set decorations: Emile Kuri, Hal Gausman. Costumes: Chuck Keehne, Gertrude Casey. Music: Paul J. Smith. Associate producers: Bill Walsh, Ron Miller. Assistant director: Joseph L. McEveety. Special effects: Eustace Lycett. Special ti-tles: Bill Justice, Xavier Atencio. French production supervisor: Sacha Kamenka. Makeup: Pat McNalley. Hairstyling: Ruth Sandifer. Sound: Robert O. Cook, Dean Thomas. Music editor: Evelyn Kennedy. Run-ning time: 130 minutes.

Title song by Richard M. Sherman, Robert B. Sherman.

Cast: Fred MacMurray (Harry Willard), Jane Wyman (Katie Willard), Michael Callan (Nick O'Mara), Deborah Walley (Amy Willard), Tommy Kirk (Elliott Willard), Kevin Corcoran (Skipper Willard), Jessie Royce Landis (La Contessa), Georgette Anys (Madame Clebert), Ivan Desny (Ru-dolph), Francoise Prevost (The Girl), Carol White (Penelope), Marie Sirago (Florelle), Alex Gerry (Horace), Howard I. Smith (Judge Henderson), Casey Adams (The Tight Suit), James Millhollin (librarian), Marcel Hilaire (sewer guide), Richard Wattis (Englishman), Doris Packer (Mrs. Hender-son), Ana Maria Majalca (Shamra), Hassan Khay-yam (Shamra's father).

Bon Voyage! sounds like a good idea for a Disney film: the adventures of a typical American family on their first trip abroad. Any possibilities that may have been inherent in the idea were dissolved in the transi-tion to film, however. *Bon Voyage!* is a dull, hack-neyed, and tremendously overlong film. What is more (and this is especially odd for a Disney movie) it is aimed at the wrong audience.

The crafters of the screenplay and production obviously thought that by having an attractive middle-aged couple, a teen-age daughter, a teen-age son, and a mischievous younger son, the film would have appeal for the entire family. What they didn't count on was the fact that while they were concentrating on the parents, the kids in the audience would be bored stiff, and vice versa. This is perhaps the first Disney film where parents had to keep their kids quiet in the theatres, instead of the other way around.

The titles feature a travel montage of postcards, baggage, brochures, etc., concluding with an aerial view of the Statue of Liberty, and then swings over to Manhattan Island where we join the Willard family in a cab en route to the pier. The exposition is flatly laid out in conversation in the cab. (They're from Terre Haute, they've been meaning to do this for twenty-two years but the kids were growing up, etc.)

Misadventures start at the dock, with young Skipper running off, Amy meeting a handsome boy, Elliott moping, and Father being his usual bumbling self. There is a bon voyage party sequence, and then considerable time on the crossing itself, during which Amy starts to get serious with the new boyfriend, Nick O'Mara, and formerly "square" Elliott takes up with an Indian girl. A perplexed parent, Harry asks his wife if she's ever read *State Fair,* and makes an analogy to their current situation.

Once in Paris, everyone goes his separate way, prime problems being Harry getting lost in the Paris sewer system, the family meeting Nick's mother, a countess, whose pampering has left Nick a spoiled, confused young man, and a gigolo pursuing Katie, much to the chagrin of her husband, who winds up socking the swain in the jaw at a Riviera casino, causing considerable havoc.

All's well that ends well, however, and on their last night in France, the parents are finally left alone by their children, and they enjoy the romance in the air as fireworks go off in the sky.

Bon Voyage! might have been easier to take were it not so overdrawn and overlong. Unnecessary and repetitive scenes abound, with Deborah Walley's hot-and-cold romance with Michael Callan reversing itself so many times that the viewer finally gets tired of the whole thing.

Bosley Crowther noted in the *Times:* "Everything possibly unearthable in the way of an obvious cliché involving the hick behavior of American tourists abroad seems to have been dug out from somewhere by the screen-playwright and made to fit into this enactment of a family's vacation odyssey." *Time* said it moved "at a snail's pace."

Though Disney was certainly counting on whole families coming to enjoy the film, it was unforgivable to desert his juvenile audience so much in this screenplay. Children who went to see the film when it was released (during the summertime) felt cheated at having to sit through endless sequences of teen-age love, marital jealousy, and such. A scene where Fred MacMurray is confronted by a French mother who claims that Tommy Kirk despoiled her daughter's

virtue couldn't have meant much to the tots in the audience.

Even the expertise of Fred MacMurray could not save some scenes, such as the one at the going-away party where after twenty-two years of marriage, he still doesn't know how to address his father-in-law.

Still, *Bon Voyage!* had family appeal, in anticipation if not in realization, and it grossed $5 million in its domestic release.

The Willard family passport: Tommy Kirk, Deborah Walley, Fred MacMurray, Kevin Corcoran, and Jane Wyman. © *1964 Walt Disney Productions*

Mother and Father finally get some peace and quiet near the end of *Bon Voyage!* © *1964 Walt Disney Productions*

BIG RED

RELEASED BY BUENA VISTA ON JUNE 6, 1962. TECH-nicolor. Coproducer: Winston Hibler. Director: Nor-man Tokar. Screenplay: Louis Pelletier, based on novels by Jim Kjelgaard. Photography: Edward Col-man. Editor: Grant K. Smith. Art directors: Carroll Clark. Marvin Aubrey Davis. Set decorations: Emile Kuri, Hal Gausman. Costumes: Chuck Keehne. Mu-sic: Oliver Wallace. Orchestrations: Walter Sheets. Associate producer: Erwin L. Verity. Assistant direc-tor: Arthur J. Vitarelli. Makeup: Pat McNalley. Irish setters trained by William R. Koehler. Sound: Robert O. Cook, Dean Thomas. Music editor: Evelyn Ken-nedy. Running time: 89 minutes.

Songs: "Mon Amour Perdu," "Emile's Reel" by Richard M. Sherman, Robert B. Sherman.

Cast: Walter Pidgeon (James Haggin), Gilles Payant (Rene Dumont), Emile Genest (Emile Fornet), Janette Bertrand (Therese Fornet), Doris Lussier (Farmer Mariot), Rolland Bedard (conductor), Georges Bouvier (baggageman), Teddy Burns Goulet (engineer).

Big Red is a simple story, well told, using Dis-ney's strong point of matching charismatic human beings with irresistible animal stars.

Rene Dumont, an orphan boy, obtains a job at the home of a lonely, wealthy dog fancier named James Haggin; the boy works and lives with Haggin's overseer, Emile. There is a beautiful dog named Big Red in the kennel whom Haggin thinks will become a prizewinner, but he is unable to do anything with the dog, who is incorrigible. The boy, however, creates an instant rapport with the animal, and not only trains him, but grows to love him. Haggin then realizes that the dog may become totally dependent on the boy, and orders Rene to stay away from Red until after the big dog show. The night before the show, Rene can-not resist saying hello to his pet. He waves to him through a window of the house, and the canine be-comes so excited that he crashes through the window to be with the boy, cutting himself seriously in the process.

Haggin reluctantly orders Emile to put the dog out of its misery, but rather than see that happen, Rene runs off with Red and nurses him back to health. When he returns the dog to Haggin, the owner is overwhelmed, and asks Rene to stay with him, but the boy says no, and takes off on his own.

Some time later Haggin ships Red and his newly found mate out of town on a train; along the way the two dogs escape and run off into the woods. It seems impossible that they will ever be found, but when Rene hears of it, he goes off after the dogs. When Haggin learns what Rene has done, he fears for the boy's safety and goes after him. Rene finds Red, and discovers that his mate is giving birth to puppies; he heads home with Red so they can return with help. Meanwhile, Haggin has an accident and tumbles down a slope, getting his foot locked among several rocks. A mountain lion shows up and hovers around him menacingly. Just then, Rene comes by; Red im-mediately goes for the mountain lion, but before any harm can be done, Rene manages to shoot the predator.

Rene frees Haggin, and helps him to walk home; reunited, they realize how much they mean to each other, and Haggin tells the boy that he's going to live with him from now on.

Big Red does not read well on paper, but it plays well, thanks to strong performances and a sense of quiet realism and understatement on the part of di-rector Norman Tokar. Unlike some later Disney efforts, this one gives its main characters some dimen-sion, and acts out its story against charming and natural backgrounds. There is a delightful sequence, for instance, where Rene, overseer Emile, and his wife have an informal musicale. It's totally spontaneous, and has a natural, unaffected air that gives it a very special flair. Contrast this to a contrived barn-dance scene in Tokar's later film *Those Calloways*, where every move, every utterance, seems wholly preplanned.

Pidgeon's character is nicely sketched here as well. We learn about him bit by bit, and, even then, only in hints. Apparently his son was killed in action, and his housekeeper continually tells him he shouldn't be living alone. The main theme of the film, in fact, is the humanization of the Pidgeon character, who grows from a man obsessed with materialism (in the form of prize canines) to a man capable of loving someone as he once did.

Norman Tokar became a prolific Disney director in the 1960s; this, his initial effort for the studio, re-mains one of his best, for sincerity of approach and

Walter Pidgeon, Gilles Payant, and Red, against a beautiful Canadian backdrop. © *1961 Walt Disney Productions*

Payant and Pidgeon clean up Red after he's returned from wandering off. © *1961 Walt Disney Productions*

the whole general feel of underplaying. There is no grand finale, just Pidgeon and the boy walking home together, when the The End title appears. This is just one example of many where restraint makes something work in *Big Red*.

Critics were not overly enthusiastic about the film, however. *Variety* called it a "lesser Disney effort." The *Times* said it "does not rate a blue ribbon." Robert Salmaggi in the *Herald Tribune* had the kindest words to say, calling it "charming. . . . To be sure, the usual quota of sentiment and tears is present, but in nicely restrained doses . . . moviegoers will find it difficult not to warm up to Big Red, a magnificent Irish Setter."

ALMOST ANGELS

They may be choirboys, but they're still just kids.
© *1962 Walt Disney Productions*

Sean Scully takes a bow after conducting the choir on their concert tour.   © *1962 Walt Disney Productions*

RELEASED BY BUENA VISTA ON SEPTEMBER 26, 1962. Technicolor. Production supervisor: Peter V. Herald. Director: Steve Previn. Screenplay: Vernon Harris, based on an original idea by R. A. Stemmle. Photography: Kurt Grigoleit. Editor: Alfred Srp. Art directors: Werner and Isabell Schlichting. Costumes: Leo Bei. Musical director: Heinz Schreiter, with the Wiener Symphoniker Orchestra, conducted by Helmuth Froschauer. Choreography: Norman Thomson. Production managers: Willy Egger, Robert Russ. Assistant director: Rudolf Nussgruber. Studio representative: Harry Tytle. Camera operator: Herbert Geier. Second unit photography: Hermann Mergth. Dialogue coach: Kent McPherron. Makeup: Rudolph Ohlschmidt, Leopold Kuhnert. Sound: Heinz Janeozka, Kurt Schwartz. Running time: 93 minutes.

Cast: Peter Weck (Max Heller), Hans Holt (Director Eisinger), Fritz Eckhardt (Father Fiala), Bruni Lobel (Frau Fiala), Gunther Phillipp (radio commentator), Vincent Winter (Toni Fiala), Sean Scully (Peter Schaefer), Denis Gilmore (Friedel Schmidt), Henny Scott (Ferdy), Heinz Grohmann (music teacher), Rose Renee Roth (wardrobe mistress), Heidi Grubl (seamstress), Ferda Maren (sisternurse), Liselotte Wrede (woman), Bernhard Hindinger (Felix Meinl), Oskar Willner (Misignore), Walter Varndel (mathematics teacher), Anni Schoenhuber (woman), Elizabeth Stiepl (mother), Hermann Furthmosek, Hans Christian, Walter Regelsberger (choirmasters), and the Vienna Boys' Choir.

Filmed entirely in Austria, this lightweight film is heavy on schmaltz, but generally well done, placing a close-up story of several boys against the background of the Vienna Boys' Choir.

The titles appear over lovely views of a train winding through the lovely landscapes of Austria. The train is bringing the choirboys home from a European tour, and little Toni, the son of the train's engineer, is intrigued. He decides he would like to join the choir, too. His mother helps to arrange an audition, and he is accepted. His father is tougher to convince; he finally agrees to go along with the idea, as long as Toni's schoolwork is up to par.

Toni admires Peter, the oldest member of the group; the choirmaster's attention to Toni creates something of a rivalry, but it grows into a friendship before too long.

A crisis arrives when Peter's voice cracks one day; he is losing his youthful soprano, and he is disconsolate, since the choir is about to leave on an extended tour. Toni cooks up a scheme to help him, however. During the dress rehearsal the next evening, before an invited audience, another boy sings for Peter backstage; the boys figure that when Peter's handicap is discovered on the road, it will be too late to send him back. But Peter gives up in the middle of the performance, running from the stage, shamefully embarrassed.

The choir director goes to see Peter and console him. Then, the next day, he convinces the board of directors that since Peter has been so exceptional over the years, he should go on tour as his assistant conductor. They agree. The finale is a montage of the boys' international tour, concluding in a great symphony hall where Peter conducts "The Blue Danube," giving the featured solo to Toni and his little friend Friedel. Peter receives a great ovation.

Almost Angels sets out to "humanize" the Vienna Boys' Choir to prove to the largely American audience of youngsters bound to see this film that choirboys are "regular guys" too. Thus, the story is neatly woven around a few central characters, emphasizing schoolboy mischief (there is a large-scale pillow fight), youthful competition, and such. In one scene where Toni is discouraged about low grades, the choir director shows him busts of great composers who were once members of this same choir, and whose grades in arithmetic were no better than his.

In stressing this aspect of the choirboys' lives (as well as their dedication to music), it seems odd that a performance would be shown in which several of the boys must dress as little girls—the very kind of thing the filmmakers had tried to steer away from in portraying the youths throughout the film.

The music itself is, as might be expected, excellent, and the performances are well spaced in the narrative to avoid monotony and keep the story moving at all times.

The performances, particularly those of the children, are fine, and played against authentic locations, both interior and exterior, lend the film a credibility it might otherwise lack. Sean Scully, who plays Peter, became a temporary Disney protégé, starring in an elaborate TV version of *The Prince and the Pauper* at this time.

Almost Angels received unusually enthusiastic reviews in the New York press. Thompson in the *Times* called it "a wholesome little family film, attractive to the eye and ear," and Salmaggi in the *Herald Tribune* thought it "charming." Only hard-boiled *Variety* had a discouraging word or two, writing that "*Almost Angels* is almost unbearably saccharine in story style, and the singing interludes, at first a tonic for tired ears, eventually overstay their welcome."

But as double-feature fodder, the film enjoyed modest success, enough to make it worth Disney's while to continue planning to shoot feature films abroad.

THE LEGEND OF LOBO

RELEASED BY BUENA VISTA ON NOVEMBER 7, 1962. Technicolor. A Walt Disney-Calgary Ltd. Production. Coproducer: James Algar. Screenplay: Dwight Hauser, James Algar, based on a story by Ernest Thompson Seton. Photography: Jack Couffer, Lloyd Beebe. Editor: Norman Palmer. Music: Oliver Wallace. Orchestrations: Walter Sheets. Narrator: Rex Allen, with music by Allen and the Sons of the Pioneers. Field producer: Jack Couffer. Production manager: Erwin L. Verity. Sound: Robrt O. Cook. Running time: 67 minutes.

Title song by Richard M. Sherman and Robert B. Sherman.

In the tradition of *Perri* and *Nikki* comes *Lobo*, "a tale of the old West told in song and story." Lobo is a wolf, and we follow his life from birth (he is one of five children) to adulthood, when he must make it on his own against the hazards of life. His mother has been killed, and his father trapped; Lobo is determined to avoid these fates.

He tries to join a new pack, and must prove his worth; when he does, he becomes the new leader. He finds himself a mate, who is captured by a rustler, knowing that Lobo will follow. He does, but brings his whole pack with him, and although the human is an expert hunter, he is no match for the cunning Lobo, who manages to elude him. Unfortunately, the episode teaches Lobo for good that he must move on to a place where man will not interefere with his life.

Lobo is put together with the expertise one would expect from the experienced Disney team. At sixty-seven minutes it moves well and has few dead spots. If it seems somewhat less compelling than others in this series, it is probably because a wolf has less attraction than a cute squirrel like Perri, and no human beings to interact with as in *Nikki*.

Lobo's biggest asset, aside from the always first-rate raw footage, is the sound track with Rex Allen and the Sons of the Pioneers. Allen, a former cowboy star, became a Disney favorite in the 1960s, and with good reason. His friendly, easygoing approach to the script brings a great deal of life to any subject; and the musical interpolations are a welcome addition.

Bosley Crowther pointed out that ". . . the theme and the drama, what little of the latter there is, is carried in the narration, which cheerily endows the wolf with a great deal more charm and character than is evidenced on the screen. However, to the youngsters, this may not be apparent at all."

Field producer/cameraman Jack Couffer put his experience with wolves to good use some twenty years later, when he coproduced the more ambitious Disney feature *Never Cry Wolf*, which managed to explore human nature as well as animal behavior.

Lobo and friend in a meditative moment on the prairie. © *1961 Walt Disney Productions*

IN SEARCH OF THE CASTAWAYS

RELEASED BY BUENA VISTA ON DECEMBER 19, 1962. Technicolor. Director: Robert Stevenson. Screenplay: Lowell S. Hawley, based on the novel *Captain Grant's Children* by Jules Verne. Photography: Paul Beeson. Additional photography: Ray Sturgess, Michael Reed, David Harcourt. Editor: Gordon Stone. Art director: Michael Stringer. Set decorations: Vernon Dixon. Costumes: Margaret Furse. Music: William Alwyn. Conductor: Muir Mathieson. Second unit director: Peter Bolton. Associate producer: Hugh Attwooll. Production manager: Peter Manley. Assistant director: Eric Rattray. Special photographic effects: Peter Ellenshaw. Special effects: Syd Pearson. Casting: Maude Spector. Continuity: Pam Carlton. Makeup: Harry Frampton. Hairstyling: Barbara Ritchie. Animals by Jimmy Chipperfield. Sound editor: Peter Thornton. Sound recordists: Dudley Messenger, Gordon McCallum. Running time: 100 minutes.

Songs: "Merci Beaucoup," "Grimpons," "Enjoy It," "The Castaways Theme" by Richard M. Sherman, Robert B. Sherman.

Cast: Hayley Mills (Mary Grant), Maurice Chevalier (Professor Paganel), George Sanders (Thomas Ayerton), Wilfrid Hyde-White (Lord Glenarvan), Michael Anderson, Jr. (John Glenarvan), Keith Hamshire (Robert Grant), Jack Gwillim (Captain Grant), Antonio Cifariello (Indian chief), Wilfrid Brambell (Bill Gaye), Ronald Fraser (guard), Iniate Wiata (Maori chief), George Murcell, Mark Dignam, Michael Wayne, David Spenser, Milo Sperber, Roger Delgado, Barry Keegan, Maxwell Shaw, Andreas Malandrin.

For his first fantasy venture in a while, Disney chose to return to the writings of Jules Verne. The confusing, many-faceted story has to do with a searching party seeking out the long-lost Captain Grant, their only clue being a note found in a bottle. A professor, Grant's two children, the owner of the boat Grant was commanding, and his son engage in the difficult task of tracking down the captain.

They journey to South America, where they endure an earthquake, a ride through an ice cavern on a broken ledge that becomes a bobsled, a giant condor snatching young Robert Grant, a massive flood that strands them in a giant tree, a fire in the tree, a jaguar roaming among the branches, and a waterspout. After all this they discover that they shouldn't have been in South America at all, but in Australia.

Off they go, and upon arrival they advertise for anyone having information leading to the whereabouts of Captain Grant. Thomas Ayerton, a former

Ayerton (George Sanders) threatens his captive, Captain Grant (Jack Gwillim, with back to camera) in *In Search of the Castaways*. © *1962 Walt Disney Productions*

Hayley Mills hugs Maurice Chevalier, who makes their adventures just a bit livelier than normal. © *1962 Walt Disney Productions*

member of his crew, shows up and offers to take them to New Zealand, where Grant is being held. He loads "trinkets" on board their ship to trade with the natives. It soon turns out that he is a gunrunner who had set the captain adrift in the first place. He casts *them* adrift, and when they reach shore they are held captive in a tribal village, where they meet Bill Gaye, a half-crazed member of Grant's crew. He leads them to an escape route, over the volcanic mountains nearby. When they climb over the mountains and into an adjacent cove, they discover Grant himself, who has just been visited by Ayerton, with more illegal guns. While he is ashore, our heroes climb aboard Ayerton's ship, subdue the crew, and get the drop on Ayerton when he returns, putting an end to the mystery and reuniting the children with their father.

Castaways is a briskly paced, lavishly filmed adventure, but a curious one at the same time. Because the opening sequences are realistic, and the search for Grant a logical one, the audience is totally unprepared for the sudden burst of fantasy that propels the film into an ever-mounting collage of impossible happenings. The rescue party is spending the night on a ledge high `in the Andes Mountains, when suddenly there is an earthquake and the ledge breaks off, turning into a giant sled! From this point on, the bizarre fantasy elements never stop coming. Ordinarily, this would be prime Disney material, but here somehow the effect is diminished. There is not only the suddenness, but the total lack of rhyme or reason, unlike the earlier Disney/Verne endeavor, *20,000 Leagues under the Sea*, where everything fit into place.

There seems no earthly purpose for throwing in a giant condor or a massive flood, and the slightly off-center feeling is only amplified when Maurice Chevalier starts to sing about their troubles! Any credibility or tenacity on the part of the viewer is thrown out the window when after all this, Chevalier suddenly realizes that they have traced the note to the wrong part of the world—negating everything that has happened up to that point.

Castaways is all form and no substance; this is not to say that the various elements don't work, just that they don't work *together*. There is puppy-love romance between Hayley Mills and Michael Anderson, Jr., scene-stealing and buoyant songs from Maurice Chevalier, bumbling comedy relief from Wilfrid Hyde-White—but it never meshes.

The effects themselves range from very good, in the case of some complicated ones like the flood, to unconvincing, as in the sledding sequence, which does take the party through a dazzling ice cavern. A major handicap is the heavy reliance on obviously indoor sets and substandard matte work, as when the party is climbing up the mountain ledges on mules.

Bosley Crowther in the *New York Times* said the film was "good for children of all ages—between 6–12, that is. . . . It is, as we say, a whopping fable, more gimmicky than imaginative, but it doesn't lack for lively melodrama that is more innocent and wholesome than much of the stuff the children see these days on television."

Yet, considering what the Disney studio was capable of, *In Search of the Castaways* must be rated a disappointment.

SON OF FLUBBER

RELEASED BY BUENA VISTA ON JANUARY 18, 1963. DIrector: Robert Stevenson. Associate producers: Bill Walsh, Ron Miller. Screenplay: Bill Walsh, Donald Da Gradi, based on a story by Samuel W. Taylor, and the Danny Dunn books. Photography: Edward Colman. Editor: Cotton Warburton. Art directors: Carroll Clark, William H. Tuntke. Set decorations: Emile Kuri, Hal Gausman. Costume designer: Bill Thomas. Costumers: Chuck Keehne, Gertrude Casey. Music: George Bruns. Orchestrations: Walter Sheets. Second unit director: Arthur J. Vitarelli. Assistant director: Joseph McEveety. Special effects: Eustace Lycett, Robert A. Mattey, Jack Boyd, Jim Fetherolf. Makeup: Pat McNalley. Hairstyling: Ruth Sandifer. Sound supervision: Robert O. Cook. Sound mixer: Dean Thomas. Music editor: Evelyn Kennedy. Running time: 100 minutes.

Cast: Fred MacMurray (Professor Ned Brainard), Nancy Olson (Betsy Brainard), Keenan Wynn (Alonzo Hawk), Tommy Kirk (Biff Hawk), Elliott Reid (Shelby Ashton), Joanna Moore (Desiree de la Roche), Leon Ames (President Rufus Daggett), Ed Wynn (A. J. Allen), Ken Murray (Mr. Hurley), Charlie Ruggles (Judge Murdock), William Dema-rest (Mr. Hummel), Bob Sweeney (Mr. Harker), Paul Lynde (sportscaster), Stuart Erwin (Coach Wilson), Edward Andrews (defense secretary), Alan Hewitt (prosecutor), Leon Tyler (Humphrey), Forrest Lewis (Officer Kelly), James Westerfield (Officer Hanson), Alan Carney (referee), Lee Giroux (newscaster), Jack Albertson (Mr. Barley), Eddie Ryder (Mr. Osborne), Harriet MacGibbon (Mrs. Daggett), Beverly Wills (woman in television commercial), Wally Boag (man in television commercial), Walter Elias Miller (baby Walter in commercial), Joe Flynn (announcer in commercial), Harvey Korman (husband in commercial), Mari Lynn (wife in commercial), Belle Montrose (mother in commercial), Henry Hunter (admiral), Hal Smith (bartender), J. Pat O'Malley (sign painter), John Olsewski (Rutland football player #15), Norman Grabowski (Rutland football player #33), Gordon Jones (Rutland coach), Lindy Davis (newsboy; first hobgoblin), Darby Hinton (second hobgoblin), Hope Sansberry (secretary), Byron Foulger (proprietor), William H. O'Brien (attendant), Jack Rice (second juror), Dal McKennon (first juror), Burt Mustin (first bailiff), Ned Wynn (Rutland student manager), Brad Morrow (first football player), Robert Shayne (assistant to the defense attorney).

Until this time Disney had never produced a sequel to any of his theatrical features, restraining such activities to TV production, where if something paid off, it was followed through. The success of *The Absent Minded Professor,* however, and the possibilities for wacky inventions and special effects its formula presented, were too good to resist, so two years after the release of the first film, *Son of Flubber* followed.

It is a formula film in the strictest sense of the word. The Disney staff looked at *The Absent Minded Professor,* analyzed what made it "work," and then repeated every element in *Son of Flubber,* right down to casting many of the same people—not just the stars, but supporting players as well.

What the film lacks, however, is a story. It meanders from one subplot to another, working in as many gimmicks as possible along the way. Generally speaking, it has to do with Professor Brainard's new discovery, "dry rain," which he feels will make him enough money to subsidize Medfield College, which is about to be repossessed by financier Alonzo Hawk. "Dry rain" involves aiming a shotgun device at a certain area, which produces an artificial rain cloud. Unfortunately, it is very difficult to aim, and it has

one unfortunate side effect: it breaks every piece of glass within range of the ray gun. Meanwhile, two other events are taking place: Biff Hawk is experimenting with the Professor's equipment, and discovers "flubbergas," which he uses to help Medfield win a far-out football game (the inflated player, instead of the football, is hurled down the field) ; and the Professor's wife, Betsy, walks out on him because she is jealous of Ned's old flame, Desiree de la Roche, who has her eyes on him.

The damage "dry rain" has caused brings the Professor to court, and just when all looks bleak, a county agricultural agent comes in to testify that the artificial rain has produced *good* effects that far out-

When the Professor is dragged into court, his wife appears as a witness; Charlie Ruggles tries to preside over the unorthodox proceedings in *Son of Flubber.* © *1962 Walt Disney Productions*

Flubbergas is what's responsible for Medfield's football team soaring to victory, as evidenced in this photo. © *1962 Walt Disney Productions*

weigh the damage. As evidence, he brings into the courtroom a dazzling display of oversized vegetables that grew that way thanks to the Professor's invention. The courtroom also provides a background for a reconciliation between the Professor and his wife, for a truly happy ending.

On the whole, *Son of Flubber* is silly and disjointed. Its strength lies in individual scenes, such as the opening sequence which shows what has happened to the Brainards since the discovery of flubber. He is hounded by an Internal Revenue Service man who holds him responsible for money he never received from the government for his discovery, and then he and his wife are visited by some hucksterish advertising men who want to buy commercial rights to flubber. As an inducement they show proposed TV commercials for some flubber products (such as "flubber-oleum," which enables a tired family to bounce back to life on their flubberized floors). All this is fast, funny, and nicely satirical.

There is some obvious but surefire stuff involving the Prof's rain clouds and the breaking glass, including a funny scene with Keenan Wynn on the phone in his office as the entire place, lined with plate glass, falls apart.

Then there are parallel sequences lifted from *The Absent Minded Professor.* The first occurs when Betsy goes to a costume party where Shelby Ashton, her old beau, flirts with her. The jealous Professor follows him outside in his car, and flies overhead as he's driving home in his Neptune costume. With a flick of his switch he causes it to rain inside Shelby's car, driving him crazy and causing him to run his car smack into the police car he had hit in the earlier film, containing the same befuddled officers.

The second repeat is the football game, closely patterned after the hilarious basketball contest in the first film. Even the coaches and referees (Alan Carney, Gordon Jones) are played by the same people. This is prime sight-gag material, of course, and the movie's strongest asset. It also provides a first-rate finale. In

the midst of the game one of the players hurls a flubberized ball downfield. Since it's been "souped up," it doesn't land, continuing to fly off into the horizon. At the end of the film we see a panoramic shot of the stratosphere, with satellites in orbit among the various stars. And there, flying through outer space, is the very same football.

The technical credits are, again, first-rate, and in some ways even better than those on *Professor,* since there is less emphasis on the car and more footage devoted to other kinds of trickery: the indoor rainclouds, breaking glass, oversized vegetables, flying football players, etc. Still, it was felt that this could be carried off more convincingly in black and white than in color.

The other aspect of *Son of Flubber* that gives it merit is the cast, certainly one of the best ensembles of comic actors ever put together for one film. At every turn there is another amusing vignette: Joe Flynn as the commercial announcer, Paul Lynde as the sportscaster calling the flubber game, Alan Carney as the referee, Charlie Ruggles as the judge, Ed Wynn as the the agricultural agent, to name just a few. Most of these players came to be regarded as Disney's stock company in the 1960s, for every film the studio made seemed to include at least a few of them in the cast. This was part of Disney's audience-priming, counting on the familiarity of such character actors to ensure built-in laughs in every situation.

As might have been expected, the critics found this sequel less enchanting than the original, but most had some good words to say. Bosley Crowther in the *Times* called it "good entertainment. . . . It is crazy, of course, in the spirit of old-fashioned sight-gag slapstick farce, but it is fun . . ." *Time* recommended the film for "any moviegoer who needs a good, old-fashioned locomotive laugh."

Equally predictable, *Son of Flubber* followed in the footsteps of its ancestor and grossed some $9 million in its domestic release—which explains why sequels are made.

MIRACLE OF THE WHITE STALLIONS

RELEASED BY BUENA VISTA ON MARCH 29, 1963. Technicolor. Director: Arthur Hiller. Associate producer: Peter V. Herald. Screenplay: A. J. Carothers, based on the book *The Dancing White Horses of Vienna* by Colonel Alois Podhajsky. Photography: Guenther Anders. Second unit photography: Peter Pochlatko.

Editors: Alfred Srp, Cotton Warburton. Art directors: Werner and Isabell Schlichting. Costumes: Leo Bei. Music: Paul J. Smith. Orchestrations: Franklyn Marks. Production managers: Walter Tjaden, Robert Russ. Assistant director: Laci Ronay. Technical adviser and special effects: Paul Waldherr. Makeup:

Rudolph Ohlschmidt. Sound: Kurt Schwarz, Robert O. Cook. Music editor: Evelyn Kennedy. Running time: 117 minutes.

Song: "Just Say Auf Wiedersehen" by Richard M. Sherman, Robert B. Sherman.

Cast: Robert Taylor (Colonel Podhajsky), Lilli Palmer (Vedena Podhajsky), Curt Jurgens (General Tellheim), Eddie Albert (Rider Otto), James Franciscus (Major Hoffman), John Larch (General Patton), Brigitte Horney (Countess Arco-Valley), Philip Abbott (Colonel Reed), Douglas Fowley (U.S. general), Charles Regnier (General Stryker), Fritz Wepper (Rider Hans), Guenther Haenel (Groom Sascha), Philo Hauser (dispatcher), Michael Janisch (refugee leader), Margarethe Dux (woman railroad official), Max Haufler (engineer), Robert Dieti (German M.P. captain), Josef Krastl (Att. Carl), Peter Jost (Kreisleiter), Kurt Jager, Olaf Tschierschke (riders), Herbert Prilopa (Orderly Tellheim), Erik Schumann (Captain Ranhoff), Helmut Janatsch (intruder), Michael Tellering (Stryker's adjutant), Hal Gallili (Brooklyn G.I.), Harry Hornisch (first rider), James Dobson (southern G.I.).

Miracle of the White Stallions is one of Disney's most unusual films, because it is so un-Disneyesque. The production, the story, the cast, the whole atmosphere of the production give no clue that the Disney studio was behind it.

The story is a basically true one, about the famed Spanish riding school in Vienna, which breeds the stately Lippizan horses. In 1945, with Vienna caught in the middle of two indecisive powers, it seems a great risk to keep the horses sheltered at the riding hall. Colonel Podhajsky, the head of the school, re-

Robert Taylor and Lilli Palmer, as husband and wife in *Miracle of the White Stallions*. © *1962 Walt Disney Productions*

A magnificent Lippizan goes through its paces in the finale of *Miracle of the White Stallions*. © *1962 Walt Disney Productions*

quests permission from the Germans to evacuate his prized animals, but the request is denied. Podhajsky then goes to a friend, General Tellheim, to ask if he can use his influence; Tellheim replies that it is impossible, but notes that there has been clearance to remove "art treasures" from the city, and tells Podhajsky that if he wanted to use his judgment in interpreting that phrase, nothing could be done to stop him.

With this encouragement Podhajsky, his wife, and some of his men set to work in the involved task of taking the horses out of the city without arousing undue suspicion. They stay at the country estate of Countess Arco-Valley, where things are relatively peaceful and the horses are free to roam. The only problem is that the mares have been separated from the stallions, meaning that the breed may die out.

When American troops move into Austria, Podhajsky begs the commanding officer to give his horses priority, and to rescue his stallions from Czechoslovakia when they cross the border to bring back allied prisoners. The final die is cast when Podhajsky hastily assembles a performance in order to impress General Patton and win his sympathy. It works, the mares are returned, and Podhajsky's battle is won.

The story ends in 1955, the 212th Anniversary of the riding hall, with a performance of the Royal Lippizans, attended by many of the people, from ex-soldiers to train engineers, who helped save the white stallions.

This is another example of a film whose audience seems hazily defined. The narrative of *Miracle of the White Stallions* is simply too confusing and too demanding for young minds, and at 117 minutes it goes on far too long to hold a child's interest with merely pretty pictures of horses. For adults there is more value, but the oversimplicity of the dialogue and characterizations in many cases would tend to negate much of its appeal to that sector of the audience as well. The result is a film that succeeds in neither area; a pity, since the raw material for a more compelling film is obviously here.

A major shortcoming is the Robert Taylor characterization. Podhajsky is uncompromisingly serious and dedicated to his horses. As a result he comes off as

cold and distant; there is no audience empathy in his fervent working to save the horses, because he never earns the viewer's sympathy. The German general, played by Curt Jurgens, who dislikes war and helps Podhajsky, is a much more likable character from the start.

Another problem is the script, which has too much talk and too little action. At times it is difficult to understand the situation at hand, since so many factors come into play. One suddenly finds oneself asking where we are, which side is where, what country were they just talking about? A clearer concept of the whole story would have undoubtedly added excitement and sweep to the film.

This was the first major movie credit for director Arthur Hiller, who had previously done television shows (and one B-movie), and who has since gone on to greater success with such films as *Love Story, The Hospital,* and *Silver Streak.* He has also acquired a reputation of being only as good as his script. Goodness knows, *Stallions* could have used a better script—and some visual stimulation—to make it more compelling.

The cast does its best with the script. Lilli Palmer's sincerity and warmth help a great deal, and Curt Jurgens's skilled performance all but steals the film. Alas, the pivotal role is Taylor's, and with it the film falls flat.

Variety called the film "inept. . . . Very likely there was a deeply moving story in the rescue of Austria's renowned Lippizan horses during World War Two, but it doesn't materialize in *Miracle of the White Stallions,* a fuzzy, laborious and generally undistinguished dramatization of that story in a confusing and insensitive scenario, plus turtle-tempoed direction by Arthur Hiller . . ." Robert Salmaggi in the *Herald Tribune* wrote that *"Miracle of the White Stallions* falls between two stools: not schmaltzy enough for the kiddies, too pallid for the adults." *Time* added: "They [the horses] are . . . more intelligent than most of the people connected with this picture."

Miracle of the White Stallions did not seem miraculous to many moviegoers, and the film died at the box office.

SAVAGE SAM

RELEASED BY BUENA VISTA ON JUNE 13, 1963. TECHnicolor. Coproducer: Bill Anderson. Director: Norman Tokar. Screenplay: Fred Gipson, William Tunberg, based on the book by Fred Gipson. Photography: Edward Colman. Editor: Grant K. Smith. Art directors: Carroll Clark, Marvin Aubrey Davis. Set decorations: Emile Kuri, Hal Gausman. Costumes: Chuck Keehne, Gertrude Casey. Music: Oliver Wallace. Orchestrations: Walter Sheets. Assistant to the producer: Louis Debney. Assistant director: Joseph L. McEveety. Special effects: Eustace Lycett, Jim Fetherolf. Makeup: Pat McNalley. Hairstyling: Ruth Sandifer. Sound: Robert O. Cook. Music editor: Evelyn Kennedy. Running time: 103 minutes.

Song: "The Land of the Wild Countree" by Terry Gilkyson.

Cast: Brian Keith (Uncle Beck), Tommy Kirk (Travis Coates), Kevin Corcoran (Arliss Coates), Dewey Martin (Lester White), Jeff York (Bud Searcy), Royal Dano (Pack Underwood), Marta Kristen (Lisbeth Searcy), Rafael Campos (young warrior), Slim Pickens (Wily Crup), Rodolfo Acosta (Bandy Legs), Pat Hogan (Broken Nose), Dean Fredericks (Comanche chief), Brad Weston (Ben Todd).

Officially a sequel to *Old Yeller*, *Savage Sam* has little in common with the earlier film, except the same author, and repetition of the character names of the principals.

Again, Tommy Kirk and Kevin Corcoran play brothers who must fend for themselves, but this time the film does not center around their dog; Sam, the son of Yeller, is a key figure in the story, not the story itself. After some meandering footage devoted to establishing the characters and their home life, the central plot element comes to the fore. Travis, Arliss, and neighbor Lisbeth Searcy are kidnapped by Indians. The boys' Uncle Beck gathers a searching party to follow them when the cavalry is defeated in its attempt. By now much time has gone by, and only the sharp sense of smell belonging to Savage Sam will locate the tribe, which has moved on.

In transit Travis has been left behind, stranded out in the wilderness. Once the rescue party locates him, they must all join forces to find the Indians, lure them away from their camp long enough to subdue them, and move in to snatch away Lisbeth and Arliss. An attempt to do this quietly backfires, and the encounter turns into a full-scale battle, with the white men coming out on top, and the children saved.

Savage Sam is an exciting, colorful film, very different from *Old Yeller*, whose major qualities were warmth and depth of characterization. *Sam* is not quite so skillful in the latter department, for young Arliss, as played by Kevin Corcoran, is now an obstinate, loudmouthed brat, responsible for occasional havoc, as when he taunts an Indian to the point of aggravation and stirs up a minor skirmish. Jeff York, as shiftless Bud Searcy, is also less appealing than he was in the earlier film, perhaps because there is more at stake here, and his so-called comic relief only gets in the way of the plot. (He is redeemed somewhat in the end, when he pulls the trigger that kills one of the Indian leaders holding his daughter captive.)

Sam benefits mostly from the colorful scenery and pulsating excitement of its action scenes, which are many. The final clash is particularly vivid and quite violent, with Corcoran smashing an Indian on the head with the butt of a rifle as he rides past him, and later hurling a rock at an adversary's eye!

Some of this is rather odd, considering Disney's usual attitude toward Indians. The sentiments ex-

Brian Keith restrains Savage Sam. © *1962 Walt Disney Productions*

Tommy Kirk and Sam in the film's climactic segment. © *1962 Walt Disney Productions*

pressed throughout this film vary from character to character (one calling them "dirty murderin' savages"), but from their actions, and from the harshness of the Indians themselves, the overall result is negative. Certainly the glee with which young Corcoran bats an Indian on the head would have been out of place in most other Disney tales of the Old West.

There is also a bit of romance, or more properly puppy love, in this film between Tommy Kirk and Marta Kristen, just hinted at in the earlier endeavor. Kirk again contributes a strong performance, his last before returning to the screwball-comedy mold. Brian Keith's rugged manliness fills out his role perfectly, setting the tone for *his* future Disney films.

Though an unlikely film to have special effects, *Savage Sam* has a few, most notably a thunderous hailstorm, which is carried out beautifully, along with all other technical credits on the film.

Critical reaction was mixed and lukewarm at best. Eugene Archer in the *New York Times* singled out Corcoran as an "obnoxious brat," and opined that "Fred Gipson and William Tunberg have written

abundant clichés, and Norman Tokar has directed every scene as if it were his last." Robert Salmaggi in the *Herald Tribune* was kinder, calling the film "typical Walt Disney adventure offering—clean, wholesome, family-type fare . . ." *Variety* wrote: "*Savage Sam* is one of the least satisfactory items to emerge from the Buena Vista hopper in years. . . . At the root of the picture's problem is the incongruous air of levity with which the scenarists and the director have approached what is obviously a dead-serious situation. This clash confuses the audience throughout and makes it impossible to take the story seriously." The publication predicted that "it will take all the intrinsic drawing power of the Walt Disney banner to counteract the inadequacies of this undernourished Western . . ."

The box-office returns were equally "undernourished," for *Savage Sam* was not much of a financial success. Perhaps its (admittedly minor) linkage to *Old Yeller* was not stressed enough; or perhaps the word "Savage" kept some people away. In any event this was one Disney sequel that really didn't pay off.

SUMMER MAGIC

RELEASED BY BUENA VISTA ON JULY 7, 1963. TECHnicolor. Director: James Neilson. Screenplay: Sally Benson, based on the novel *Mother Carey's Chickens* by Kate Douglas Wiggins. Photography: William Snyder. Special photographic effects: Peter Ellenshaw. Editor: Robert Stafford. Art directors: Carroll Clark, Robert Clatworthy. Set decorations: Emile Kuri, Frank R. McKelvy. Costumes: Bill Thomas, Chuck Keehne, Gertrude Casey. Music: Buddy Baker. Orchestrations: Walter Sheets, Bobby Hammack. Vocal supervision: Camarata. Associate producer: Ron Miller. Assistant director: Austen Jewell. Special effects: Eustace Lycett. Makeup: Pat McNalley. Hairstyling: Ruth Sandifer. Sound: Robert O. Cook, Dean Thomas. Music editor: Evelyn Kennedy. Running time: 100 minutes.

Songs: "Flitterin," "Beautiful Beulah," "Summer Magic," "The Ugly Bug Ball," "The Pink of Perfection," "On the Front Porch," "Femininity" by Richard M. Sherman and Robert B. Sherman.

Cast: Hayley Mills (Nancy Carey), Burl Ives (Osh Popham), Dorothy McGuire (Margaret Carey), Deborah Walley (Cousin Julia), Eddie Hodges (Gilly Carey), Jimmy Mathers (Peter Carey), Michael Pollard (Digby Popham), Wendy Turner (Lallie Joy),

Una Merkel (Maria Popham), Peter Brown (Tom Hamilton), Jim Stacy (Charles Bryan), O. Z. Whitehead (Mr. Perkins), Eddie Quillan (mailman), Norman Leavitt (barber), Paul E. Birns (drinker).

Summer Magic is the kind of film usually described as "lightweight entertainment." Based on the old war-horse *Mother Carey's Chickens* (which was filmed before in 1938), the story—such as it is—deals with the recently widowed Margaret Carey discovering that she has no money, and moving her family to a run-down house in Maine. Gregarious Osh Popham, the town postmaster, helps them fix it up, and doesn't press them for any rent; that's because the house's owner, a Mr. Hamilton, is away in Europe and not expected for a long time. Hamilton shows up unexpectedly, but keeps his identity quiet when he meets and is attracted by Nancy Carey. By the time he explains who he is, everyone is friendly and the Careys look forward to continuing their happy life in Maine.

Told compactly, this story might take up about twenty minutes. The remaining eighty of this film are taken up with a subplot about a snobbish cousin who comes to stay with the family, a heartrending plot that is resolved with the girl, who comes to her senses, crying, "it's all been my fault," and seven songs contributed by the Sherman brothers. Most of these are unmemorable, but they do serve the purpose at hand, and the entire cast gets to join in at one time or another. The most ingenious (if incongruous) number is Burl Ives's rendition of "The Ugly Bug Ball," accompanied by what looks like leftover material from the True-Life nature films.

The cast is attractive and congenial, with Dorothy McGuire as Margaret Carey, Hayley Mills (in her least challenging role) as her daughter, Eddie Hodges and Jimmy Mathers as her sons, Burl Ives as the friendly postmaster/merchant who helps the Careys, Michael Pollard as his funky son, and Una Merkel as his stern wife, with Peter Brown as the young Mr. Hamilton.

If the viewer finishes watching the film and then cannot remember a thing about it, that's all right, because apparently no attempt was made to put any-

Jimmy Mathers and Dorothy McGuire, about to leave their Boston home for the "wilderness."   © *1962 Walt Disney Productions*

The cast of *Summer Magic* in an impromptu front-porch musicale: Peter Brown, Deborah Walley, Dorothy McGuire, Jimmy Mathers, Wendy Turner, Una Merkel, Eddie Hodges, Burl Ives, and Hayley Mills.   © *1962 Walt Disney Productions*

thing of lasting value into it . . . even though screen-writer Sally Benson was the author whose stories had inspired an earlier family classic *Meet Me in St. Louis*. The title, *Summer Magic*, certainly revealed the studio's modest intentions for this film, however: untaxing entertainment for summer vacationers. *Time* magazine speculated, " . . . kids may be lured into dark, cool caverns with promises of sugar-coated escapism—escape from the traumas of the Little League, respite from the tyranny of the report card, surcease from the torments of the tooth brace and the training bra."

Wrote Judith Crist in the *Herald Tribune*:

"Under the sugar-coated pen of Sally Benson, Kate Douglas Wiggins' turn-of-the-century widow and three little orphans emerge as a ragtime quartet, one of those obnoxious families who are perpetually gathering around the piano and singing their hearts out in time of crisis." Eugene Archer in the *Times* ventured to say that "six-year-olds may love it."

There is no record on how many youngsters did "love" the movie, but a good many went to see it, at least $4 million worth; not enough to declare the film a success in the terms of *Mary Poppins*. But then, who said anyone was trying to make a *Mary Poppins*?

THE INCREDIBLE JOURNEY

RELEASED BY BUENA VISTA ON OCTOBER 30, 1963. Technicolor. *For Calgary Ltd.:* Field producer: Jack Couffer. Photography: Jack Couffer, Lloyd Beebe. *For Walt Disney Productions:* Coproducer: James Algar. Director: Fletcher Markle. Screenplay: James Algar, based on the book by Sheila Burnford. Photography: Kenneth Peach. Narrator: Rex Allen. Editor: Norman Palmer. Art directors: Carroll Clark, John B. Mansbridge. Set decorations: Emile Kuri, Charles S. Thompson. Costumes: Chuck Keehne. Music: Oliver Wallace. Orchestrations: Walter Sheets. Production manager: Erwin L. Verity. Unit manager: William O. Sullivan. Assistant director: Mickey McCardle. Makeup: Pat McNalley. Animal supervision: William R. Koehler, Halleck H. Driscoll, Al Niemela. Sound: Robert O. Cook. Music editor: Evelyn Kennedy. Running time: 80 minutes.

Cast: Emile Genest (John Longridge), John Drainie (Professor Jim Hunter), Tommy Tweed (The Hermit), Sandra Scott (Mrs. Hunter), Syme Jago (Helvi Numi), Marion Finlayson (Elizabeth Hunter), Ronald Cohoon (Peter Hunter), Robert Christie (James MacKenzie), Beth Lockerbie (Nell MacKenzie), Jan Rubes (Carl Numi), Irena Meyeska (Mrs. Numi), Beth Amos (Mrs. Oakes), Eric Clavering (Bert Oakes), and Muffey (Bodger), Syn Cat (Tao), Rink (Luath).

Once again, Disney employed the services of Calgary Ltd. to help him film an animal adventure tale against the beautiful background of Canada. In *The Incredible Journey* a family going away for the summer leaves their three pets, two dogs, and a cat with a friend, John Longridge, who lives 250 miles away. He is very fond of the animals, and treats them well, but one day he goes off for a hunting trip alone, and the animals misunderstand. They decide to wend their

way back home, clear across Canada. The balance of the film follows their adventures, both collectively and (when Tao, the cat, is separated from the others) individually, before they miraculously reach their destination.

Blending elements of the True-Life films, with Rex Allen narrating, and pure fiction, *The Incredible Journey* tells a fascinating yarn that is particularly appealing to younger viewers. Each of the animals, Bodger, a bull terrier, Tao, a Siamese cat, and Luath, a Labrador retriever, is given a distinctive personality from the very start of the journey. Most of the encounters along the trip involve all three, but even here their own traits come through in how they handle the situation. Tao is seemingly the wisest, and the most practical; because of his litheness, he is also most capable of getting in and out of difficult spots. It is one of the dogs who is too dumb, or too slow, to realize what he is getting into when he investigates a porcupine, and gets covered with quills. Fortunately, the animals meet a friendly old hermit who invites them into his home and offers them food and shelter along their way. When Tao is washed away by a river current, he is found almost lifeless by a young girl who brings the cat home and nurses him back to health.

All these escapades combine to produce an interesting tale. Not surprisingly, it is the human element that comes off the weakest in the film. Emile Genest is sincere as Longridge, and his sorrow and concern over the loss of the animals is convincing. But the final sequences, in which the Hunter family returns, and the children are disconsolate at the news of their pets, do not come across quite so well, because we have seen so little of the family before that their sudden lapse into emotionalism, especially on the part of the young boy who apparently can't go on without his pet, doesn't really affect the viewer as it should.

Tao, Bodger, and Luath in *The Incredible Journey*.
© *1963 Walt Disney Productions*

Emile Genest asks housekeeper Beth Amos about the animals' disappearance. © *1963 Walt Disney Productions*

Still, *The Incredible Journey* is a beautiful film to watch, and an entertaining one as well. The film was greeted with enthusiastic reviews. Howard Thompson, who had some reservations about certain aspects of the film, still called it "an ideal live-action picture for the small fry . . . about as gentle, warm and lovely a color movie as any pet owner could wish, at least for the kids . . . the expressive animal faces often convey more than the kindly utterances of random humans along the way." *Variety* called the film "an exceptionally good, colorful adventurous tale for the younger element." And even usually cynical *Time* labeled it "a really charming little picture about pets."

Journey wasn't a blockbuster hit, but as one of Disney's bread-and-butter pictures, it did well. It inspired a remake in 1993, *Homeward Bound: The Incredible Journey*, in which the animals talked (in voice-over); that film, in turn, spawned a 1996 sequel.

THE SWORD IN THE STONE

RELEASED BY BUENA VISTA ON DECEMBER 25, 1963. Technicolor. Production supervisor: Ken Peterson. Director: Wolfgang Reitherman. Art director: Ken Anderson. Directing animators: Franklin Thomas, Milt Kahl, Oliver Johnston, Jr., John Lounsbery. Story: Bill Peet, based on the book by T. H. White. Character animators: Hal King, Eric Larson, Cliff Nordberg, Hal Ambro, Dick Lucas. Character design: Milt Kahl, Bill Peet. Backgrounds: Walt Peregoy, Bill Layne, Albert Dempster, Anthony Rizzo, Ralph Hulett, Fil Mottola. Layout: Don Griffith, Basil Davidovich, Vance Gerry, Sylvia Cobb, Dale Bernhart, Homer Jonas. Effects animation: Dan MacManus, Jack Boyd, Jack Buckley. Music: George Bruns. Orchestrations: Franklyn Marks. Film editor: Donald Halliday. Sound supervision: Robert O. Cook. Music editor: Evelyn Kennedy. Running time: 75 minutes.

Songs: "A Most Befuddling Thing," "Blue Oak Tree," "Mad Madame Mim," "That's What Makes the World Go Round," "Higitus Figitus," "The Legend of the Sword in the Stone" by Richard M. Sherman, Robert B. Sherman.

Voices: Ricky Sorenson (Wart), Sebastian Cabot (Sir Ector), Karl Swenson (Merlin), Junius Matthews (Archimedes), Alan Napier (Sir Pelinore), Norman Alden (Kay), Martha Wentworth (Madame Mim, Granny Squirrel), Ginny Tyler (little girl squirrel), Barbara Jo Allen (scullery maid), Richard and Robert Reitherman, and The Mello Men.

The Sword in the Stone was welcomed as Disney's first animated cartoon feature in two years. Though it was fairly well received and moderately successful at the box office, few could resist commenting how different this film seemed from the earlier animated endeavors, not only in drawing style, but in the whole atmosphere of the film, which was telling a medieval tale with a bit too much of its head in the 1960s. In fact, the opening title music is incongruously jazzy in nature, before settling down to more appropriate period music for the storybook introduction.

A volume of *The Sword in the Stone* by T. H. White is opened to the first page, with a troubadour singing the background of the story, illustrated by a series of tableaux, explaining the sword imbedded in the stone, which would determine the next king—whoever would be able to pull the sword out of its rigid position.

We next meet Merlin the Magician, and his pet owl Archimedes, in their forest retreat. Merlin foresees a visitor coming to join him; it turns out to be young Wart, who is running after an arrow lost in a hunting expedition by his knight, Kay. Wart drops in on Merlin, who announces with a flourish that he is now going to assume responsibility for Wart's education. He returns to the castle to live with Wart, and immediately takes the boy out for a series of unusual adventures.

Merlin turns the boy into various animals, to get an idea of how they live, and to prove his general theory that brains always conquer brawn. First he changes Wart into a fish, precipitating an exciting battle with a killer pike, in which Wart is forced to use his brains (with a little help from Archimedes). Then he becomes a squirrel, which gets awkward when a female squirrel falls in love with him and refuses to accept his rejection. Finally, he becomes a bird, and as such is chased by a hawk into the cabin of Madame Mim. When she learns that he is one of Merlin's friends, she decides to do away with him. Just then, Merlin shows up, and challenges Madame Mim to a wizard's duel, in which the two opponents can turn themselves into anything at all in order to undo the other. Mim plays dirty, but Merlin is too crafty to fall for her tricks. When she becomes a fire-breathing dragon, it looks as if all is lost, but Merlin uses his brains, and becomes a germ, which spreads a disease throughout the dragon's system and kills her.

These adventures have done Wart no good in his duties as a squire, however, and just before the big jousting match, he realizes he has forgotten to bring Kay's sword. Running off to find a replacement, he spots the sword in the stone and pulls it out easily. When the others see the fabled sword, they ask where he got it, and refuse to believe his story. They return to watch Wart pull the sword from the stone once more, and awed by the spectacle, dub him their king.

Merlin leaves, and Wart, now King Arthur, is uncomfortable on the throne. But Merlin returns to predict his illustrious future—adding that some day they may even make a motion picture about him!

The Sword in the Stone is a good film, but it falls far short of greatness. One would think that with a story as good as T. H. White's, transference to the realm of animated cartoon would have been relatively simple. But instead of playing up the wonder and awe of Merlin and the boy he takes under his wing, the

One of *The Sword in the Stone*'s tableaux, illustrating the legend of King Arthur and the sword that made him king. © *1962 Walt Disney Productions*

Wart, the boy-king, and his mentor, Archimedes. © *1962 Walt Disney Productions*

Disney screenplay does everything it can to bring them down to earth. Merlin's magic is a matter-of-fact thing, and the life to which Wart aspires is treated in a mundane fashion.

Most distressing of all is the attempt to make the jokes "relevant" to the 1960s, with Merlin constantly dropping throwaway lines about seeing into the future. At the end, when Merlin returns to visit the new King Arthur, he announces that he's just been to Bermuda, and he sports sunglasses, a flowered shirt, and shorts. The final gag in the film is a spoof of a then-current television commercial! This only cheapens the film, instead of making it funnier or more appealing. It also leaves it in danger of dating badly in years to come.

In addition to the obvious, there *is* considerable wit in *The Sword in the Stone*, both in Merlin's dialogue, and especially in that of his pet owl, Archimedes. But in the opening portion of the film, there is an overreliance on dialogue that would tend to make many young viewers restless. It is well into the film before there is a purely visual sequence, such as

Merlin using magic to have all the dirty dishes in the castle wash themselves, or shrinking his belongings and having them find their way into his traveling case when he goes to join Wart. Most of the visual humor in this part of the film is in the manner of little touches, such as Merlin pouring his tea down his beard, accentuating his absentmindedness.

The film's real highlight is the wizard's duel. Here is the kind of sequence that remains in one's memory (more than can be said for the rest of the film), with a whole series of ingenious visual ideas as Madame Mim continually tries to top Merlin by changing herself into progressively more vicious animals, concluding with her pièce de résistance, a fire-breathing dragon. Even her dirty pool is shown visually, with Merlin using his wits to avoid her trickery.

The scenes in which Wart becomes various animals hark back most closely to the Disney of yore, as well as providing more movement and excitement than any other segments in the film. The sequence where Wart, as a fish, is pursued by a shark, has genuine thrills; its conception and timing are superb, making the most of the situation. Meanwhile, the squirrel sequence provides some truly charming moments, as the determined female squirrel pursues her potential mate. There is an amusing punch line as Merlin, who has turned himself into a somewhat older squirrel, finds an older female coming after *him!*

There are the obligatory "beauty shots" throughout *Sword,* scenes played in the reflection of a stream, the stylized tableaux at the beginning of the film, and inventive visual concepts such as the rickety tower of the castle where Merlin is sent to live.

But *The Sword in the Stone* more closely resembles the Disney live-action product of this era than the classic animated cartoons that one associates with the studio. Like so many of the live movies, it provides

thoroughly pleasant entertainment for seventy-five minutes, but it leaves the audience with nothing to take out of the theatre. It's difficult to remember very much about the film even when one tries, unlike most of the good Disney cartoon features, which have an indelible stamp on the memory.

Most reviewers were grateful for even half-steam Disney animation at this point, and the film, released at Christmastime, garnered generally favorable reviews. Judith Crist in the *Herald Tribune* found it "a thorough delight. . . . The songs are bright and singable, the art work lovely and the plot charming in its twists and turns." Howard Thompson in the *Times* called it "a warm, wise and amusing film. . . . The humor sparkles with real, knowing sophistication—meaning for all ages—and some of the characters on the fifth-century landscape of Old England are Disney pips . . ."

Not that these critics were wrong. The film *is* charming, and enjoyable, but it lacks the spark that set so many other Disney films out of the ordinary. Stanley Kauffmann in *The New Republic* wrote a dissenting opinion: "A huge coast-to-coast malted milk made of pasteurized Arthurian ingredients. Every element in it, pictorial and musical, is derivative of earlier and better Disney pictures, and the whole has a factory-line feeling devoid of joy."

Proof of the pudding came at the box office. The film grossed $4½ million, not bad by any means, but hardly up to par for a Disney Christmas release. More interestingly, the film has left no traces; its characters have not evolved into Disney "classics" that are worthy of merchandising or following up on the printed page. In discussions of Disney's work the film is seldom, if ever, mentioned. Despite periodic reissues, the film has never achieved the lasting affection audiences feel for other Disney cartoon features.

THE MISADVENTURES OF MERLIN JONES

Released by buena vista on january 22, 1964. Technicolor. Director: Robert Stevenson. Screenplay: Tom and Helen August, based on a story by Bill Walsh. Photography: Edward Colman. Editor: Cotton Warburton. Art directors: Carroll Clark, William H. Tuntke. Set decorations: Emile Kuri, Hal Gausman. Costumes: Chuck Keehne. Music: Buddy Baker. Orchestrations: Bob Brunner. Associate producer: Ron Miller. Assistant director: Joseph McEveety. Special titles: Bill Justice, Xavier Atencio.

Makeup: Pat McNalley. Hairstyling: La Rue Matheron. Sound: Robert O. Cook. Music editor: Evelyn Kennedy. Running time: 88 minutes.

Song: "Merlin Jones" by Richard M. Sherman, Robert B. Sherman.

Cast: Tommy Kirk (Merlin Jones), Annette Funicello (Jennifer), Leon Ames (Judge Holmby), Stuart Erwin (Police Captain Loomis), Alan Hewitt (Professor Shattuck), Connie Gilchrist (Mrs. Gossett), Dal

McKennon (Detective Hutchins), Norman Grabowski (Norman), Michael Fox (Kohner), Bert Mustin (Bailiff).

More than once Disney had taken television shows and released them to theatres; the transference was usually undetectable, such was the quality of the product. *The Misadventures of Merlin Jones* marked the first time a feature film from the studio looked as if it belonged on television!

The Misadventures of Merlin Jones is an inexpensive film, with little or no action, broken evenly into two sections that look suspiciously like divisions between segments of the Disney TV hour. In the first section, brainy student Merlin Jones develops the ability to read minds, and eavesdrops on Judge Holmby, who is plotting a robbery! Merlin tries to tell the police, but they don't believe him, so he sets out with his girl friend Jennifer to foil the judge in his dastardly plot. It turns out that the judge has been leading a double life—as a mystery novelist. What Merlin heard was the plot of his newest book. End of part one.

Part two has Merlin running headlong into thick-witted Norman, a school lunkhead who has charge over the science department's chimpanzee. Merlin is experimenting with hypnotism, and wants to use the animal as a guinea pig, but he is ordered to stay away by the judge after causing considerable havoc in the science lab. Then the judge asks Merlin to come to see him one night; he wants to be hypnotized himself, and Merlin agrees. He mesmerizes the judge into going to school and stealing the monkey. The next day Merlin is held responsible, and the judge has no memory of the hypnotic trance! Finally, in private, Merlin manages to explain what happened, and all ends happily. End of part two.

If the plot elements of *Merlin Jones* sound a bit thin for a feature film, that's just because they are. Add to this the stupidest collection of characters ever devised for one film, and you have the ingredients for this Disney package.

Merlin Jones, supposedly a brain, has some oddly incoherent moments, particularly when trying to get out of a jam with his girl friend. His science professor, presumably an intelligent man, learns of Merlin's discovery that he can read minds, but fails to find anything remarkable in that, worried only that Merlin knows the name of a teacher he's trying to date. The less said about the "judge" the better.

So little of consequence happens in *Merlin Jones* that it's difficult to conceive of it being planned as a feature film. Virtually the whole takes place indoors, or on studio interiors, with only one elaborate prop (Merlin's electronic headgear). The animated opening titles, using paper cutouts, probably took more time and imagination to work out than the rest of the film.

Yet the credits match those of any top-drawer Disney feature. Certainly Robert Stevenson was get-

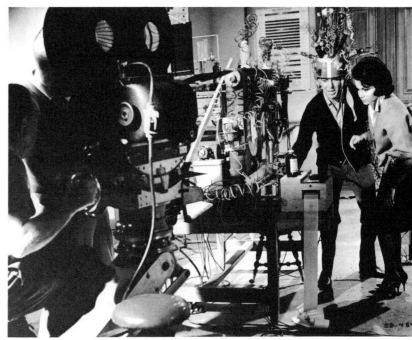

A production scene from *The Misadventures of Merlin Jones,* showing Tommy Kirk and Annette Funicello. © *1963 Walt Disney Productions*

ting the most choice assignments from the studio at this time. The whole project is difficult to understand.

As for the players, there is little to criticize when one considers the level of writing in the script. For some reason it was decided to make Tommy Kirk look as square and unappealing as possible, hence a most unbecoming crew cut and outmoded clothes. Annette Funicello's most challenging moment comes when she sings the title song, a ricky-ticky number written by the Sherman brothers.

The reviewers were thoroughly perplexed by the film. Robert Salmaggi wrote in the *Herald Tribune:* "We have a sneaking suspicion that *The Misadventures of Merlin Jones* was originally slated for Disney's weekly television series. . . . The only thing missing is the commercials. . . . Let's skip the plot detail. In fact, skip this one altogether." Eugene Archer in the *Times* wrote: ". . . the quality is low even by television standards. . . . Performances are as perfunctory as the script, the color photography and Robert Stevenson's direction." Archer asked, rhetorically, "Who is expected to spend the $2 [to see this film]?"

The answer: several million kids. The film grossed $4 million in its domestic release, not bad for a picture that probably cost less to make than any other Disney film in the past year. It did well enough to warrant a sequel, if that can be imagined, and even rated a reissue in 1972, proving once again the unpredictability of the moviegoing masses, especially where Disney is concerned.

A TIGER WALKS

RELEASED BY BUENA VISTA ON MARCH 12, 1964. Technicolor. Coproducer: Bill Anderson. Director: Norman Tokar. Screenplay: Lowell S. Hawley, based on a novel by Ian Niall. Photography: William Snyder. Editor: Grant K. Smith. Art directors: Carroll Clark, Marvin Aubrey Davis. Set decorations: Emile Kuri, Frank R. McKelvy. Costumes: Chuck Keehne, Gertrude Casey. Music: Buddy Baker. Orchestrations: Bob Brunner. Associate producer: Ron Miller. Assistant director: John C. Chulay. Makeup: Pat McNalley. Hairstyling: La Rue Matheron. Sound: Robert O. Cook. Music editor: Evelyn Kennedy. Running time: 91 minutes.

Cast: Brian Keith (Pete Williams), Vera Miles (Dorothy Williams), Pamela Franklin (Julie Williams), Sabu (Ram Singh), Kevin Corcoran (Tom Hadley), Peter Brown (Vern Goodman), Edward Andrews (governor), Una Merkel (Mrs. Watkins), Arthur Hunnicutt (Lewis), Connie Gilchrist (Lewis's wife), Theodore Marcuse (Josef Pietz), Merry Anders (Betty Collins), Frank McHugh (Bill Watkins), Doodles Weaver (Bob Evans), Frank Aletter (Joe Riley), Jack Albertson (Sam Grant), Donald May (Captain Anderson), Robert Shayne (governor's adviser), Hal Peary (Uncle Harry), Ivor Francis (Mr. Wilson), Michael Fox, Richard O'Brien.

A Tiger Walks is a very strange film, not the least because it paints a fantastically ugly portrait of small-town American life, zeroing in on oily politicians and greedy, grasping people who take advantage of a situation for personal gain.

The story deals with a tiger who escapes from a circus truck passing through a small town. Panic arises as the tiger roams free in the nearby woods. Julie Williams, the sheriff's daughter, takes an interest in the tiger and begs her father not to kill it, but merely to capture it so it can be turned over to a zoo. Though her father is trying to keep control of the situation, the small town becomes a headline attraction, and the tiger hunt big news. When Julie is interviewed on TV, she expresses her feelings for the tiger, which has been severely mistreated during its life with the circus. She proposes that a fund be started to purchase the tiger and give it a good home in the zoo.

Though the tiger hunt becomes a political football for the state governor, who is due for reelection, and family relations are strained between Julie and her father, the girl's TV appearance sparks a nationwide movement on the part of children to "save that tiger," by raising money to buy it. Julie's father is finally won over to the cause, and he joins with Ram Singh, a circus trainer, in outwitting the governor and the National Guard in capturing the tiger without hurting it, and turning it over to the local zoo, where, on dedication day, Julie is the heroine of the hour.

Woven into this offbeat story is a myriad of bitter vignettes: the local hotel owner doubles her rates when she learns that reporters and curiosity seekers will be coming to town; a local hotshot reporter sees his chance for fame and fortune by getting a scoop on the story; the sheriff asks the other reporters to hold back the story overnight to avoid creating a panic, but they refuse; the National Guard fail to heed the sheriff's warning about sending men into the woods on a foggy night, and ends up shooting an innocent man; when the sheriff organizes a searching party to find a man who's out in the woods with the tiger, and they discover his companion dead, the volunteers desert the sheriff, rather than try to help the poor fellow; when the "save that tiger" campaign becomes popular, it is picked up and exploited by a greasy kiddie-show host.

Presumably, the justification for this large-scale attack at modern America is that the forces of good (represented by Julie and her peers) come out on top, while the "bad guys" (the governor, who doesn't get reelected, the National Guard, which can't take credit for the capture, etc.) lose. Still, it's surprising to find the Disney folks dishing out such pungent (if unsubtle) material. Perhaps they were taking a cue from Frank Capra, who managed to expose the underside of human nature even while championing the "little man" in his famous films of the 30s and 40s.

Behind all this is the decidedly offbeat premise of a girl leading the country's juvenile population on a campaign promoting sympathy toward a man-eating tiger! The film is supposed to teach compassion toward all living things, but, as some critics pointed out, it remains difficult to muster up as much love for a Bengal tiger, as one would for an Irish Setter.

A Tiger Walks was greeted with no little curiosity by the critics, but in the end most of them found it uncompelling, particularly in its preachings. Robert

Frank Aletter, Doodles Weaver (partially hidden), Sabu, and Brian Keith in *A Tiger Walks*. © *1963 Walt Disney Productions*

Pamela Franklin questions her father, Brian Keith, about the capture of the tiger, while her mother (Vera Miles) looks on. © *1963 Walt Disney Productions*

Salmaggi in the *Herald Tribune* called it "a kittenish case of too much tempest in a teacup." Bosley Crowther in the *Times* said it was "angled towards zoophiles, especially those of the younger generation who are usually more compassionate than critical." *Variety* noted that "the Buena Vista release does not succeed in its bid for adult enjoyment, principally because the film's center of comic and dramatic gravity is synthetic and childish. But most kids will probably get a boot out of it . . . ."

Aside from the plot elements, *A Tiger Walks*'s chief point of interest is its cast. The sheriff is played by Disney regular Brian Keith; his wife is played by Vera Miles, a talented and versatile actress who became a Disney stalwart through the rest of the decade. For the role of Julie, Disney chose a young British girl who had made an impressive debut earlier in the dec-

ade; Pamela Franklin went on to earn an Academy Award nomination for her superb work in *The Prime of Miss Jean Brodie*.

The supporting cast is full of interesting people: Sabu, in his last film role, as the kindly circus animal trainer; Edward Andrews, typecast as the slimy governor; Una Merkel as the money-grasping hotel owner; veteran comic Doodles Weaver as the ambitious would-be reporter; Frank McHugh as one of the townspeople who deserts sheriff Keith; and "Great Gildersleeve" Hal Peary as the silly kiddie-show host, to name just a few.

This marked director Norman Tokar's third venture for Disney in a string of generally well-made, well-thought-out films. Unfortunately, it was not a major success at the box office, landing on the Disney TV show a few years later.

THE THREE LIVES OF THOMASINA

RELEASED BY BUENA VISTA ON JUNE 3, 1964 (PRE-release engagements, December 11, 1963). Technicolor. Director: Don Chaffey. Associate producer: Hugh Attwooll. Screenplay: Robert Westerby, based on the book *Thomasina* by Paul Gallico. Photography: Paul Beeson. Additional photography: Ray Sturgess, Michael Reed. Editor: Gordon Stone. Art director: Michael Stringer. Set decorations: Vernon Dixon. Costumes: Margaret Furse. Music: Paul J. Smith. Conductor: Eric Rogers. Orchestrations: Walter Sheets. Production manager: Peter Manley. Special effects: Ub Iwerks, Jim Fetherolf. Makeup: Harry Frampton. Hairstyling: Betty Sheriff. Sound: Jonathan Bates, C. C. Stevens, Gordon K. McCallum. Music editor: Evelyn Kennedy. Running time: 97 minutes.

Song: "Thomasina" by Terry Gilkyson.

Cast: Patrick McGoohan (Andrew MacDhui), Susan

Karen Dotrice and Thomasina.   © 1963 Walt Disney Productions

Patrick McGoohan slowly finds himself falling in love with the unusual girl in the woods, Susan Hampshire.   © 1963 Walt Disney Productions

Hampshire (Lori MacGregor), Karen Dotrice (Mary MacDhui), Vincent Winter (Hughie Stirling), Denis Gilmore (Jamie McNab), Laurence Naismith (Reverend Angus Peddie), Finlay Currie (Grandpa Stirling), Wilfrid Brambell (Willie Bannock), Jean Anderson (Mrs. MacKenzie), Francis De Wolff (Targu), Jack Stewart (Birnie), Ewan Roberts (Constable McQuarrie), Oliver Johnston (Mr. Dobbie), Mathew Garber (Geordie), and Elspeth March as the voice of Thomasina.

Like director Don Chaffey's earlier effort for Disney, *Greyfriars Bobby,* this is a delicate and charming film, far better than its predecessor in its wealth of imaginative ideas, its excellent cast, and the basis of it all, Paul Gallico's lovely story.

The setting is Scotland in 1912. Widower Andrew MacDhui is the town veterinarian; he has no feeling for the simple, naïve, and often emotional townspeople who bring their pets to him. They would prefer some soft-soaping, but he remains cold and efficient. His daughter Mary is utterly devoted to her cat, Thomasina, and when the pet is injured one day, her father sadly diagnoses the problem as tetanus, and tells her that Thomasina will have to be killed. Mary is distraught, while her father cannot understand why the logic of the situation should not be clear to the girl. Her friends help her to arrange an elaborate funeral for the cat, but just as they are about to bury the feline, Lori MacGregor shows up.

Lori lives in the woods, where she takes in injured animals and nurses them back to health, without medicine or special cures—merely with common sense and love. The children think she is a witch, and the sight of her sends them scurrying. But Lori notices that Thomasina is not really dead at all; she takes the cat home with her, and slowly helps her to recover. In the process, however, Thomasina goes to Cat Heaven, and when she is miraculously brought back to life, it is as if she is starting anew; she has no memory of her former existence.

MacDhui's heartlessness in killing his daughter's pet earns him a bad reputation, and the townspeople stop coming to him, going instead to the girl in the woods. MacDhui finally goes to see her, and is slowly won over, not only by her amazing skills, but by her beauty and love of life. One night, Mary MacDhui sees Thomasina walking outside her house, and frantically runs after her, through a driving storm. She contracts pneumonia, and becomes gravely ill. Doctors can do little, and in desperation MacDhui sends for Lori. Lori tells MacDhui that only he can help Mary recover, with *his* love. When Thomasina appears outside Mary's window, MacDhui goes to bring her in, and this sight restores Mary's desire to live. She recovers, and soon acts the role of bridesmaid as her father is wed to Lori.

Thomasina is one of Paul Gallico's best stories, in the tradition of such other classics as *The Snow Goose.*

But it also has, at least in this film version, several of the elements that had become standard in Disney movies. First, there is the theme of the humanization of a cold adult, convincingly portrayed by Patrick McGoohan, who makes the transformation totally believable. Then, there is the whole idea of seeing a situation from a child's point of view, which takes in much of the film, and which becomes a major point in Lori MacGregor's attempt to get through to Dr. MacDhui. The children's arranging of a town funeral, and subsequent boycotting of the veterinarian, are delightful sequences in keeping with this theme.

There is a unique Disney touch in the sequence of Thomasina's trip to Cat Heaven, a wondrous piece of movie magic with Thomasina floating through space before arriving at this feline Valhalla, walking through a procession of statues of great cats, and arriving at the pinnacle where rests a giant Cat Goddess, with luminescent stars twinkling in the background.

Another delightful idea is that of giving Thomasina a voice for expressing her thoughts at various points throughout the story; it is particularly opportune when she is brought back to life a second time, for no outside narration, or exposition by humans, could get across the point as convincingly (or with as much charm) as Thomasina herself.

The cast is uniformly excellent, with fine support for the leads from such old reliables as Finlay Currie and Laurence Naismith. Disney was so pleased with Susan Hampshire that he signed her again two years later to do the female lead in *The Fighting Prince of Donegal*. Young Karen Dotrice (the daughter of actor Roy Dotrice) won over everyone, and Disney brought her to America to play one of the juvenile leads in *Mary Poppins* after seeing her work in this film. He also liked a young boy who appeared as one of her friends, Matthew Garber, and he became Miss Dotrice's younger brother in *Poppins*.

Most critics found something to admire in *The Three Lives of Thomasina*, but on the whole considered the film too sluggish. Howard Thompson in the *New York Times* said: "This sentimental and extremely genteel little movie seems best suited for small girls. . . . Mr. Gallico's fable is a genuinely endearing one in spirit and flavor. If only the picture were as succinct and tangy." He added: ". . . how anybody, young or old, could mistake the beautiful, silver-voiced Susan Hampshire for a witch is a stumper." Robert Salmaggi in the *New York Herald Tribune* wrote: "While it does have a certain charm and a good deal of the Disney stamp about it, this live-action entry tends to sag noticeably after the first few scenes and does not pick up until the final segments." *Variety* felt that "it lacks excitement."

"Excitement" may well be all this lovely film lacks, however. Especially considering the subsequent success of lead players McGoohan and Hampshire, *The Three Lives of Thomasina* may find an even larger audience in the near future, if reissued. It certainly deserves it.

THE MOON-SPINNERS

RELEASED BY BUENA VISTA ON JULY 2, 1964. TECHnicolor. Coproducer: Bill Anderson. Director: James Neilson. Associate producer: Hugh Attwooll. Screenplay: Michael Dyne, based on the novel by Mary Stewart. Photography: Paul Beeson. Additional photography: John Wilcox, Michael Reed. Editor: Gordon Stone. Art director: Tony Masters. Costumes: Anthony Mendleson. Music composer, conductor: Ron Grainer. Second unit director: Arthur J. Vitarelli. Production manager: Peter Manley. Assistant director: John Peverall. Camera operator: David Harcourt. Continuity: Yvonne Axworthy. Casting: Maude Spector. Makeup: Harry Frampton. Hairstyling: A. G. Scott. Animals: Jimmy Chipperfield. Sound editor: Jonathan Bates. Sound recording: Dudley Messenger, Gordon McCallum. Running time: 118 minutes.

Song: "The Moon-Spinners Song" by Terry Gilkyson.

Cast: Hayley Mills (Nikky Ferris), Eli Wallach (Stratos), Pola Negri (Madame Habib), Peter McEnery (Mark Camford), Joan Greenwood (Aunt Frances), Irene Papas (Sophia), Sheila Hancock (Mrs. Gamble), Michael Davis (Alexis), Paul Stassino (Lambis), John LeMesurier (Anthony Gamble), Andre Morrell (yacht captain), George Pastell (police lieutenant), Tutte Lemkow (Orestes), Steve Plytas (hearse driver), Harry Tardios (bus driver), Pamela Barrie (Ariadne).

The Moon-Spinners is much ado about nothing, as it turns out at the end of nearly two hours of melodrama, but it's the kind of film that is so engaging along the way that one hardly minds the fact that there is no foundation to the whole effort.

Told as simply as possible, the story deals with a girl named Nikky Ferris who is vacationing with her Aunt Frances in Greece. When they arrive at a hotel in Crete, their reservations are ignored, until sheer persistence wears down the woman who runs the establishment. Her husband, Stratos, is not pleased at the prospect of two strangers staying there at this particular time, and obviously something fishy is going on. Nikky meets a young man named Mark Camford

Peter McEnery tries to stop Hayley Mills from becoming involved in the dangerous goings-on in *The Moon-Spinners.* © *1963 Walt Disney Productions*

Pola Negri and her henchman, Eli Wallach.   © *1963 Walt Disney Productions*

who is also mixed up in this strange business, but he remains vague when she questions him.

Next morning, Nikky has a date with Mark, but he is nowhere to be found. Stratos tells her that he left on an early bus. As she strolls along the beach and peers inside an ancient church, she finds Mark there, wounded! It seems he was fired from a London bank, accused of a jewel robbery he didn't commit. Mark is certain that Stratos pulled the job, and is trailing him in hope of getting proof. When Nikky leaves the church, she bumps into Stratos, who suspects that she knows too much; he locks her inside a windmill, and it is for a friendly native boy, Alexis, to free Nikky in an exciting escape attempt.

Fleeing from Stratos, Nikky and Mark are rescued by Anthony Gamble, the British consul, who takes them to his home. It soon develops that he too is involved in this ring, and is decidedly not the British consul. Mark spots a boat offshore belonging to famed jewel collector Madame Habib, and figures out that she is there to purchase the jewels from Stratos. Mark

runs off in pursuit of Stratos, while Nikky goes out to the yacht to talk the eccentric millionairess out of buying the stolen jewels. All the principals converge on the yacht in a confusing melee, but the police arrive in time to nab Stratos, whose arrest exonerates Mark, leaving him free to spend all his time with Nikky.

The Moon-Spinners is a fun film. From the red herrings and furtive glances at the start, it's clear that this is going to be a slam-bang mystery melodrama, with all the stops pulled out. And that's just what it is, along with dashes of romance, comedy, and the beautiful scenery of Crete.

Taking a page from Hitchcock, director Neilson decided to play the story for all it was worth, and in many ways the film is reminiscent of the Hitchcock formula that worked for the master time and time again. Neilson's film lacks the insouciance of a Hitchcock movie, but there is room for light moments, in Joan Greenwood's (Hayley Mills's aunt), droll delineation of her character, and in the showdown with Pola Negri (Madame Habib).

The Hitchcocklike sequence with young Alexis helping Nikky to escape from the windmill, by climbing through a window onto one of the blades, and hanging on before dropping to the ground, is masterfully done, with some hair-raising shots from their point of view taken from the air.

The scenery is one of the film's major assets, with the sea and sky, and coastal landscapes, providing impressive backgrounds that would almost make anything in front of them look good. The on-land scenery is equally diverting, although it's interesting to note that the ancient Greek church, which is very striking, was built by the Disney staff especially for the movie.

The trick in carrying out a fanciful story such as this is knowing when to stop toying with the audience and when to give them something to sink their teeth into. *The Moon-Spinners* plays around a bit too much, for every time one chase is over, another begins, and every climax is topped with another. It really is too much of a good thing.

The film does relieve occasional monotony by introducing new characters at strategic points. Well into their adventure together, Nikky and Mark meet the "British consul," and in a clever piece of yarn-spinning, he is undone by his wife, who at first seems to be a pleasant woman, but who turns out to be an alcoholic who indirectly does the youngsters a good turn by exposing her husband.

Last, but not least, there is Madame Habib. It is a little unnerving to have such a broad tongue-in-cheek character appear near the end of the film, in which everyone else has been taking themselves most seriously, but her characterization still comes as a welcome relief. Nikky is fished out of the water onto Madame's yacht, and when she is shown in to see the lady, her only comment is a sullen "You are dripping all over my carpet." Madame has a pet cheetah named Shalimar, who shares her ornate parlor on the luxury yacht. The lady is indecisive about how to deal with Nikky who begs her not to buy the jewels, but the subsequent confusion with Stratos, Mark, the police, and assorted others makes up her mind for her, as much as anything else.

Getting Pola Negri to play the part of Madame Habib was no small coup for the Disney company. The silent-screenstar had made her last film in 1943, but her name still spelled glamour and the exotic to millions of people around the world. Bill Anderson phoned the star at her home in Texas, and persuaded her at least to read the script. Miss Negri was warming to the subject when her closest friend and companion, Margaret West, died. She reluctantly agreed to go to Hollywood a short time later, to discuss the project further, but as she recalled in her autobiography, it was Walt Disney himself who finally convinced her to do the role.

Mr. Disney was a truly wonderful gentleman,

fully aware of what I was going through and responding to my situation with warmth and sympathy. . . . I was still hesitant to make a commitment. "To go through all that again—Mr. Disney, I don't think I have the strength." "I'll take the responsibility for making things easy for you," he responded. "If you come to London, you won't have to do anything but give your performance."

Miss Negri capitulated, and went beyond the call of duty to make sure that Madame Habib's full potential as a character was realized. In the script she was to have a pet Siamese cat. The star suggested the substitution of a cheetah, which made her sequence all the more fun.

The other main object of attention in *The Moon-Spinners* was a grown-up Hayley Mills. Now eighteen, it was clear that the young actress was ready for more mature roles. Thus, in the film, she is something of a man-chaser (revealed in dialogue with her aunt), rather worldly, and even capable of wearing a dress with some decolletage. To make the role complete, she and leading man Peter McEnery finish the film in a time-honored Hollywood clinch. Fortunately, age had not diminished Miss Mills's acting ability or her natural charm; her performance in *The Moon-Spinners* is excellent.

The film also marked the debut of a new Disney protégé, Peter McEnery, who had already achieved some measure of success on the London stage and in some British films. Disney later gave him his own vehicle, *The Fighting Prince of Donegal*, but he never achieved the worldwide success of his female costar, Hayley Mills.

Most critics found *The Moon-Spinners* too juvenile in its playing and plotting. Bosley Crowther in the *Times* called it "essentially an entertainment for the younger set. That is to say, it is a picture in which standard melodrama abounds—the kind that the older observer may find just too bubbling with clichés." Robert Salmaggi in the *Herald Tribune* wrote that *The Moon-Spinners* offers an intriguing title, the fine talent of bubbly Hayley Mills (now grown up and sexy at 18), some interesting shots of the isle of Crete and its people, and not much else . . ."

Unfortunately, though adult audiences found the film too juvenile, juvenile audiences stayed away, thinking perhaps that it was too adult. Most successful Disney films have had a solid premise, which can be promoted not only by advertising and publicity, but by all-important word of mouth. The fact that the question "What is *The Moon-Spinners* about?" requires a twenty-minute answer may account for its box-office failure.

So that the expensive production should not be a total loss, Disney cut it into a three-part story for his TV program, and lavished unusual advertising money on its television debut. The confusion of the story was only accentuated by the weekly intermissions.

MARY POPPINS

RELEASED BY BUENA VISTA IN OCTOBER 1964 (PRE-release engagements, August 29, 1964). Technicolor. Coproducer: Bill Walsh. Director: Robert Stevenson. Screenplay: Bill Walsh, Donald Da Gradi, based on the *Mary Poppins* books by P. L. Travers. Photography: Edward Colman. Editor: Cotton Warburton. Art directors: Carroll Clark, William H. Tuntke. Set decorations: Emile Kuri, Hal Gausman. Costume and design consultant: Tony Walton. Costume designer: Bill Thomas. Costumers: Chuck Keehne, Gertrude Casey. Consultant: P. L. Travers. Music supervisor, arranger, conductor: Irwin Kostal. Choreography: Marc Breaux, Dee Dee Wood. Assistant directors: Joseph L. McEveety, Paul Feiner. Makeup: Pat McNally. Hairstyling: La Rue Matheron. Sound supervision: Robert O. Cook. Sound mixer: Dean Thomas. Music editor: Evelyn Kennedy. Dance accompanist: Nat Farber. Assistant to the conductor: James MacDonald. Live-action second unit director: Arthur J. Vitarelli. Animation director: Hamilton Luske. Animation art director: McLaren Stewart. Nursery sequence design: Bill Justice, Xavier Atencio. Animators: Milt Kahl, Oliver Johnston, Jr., John Lounsbery, Hal Ambro, Franklin Thomas, Ward Kimball, Eric Larson, Cliff Nordberg, Jack Boyd. Backgrounds: Albert Dempster, Don Griffith, Art Riley, Bill Layne. Special effects: Peter Ellenshaw, Eustace Lycett, Robert A. Mattey. Running time: 140 minutes.

Songs: "Spoonful of Sugar," "Jolly Holiday," "I Love to Laugh," "Chim-Chim-Cheree," "Feed the Birds (Tuppence a Bag)" "Step in Time," "Stay Awake," "Sister Suffragette," "A Man Has Dreams," "The Life I Lead," "Let's Go Fly a Kite," "Fidelity Feduciary Bank," "The Perfect Nanny," Supercalifragilistic-expialidocious" by Richard M. Sherman, Robert B. Sherman.

Cast: Julie Andrews (Mary Poppins), Dick Van Dyke (Bert; Mr. Dawes, Sr.) David Tomlinson (Mr. Banks), Glynis Johns (Mrs. Banks), Ed Wynn (Uncle Albert), Hermione Baddeley (Ellen), Karen Dortice (Jane Banks), Matthew Garber (Michael Banks), Elsa Lanchester (Katie Nanna), Artur Treacher (Constable Jones), Reginald Owen (Admiral Boom), Reta Shaw (Mrs. Brill), Arthur Malet (Mr. Dawes, Jr.) Jane Darwell (The Bird Woman), Cyril Delevanti (Mr. Grubbs), Lester Matthews (Mr. Tomes), Clive L. Halliday (Mr. Mousley), Don Barclay (Mr. Binnacle), Marjorie Bennett (Miss Lark), Alma Lawton (Mrs. Corry), Marjorie Eaton (Miss Persimmon), Paul Frees, Bill Lee, Thurl Ravenscroft (animal voices).

There really is only one word to describe *Mary Poppins,* and that is supercalifragilisticexpialidocious. To attempt a more complete assessment would exhaust a library full of adjectives.

Many people regard *Mary Poppins* as Walt Disney's crowning achievement, and that it may well be. Certainly it was the biggest hit in the history of the studio, both critically and financially; it is the kind of movie that will play forever. *Mary Poppins* does have the feeling of a masterwork; that is to say, the film is really the culmination of thirty-five years' work, for no amount of enthusiasm or capability could ever have taken the place of the experience of the Disney staff, under the guidance of Walt himself, who worked together to make this film. Of equal importance is the fact that Disney went out and hired new blood to work with his veteran staff, in what was obviously a perfect blend of veteran know-how and youthful imagination.

The film begins quietly, on a panoramic view of London at dawn (the year is 1910) ; in our aerial view of the city, over which the titles appear, we get our first glimpse of Mary Poppins, sitting atop a cloud with her umbrella and carpetbag. Gradually zeroing in on a particular neighborhood, we see a one-man band entertaining some people outside the local park. This is Bert, a happy-go-lucky fellow who says hello to us and gives us a brief tour of the street, which houses Admiral Boom, a precise military man who fires his rooftop cannon at eight every morning and every evening at six. Then we see the Banks home, where a frustrated nanny is walking out, fed up with the two "incorrigible" Banks children.

That evening, Mr. Banks, a very precise man, places an advertisement in the newspaper for a very strict governess. His children compose their own ad for a nanny, which Banks regards as foolish and tears up, tossing the pieces into the fireplace. The fragments of paper miraculously fly up the chimney and into the sky, where they are transmitted to Mary Poppins. The next morning a group of nannies waiting outside the

Dick Van Dyke, Julie Andrews, Matthew Garber, and Karen Dotrice in *Mary Poppins*. © *1963 Walt Disney Productions*

house are suddenly blown away by a strong gust of wind, leaving the path clear for Mary Poppins to float down from the sky, her umbrella providing a natural parachute.

The children soon discover that Mary Poppins, who describes herself as "practically perfect," is a very unusual woman. For their first game she tells the children that they must clean up their room; their dour expressions turn to smiles when Mary actually turns the chore into a game, with the toys and clothes arranging themselves at the snap of a finger.

Out for a walk they find Bert drawing chalk paintings on the sidewalk. When one picture of a lovely countryside captures the children's fancy, Mary,

Bert, and the youngsters hop into the picture, and suddenly find themselves in a magical world of make-believe. As the kids go off to the merry-go-round, Bert and Mary stroll along and stop at an outdoor café where Bert dances with their penguin waiters. Later they join Jane and Michael on the merry-go-round, as the horses break loose for a jaunt in the country. First they become part of a hunting party, and then join a horse race, which Mary wins! Asked for her reaction, she says that it's supercalifragilisticexpialidocious, joined in song by a group of local buskers. Just then, it starts to rain, "melting" the drawings and causing the foursome to return home.

Every day brings new adventures. The children

Bert and Mary Poppins get an assist from some animated
friends. © 1964 Walt Disney Productions

Richard (*left*) and Robert (*right*) Sherman, the brother-songwriting team responsible for *Mary Poppins*'s delightful score, pose on the set of the film with its two stars. © *1963 Walt Disney Productions*

go with Mary to see her Uncle Albert, who rises to the ceiling every time he starts to laugh—and, unfortunately, he can't stop laughing. They join him for tea, and find his laughter so contagious that soon they too are floating near the roof. To Mr. Banks's complaint that the children are having nothing but fun and not learning anything, Mary suggests that he take them to the bank with him. That evening, however, she sings to the children of the old bird woman who sits on the steps of a building near the bank, selling food for the birds at tuppence a bag. When the children go to the bank the next day, Father wants Michael to open an account with his tuppence, but the boy wants to feed the birds instead. A misunderstanding with the chairman of the bank, aging Mr. Dawes, attracts attention, and confusion starts a run on the bank. The children run away as fast as they can, getting lost in a dingy part of town; they are discovered by Bert, who explains his sooty condition by telling them of his life as a chimney sweep. He and Mary take them to the London rooftops to meet the fraternity of chimney sweeps, who revel in a boisterous song and dance.

That night their father is called to the bank, where he is fired. Suddenly a change comes over him. His eyes are opened for the first time, as he realizes that in his effort to be precise, and run his life as the bank is run, he has been cold and unloving. He tells off the board of directors of the bank, and disappears into the night. The next morning he appears from the basement of the house, having repaired a kite that the children broke earlier that week. They are astonished

at the change in their father, who insists that they run to the park and fly their wonderful kite. For the first time he really *is* their father. Her work done, Mary Poppins bids the children good-bye, and flies off into the sky for new adventures.

Mary Poppins is a film rich in detail, but its universal appeal is due to the fact that it blends so many elements together: there is wit in the subplot of Mrs. Banks's suffragette movement, and individual jokes (when Banks is fired at the bank, the ceremony is marked by turning his umbrella inside out and punching a hole in his bowler hat); there is whimsy in the presence of Admiral Boom, who keeps his house "ship-shape" (which is to say, exactly like a ship!); there is fantasy in the key sequences like the long excursion into the cartoon world of Bert's painting; there is sentiment in the basic theme of making Mr. Banks realize his neglect of his children, as well as in specific ideas such as the Bird Woman; and, of course, there is music.

There is so much in the film that the result is almost overpowering. The whole long "Jolly Holiday" segment is a brilliant set piece in itself. Mary and Bert stroll along through cartoon fields, stopping at a roadside barnyard where the animals join in a musical tribute to Mary. At the outdoor café, four busy penguins wait on the couple, prompting Bert to get up and imitate their funny walk. This segues into a soft-shoe dance routine featuring Bert and the four animated penguins. Then, at the merry-go-round, when the horses break loose, Mary, Bert, Jane, and Michael find themselves riding to hounds along with a host of cartoon horsemen. The finale is the animated horse race, into which our live-action friends intrude, followed by a prize ceremony when Mary wins the race.

This whole sequence is filled to overflowing with fantastic detail. There is one astounding shot where we see Mary and Bert walking over a mill bridge, their images reflected in the water below; on top of this comes a family of animated ducklings, rippling through the live-action reflection! In this early part of the segment Bert presents Mary with a cartoon bouquet, which flies away in a hundred directions (it was comprised of butterflies); later, at the end of the horse race, a cartoon judge gives Mary a live-action bouquet, for a neat parallel.

Even the transitions opening and closing the sequence are ingenious. When the foursome jumps into the sidewalk, they raise a cloud of chalk dust. At the end, when it begins to rain, the cartoon backgrounds start to blur around the live-action characters in the foreground, signaling their return to reality.

To record every magical moment of the film on paper would be to reproduce a detailed account of the entire script. But it is important to note that there is no repetition in *Mary Poppins;* its wonders emerge from an apparently bottomless bag of tricks. On the one hand there is the brilliantly exuberant chimney-sweep segment (which critic Judith Crist said showed "why movies were invented"), not only choreographed to perfection, but *designed* and arranged cinematically to a tee. Then there is the uncommonly beautiful and haunting sequence where Mr. Banks is called to his office at night to be fired. There has been a buildup to this, where Bert has explained to the children that their father, for all his gruffness, is a good man. He has also asked them to consider how lonely he is; when they need help, they can go to him, but he has no one to go to. With this thought freshly planted, we see Banks walking to the bank that night, all alone, through the deserted park, the empty lamp-lit streets, and through the cavernous bank entrance itself. The segment accentuates once again the reason for *Mary Poppins*'s success: it has humanity, as well as fantasy, in its makeup.

One of the amazing things about this film is its total stylization. Nothing in it is real; every square inch is designed, and designed with a purpose in mind. Even the opening panorama of London, one soon discovers, is a painting, which is artfully blended into live action when the camera closes in on the neighborhood where the Bankses live. Some of the design ideas are flamboyant, such as the rooftops where the chimney sweeps perform; some are more subtle, but just as vital, such as the ominous conference room where the bank board of directors waits to fire Mr. Banks.

The color, needless to say, is dazzling, particularly in the "Jolly Holiday" sequence, which also features some of the most delightfully executed car-

toon animals to appear in any Disney film. The barn-yard chorus that sings "It's a Jolly Holiday with Mary" is sheer joy.

The songs, written by the Sherman brothers, are without qualification their best ever, in turns witty, sentimental, formularized, and unique. Mr. Banks's patter songs are a direct descendant of Rex Harrison's from *My Fair Lady,* but there are no antecedents for the joyful "Spoonful of Sugar" or the haunting "Chim-Chim-Cheree." Every song in the film suits its context perfectly and conveys emotions and ideas otherwise unexpressed in dialogue.

As good as the songs are, however, it is the delivery that puts them over. Reading the lyrics of "Feed the Birds (Tuppence a Bag)," one finds a simplistic and cloying piece of material that is transformed into a song of depth and meaning by Julie Andrews's beautiful rendition and the tasteful arrangements of Irwin Kostal. The entire score is given 200 percent performances by Julie Andrews, Dick Van Dyke, and the other players.

Which brings us to the cast of the film. Again, it is impossible to say too much in praise of the entire troupe. The character of Mary Poppins is supposed to be enigmatic. When performing some nifty feat of magic, like sliding *up* a banister, she does it with nonchalance. In any discussion of herself, she uses the term "practically perfect." And when confronted with questions or pleas about the things she can do (as when the children try to relive their day's adventure in the chalk drawing), she denies knowledge of what they are talking about. Yet she *is* sweet, and she *does* bowl everyone over with her charm and sense of fun.

Julie Andrews captures every nuance of the character; those who scoffed at her Academy Award for the performance, explaining it off as a sentimental gesture, or a backhanded insult at Jack Warner (who decided not to use her in the film of *My Fair Lady*), ought to look at her work in *Poppins* once again. It truly is inspired.

Dick Van Dyke has never been better. He has never had a better vehicle for his talents, which are more considerable than many TV viewers might think. He captures the carefree nature of Bert to perfection, with particular highlights coming in his two big dance scenes, with the cartoon penguins and with the chimney sweeps. But he also conveys a warmth and genuine friendliness that goes beyond the geniality of a good song-and-dance man. He has the rare ability to talk to children (as he does in several key scenes of the film) without ever talking down to them.

Cute children have murdered many a promising film, but there is a difference between children who *are* cute and children who *act* cute. Watch the two youngsters as they read their rhyming advertisement for a nanny in the early part of this film; they are as appealing as any child performers who ever worked on the screen. Both Karen Dotrice and Matthew Garber had proven their worth in Disney's *Three Lives of Thomasina* earlier that year; *Mary Poppins* reaffirmed their talent.

David Tomlinson and Glynis Johns are perfectly suited to their roles as the children's parents. Tomlinson never makes the father a villain; even children can see that he is merely cold and aloof, not wicked. His extroverted performance is exactly what the role calls for, and his delivery of the patter songs is a treat. Glynis Johns's role is relatively small, but she is the kind of performer who lights up a screen the minute she appears. She makes every minute count, and her amusing suffragette song is most enjoyable.

The supporting cast could not possibly be improved. Two veteran scene stealers, Arthur Treacher and Reginald Owen, make their admittedly minor roles stand out. Ed Wynn is, as always, Ed Wynn, in a role tailormade for him, as the man who can't stop laughing.

What is there to say of Robert Stevenson's direction and the work of his many collaborators? It is very seldom that a movie shows so much thought and imagination and planning in the execution of every square inch of film. All that can be said is that everything works beautifully.

Is there, then, *anything* wrong with *Mary Poppins*? Well, the film, like Mary herself, is practically perfect. It misses perfection just by a hair. Its largest flaw is overlength. While millions of children have sat in rapt attention through the whole film, few people could help but squirm at one point or another through the two hours and twenty minutes. Though it would be a shame to touch this film, it does seem likely that some trimming could have made the film just a little bit better by sharpening its impact. Probably the easiest thing to cut would have been the whole Ed Wynn laughing sequence, but this might have been retained if some judicious cutting had been done in several existing sequences. In any event the length is not fatal to *Mary Poppins*; just something that takes a little bit away from its overall strength.

Another point applies more to film buffs and adults than to children, but it is worth noting. In the "Spoonful of Sugar" sequence, stop-motion live-action photography is used, and even played backward, with the children, and Mary Poppins, superimposed on top. This is responsible for a scene of Jane snapping her fingers and watching her toys, strewn all over the floor, leap back onto the shelf in perfect array.

Though the average viewer would not understand how this movie magic had been accomplished, even an untrained eye can see the graininess of the stop-action film, and the contrast of the players matted in on top. The point is, this is the only sequence in the entire film where one is *aware* of special effects. Even a trained eye is stumped for the rest of the film, and what is more, the viewer doesn't *care* about how the other tricks were accomplished. The illusion is complete, because one is willing to let oneself believe what he sees on the screen. The "Spoonful of Sugar" sequence merely reminds the astute viewer that he is watching some sort of special effects.

Some will say this is carping, and perhaps it is. But it in no way changes the fact that *Mary Poppins* is an outstanding film. Such was the opinion of nearly every critic who saw the movie. Not since the early days of animation had Disney received such laudatory reviews. Critics found that two anticipated brickbats would have to be laid aside; first, the film had not destroyed P. L. Travers's character, although there was some change in the transition from book to film; second, the film was not an icky piece of sentiment—indeed, such qualities were nicely restrained.

So, Hollis Alpert in *Saturday Review* called it "one of the most magnificent pieces of entertainment ever to come from Hollywood." Bosley Crowther wrote that ". . . as Mary Poppins says, 'Practically perfect people never permit sentiment to muddle their feelings.' But being not practically perfect, I find it irresistible."

Judith Crist wrote in the *New York Herald Tribune*:

> The performers surpass even the technical wizardry of the film. . . . Miss Andrews is superb at song and dance and comedy and the heart of the matter (Too beautiful to be Mary Poppins? This is a carp by the old-in-heart who don't know that Mary Poppins is young and beautiful because anyone beloved by children is). And Dick Van Dyke's Bert reveals that this young performer's gifts have never been truly exploited before—obviously because they're limitless. Watch the final cast credits for further proof.

Miss Crist refers to the fact that Van Dyke plays a second role in the film, which is not revealed until the end. He renders a hilarious performance as the very, very old chairman of the bank board of directors, Mr. Dawes, Sr.

Time commented:

> Although she [Mary] pokes her pretty fingers into a world of sticky sweetness, she almost invariably pulls out a plum. All speeches and cream, with a voice like polished crystal, she seems the very image of a prim young governess who might spend her free Tuesdays skittering off to Oz. To make a good show better, Disney employs all the vast magic-making machinery at his command. The sets are luxuriant, the songs lilting, the scenario witty but impeccably sentimental, and the supporting cast only a pinfeather short of perfection.

The public responded to *Mary Poppins* as it had to no previous Disney film. Bolstered by these enthusiastic reviews, as well as the most high-powered promotional campaign ever launched by the studio, the film earned an unbelievable $31 million in domestic release and a reported total of $45 million from worldwide showings. It is impossible to tell how much additional revenue was realized from the sale of records, sheet music, and the hundreds of licensed items that accompanied the film.

The film earned thirteen Academy Award nominations, winning in five categories: Best Actress, Film Editing, Original Score, Song ("Chim-Chim-Cheree"), and Special Visual Effects.

But when one speaks of *Mary Poppins*'s success, it isn't the number of awards, or the amount of box-office revenue, that really come to mind. It's the fact that this one film managed to synthesize—so brilliantly—all the elements of entertainment and moviemaking magic that Disney had developed and refined throughout his career.

If he had made no other film in his lifetime, *Mary Poppins* would have earned Walt Disney the gratitude of the world—and the envy of his Hollywood colleagues. Instead, this was the pinnacle of an already fantastic career.

EMIL AND THE DETECTIVES

RELEASED BY BUENA VISTA ON DECEMBER 18, 1964. Technicolor. Director: Peter Tewksbury. Associate producer: Peter V. Herald. Screenplay: A. J. Carothers, based on the book by Erich Kastner. Photography: Gunther Senftleben. Editors: Thomas Stanford, Cotton Warburton. Art directors: Werner and Isabell Schlichting. Costumes: Leo Bei, Josef Wanke. Music: Heinz Schreiter, played by the Berliner Symphoniker. Production manager: Paul Waldherr. Assistant director: Brigitte Liphardt. Camera operator: Franz Hofer. Makeup: Jupp Paschke, Joachim Schmalor. Sound: Bernhard Reicherts. Running time: 99 minutes.

Cast: Walter Slezak (Baron), Bryan Russell (Emil), Roger Mobley (Gustav), Heinz Schubert (Grundeis), Peter Erlich (Muller), Cindy Cassell (Pony), Elsa Wagner (Nana), Wolfgang Volz (Stucke), Eva-Ingeborg Scholz (Frau Tischbein), Franz Nicklisch (desk sergeant), Brian Richardson (professor), David Petrychka (Dienstag), Robert Swann (Hermann), Ann Noland (Frieda), Ron Johnson (Rudolf), Rick Johnson (Hans).

Erich Kastner's story of a young boy who is robbed on his way to visit a relative is a worldwide classic; it was previously filmed in Germany in 1931. It would seem a perfect choice for refilming by the Disney company. But this dreary film comes as a severe disappointment.

The story is fairly simple. While on the bus that will take him to his aunt, a not-so-subtle crook steals an envelope of money pinned inside Emil's jacket. Instead of enlisting the aid of police, Emil joins with an underground syndicate of would-be detectives, average age around ten. They trail the thief and discover that he is working with two others, one a self-styled criminal mastermind who is after bigger things than Emil's pocket money.

The balance of the film involves the boys' attempt to trap the crooks with evidence, convince the police that they aren't fooling, and recover Emil's money.

What's the problem? The film moves at a snail's pace, crawling along for ninety-nine minutes, far too much time to spend on such a basic story. There are interminable scenes involving the crooks' plotting an underground tunnel leading to a bank; scenes where something is supposed to happen any minute, but never does. There is also undue emphasis on the chief crook (Walter Slezak) and his high style of living, with dialogue that could have little meaning for a youthful viewer.

Although filmed in West Germany and decidedly European in flavor, the script has been heavily Americanized, and there are some key Disney touches, particularly in the main titles (whose amusing animated ideas show more verve than the rest of the film), where the trio of crooks are referred to as "The Three Skrinks." A narrator tells us in stentorian tones that "this is the story of a crime, just as it happened." Perhaps if such a satirical tone had been maintained for the rest of the film, it would be more digestible, but instead the alleged tongue-in-cheek touches are weighted down to the extent that they are neither funny nor realistic, failing on both counts.

There seems to have been an attempt to jazz up the movie somewhat after it had been completed—hence the animated titles and "the three skrinks." Apparently there was concern for American acceptance of the whole enterprise; the main title even tells the youngsters how to pronounce "Emil!"

But pronunciation is hardly *Emil*'s major drawback. It has the raw material for a good movie, but in the end what kills it is the sluggish pace and needlessly padded script.

Reviewers were kind to the film.

Emil (Bryan Russell) is immediately suspicious of the man (Heinz Schubert) sitting next to him on his bus trip.
© 1964 Walt Disney Productions

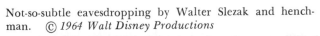

Not-so-subtle eavesdropping by Walter Slezak and henchman. © 1964 Walt Disney Productions

THOSE CALLOWAYS

RELEASED BY BUENA VISTA ON JANUARY 28, 1965. Technicolor. Coproducer: Winston Hibler. Director: Norman Tokar. Screenplay: Louis Pelletier, based on the book *Swiftwater* by Paul Annixter. Photography: Edward Colman. Editor: Grant K. Smith. Art directors: Carroll Clark, John B. Mansbridge. Set decorations: Emile Kuri, Hal Gausman. Costume designer: Bill Thomas. Costumers: Chuck Keehne, Gertrude Casey. Music: Max Steiner. Orchestrations: Murray Cutter. Assistant director: Tom Leetch. Matte artist: Jim Fetherolf. Special effects: Eustace Lycett. Makeup: Pat McNalley. Hairstyling: La Rue Matheron. Animal unit: Lloyd Beebe, William R. Koehler. Wild geese sequences: Dick Borden. Sound supervision: Robert O. Cook. Sound mixer: Dean Thomas. Music editor: Evelyn Kennedy. Running time: 131 minutes.

Songs: "The Cabin Raising Song," "Rhyme-Around" by Richard M. Sherman, Robert B. Sherman.

Cast: Brian Keith (Cam Calloway), Vera Miles (Liddy Calloway), Brandon de Wilde (Bucky Calloway), Walter Brennan (Alf Simes), Ed Wynn (Ed Parker), Linda Evans (Bridie Mellot), Philip Abbott (Dell Fraser), John Larkin (Jim Mellot), Parley Baer (Doane Shattuck), Frank de Kova (Nigosh), Roy Roberts (E. J. Fletcher), John Qualen (Ernie Evans), Tom Skerritt (Whit Turner), Paul Hartman (Charley Evans), Russell Collins (Nat Perkins), John Davis Chandler (Ollie Gibbons), Chet Stratton (Phil Petrie), Renee Godfrey (Sarah Mellot), Frank Ferguson (doctor).

Those Calloways is a long, episodic film, but it has many rewards for a patient audience. Although it gets sidetracked on various subplots, the film basically deals with the Calloway family, who live in the woods outside the small town of Swiftwater in New England.

Cam, the individualistic head of the family, dreams of building a bird sanctuary to protect the geese that fly through the area every year. Some of the townspeople find Calloway to be an eccentric for his protective views about the geese, which others revel in shooting.

Cam and his son Bucky hope to trap enough furs that winter to raise the money to buy a nearby lake for Cam's sanctuary, but after much hardship in getting the furs the market drops drastically, and they receive a tiny sum for their efforts. To wife Liddy's chagrin, he uses the money to make a down payment on the lake, meaning they must forfeit their mortgaged home.

The whole town shows up to help Cam raise a new cabin on the lake site. Then an ambitious young salesman stops by; he has plans to turn Swiftwater into a resort area, but he pitches Cam a bill of goods that his boss, a wealthy man, wants to help establish this sanctuary. He gives Cam enough money to plant corn, which will attract the birds. When Cam realizes that this boss is really interested in attracting the birds in order to shoot them, he goes on a rampage. He confronts the wealthy hunter, and in a struggle is accidentally shot.

Meanwhile, a town meeting is held to debate the question of keeping Swiftwater "pure" or selling out to the men who want to make it a tourist spot. The shooting adds an emotional tone to the meeting, which, after a long tussle, decides in favor of rejecting the businessmen. Town crier Alf Simes goes out to see Cam the next morning, and with the good news comes another happy turn of events: the crisis is past, and Cam will recover to see his dream come true.

Those Calloways is a warm and lovely film. There is a constant danger of losing touch with reality and identification, but the main characters are so skillfully played that they always come across, and even the flamboyant supporting actors like Walter Brennan and Ed Wynn make their performances seem real.

Brian Keith's role is particularly difficult. Cam Calloway is a good man, but when things haven't gone well before he has turned to drink. He has never really made good, although his son reveres him and embodies all his best qualities, with none of his worst. Having been raised by a local Indian Tribe, Calloway has a deep-rooted commitment to the wilderness, and to animal life, which takes precedence in his mind over everything else. These are delicate qualities to convey convincingly, but Keith does it quite well.

Vera Miles is equally good as Liddy Calloway, who has grown accustomed to her husband's ways, and leads a largely unrewarding life as a frontier-type wife. There is a telling scene between the couple as they recall their first meeting, and their youthful hopes, but Miss Miles's most striking moment in the film comes when her husband and son present her with a surprise Christmas gift—a white ermine jacket made up from furs they caught. She is completely overcome with joy, and cries uncontrollably. It is a moving and memorable scene.

Brandon de Wilde has just the right combination of confidence and immaturity as Keith's son, who falls in love with pretty Bridie Mellot, played by Linda Evans. A subplot of the film concerns his reticence to fight; in an opening scene he is beat to a pulp by a town bully, and much later, after constant practice, he turns the tables on the astonished fellow.

Director Norman Tokar's chief concern was atmosphere; whole vignettes are built around creating a certain mood, and in nearly every case they succeed. The cracker-barrel sessions at the general store are real and vivid, with Ed Wynn as a genial but hard-of-hearing participant; the cabin-raising is a spirited and naturally invigorating sequence; Bucky's lengthy foray into the woods in search of a wolverine who is raiding his traps is suspenseful, as the boy becomes trapped inside a woodpile without his gun, the fierce animal ready to maul him to death; the Calloways' Christmas party is warm and appealing.

Only the hoedown, after the cabin is raised, smacks of contrivance. Though every effort is made to give a feeling of spontaneity to the scene, the Sherman brothers' song "Rhyme-Around" comes off as what it is—a song with planned verses.

The breathtaking Vermont scenery is as important to the film as any of the actors; after seeing the beautiful settings, it would be difficult not to side with Cam Calloway in his fight against the exploiters.

Another great plus in the film is the music by Max Steiner. This was the only time the great film composer ever worked for Disney. Though it seems a shame that further assignments didn't follow, it is good that Steiner worked on this particular film, which inspired a rich and lovely score that never would have come from working on, say, *The Monkey's Uncle.*

Those Calloways is the kind of film that one either loves or hates. The cynical-minded will resist it from the very start, while others who allow themselves to go along with it may well find themselves beguiled. Such was the case with critics who saw the film. Some, like Judith Crist, liked it. She felt that it could "provide even the sourest-toothed with some remarkable movie moments. . . . [At one point] you're up to your neck in Vermont syrup. That you don't drown in

Linda Evans watches helplessly as Brandon de Wilde is beaten up by the town bully. © *1964 Walt Disney Productions*

Father and son in a friendly tussle: Brandon de Wilde and Brian Keith. © *1964 Walt Disney Productions*

the stuff is to the credit not only of the wildlife but of an excellent cast." Other critics, like Eugene Archer in the *New York Times,* found it "a conventional domestic chronicle . . . undistinguished but not without a certain rustic charm." *Time* found it a bit much: "*Those Calloways,* as depicted by Walt Disney's elfin helpers, demonstrate conclusively that not every rural New England community is Peyton Place. These Calloways are wholesome folks, and their struggles to provide a sanctuary for migratory geese make the high-flying fancies of Disney's *Mary Poppins* seem quite worldly, if not downright cynical."

Unfortunately, *Those Calloways* didn't have the kind of instant appeal necessary for Disney success, and audiences did not flock to see it. It was yet another quality film that failed to find financial success, but Disney knew that director Tokar and screenwriter Pelletier had hit their stride with this film, and he wisely assigned them to work together again on another film, *Follow Me, Boys!*

THE MONKEY'S UNCLE

RELEASED BY BUENA VISTA ON JUNE 23, 1965. TECHnicolor. Coproducer: Ron Miller. Director: Robert Stevenson. Screenplay: Tom and Helen August. Photography: Edward Colman. Editor: Cotton Warburton. Art directors: Carroll Clark, William H. Tuntke. Set decorations: Emile Kuri, Hal Gausman. Costumes: Chuck Keehne, Gertrude Casey. Music: Buddy Baker. Orchestrations: Walter Sheets. Second unit director: Arthur J. Vitarelli. Assistant director: Joseph L. McEveety. Special effects: Robert A. Mattey, Eustace Lycett. Makeup: Pat McNalley. Hairstyling: La Rue Matheron. Sound: Robert O. Cook. Music editor: Evelyn Kennedy. Running time: 87 minutes.

Song: "The Monkey's Uncle," sung by the Beach Boys; written by Richard M. Sherman, Robert B. Sherman.

Cast: Tommy Kirk (Merlin Jones), Annette Funicello (Jennifer), Leon Ames (Judge Holmsby), Frank Faylen (Mr. Dearborne), Arthur O'Connell (Darius Green III), Leon Tyler (Leon), Norman Grabowski (Norman), Alan Hewitt (Professor Shattuck), Connie Gilchrist (housekeeper), Cheryl Miller (Lisa), Gage Clarke (college president), Mark Goddard (Haywood), Harry Holcombe, Alexander Lockwood, Harry Antrim (board of regents).

To say that *The Monkey's Uncle* is better than *The Misadventures of Merlin Jones* is not much of a compliment, but it's the best one can do. Once again,

so-called genius Merlin Jones is up to his ears in experiments, and once again his feature film divides into two separate and distinct segments. In the first Merlin arranges to adopt Stanley, a chimpanzee, in order to conduct experiments at home. He finds that sleep learning actually works with the chimp, and later puts it to use on two lunkheads at school who must pass an English exam in order to stay on the team. Merlin and the boys are accused of cheating, but they are exonerated when Merlin explains his system, and he is the hero of the hour.

Judge Holmsby, on the Midvale College Board of Regents, calls on Merlin again in the second segment. It seems that another member of the board, Mr. Dearborne, hates football, and has found a man who will give the school a million dollars if they will discontinue the sport. Then the judge meets an eccentric fellow named Darius Green III, who guarantees *ten* million to the school if they can carry out an ancestor's wish to see man fly.

Merlin is charged with carrying the project through, and he engages one of the football players, Leon, to be his guinea pig. The bicycle-propelled birdman operation works, but as soon as Leon's legs give out, he crashes into a hog wallow. Merlin is forced to take over himself, after determining that what is needed is additional strength to power the pedals; he uses a form of adrenaline to do the trick. While he is up in the air, the regents watching, two men in white suits come after Darius Green III to take him back to the nut house! All seems lost, until Mr. Dearborne reveals that Green was his source too. Football re-

Tommy Kirk takes to the air in *The Monkey's Uncle.*
© *1964 Walt Disney Productions*

mains at Midvale, and Merlin comes out on top once more.

This film's advantage over the previous one is that at least this has some movement. While the first half of the film is obvious situation-comedy pap, the flying machine has its moments, especially in a funny dream sequence where Leon envisions himself a member of the bird fraternity.

The flying sequences are obviously the film's strongest point, for once again we have to contend with Merlin, a so-called brain who refuses to leave his chimpanzee with a baby-sitter. ("Try to understand," he says to his girl friend, who can't.) When he finally *does* get a baby-sitter, she turns out to be a curvy blonde, causing some friction for Merlin with girl friend Jennifer.

Then there is the judge, another man of remarkable intelligence who displays his brainpower even more than in the first film. In addition to trying to find a way for the football players to "cheat, without really cheating," he fails to check out the eccentric Darius Green III to see if he can back up what he says.

Adding to the intellectual fun is an erudite theme song sung by Annette and the Beach Boys, including the line "I love the monkey's uncle and I wish I were the monkey's aunt."

Still, *The New York Times*'s Richard F. Shepherd was philosophical about it. "In all, the film is a quick refresher for a hot day, a cooling soft drink that may not linger long but does just what it professes to do."

Annette Funicello, Tommy Kirk, and Leon Ames after an unsuccessful launching. © *1964 Walt Disney Productions*

THAT DARN CAT!

RELEASED BY BUENA VISTA ON DECEMBER 2, 1965. Technicolor. Coproducers: Bill Walsh, Ron Miller. Director: Robert Stevenson. Screenplay: The Gordons, Bill Walsh, based on the book *Undercover Cat* by the Gordons. Photography: Edward Colman. Editor: Cotton Warburton. Art directors: Carroll Clark, William H. Tuntke. Set decorations: Emile Kuri, Hal Gausman, Costume designer: Bill Thomas. Costumers: Chuck Keehne, Gertrude Casey. Music: Bob Brunner. Orchestrations: Franklyn Marks. Second unit director: Arthur J. Vitarelli. Assistant director: Joseph L. McEveety. Matte artist: Jim Fetherolf. Special effects: Eustace Lycett. Makeup: Pat McNalley, La Rue Matheron. Animal supervision: William R. Koehler. Sound supervision: Robert O. Cook. Sound mixer: Dean Thomas. Music editor: Evelyn Kennedy. Running time: 116 minutes.

Song: "That Darn Cat" by Richard M. Sherman, Robert B. Sherman. Sung by Bobby Darin.

Cast: Hayley Mills (Patti Randall), Dean Jones (Zeke Kelso), Dorothy Provine (Ingrid Randall), Roddy McDowall (Gregory Benson), Neville Brand (Dan), Elsa Lanchester (Mrs. MacDougall), William Demarest (Mr. MacDougall), Frank Gorshin (Iggy), Richard Eastham (Supervisor Newton), Grayson Hall (Margaret Miller), Tom Lowell (Canoe), Richard Deacon (drive-in manager), Iris Adrian (landlady), Liam Sullivan (Graham), Don Dorrell (Spires), Gene Blakely (Cahill), Karl Held (Kelly), and Ed Wynn (Mr. Hofstedder), with Ben Lessy (candy man), Larry J. Blake (police officer).

That Darn Cat! refers to D.C., a slithery Siamese belonging to Patti Randall and her sister Ingrid. One night D.C. comes home from a nocturnal with a wristwatch around his neck, the letters HEL written on the back. They were scrawled by Margaret Miller, a bank teller being held prisoner by two robbers holed up in an apartment in town; it was a desperate (and incomplete) plea for help. Patti recognizes it right away and runs to the FBI, where she persuades agent Zeke Kelso that it just might be a definite lead. Kelso, who is allergic to cats, is given the unenviable task of trying to trail the feline when he goes out again that night.

The situation is complicated by a nosy neighbor, a curious boyfriend of Patti's, a fussy man down the street who is ready to shoot the mischievous D.C. on sight, and other intruders. A sidetrack to a local drive-in movie leaves the establishment, and most of its customers, a mess.

The FBI is ready to give up, but Kelso, buoyed by a phony tip from jeweler Mr. Hofstedder (prodded by Patti, of course) that the watch definitely belongs to Margaret Miller, the bank teller, gives it one more try. This time he is led right into the apartment hideout of the two robbers, where there is a fight to the finish. Patti, who has been trailing Kelso, comes in after him to join in the struggle, until the other FBI men show up. The news in next morning's paper explains the Randall family's mysterious behavior to everyone, and there is a happy reunion between Patti and her suspicious boyfriend Canoe, as well as a new twosome, Ingrid and FBI man Zeke.

That Darn Cat! is a protracted but well-made, entertaining suspense comedy. What sets it apart from most other Disney comedies is that its alternate theme, the serious side of the story involving the two robbers and their hostage, is *not* played for laughs, but is done instead in a most serious and suspenseful manner. Naturally, this makes for a much better film.

What's more, the slapstick comedy in the film, though sometimes gratuitous, is genuinely clever in staging and concept, providing many surprise laughs and some very ingenious sight gags—such as Patti's boyfriend, sneaking along after her in front of a garage, being propelled upward as the garage door electronically opens, trapping him inside!

That Darn Cat! has a lot going for it, including an impressive cast that makes the most out of every situation. Hayley Mills's cuteness is just about worn out by now (this was her last Disney film), and Dorothy Provine's sure comedy playing is far more interesting. Roddy McDowall has the broadest, most obvious role in the film, but he carries it through with polish. Best of all are the character vignettes by Elsa Lanchester as a relentlessly nosy neighbor, William Demarest as her crabby husband, and Ed Wynn as the befuddled jeweler who is duped into going along with Hayley Mills's scheme to inform the FBI about a watch.

Neville Brand is slickly menacing (without ever becoming a caricature) as Dan, the brains of the holdup duo, and Frank Gorshin is perfect in a nicely subtle spoof of a neurotic thief, Brand's partner. Grayson Hall is excellent as the nerve-shattered

Hayley Mills and Dorothy Provine, with feline friend.
© *1964 Walt Disney Productions*

Comic relief par excellence: William Demarest and Elsa
Lanchester.   © *1964 Walt Disney Productions*

woman they hold prisoner, and Iris Adrian is her usual hilarious self as their suspicious landlady. (When they make an alibi for having a woman in their room, she snaps: "Do you think I got off the bus from Stupidsville last night?", as only she can.)

Robert Stevenson's direction, aided immeasurably by the superb editing of Cotton Warburton, enhances the possibilities inherent in every scene. Most of the laughs in the film come not just from the situations, but from the way they are presented cinematically. This film displays Stevenson's comedy expertise far better than his other Disney efforts, which relied more on gimmickry.

That Darn Cat! marks one of the few occasions when Disney actually hired an original author (in this case, two) to work on his own screenplay; this clearly sets the film a notch above most other animal comedies from the studio, thanks to the Gordons' collaboration with Bill Walsh. If only they had restrained themselves somewhat, and allowed one less prowl by D.C., the film would have been shorter than the nearly two hours it now is—and it would have been that much better.

As it was, *That Darn Cat!* received good notices, Bosley Crowther in the *Times* speaking for most when he called it "an entertaining picture." He went on to note that "in these frenziedly farcical activities, it is not surprising to find the cat the coolest, most controlled, intelligent, and indeed, believable participant. . . . Alongside of D.C. the people are—well, people in a Disney film, which is something between delightful fictions and unendurable freaks."

The sprightly picture, which looked like fun just from the TV commercials, attracted a tremendous Christmastime audience, and the film grossed $9½ million in domestic release alone. Which says something for cats, and a bit for the people surrounding them in this film.

That Darn Cat! was remade by the studio in 1997, with the talented Christina Ricci in the leading role, and comic actor Doug E. Doug as the agent on the cat's trail. Dean Jones made a welcome return to Disney in a costarring role.

THE UGLY DACHSHUND

RELEASED BY BUENA VISTA ON FEBRUARY 4, 1966.
Technicolor. Coproducer: Winston Hibler. Director:
Norman Tokar. Screenplay: Albert Aley, based on
the book by G. B. Stern. Photography: Edward Col-
man. Editor: Robert Stafford. Art directors: Carroll
Clark, Marvin Aubrey Davis. Set decorations: Emile
Kuri, Frank R. McKelvy. Costumes: Chuck Keehne,
Gertrude Casey. Music: George Bruns. Orchestrations: Franklyn Marks. Second unit director: Arthur
J. Vitarelli. Assistant director: Tom Leetch. Special
effects: Eustace Lycett. Makeup: Pat McNalley. Hairstyling: La Rue Matheron. Dogs trained by William R.
Koehler, Glenn Randall, Jr. Sound supervision: Robert O. Cook. Music editor: Evelyn Kennedy. Running
time: 93 minutes.

Cast: Dean Jones (Mark Garrison), Suzanne Pleshette
(Fran Garrison), Charlie Ruggles (Dr. Pruitt), Kelly
Thordsen (Officer Carmody), Parley Baer (Mel
Chadwick), Mako (Kenji), Charles Lane (judge),
Robert Kino (Mr. Toyama), Gil Lamb (milkman),
Dick Wessel (garbage man), Hal Smith.

The Ugly Dachshund is one of those silly cute-
animal comedies that seems to have been conceived
and executed on someone's lunch hour. Yet movies
such as this continued to attract a wide audience, so
the Disney studio continued to make them.

This one concerns a young commercial artist,
Mark Garrison, whose wife Fran dotes on her dachshund. When the dog gives birth to puppies, the
veterinarian, Dr. Pruitt, convinces Mark that he
should also take home a baby Great Dane who has
been abandoned. The Dane grows up with the dachshund puppies, often causing problems because of his
size; he is as frisky as the other puppies, but when he
jumps around damage ensues. What's more, his reputation as a troublemaker earns him the blame for the
mischief the other puppies get into.

Mark and Fran become chauvinistic about their
respective dogs, and as Fran trains one of her puppies
to enter the dog show, Mark decides to do the same
with the Dane, without telling her. The trick is to get
the dog not to act like a dachshund—no mean feat.
But at the dog show Fran's puppy is an also-ran, while

the Great Dane takes the Blue Ribbon. At this, husband and wife decide to stop competing, and stop
pushing their dogs to be something they aren't.

At one time it was said that television was aimed
at a twelve-year-old mind; if so, this film must have set
its sights somewhat lower. But there is no denying
that its obvious story line, unsubtle acting, and visual
comedy are surefire fodder for the younger set. It is
precisely that formula that made the film a hit.

Yet with films such as this, one always wonders
why they *couldn't* be better, coming from a studio
with so much talent and imagination in every corner.
Must the scenarists *always* take the easy way out of
every situation; must predictability reign supreme?
Apparently, the answer is yes.

There are several major scenes of doggy destruction in the film. The most awesome, though not the
largest in scale, is when the puppies get loose in
Mark's art studio, emptying every tube of paint,
dumping every can of liquid and every colorful com-
modity in the room, as they slip and slide around the
floor, adding to the mess. Many adults might find this
sequence heartrending, rather than amusing. A second
such scene is at least clever, where the dogs unravel a
ball of yarn around the living room, tying up every
piece of furniture in the vicinity. The third, and most
epic in nature, takes place at the Garrisons' lawn
party, where the dogs run loose and create a holocaust, in which tables are overturned, a waiter trips
into a gooey cake, and (of course) everyone falls into
the fishpond.

The most ingenious touch in the whole film is at
the dog show, where, in a scene reminiscent of *101
Dalmatians*, we see dogs and their owners whose faces
and expressions match perfectly: a tough bulldog with
a gruff master, a fluffy poodle with a frilly mistress,
etc.

The performances are capable enough, considering the superficiality of the characters. Both Dean
Jones and Suzanne Pleshette, who embody the all-
American wholesomeness requisite for such roles, were
called upon for further Disney assignments, whereas
Charlie Ruggles as the vet was making a return engagement. This marked the first of many unbilled
cameo spots by veteran comic Gil Lamb, here portraying a milkman.

Knowing the capabilities of director Norman Tokar, it seems a shame that he should have wasted his time on trivia such as this.

Time magazine provided the best capsule: "Such comedies as this one are too wholesome for kids, too foolish for dog fanciers, and a sure way to persuade young adults that movies filled with sex and violence can't be all bad."

Yet no one went to see the lovely *Those Calloways,* and an eager audience racked up earnings of $6 million for this film! It is very difficult to argue with that kind of success.

Suzanne Pleshette excitedly consults with her veterinarian, Charlie Ruggles. © *1965 Walt Disney Productions*

Dick Wessel, Suzanne Pleshette, Dean Jones, and the ugly dachshund. © *1965 Walt Disney Productions*

LT. ROBIN CRUSOE U S N

RELEASED BY BUENA VISTA ON JUNE 29, 1966. TECHnicolor. Coproducer: Bill Walsh, Ron Miller. Director: Byron Paul. Screenplay: Bill Walsh, Donald Da Gradi, based on a story by Retlaw Yensid. Photography: William Snyder. Editor: Cotton Warburton. Art directors: Carroll Clark, Carl Anderson. Set decorations: Emile Kuri, Frank R. McKelvy. Costume designer: Bill Thomas. Costumers: Chuck Keehne, Neva Rames. Music: Bob Brunner. Orchestrations: Cecil A. Crandall. Second unit director: Joseph L. McEveety. Animation styling: McLaren Stewart. Animation effects: Jack Boyd. Unit manager: Marvin Stuart. Assistant director: Tom Leetch. Special effects: Peter Ellenshaw, Eustace Lycett, Robert A. Mattey. Makeup: Pat McNalley. Hairstyling: La Rue Matheron. Animal supervision: Stewart Raffill. Sound supervision: Robert O. Cook. Sound mixer: Larry Jost. Music editor: Evelyn Kennedy. Running time: 110 minutes

Cast: Dick Van Dyke (Lt. Robin Crusoe), Nancy Kwan (Wednesday), Akim Tamiroff (Tanamashu), Arthur Malet (umbrella man), Tyler McVey (captain), P. L. Renoudet (pilot), Peter Duryea (copilot), John Dennis (crew chief), Nancy Hsueh, Victoria Young, Yvonne Ribuca, Bebe Louie, Lucia Valero (native girls).

Dick Van Dyke and Nancy Kwan in *Lt. Robin Crusoe,
U.S.N.*   © 1965 Walt Disney Productions

Nancy Kwan leads a group of angry islanders, as chief Akim
Tamiroff demands the attention of Dick Van Dyke (off
camera).   © 1965 Walt Disney Productions

The story credit for this film reads "Retlaw
Yensid." If you spell that backwards, it's Walter Disney. Obviously, Walt himself came up with the premise of a modern-day Robinson Crusoe tale to star Dick
Van Dyke. It sounds like a fine idea, but no one
bothered to embellish it to any great extent, and what
subplots there are fail miserably. *Lt. Robin Crusoe*
really should have been a short, or at best a Disney
TV hour. As a feature film it is completely without
merit.

Crusoe is a navy pilot who is forced to bail out of
his plane. He lands at sea, inflates his life raft, and
struggles to exist before finally sighting land. Apparently alone on the island, he seeks shelter and slowly
builds a very comfortable domicile. He discovers the
wreckage of an old submarine, from which he borrows
tools and useful materials. At the same time he discovers a companion—a chimpanzee who had been in
the space program, and thought lost at sea.

Soon thereafter, he finds another human—a
native girl named Wednesday, who has been exiled to
the island while her chieftain father prepares her
wedding. Complications arise with the angry father
and a flock of other island girls, especially when they
get the impression that Crusoe is going to marry
Wednesday. He has no such intention, and quickly
becomes a human target as the girls run after him.
Just in the nick of time, a navy helicopter comes to
rescue Robin, pulling him just out of reach of the
warring native females. He returns to his ship, where
a hero's welcome is prepared; alas, it isn't for him, but
instead for the long-lost chimp.

Dick Van Dyke is a talented and creative performer, but *Lt. Robin Crusoe* hardly shows him off to
best advantage. It's pretty dreary going, and Van
Dyke's solo comedy is labored and largely unfunny;
apparently, he works best in situations where he has
other comic actors surrounding him, with good material backing them all up. This film certainly didn't
present that kind of situation, even though Van
Dyke's old friend Byron Paul handled the direction.

Arthur Knight, an admirer of the comedian,
wrote in *Saturday Review:* "There is no variety to his
playing, no zest (or possibly too much zest) to his
performance. Inevitably, some things work out nicely,
such as a protracted bit of charades played with
Nancy Kwan; but this seems to be one of the few
sustained scenes that permit the buoyant Van Dyke
personality to bubble through."

Howard Thompson wrote in the *New York
Times:* "Most of the picture has Mr. Van Dyke mugging and tripping over the lush scenery. It's neither
very funny nor new and the picture is recommended,
with reservations, only for the very, very young and
for television fans who think Mr. Van Dyke can do no
wrong."

Apparently a lot of people fell into the latter
category, for *Lt. Robin Crusoe,* perhaps the flimsiest
Disney film of all time, grossed nearly $8 million in its
domestic release, an impressive latter-day example of
star power.

THE FIGHTING PRINCE OF DONEGAL

RELEASED BY BUENA VISTA ON OCTOBER 1, 1966. Technicolor. Coproducer: Bill Anderson. Director: Michael O'Herlihy. Screenplay: Robert Westerby, based on the book *Red Hugh, Prince of Donegal* by Robert T. Reilly. Photography: Arthur Ibbetson. Special photographic effects: Peter Ellenshaw. Editor: Peter Boita. Art director: Maurice Carter. Costumes: Anthony Mendleson. Music: George Bruns. Orchestrations: Walter Sheets. Associate producer: Hugh Attwooll. Production manager: David Anderson. Assistant director: David Bracknell. Camera operator: Freddy Cooper. Continuity: June Faithfull. Casting: Maude Spector. Makeup: Harry Frampton. Hairstyling: Eileen Warwick. Sound editor: Peter Keen. Sound recordists: Ken Rawkins, Gordon McCallum. Running time: 112 minutes.

Cast: Peter McEnery (Hugh O'Donnell), Susan Hampshire (Kathleen MacSweeney), Tom Adams (Henry O'Neill), Gordon Jackson (Captain Leeds), Andrew Keir (Lord MacSweeney), Donal McCann (Sean O'Toole), Maurice Roeves (Martin), Richard Leech (head of O'Neill clan), Maire NiGhrainne, Moire O'Neill, Fidelma Murphy (daughters of Irish woman who shelter O'Donnell), Norman Wooland, Peter Jeffrey, Marie Kean, Bill Owen, Peggy Marshall, John Forbes Robertson, Patrick Holt, Robert Cawdron, Roger Croucher, Keith McConnell, Inigo Jackson, Peter Cranwell.

Disney had not made a British swashbuckler since 1953's *The Sword and the Rose*, and *The Fighting Prince of Donegal* marked a welcome return to the genre. The film bears more than a passing resemblance to *Rob Roy, The Highland Rogue* in spirit and subject matter, but it far outdistances the earlier film.

In the sixteenth century there was a legend in Ireland: "When Hugh succeeds Hugh, Ireland shall be free." When Hugh O'Donnell, the Prince of Donegal, dies, his son Red Hugh inherits the title, and with it the responsibility of living up to the legend.

Hugh meets with the heads of other clans and urges them to join together, not to fight, but to make a treaty with the British. Then, if that should fail, to unite in one solid show of strength. The clan leaders agree. Hugh becomes especially close to Lord Mac-

Our hero has his hands full in this climactic swordfest; Gordon Jackson and Peter McEnery in *The Fighting Prince of Donegal*. © *1966 Walt Disney Productions*

Virtue has its own reward: McEnery and Susan Hampshire in the final clinch. © *1966 Walt Disney Productions*

Sweeney, and falls in love with his daughter Kathleen. One day they spot an English merchant ship offshore; the captain invites Hugh and MacSweeney for dinner that evening. They go, only to discover that it's a trap. MacSweeney is let go, but O'Donnell is held hostage to ensure that the clans will not mount an attack. He is taken to Dublin Castle as prisoner.

The wicked Captain Leeds, in charge of the prison, taunts O'Donnell and challenges him to a quarter-staff fight, which Hugh wins handily, embarrassing the captain. They become bitter enemies. A sympathetic prisoner named Sean O'Toole plans an escape with Hugh; their first attempt fails, but later when joined by Henry O'Neill, who has been jailed after trying to present a treaty to Captain Leeds (temporary substitute for the viceroy), the three of them manage to escape, with the help of a young prison boy.

When they learn that Leeds has captured Donegal Castle, and is holding Kathleen and Hugh's mother prisoner, Hugh and the clansmen spring into action. By clever subterfuge, they manage to break into the castle courtyard where they subdue the enemy. Hugh confronts Captain Leeds on a staircase leading to the tower, where Kathleen and Hugh's mother are barricaded. An exciting duel ends with Hugh victorious, but instead of killing his opponent, he makes him agree to accept an Irish treaty and be held as prisoner until the whole matter is settled. Hugh is reunited with Kathleen on the happy occasion of a peaceful and united Ireland coming into being.

The Fighting Prince of Donegal is a rousing and suspenseful swashbuckler, with a young and dashing hero, a beautiful heroine, a thoroughly despicable villain, plenty of color and atmosphere, and a clear-cut story line with good guys winning out over the bad guys. What more could one ask?

As with the earlier Disney British endeavors, this film is mounted on a lavish scale, with magnificent interiors perfectly complementing the beautiful outdoor surroundings. The action is staged for maximum impact, and the final duel is fought in a manner fondly reminiscent of the classic battle between Errol Flynn and Basil Rathbone in *The Adventures of Robin Hood*.

Yet this is no tongue-in-cheek affair. It is played for all it's worth, and some of the battling is vividly violent and exciting. In short, the film has everything going for it.

The cast is splendid, all the way down the line. Though publicity for the film treated Peter McEnery as a Disney protégé, the young actor never appeared in any further films for the studio, concentrating instead on a promising stage career, with some British films sandwiched in between roles. Susan Hampshire has continued to enjoy international acclaim for her stage, film, and television work. The supporting roles are perfectly cast, from boisterous Andrew Keir as Lord MacSweeney to the versatile Gordon Jackson, a prolific actor giving his all as the evil Captain Leeds. Tom Adams was a last-minute replacement for actor Mark Eden, who injured himself in the early stages of shooting.

This was Irish-born director Michael O'Herlihy's first feature film, after considerable experience as a TV director in Hollywood. He subsequently piloted several other films for the studio, with the same skill and sense of pacing shown in this initial effort.

The blame for the movie's one fault lies with the screenwriter, who could have cut some of the extraneous plot action to obtain a tighter script. At 112 minutes the film is a bit long, and certainly one escape attempt from Dublin Castle would have done as well as two.

Critics fell into two camps: on the one hand, those who found nothing new to offer in the film, besides a distortion of history; and on the other hand, those who just sat back and had fun. In the former category, *Variety* called it a "tame and cliché programmer with little appeal to grownups, not much more for the very young," and *Time* wrote that "in the new movie, one of the great fighting Irishmen is transformed into a priggish Prince Valiant and his complex politico-military career made into the sort of primary colored comic strip that parents consider safe and children consider dull."

But Howard Thompson in the *New York Times* called it "a good little adventure movie," and Judith Crist wrote in the *New York Herald Tribune* that the *"Fighting Prince of Donegal* is a great film for the Irish and the kids and those of us who simply can't resist all the swash and buckle that goes with a sixteenth century fight for freedom, complete with castles and moats and gathering clans and lovely colleens and two-fisted lads fighting for the glory of the Auld Sod against Good Queen Bess' evil envoys."

No great shakes at the box office, *Donegal* provided Disney with a most engaging potboiler to keep up his flow of films.

FOLLOW ME, BOYS!

RELEASED BY BUENA VISTA ON DECEMBER 1, 1966. Technicolor. Coproducer: Winston Hibler. Director: Norman Tokar. Screenplay: Louis Pelletier, based on the book *God and My Country* by MacKinlay Kantor. Photography: Clifford Stine. Editor: Robert Stafford. Art directors: Carroll Clark, Marvin Aubrey Davis. Set decorations: Emile Kuri, Frank R. McKelvy. Costume designer: Bill Thomas. Costumers: Chuck Keehne, Neva Rames. Music: George Bruns. Orchestrations: Walter Sheets. Assistant to the producer: Jerome Courtland. Assistant director: Terry Morse, Jr. Matte artist: Jim Fetherolf. Special effects: Eustace Lycett. Makeup: Pat McNalley. Hairstyling: La Rue Matheron. Sound supervision: Robert O. Cook. Sound mixer: Robert Post. Music editor: Evelyn Kennedy. Running time: 131 minutes.

Song: "Follow Me, Boys!" by Robert B. Sherman, Richard M. Sherman.

Cast: Fred MacMurray (Lemuel Siddons), Vera Miles (Vida Downey), Lillian Gish (Hetty Seibert), Charlie Ruggles (John Everett Hughes), Elliott Reid (Ralph Hastings), Kurt Russell (Whitey), Luana Patten (Nora White), Ken Murray (Melody Murphy), Donald May (Edward White, Jr.), Sean McClory (Edward White, Sr.), Steve Franken (P.O.W. lieutenant), Parley Baer (Mayor Hi Plommer), William Reynolds (Hoodoo Henderson as a man), Craig Hill (Leo as a man), Tol Avery (Doctor Ferris), Willis Bouchey (judge), John Zaremba (Ralph's lawyer), Madge Blake (Cora Anderson), Carl Reindel (tank captain), Hank Brandt (Frankie Martin as a man), Richard Bakalyan (umpire), Tim McIntire (corporal), Willie Soo Hoo (Quong Lee as a man), Tony Regan (Hetty's lawyer), Robert B. Williams (Artie), Jimmy Murphy (first P.O.W. soldier), Adam Williams (P.O.W. sergeant), and Lem's Boys: Dean Moray (Hoodoo Henderson), Bill Booth (Leo), Keith Taylor (Beefy Smith), Rickey Kelman (Frankie Martin), Gregg Shank (Mickey Doyle), Donnie Carter (Red), Kit Lloyd (Oliver), Ronnie Dapo (Tiger), Dennis Rush (Jimmy), Kevin Burchett (Eggy), David Bailey (Duke), Eddie Sallia (Harry), Bill "Wahoo" Mills (David), Warren Hsieh (Quong Lee), Duane Chase (Joe), Mike Dodge (Phil), Gregor Vigen (Ronnie Larsen), Michael Flatley (scout #1, troop #1), Sherwood Ball (scout #3, troop #1), Colyer Dupont (scout at cliff), Dean Bradshaw (first scout in war games), Chris Mason (second scout in war games), Johnny Bangert (third scout in war games).

Follow Me, Boys! tells the story of Lemuel (Lem) Siddons, a saxophone player with Melody Murphy's Collegians in the 1930s. He is tired of constantly traveling, and tells Murphy that he'd give anything to settle down in a nice, small town and get married. When the band bus stops in just such a town, called Hickory, Lem decides to make his move, and lets the band go on without him. In a few minutes' time he procures a job in the local general store, and meets a pretty bank cashier named Vida Downey; although she wants nothing to do with him, Lem knows instantly that this is the girl he's been looking for. His competition is Ralph Hastings, the vice-president of the bank, and nephew of the town's wealthiest woman, Hetty Seibert.

Lem overhears Vida saying what a shame it is that there isn't some activity for the local boys to get involved with, instead of running around on the streets. At a civic club meeting soon thereafter, Lem volunteers to start a Boy Scout troop, winning Vida's favor at last. Before long, the troop is a reality, and after a few bumpy moments, Lem and Vida are married. When Vida learns that she cannot have children, she and Lem devote themselves even more to the scouts—"their" boys. When Whitey, a troublesome boy who has "reformed" as a scout, loses his father, Lem and Vida adopt him, making their happiness complete.

All along, Lem plugs away at his longtime ambition to become a lawyer. But as he becomes more and more involved with the scouts, he has less time to devote to studying.

Time passes, and during World War II Whitey becomes a doctor in the Army Medical Corps, while at home, Lem's new group of scouts participates in war games with an unwitting army squadron.

One day banker Ralph Hastings announces that the scouts will have to leave their lakeside headquarters, owned by his aunt Hetty. Hastings realizes the value of the land, and sets out to prove his aunt incompetent, so he can reclaim the property. Lem defends Miss Seibert in court, where she proves to be as astute as her nephew, perhaps even more so.

When war ends, Whitey returns home with a bride, Nora, and establishes a practice in Hickory. His

"Lift 'em up, put 'em down," cries scout leader Fred Mac-Murray in *Follow Me, Boys!* © 1966 Walt Disney Productions

Fred MacMurray and Vera Miles take orphaned Kurt Russell into their home.   © 1965 Walt Disney Productions

most difficult patient, however, is Lem, who is getting old, but who refuses to slow down. Eventually, he is forced to turn over scout leadership to another man, and ease up on his activities. His final achievement is to be the dedication of the new scout camp at Seibert Lake. The ceremony turns out to be a townwide tribute to Lem Siddons, with the entire population, including many of his former scouts, in attendance. One of them, now the governor, thanks Lem on behalf of everyone. He replies that it has been "the happiest life a man can have."

There are two ways to look at *Follow Me, Boys!* Objectively speaking, it is the biggest barrel of corn ever put together by the Disney studio. Not a cliché has been overlooked in the situations (Lem and Vida "meeting cute"; the bad boy with a drunken father who is redeemed by scouting, etc.); and dialogue ("Come on, guys," urges novice scout leader Siddons). Every movement is calculated either for laughter, adventure, or heart tugs.

That's objectively speaking. However, if one is sentimental and willing to let the movie work on one's emotions, it's possible to be taken in, so that even the clichés serve their purpose—and when aging Lem Siddons looks around him at the end of the film and sees a throng of happy, grateful people, one can be genuinely moved.

Certainly the film is unabashed corn; but it is laid out with such conviction and sincerity that it is quite possible for a viewer to lose all perspective and warm to the sentimental tale.

Even Bosley Crowther, who found it unbearably sloppy, had to add that ". . . it's only fair to inform you that the audience yesterday (made up largely, it appeared, of older people) was chuckling and sniffling all through the film."

This was the formula that had worked before for director Norman Tokar and scenarist Louis Pelletier in *Those Calloways,* and in a different vein in *Big Red.* Again, they worked toward creating an atmosphere, and used a variety of vignettes to achieve this goal.

The film even has an obligatory boy-dangling-over-cliff-on-a-rope sequence. This seems to have been a prerequisite for every Boy Scout movie in the history of Hollywood (*Scouts to the Rescue, Henry Aldrich Boy Scout, Mr. Scoutmaster,* etc.).

The performances are all very good, with the character actors outdistancing the leads in most departments. Lillian Gish is delightful as the benevolent Hetty Seibert, particularly in her courtroom scenes; Charlie Ruggles exudes his usual geniality as the store owner who gives Lem his first job in town; Sean McClory is excellent as Whitey's well-meaning father who hits the bottle once too often. Young Kurt Russell is also quite good in a role that could have been thoroughly obnoxious, as the bad boy who makes good.

As always, Fred MacMurray's simple, honest approach to his role breathes life into lifeless dialogue and enables one to believe the hokiest lines. Vera Miles does nicely as his sympathetic wife.

Former Disney child star Luana Patten returned to the fold once more as Whitey's bride, a minor but noticeable role.

Follow Me, Boys! suffers from the malady common to many Disney films of this time, overlength. Its leisurely pace is part of its charm, of course, but the film's episodic nature points up the padding all the more. An extended sequence in which Lem's scouts inadvertently become involved in army war games is nicely done, but hardly compelling or relevant to the story; it is this kind of segment that pushes the film toward two hours and ten minutes of running time. (It was cut by ten minutes for its 1976 reissue.)

The film provided Disney with a perfect family release for Christmastime, playing to great success at New York's Radio City Music Hall and around the country.

Critics, however, cringed at the syrupy assault. Bosley Crowther in the *New York Times* wrote that the film was "such a clutter of sentimental blubberings about the brotherhood of the Boy Scouts and indiscriminate ladling of cornball folksy comedy that it taxes the loyalty and patience of even a one-time ardent member of the Beaver Patrol." Judith Crist in the *New York World Journal Tribune* noted: "This two-hour commercial for the Boy Scouts of America and ecstatic eulogy to The Clichés of Pure-Hearted Simple-Minded Americana is the kind of movie that has tended to give Walt Disney films a frequently

undeserved reputation for gooery among diabetics, dieters and other thinking members of the adult community. There's nothing undeserved about it this time, though." *Time* thought the film was "likely to restore public faith in juvenile delinquency."

Variety, with an eye toward public reaction rather than private taste, called it a "topnotch Walt Disney drama which should strike a respondent chord with every audience regardless of how sophisticated. The production catches the spirit of rural America in the '30s with moving charm, blending comedy, drama and romance in a buildup toward an emotionally-charged climax."

Public reaction *was* good, despite the critical roasting, and *Follow Me, Boys!* earned $5½ million in its domestic release—not as much as it might have with better reviews and a less sticky approach, but enough to prove that a sizable audience for this kind of film did exist.

MONKEYS, GO HOME!

RELEASED BY BUENA VISTA ON FEBRUARY 2, 1967. Technicolor. Coproducer: Ron Miller. Director: Andrew V. McLaglen. Screenplay: Maurice Tombragel, based on the book *The Monkeys* by G. K. Wilkinson. Photography: William Snyder. Editor: Marsh Hendry. Art directors: Carroll Clark, John B. Mansbridge. Set decorations: Emile Kuri, Frank R. McKelvy. Costume designer: Bill Thomas. Costumers: Chuck Keehne, Neva Rames. Music: Robert F. Brunner. Orchestrations: Cecil A. Crandall. Assistant to the producer: Louis Debney. Dialogue coach: Flora Duane. Assistant director: Tom Leetch. Matte effects: Peter Ellenshaw, Jim Fetherolf. Makeup: Pat McNalley. Hairstyling: La Rue Matheron. Animal supervision: Stewart Raffill. Sound supervision: Robert O. Cook. Sound mixer: Robert Post. Music editor: Evelyn Kennedy. Running time: 101 minutes.

Song: "Joie de Vivre" by Richard M. Sherman, Robert B. Sherman.

Cast: Maurice Chevalier (Father Sylvain), Dean Jones (Hank Dussard), Yvette Mimieux (Maria Riserau), Bernard Woringer (Marcel Cartucci), Clement Harari (Emile Paraulis), Yvonne Constant (Yolande Angelli), Marcel Hillaire (Mayor Gaston Lou), Jules Munshin (M. Piastillio), Alan Carney (grocer), Maurice Marsac (Fontanino), Darleen Carr (Sidoni Riserau).

Easygoing Maurice Chevalier tries to calm down Dean Jones, who seems to be taking out his anger on Yvette Mimieux. © *1967 Walt Disney Productions*

No comment. © 1966 Walt Disney Productions

The *New York Times*'s Vincent Canby saw *Monkeys, Go Home!* with an audience of children, and he wrote that "their fun, it seems, is derived in direct proportion to the number of chimpanzees on hand."

No one knew this better than the Disney staff, in conceiving this film to provide as many funny scenes of monkeys as the script would allow. The story, apparently, was just a necessary evil. It deals with a young American, Hank Dussard, who goes to France to see an olive farm he has inherited from his late uncle. The local priest, Father Sylvain, warns him that the economics of running such an enterprise are hazardous; one must have a large family to harvest the olives after the seasonal wind has blown them off the trees, or the wages one would pay would make it unfeasible.

Father Sylvain sends Maria Riserau to help Hank get settled, and straighten out the neglected house. She also helps Hank when he concocts a scheme to train four monkeys to pick his olives for him. A local real-estate dealer who wants to buy Hank's property learns about the monkeys, and mounts a local campaign to drive them, and Hank, away; he is aided by Cartucci, who joins the fight because he doesn't want Hank to take Maria away from him.

Hank exposes this conspiracy with Father Sylvain's help, and then finds another obstacle: a woman claiming to be Hank's cousin, and coowner of the farm. Maria uses the monkeys to scare her off, and she confesses to the priest that she was hired by the crooked realtor.

The wind blows, and the olives are ready to be picked up. Hank sets his monkeys to work, but Maria has brought a male chimpanzee with her, and the four females are more interested in chasing him than in picking up olives. Father Sylvain asks the townspeople to help out poor Hank, and they eagerly join in for a happy ending.

There isn't much to say for *Monkeys, Go Home!* It is what it is. William Peper wrote in the *World Journal Tribune:* "If a chimpanzee is cute, does it not follow that a quartet of them will be four times as cute? Obviously, the makers of this movie believe it with all their hearts. This situation has inspired director Andrew V. McLaglen to create scenes of monkeys eating lots and lots of bananas, of monkeys dressed as ghosts, or monkeys carrying picket signs. Clearly, the man is in love with his work . . ."

For non-monkey-lovers, there is little to recommend in the film. Dean Jones and Yvette Mimieux are a healthily attractive couple, but they don't emit fireworks, and Maurice Chevalier is his usual effervescent self, singing an unmemorable song by the Sherman brothers, "Joie de Vivre," with a young Disney discovery, Darleen Carr.

But the only raison d'être for this film is that barrel of monkeys, who scamper about creating all sorts of mischief. If you like them, you'll like this film. But apparently, Disney had wrung the monkey market dry, for *Monkeys, Go Home!* did not perform especially well at the box office.

It was director Andrew McLaglen's first feature film for the studio, having graduated from television to such Westerns as *Shenandoah* and *McClintock*, the latter displaying a broad sense of comedy not unlike that in *Monkeys, Go Home!* Screenwriter Maurice Tombragel, who had won kudos for his scripting of *Moon Pilot* a few years earlier, strictly adhered to formula in laying out this obvious story line.

William Peper concluded: "It was photographed on the back lot of the Disney studios [on the refurbished *Zorro* set, incidentally] so don't look for any authentic Gallic backgrounds." Just monkeys in the foreground.

THE ADVENTURES OF BULLWHIP GRIFFIN

RELEASED BY BUENA VISTA ON MARCH 3, 1967. TECH-
nicolor. Coproducer: Bill Anderson. Director: James
Neilson. Screenplay: Lowell S. Hawley, based on the
novel *By the Great Horn Spoon* by Sid Fleischman. Photography: Edward Colman. Editor: Marsh Hendry.
Art directors: Carroll Clark, John B. Mansbridge. Set
decorations: Emile Kuri, Hal Gausman. Costume designer: Bill Thomas. Costumers: Chuck Keehne,
Neva Rames. Music: George Bruns. Orchestrations:
Walter Sheets. Titles and things: Ward Kimball. Second unit director: Arthur J. Vitarelli. Associate
producer: Louis Debney. Choreographer: Alex Plass-
chaert. Assistant director: John C. Chulay. Matte artist: Peter Ellenshaw. Special effects: Eustace Lycett.
Makeup: Pat McNalley. Hairstyling: La Rue Matheron. Sound supervision: Robert O. Cook. Sound
mixer: Dean Thomas. Music editor: Evelyn Kennedy.
Running time: 110 minutes.

Songs: "Girls of San Francisco," "Whoever You Are,"
"California Gold" by Richard M. Sherman, Robert B.
Sherman. Additional songs by Mel Leven and George
Bruns.

Cast: Roddy McDowall (Bullwhip Griffin), Suzanne
Pleshette (Arabella Flagg), Karl Malden (Judge
Higgins), Harry Guardino (Sam Trimble), Richard
Haydn (Quentin Bartlett), Hermione Baddeley
(Miss Irene Chesney), Bryan Russell (Jack Flagg),
Liam Redmond (Captain Swain), Cecil Kellaway
(Mr. Pemberton), Joby Baker (bandido leader),
Mike Mazurki (Mountain Ox), Alan Carney (Joe
Turner), Parley Baer (chief executioner), Arthur
Hunnicutt (referee), Dub Taylor (timekeeper),
Pedro Gonzalez-Gonzalez (bandido), Gil Lamb, Burt
Mustin, Dave Willock, John Qualen.

The Adventures of Bullwhip Griffin is a bouncy
spoof of the California gold-rush saga, with Roddy
McDowall as a butler forced to abandon his proper
Boston setting when his young master Jack Flagg runs
away to join the gold hunt. Griffin, the butler, stows
away on ship with the boy, where they meet a would-
be actor named Quentin Bartlett who owns a treasure
map. He offers to cut the two in as partners if they
will protect him. They agree, but soon thereafter a sly
crook named Judge Higgins steals the map from
Bartlett.

When the ship docks at San Francisco, Griffin and

Roddy McDowall finds that Suzanne Pleshette has become
an entertainer in Harry Guardino's sawdust saloon. ©
1965 Walt Disney Productions

Jack go after Higgins, and engage in a wide variety of
adventures in which they leap from destitution to
riches and back again, through the machinations of
Higgins. They return to San Francisco broke, and
discover Jack's sister Arabella working in Sam Trimble's saloon as a singer/dancer. Griffin is shocked to
see the former debutante in such an undignified position, and determines to get enough money to send her
home.

When in San Francisco before, a lucky punch on
the jaw of Mountain Ox, a bouncer in the saloon,
earned Griffin the nickname Bullwhip. Now he capi-
talizes on that and accepts Trimble's offer of $1,000
for winning a boxing match with the Ox. Griffin goes
into training, and when the great event is held, he is
in agile form. Knocked out at one point, a kiss from
Arabella revives him and sends him back into battle,
triumphant.

Meanwhile, Higgins, in one of his innumerable
disguises, is robbing Sam Trimble's safe. He is caught
in the nick of time, Bullwhip is a hero, and he and

The long-awaited battle between Bullwhip Griffin (Mc-Dowall) and Mountain Ox (Mike Mazurki). Guess who wins. © *1965 Walt Disney Productions*

Arabella realize at last that they love each other.

Bullwhip Griffin's plot takes an endless number of twists and turns, but constantly comes up with new surprises to maintain a peak of interest throughout the film. The situations, the characters (particularly the roguish villainy of Karl Malden as Higgins), and the film's considerable bag of tricks make it a most entertaining treat.

One of the film's strongest assets is the visual gimmickry of Ward Kimball, who provided the transitional animation in appropriately rococo style, with cupids, engravinglike drawings, and such, with a good many punny ideas. There are other bright thoughts, such as having a cupid fly across the screen to muted trumpet sounds every time Bullwhip is knocked cold. When he is practicing with a punching bag, he sees the face of Sam Trimble in the bag and sends it off its foundation, clear up into the sky. (In a typical Disney touch the image of Trimble is not only superimposed on the bag, but the smoke from his cigar floats off the perimeter of the bag into the air.)

Atmosphere is vivid throughout the film, with a nice flavor of the sawdust city inhabited by scraggly miners. The saloon itself is ideal, with Suzanne Pleshette leading a quartet of chorines through some bright song numbers.

The film's pièce de résistance is the climactic fight between Bullwhip Griffin and Mountain Ox. Here the special effects come thick and fast, with Griffin literally bouncing around the ring, outwitting his brawny opponent with a series of rapid-fire moves that not only defy gravity, but defy credibility. The fight is staged in the best sight-gag tradition, and comes across beautifully.

The cast is spirited and well chosen, with Roddy McDowall perfect as the very proper butler who learns how to take care of himself in the wild and woolly West; Suzanne Pleshette as Arabella, who is spunky enough to accept a job in Trimble's saloon when she learns she is penniless; Karl Malden as the tricky Judge Higgins; Richard Haydn as the actor who holds the treasure map; and Harry Guardino as slick Sam Trimble, who has an eye for his new singing star. Bryan Russell is good as the young boy in McDowall's charge. And naturally, the character bits are played by seasoned professionals, several of them Disney regulars by now.

Bullwhip Griffin didn't wow any of the critics. Howard Thompson in the *Times* thought it "slow, overdrawn, and tame to the point of gentility. . . . The best thing about the film, keying what it might have been, are the delightful, sprightly animated inserts threading the story and tuned up by a barbershop quartet." William Peper in the *World Journal*

Tribune concurred, with somewhat kinder sentiments toward the film as a whole, calling it "the family picture at its most palatable." Only *Variety* was really enthusiastic, dubbing it "excellent . . . zesty direction, solid performances, first-rate production values and broad comedy angles make this production particularly strong for all-age audiences."

Few people of any age came to see the film, however, and it was not a financial success. Just a short time later it was shown on the Disney TV show.

THE GNOME-MOBILE

RELEASED BY BUENA VISTA ON JULY 12, 1967. TECHnicolor. Coproducer: James Algar. Director: Robert Stevenson. Screenplay: Ellis Kadison, based on the book by Upton Sinclair. Photography: Edward Colman. Editor: Norman Palmer. Art directors: Carroll Clark, William H. Tuntke. Set decorations: Emile Kuri, Hal Gausman. Costume designer: Bill Thomas. Costumers: Chuck Keehne, Neva Rames. Music: Buddy Baker. Orchestrations: Wayne Robinson. Second unit director: Arthur J. Vitarelli. Unit manager: Joseph L. McEveety. Assistant director: Paul Cameron. Matte artist: Peter Ellenshaw. Special effects: Eustace Lycett, Robert A. Mattey. Art styling: Sam McKim, David Jonas. Makeup: Pat McNalley. Hairstylng: La Rue Matheron. Sound supervision: Robert O. Cook. Sound mixer: Dean Thomas. Music editor: Evelyn Kennedy. Running time: 90 minutes.

Song: "The Gnome-Mobile" by Robert B. Sherman, Richard M. Sherman.

Cast: Walter Brennan (D. J. Mulrooney; Knobby), Matthew Garber (Rodney), Karen Dotrice (Elizabeth), Richard Deacon (Ralph Yarby), Tom Lowell (Jasper), Sean McClory (Horatio Quaxton), Ed Wynn (Rufus), Jerome Cowan (Dr. Ramsey), Charles Lane (Dr. Scoggins), Norman Grabowski (nurse), Gil Lamb (gas attendant), Maudie Prickett (Katie Barrett), Cami Sebring (Violet), Ellen Corby (Etta Pettibone), Frank Cady (Charlie Pettibone), Pamela Gail, Susan Gates, Jacki Ray, Joyce Menges, Susan and Bunny Henning (Gnomes).

It had been quite some time since Disney returned to his true métier, the fantasy, but *The Gnome-Mobile* brought him back in style. In addition, the film embodies many of the key elements in the Disney philosophy (as expressed in his films): children are smarter than most adults; man constantly destroys the beauty of nature; big business is cold and cruel.

The story has lumber tycoon D. J. Mulrooney taking his visiting niece and nephew into the great redwood forest for a picnic. Young Elizabeth wanders off and meets a two-foot gnome named Jasper, who asks her for help. It seems that his tiny clan is cut off from all other gnomes, although they know that others must exist. But Jasper's 943-year-old grandfather, Knobby, is upset that the breed might be dying, and is losing his will to live.

Elizabeth enlists the aid of D.J., who offers to drive Jasper and Knobby to another part of the forest untouched by man, where other gnomes might live. As they ride along in D.J.'s pride and joy, his 1930 Rolls Royce, they redub the car a Gnome-Mobile. The irascible Knobby harangues the others about how the forest has been ruined by lumbermen—Mulrooney in particular.

When the party stops for the night at a motel, D.J. hides the gnomes in a picnic basket, but hearing that his benefactor is the same Mulrooney who runs the lumber company, Knobby raises a racket, attracting a nearby spectator, Horatio Quaxton, who runs a freak show. That night he manages to steal the two gnomes and run off without being noticed. When D.J. realizes what has happened, he calls his office and tells them to send the company's security forces to search for the gnomes. Mulrooney's vice-president, Ralph Yarby, fears that D.J. has lost his marbles, and, using deception, takes D.J. to a nearby sanitarium.

When Rodney discovers where they've taken his grandfather, he and Elizabeth help him escape. They drive off in their car, with Yarby and the sanitarium men in hot pursuit. There follows a mad chase, which leaves the pursuants' car a shambles, as D.J. and the kids drive on in search of Jasper and Knobby.

They rescue Jasper, who tells them that Knobby got off on his own. They discover the old codger in the woods with a group of other gnomes, including Rufus, the 1,100-year-old gnome king. When Jasper arrives, Rufus brings on a gaggle of beautiful female gnomes,

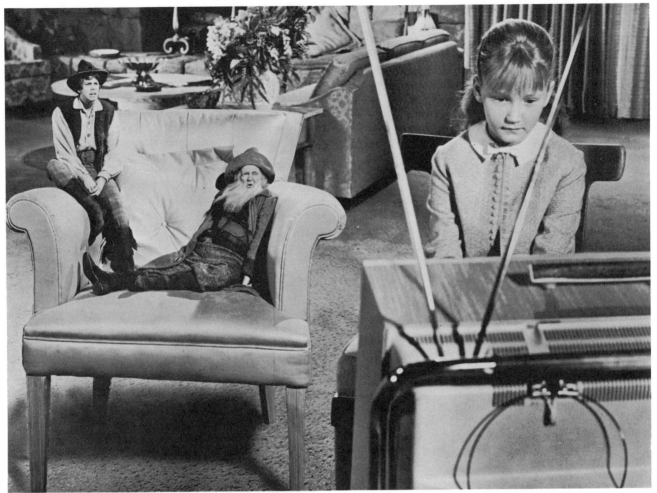

Tom Lowell and Walter Brennan, as two of the gnomes, try to get Karen Dotrice's attention. © 1967 Walt Disney Productions

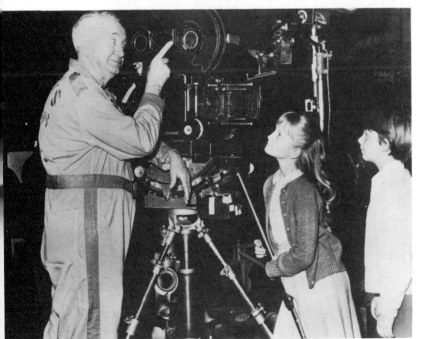

Walter Brennan hams it up with Karen Dotrice and Matthew Garber on the set of *The Gnome-Mobile.* © 1966 *Walt Disney Productions*

all eager to win the hand of the one eligible male in sight. Jasper is dipped in a foamy pool, making him a slippery subject, and a Sadie Hawkins-type race is on. Jasper likes one girl named Shy Violet, but the others are more aggressive. Luckily, after an exhausting race, Violet wins her man, and they are married. In honor of the occasion D.J. bequeaths to the gnomes 50,000 acres of redwood forest for their own, and then offers them all a ride in his Gnome-Mobile for a happy finale.

The Gnome-Mobile is a colorful delight, with no lulls in its swift-moving story. There are definite highlights, however: the frantic car chase, in which the sanitarium limousine falls apart piece by piece as it jumps over the rugged terrain; the gnome chase at the end; and an eye-popping, hair-raising scene in which Quaxton tries to stop Jasper from escaping.

Needless to say, the special effects are impeccable, reminiscent in some ways of *Darby O'Gill and the Little People,* with absolutely undetectable blending of the life-sized actors and the two-foot gnomes. When the going gets tricky, as in the escape scene where

Quaxton uses a net and then a fishing rod to capture his elusive gnome, the results are really incredible.

Along with the gnomes, there are talking animals in the forest, and these are represented by Disney's latest piece of magic, Audio-animatronics. In effect, they are robots, or three-dimensional cartoons, if you wish. By any name they are a treat to watch in action, conversing with Jasper and warning him not to trust the humans.

The color styling for the film is dazzling, making even the simplest scene in the forest a visual bonanza.

The performances are all perfectly in tune with the mood of the film. Walter Brennan is just right as the big businessman with a heart of gold, as well as in his dual role of Knobby, the crusty old gnome who has started to fade away because he has nothing to live for. Matthew Garber and Karen Dotrice are as appealing here as they were in *Mary Poppins,* and Tom Lowell, who debuted for Disney as Hayley Mills's boyfriend in *That Darn Cat,* is ideal as Jasper. The supporting cast is well rounded out, as one had come to expect in every Disney film, with seasoned pros.

Once again, it is clear that Robert Stevenson has

a special knack for this kind of material, much more so than for everyday situation comedy. His Disney fantasies (*Darby O'Gill, Mary Poppins,* this film, and to an extent *The Absent Minded Professor*) are among the screen's all-time best. He knows, most of all, how to root the film's fantasy elements in reality, so they will seem real to young viewers.

Most critics liked the premise of the film, but some thought it missed the mark, like the *Times*'s Howard Thompson, who called it "good-natured but heavy-handed . . . the action and light-hearted spirit sag under a crisscross jumble of slapstick and broadly handled locomotion that flattens the fun." *Variety* thought it "amusing, if somewhat uneven." But Judith Crist overlooked the flaws and called it "a lot of fun."

It *is* a lot of fun, and done with the expertise only Disney could have provided. Even though it was a medium success at the box office, the film has no lasting reputation, which it most certainly deserves. Perhaps time will open more people's eyes to the excellence of this zesty comedy-fantasy, which ranks among Disney's best.

THE JUNGLE BOOK

RELEASED BY BUENA VISTA ON OCTOBER 18, 1967. Technicolor. Director: Wolfgang Reitherman. Directing animators: Milt Kahl, Franklin Thomas, Oliver Johnston, Jr., John Lounsbery. Story: Larry Clemmons, Ralph Wright, Ken Anderson, Vance Gerry, inspired by the Rudyard Kipling *Mowgli* stories. Character animation: Hal King, Eric Larson, Walt Stanchfield, Eric Cleworth, Fred Hellmich, John Ewing, Dick Lucas. Background styling: Albert Dempster. Backgrounds: Bill Layne, Art Riley, Ralph Hulett, Thelma Witmer, Frank Armitage. Layout: Don Griffith, Basil Davidovich, Dale Barnhart, Tom Codrick, Sylvia Roemer. Effects animation: Dan MacManus. Music: George Bruns. Orchestrations: Walter Sheets. Production manager: Don Cuckwall. Film editor: Tom Acosta, Norman Carlisle. Sound: Robert O. Cook. Music editor: Evelyn Kennedy. Running time: 78 minutes.

Songs: "I Wanna Be Like You," "Trust in Me," "My Own Home," "That's What Friends Are For," "Colonel Hati's March" by Richard M. Sherman, Robert B. Sherman. "The Bare Necessities" by Terry Gilkyson.

Voices: Phil Harris (Baloo the Bear), Sebastian Cabot (Bagheera the Panther), Louis Prima (King Louis of the Apes), George Sanders (Shere Khan, the tiger),

Sterling Holloway (Kaa, the snake), J. Pat O'Malley (Colonel Hati, the elephant), Bruce Reitherman (Mowgli, the man-cub), Verna Felton, Clint Howard (elephants), Chad Stuart, Lord Tim Hudson, J. Pat O'Malley (vultures), John Abbott, Ben Wright (wolves), Darleen Carr (girl).

The Jungle Book was the last animated cartoon feature that bore Disney's personal stamp. For the second time in a row he decided to base a cartoon feature on a well-known book (in this case a collection of stories), although the adaptation was, predictably enough, quite freewheeling.

It deals with Mowgli, an Indian boy abandoned at birth, who is raised as a wolf cub, after being discovered by Bagheera, the panther. Ten years later Bagheera decides to return Mowgli to his people when he learns that the tiger Shere Khan is coming back to his home territory. Their trip through the jungle is interrupted by a variety of encounters, which Mowgli (who doesn't want to leave the jungle) is only too happy to find.

Bagheera finally walks out in disgust, and Mowgli is befriended by Baloo, a happy-go-lucky bear whose philosophy of life is to sit back and relax. Mowgli follows his example, but soon finds himself kidnapped by monkeys, who take him to their leader, King Louis.

Mowgli takes the advice of Baloo the Bear and enjoys the leisurely life. © *1965 Walt Disney Productions*

Mowgli arouses the ire of both Colonel Hathi and the vicious Shere Khan. © *1965 Walt Disney Productions*

Baloo goes to Bagheera for help, and the two of them manage to rescue Mowgli from the overly enthusiastic orangutan.

Mowgli runs off on his own, rather than be taken away from the jungle. He meets four vultures who befriend him when they see he is all alone. Then Shere Khan appears, and Mowgli is on his own once more to face the vicious predator. Baloo jumps in and tries to interfere, but Shere Khan knocks him cold. Then the vultures offer their help, and keep the tiger occupied long enough for Mowgli to tie a burning branch to his tail. Fire is the one thing that frightens tigers to death, and Shere Khan takes off instantly for parts unknown.

Now Mowgli can remain in the jungle without any problems. Just then, however, he spies an Indian girl on the edge of the forest; his human instincts return to him, and he forsakes his jungle life to go with her. Mowgli's animal friends realize that it's all for the best.

The Jungle Book is a very easygoing film. The trouble is, it's *too* easygoing. Though it has a lot of fun to offer, and the characters are very likable, the film is singularly lacking in excitement. It ambles along in a genial fashion, but one keeps waiting for something to happen.

Visually, it is a most impressive work. The variety of jungle settings and the opportunities for effects animation (reflection in the water, glimmering moonlight, etc.) are fully realized. More importantly, the character design is excellent. Baloo, King Louie, the elephants, and other "funny" characters in the narrative are all designed amusingly, while the other characters reflect their own personality traits in the way they look: the menacing Shere Khan, the sly, hypnotic snake Kaa, the very proper panther Bagheera. This is the essence of an animated cartoon, and it is good to see the potential being utilized to the fullest extent.

On the other side of the coin there is the question of voice characterization. Seldom before had the Disney people allowed a strong voice personality to dominate a character as in *The Jungle Book*. This does not apply as strongly to children as it would to adults, but when one is watching (and listening to) Baloo, one is not thinking about a bear, one is thinking about Phil Harris. Similarly, Louis Prima and George Sanders are so striking on the sound track that it's difficult to get involved with their animal characters on screen.

The animators claimed that these performers helped shape and define the characters, but some people accused them of using the actors' well-known personalities as crutches—instead of creating full-bodied characters *first* and then finding suitable actors to portray them on the soundtrack, as had been done for most of Disney's earlier cartoon features. (The problem became more acute when Phil Harris was brought back to do voices for *The Aristocats* and *Robin Hood*, playing essentially the same character every time.)

In many ways the best voice in the film is Sterling

A recording session for *The Jungle Book;* storyman Larry Clemmons, veteran Disney voice man Sterling Holloway, director Wolfgang Reitherman, and Sebastian Cabot. © *1965 Walt Disney Productions*

Holloway's, used for the slithery snake, Kaa. The Sherman brothers concocted a clever song to emphasize Kaa's lingering "s" sound, as did most of his dialogue. The versatile Holloway, of course, contributed voices to more Disney cartoons than any other actor.

The songs themselves are hardly memorable, although they suit the plot situations fairly well. The most enjoyable is "I Wanna Be Like You," which the chimp King Louis sings to Mowgli, the man-cub, followed closely by Baloo's "The Bare Necessities," which explains his philosophy of life. (This song, contributed by Terry Gilkyson, was nominated for an Academy Award.)

The Jungle Book is not a bad film by any means, but it lacks a certain spirit, a certain momentum that might have made it special. Its chief asset is its utter likability, but it remains one of the more forgettable Disney cartoon features.

Yet *The Jungle Book* garnered some very impressive reviews . . . colored no doubt by a certain wistfulness over the knowledge that it was Walt's last animated film. (It was released some ten months after his death.) *Time* magazine, always wary in its enthusiasm for Disney projects, noted that the film had little to do with Kipling, but added that "the result is thoroughly delightful. The reasons for its success lie in Disney's own unfettered animal spirits, his ability to be childlike without being childish . . . it is the happiest possible way to remember Walt Disney." Howard Thompson in the *New York Times* called it "a perfectly dandy cartoon feature . . . grand fun for all ages," *Life*'s Richard Schickel thought it "the best thing of its kind since *Dumbo*."

But Judith Crist said the film was "completely devoid of mood or atmosphere . . . a middle-brow cartoon of middling quality." And *Variety,* in a generally favorable review, noted that "the story development is restrained—the potential dangers are suggested and there is an overriding upbeat end in sight from the beginning—so moppet audiences may squirm at times."

They did not hesitate to give it a try, however, and *The Jungle Book* became a sensational box-office hit, earning $13 million in its domestic release alone, ranking sixth of Disney's films on *Variety*'s list of all-time box-office champs. Apparently the combination of Disney and the familiar Kipling tales was enough to pull children and their parents into theatres, especially during the holiday season.

The Jungle Book was released exactly thirty years after the debut of Disney's first animated feature, *Snow White and the Seven Dwarfs.* In the ensuing years the Disney staff had conquered the field of animation so thoroughly that there seemed nowhere else to go. The challenge facing this production team, which had worked together on so many films, was how not to go stale or simply tread water. And now they would have to confront that challenge without their leader.

THE HAPPIEST MILLIONAIRE

RELEASED BY BUENA VISTA IN JANUARY 1968 (PRE-miere, June 23, 1967; prerelease engagements, October 1967). Technicolor. Coproducer: Bill Anderson. Director: Norman Tokar. Screenplay: A. J. Carothers, based on the book and play by Kyle Crichton and Cordelia Drexel Biddle. Photography: Edward Colman. Editor: Cotton Warburton. Art directors: Carroll Clark, John B. Mansbridge. Set decorations: Emil Kuri, Frank R. McKelvy. Costume designer: Bill Thomas. Costumers: Chuck Keehne, Neva Rames. Music supervisor, arranger, conductor: Jack Elliott. Choreography: Marc Breaux, Dee Dee Wood. Special effects: Eustace Lycett, Peter Ellenshaw. Titles: Alan Maley. Assistant to the producer: Tom Leetch. Assistant director: Paul Cameron. Makeup: Gordon Hubbard. Hairstyling: Vivienne Zavitz. Sound supervision: Robert O. Cook. Sound mixer: Dean Thomas. Music editor: Evelyn Kennedy. Running time: 164 minutes.

Songs: "I'll Always Be Irish," "Detroit," "Fortuosity," "It Won't Be Long 'Til Chrismas," "What's Wrong with That?", "Watch Your Footwork," "Bye-Yum Pum Pum," "Are We Dancing?", "There Are Those," "Let's Have a Drink on It," "Valentine Candy," "Strengthen the Dwelling" by Richard M. Sherman, Robert B. Sherman.

Cast: Fred MacMurray (father), Tommy Steele (John Lawless), Greer Garson (mother), Geraldine Page (Mrs. Duke), Gladys Cooper (Aunt Mary), Hermione Baddeley (Mrs. Worth), Lesley Ann Warren (Cordelia Drexel Biddle), John Davidson (Angie Duke), Paul Peterson (Tony), Eddie Hodges (Liv), Joyce Bulifant (Rosemary), Sean McClory (Sergeant Flanagan), Jim McMullan, William Wellman, Jr.,

Jim Gurley (marine lieutenants), Aron Kincaid (Walter Blakely), Larry Merrill (Charlie Taylor), Frances Robinson (Aunt Gladys), Norman Grabowski (Joe Turner).

Still reeling at the success of *Mary Poppins,* Disney decided to mount another expensive musical extravaganza to compete with the then-current flood of three-hour movie musicals playing around the country to reserved-seat audiences. For a subject he chose *The Happiest Millionaire,* which had been produced on

Fred MacMurray, Tommy Steele, and Greer Garson in *The Happiest Millionaire.*   © *1966 Walt Disney Productions*

Broadway in 1956 as a straight narrative play. He put his prolific songwriters, Richard and Robert Sherman, to work, and rehired the duo responsible for the choreography in *Poppins*, Marc Breaux and Dee Dee Wood. He assigned Norman Tokar to direct the film, and put together an impressive cast to fill the large number of principal roles.

The Happiest Millionaire was the last film to bear Walt Disney's personal imprint, although it was released almost a year after his death. It would be nice to say that his last film was a rousing success, but it was not.

The central character is Anthony J. Drexel Biddle, an eccentric millionaire who shares his Philadelphia mansion with pet alligators, members of his Bible class (who incongruously wear boxing gloves, part of the Biddle philosophy of physical fitness), and a bewildered staff, headed by a new addition, Irish-born John Lawless, the butler. Biddle and his wife send their daughter Cordy to finishing school in New Jersey, where she meets the offspring of another wealthy family, Angie Duke of New York. She falls in love with him, and all seems well for an early wedding.

But the youngsters have not reckoned with their families, who create a rivalry that all but destroys the love match. Angie can't take any more, and he stalks out of the Biddle home, followed by John Lawless, They go to an Irish pub, where a drinking spree leads to a brawl that puts Angie in jail. Both the Dukes and the Biddles come down to bail him out, the incident bringing the families together again on common ground. They decide to forget their differences, and the wedding is on again.

It is a tribute to the director and scenarist that while this elementary story is stretched out to nearly three hours, it moves along quite briskly. The film has few lulls, although if one examined it objectively to prune out extraneous matter, two-thirds of the film might go down the drain.

That it is a lightly enjoyable film is not much to say about such an ambitious production, but that is about the best one can do. The first problem is the characters, usually the strong point in director Tokar's work.

Of Fred MacMurray's "lovable eccentric," *Time*'s critic wrote: "The main trouble . . . is that Fred MacMurray's impersonation is eccentric but not lovable. He is, in fact, a boor. . . . MacMurray dashes around his vast house conducting calisthenic Bible classes, honking at his ambulatory alligators, roughing up his guests with show-off fisticuffs, show-off opera arias, show-off opinions." Only the actor's natural likability saves the characterization from total disaster.

The young lovers are—well, young lovers, who traditionally are on hand for obligatory reasons, and are hardly expected to generate much excitement. There is an attempt to give John Davidson's character some dimension by stressing his fascination with the

Lesley Ann Warren is introduced to her future mother-in-law, Geraldine Page, by fiancé John Davidson. © *1967 Walt Disney Productions*

Walt Disney poses on the set with Gladys Cooper, Lesley Ann Warren, Greer Garson, Fred MacMurray, Geraldine Page, John Davidson, and Tommy Steele. © *1966 Walt Disney Productions*

automobile and Detroit (recall that this takes place in 1916), but it's difficult for the audience to share his enthusiasm.

The two matriarchs, Mrs. Duke, played by Geraldine Page, and Aunt Mary, played by Gladys Cooper, are caricatures, especially the former, whose presence merely reinforces the idea that this is all a cardboard charade and not an indication of real life. Even a song—"There Are Those"—intended to be a great moment of confrontation between the two ladies—is hopelessly contrived.

Most reviews agreed that Tommy Steele as John Lawless was one of the film's saving graces, but he too throws things off balance, for his singing and dancing, music-hall style, and comic antics with the alligators make it more difficult to understand whether this is supposed to be realistic or whimsical. The film, as a result, fails in both departments.

What keeps the film from folding up altogether is the musical numbers, not just the major productions like "Let's Have a Drink on It," with a bar full of Irish rowdies kicking up their heels, but small-scale sequences as well, such as the charming one built around the song "Bye-Yum Pum Pum," in which Lesley Ann Warren's roommate, played by Joyce Bulifant, teaches her naive young friend how to flirt with a man.

Tommy Steele's exuberance carries a lot of the film, from the opening introductory number to his duet of "Fortuosity" with one of Mr. Biddle's alligators. (Reportedly, one of Disney's audio-animatronics was used for the alligator, until Walt saw the rushes and decided that it looked too phony, at which point the real animal was brought in.)

Every actor with a reasonable part in the film participates in at least one song; in the case of Eddie Hodges and Paul Peterson, it gives them their only chance in the spotlight when they do "Watch Your Footwork."

Included in the songfest is Fred MacMurray himself, who has a patter song called "What's Wrong with That?" as well as several other more melodic tunes. It must have come as quite a surprise to many viewers that he could sing at all; in fact, he has a very pleasant singing voice. (Film buffs may recall his rendition of the deathless song "My Concertina" in *The Princess Comes Across* in 1936.)

Since the film totters so uneasily between the real and the unreal, the characters make no imprint whatsoever, and at the end of the film one is left with nothing.

The only conclusion one can draw from this is that *The Happiest Millionaire* was a bad choice for Disney to produce. Most of his other musicals were either outright fantasies, like *Mary Poppins,* or lighthearted stories done on a modest scale, like *Summer Magic.* The characters and situations of *Millionaire* left him hanging in between, and, in trying to top *Mary Poppins,* it was arbitrarily decided to spend freely on sets, costumes, and other appointments.

The Happiest Millionaire was also intended as a road-show attraction. This turned out to be something of a blunder, but it was one which Disney shared with every other producer in Hollywood. After the enormous success of *Mary Poppins* and *The Sound of Music,* every studio rushed into preparation of large-scale musical films, which all seemed to hit the market within a year's time. The public was oversaturated, and before long they stopped going to see them—at least at reserved-seat prices.

Except for New York's Radio City Music Hall, where it was the Christmas attraction (trimmed, incidentally, to 141 minutes), the film played reserved seat around the country with extremely disappointing results. With this attempt the Disney company swore off road-show films, realizing that with their kind of product, they could reach more people and make more money through neighborhood theatres. *Millionaire*'s gross, when national release was completed, was $5 million, hardly anything to sneeze at, but a far cry from *Mary Poppins*'s $31 million, and not all that much considering the higher tariffs charged.

Of course, better reviews would have helped. Bosley Crowther in the *New York Times* called it a "laboriously low-brow, high-hat film. . . . It's a good thing the title character in *The Happiest Millionaire* is loaded with money and social standing, because he hasn't got anything else to justify his being given houseroom, even in a Walt Disney musical comedy." Judith Crist dubbed the film "a sickly-sweet superdeluxe marshmallow of a musical with so much of everything good turned saccharine that it is guaranteed to turn the most juvenile stomach." *Life*'s Richard Schickel wrote: "The best things about Disney have always been impeccable, innovative technical work, crisp stories, superb physical comedy. Without them the faults of the studio style are too readily apparent—a fatal attraction to fake nostalgia, the insistence on smoothing characters into types and life into a series of 'situations.' *Millionaire* is a parody of the Disney product in its late commercial phase."

Only *Variety* had good words for the film: "Outstanding . . . a family comedy, blending creative and technical elements, scripting, excellent casting, direction, scoring, choreography, and handsome, plush production. . . . Fred MacMurray, snug in an excellent characterization, is well teamed with Greer Garson, long absent from the screen."

Variety's reviewer was one of the few to see an uncut 164-minute print, however. It was trimmed to 159 for its Los Angeles opening (excising one musical number, "It Won't Be Long 'Til Christmas"), 141 for New York, and 118 minutes for general release. A restored version was prepared by the studio archive and ultimately released in video.

The Happiest Millionaire is no classic. It is, however, a lively and largely entertaining film. When one considers the ratio of good to bad films in Disney's career, one misfire isn't such a disgrace.

3 · Without Walt

Walt DISNEY'S DEATH, IN DECEMBER OF 1966, RAISED SERIOUS QUESTIONS about the future of his organization. But Disney left behind a solid management team that was—even during his lifetime—making many of the day-to-day decisions about everything from new rides at Disneyland to the casting of an upcoming TV episode. Virtually every one of these excutives was a "career employee," steeped in the Disney tradition. President E. Cardon "Card" Walker started at the company as a traffic boy in 1938. Irving Ludwig, president of the Buena Vista distribution firm, first came to work as a field salesman for *Fantasia* in 1940. Donn Tatum (who succeeded Roy Disney as chairman after Roy's death in 1971) and movie division vice president Ron Miller, the relative newcomers, joined Walt Disney Productions in the 1950s . . . with Miller boasting an even more personal association—he married Walt's daughter Diane. So it was with understandable confidence that Walker told *Business Week* magazine in 1978, "What we are doing is intuitively based on a hell of a lot of experience."

Such was their experience that it was almost impossible to distinguish a Disney studio film of the 1970s from one made prior to Walt's death in the 1960s. Indeed, this presumed asset proved to be the company's biggest problem in years to come.

The final years of the 1960s saw "business as usual" on the Disney release calendar. *Blackbeard's Ghost* (1968) was an entertaining comedy-fantasy starring Disney regulars Dean Jones and Suzanne Pleshette, with the added prestige of Peter Ustinov in the leading role of Blackbeard the Pirate, who comes into the life of a harried track coach and uses his invisibility to help the coach's team. *The One and Only Genuine Original Family Band* (1968) featured a three-generation musical family in this story set in the late 1800s. Again, the cast was filled with familiar faces: Walter Brennan, Buddy Ebsen, Lesley Ann Warren, and John Davidson (who'd appeared together in *The Happiest Millionaire*), and young Kurt Russell, who was soon to become the studio's leading juvenile star. *Char-*

Peter Ustinov and Dean Jones spruce up in a scene from *Blackbeard's Ghost*. © 1968 Walt Disney Productions

Glenn Ford expresses his friendship for Chief Dan George in *Smith!* © 1969 Walt Disney Productions

lie the Lonesome Cougar (1968) and *Rascal* (1969) upheld the friendly animal tradition, while *Never a Dull Moment* (1968) gave Dick Van Dyke another clean-cut comedy vehicle. (Just as typically, a good, solid little film without an easy handle, but bearing the Disney name got lost in the shuffle. *Smith,* starring Glenn Ford and a first-rate supporting cast, including Nancy Olson, Dean Jagger, Keenan Wynn, Warren Oates, and Chief Dan George, had an interesting story, a timely pro-Indian theme, and a mature romantic relationship between its stars. But it was ignored or dismissed by critics, and even the Disney company didn't seem to know quite what to do with it.)

No one at the studio was quite prepared for the response to *The Love Bug,* however. This engaging comedy-fantasy, released in 1969, had the kind of Disney premise that usually spelled success: a car with a mind of its own. In this case, it's a Volkswagen Beetle that's attracted to racing driver Dean Jones and his mechanic Buddy Hackett and repulsed by their rival, David Tomlinson. The film is full of wild chases, special effects, and slapstick, plus ingratiating performances, but it's the central idea of a live-action car with an actual personality that makes *The Love Bug* work.

The Love Bug became the biggest American box-office hit of 1969—and the second-biggest grossing film in Disney history, after *Mary Poppins.* It eventually inspired three theatrical sequels and a limited TV series. The original film was remade for TV in 1999.

But it would be some time before the company experienced a box-office hit of that magnitude again in the live-action field. Animation was another matter, and in 1970 the company unveiled its first full-length animated film produced without the participation of Walt Disney.

The Aristocats came as a pleasant surprise to those who were disappointed with *The Jungle Book.* It's a winning, carefree cartoon about a cat and her offspring who inherit a fortune from their late mistress and fall prey to a scheming butler who is next in line for the inheritance. They are rescued by a free-swinging alley cat named Thomas O'Malley.

The film bears more than a passing resemblance to *101 Dalmatians,* taking its most successful ingredients and adapting them to this new story, making animals the main characters, with human beings in subordinate roles, and emphasizing the communication within the animal fraternity. Although, as Mike Barrier pointed out in a lengthy review of the film in *Funnyworld,* there is no plot device as ingenious as the "twilight bark" in *Dalmatians, Aristocats* does have substantial charm and humor of its own, which helps to make up for the less-than-inspired storyline.

Herbie in action, with his owners on board, more or less, in *The Love Bug*. © 1969 Walt Disney Productions

Duchess and O'Malley in characteristic poses from *The Aristocats*. © 1970 Walt Disney Productions

Roy Snart meets a genteel underwater creature en route to the Isle of Naboombu in *Bedknobs and Broomsticks*. © 1971 Walt Disney Productions

As with *The Jungle Book*, the Hollywood stars who provided voices helped to shape their characters' personalities. Phil Harris *was* Thomas O'Malley, and Eva Gabor seemed ideal as The Duchess. Unfortunately, the studio was unable to get Louis Armstrong to do the voice of Scat Cat, a jazzy character who was designed with Satchmo in mind; his infectious ad-libbing might have been a real plus, though Scatman Crothers did a fine job in the role.

The worst that one could say of *The Aristocats* is that it is unmemorable. It's smoothly executed, of course, and enjoyable, but neither its superficial story nor its characters have any resonance. Still, the film was a box-office success, even more so in Europe than in America (its reception in France was nothing short of ecstatic) and served as a healthy affirmation that the Disney animation department was till preeminent.

Animation helped contribute to the success of *Bedknobs and Broomsticks*, the studio's most ambitious live-action feaure since Disney's death, and the first to consciously emulate the ingredients that made *Mary Poppins* a hit. This was no coincidence, as the songwriting Sherman brothers explained in an interview with Doug McClelland for *Record World* magazine:

> Actually, he [Walt] bought the Mary Norton book before *Mary Poppins*. I remember just before everything got going on *Poppins*, we were having some trouble getting okays from P. L. Travers, the author of the stories, on the songs we had written. It was very exasperating. One day Walt came to us and said, "Don't worry, boys. I've bought another story that deals with magic. If we can't work things out with Travers, we'll be able to use your stuff in the other picture."

It was deliberately decided not to move ahead with *Bedknobs* for a while, however, because of its similarities to *Poppins*. Nevertheless, the story was developed in 1964, at which time the Shermans started writing their score. After a dormant period, production resumed on a major scale in 1970. Lynn Redgrave, Leslie Caron, and Judy Carne (along with Julie Andrews) were all considered for the leading role of Eglantine, an amateur witch in wartime England, but, very wisely, Angela Lansbury was finally chosen for what is, after all, a rather mature role. Ron Moody was originally slated to play her vis-à-vis Emelius Browne, but he was replaced by David Tomlinson, marking an even stronger resemblance to *Poppins*, despite the major difference in his characterization.

The film did not cause anthing close to the sensation of its predecessor, which is easy to understand; its story is not as universal, its songs are not as good, and its ingredients are not as fresh. But *Bedknobs and Broomsticks* is a thoroughly entertaining fantasy that deserves to stand on its own, quite apart from *Mary Poppins* (despite those moments—particularly songs—that bring to mind specific elements of the earlier film). The film also boasts one sequence that ranks alongside the best of Disney, a blend of live action and animation that in many ways surpasses all previous endeavors of this kind.

In this sequence, a highlight of the film, Eglantine and friends journey into the pages of a storybook to the Isle of Naboombu, a kingdom ruled by animals. Traveling on their magic brass bed, they land first in a lagoon where Eglantine and Emelius win a dance competition at the Beautiful Briny Ballroom. Then, on land, they meet the overbearing lion king of Naboombu (whose voice and demeanor parody Robert Newton's Long John Silver from the Disney *Treasure Island*). He's looking for a sucker to referee the Royal Cup soccer match, and Emelius volunteers—so he can have a chance to steal the king's amulet—but finds himself in the midst of a wild, no-holds-barred free-for-all in which the King makes up rules as he goes along.

The action is fast paced and frenzied, and the interaction between live characters and the cartoon figures is truly impressive. What's more, the characters are fun to watch because they're designed in an amusing way (the fishy musicians in the Ballroom, the mismatched soccer teams whose members range from a namby-pamby hippo to a ferocious alligator). It's significant to note that this sequence was directed by Ward Kimball, who deviated from the current house style of animation and design, with these marvelous results. This sequence is seldom excerpted in compilations of Disney's work; if it were, it would certainly elicit greater interest in *Bedknobs and Broomsticks* in general.

But the film was not a major box-office hit—it was cut by twenty minutes and stripped of all but two of its songs for its 1979 reissue. (Finally, in the 1990s, the studio restored the film as best it could, and released that version on home video.) The film's poor reception dampened the studio's interest in doing musicals, or large-scale productions of any kind. Instead, the company was content to continue turning out an average of four films a year, alternating between gimmicky slapstick comedies (*$1,000,000 Duck; Now You See Him, Now You Don't*) and homespun stories about nature, children, and animals (*The Wild Country; The Biscuit Eater.*)

In 1973 James Garner signed on for two films with Disney. It was a mutually promising agreement; Garner was looking for good movie vehicles, and Disney was happy to have a star of his stature on board. (Though the studio's films were always well cast, it was rare to find a box-office name above the title. Audiences generally went to see "a Disney film," not "the new Dean Jones comedy." Garner even acknowledged the unlikelihood of his working for the studio in an amusing coming-attractions trailer for his first film.) But neither *One Little Indian* nor *Castaway Cowboy* fulfilled anyone's expectations.

James Garner and Clay O'Brien are fugitives from the U.S. Cavalry in *One Little Indian*. © 1972 Walt Disney Productions

Robin takes on Prince John's guards in the Disney studio's animated version of *Robin Hood* © Walt Disney Productions

The next real studio event was the release of another full-length animated feature, *Robin Hood,* at the end of 1973. The basic twist on this classic story was to cast animals in all the familiar roles: thus, Robin Hood and Maid Marian are foxes, Little John is a bear, villainous Prince John is a tiger, and his sinister aide-de-camp is a snake. A rooster balladeer named Allan-a-dale narrates the story in song.

Alas, those are the major innovations in *Robin Hood,* which otherwise stands as an undistinguished Disney achievement. The animation is first-rate, as always, and there are bravura scenes of character animation that were rendered by some of the studio's now-legendary Nine Old Men. But the overall film carries a sense of déjà vu in its story (filmed so many times before, even once by Disney) and characters (from the now-too-familiar supporting role voiced by Phil Harris to the physical design of other key figures like Sir Hiss, the snake). Some sharp-eyed animation buffs even recognized reuse of actual animation, as when the staff took a shortcut by tracing the dance movements from a famous scene in *Snow White* for a brief dance inerlude with Maid Marian and some of her forest friends.

Perhaps the biggest problem with *Robin Hood* was in its story development—or lack of it. Individual set-pieces, like Robin's disruption of Prince John's tournament, actually play better when seen on their own than they do in the context of the film, which doesn't provide a strong enough thread to hold these pieces together. The film brought to mind Ward Kimball's description of an earlier Disney feature as "a loud-mouthed vaudeville show."

There's also something wrong when Robin Hood is the dullest character in the film.

But none of this criticism—voiced mainly by animation buffs, not the general press—had any effect on the public (except to erase all memory of Disney's delightful live action version of the same story, made in 1952). *Robin Hood* was a tremendous success; in fact, it was the biggest box-office hit of any Disney animated feature to date.

This success reinforced the company's renewed commitment to animation that blossomed in the 1970s. Just a few years earlier, it had seemed as if the animation department of Walt Disney Productions was going to be allowed to die—slowly, but surely—through attrition. The Nine Old Men were getting Older, some were no longer actively involved with animated features, and many of their equally important colleagues, the people who had built that incredible library of animated film, were retiring. There was no organized plan to train a younger generation, to pass on the incredible amount of experience that had been learned by these dedicated men and women. It was literally possible that like some ancient masters of black magic, their secrets would die with them.

Fortunately, a greater wisdom prevailed, and the company embarked on a full-scale program to seek out and enlist young talent. Eventually, the training and apprenticeship of these recruits was absorbed by the California Institute of the Arts, or Cal Arts as it's popularly known, the university endowed by Walt Disney (incorporated in 1961, it finally opened its doors in Valencia, California, ten years later).

The first group of young people to join the Disney staff not only embraced the values and traditions of their elders, but did them one better, by pushing for a return to the full-bodied brand of animated filmmaking that Disney had pioneered with them in decades past.

"The pictures now are entertaining, they're fast-paced, and they're clear. Walt had all those things, and he touched you besides," the studio's newest animating director, Don Bluth, told John Culhane in a *New York Times* article.

Acknowledging the outstanding personality animation still being done by some of the Disney veterans, newcomer Andy Gaskill remarked, "Lately, our features have resembled an empty rehearsal hall where these master actors come out and sort of kibitz with each other. We've got to have some convincing framework for all these great characters."

Unity of purpose, restoration of certain graphic "frills" that had been foresaken in recent years, and a striving for more heart in the stories—these were the goals of the younger generation. And their fondest dream was to bring to life a medieval fantasy-quest called *The Black Cauldron,* based on a prestigious 1968 book by Lloyd Alexander. Executive producer Ron Miller promised that they would have their chance—after proving themselves on other more traditional projects.

Don Bluth was given the opportunity to direct a short-subject with the new corps of Disney artists. A parable about a boy who sells his donkey to two travelers named Joseph and Mary, *The Small One* was released in time for Christmas 1976, and while it was criticized for being too saccharine, it did verify the skills of the new Disney team. Some of the younger crew then got to work side by side with three of the formidable studio masters—Frank Thomas, Ollie Johnston, and Milt Kahl—on the next full-length feature, *The Rescuers.*

The Rescuers was a breath of fresh air for everyone who had been concerned about the future of animation at Walt Disney's. Here, for the first time in years, was a feature film that had humor and imagination and *heart* expertly woven into a solid story structure . . . with a delightful cast of characters. The story was simple: a little girl is held captive by a wicked woman who needs her to help procure a precious diamond. The task of finding the youngster is taken up by two mice detectives named Bernard and Bianca.

Orville the albatross prepares his passengers—Bernard and
Bianca—for takeoff in one of the highlight scenes from *The Rescuers*. © Walt Disney Productions

The beauty of the film is that so many of its animal characters—
Orville the albatross, who operates an air-carrier service, Evinrude the
dragonfly, who assists our heroes in the swamp—and its key human
cast—the flamboyantly evil Madame Medusa, and her oafish henchman
Mr. Snoops—are *pure cartoon creations*, not mere imitations of live actors
on screen. (What's more, they aren't overwhelmed by their real-life alter
egos, even though talented and recognizable performers were doing
their voices.) This alone would have set *The Rescuers* apart from other
recent Disney fare, but the combination of this and other proven ingredients made this film the most satisfying animated feature to come from
the studio since *One Hundred and One Dalmatians*.

The timing of its debut was interesting, as well, because it invited
comparison with two features completed that same year by younger,
equally dedicated animation talents. But *The Rescuers* left Richard Williams's *Raggedy Ann and Andy* and Ralph Bakshi's *Wizards* at the starting
gate . . . and climbed ahead of Disney's own *Robin Hood* to become the
highest grossing animated feature in film history.

The animation team scored another bull's-eye with its contribution
to the studio's big Christmas release, *Pete's Dragon*. The first Disney musical in six years, it was heralded with a campaign that virtually duplicated

Pete, played by Sean Marshall, asks his dragon friend Elliott for help in this scene from *Pete's Dragon.* © Walt Disney Productions

the look of the original *Mary Poppins* ads—an unwise reminder of the earlier film, for though this one also premiered at New York's Radio City Music Hall, it simply wasn't in the same league.

Pete's Dragon should have been that good. The story is perfect Disney fodder: an orphan boy named Pete flees from his cruel guardians and comes to a Maine fishing town, where he's taken in by a young woman who lives in a lighthouse with her father. The lonely youngster's best friend turns out to be a dragon named Elliott—which causes Pete to be pursued by a number of people who want to exploit the animal.

Unfortunately, the film has more than its share of problems. First, it's too long. It even starts slowly. It also shares one problem with all of Disney's musicals since *Poppins:* a pedestrian music score. There are a couple of agreeable songs, but not one that might be remembered after the film is over. Another equally serious problem is a leading lady, pop singer Helen Reddy, with no screen charisma. (The studio was able to modify one of these faults after the film's premiere engagements, by cutting 13 minutes from its running time.)

But *Pete's Dragon* does have one major asset: the animated title character, designed by Ken Anderson and brought to life with verve and humor by director Don Bluth and his crew. Every scene involving young actor Sean Marshall and his cartoon friend is a winner—making the antics of the other cast members seem all the more tiresome.

Pete's Dragon did respectable business, but proved to be another discouraging endeavor for the Disney studio, which inevitably measured this film against the enormous success—both financial and artistic—of *Mary Poppins.*

The decision to cast a singer with little film experience in the lead, the inclusion of a coined-word song ("A Brazzle Dazzle Day"), and of course the duplication of *Poppins*'s ad campaign not only invited comparisons to the 1964 movie, but seemed to confirm a general feeling within the film industry that most decisions at the Disney studio were still being made on the basis of the question, "What would Walt have done?"

The answer, one liked to think, was "something better." Disney veteran Ward Kimball recalled, "Walt was criticized by the banks and the financial empires through the years—'That crazy Disney, blowing all that money.' [But] he had a way of saying, 'This is different, this is new, this is worth a try.'" It was that willingness to take risks that apparently died with Walt.

Looking at the general studio output from the late 1960s through the early 1980s, one would think that time had stood still. There was no real way of identifying *Charley and the Angel* or *Herbie Goes to Monte Carlo* as being films made in 1973 or 1977 . . . especially given the studio's habit of rehiring the same actors, not only for the leads but supporting roles as well. (In fact, Disney became a haven for veteran character actors—though they were generally called on to give the same performance in every film.)

This is not to dismiss the entirety of Disney's live-action product. There were some entertaining gimmick comedies, such as *The World's Greatest Athlete, Gus,* and *The Shaggy D.A.* (the successful sequel to the 1959 comedy *The Shaggy Dog*), but even here, familiarity began to breed a certain degree of contempt. The studio relied on the same few producers, directors, and writers for most of these films, and it was difficult to dispel the feeling that they were being turned out with a cookie-cutter. The perpetual involvement of tow-headed children, the somewhat mechanical slapstick mayhem, the inevitable crackup of police cars (a favorite gag), made it difficult to generate much enthusiasm for these films year after year after year.

The studio's most eagerly awaited live-action film of the mid-70s was *The Island at the Top of the World,* a large-scale fantasy adventure about an expedition by dirigible to a hidden Arctic civilization in search of a wealthy man's missing son. But *Island* turned out to be disappointingly ordinary; its main characters had no particular appeal, which made it difficult to become involved in their adventure. The special effects ranged from spectacular (a volcanic eruption) to obvious. It was not a *bad* film by any means, but it wasn't thrillingly good, either, a considerable letdown for Disney fans. The studio fared better with a less ambitious venture the following year called *Escape to Witch Mountain,* about two children with psychic powers. British director John Hough (who'd made an excellent horror film called *The Legend of Hell House*) was hired to direct, and the results were successful enough to warrant a sequel three years later.

Some of the studio's most satisfying films were made abroad during the 1970s: *Ride a Wild Pony,* made in Australia, and two British productions, *The Littlest Horse Thieves,* a turn-of-the-century story, and *Candleshoe,* starring Helen Hayes, David Niven, and Jodie Foster.

But even the better Disney productions were yielding diminishing returns, for reasons the company was slow to comprehend. The most obvious cause was an erosion of trust in the Disney name, caused by too many mediocre films.

Tim Conway tries to grill his sheepdog while Pat McCormick and Herb Vigran look on in *The Shaggy D.A.* © Walt Disney Productions

David Hartman hovers over the other members of a frightened party surrounded by molten lava: David Gwillim, Agneta Eckemyr, Mako, and Donald Sinden, in *The Island at the Top of the World.* © Walt Disney Productions

Ike Eisenmann demonstrates his levitation powers for Bette Davis
and Christopher Lee in *Return from Witch Mountain*. © Walt Disney
Productions

Another, subtler reason was a change in the studio's target audience. For one thing, kids of the 1970s were not growing up under the
Disney influence the way their parents had some years earlier. On TV,
Disney had been supplanted by *Sesame Street* and The Muppets; a revival
of the original *Mickey Mouse Club* in 1975 was only a middling success,
and a more ambitious attempt to rekindle the original magic with a
brand-new Club was a conspicuous failure.

Moreover, America's young people were changing, growing up a
little faster, shedding their innocence a bit sooner than earlier generations. Young people's tastes were changing, and the Disney product was
not changing along with it. One of the biggest hits of 1976 was Paramount's *The Bad News Bears*, about a hard-luck little league team with a
lackadaisical, beer-swilling coach (Walter Matthau) and a girl as its star
pitcher (Tatum O'Neal). This entertaining comedy might have been
made by Disney, except that it involved a caliber of star talent that the
studio wouldn't have hired, and it was rated PG, mostly because its juvenile characters had a habit of using four-letter words. Nonetheless, the
film became a smash success with adults *and* kids—who probably weren't
as shocked by the language as were their parents.

The following year, 1977, saw the release of another film that
pointed the movie industry in a new direction, and underscored the
need for change at Disney. The film was *Star Wars*, and it not only captivated children, but "grown-up children," an audience Disney had lost
years ago. The outer-space saga was simply *Flash Gordon* brought up to
date, and carried out with style—plus state-of-the-art special effects. Yet
its appeal was enormous, and more than one observer commented that it
was the kind of film Disney *should* have made.

(Even its rating told something about the changing movie audience.
Reportedly, the Motion Picture Association of America's Ratings Board
split its initial vote on *Star Wars* between G and PG. The studio instantly
opted for a PG, because G ratings had become such a turnoff to young

Barbara Harris and Jodie Foster are the mother and daughter who switch personalities—with delightful results—in *Freaky Friday,* one of the studio's best contemporary comedies. © 1977 Walt Disney Productions

people—on whom they were depending to make this film a hit.)

It would be two years before the public saw Disney's "response" to this movie phenomenon.

Meanwhile, very little of the public saw one of the studio's best films in years, *Freaky Friday.* For once, the company had something that might have been promoted as a contemporary film and not "just another Disney picture." But by the time word started spreading about this sleeper, it was already gone from most theaters.

The premise made this film seem like typical Disney fare: a mother and daughter magically exchange identities for a day. But producer Ron Miller commissioned the author of the original novel, Mary Rodgers, to adapt her own screenplay (itself an unusual move for Disney) and then hired two exceptional actresses to play the leads. Directing chores went to another studio newcomer, Gary Nelson. The film was far from perfect (certain formula devices were shoe-horned into the script, including a slapstick chase finale and—yes—a police car crackup), but it had so much verve and originality that these seemed minor quibbles.

What the studio failed to realize was the appeal of its two stars, Jodie Foster, who had made one of her earliest TV appearances in a Disney TV show, *Menace on the Mountain,* and her feature debut in the studio's *Napoleon and Samantha* and had gone on to become one of the hottest young actresses in Hollywood, and Barbara Harris (a premier Broadway actress who never quite found her niche in films). Their performances made *Freaky Friday* something to see—as a number of leading critics pointed out. Watching Harris transform herself into a skateboarding, bubble-gum chewing adolescent and Foster become a harried suburban mother was sheer delight.

But Buena Vista marketed the film the same way it would any studio comedy, failing to make hay with a handful of good reviews and settling for normal kiddie matinee business instead of exploring this film's real potential with a larger audience.

The company tried to make amends during the next few years, with such films as *Candleshoe* and, particularly, *The North Avenue Irregulars,* which had good promotable casts, but both films—while enjoyable— didn't break out of the Disney mold enough to win very broad appeal. Disney's share of the U.S. and Canadian film market was eroding year by year—from 6 percent in 1977 to 5 percent in 1978 and 4 percent in 1979. The film division's contribution to overall corporate profits fell even more sharply during the 1970s (from one-half to one-quarter) as theme parks, merchandising, and the like accounted for an ever-growing share.

Disney executives were painfully aware of these statistics, and realized that something had to be done. Their first experiment was to acquire an independently produced feature film called *Take Down* for release by Buena Vista. The film was rated PG—not for anything particularly offensive—and the studio took no chances, making sure the Disney name did not appear on screen or in any advertising for *Take Down,* the story of a high school wrestling coach and his prickly protégé. Unfortunately, the film was not a success, and another Great Experiment died at birth.

There was a lot more riding on the studio's 1979 Christmas release. Budgeted at a record $20 million, *The Black Hole* was the studio's answer to *Star Wars* and the flurry of interest it had generated in outer-space adventure. The film was eagerly anticipated, and its production was followed closely by the general press and science-fiction fandom. For the first time, the studio shone a spotlight on its special effects wizard Peter Ellenshaw (whose son P. S. Ellenshaw, also known as Harrison, had been a major contributor to *Star Wars*), promoting him as if he were the star of *The Black Hole*—which in a sense, he was. He designed and supervised the elaborate visual effects for this story about a space station of the future and one man's determination to explore a void in space known as a black hole.

That Christmas *The Black Hole* appeared—only to be greeted by a collective sigh of disappointment. For an epic film it seemed awfully flat,

Production design is the star of *The Black Hole*—not to mention a pair of robots, V.I.N.CENT (seen in mid-air) and Maximillian. The humans on hand are Ernest Borgnine, Anthony Perkins, Yvette Mimieux, and Robert Forster. © 1979 Walt Disney Productions

with dialogue left over from a 1950s B-movie. The film as a whole was reminiscent of Disney's own *20,000 Leagues under the Sea,* with Maximilian Schell in a rehash of the Captain Nemo character . . . except it wasn't as entertaining. Worst of all, the climactic trip through a black hole was notably unexciting.

The film did boast superior special effects, by and large, though it was distressing to notice black strings suspending a "floating" robot in at least one scene. The robot, a cute little fellow named V.I.N.CENT, was awfully reminiscent of *Star Wars*'s now-famous R2D2.

To some people, the saddest part was that Disney was jumping on a bandwagon instead of leading the parade. To others, it was a blow to find that the Disney team couldn't match the entertainment and expertise of its young competitors.

The Black Hole, released at the same time as another space saga, *Star Trek—The Motion Picture,* didn't fare that badly at the box office, taking in some $25 million domestically. That would have been a bonanza for a (typically) less expensive Disney film, but in this case it wasn't enough to recover costs—and it was many millions behind the outer-space competition.

It was followed, in rapid order, by another less ambitious—but equally significant—failure. In an effort to bring Disney up to date, Ron Miller hired two young writer-directors, David Wechter and Michael Nankin, whose only credit was an independently produced short subject, and gave them free rein to make a contemporary PG-rated youth comedy. The result, *Midnight Madness,* did not capture the *Animal House* crowd, being too tame for the marketplace, though a bit wild for Disney, and headed straight for box-office oblivion.

The company's next move was to participate in coproductions with other studios, sharing both the investment responsibility and the profits. Only cartoon buffs caught the irony of Disney's participation with Paramount Pictures in a feature-film of *Popeye*—which nearly fifty years earlier had been the studio's leading cartoon rival! But Disney's input was both financial and technical (some post-production work was done at the Burbank studio), not creative, which in this case was too bad. The film could have used some help.

A second coproduction with Paramount fared much better. *Dragonslayer* was a well made, entertaining fantasy adventure. But Disney's name in the film's advertising (including TV commercials) led many parents to believe that this was a Disney *type* of movie, leading to negative feedback when younger children found the film too realistic and frightening, especially in its depiction of the dragon.

At this point the studio decided to forgo further coproduction deals and outside product acquisitions. If risks were to be taken and mistakes to be made, they might as well be made in house.

And that's exactly what happened next. In April of 1980 *The Watcher in the Woods* premiered in New York City. It was an interesting if somewhat familiar story of the occult, with Lynn-Holly Johnson as a girl haunted by the spirit of another girl who supposedly died some years ago. It had a good cast, headed by Bette Davis, and a good director, John Hough. What it *didn't* have was an ending . . . though following its abrupt conclusion there were extensive credits for an "Other World" sequence. The explanation: this elaborate special-effects segment wasn't completed in time for the film's release date so the studio simply debuted the film without it, hoping no one would notice!

Some reviewers *didn't* notice those telltale credits, but most of them did comment on the weakness of the dénouement. (Vincent Canby wrote in the *New York Times,* "I challenge even the most indulgent fan to give a coherent translation of what passes for an explanation at the end.") To save face, the studio announced that it was withdrawing the

Bette Davis plays an elderly woman mourning the long-ago disappearance of her daughter in *The Watcher in the Woods.* © 1980 Walt Disney Productions

No one can top the Disney team for cute characters, as witness the young stars of *The Fox and the Hound.* © 1980 Walt Disney Productions

film from circulation in order to "refilm" the ending. But when the picture finally saw national release, a year and a half later, the sequence still wasn't there. It simply hadn't worked. (The film *did* have a new, much improved closing scene, but apparently this didn't alter the general air of apathy that greeted *Watcher in the Woods*.)

However, the company's biggest public embarrassment was caused not by a movie, but by a move. In September of 1979 a number of artists left the animation department of Walt Disney Productions, in a bitter exodus that received major news coverage around the world. Leading the walkout was Don Bluth, one of the key figures in Disney's "new generation" of animation talents; he was followed by seven animators and four assistants, who bound together to form their own company, Don Bluth Productions. Their departure was caused by creative, as well as financial, differences.

"We felt like we were animating the same picture over and over again with just the faces changed a little," Bluth complained. "For example, they've gutted all of the meaning from *The Fox and the Hound*. It's become a cute story instead of a meaningful one."

It would now take longer for the public to judge. The walkout cost Disney its Christmas release for 1980—and an undetermined amount of good will.

The Fox and the Hound didn't appear until the summer of 1981. It's the simple story of a pair of young animals who are raised together as best friends until, at adulthood, they learn that they are by nature sworn enemies. The film generated a kind of "good news/bad news" reaction. The good news was that Disney's young animators were in firm control. At a time when other studios were trying to create a niche in the field of animated feature films, *The Fox and the Hound* showed that the Disney crew was still without peer in its ability to bring appealing animal characters to life. A full-blooded fight scene between a dog and a bear, animated by Glen Keane, drew particular praise as an animation tour-de-force.

The bad news had more to do with conception than execution. *The Fox and the Hound* is a pleasant but extremely low-key film that relies far too much on formula cuteness, formula comedy relief, even formula characterizations. Those formulas are time worn, and time proven, too (the public certainly responded to them—the film was a box-office smash), but to some observers they represented a backward step, or at best a stagnation, for the Disney studio. Many people were counting on the younger generation to bring new life and new ideas to their work; this film was just a synthesis of old ideas that had worked before, and that smacked of executive-level "What would Walt have done?" fears.

At least *The Fox and the Hound* was a respectable endeavor. Disney's track record, after more than a decade without Walt at the helm, was not. But the 1980s began on a note of genuine change that took even jaded film industry pundits by surprise. The studio appointed twenty-seven-year-old Tom Wilhite, who'd worked his way to the top of the publicity department, to be the new Vice President in charge of development for feature films and television.

Wilhite made it clear that he was interested in genuine, not cosmetic, change. He began soliciting scripts, properties, and ideas from every corner of the film industry—an industry from which the Disney studio had remained isolated for more than fifty years. He persuaded studio executives to let him give "points" (profit participation) to major creative talents, a precedent-shattering move that enabled the company to talk seriously with important stars, producers, directors, and writers who otherwise might refuse to work with Disney. And he encouraged new ideas from within the company itself, personally giving the green light for some young animators to make experimental shorts on studio

Jeff Bridges disappears into the high-tech landscape of *Tron*.
© 1982 Walt Disney Productions

time and expense. Tim Burton and Rick Heinrich's *Vincent,* a comically macabre clay-animation film, and Daryl Van Citters's *Fun with Mr. Future,* a zany comedy, were widely praised, if not widely seen. Wilhite chalked it up to "research and development."

In the summer of 1982 the "change" at Disney was made complete by the release of *Tron.* For the first time since anyone could remember, the studio was actually riding the crest of a wave, capitalizing on a trend as it was peaking—not after it had faded. The trend was video games, and *Tron* seemed like the perfect summertime movie for kids who were hooked on electronic games. Writer-director Steven Lisberger called on the expertise of many different computer-image companies and experimental laboratories to develop the look of *Tron.* And he created a film that was as visually exciting and new as anything to come from Hollywood that year.

Where *Tron* fell short was in the story department. The idea was certainly sound: a computer whiz is sucked into an elaborate computer system where he must battle for his life in a giant video game. Judging by luke-warm audience response, the film's biggest problem was failing to pull viewers into the adventure and make them feel as if they were in Jeff Bridges's place. In many scenes the actors were so camouflaged by high-tech accouterments that it was difficult to identify who was the hero and who was the villain! Some critics felt that the film as a whole was too "inside," its appeal limited to those who already knew and understood the world of computers. (The script does include a number of inside jokes, but the best of all is a computer-graphic image of Mickey Mouse which can be seen, fleetingly, as part of the "landscape" in one shot.)

Whatever the case, the ingredients of *Tron* turned out to be more impressive than the film itself. And while it was far from a flop at the boxoffice, its failure to become a blockbuster of the George Lucas/ Steven Spielberg variety made it seem that way.

Still, *Tron* showed the Disney studio daring to try something exciting and new; that was more than could be said for most of the studio's recent product. In truth, wunderkind Wilhite was prouder of his other 1982 release, *Tex.* This was the first film to be made from a novel by S. E. Hinton, the best-selling author of young adult fiction—and the first Disney picture to be selected for inclusion in the prestigious New York Film Festival. As with *Tron, Tex* was made in an atmosphere of creative freedom unusual for Disney. It was filmed entirely on location in Oklahoma, for a very modest budget by 1980s Hollywood standards ($5 million), and showed—in every pore—a kind of integrity one found difficult to attach to *Herbie Goes Bananas.*

Tex, a low-key story of a motherless teenager's coming of age, proved to be a tough sell for Disney (no fault of the studio's—two other companies had similar problems with Francis Ford Coppola's subsequent adaptations of Hinton's *The Outsiders* and *Rumblefish*) and failed to score at the box office, despite some excellent reviews and the notoriety that came from a Disney picture that actually acknowledged the existence of sex and drugs.

The company's next ambitious project also proved to be a disappointment: *Something Wicked This Way Comes* was a Ray Bradbury story that should have been filmed when it was written, in the early 1960s. By the time Disney got to it, the bloom was off the rose, and its images—not to mention its plot—had been undercut by too many other films. (The central "revelation" about a mysterious traveling carnival could only have come as a surprise to people who had never watched a *Twilight Zone* episode in their lives.) Despite Bradbury's own script, a good cast, and an ideal director (Jack Clayton, who made the well-remembered British shocker *The Innocents*), *Something Wicked* was only fitfully satisfying. At the box office it laid an egg.

The biggest problem for Tom Wilhite and his colleagues may have been the fact that they were limited to three or four movies a year (most of the major Hollywood studios average fifteen to twenty). With so much riding on each picture, the failures seem more pronounced . . . especially at a time when Hollywood is no longer satisfied with modest success, and anything less than a "megahit" is a flop. In the fall of 1983, Richard Berger was named to head the newly christened Walt Disney Pictures, hastening Wilhite's resignation after four years in his production post.

Matt Dillon (center) has the title role in *Tex,* as a teenaged boy experiencing extreme growing pains. Bill McKinney is his absentee father, and Jim Metzler is his harried brother. © 1982 Walt Disney Productions

Fortunately, studio executives knew they had something out of the ordinary in *Never Cry Wolf* and nurtured it into nation-wide release instead of following a hit-and-run pattern. It was a well-considered plan for a film that had been literally years in the making. Director Carroll Ballard was signed by Disney on the heels of his great success with *The Black Stallion* (a movie that—like so many others—people said the Disney studio *should* have made), though coproducer Jack Couffer's association with Disney went back more than twenty years, to such films as *Nikki, Wild Dog of the North* and *The Incredible Journey*.

To film Farley Mowat's account of his experiences observing wolves' behavior in the Yukon, Ballard decided that it was crucial to experience a change of seasons. This meant an unusually lengthy shooting schedule, followed by an even lengthier editing period, to get the film just right. Its release was postponed more than once.

But *Never Cry Wolf* was worth the wait. From the opening moments, Charles Martin Smith (who collaborated on the narration spoken by his character) elicits our empathy, and we experience the rest of the film *with* him . . . as he learns about the wolves, and about himself. It's particularly amusing to consider that in a Walt Disney film the main character is obliged to eat mice.

Never Cry Wolf made many critics' Ten-Best lists for 1983, and though it was not an immediate box-office smash, it persevered through the early months of 1984 to find an audience and become a moneymaker.

The Disney studio wound up 1983 on an even higher note when it released *Mickey's Christmas Carol*. This twenty-seven-minute featurette was inspired by a 1975 children's record with Alan Young as the voice of Scrooge. Studio story man Burny Mattinson got the green light to turn this recording into a full-fledged film—and had the distinction of directing Mickey Mouse in his first new film since 1953's *The Simple Things*. There was some question of why the studio would want to pursue yet another version of Charles Dickens' *A Christmas Carol*, but Mattinson and his colleagues provided enough ingenious twists, turns, and embellishments to make it all worthwhile. As frosting on the cake, they decided to include as many Disney cartoon characters as possible in the cast, not only in leading roles but in cameo appearances as well. So, while the leads are played by Mickey, Minnie, Donald, Daisy, Goofy, Pegleg Pete, Willie the Giant, Jiminy Cricket, and Scrooge McDuck (the comic-book character in only his second film appearance) everyone from the Three Little Pigs to Gus Goose turn up on screen.

Mickey's Christmas Carol attracted considerable attention, and the film's release harked back to a tradition of fifty years ago: a Disney short winning top billing, over its accompanying feature film (in this case, a reissue of *The Rescuers*).

Reaction to the short was so positive that the studio began considering other films to feature its timeless character. And the greatest recognition of all came when *Mickey's Christmas Carol* was nominated for an Academy Award as Best Animated Short Subject. Walt would have been proud.

(There was another, less publicized short-subject event in 1983, when the studio released *Winnie the Pooh and a Day for Eeyore*. The news had nothing to do with the film itself—which was much inferior to the earlier Pooh cartoons—but with the fact that while it bore the Disney name, it was actually made by an outside animation studio, Rick Reinert Productions. Disney had farmed out animation before, for TV commercials and more recently for its satellite TV channel, but not since *Merbabies* in 1938, which was produced by Walt's former colleagues Hugh Harman and Rudolf Ising, had there been an entire film animated by

Charles Martin Smith is left on his own in the Arctic in this memorable scene from *Never Cry Wolf*. © 1983 Walt Disney Productions

Scrooge McDuck appears on screen for just the second time, in the role of Ebeneezer Scrooge, with Mickey Mouse as beleaguered Bob Cratchit, in *Mickey's Christmas Carol*. © 1983 Walt Disney Productions

outsiders—though lead animator Nancy Bieman *was* a graduate of Cal Arts.)

As 1984 began, with Mickey Mouse back on movie screens, Walt Disney Productions made a momentous decision: to inaugurate a new division called Touchstone Films, with its own identity, for the purpose of releasing more adult movie fare and attracting major Hollywood talent. This decision had been mulled over for some years, but was brought to a head by the completion of a delightful comedy called *Splash*. The film was destined for a PG rating, and to have diluted the mild ingredients that earned it that tag would have also killed its chances with a contemporary audience. It's also possible that Disney's name on the film might have given some people the idea that it was a kiddie movie.

"With Touchstone we are making a very clear distinction between the classical, customary Disney entertainment for the entire family and our diversification into a wider spectrum of films," Ron Miller declared in a press announcement. "The name Walt Disney Pictures on a production will signal that the film is designed as family entertainment, while the Touchstone name will identify those films appealing to other segments of the audience."

Splash captured the best reviews of any Disney film in years, and the biggest opening weekend business in the company's history—deservedly so.

It's the story of a mermaid who pursues her one true love by temporarily turning human and stalking him on dry land. With appealing performances by Daryl Hannah, Tom Hanks, and John Candy, a truly funny script by Lowell Ganz, Babaloo Mandel, and Bruce Jay Friedman, and imaginative direction by Ron Howard (who'd worked for Disney as a young actor in 1971's *The Wild Country*) *Splash* is the kind of bull's-eye hit that Disney—under any name—had been looking for . . . and an auspicious beginning for the Touchstone banner.

Daryl Hannah is everyone's ideal of a mermaid come to life in *Splash*. © 1984 Walt Disney Productions

Films have become just one facet of the Walt Disney empire. Walt did not live to see the opening of Walt Disney World or Epcot Center in Florida, but he launched those ideas . . . just as he did the California Institute of the Arts.

But it's not likely that Walt could have foreseen a day when his company would be transmitting daily television programming from a satellite (on The Disney Channel) or selling its movies over-the-counter on videotape.

Could he have imagined that one day his weekly TV show would be considered passé, after more than twenty years on the air? Or that the soundtrack for his beloved *Fantasia* would be labeled obsolete because it wasn't recorded in something called Dolby?

Who can say how Walt Disney would have reacted to all of this? And who can guarantee that he would have cleared the many hurdles his company came up against in the 1970s and 80s?

For many years, the answer to any question at the studio was, "What would Walt have done?" Critics of the company cited this as evidence that Disney's successors lacked the guts and imagination to serve as real leaders.

But Walt Disney was no ordinary executive. He and the company were one in the same. He was the brains, the heart, the backbone of the outfit. And he was touched with genius.

What's more, his timing was right. Disney was a child of the twentieth century. He and the movies grew up at the same time. When he'd conquered that medium, there were others awaiting him. He never looked back.

It isn't fair to criticize anyone for not being able to fill Walt Disney's shoes. No one could fill them but Walt.

Indeed, when "outsiders" took over the Disney company in 1984, they tried not to look over their shoulders, deciding instead to lead their company into the future.

4·The Rest of the Story

THIS WAS JUST THE BEGINNING, AS IT TURNED OUT. IN LATE 1984, RON Miller was ousted from office and in a complicated corporate maneuver, leadership of the Disney company changed hands. (The process was so complicated—and so dramatic—that it inspired a book-length chronicle, *Storming the Magic Kingdom,* by John Taylor.) Its new president was Frank Wells, formerly of Warner Bros.; its new chief executive officer and chairman was Michael Eisner, a one-time TV network wunderkind who'd recently had a long string of successes as vice-president of production at Paramount Pictures. For some traditionalists, the idea of Eisner—an unabashedly ambitious executive—following in Walt's footsteps was difficult to swallow. For his part, Eisner faced that image problem head-on by later hosting the weekly Disney TV show on ABC, along with Mickey Mouse and other studio characters.

The new Disney "image" was transformed even further when Eisner recruited several of his closest associates from Paramount to join him, including Richard E. Frank, Bill Mechanic, and Jeffrey Katzenberg. This sent a signal, loud and clear, to the Hollywood community that there would be a whole new ballgame in Burbank.

The difference started showing up on movie screens in 1986, when Touchstone released such films as the R-rated *Down and Out in Beverly Hills* and *Ruthless People,* both starring Bette Midler, and *The Color of Money,* starring red-hot Tom Cruise with Paul Newman, directed by Martin Scorsese. At the end of 1987 the company released two smash hits in a row: *Three Men and a Baby* (a remake of a popular French comedy) starring Tom Selleck, Ted Danson, and Steve Guttenberg, which made $167 million in the U.S. and Canada; and *Good Morning, Vietnam* starring Robin Williams, which made $123 million domestically. Those were unprecedented box-office returns for the Disney company—two to three times more than even their recent successes had earned. They also involved talents on both sides of the camera that wouldn't have been associated with the studio just a few years earlier. (Newman won an Academy Award for *The Color of Money,* and Williams was nominated as Best Actor for *Good Morning, Vietnam,* further evidence that Disney was moving closer to the mainstream of Hollywood studios.)

Those films reinforced the identity of Touchstone Pictures, but Walt Disney Pictures was not faring nearly as well in the live-action arena. Two 1985 releases essentially completed before the new regime's arrival at

Disney, *Return to Oz* (an ambitious but cold and distant sequel to *The Wizard of Oz*) and *Baby . . . Secret of the Lost Legend* (a baby dinosaur saga) were major disappointments, although both films boasted some impressive special effects. (In fact, the best thing about *Oz* was some ingenious clay animation contributed by Will Vinton Productions.) *One Magic Christmas*, released at holiday time in 1985, was an unusually bleak seasonal film, though a good one. It was not a success.

Over the next few years, as if to acknowledge the problem of producing first-rate family films, the studio barely released any under the Walt Disney banner, and of those few, *Benji the Hunted* (1987) and *Return to Snowy River, Part II* (1988) were acquisitions, not home-grown Disney productions. Instead, the company found itself tapping into a new audience via Touchstone: teenagers and young adults. Such PG and PG-13–rated films as *Adventures in Babysitting* (1987), *Can't Buy Me Love* (1987), and the Ernest movies starring professional lamebrain Jim Varney—*Ernest Goes to Camp* (1987), *Ernest Saves Christmas* (1988), *Ernest Goes to Jail* (1990), *Ernest Scared Stupid* (1991)—all modestly produced and surprisingly successful at the box-office, seemed to satisfy a portion of the public that at one time would have been awaiting release of the newest Hayley Mills or Tommy Kirk movie.

Such blurring of lines between Disney- and Touchstone-type product didn't seem to trouble anyone at the studio until 1988 and the imminent release of *Who Framed Roger Rabbit.* This ambitious and expensive picture was a joint venture with Steven Spielberg's Amblin company, and that in itself was a major coup for Disney. (More than one pundit had remarked that Spielberg *was* the modern-day Walt Disney. A marriage of this kind was highly desirable to the Burbank brigade . . . and, apparently, an exciting prospect for Spielberg, too, as a lifelong Disney fan.)

The concept of the film, about a hard-boiled L.A. detective in the late 1940s, was to combine live-action and animation in a more sophisticated manner than had ever been attempted before. Although the story was fanciful, its ideas and sensibilities were adult in nature. The animated leading lady of the piece, Jessica Rabbit, was an impossibly buxom, breathy-voiced siren inspired by Tex Avery's Red Hot Riding Hood character from 1940s MGM cartoons—about as distant from a Disney heroine as one could imagine.

What's more, the script called for appearances by a variety of classic cartoon characters, from Disney icons like Mickey and Donald to other studios' creations including Betty Boop, Bugs Bunny, and Daffy Duck. (In fact, this film marked the first-ever meeting between those two immortal mallards, Donald and Daffy.)

The trouble was, *Who Framed Roger Rabbit,* in spite of its cartoon content, was not meant for kids. Some within the Disney organization thought it was risky to allow Mickey Mouse and Co. to appear in such a film, let alone produce it under the Disney banner. (In point of fact, animation director Richard Williams farmed out the artwork to a variety of shops in the U.S. and England. Relatively little was done by Disney artists.) As the film neared release, a concerted effort was made to disassociate the Disney name from this production. It didn't work: a June 27, 1988, *Newsweek* magazine cover story blurted, "Spielberg and Disney take a $45-million gamble." Virtually every reviewer and entertainment reporter referred to it as a Disney film.

Still, the studio kept its corporate distance from the PG-rated comedy—until the picture opened to land-office business and rave reviews. Within a few weeks, not only were Mickey and friends being exposed to the public, but newspaper ads featuring a gaggle of familiar cartoon faces were promoting the film as if it were a family picture! Some gullible parents were heard to complain, but the cash registers rung up $154 million in receipts.

Private eye Eddie Valiant (Bob Hoskins) grapples with a gangly animated nemesis in *Who Framed Roger Rabbit.* © *1988 The Walt Disney Company and Amblin Entertainment, Inc.*

There was inevitable talk about a sequel, but such a project never came to pass. Disney and Amblin did decide to make several subsequent Roger Rabbit short-subjects—*Tummy Trouble* (1989), *Roller Coaster Rabbit* (1990), *Trail Mix-Up* (1993)—which, if anything, were even more hyperkinetic than the animated sequences in the feature film.

Disney's turnabout in embracing the film had amusing and unexpected repercussions six years later when Michael Fleming reported in the trade journal *Variety* on March 14, 1994, that in several frames of the film one could see up Jessica's dress to reveal her private parts. Both print and electronic media picked up this story as if it was news, and gleefully reported it, never questioning its veracity. Examining the frames in question proved inconclusive; to most observers the area in question between Jessica's legs was merely a shadow. There were certainly no details to be seen. In no story that appeared in print was *Who Framed Roger Rabbit* identified as anything but "a Disney film." A freelance animator later claimed that he had indeed drawn those frames, in pencil, but ink and paint had filled them in so as to obscure his little joke.

But *Variety*'s blithe comment that the Jessica Rabbit incident was just the latest in a long line of scandalous shots—dating back to forest-animal hijinks in *Snow White and the Seven Dwarfs*—caused longtime Disney buffs to scowl. Veteran Disney animator Ward Kimball said that many of the animators made off-color drawings for their own amusement, and sometimes even slipped one into pencil-test reels, but confirmed that it would have been impossible to "sneak" even one frame into a finished film. Kimball's wife, Betty, who worked in ink and paint years ago, explained that since the department was staffed primarily by women, their supervisor Hazel Sewell was especially sensitive to this sort of prank and "would have immediately gone to Walt" with it. It was more than her job to protect both the girls and the Disney reputation; it was a matter of family honor. Hazel also happened to be Walt's sister-in-law.

When Michael Eisner and his associates arrived at the Disney studio, the company's newest and most unusual animated feature was in its final stages of production: *The Black Cauldron* (1985). This project had been championed for years by a younger element within the animation department, eager to break away from Disney tradition and try something entirely different. What finally emerged was a juvenile-themed sword-and-sorcery tale that struck many as neither fish nor fowl: not full-blooded enough to satisfy an older audience, yet too intense to appeal to very young children. The most likable characters in the film—as everyone seemed to recognize—were the cute/funny supporting players, Gurgi (a good guy with an endearingly silly voice by John Byner) and Creeper (a comic bad-guy henchman), not the pallid young boy who propels the story, or the deep-voiced villain (The Horned King) who tries to thwart the boy's quest for the Black Cauldron.

The Black Cauldron was no disgrace; the story was well told, and the film expertly animated, under the direction of Ted Berman and Richard Rich. It was the first animated feature since *Sleeping Beauty* to be filmed in 70mm. But there was nothing memorable about the picture, and the presence of funny supporting characters provided just enough of an echo of earlier Disney films to make one wish the rest of the film had followed a similar path. It made $21 million, but a reissue of *101 Dalmatians* later that year made $33 million, which seemed to say it all.

The one distinction of *The Black Cauldron* was that it marked the Disney studio's entry into the field of computer-generated images. Earlier, animators John Lasseter and Glen Keane had spent some time working on a brief computer experiment using characters from Maurice Sendak's *Where the Wild Things Are*. In *Cauldron*, baubles, a boat, and the cauldron itself were manipulated by computer, as the animators experimented with moving geometric images, attempting to maintain their feeling of volume from different angles.

There was, at this time, a pall cast over the animation department at Disney. Most of the studio's celebrated veterans had retired or passed on by now. The younger generation—what there was of it—now had reason to wonder what the future of animation might be at the studio. Although Eisner and Katzenberg had "green-lighted" the long-delayed *The Great Mouse Detective* within weeks of their takeover, there was still a lack of enthusiasm in the air. When the staff was exiled from the Animation building, and moved off the lot to annex buildings in nearby Glendale, the message seemed clear: cartoons were no longer a top priority for Disney.

The Great Mouse Detective (1986), based on Eve Titus' book *Basil of Baker Street,* was the story of a Sherlock Holmesian mouse who's charged with solving a mystery and besting the beastly villain known as Ratigan. This brisk and enjoyable feature was credited to four directors—John

Musker, Ron Clements, Dave Michener, and Burny Mattinson—and emerged as an amiable blend of old- and new-style Disney. Its center-piece was the vocal performance of Vincent Price as the very theatrical Ratigan, whose character was summed up in a signature song, "The World's Greatest Criminal Mind."

The "new" Disney was represented by the studio's most ambitious use of computer imaging to date in the climactic sequence which takes place inside London's famous Big Ben. As Basil attempted to wend his way through the complex mechanical workings of the clock, his character was hand-drawn, but all the machinery was created using computer-generated imagery. It *looked* that way, but given the nature of the assign-ment—with ratchets and gears galore, and an ever-changing perspec-tive—the application seemed appropriate. The film earned favorable reviews, although its box-office take of $21 million was mild. (*Lady and the Tramp,* reissued that Christmas, made $31 million.) The studio re-issued it in 1992 as *The Adventures of The Great Mouse Detective.*

It was two years before the next animated feature was ready: a cartoon update of Charles Dickens' *Oliver Twist* with Oliver as a cute orphaned kitten who falls in with a pack of roguish dogs and their human master, Fagin. Like its predecessor, *Oliver & Company* (1988) was a hybrid of old-fashioned and newly minted Disney. Direction was in the hands of animator/storyman George Scribner, but two of the film's major assets came from intervention at the executive level: it was Jeffrey Kat-zenberg who wooed popular performer/songwriter Billy Joel to act in the role of Dodger, and to perform the film's best song, the jaunty "Why Should I Worry?", on the soundtrack. He also invited the company's

A dramatic moment with Dr. Dawson, Olivia Flaversham, and Basil (of Baker Street) in *The Great Mouse Detective.* © 1986 The Walt Disney Company.

newest live-action star, Bette Midler, to sing a featured number, "Perfect Isn't Easy," as self-possessed French poodle Georgette. Adding contemporary name value to the project certainly gave *Oliver & Company* an important boost.

There was some debate over the intensity of scenes in the film depicting vicious guard dogs (and their owner, the evil Sykes), and their appropriateness for young children, which echoed the kind of arguments associated with Disney since the days of the Wicked Witch in *Snow White*.

Once more, computers were put into play to enhance certain scenes in *Oliver & Company*—a total of eleven minutes in all. Fagin's trike (which had eighteen moving parts), a piano, a cityscape, and a series of cars in a traffic jam were among the components of the film generated by animators working directly on computer. The difference was visible to the educated eye, especially as the hand-drawn animated characters scurried over, under, and alongside those vehicles. However, blending of traditional and computerized artwork did yield interesting and in some cases spectacular results, as in the subway tunnel climax and the Brooklyn Bridge finale. The computer enabled the director and his layout team to use dramatic camera angles and flamboyant cinematic devices that would have been deemed unfeasible (or just too darned difficult) in earlier times.

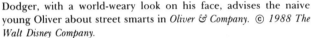

Dodger, with a world-weary look on his face, advises the naive young Oliver about street smarts in *Oliver & Company*. © 1988 The *Walt Disney Company*.

Another facet of the film's look harked back to the early 1960s, when Xerography influenced the style of *101 Dalmatians*. Xerox overlays were used over the painted backgrounds of New York City to give the urban backdrop a modern, sharply defined look.

The combination of a sure-fire story source (Dickens), an appealing cast of Disneyfied cat characters, and the name value of Billy Joel and Bette Midler helped to make *Oliver & Company* the studio's most successful animated feature in years. The $53-million gross restated Disney's predominance in the field of theatrical animation—both to outsiders, and perhaps insiders as well. It was at this time that the company reaffirmed its commitment to animation, thanks to the prodding of Vice Chairman of the Board Roy E. Disney and the growing participation of Katzenberg. Peter Schneider, named senior vice-president of production for animation, joined his colleagues in promising a new animated feature every year. They were soon to learn, as Walt did forty years earlier, that this was easier said than done. Still, it augured well for the studio to have that drive and desire.

On May 1, 1989, the company opened a Feature Animation studio in Orlando, Florida, as part of the Disney-MGM Studio theme park. Tourists were invited to watch animators at work (through a glass partition) and learn about the animation process from Walter Cronkite and Robin Williams in special films shown in a theatre and on a battery of TV monitors. There was some speculation that this was less a studio than a setup for Florida vacationers, but in fact the studio has grown and thrived. Mark Henn was among the first senior animators to move there, and he has contributed major work to the studio features ever since. The facility has expanded twice, and in 1995 houses a staff of more than two hundred twenty-five. The second and third Roger Rabbit shorts were produced in their entirety at the Florida facility, which by the 1990s was supplying between ten and twenty minutes of finished animation for each Disney feature.

One of the songs in *Oliver & Company,* "Once Upon a Time in New York City", was penned by Howard Ashman, a young show-music composer who with his partner Alan Menken had written the successful off-Broadway musical *Little Shop of Horrors* (filmed in 1986). Ashman and Menken had been signed by Disney to write the score for *The Little Mermaid,* a free adaptation of Hans Christian Andersen's classic story, which Ashman also coproduced. He and his colleagues were to lead the company to new heights of recognition and success in the cartoon field.

The Little Mermaid (1989) didn't seem, from a distance, to be anything revolutionary. It featured a classical Disney fairy-tale storyline: Ariel, the headstrong, teenaged daughter of the undersea world's King Triton, longs to live in the exotic world of the creatures on land. Despite warnings from her protectors and friends, she succumbs to temptation offered by the evil sorceress Ursula, who promises to make her human if she will sacrifice her voice. When, as a human, she meets the man of her dreams, she's unable to speak!

The film was written and directed by a two-man team, John Musker and Ron Clements—a studio first. A graduate of the animation program at CalArts, Musker joined the Disney staff in 1977, starting out as an assistant animator on *The Small One,* and contributing story material to *The Black Cauldron.* His rise was rapid, and in 1986 he had both codirecting and co-story credits on *The Great Mouse Detective.* His partner Clements is, like Musker, a Midwesterner who fell in love with animation as a child. In his teens, he fashioned his own Super 8mm animated films, one of which (a Sherlock Holmes story) helped get him a job at Disney years later—and served as the springboard for *The Great Mouse Detective.* Clements was accepted in the studio's Talent Development Program,

Ariel, her hair, and her faithful friend Flounder in *The Little Mermaid.*
© *1989 The Walt Disney Company.*

and then spent two years apprenticing under master animator Frank
Thomas, graduating from in-betweener to assistant animator before
becoming an animator/storyman on such films as *The Rescuers, Pete's
Dragon, The Fox and the Hound,* and *The Black Cauldron.*

Musker and Clements were both dazzled by Disney in their boyhood, and steeped in studio tradition. They were lucky enough to join
the studio at a time when they could learn from some of the remaining
"old masters," but they were young enough to have ideas of their own
that they were eager to implement.

In Howard Ashman the duo found an ideal collaborator; indeed,
Ashman and Musker produced *The Little Mermaid* together, an unusual chore for either an animation director or a lyricist to take on—
and even more unusual for the Disney studio to allow. Because of
this, the songs and story for *The Little Mermaid* were conceived
together in unusual (pardon the pun) harmony. Composer Menken
later explained, "Because Howard was involved as a producer, as well
as a lyricist, he had a strong concept for the music, as well as for
the lyrics. He would come in with not only the words but the whole
dramatic thrust and style of the song, and how we were going

to use the underscore." (That underscore would earn Menken an Oscar.)

It was Ashman and Menken who had the notion to make the mermaid's official guardian, a crab named Sebastian, a Jamaican character so they could use calypso and reggae rhythms in their songs. "It was a way of adding energy, spice, and a little bit of contemporary pop feeling" to the score, Ashman explained. It also won the songwriters an Academy Award for the infectious and upbeat "Under the Sea." The presentation of the song in the film was so dynamic and exciting that its finale seemed to invite applause—as if it were a Broadway performance.

It was also their idea to have Ariel, the title character, express her hopes and dreams in a song early on, and this is where the influence of Broadway came in. "In almost every musical ever written," Ashman explained, "there's a place usually early in the show where the leading lady sits down on something—in *Brigadoon* it's a tree stump; in *Little Shop of Horrors* it's a trash can—and sings about what she wants most in life. We borrowed this classic rule of Broadway musical construction for 'Part of Your World.' Because Jodi Benson (the voice of Ariel) is an actress who sings, she was able to convey a tremendous amount of soul and specificity in her performance." Indeed, Benson was just the first of many Broadway performers who would lend their acting and singing skills to this new generation of Disney musicals.

If the Broadway tradition had simply been grafted onto a classic Disney fairy-tale story, that might have been enough, but what these collaborators added was something else: a contemporary sense of humor. Some of this came through in the songs (the 50s' doo-wop–style "Kiss the Girl," in which Sebastian tries to encourage Eric in his reluctant wooing of Ariel, or the elegantly witty lyrics of villainess Ursula's "Poor Unfortunate Souls"); some of it in the visuals (a blowfish in "Under the Sea" who puffs his cheeks out when playing trumpet like Dizzy Gillespie, another underwater musician who looks like Duke Ellington, expressing John Musker's longtime love of caricature); some of it in the voice work (especially the casting of Buddy Hackett as the addle-brained seagull, Scuttle).

The musical/comedy/storytelling mix struck moviegoers as ideal, and *The Little Mermaid* attracted moviegoers of all ages in record numbers, earning $84 million in domestic theatrical ticket sales and uncounted additional income from a merchandising boom that followed. (Much of that "boom" played out a bit slower than it should have, because licensees weren't prepared for the enormous success of the picture. Neither was the Disney company itself; the studio hadn't generated this level of interest in newly created characters for quite some time. *Mermaid* started a snowball of new-generation merchandising that hasn't peaked yet—and likely never will. With the Disney company now operating its own chain of retail stores, and a mail-order catalog, its animated features have provided many millions of dollars in merchandise opportunities by adding all-new characters to the Disney "family." The characters have also been embraced, alongside Mickey and pals, at the company's theme parks.)

Praise for *The Little Mermaid* was not unanimous: some women questioned the use of cleavage in the character design of a 16-year-old girl, and the potency of a leading female character who's robbed of her voice for more than half the story. Others thought the broadly comic "Les Poissons" number, in which a zealous French chef tries to make a meal of Sebastian, was in questionable taste for Disney (which has always specialized in anthropomorphized creatures).

But these were minor quibbles compared to the enormous wave of acclaim—and box-office coin—that greeted *The Little Mermaid.* Now there was no question: Disney was rewriting animation history.

Flush with success, and determined to meet its goal of one new film a year, the studio released *The Rescuers Down Under* in 1990, along with three other properties: a Roger Rabbit short, *Roller Coaster Rabbit* (which appeared with Touchstone's live-action feature *Dick Tracy*), an ersatz feature produced by the company's television division and intended to take advantage of its latest TV success; *Ducktales—The Movie: Treasure of the Lost Lamp;* and a brand-new Mickey Mouse featurette, *The Prince and the Pauper,* which accompanied *The Rescuers Down Under* in theatres at the end of the year.

Ironically, or perhaps fittingly, the strongest reception was given to Mickey and friends. Like the earlier *Mickey's Christmas Carol,* this half-hour film was a short-and-sweet adaptation of a classic, can't-miss story (by Mark Twain), with a perfect role—two, in fact—for the indomitable Mickey, and enough supporting parts to enable other Disney favorites like Donald, Goofy, et al., to make appearances as well. (It also gave the younger generation of Disney animators a chance to work with these classic characters.)

The Rescuers Down Under, directed by animators Hendel Butoy and Mike Gabriel, brought back the intrepid mouse duo Bernard and Bianca (voiced by Bob Newhart and Eva Gabor) first seen in the 1977 feature *The Rescuers.* Their new adventure offered a change of scenery, a good balance of comedy and adventure, some colorful supporting characters including Wilbur the Albatross, introduced as the brother of Orville from the previous film, and voiced by comic actor John Candy, and a few set-pieces boasting bravura animation work. Glen Keane's animation of an eagle was particularly impressive, but he had to compete for honors with the work of a computer, responsible for rendering and animating villainous McLeach's demon tractor—a vehicle with a formidable personality. Plottier than it had to be, *The Rescuers Down Under* didn't win anywhere near the raves—or the business—that greeted *Mermaid,* but it did provide good family entertainment, and earned a respectable $27 million.

The best was yet to come. In the fall of 1991, the studio offered the New York Film Festival an opportunity to show an unfinished print of *Beauty and the Beast* as a "work in progress." Members of the press were long accustomed to seeing Disney cartoon features this way, with the soundtrack nearly complete and much of the animation intact, but with sections still in penciled form and other sequences not animated at all, shown instead as a series of storyboard drawings. For Disney to expose such an unfinished work to the public, however, and at a prestigious filmmakers' forum such as this one, was unprecedented . . . and very, very canny. It signaled that this film was different—that it was, in fact, a *film,* not just a cartoon. It underscored, to a lay audience, the enormous amount of work involved in crafting such a motion picture. And, in the city that was home to the Broadway theatre, it sent a clarion call that the long-ailing Broadway musical was alive and well, in a brand-new form. (Indeed, *The New York Times'* powerful theatre critic, Frank Rich, called *Beauty* "the best Broadway musical comedy score of 1991.")

The media seized on this story, and so did the film industry. *Beauty and the Beast* became the most eagerly anticipated Disney cartoon feature in years. What's more, for perhaps the first time since Walt's heyday, the audience anticipating its arrival was not comprised solely of children.

Building on the Broadway musical foundation that served *The Little Mermaid* so well, this one had an even more elaborate—and intricately plotted—"character statement" song near the beginning: "Belle." Here, in one fell swoop, the audience was introduced to its leading lady, learned of her desires and frustrations (being a bookish girl in a village filled with simple people who didn't understand her), and became acquainted with the setting of the story. David Friedman, who conducted the songs and provided the vocal arrangements for the film, said " 'Belle' is like the *Pastoral Symphony* with the entire town waking up. It has a classicality about it and is very symphonic in structure. We used a 62-piece orchestra with a lot of strings."

Howard Ashman was credited as executive producer this time around, and worked with a new team of Disney directors, Gary Trousdale (a CalArts graduate who joined the studio in 1984 and found his niche in the story department) and Kirk Wise (another CalArts grad who, like Trousdale, started out as an animator but gravitated to story and character development instead). They were joined by producer Don Hahn, who started at Disney in 1976 and moved from assistant director to production manager, learning every aspect of producing animated cartoons.

It is significant that *Beauty* was the first animated Disney feature to be scripted by a woman: Linda Woolverton, a former actress, TV animation scriptwriter, and author of novels for children. Woolverton, who helped define Belle as a strong and sympathetic character, was given credit for "Animation Screenplay," a new coinage at Disney. (Ten others were credited with "Story," which in the traditional Disney sense meant development of sequences, characters, and bits of business.) Woolverton had written four drafts of *Beauty* as a non-musical film when she began working with Howard Ashman on reshaping it as a musical production. She later said, "I learned more about movies from Howard than any single person I have ever worked with. He knew how to fill every scene with emotional content."

Beauty marked another first in Disney history: crediting each animator on-screen for the character he brought to life, and citing others' contributions according to the character "unit" in which they worked. Now, for the first time, moviegoers as well as animation buffs could connect the names of Disney's new team of supervising animators with the work they did: James Baxter, Michael Cedeno, and Mark Henn (Belle), Glen Keane (Beast), Andreas Deja (Gaston), Nik Ranieri (Lumiere), Will Finn (Cogsworth), Dave Pruiksma (Mrs. Potts and Chip), Ruben A. Aquino (Maurice), Chris Wahl (Le Fou), and Russ Edmonds (Philippe).

Computer-generated animation also had its place, in the "Be Our Guest" number, and most notably in the ballroom sequence, where sweeping, swirling camera movement was accomplished while Beauty and the Beast danced together. Their hand-drawn movements were composited against a constantly changing background perspective that high-tech machinery made possible.

For the audience, the innovation in *Beauty and the Beast* was a turnabout of expectations. For the first time, a handsome character—the jut-jawed Gaston—was shown to be a villain, while the beastly looking character was revealed to have the heart of a hero underneath his fearsome hide.

As in *Mermaid,* key songs became showpieces: the boisterous "Gaston," establishing the braggadocio and unpleasantness of the beefy bad guy; "Beauty and the Beast," tenderly sung by Angela Lansbury as Mrs. Potts, the motherly teapot; and the flashy, Ziegfeldian "Be Our Guest," an all-stops-out production number sung by ze very French candelabra Lumiere, voiced by Jerry Orbach (as a cross, he said, between Maurice Chevalier and Pepe Le Pew). It is worth noting that both Orbach and Lansbury were Broadway musical veterans who knew how to "sell" a song.

Once again, Alan Menken won an Oscar for his music score, while the team of Ashman and Menken earned an Academy Award for the title song. But sadly, Ashman was not present at the ceremony to enjoy the fruits of his success: he was felled by the AIDS virus shortly before the

The beast has been transformed on the inside, though the harsh
exterior remains in this dreamy-eyed scene from *Beauty and the Beast*.
© *1991 The Walt Disney Company.*

film's release. As one of the architects of Disney's animation renaissance, his loss hit colleagues especially hard.

Even more than *Mermaid, Beauty and the Beast* generated interest from grown-up moviegoers as well as children, which explains its soaring box-office net of $145 million. That adult appeal was reflected in another tangible way: the film was nominated for an Academy Award for Best Picture. Hollywood cynics remarked that if there had been more outstanding movies that year, *Beauty* wouldn't have stood a chance. But good year or bad, the honor was unprecedented, and the Disney organization had every right to be proud. Walt Disney earned more Oscars than anyone else in movie history, but he'd never seen one of his cartoons honored alongside live-action, mainstream feature films this way. It was, by any standards, a milestone.

(In 1994, the Disney company produced its first full-fledged Broadway musical—on Broadway. It was, appropriately, *Beauty and the Beast.*)

Meanwhile, Musker and Clements, the writer-director duo who'd spun the studio into high gear with *The Little Mermaid,* had something very different up their sleeves. In preparing their next film, *Aladdin* (1992), they decided to invoke the spirit of non-Disney cartoons! With the more irreverent Warner Bros. spirit in mind, they set about writing a comedy-oriented screenplay that would still rest on the foundation of a classic story (in this case, one from the Arabian Nights): Aladdin, a wiry thief who lives by his wits, yearns to be worthy of the beautiful Princess Jasmine, but when he gets his wish (thanks to an obliging Genie) he disguises his identity, and falls prey to the machinations of the Sultan's evil advisor, Jafar. Moral: it's not who you are, but what you are inside, that counts.

Again, the writer-directors relied on the musical-comedy grounding of a good score. Before his death, Howard Ashman had composed several songs with Alan Menken—including the introductory "Arabian Nights," the show-stopping "Friend Like Me," and the grandiose "Prince Ali"—which once again set the tone for the film. British lyricist Tim Rice, best known for his collaboration with Andrew Lloyd Webber on *Jesus Christ Superstar* and *Evita,* was asked to complete the job left behind by Ashman, and contributed the film's biggest hit, the romantic ballad "A Whole New World," sung by Aladdin and Princess Jasmine as they soar above Baghdad on a magic carpet.

A new member of the Disney team, animator Eric Goldberg (veteran of his own animation studio in London, and one of the few recruits *not* to have come through CalArts), was assigned the character of the Genie, and he drew his visual inspiration from another non-traditional source: the drawing style of master caricaturist Al Hirschfeld. Borrowing Hirschfeld's flowing lines, Goldberg helped develop a character who looked quite different from any in Disney history.

But perhaps the strongest influence on *Aladdin* was the man chosen to provide the voice of the Genie, Robin Williams. A comic improviser without peer, he was encouraged to depart from the script whenever the spirit moved him, and his quicksilver comedy riffs inspired (demanded?) a rapid-fire approach to drawing, staging, and editing his scenes—including his showcase song, "Friend Like Me." Wild distortion, nonsequitur transitions, even mimicry (accompanied by caricatures of such contemporary figures as TV host Arsenio Hall) were blasted at the audience with tommy-gun bursts of hilarity. Even some Disney references (from *Pinocchio* to Disneyland) made their way into the melange. Not since the manic treatment of the title song from *The Three Caballeros* had a studio feature ventured so far into this comic territory.

There were some who felt that Williams' comedy was so overpowering that it made the rest of the story seem ordinary in comparison. (In fact, there was a *second* comic character in the story, the villainous Jafar's parrot sidekick Iago, whose sardonically hilarious wisecracks were voiced by screechy comedian Gilbert Gottfried.) Indeed, Aladdin and Jasmine, while pleasant to be sure, couldn't hold a candle to their more flamboyant costars.

One costar proved to be unique in the annals of Disney animation: the magic carpet. This inanimate object was given life, and an astonishing range of expression, by animator Randy Cartwright, without resorting to the anthropomorphized trick of imposing a face on the design. Instead, what might best be described as body english was brought into play to make this flexible fellow seem almost human. (One clever idea: using his corner tassels as if they were hands and feet.)

Adding further to the distinction of the carpet was the fact that his mock-Persian design was rendered completely by computer. Manipulating such a complicated design frame by frame would have been deemed impossible (or at best impractical) just a few years earlier. Now, computer artist Tina Price was able to impose the carpet's ingenious pattern onto Cartwright's animated outline no matter how it was bent, rolled, or scrunched. Here, truly, was the best collaboration to date between handdrawn and computer-generated animation. CGI (Computer Generated Imagery) was also utilized to dramatic effect in the Cave of Wonders sequence, in particular the meltdown.

Aladdin proved to be a tremendous crowd-pleaser, and also had adults paying to see it as much as children; many of them went back a second or third time (just to catch all of Robin Williams' lines!). The result was a staggering $217 million at the box office. That daunting figure was *exceeded* by the revenue from home video sales the following year, when the film sold twenty-four million copies. (Those editions of the film bore a minor change from the one shown in theatres. Responding to protests from the American-Arab Anti-Discrimination Committee, a lyric in the introductory song "Arabian Nights" describing Arabia as a place "where they cut off your hand if they don't like your face" was changed to "where it's flat and immense and the heat is intense." The following line, "It's barbaric, but hey—it's home," was untouched.)

Aladdin was so profitable, in fact, that it not only spun an animated TV series, as had *The Little Mermaid* before it, but inspired the company to create a "feature film" released direct to video. Despite the absence of Robin Williams (replaced by comic actor Dan Castellaneta, of *The Simpsons* cast) and a brace of serviceable, but unmemorable songs, *The Return of Jafar* was a home-video hit in 1994, selling more than seven million copies . . . and becoming one of the top-ten video sellers of all time! Robin Williams returned for the next video sequels.

(In a world laced with ironies, Disney also acquired, first for showing on The Disney Channel and then for release on home video, *The Brave Little Toaster,* a first-rate animated feature completed in 1987. The film had been developed at Disney in the early 1980s; when production exec Tom Wilhite left the studio, he took the project with him and formed Hyperion Films, named after the street where Walt Disney had his very first studio in Los Angeles. It was directed by another ex-Disneyite, Jerry Rees.)

Home video significantly affected the way every movie studio did business in the 1980s and 90s, but it had its greatest impact on The Walt Disney Company. At a time when rental of cassettes was Hollywood's principal source of video revenue, Disney tested the waters of video sales and soon found that millions of families felt they had to *own* such classics as *Pinocchio* as well as modern hits like *The Little Mermaid.* It seemed, in fact, as if everything Disney touched on video turned to gold. (This success was not without its pitfalls: the studio became a target of lawsuits from such varied ex-collaborators as The Philadelphia Orchestra, over *Fantasia,* Peggy Lee, concerning *Lady and the Tramp,* and the author of

The Genie overpowers Aladdin (not to mention Abu and the Magic Carpet) as he takes center stage, Vegas-style, in this razzle-dazzle comic moment from *Aladdin*. © *1992 The Walt Disney Company.*

the book on which *The Fox and the Hound* was based. Each of them claimed that the studio didn't have the right to sell their work on video.)

This triggered the question of what to do about the studio's decades-old policy of reissuing its animated classics to theatres. In the late 1980s the company hit on the ingenious plan of following each theatrical rerelease—*Cinderella* (1987), *Bambi* (1988), *Peter Pan* (1989), *The Jungle Book* (1990), etc. with that movie's video debut the following season, taking advantage of its renewed public awareness. Maintaining a policy of releasing these classics for a limited time on video, and then withdrawing them from the marketplace, Disney managed to reap maximum returns from both the theatrical and video arenas.

There was just one hitch: eventually, they would run out of titles. In 1992 Disney experimented with reissuing *Pinocchio* to theatres. It had been one of the first classics to go to home video, in 1985, following its last go-round in theaters the previous year. That meant that VHS copies of the film had not been available to customers in seven years. Would enough parents of young children, unable to buy video copies, take those kids to see it in a theatre? And would they be joined by others who simply wanted to have the theatrical experience of seeing this great Disney feature? The answer was yes, but only in modest numbers. *Pinocchio* netted $18 million in its 1992 reissue. Thus, in 1994, for the first time in the company's history, there was no Disney classic on theatre screens. Clearly, video was now the medium of choice.

Two of Disney's greatest films did have "last hurrahs" on screen, however. In 1990 the studio undertook a major restoration of *Fantasia,* cleaning the original negative material one frame at a time, and attempting to replicate the Fantasound experience with modern sound technology. (The company also took the liberty of adding something the film had never had before: credits for all the artists who worked on it.) The brilliant-looking and -sounding result generated a great deal of publicity, and on its fiftieth anniversary, *Fantasia* made more money at the box office than it ever had before: $25 million, to be exact. It was followed by an even more successful video release; at holiday time in 1991 *Fantasia* was the video everyone "had to have." Finally, after half a century, Walt Disney's dream of reaching a wide audience with this bold and experimental film came true.

Snow White and the Seven Dwarfs had undergone a careful restoration for its fiftieth-anniversary reissue in 1987, but in 1993 the company decided to go one step further. Eastman Kodak had opened a division called Cinesite that specialized in the brave new world of digital special effects for movies. Its technicians also tried to interest the Hollywood studios in using this technology to restore older films. Disney was intrigued enough to run a test on *Snow White,* and then committed to Cinesite the task of inspecting and upgrading every frame of film under the watchful eye of Disney representatives, including special effects master Harrison Ellenshaw (son of fabled Disney matte artist Peter Ellenshaw). Figures that had been out of registration when the film was photographed in 1937 were now adjusted. Occasional light flares and other flaws were fixed, along with overall color-correction. A side-by-side comparison of the earlier print and the new version was simply eye-popping. Ellenshaw was careful not to attempt to "improve" the original artists' work; his goal was to make it look as good as it did in 1937. (As film buffs know, nothing looks exactly as it did back then. There was silver in the nitrate film base of that period, and "silver screens" in theatres as well; when a three-strip Technicolor print was projected it was positively dazzling. No one can replicate that look—not even digitally.)

There were concerns that a generation of youngsters turned on by *Aladdin* might not accept the pastel storybook look of *Snow White,* or its old-fashioned sentiment. But $41 million worth of children and parents turned out to see it in theatres, and when it was released on video in 1994 it outsold *Jurassic Park,* upsetting predictions of most video industry sages. What those people didn't take into account is that *Snow White* isn't simply a successful or popular film; it is beloved.

An unexpected source of revenue—and attention—was derived from Disney's animation in the 1980s: original artwork. For years, a coterie of collectors had traded in animators' drawings and finished cels (especially since thousands of those cels had been put into circulation by Disney, first in the 1940s through Courvoisier Galleries, and then from the 1950s on through the Art Corner at Disneyland). Now, a series of auctions at prestigious auction houses in New York, Los Angeles, and London brought record-breaking five-figure prices for vintage Disney pieces. It was only a matter of time before the Disney company would get into the business themselves, creating new "limited edition" cels and backgrounds from the original artwork in their archives.

The irony here is that cels became a big business just as the studio stopped using them! Animators continue to work, as they always have, with pencil and paper, but beginning with *The Rescuers Down Under,* the studio found that there was no longer a need to use clear acetate sheets to trace and color those drawings. The same job could be done even more efficiently on a computer screen. It still requires an artist to supervise this process; hence, the term "Ink and Paint" is still used at Disney, even though both ink and paint are now provided by a machine.

Where cel animation still exists is in the TV division, a thriving enterprise the likes of which Walt Disney could never have envisioned. It was 1985 when, under Roy E. Disney's wing, the company made its first foray into weekly animated television output. Mindful (to say the least) of what was at risk—the reputation of a studio known the world over for the very best in animation—Disney and his executive staff "auditioned" production houses around the world to find ones that could meet their standards. Like every other TV production company in Hollywood, Disney generated its stories, soundtracks, and key drawings at home, but was obliged to farm out the actual production to cartoon factories abroad. The difference here is that Disney was prepared to forego short-term profits in return for quality work.

(In 1989 the company acquired controlling interest in an existing animation studio outside of Paris, where animation was generated for a number of television projects and *DuckTales The Movie.* In 1994, however, it was decided to retool the operation as a feature animation facility, and animator Andreas Deja was sent there to work on the Mickey Mouse theatrical featurette *Runaway Brain,* to help bring the European animators up to speed. The studio was then set to contribute to Disney's upcoming feature film *The Hunchback of Notre Dame.*)

When they debuted in September of 1985, *Disney's Adventures of the Gummi Bears* (on NBC) and *The Wuzzles* (on CBS) were easily the best-looking cartoons on Saturday morning television: not at the level of feature-film animation, to be sure, but several giant notches above the norm for TV. (Cartoon buffs also delighted in hearing Bill Scott and June Foray—the voices of beloved TV cartoon stars Bullwinkle and Rocky—reunited in the cast of *Gummi Bears.* Alas, Bill Scott, who also lent his voice to *The Wuzzles,* died after that first season.)

Emboldened by its success, the company then took on an even greater challenge: producing a daily half-hour series, *DuckTales,* in 1987. Updating the characters of Scrooge McDuck and Donald Duck's nephews Huey, Dewey, and Louie, and adding new characters alongside them, this story-driven adventure show (based on the much-loved comic-book adventures written and drawn years earlier by Carl Barks) managed to maintain an admirable level of quality in both writing and visuals. Now poised to become a major supplier of television animation, Disney added *The New Adventures of Winnie the Pooh* to its weekly roster in 1988 (with new actors simulating the familiar voices of Sterling Golloway, et al.) and *Chip 'n' Dale's Rescue Rangers* to its daily lineup of 1989. In 1990 a daily two-hour block called "The Disney Afternoon" was launched with *Tale Spin* (mating new characters with Baloo of *Jungle Book* fame) and reruns of Gummi Bears joining the existing daily programs.

Since that time, the company has produced *Darkwing Duck* (beginning in 1991), *Goof Troop* (1992, with Goofy and the former Pegleg Pete acquiring lookalike sons), *Disney's The Little Mermaid* (1992), *Raw Toonage* (1992-93), *Bonkers* (1993), *Marsupilami* (1993), *Disney's Aladdin* (1994), the dark and decidedly un-Disneylike *Gargoyles* (1994, inspired no doubt by the success of Warner Bros.' Batman series), and the anarchic, Ren & Stimpy-ish *The Schnookums & Meat Funny Cartoon Show* (1995).

Disney's relationship with television in general expanded during the 1980s and '90s. In 1982–83 the studio, in its first throes of change, tried mining its library for new series material, but *Herbie the Love Bug* and *Zorro and Son* lasted just five episodes each. Under the Eisner regime, *The Disney Sunday Movie* returned the studio to its longtime family time slot, first on ABC, then on NBC, from 1986 to 1990. Since that time the company's television division has produced and/or distributed a wide variety of programs, ranging from *Siskel & Ebert at the Movies* and *Live With Regis and Kathy Lee* to such successful sitcoms as *Empty Nest, Blossom, Dinosaurs, Home Improvement*, and *Ellen*. Not forgetting the value of its library properties, Disney has also revived, with varying degrees of success, *Davy Crockett, The Absent-Minded Professor* (with Harry Anderson), and *The Shaggy Dog* (with Ed Begley, Jr.) in TV movies aired both on broadcast TV and cable's The Disney Channel. They were followed by *The Lion King's Timon and Pumbaa* (1995), *The Mighty Ducks* (1996), *Quack Pack* (1996), *Disney's Doug* (1996), *Jungle Cubs* (1996), *Gargoyles: The Goliath Chronicles* (1996), *Nightmare Ned* (1997), *101 Dalmatians* (1997), *Pepper Ann* (1997), *Recess* (1997), *Hercules* (1998), *Disney's Mickey Mouseworks* (1999), *Clerks* (2000, for prime time), and *The Weekenders* (2000, for prime time).

The Disney Channel has acquired and produced its own shows, notably a highly contemporary *The Mickey Mouse Club*, abbreviated to MMC (which introduced such future young stars as Britney Spears, Kerri Russell, Christina Aguilera, and J. C. Chasez and Justin Timberlake of the rock group 'NSYNC) and one of the best shows in television history, *Disney's Adventures in Wonderland*, a daily program with a Broadway-caliber cast, superior comedy writing, bright, original songs, and a soft-sell lesson in every episode. Both shows were taped at the Disney Studios near Orlando, Florida, where an animation studio annex was also opened in the 1980s. It was there that a pair of charming computer-generated short subjects was hatched by a group of artists after hours, *Oilspot and Lipstick* (1987), later shown in the touring theatrical program The International Tournee of Animation, and *Off His Rockers* (1992), which was released theatrically with *Honey, I Blew Up the Kid*.

The company's limitless expansion into new areas of entertainment took it into book and magazine publishing, music, and computer software. In 1991 the studio entered into a three-picture deal with Pixar, a prestigious studio in Northern California that had made its name with a pair of innovative computer-animated short-subjects, *Luxo, Jr.* and *Tin Toy*. Pixar's John Lasseter had in fact been a Disney animator. In 1995 he directed the studio's first all-computer-animated feature, *Toy Story*.

In 1993 Disney acquired Miramax, the daring and successful young company responsible for finding, co-financing, distributing, and nurturing the finest in American and international filmmaking. It seemed an odd marriage, especially since Miramax was known for taking on controversial, adult movies—from *The Crying Game* to *Pulp Fiction*—and fighting highly publicized battles over censorship. Miramax has retained its own identity and apparently its autonomy, however. (In fact, the company acquired an animated feature for release in 1995 that had been started as a labor of love by animator Richard Williams in the 1970s, *The Thief and the Cobbler.* It was later restructured and reanimated by others.)

An earlier, even more eagerly anticipated merger between Disney and Jim Henson Productions never came to pass, although after Henson's death the two sides patched up their differences and while remaining separate, have gone into business together on a number of ventures, including a home video line and the production of such movies as *The Muppet Christmas Carol.*

The Disney Company's position in the entertainment world changed dramatically with its acquisition of the ABC television network in 1996. What irony that the studio should now own the network that had put Walt into the TV business in the first place—and had been instrumental in financing Disneyland.

The live-action side of Walt Disney Pictures finally had its first bona fide hit in 1989 with *Honey, I Shrunk the Kids.* This fanciful comedy starred Rick Moranis as a bumbling inventor whose experimental ray-gun zaps his two kids, and some neighborhood friends, down to microscopic size.

One of the memorable special effects images in *Honey, I Shrunk the Kids*: adrift in a bowl of breakfast cereal. © 1989 *Buena Vista Pictures.*

A perfect kids'-eye view fantasy/adventure filled with imaginative special effects (including stop-motion animation by such experts as David Allen, who worked on the ant, and Phil Tippett, who was responsible for the oversized scorpion), the lighthearted film made $130 million. In a perfect example of studio "synergy," the film's success inspired a giant-sized playground attraction at Walt Disney World.

The studio inaugurated another "brand name," Hollywood Pictures, in 1990, to release a varied slate of pictures. Walt Disney Pictures remained the least active product line in the theatrical arena. Its ongoing releases included *Cheetah* (1989), a good film for children about friendship, and respect for other cultures, set in Africa; a remake of Jack London's *White Fang* (1991); the seagoing adventure *Shipwrecked* (1991); and the underrated (and too-little-seen) *Wild Hearts Can't Be Broken* (1991), a lovely, well-made film about a real-life woman named Sonora Webster who rode a diving horse in 1930s sideshows—even after she was blinded in an accident.

By now, most Disney movies were carrying a PG rating, once unheard of for this studio, but now reflecting changing times and tastes even for the family audience. *The Rocketeer* (1991), adapted from Dave Stevens' nostalgic comic-book story set in the 1930s, was handsomely made but ultimately a disappointment. *Newsies* (1992) was a well-intentioned effort to make a new live-action movie musical; melding that idea to a story of striking newsboys in 1899 led toward disaster. The film was both a flop and an embarrassment. But *The Mighty Ducks* (1992) caught the brass ring with its sure-fire story of a misfit/underdog hockey team and its loser of a coach, played by Emilio Estevez. It not only made $50 million, but it gave the Disney company the idea of buying a real-life hockey team in Anaheim (home of Disneyland) and naming them The Mighty Ducks. (A 1994 sequel, *D2: The Mighty Ducks,* was not nearly as good.) Disney's other hit of 1992 was the inevitable sequel *Honey, I Blew Up the Kid,* with Rick Moranis repeating his role as crackpot inventor and dad, this time responsible for his infant son growing to gigantic proportions and stalking around Las Vegas! (The film's youthful leading lady, Keri Russell, was plucked from the cast of the new *The Mickey Mouse Club.*)

Homeward Bound: The Incredible Journey (1993) was a remake of the 1963 movie *The Incredible Journey,* but this being the 90s, it was decided that the animals should talk. Fortunately, the script by Caroline Thompson and *Beauty and the Beast*'s Linda Woolverton, and the vocal performances by Michael J. Fox, Sally Field, and Don Ameche were excellent. This was Disney entertainment in the truest sense of the term. Other Disney films of 1993—the African adventure *A Far Off Place,* the Mark Twain classic *The Adventures of Huck Finn,* and the Bette Midler–produced special-effects comedy about witches, *Hocus Pocus*—all took hits from critics and parents who found them a bit more intense for younger children than the Disney family label might have led them to expect. The year rounded out with another film built on a sure-fire formula, *Cool Runnings* (1993), based on the irresistible true story of a Jamaican bobsled team determined to enter the 1988 Winter Olympics—and their once-disgraced coach (played to perfection by comic actor John Candy) who finally has a chance to redeem himself.

That fall, Touchstone released a film that might have gone out under the Disney label: *Tim Burton's The Nightmare Before Christmas,* a dark and inventive fable from the dark and inventive filmmaker who a decade earlier toiled as a Disney employee. Directed by Henry Selick, *Nightmare* told its story of Jack Skellington, The Pumpkin King, and his attempt to take over Christmas, in the technique known as stop-motion animation. With incredible stylized sets, and imaginatively designed characters manipulated one frame at a time, *Nightmare* marked a milestone in American animation. Its computer-controlled cameras permitted a degree of

An unwilling coach meets his unruly team: Emilio Estevez and friends in *The Mighty Ducks.* Even Disney executives never dreamed that this film's success would lead to them purchasing an actual hockey team. © *1992 Buena Vista Pictures.*

cinematic flexibility that earlier animators, from George Pal to Ray Harryhausen, would have envied . . . although this project did use Pal's "replacement head" system of substituting character heads with different facial expressions rather than manipulating mouth and eye movements from frame to frame. Topping it all off was a brilliant score by Danny Elfman, who also sang the leading role of Jack. A hit at the New York Film Festival, *Nightmare* made $50 million, but perhaps its fright-wig look at Christmas kept it from being even more successful. (The sight of a giant snake devouring a Christmas tree may have made it a more appropriate Touchstone release than a Disney title after all.) When it was released on laserdisc in 1994, *Nightmare* was accompanied by the short films that Tim Burton made for Disney in the early 80s, when the studio never knew quite what to do with them: *Vincent* and *Frankenweenie.*

When Disney's new production partners, Caravan Pictures (headed by producers Joe Roth and Roger Birnbaum), developed an updated version of *The Three Musketeers* (1993), Disney decided to "co-present" the PG-rated adventure yarn. The same collaborators were linked for 1994's baseball fantasy *Angels in the Outfield,* a remake of the 1951 MGM picture. (In the 50s version, the angels were invisible; in the 90s version, they were a function of souped-up special effects.) Other 1994 releases from Walt Disney Pictures: the action adventure *Iron Will,* the *Home Alone*–inspired comedy *Blank Check, D2: The Mighty Ducks, White Fang 2: Myth of the White Wolf,* and the underrated Thanksgiving saga *Squanto: A Warrior's Tale.* Then, for Christmas, Disney presented Tim Allen, star of the company's top-rated television series *Home Improvement,* in a holiday-themed fantasy, *The Santa Clause.* It opened in theatres at the same time as 20th Century-Fox's remake of the beloved Christmas classic *Miracle on 34th Street,* but Tim Allen's potent name, combined with the contemporary story spin of this Santa tale, left the rival picture in the dust. *The Santa Clause* leaped over the $100 million mark in a matter of weeks, and delighted viewers young and old. The story deals with an uncaring, divorced dad who accidentally causes Santa to fall off his roof—and then, unwittingly, assumes the fat man's identity. Gradually, he is transformed into Santa Claus—first on the outside, and then, more significantly, on the inside. What begins as a somewhat cynical, modern-day comedy evolves into the reaffirmation of belief and wonder so vital to the Christmas spirit. Allen, in his film debut, delivered a terrific and completely credible comedic performance.

Disney's triumph for 1994, however, was the release of *The Lion King,* which at year's end nosed out *Forrest Gump* to take its place as the most successful movie of the year, grossing more than $300 million in the U.S. and Canada alone.

The Lion King took the studio back more than fifty years, to *Bambi* territory. In fact, it might be described as *Bambi* for the 90s. It deals with the same essential truths: the continuity of life, and the importance of the family unit. *The Lion King,* however, is a much tougher film than *Bambi*—and considering the potency of the earlier film, that's a formidable statement.

The picture opens with a dazzling set-piece: as the sun rises on a majestic day in Africa, all of nature awakens, and a new crown prince is presented to the animal kingdom. He is Simba, the newborn lion cub and son of Mufasa, King of the Jungle, and Sarabi. This awakening of flora and fauna is accompanied by a commanding song, "The Circle of Life," sung by offscreen voices and building to a crescendo at the end of the sequence.

What an opening! (It was so good—and so strong—that Disney executives decided to use it, intact, as the preview trailer for *The Lion King.* Audiences who saw it were clearly primed to pay their money to see the entire film—and did.)

That said, *The Lion King* is less dependent on the Broadway musical structure than other recent Disney features. Not that the songs aren't effective in telling the story, or enhancing one's enjoyment of the film. But, for the first time since Ashman and Menken arrived at Disney, an animated feature was built on a foundation of drama rather than music.

The story is almost primal in its appeal. King Mufasa is burdened by an evil, jealous brother, Scar, who plots a deadly scheme. Sending young Simba to a remote valley, he causes a wildebeest stampede. Mufasa risks his life to rescue his son, but Scar cold-bloodedly kills his brother, then makes young Simba believe that *he* was the cause of his father's death. Ridden by guilt and shame, Simba runs away to a distant land, and grows up in the carefree company of a warthog and a meercat, Pumbaa and Timon. Eventually, his childhood friend Nala, a lioness, and a tribal shaman, Rafiki, convince him that he must return to his home-

"If the suit fits . . ." Tim Allen inherits a job he didn't ask for in the comedy hit *The Santa Clause.* © *1994 The Walt Disney Company.*

land, to take his father's place as King and avenge himself against the wicked Scar.

In *Bambi*, the young deer's mother is killed off-camera; in *The Lion King*, the cub's father is murdered, and the young boy is confronted with his lifeless body. He can't believe it's true; he tries to get his father to cradle him. Alone in the now-desolate valley, he cries out in anguish. Then, when his uncle shows up, the evil lion convinces Simba that he was responsible for his father's death.

This is a chilling scene, as dramatic as any ever animated at the Disney studio, and perhaps more so. It caused younger children to cry, and understandably so. Yet the film's ultimate message is the same as that in *Bambi:* life must go on.

To achieve the required impact in a scene like this, all the elements must be orchestrated just right: writing, staging, acting. *The Lion King* doesn't miss a beat. The screenplay, by Irene Mecchi, Jonathan Roberts, and Linda Woolverton (with additional story work by twenty-five others) is perfectly realized by directors Roger Allers and Rob Minkoff, who jointly made their feature directing debuts on this project. Artist and animator Allers worked on such features as *Animalympics*, *Rock & Rule*, and *Little Nemo in Slumberland* before joining the Disney studio, where he became a senior storyman on *Oliver & Company* and all subsequent animated features. Minkoff studied character animation at (where else?) CalArts, and interned with Eric Larson at the studio before moving into character design on *The Great Mouse Detective* and story development on later feature films. He made his directing debut with the Roger Rabbit shorts *Tummy Trouble* and *Roller Coaster Rabbit*.

As for performances, *The Lion King* drew on an "A-list" of actors to bring its characters to life, including James Earl Jones as Mufasa, Jeremy Irons as the Shakespearean Scar, Matthew Broderick as the grown-up Simba, Whoopi Goldberg, Cheech Marin, and Jim Cummings as the lowlife hyenas, Rowan Atkinson as the stuffy Zazu, and a pair of boisterous Broadway performers, Nathan Lane and Ernie Sabella, as Timon and Pumbaa.

The wonder of *The Lion King* is that it shifts emotional gears so easily, from the stark terror of the stampede and Mufasa's death to the sidesplitting comedy of Timon and Pumbaa, and then back again to mysticism and drama. It is, arguably the most adult of all Disney cartoon features, particularly in its sense of humor. Timon's nonstop patter is reminiscent of nightclub standup comedy. Scar's scenes are filled with in-jokes that invoke everything from *Gone With the Wind* ("I'll never go hungry again!") to Jeremy Irons' Oscar-winning performance in *Reversal of Fortune* ("You have no idea."). In a later scene there's even a sly dig at Disneyland's "It's a Small World" anthem!

Each of the songs contributes another specific emotion, from the youthful exuberance of "I Just Can't Wait to Be King" to the light-hearted mindset of "Hakuna Matata." Best of all, the potentially sappy romantic notions in "Can You Feel the Love Tonight" are neatly countered by the coda, as sung by Timon and Pumbaa, in which they decry their friend Simba's descent into mushiness, where he is "doomed."

The five songs for *The Lion King* were written by perennial chart-topper Elton John (who also sings a reprise of "Can You Feel the Love Tonight" over the closing credits) in collaboration with Sir Tim Rice. Securing the services of a pop superstar like John was a coup indeed, but even he was impressed with the way his songs were orchestrated and produced by Hans Zimmer. Zimmer's original score, and orchestral treatment of the John/Rice songs, is nothing short of masterful—one of the finest musical achievements in the whole of Disney history. Both Zimmer and the songwriting team won Oscars for their work; "Can You Feel the Love Tonight" was honored as Best Original Song. From the

Rafiki cuddles the baby Simba as his parents (Mufasa and Sarabi) proudly look on in the opening sequence of *The Lion King*. © 1994 *The Walt Disney Company.*

film's "cold" opening, an African chant, to its choral work and dramatic underscoring, the score adds depth and dimension to an already impressive film.

Perhaps the most impressive single moment in *The Lion King* is the wildebeest stampede. This awesome spectacle was largely the work of a computer program developed by the studio's CGI team (Computer Generated Imagery). CGI supervisor Scott Johnston explained, "Since the scene called for a stampede, we had to come up with a way that our animators could control the behavior of herds of wildebeests without having them bump into each other. We developed a simulation program that would allow us to designate leaders and followers within each group. We were also able to individualize and vary the movement of each animal within a group to give them a certain random quality. Effectively they could all be doing different things with the library of behavior, including slow and fast gallops, various head tosses, and even a few different kinds of leaps."

For the key animators who still worked in pencil, *The Lion King* harked back to *Bambi* in its fundamental challenge: to create four-legged jungle creatures who looked realistic enough to be convincing, yet human enough to incorporate a recognizable range of facial expressions and characteristics. As always, the animators leaned on the visual and vocal expressiveness of the actors playing those parts, but they also spent a great deal of time studying real-life lions and other animals.

The most telling fact about the success of *The Lion King* is that in the same year, 1994, five other animated features were released theatrically in the U.S.: *The Princess and the Goblin, Thumbelina, A Troll in Central Park, The Pagemaster,* and *The Swan Princess.* Not one of them enjoyed a fraction of the impact, or success, of *The Lion King,* but more important, not one of them had the film's strength—of narrative, music, or general appeal—in spite of the fact that most of them were directed and/or produced by former Disney staffers. Industry pundits wrote off their collective failure as an inability to buck the Disney marketing "machine," but the real reason was much more basic: they didn't deliver the goods. *The Lion King* did.

The crucial weakness of most animated features is not the animation itself, which is often quite good, but the story. There are, in almost every non-Disney film, moments of dead air when a scene comes to an end, as if all the air has just been let out of a tire. It is precisely that feeling the Disney staff strives to avoid.

"If only they knew how hard we worked," says veteran storyman Joe Grant. He worked for Walt in the "golden age," left the company in 1949, and returned in 1987 to help out with character development. The same man who cowrote *Dumbo* received story credit on *Beauty and the Beast, The Lion King,* and *Pocahontas.* But he is just one of many artists and writers who contribute to these films, making conceptual drawings, fleshing out characters, working up bits of business and gags, helping to find story solutions that strengthen the overall picture. There is no magic ingredient to success at Disney, just a lot of hard work by people with imagination and experience.

There is one other ingredient that rivals often overlook: the willingness to scrap finished work if the film isn't going as well as it should. There were tremendous cost overruns on *The Black Cauldron* because of constant changes. *Aladdin* hit a stone wall at one point, and many Ashman-Menken tunes were jettisoned. Even *The Lion King* had its share of problems.

The studio's newest animated feature, *Pocahontas,* had a similarly rocky road to completion. The film was sold to studio executives on the basis of its name, nothing more, when director Mike Gabriel suggested the topic of Pocahontas and John Smith at a meeting with Jeffrey Katzenberg in the early 1990s. Then came the task of developing a story and a set of characters that would work in a Disney cartoon context. How to introduce humor to an essentially serious story—and how to meet the challenge of animating realistic human characters?

This formidable assignment was placed in the hands of a relatively new Disney team. Animator Eric Goldberg, who scored such a hit with the Genie in *Aladdin,* was selected to codirect *Pocahontas* with Gabriel. They worked from a screenplay by Carl Binder, Susannah Grant, and Philip LaZebnik, with story work supervised by young studio veteran Tom Sito. The project was produced by James Pentecost, a newcomer to Disney with substantial stage credits. For songs, the studio teamed Alan Menken with a new collaborator, Stephen Schwartz, whose Broadway scores include *Pippin* and *Godspell.*

First, Little Hiawatha, then Tonka, and now, Pocahontas: the studio's newest (but not first) native American star. © *1995 The Walt Disney Company.*

Walt Disney Pictures: Filmography

Following is a list of all the feature films released under the Walt Disney banner since Walt's death. All were released by Buena Vista, and rated G unless otherwise noted. Release dates (by month) are those on the official Disney records and differ in some cases from listings in other sources. In 1984 the company initiated the Touchstone banner, and in 1990 Hollywood Pictures; this filmography concentrates only on the features released as Walt Disney Pictures.

This is intended as a capsule guide, so only selective credits for cast, producer, director, writer, animators, and composers have been included.

1967

Charlie the Lonesome Cougar

Released October. Producer: Walt Disney. Coproducer: Winston Hibler. Field producers: Lloyd Beebe, Charles L. Draper, Ford Beebe. Story: Jack Speirs and Winston Hibler. Screenplay: Jack Speirs. Cast: Ron Brown (Jess Bradley), Brian Russell (Potlatch), Linda Wallace (Jess's fiancée), Jim Wilson (farmer), Clifford Peterson (mill manager). Narrator:

Rex Allen. Running time: 75 minutes.

A forester finds an orphaned cougar kitten and raises it as a pet.

1968

Blackbeard's Ghost

Released February. Producer: Walt Disney. Coproducer: Bill Walsh. Director: Robert Stevenson. Screenplay: Bill Walsh, Don Da Gradi. Cast: Peter Ustinov (Blackbeard), Dean Jones (Steve Walker), Suzanne Pleshette (Jo Anne Baker), Elsa Lanchester (Emily Stowecroft), Joby Baker (Silky Seymour), Elliott Reid (TV commentator), Richard Deacon (Dean Wheaton). Running time: 107 minutes.

A track coach accidentally conjures up the spirit of Blackbeard the Pirate and uses him to help his inept track team and rid the town of local gangsters.

The One and Only, Genuine Original Family Band

Released March (general release: June). Producer Bill Anderson. Director: Michael O'Herlihy. Story and Screenplay: Lowell S. Hawley. Based on the autobiographical novel *Nebraska 1888* by Laura Bower Van Nuys. Music and lyrics by Richard M. Sherman, Robert B. Sherman. Cast: Walter Brennan (Grandpa Bower), Buddy Ebsen (Calvin), Lesley Ann Warren (Alice), John Davidson (Joe Carder), Janet Blair (Katie), Wally Cox (Mr. Wampler). Goldie Hawn is one of the dancers; by the time the film was in release she was already a star of television's *Laugh-In.* Running time: 110 minutes.

Grandpa Bower organizes his ten-member family into a family band to perform at the 1888 Democratic convention.

Never a Dull Moment

Released June. Producer: Ron Miller. Director: Jerry Paris. Screenplay: A. J. Carothers. Based on a book by John Godey. Cast: Dick Van Dyke (Jack Albany), Edward G. Robinson (Smooth), Dorothy Provine (Sally), Henry Silva (Frank Boley), Joanna Moore (Melanie), Tony Bill (Florian). Running time: 100 minutes.

An actor is mistaken for a notorious killer and gets involved with an art museum robbery. Jerry Paris also directed Van Dyke in his hit television series.

The Horse in the Gray Flannel Suit

Released December. Producer: Winston Hibler. Director: Norman Tokar. Screenplay: Louis Pelletier. Based on the book *The Year of the Horse* by Eric Hatch. Cast: Dean Jones (Frederick Bolton), Diane Baker (Suzie Clemens), Lloyd Bochner (Archer Madison), Fred Clark (Tom Dugan), Ellen Janov (Helen Bolton), Morey Amsterdam (Charlie Blake), Kurt Russell (Ronnie Gardner), Lurene Tuttle (Aunt Martha). Running time: 113 minutes.

An advertising executive arranges for his firm to buy his teen-age daughter a horse and names it after a client's product.

1969

Smith!

Released March. Producer: Bill Anderson. Director: Michael O'Herlihy. Screenplay: Louis Pelletier. Based on a book by Paul St. Pierre. Cast: Glenn Ford (Smith), Nancy Olson (Norah), Dean Jagger (Judge), Keenan Wynn (Vince Heber), Warren Oates (Walter), Chief Dan George (Ol' Antoine). Running time: 102 minutes.

A rancher tries to help a young Indian suspected of murder.

The Love Bug

Released March. Producer: Bill Walsh. Director: Robert Stevenson. Screenplay: Bill Walsh, Don Da Gradi. Based on a story by Gordon Buford. Cast: Dean Jones (Jim Douglas), Michele Lee (Carole), David Tomlinson (Thorndyke), Buddy Hackett (Tennessee), Joe Flynn (Havershaw), Benson Fong (Mr. Wu). Running time: 107 minutes.

An unsuccessful racing driver has a change of luck when he purchases a white Volkswagen (nicknamed Herbie) with a mind of its own. This led to three sequels and a limited TV series.

Rascal

Released June. Producer: James Algar. Director: Norman Tokar. Screenplay: Harold Swanton. Based on the book by Sterling North. Cast: Steve Forrest (Willard North), Bill Mumy (Sterling), Pamela Toll (Theo), Bettye Ackerman (Miss Whalen), Elsa Lanchester (Mrs. Satterfield), Henry Jones (Garth). Narrator: Walter Pidgeon. Running time: 85 minutes.

A baby raccoon becomes a boy's only companion during his father's absence.

The Computer Wore Tennis Shoes

Released December. Producer: Bill Anderson. Director: Robert Butler. Screenplay: Joseph L. McEveety. Cast: Cesar Romero (A. J. Arno), Kurt Russell (Dexter), Joe Flynn (Dean Higgins), William Schallert (Professor Quigley), Alan Hewitt (Dean Collingsgood), Richard Bakalyan (Chillie). Running time: 90 minutes.

The mind of Medfield college student Dexter becomes infused with the college computer's memory bank when he attempts to repair the machine.

1970

King of the Grizzlies

Released February. Producer: Winston Hibler. Director: Ron Kelly. Screenplay: Jack Speirs. Adaptation: Rod Peterson, Norman Wright. Based on *The Biography of a Grizzly* by Ernest Thompson Seton. Cast: John Yesno (Moki), Chris Wiggins (Colonel), Hugh Webster (Shorty), Jan Van Evera (Slim), and Wahb, the grizzly bear. Narrator: Winston Hibler. Running time: 93 minutes.

An Indian, working as a ranch foreman, has a mystical tie with a grizzly bear who invades the ranch.

The Boatniks

Released July. Producer: Ron Miller. Director: Norman Tokar. Screen story and Screenplay: Arthur Julian. Cast: Robert Morse (Ensign Garland), Stefanie Powers (Kate), Phil Silvers (Harry Simmons), Norman Fell (Max), Mickey Shaughnessy (Charlie), Wally Cox

(Jason), Don Ameche (Commander Taylor). Running time: 100 minutes.

An incompetent Ensign matches wits with a trio of jewel thieves at a California harbor.

The Aristocats

Released December. Producers: Winston Hibler, Wolfgang Reitherman. Director: Wolfgang Reitherman. Story: Larry Clemmons, Vance Gerry, Ken Anderson, Frank Thomas, Eric Cleworth, Julius Svendsen, Ralph Wright. Based on a story by Tom McGowan and Tom Rowe. Directing Animators: Milt Kahl, Frank Thomas, Ollie Johnston, John Lounsbery. Music: George Burns. Songs: Richard M. Sherman and Robert B. Sherman, Terry Gilkyson, Floyd Huddleston and Al Rinker. Voice Cast: Eva Gabor (Duchess), Phil Harris (Thomas O'Malley), Sterling Holloway (Roquefort), Scatman Crothers (Scat Cat), Paul Winchell (Chinese cat), Lord Tim Hudson (English cat), Vito Scotti (Italian cat), Thurl Ravenscroft (Russian cat), Nancy Kulp (Frou Frou), Pat Buttram (Napoleon), George Lindsey (Lafayette), Monica Evans (Abigail), Carole Shelley (Amelia), Hermione Baddeley (Madame), Roddy Maude-Roxby (Edgar the Butler), Bill Thompson (Uncle Waldo). Running time: 78 minutes.

Duchess, a cat, and her three kittens, heirs to a great fortune, search for the way home to Paris, after a jealous butler abandons them in the countryside. (Animated.)

1971

The Wild Country

Released January. Producer: Ron Miller. Director: Robert Totten. Screenplay: Calvin Clements, Jr., Paul Savage. Based on the book *Little Britches* by Ralph Moody. Cast: Steve Forrest (Jim), Jack Elam (Thompson), Ronny Howard (Virgil), Frank de Kova (Two Dog), Vera Miles (Kate), Morgan Woodward (Ab). Running time: 100 minutes.

The joys and hardships of a family establishing a homestead in Wyoming of the 1880s.

The Barefoot Executive

Released March. Producer: Bill Anderson. Director: Robert Butler. Screenplay: Joseph L. McEveety. Story: Lila Garrett, Bernie Kahn, Stewart C. Billett. Cast: Kurt Russell (Steven Post), Joe Flynn (Wilbanks), Harry Morgan (Crampton), Wally Cox (Mertons), Heather North (Jennifer), Alan Hewitt (Farnsworth). Running time: 96 minutes.

With the help of a chimp who can pick the top-rated shows, a television page becomes the network Vice President.

Scandalous John

Released June. Producer: Bill Walsh. Director: Robert Butler. Screenplay: Bill Walsh, Don Da Gradi. Cast: Brian Keith (John McCanless), Alfonso Arau (Paco), Michele Carey (Amanda), Rick Lenz (Jimmy), Harry Morgan (Hector Pippin), Simon Oakland (Whitaker). Running time: 113 minutes.

A cantankerous old cowboy tries to save his ranch from a land developer in this modern version of *Don Quixote*.

$1,000,000 Duck

Released June. Producer: Bill Anderson. Director: Vincent McEveety. Screenplay: Roswell Rogers. Based on a story by Ted Key. Cast: Dean Jones (Professor Albert Dooley), Sandy Duncan (Katie), Joe Flynn (Finley Hooper), Tony Roberts (Fred), James Gregory (Rutledge), Lee Harcourt Montgomery (Jimmy). Running time: 92 minutes.

A family cashes in when a pet duck lays eggs with a golden yolk.

Bedknobs and Broomsticks

Released November (world premiere in London, October). Producer: Bill Walsh. Director: Robert Stevenson. Screenplay: Bill Walsh, Don Da Gradi. Based on a book by Mary Norton. Songs: Richard M. Sherman, Robert B. Sherman. Animation Director: Ward Kimball. Cast: Angela Lansbury (Eglantine Price), David Tomlinson (Emelius Browne), Roddy McDowall (Mr. Jelk), Sam Jaffe (Bookman), Ian Wieghill (Charlie), Cindy O'Callaghan (Carrie), Roy Snart (Paul). Running time: 117 minutes. (Reissued in 1979 in a 98 minute version, minus most musical numbers.)

Musical adventure about an apprentice witch searching for a magic spell with which to aid the British effort during World War II. Features a twenty-minute live action/animation sequence.

1972

The Biscuit Eater

Released March. Producer: Bill Anderson. Director: Vincent McEveety. Screenplay: Lawrence Edward Watkin. Based on a story by James Street. Cast: Earl Holliman (Harve McNeill), Lew Ayres (Mr. Ames), Godfrey Cambridge (Willie Dorsey), Patricia Crowley (Mrs. McNeill), Bea Richards (Charity), Johnny Whitaker (Lonnie). Running time: 90 minutes.

Two boys take on an unwanted pup and devote themselves to training a champion bird dog. This story was filmed before in 1940.

Now You See Him, Now You Don't

Released July. Producer: Ron Miller. Director: Robert Butler. Screenplay: Joseph McEveety. Based on a story by Robert L. King. Cast: Kurt Russell (Dexter), Cesar Romero (A. J. Arno), Joe Flynn (Dean Higgins), Jim Backus (Forsythe), William Windom (Lufkin), Michael McGreevey (Schuyler). Running time: 88 minutes.

Medfield college student Dexter invents an invisability liquid, and a gang of local crooks are determined to get it. A sequel to *The Computer Wore Tennis Shoes*

(1970). Followed by *The Strongest Man in the World* (1975).

Napoleon and Samantha

Released July. Producer: Winston Hibler. Director: Bernard McEveety. Screenplay: Stewart Raffill. Cast: Michael Douglas (Danny), Will Geer (Grandpa), Jodie Foster (Samantha), Johnny Whitaker (Napoleon), Arch Johnson (Chief of Police). Running time: 91 minutes.

Two children, along with a pet lion, run away and take refuge at a friend's mountain retreat. This was Jodie Foster's feature film debut.

Snowball Express

Released December. Producer: Ron Miller. Director: Norman Tokar. Screenplay: Don Tait, Jim Parker, Arnold Margolin. Based on *Chateau Bon Vivant* by Frankie and John O'Rear. Cast: Dean Jones (Johnny Baxter), Nancy Olson (Sue), Harry Morgan (Jesse McCord), Keenan Wynn (Martin Ridgeway), Johnny Whitaker (Richard). Running time: 93 minutes.

An accountant quits the rat race and moves his family to the Rockies when he learns he's inherited a ski resort.

1973

The World's Greatest Athlete

Released February. Producer: Bill Walsh. Director: Robert Scheerer; Screenplay: Gerald Gardner, Dee Caruso. Cast: John Amos (Coach Archer). Jan-Michael Vincent (Nanu), Roscoe Lee Browne (Gazenga), Tim Conway (Milo), Dayle Haddon (Jane), Nancy Walker (Mrs. Petersen), Billy DeWolfe (Maxwell). Running time: 93 minutes.

A hard-luck athletic coach finds a super-athlete living in the African jungle and brings him to civilization.

Charley and the Angel

Released March. Producer: Bill Anderson. Director: Vincent McEveety; Screenplay: Roswell Rogers. Based on *The Golden Evenings of Summer* by Will Stanton. Cast: Fred MacMurray (Charley), Cloris Leachman (Nettie), Harry Morgan (The Angel), Kurt Russell (Ray), Kathleen Cody (Leonora), Vincent Van Patten (Willie). Running time: 93 minutes.

An angel, warning a sour businessman that his time on earth is short, helps him to change his hard ways.

One Little Indian

Released June. Producer: Winston Hibler. Director: Bernard McEveety. Screenplay: Harry Spalding. Cast: James Garner (Clint), Vera Miles (Doris), Clay O'Brien (Mark), Pat Hingle (Captain Stewart), Andrew Prine (Chaplain), Jodie Foster (Martha). Running time: 90 minutes.

An AWOL trooper helps a boy escape from Indians by using a disagreeable camel.

Robin Hood

Released November. Producer: Wolfgang Reitherman. Director: Wolfgang Reitherman. Story: Larry Clemmons. Based on character and story conceptions by Ken Anderson. Directing Animators: Milt Kahl, Frank Thomas, Ollie Johnston, John Lounsbery. Songs: Roger Miller, Floyd Huddleston, George Bruns, Johnny Mercer. Voice Cast: Brian Bedford (Robin Hood), Phil Harris (Little John), Monica Evans (Maid Marian), Peter Ustinov (Prince John), Terry-Thomas (Sir Hiss), Andy Devine (Friar Tuck), Roger Miller (Allan-a-Dale), Pat Buttram (Sheriff), George Lindsey (Trigger), Ken Curtis (Nutsy), Carole Shelley (Lady Kluck). Running time: 83 minutes.

An animated retelling of the classic legend with animals playing the parts (i.e., Robin Hood is a fox; Little John, a bear; etc.).

Superdad

Released January 1974 (world premiere December 1973). Producer: Bill Anderson. Director: Vincent McEveety. Screenplay: Joseph L. McEveety. Based on a story by Harlan Ware. Cast: Bob Crane (Charlie), Kurt Russell (Bart), Barbara Rush (Sue), Joe Flynn (Hershberger), Kathleen Cody (Wendy). Running time: 96 minutes.

A father competes with his daughter's fiancé in an effort to prove his worth to his future son-in-law.

1974

Herbie Rides Again

Released June (released in England, February). Producer: Bill Walsh. Director: Robert Stevenson. Screenplay: Bill Walsh. Based on a story by Gordon Buford. Cast: Helen Hayes (Mrs. Steinmetz), Ken Berry (Willoughby), Stefanie Powers (Nicole), John McIntire (Mr. Judson), Keenan Wynn (Alonzo Hawk), Huntz Hall (Judge). Running time: 88 minutes.

Herbie, the Volkswagen, helps Mrs. Steinmetz thwart Alonzo Hawk, who needs her property to build a skyscraper. A sequel to *The Love Bug* (1969).

The Bears and I

Released July. Producer: Winston Hibler. Director: Bernard McEveety. Screenplay: John Whedon. Based on the book by Robert Franklin Leslie. Narration written by Jack Speirs. "Sweet Surrender" composed and sung by John Denver. Cast: Patrick Wayne (Bob), Chief Dan George (Chief Peter), Andrew Duggan (Commissioner), Michael Ansara (Oliver), Robert Pine (John). Running time: 89 minutes.

Vietnam Vet retreats to the North Woods, where he becomes a foster parent to three bear cubs.

The Castaway Cowboy

Released August. Producers: Ron Miller, Winston Hibler. Director: Vincent McEveety. Screenplay: Don Tait. Story by Don Tait, Richard Bluel, Hugh Benson. Cast: James Garner (Costain), Vera Miles (Henrietta), Robert Culp (Bryson), Eric Shea (Booton), Elizabeth Smith (Liliha). Running time: 91 minutes.

A ship-wrecked cowboy finds romance and adventure on a Hawaiian island.

The Island at the Top of the World

Released December. Producer: Winston Hibler. Director: Robert Stevenson. Screenplay: John Whedon. Based on *The Lost Ones* by Ian Cameron. Cast: David Hartman (Professor Ivarsson), Donald Sinden (Sir Anthony Ross), Jacques Marin (Captain Brieux), Mako (Oomiak), David Gwillim (Donald Ross), Agneta Eckemyr (Freyja). Running time: 94 minutes.

A team of explorers use a giant airship to search the Arctic for a missing person; they discover a volcanic island filled with incredible dangers.

1975

The Strongest Man in the World

Released February. Producer: Bill Anderson. Director: Vincent McEveety. Screenplay: Joseph McEveety, Herman Groves. Cast: Kurt Russell (Dexter), Joe Flynn (Dean Higgins), Eve Arden (Harriet), Cesar Romero (A. J. Arno), Phil Silvers (Krinkle), Dick Van Patten (Harry). Running time: 92 minutes.

Medfield college student Dexter gains superhuman strength when he eats cereal accidentally containing a chemical compound he has been working on. A sequel to *The Computer Wore Tennis Shoes* (1970) and *Now You See Him, Now You Don't* (1972).

Escape to Witch Mountain

Released March. Executive Producer: Ron Miller. Producer: Jerome Courtland. Director: John Hough. Screenplay: Robert Malcom Young. Based on the book by Alexander Key. Cast: Eddie Albert (Jason), Ray Milland (Bolt), Donald Pleasance (Deranian), Kim Richards (Tia), Ike Eisenmann (Tony). Running time: 97 minutes.

Pursued by an evil millionaire, two orphaned children with psychic powers try to discover their origins. Followed by a 1978 sequel, *Return to Witch Mountain*.

The Apple Dumpling Gang

Released July. Producer: Bill Anderson. Director: Norman Tokar. Screenplay: Don Tait. Based on a book by Jack M. Bickham. Cast: Bill Bixby (Russell Donavan), Susan Clark (Magnolia), Don Knotts (Theodore), Tim Conway (Amos), David Wayne (Colonel T. T. Clydesdale), Slim Pickens (Frank Stillwell). Running time: 100 minutes.

A gambler inherits the responsibility of three orphaned youngsters who co-own a gold mine. Followed by one sequel, *The Apple Dumpling Gang Rides Again* (1979) and a limited TV series.

One of Our Dinosaurs is Missing

Released July. Producer: Bill Walsh. Director: Robert Stevenson. Screenplay: Bill Walsh. Based on *The Great Dinosaur Robbery* by David Forrest. Cast: Peter Ustinov (Hnup Wan), Helen Hayes (Hettie), Clive Revill (Quon), Derek Nimmo (Lord Southmere), Joan Sims (Emily). Running time: 93 minutes.

A group of English nannies set out to retrieve a piece of top-secret microfilm hidden inside a dinosaur skeleton.

The Best of Walt Disney's True Life Adventures

Released October. Director: James Algar. Narrator: Winston Hibler. Running time: 89 minutes.

A compilation feature taken from the award-winning short-subject series.

Dr. Syn, Alias The Scarecrow

Released November. Producer: Walt Disney. Coproducer: Bill Anderson. Screenplay: Robert Westerby. Based on "Christopher Syn" by Russell Thorndike and William Buchanan. Cast: Patrick McGoohan (Dr. Syn), George Cole (Mr. Mipps), Tony Britton (Bates), Michael Hordern (Squire), Geoffrey Kean (General Pugh). Running time: 84 minutes.

This film was originally made for the Disney TV show, as a three-parter. It was released theatrically abroad in 1963, but given its first American showing at this time.

1976

No Deposit, No Return

Released February. Producer: Ron Miller. Coproducer: Joseph McEveety. Director: Norman Tokar. Screenplay: Arthur Alsberg, Don Nelson. Story: Joseph McEveety. Cast: David Niven (J. S. Osborne), Darrin McGavin (Duke), Don Knotts (Bert), Herschel Bernardi (Sergeant Turner), Barbara Feldon (Carolyn), Kim Richards (Tracy). Running time: 112 minutes.

Two bumbling crooks get involved with a pair of children who want to be kidnapped as part of a scheme to rejoin their mother overseas.

Ride a Wild Pony

Released March (world premiere December 1975). Executive Producer: Ron Miller. Producer: Jerome Courtland. Director: Don Chaffey. Screenplay: Rosemary Anne Sisson. From the novel *A Sporting Proposition* by James Aldridge. Cast: Michael Craig (James), John Meillon (Charles Quayle), John Meillon, Jr. (Kit Quayle), Robert Bettles (Scott), Eva Griffith (Josie), Graham Rouse (Bluey). Running time: 91 minutes.

In Australia, a poor farm boy and a crippled rich girl vie for the love and ownership of a pony.

Gus

Released July. Producer: Ron Miller. Director: Vincent McEveety. Screenplay: Arthur Alsberg, Don Nelson. Based on a story by Ted Key. Cast: Edward Asner (Hank Cooper), Don Knotts (Coach), Gary Grimes (Andy), Tim Conway (Crankcase), Liberty Williams (Debbie), Dick Van Patten (Cal). Running time: 96 minutes.

An inept football team welcomes its newest member—a place-kicking mule!

Treasure of Matecumbe

Released July. Executive Producer: Ron Miller. Producer: Bill Anderson. Director: Vincent McEveety. Screenplay: Don Tait. Based on *A Journey to Matecumbe* by Robert Lewis Taylor. Cast: Robert Foxworth (Jim), Joan Hackett (Lauriette), Peter Ustinov (Dr. Snodgrass), Vic Morrow (Spangler), Johnny Doran (David), Billy Attmore (Thaol). Running time: 117 minutes.

Shortly after the Civil War, two boys meet friend and foe during their journey to find buried treasure in the Florida swamps.

The Shaggy D.A.

Released December. Executive Producer: Ron Miller. Producer: Bill Anderson. Director: Robert Stevenson. Screenplay: Don Tait. Suggested by *The Hound of Florence* by Felix Salten. Cast: Dean Jones (Wilby Daniels), Suzanne Pleshette (Betty), Tim Conway (Tim), Keenan Wynn (John Slade), Jo Anne Worley (Katrinka), Dick Van Patten (Raymond). Running time: 92 minutes.

A lawyer, running for district attorney, finds himself in possession of an ancient ring which transforms him into a big shaggy dog. A sequel to *The Shaggy Dog* (1959).

1977

Freaky Friday

Released January (world premiere December 1976). Producer: Ron Miller. Director: Gary Nelson. Screenplay: Mary Rodgers, from her novel. Cast: Barbara Harris (Ellen), Jodie Foster (Annabel), John Astin (Bill), Patsy Kelly (Mrs. Schmauss), Vicki Schreck (Virginia), Dick Van Patten (Harold), Sorrell Booke (Mr. Dilk), Alan Oppenheimer (Mr. Joffert), Kaye Ballard (Coach Betsy), Ruth Buzzi (Opposing Coach). Running time: 95 minutes.

A harried mother and her thirteen-year-old daughter miraculously exchange bodies for a day.

The Littlest Horse Thieves

Released March (released in England as *Escape from the Dark* May 1976). Producer: Ron Miller. Director: Charles Jarrott. Screenplay: Rosemary Anne Sisson. From a story by Rosemary Ann Sisson and Burt Kennedy. Cast: Alastair Sim (Lord Harrogate), Peter Barkworth (Richard Sandman), Maurice Colbourne (Luke), Susan Tebbs (Violet), Chloe Franks (Alice), Andrew Harrison (Dave), Benjie Bolgar (Tommy). Running time: 104 minutes.

Three youngsters make a daring attempt to rescue a herd of doomed pit ponies from an English coal mine.

The Many Adventures of Winnie the Pooh

Released March. Producer: Wolgang Reitherman. Directors: Wolfgang Reitherman, John Lounsbery. Running time: 74 minutes.

Compilation of three Winnie the Pooh shorts, with new bridging animation.

The Rescuers

Released June. Executive Producer: Ron Miller. Producer: Wolfgang Reitherman. Directors: Wolfgang Reitherman, John Lounsbery, Art Stevens. Story: Larry Clemmons, Ken Anderson, Vance Gerry, David Michener, Burny Mattinson, Frank Thomas, Fred Lucky, Ted Berman, Dick Sebast. Suggested by *The Rescuers* and *Miss Bianca* by Margery Sharp. Directing Animators: Ollie Johnston, Frank Thomas, Milt Kahl, Don Bluth. Songs: Carol Connors, Ayn Robbins, Sammy Fain, Robert Crawford. Voice Cast: Bob Newhart (Bernard), Eva Gabor (Miss Bianca), Geraldine Page (Mme. Medusa), Joe Flynn (Mr. Snoops), Jeanette Nolan (Ellie Mae), Pat Buttram (Luke), Jim Jordan (Orville), John McIntire (Rufus). Running time: 76 minutes.

Two mice attempt to rescue a little girl from an evil woman, who uses the kidnapped child to search for a lost diamond. Animated.

Herbie Goes to Monte Carlo

Released June. Producer: Ron Miller. Director: Vincent McEveety. Screenplay: Arthur Alsberg, Don Nelson. Based on characters created by Gordon Buford. Cast: Dean Jones (Jim Douglas), Don Knotts (Wheely Applegate), Julie Sommers (Diane), Jacques Marin (Inspector Bouchet), Roy Kinnear (Quincey) Bernard Fox (Max), Eric Braeden (Bruno). Running time: 105 minutes.

Thieves hide a fabulous diamond in Herbie's gas tank, while Jim enters the Volkswagen in a road race between Paris and Monte Carlo. Second sequel to *The Love Bug* (1969).

Pete's Dragon

Released December (world premiere November). Producers: Ron Miller, Jerome Courtland. Director: Don Chaffey. Screenplay: Malcolm Marmorstein. Based on a story by Seton I. Miller and S. S. Field. Animation Director: Don Bluth. Elliot created by Ken Anderson. Songs: Al Kasha, Joel Hirschhorn. Cast: Helen Reddy (Nora), Jim Dale (Dr. Terminus), Mickey Rooney (Lampie), Red Buttons (Hoagy), Shelley Winters (Lena Gogan), Sean Marshall (Pete), Jane Kean (Miss Taylor), Jim Backus (the Mayor), Jeff Conaway (Willie), Charlie Callas (voice of Elliott), Gary Morgan

(Grover), Cal Bartlett (Paul). Original running time: 129 minutes; reedited version 106 minutes released in 1984.

Musical story of an orphan and his friend, a protective dragon who brings confusion to a Maine fishing village. (Live action and animation.)

1978

Candleshoe

Released February (world premiere December 1977). Producer: Ron Miller. Director: Norman Tokar. Screenplay: David Swift, Rosemary Anne Sisson. Based on *Christmas at Candleshoe* by Michael Innes. Cast: David Niven (Priory), Helen Hayes (Lady St. Edmund), Jodie Foster (Casey), Leo McKern (Bundage), Vivian Pickles (Grimsworthy). Running time: 101 minutes.

A tomboy from Los Angeles poses as a long-lost heiress to a stately English manor.

Return from Witch Mountain

Released March. Producers: Ron Miller, Jerome Courtland. Director: John Hough. Screenplay: Malcolm Marmorstein. Based on characters created by Alexander Key. Cast: Bette Davis (Letha), Christopher Lee (Victor), Kim Richards (Tia), Ike Eisenmann (Tony), Jack Soo (Yokomoto), Christian Juttner (Dazzler). Anthony James (Sickle), Dick Bakalyan (Eddie), Ward Costello (Clearcole), Brad Savage (Muscles), Poindexter (Crusher), Jeffrey Jaquet (Rocky). Running time: 94 minutes.

When the two extraterrestrial children from Witch Mountain return to visit the city, one is kidnapped by a woman determined to control their psychic powers. A sequel to *Escape to Witch Mountain* (1975).

The Cat from Outer Space

Released June. Producer: Ron Miller. Coproducer: Norman Tokar. Director: Norman Tokar. Screenplay: Ted Key. Cast: Ken Berry (Frank), Sandy Duncan (Liz), Harry Morgan (General Stilton), Roddy McDowall (Stallwood), McLean Stevenson (Link), Jesse White (Earnest Ernie). Running time: 104 minutes.

A physicist tries to help an extraterrestrial feline fix his space ship before the army can capture the alien creature.

Hot Lead and Cold Feet

Released July. Producer: Ron Miller. Director: Robert Butler. Screenplay: Joe McEveety, Arthur Alsberg, Don Nelson. Based on a story by Rod Piffath. Cast: Jim Dale (Eli, Wild Billy, Jasper), Karen Valentine (Jenny), Don Knotts (Denver Kid), Jack Elam (Rattlesnake), Darren McGavin (Mayor). Running time: 90 minutes.

Two brothers compete in a no-holds-barred endurance contest for the inheritance of a western town. (Jim Dale plays a triple role.)

1979

Take Down

Released January. This film about high-school wrestlers was Buena Vista's first outside acquisition since Walt Disney's death, and its first PG-rated release. Kieth Merrill produced, directed, and co-wrote the story, which starred Edward Herrmann and Lorenzo Lamas. Rights to the film subsequently reverted to the producer.

The North Avenue Irregulars

Released February. Producer: Ron Miller. Coproducer: Tom Leetch. Director: Bruce Bilson. Screenplay: Don Tait. Based on the book by Rev. Albert Fay Hill. Cast: Edward Herrmann (Michael Hill), Barbara Harris (Vickie), Susan Clark (Anne), Karen Valentine (Jane), Michael Constantine (Marv), Cloris Leachman (Claire), Patsy Kelly (Rose). Running time: 100 minutes.

When organized crime hits their town, a reverend and a group of disorganized ladies from the church decide to hit back.

The Apple Dumpling Gang Rides Again

Released June. Producer: Ron Miller. Coproducer: Tom Leetch. Director: Vincent McEveety. Screenplay: Don Tait. Based on characters created by Jack M. Bickham. Cast: Tim Conway (Amos), Don Knotts (Theodore), Tim Matheson (Private Jeff Reid), Kenneth Mars (Marshall), Elyssa Davalos (Millie), Jack Elam (Big Mac), Robert Pine (Lieutenant), Harry Morgan (Major Gaskill). Running time: 89 minutes.

Two incompetent western bandits land in more trouble trying to go straight. Sequel to *The Apple Dumpling Gang*, (1975), which also spawned a limited TV series.

Unidentified Flying Oddball

Released July. Producer: Ron Miller. Director: Russ Mayberry. Story and Screenplay: Don Tait. A reworking of Mark Twain's *A Connecticut Yankee in King Arthur's Court.* Cast: Dennis Dugan (Tom), Jim Dale (Sir Mordred), Ron Moody (Merlin), Kenneth More (King Arthur), John Le Mesurier (Sir Gawain), Sheila White (Alisande), Rodney Bewes (Clarence). Running time: 93 minutes.

When lightning strikes their spacecraft, an astronaut and his robot companion are launched back through time to sixth-century England during the reign of King Arthur.

The Black Hole

Released December. Producer: Ron Miller. Director: Gary Nelson. Screenplay: Jeb Rosebrook, Gerry Day. Story: Jeb Rosebrook, Bob Barbash, Richard Landau. Cast: Maximilian Schell (Dr. Reinhardt), Anthony Perkins (Dr. Alex Durant), Robert Forster (Dan Holland), Joseph Bottoms (Charles Pizer), Yvette Mimieux (Kat

McCrae), Ernest Borgnine (Harry), voice of Roddy McDowall as V.I.N.CENT. Running time: 97 minutes.

A spaceship crew are stranded on a spacecraft run by a mad scientist intent on traveling through the deadly vortex of a black hole. (First PG-rated Walt Disney Production.)

1980

Midnight Madness

Released February. Producer: Ron Miller. Coproducers: David Wechter, Michael Nankin. Directors: David Wechter, Michael Nankin. Screenplay: David Wechter, Michael Nankin. Cast: David Naughton (Adam), Debra Clinger (Laura), Eddie Deezen (Wesley), Brad Wilkin (Lavitas), Maggie Roswell (Donna), Stephen Furst (Harold). Running time: 112 minutes.

A genius grad student organizes an all-night treasure hunt in which five rival teams must decipher cryptic clues planted ingeniously around Los Angeles. (Rated PG.)

The Last Flight of Noah's Ark

Released June. Producer: Ron Miller. Coproducer: Jan Williams. Director: Charles Jarrott. Screenplay: Steven W. Carabatsos, Sandy Glass, George Arthur Bloom. Story: Ernest K. Gann. Cast: Elliott Gould (Noah Dugan), Genevieve Bujold (Bernadette), Ricky Schroder (Bobby), Tammy Lauren (Julie), Vincent Gardenia (Stoney). Running time: 98 minutes.

An unemployed pilot accepts the job of flying an old converted B-29, loaded with farm animals and an attractive young missionary, to an island in the Pacific.

Herbie Goes Bananas

Released June. Producer: Ron Miller. Director: Vincent McEveety. Screenplay: Don Tait. Based on characters by Gordon Buford. Cast: Cloris Leachman (Aunt Louise), Charles Martin Smith (D. J.), John Vernon (Prindle), Stephen W. Burns (Pete), Elyssa Davalos (Melissa), Harvey Korman (Captain Blythe), Joaquin Garay III (Paco). Running time: 100 minutes.

An orphan, with a stolen Incan treasure map, stows away in Herbie the Volkswagen's trunk, while Herbie's en route, via ocean liner, to a race in Brazil. Third sequel to The Love Bug (1969), which also led to a limited TV series.

1981

The Devil and Max Devlin

Released February. Executive Producer: Ron Miller. Producer: Jerome Courtland. Director: Steven Hilliard Stern. Screenplay: Mary Rodgers. Story: Mary Rodgers, Jimmy Sangster. Songs: Marvin Hamlisch, Carole Bayer Sager. Cast: Elliott Gould (Max Devlin), Bill Cosby (Barney), Susan Anspach (Penny), Adam Rich (Toby), Julie Budd (Stella). Running time: 95 minutes.

A corrupt landlord makes a deal with the Devil's henchman to convince three innocent people to sell their souls in order to save his own. (Rated PG.)

Amy

Released March. Executive Producer: William Robert Yates. Producer: Jerome Courtland. Director: Vincent McEveety. Screenplay: Noreen Stone. Cast: Jenny Agutter (Amy), Barry Newman (Dr. Ben Corcoran), Kathleen Nolan (Helen), Chris Robinson (Elliott), Lou Fant (Lyle), Margaret O'Brien (Hazel), Nanette Fabray (Malvina). Running time: 100 minutes.

In 1913, a woman leaves her domineering husband to teach the deaf to speak. In helping her students, she herself learns to be independent and self-reliant. Made for television, but released to theatres instead.

The Fox and the Hound

Released July. Executive Producer: Ron Miller. Coproducers: Wolfgang Reitherman, Art Stevens. Directors: Art Stevens, Ted Berman, Richard Rich. Story: Larry Clemmons, Ted Berman, Peter Young, Steve Hulett, David Michener, Burny Mattinson, Earl Kress, Vance Gerry. Based on the book by Daniel P. Mannix. Supervising Animators: Randy Cartwright, Cliff Nordberg, Frank Thomas, Glen Keane, Ron Clements, Ollie Johnston. Songs: Richard O. Johnston, Stan Fidel, Jim Stafford, Richard Rich, Jeffrey Patch. Voice Cast: Mickey Rooney (Tod), Kurt Russell (Copper), Pearl Bailey (Big Mama), Jack Albertson (Amos), Sandy Duncan (Vixey), Jeanette Nolan (Widow Tweed), Pat Buttram (Chief), John Fiedler (Porcupine), John McIntire (Badger), Dick Bakalyan (Dinky), Paul Winchell (Boomer). Running time: 83 minutes.

Two best friends, a baby fox and a puppy hunting dog, grow up and learn they must be enemies. (Animated.)

Condorman

Released August (premiere in England, July). Executive Producer: Ron Miller. Producer: Jan Williams. Director: Charles Jarrott. Screenplay: Marc Stirdivant. Suggested by The Game of X by Robert Sheckley. Cast: Michael Crawford (Woody Wilkins), Oliver Reed (Krokov), Barbara Carrera (Natalia), James Hampton (Harry), Jean-Pierre Kalfon (Morovich). Running time: 90 minutes.

A comic book artist, helping the CIA by delivering papers to a beautiful Russian agent, falls in love with her and uses comic strip devices to help her defect. (Rated PG.)

The Watcher in the Woods

Released October (an earler version premiered April 1980 in New York). Producer: Ron Miller. Coproducer: Tom Leetch. Director: John Hough. Screenplay: Brian Clemens, Harry Spalding, Rosemary Anne Sisson. Cast: Bette Davis (Mrs. Aylwood), Lynn-Holly Johnson (Jan Curtis), Carroll Baker (Helen), David

McCallum (Paul), Kyle Richards (Ellie), Ian Bannen (John Keller), Richard Pasco (Tom Colley). Running time: 83 minutes; originally 108 minutes.

A series of terrifying events haunt an American family renting a large house in England; these eerie experiences are tied to the disappearance of a teenage girl thirty years ago. (Rated PG.)

1982

Night Crossing

Released February. Executive Producer: Ron Miller. Producer: Tom Leetch. Director: Delbert Mann. Screenplay: John McGreevey. Cast: John Hurt (Peter Strelzyk), Jane Alexander (Doris), Beau Bridges (Gunther Wetzel), Glynnis O'Connor (Petra), Doug McKeon (Frank), Ian Bannen (Josef), Klaus Löwitsch (Schmalk). Running time: 106 minutes.

True story of two families' attempt to escape from East Germany in a home-made hot-air baloon. (Rated PG.)

Tron

Released July. Executive Producer: Ron Miller. Producer: Donald Kushner. Director: Steven Lisberger. Screenplay: Steven Lisberger. Story: Steven Lisberger, Bonnie MacBird. Music: Wendy Carlos. Cast: Jeff Bridges (Kevin Flynn, Clu), Bruce Boxleitner (Alan, Tron), David Warner (Dillinger, Sark), Cindy Morgan (Lora, Nori), Barnard Hughes (Dr. Walter Gibbs, Dumont). Running time: 96 minutes.

A corrupt business executive blasts a young computer genius into an electronic dimension, where computer programs are the alter egos of the programmers who created them. There, he must play computer games, for keeps, with the evil Master Control Program. (Rated PG.) (Filmed in 70mm.)

Tex

Initial release July, broad release September. Executive Producer: Ron Miller. Producer: Tim Zinnemann. Director: Tim Hunter. Screenplay: Charlie Haas, Tim Hunter. Based on the book by S. E. Hinton. Cast: Matt Dillon (Tex McCormick), Jim Metzler (Mason), Meg Tilly (Jamie), Bill McKinney (Pop), Frances Lee McCain (Mrs. Johnson), Ben Johnson (Cole), Emilio Estevez (Johnny Collins). Running time: 103 minutes.

The struggles and conflicts of two teenage brothers growing up in rural Oklahoma without parental guidance. (Rated PG.)

1983

Trenchcoat

Released March. Producer: Jerry Leider. Director: Michael Tuchner. Screenplay: Jeffrey Price, Peter Seaman. Cast: Margot Kidder (Mickey), Robert Hays (Terry), David Suchet (Inspector), Gila Von Weitershausen (Eva Werner), Daniel Faraldo (Nino), Ronald Lacey (Princess Aida). Running time: 91 minutes.

An aspiring mystery writer vacations in Malta to research her next novel and becomes involved in a conspiracy more insidious than any of her unpublished stories. (Rated PG.)

Something Wicked This Way Comes

Released April. Producer: Peter Vincent Douglas. Director: Jack Clayton. Screenplay: Ray Bradbury, from his novel. Cast: Jason Robards (Charles Halloway), Jonathan Pryce (Mr. Dark), Vidal Peterson (Will), Shawn Carson (Jim), Diane Ladd (Mrs. Nightshade), Pam Grier (Dust Witch), Royal Dano (Tom Fury). Running time: 95 minutes.

Two boys discover the supernatural secret of a traveling carnival. (Rated PG.)

Never Cry Wolf

Released September. Executive Producer: Ron Miller. Producers: Lewis Allen, Jack Couffer, Joseph Strick. Director: Carroll Ballard. Screenplay: Curtis Hanson, Sam Hamm, Richard Kletter. Based on the book by Farley Mowat. Narration written by C. M. Smith, Eugene Corr, Christina Luescher. Cast: Charles Martin Smith (Tyler), Brian Dennehy (Rosie), Zachary Ittimangnaq (Ootek), Samson Jorah (Mike). Running time: 105 minutes.

A modern man's struggle with nature in the Arctic, as he studies the behavior of wolves on assignment for the Canadian government. (Rated PG.)

Running Brave

Released September. This Ira Englander production, made in Canada, was an outside acquisition by Buena Vista. Robby Benson starred in the story of real-life Sioux Indian Olympic gold medalist Billy Mills.

1984

Splash

Released March. Executive Producer: John Thomas Lenox. Producer: Brian Grazer. Director: Ron Howard. Screenplay: Lowell Ganz, Babaloo Mandel, Bruce Jay Friedman. Screenstory: Bruce Jay Friedman. Based on a story by Brian Grazer. Cast: Tom Hanks (Allen Bauer), Daryl Hannah (Madison), Eugene Levy (Walter Kornbluth), John Candy (Freddie Bauer), Dody Goodman (Mrs. Stimler), Shecky Greene (Mr. Buyrite), Richard B. Shull (Dr. Ross), Bobby Di Cicco (Jerry), Howard Morris (Dr. Zidell). Running time: 111 minutes.

A mermaid surfaces in New York City to pursue the man she loves. (Rated PG.) (First release for Disney's new Touchstone Films division.)

1985

Return to Oz

Released June. Producer: Paul Maslansky. Director: Walter Murch. Screenplay: Walter Murch, Gill Dennis, based on the books *The Land of Oz* and *Ozma of Oz* by

L. Frank Baum. Cast: Nicol Williamson (Dr. Worley/The Nome King), Jean Marsh (Nurse Wilson/Princess Mombi), Fairuza Balk (Dorothy), Piper Laurie (Aunt Em), Matt Clark (Uncle Henry), Brian Henson (Voice of Jack Pumpkinhead), Justin Case (scarecrow), John Alexander (Cowardly Lion), Deep Roy (Tin Man), Emma Ridley (Ozma). Running Time: 109 minutes.

Dorothy Gale returns to her beloved Oz, only to find evil rulers now in charge. (Rated PG.)

The Black Cauldron

Released July. Executive Producer: Ron Miller. Producer: Joe Hale. Directors: Ted Berman, Richard Rich. Story: David Jonas, Vance Gerry, Ted Berman, Richard Rich, Joe Hale. Al Wilson, Roy Marita, Peter Young, Art Stevens. Additional dialogue: Rosemary Ann Sisson, Roy Edward Disney. Based on "The Chronicles of Prydain" series by Lloyd Alexander. Animators: Andreas Deja, Hendel Butoy, Dale Baer, Ron Husband, Jay Jackson, Barry Temple, Tom Ferriter, Ruben Aquino, Cyndee Whitney, George, Scribner, Mark Henn, Terry Harrison, Phil Nibbelink, Steven Gordon, Doug Krohn, Shawn Keller, Mike Gabriel, Phillip Young, Jessie Cosio, Ruben Procopio, Viki Anderson, David Block, Charlie Downs, Sandra Borgmeyer, David Pacheco. Key Coordinating Animator: Walt Stanchfield. Music: Elmer Bernstein. Voice Cast: Grant Beardsley (Taran), John Hurn (The Horned King), Susan Sheridan (Eilonwy), Freddie Jones (Dallben), Nigel Hawthorne (Fflewddur), Arthur Malet (King Eidilleg), John Byner (Gurgi/Doli). Prologue narrated by John Huston. Running time: 81 minutes.

A young boy sets off to stop the evil Horned King from gaining possession of the Black Cauldron, which can unleash strange forces. (Rated PG.)

The Journey of Natty Gann

Released September. Producer: Mike Lobell. Director: Jeremy Kagan. Screenplay: Jenny Rosenberg. Cast: Meredith Salenger (Natty), John Cusack (Harry), Ray Wise (Sol), Lainie Kazan (Connie), Scatman Crothers (Sherman), Barry Miller (Parker), Verna Bloom (Farm Woman). Running time: 101 minutes.

A girl travels across the country during the great Depression to join her father, with a wolf and an older boy as her unlikely companions. (Rated PG.)

One Magic Christmas

Released November. Executive Producer: Phillip Borsos. Producer: Peter O'Brian. Director: Phillip Borsos. Screenplay: Thomas Meehan. Story: Thomas Meehan, Phillip Borsos, Barry Healey. Cast: Mary Steenburgen (Ginny Grainger), Gary Basaraba (Jack Grainger), Harry Dean Stanton (Gideon), Arthur Hill (Caleb Grainger), Elizabeth Harnois (Abbie Grainger), Robbie Magwood (Carl Grainger), Michele Meyrink (Bety), Elias Koteas (Eddie), Wayne Robson (Harry Dickens), Jan Rubes (Santa), Sarah Polley (Molly Monaghan), Graham Jarvis (Frank Crump). Running time: 89 minutes.

Hard Times have caused a woman to lose the Christmas spirit, but a guardian angel and Santa conspire with her daughter to rekindle those feelings.

Touchtone releases: *Baby . . . Secret of the Lost Legend; My Science Project.*

1986

The Great Mosue Detective (later reissued as *The Adventures of The Great Mouse Detective*)

July release. Producer: Burny Mattinson. Directors: John Musker, Ron Clements, Dave Michener, Burny Mattinson. Story adaptation: Pete Young, Vance Gerry, Steve Hulett, Ron Clements, John Musker, Bruce M. Morris, Matthew O'Callaghan, Burny Mattinson, Dave Michener, Melvin Shaw. Based on the book *Basil of Baker Street* by Eve Titus. Supervising animators: Mark Henn, Glen Keane, Robert Minkoff, Hendel Butoy. Music: Henry Mancini. Animation consultant: Eric Larson. Voice cast: Vincent Price (Professor Ratigan), Barrie Ingram (Basil), Val Bettin (Dawson), Susanne Pollatschek (Olivia), Candy Candido (Fidget), Diana Chesney (Mrs. Judson), Eve Brenner (The Mouse Queen), Alan Young (Flaversham), Shani Wallis (Lady Mouse), Ellen Fitzhugh (Barmaid), Walker Edmiston (Citizen), Laurie Main (Watson), Basil Rathbone (as Sherlock Holmes-borrowed from a vintage movie soundtrack). Running time: 74 minutes.

The eminent mouse detective Basil of Baker Street is called into service when a master toymaker is kidnapped.

Flight of the Navigator

July Release. Executive Producers: Johnathan Sanger, Mark Damon, John Hyde. Co-Executive Producer: Malcolm Harding. Co-Producer: David Joseph. Producers: Robby Wald, Dimitri Vallard. Director: Randal Kleiser. Screenplay: Michael Burton, Matt MacManus, based on a story by Mark H. Baker. Cast: Joey Cramer (David Freeman), Veronica Cartwright (Helen Freeman), Cliff DeYoung (Bill Freeman), Sarah Jessica Parker (Carolyn McAdams), Matt Adler (Jeff at 16), Howard Hesseman (Dr. Faraday), Paul Mall [aka Paul Reubens] (voice of Max), Robert Small (Troy), Albie Whitaker (Jeff at 8). Running time: 89 minutes.

A twelve year-old-boy is abducted by aliens, only to return eight years later—not having aged, filled with intergalactic information, and a new friend, a robot-like creature named Max. (Rated PG.)

Touchtone releases: *Down and Out in Beverly Hills; Off Beat; Ruthless People; Tough Guys; The Color of Money*

1987

Benji the Hunted

June release. Executive Producer: Ed Vanston. Producer: Ben Vaughn. Director: Joe Camp. Screenplay: Joe Camp. Supervising Producer/Production Manager/Assistant Director: Carolyn H. Camp. Benjai's Trainers: Bryan L. Renfro, Frank and Juanita Inn. Cast: Benji (Himself), Frank Inn (Himself), Red Steagall

(Hunter), Joe Camp (Voice of TV Director). Running time: 89 minutes.

After a fishing mishap, Benji is stranded on his own and must fend for himself in a mountainous terrain filled with wild animals. The fourth Benji movie (following *Benji, For the Love of Benji,* and *Oh, Heavenly Dog!*) was the first to be made in association with Disney.

Touchstone releases: *Outrageous Fortune; Tin Men; Ernest Goes to Camp; Adventures in Babysitting; Stakeout; Can't Buy Me Love; Hello Again; Three Men and a Baby; Good Morning, Vietnam*

1988

Return to Snowy River, Part II

April release. Executive Producers: Dennis Wright, Kent Lovell, John Kearney. Producer: Geoff Burrowes. Director: Geoff Burrowes. Screenplay: John Dixon, Geoff Burrowes. Cast: Tom Burlinson (Jim), Sigrid Thornton (Jessica), Brian Dennehy (Harrison), Nicholas Eadie (Alistair Patton), Mark Hembrow (Seb), Bryan Marshall (Hawker), Rhys McConnochie (Patton Sr.). Running time: 99 minutes.

In this sequel to the hit Australian movie *The Man From Snowy River* (1982), adventurer Jim Craig returns to his home to claim Jessica Harrison as his bride—but her father and the local banker (whose son covets Jessie) have other ideas. (Rated PG.)

Oliver & Company

November release. Director: George Scribner. Screenplay: Jim Cox, Timothy J. Disney, James Mangold. Story: Vance Gerry, Mike Gabriel, Roger Allers, Joe Ranft, Gary Trousdale, Jim Mitchell, Kevin Lima, Chris Bailey, Michael Cedeno, Kirk Wise, Pete Young, Dave Michener, Leon Joosen. Inspired by Charles Dickens' *Oliver Twist.* Supervising Animators: Mike Gabriel, Hendel Butoy, Glen Keane, Mark Henn, Ruben A. Aquino, Doug Krohn. Additional Story Material: Gerrit Graham, Samuel Graham, and Chris Hubbell, Steve Hulett, Danny Mann. Music: J.A.C. Redford. Songs: Barry Mann and Howard Ashman, Tom Snow and Dean Pitchford, Ron Rocha and Robert Minkoff, Dan Hartman and Charlie Midnight, Barry Manilow, Jack Feldman, and Bruce Sussman, Rocky Pedilla, Michael Eckhart and Jon St. James, Ruben Blades. Voice Cast: Joey Lawrence (Oliver), Billy Joel (Dodger), Cheech Marin (Tito), Richard Mulligan (Einstein), Roscoe Lee Browne (Francis), Sheryl Lee Ralph (Rita), Dom DeLuise (Fagin), Taurean Blacque (Roscoe), Carl Weintraub (Desoto), Robert Loggia (Sykes), Bette Midler (Georgette). Running time: 72 minutes.

An orphaned kitten falls in with a band of pickpocket dogs, but when he's adopted by a wealthy girl, the dogs' criminal boss hatches a kidnapping scheme. (Rated G.)

Touchstone releases: *Shoot to Kill; D.O.A.; Big Business; Who Framed Roger Rabbit; Cocktail; The Rescue; Heartbreak Hotel; The Good Mother; Ernest Saves Christmas; Beaches*

1989

Honey, I Shrunk the Kids

June release. Executive Producer: Thomas G. Smith. Producer: Penny Finkelman Cox. Coproducers: Brian Yuzna, Jon Landau. Director: Joe Johnston. Screenplay: Ed Naha, Tom Schulman. Story: Stuart Gordon, Brian Yuzna, Ed Naha. Cast: Rick Moranis (Wayne Szalinski), Matt Fewer (Big Russ Thompson), Marcia Strassman (Diane Szalinski), Kristine Sutherland (Mae Thompson), Thomas Brown (Little Russ Thompson), Jared Rushton (Ron Thompson), Amy O'Neill (Amy Szalinski), Robert Oliveri (Nick Szalinski). Running time: 93 minutes.

A screwball inventor's latest contraption shrinks his kids—and the neighbor kids as well—to microscopic size. (Rated PG.)

Cheetah

August release. Executive producer: Roy Edward Disney. Producer: Robert Halmi. Director: Jeff Blyth. Screenplay: Eric Tarloff, John Cotter, Griff Du Rhone. Based on the book *The Cheetahs* by Alan Caillou. Cast: Keith Coogan (Ted Johnson), Lucy Deakins (Susan Johnson), Collin Mothupi (Morogo), Timothy Landfield (Earl Johnson), Breon Gorman (Jean Johnson), Ka Vundla (Kipoin), Lydia Kigada (Lani), Kuldeep Bhakoo (Patel), Paul Onsongo (Abdullah). Running time: 83 minutes.

Two youngsters from California join their parents in Africa and raise an orphaned cheetah as a pet.

The Little Mermaid

November release. Producers: Howard Ashman, John Musker. Directors/Writers: John Musker, Ron Clements. Based on the fairy tale by Hans Christian Andersen. Directing Animators: Mark Henn, Glen Keane, Duncan Marjoribanks, Ruben Aquino, Andreas Deja, Matthew O'Callaghan. Songs: Howard Ashman, Alan Menken. Voice Cast: Jodi Benson (Ariel), Samuel E. Wright (Sebastian), Pat Carroll (Ursula), Kenneth Mars (Triton), Buddy Hackett (Scuttle), Jason Marin (Flounder), Rene Auberjonois (Louis), Christopher Daniel Barnes (Eric), Paddi Edwards (Flotsam & Jetsam), Edie McClurg (Carlotta), Will Ryan (Seahorse), Ben Wright (Grimsby). Running time: 82 minutes.

One of King Triton's mermaid daughters yearns to be human, and gets her wish by paying a terrible price to the undersea sorceress Ursula: She gives up her voice.

Academy Award winner for Best Original Score and Song ("Under the Sea")

Touchstone releases: *Three Fugitives; New York Stories; Disorganized Crime; Dead Poets Society; Turner & Hooch; An Innocent Man; Gross Anatomy; Blaze.*

1990

Ducktales—The Movie: Treasure of the Lost Lamp

August release. A Disney Movietoons presentation of a Walt Disney Animation (France) S.A. Production.

Producer/Director: Bob Hathcock. Coproducers: Jean-Pierre Quenet, Robert Taylor. Animation screenplay: Alan Burnett. Sequence Directors: Paul Brizzi, Gaetan Brizzi, Clive Pallant, Mattias Marcos Rodric, Vincent Woodcock. Music: David Newman. Voice Cast: Alan Young (Scrooge McDuck), Terence McGovern (Launchpad), Russi Taylor (Huey, Dewey, and Louie), Richard Libertini (Dijon), Christopher Lloyd (Merlock), June Foray (Mrs. Featherby), Chuck McCann (Duckworth), Joan Gerber (Mrs. Beakley), Rip Taylor (Genie). Running time: 74 minutes.

Scrooge and his nephews embark on an archeological search for a genie's lamp.

The Rescuers Down Under

November release. Producer: Thomas Schumacher. Directors: Hendel Butoy, Mike Gabriel. Animation screenplay: Jim Cox, Karey Kirkpatrick, Byron Simpson, Joe Ranft. Suggested by characters created by Margery Sharp. Supervising Animators: Glen Keane, Mark Henn, Russ Edmonds, David Cutler, Ruben A. Aquino, Nik Ranieri, Ed Gombert, Anthony De Rosa, Kathy Zielinski, Duncan Marjoribanks. Music: Bruce Broughton. Voice Cast: Bob Newhart (Bernard), Eva Gabor (Miss Bianca), John Candy (Wilbur), Tristan Rogers (Jake), Adam Ryen (Cody), George C. Scott (McLeach), Wayne Robson (Frank), Douglas Seale (Krebbs), Frank Welker (Joanna/additional special vocal effects), Bernard Fox (Chairmouse/Doctor), Peter Firth (Red), Billy Barty (Baitmouse), Russi Taylor (Nurse Mouse). Running time: 74 minutes.

Bernard and Bianca of the Rescue Aid Society are pressed into service to help an Australian boy in trouble.

Touchstone releases: *Stella* (co-released with the Samuel Goldwyn Co.); *Where the Heart Is; Pretty Woman; Ernest Goes to Jail; Spaced Invaders; Fire Birds; Dick Tracy; Betsy's Wedding; Mr. Destiny; Three Men and a Little Lady; Green Card.*

Hollywood Pictures releases: *Arachnophobia; Taking Care of Business.*

1991

White Fang

January release. Executive Producers: Mike Lobell, Andrew Bergman. Producer: Marykay Powell. Director: Randal Kleiser. Screenplay: Jeanne Rosenberg, Nick Thiel, David Fallon. Based on the novel by Jack London. Cast: Klaus Maria Brandauer (Alex Larson), Ethan Hawke (Jack Conroy), Seymour Cassel (Skunker), Susan Hogan (Belinda), James Remar (Beauty Smith), Bill Moseley (Luke), Clint B. Youngreen (Tinker), Pius Savage (Grey Beaver), Aaron Hotch (Little Beaver). Running time: 109 minutes.

Remake of the oft-filmed Jack London story, set in Alaska, about a young man who befriends a wolf-dog. (Rated PG.)

Shipwrecked

March release. A coproduction of Filmkameratene A/S and AB Svensk Filmindustri. Executive Producer: Nigel Wooll. Producer: John M. Jacobsen. Director: Nils Gaup. Screenplay: Nils Gaup, Bob Foss, Greg Dinner, Nick Thiel. Based on the book *Haakon Haakonsen* by O. V. Falck-Ytter. Running time: 93 minutes. Cast: Stian Smestad (Hakon Hakonsen), Gabriel Byrne (Merrick), Louisa Haigh (Mary), Trond Peter Stamso Munch (Jens), Bjorn Sundquist (Mr. Hakonsen), Eva Von Hanno (Mrs. Hakonsen), Kjell Stormoen (Captain Madsen).

A young man signs on as cabin boy for an unexpectedly adventurous voyage: first the ship is beset by storm, and then by pirates. (Rated PG.)

Wild Hearts Can't Be Broken

May release. Executive Producer: Oley Sassone. Producer: Matt Williams. Director: Steve Miner. Coproducer: Robin S. Clark. Screenplay: Matt Williams, Oley Sassone. Cast: Gabrielle Anwar (Sonora Webster), Michael Schoeffling (Al Carver), Cliff Robertson (Dr. W.F. Carver), Dylan Kussman (Clifford), Kathleen York (Marie), Frank Renzulli (Mr. Slater), Nancy Moore Atchison (Arnette). Running time: 89 minutes.

In the 1930s, a girl gains notoriety by riding a horse bareback as it dives from a platform into a pool of water. She's determined to continue her performances even after a tragic accident. Based on a true story.

The Rocketeer

June release. Executive producer: Larry Franco. Producers: Lawrence Gordon, Charles Gordon, Lloyd Levin. Director: Joe Johnston. Screenplay: Danny Bilson, Paul De Meo. Story: Danny Bilson, Paul De Meo, William Dear. Based on the graphic novel created by Dave Stevens. Cast: Bill Campbell (Cliff Secord), Jennifer Connelly (Jenny Blake), Alan Arkin (Peevy), Timothy Dalton (Neville Sinclair), Paul Sorvino (Eddie Valentine), Terry O'Quinn (Howard Hughes), Ed Lauter (Fitch), James Handy (Wooly), Tiny Ron (Lothar), Robert Guy Miranda (Spanish Johnny), John Lavachielli (Rusty), Jon Polito (Bigelow), Eddie Jones (Malcolm), William Sanderson (Skeets), Clint Howard (Monk). Running time: 108 minutes.

An aspiring aviator stumbles onto a rocket-pack that turns him into The Rocketeer; he then discovers that the rocket-pack is sought after by enemy agents. (Rated PG.)

Beauty and the Beast

November release. Executive Producer: Howard Ashman. Producer: Don Hahn. Directors: Gary Trousdale, Kirk Wise. Animation screenplay: Linda Woolverton. Story Supervisor: Roger Allers. Story: Brenda Chapman, Christopher Sanders, Burny Mattinson, Kevin Harkey, Brian Pimental, Bruce Woodside, Joe Ranft, Tom Ellery, Kelly Asbury, Robert Lence. Supervising Animators: James Baxter (Belle), Glen Keane (Beast), Andreas Deja (Gaston), Nik Ranieri (Lumiere), Will Finn (Cogsworth), Dave Pruiksma (Mrs. Potts and Chip), Ruben A. Aquino (Maurice), Chris Wahl (Le Fou), Russ Edmonds (Philippe), Larry White (Wolves), Tony Anselmo (Wardrobe). Songs: Howard Ashman, Alan Menken. Music: Alan Menken. Voice Cast: Robby Benson (Beast), Paige O'Hara (Belle), Richard White (Gaston), Angela Lansbury (Mrs. Potts), Jerry Orbach (Lumiere), David Ogden Stiers (Cogsworth), Bradley Michael Pierce (Chip), Jo Anne Worley (Wardrobe), Jesse Corti (LeFou), Rex Everhart (Maurice), Frank Welker (Footstool and special vocal effects). Running time: 84 minutes.

A retelling of the classic fable about a young woman who falls in love with a hideous creature because she learns to see the person underneath his harsh exterior.

Academy Award winner for Best Original Score and Song ("Beauty and the Beast").

Touchstone releases: *Scenes from a Mall; Oscar; What About Bob?; The Doctor; True Identity; Paradise; Deceived; Ernest Scared Stupid; Billy Bathgate; Father of the Bride.*

Hollywood Pictures releases: *Run; The Marrying Man; One Good Cop; V.I. Warshawski.*

1992

Newsies

April release. Producer: Michael Finnell. Director: Kenny Ortega. Screenplay: Bob Tzudiker, Noni White. Songs: Alan Menken, Jack Feldman. Music: J.A.C. Redford. Cast: Christian Bale (Jack Kelly/Francis Sullivan), Bill Pullman (Bryan Denton), Robert Duvall (Joseph Pulitzer), Ann-Margret (Medda Larkson), Michael Lerner (Weasel), Kevin Tighe (Snyder), Charles Cioffi (Seitz), David Moscow (David Jacobs), Luke Edwards (Les Jacobs), Max Casella (Racetrack), Aaron Lohr (Mush), Ele Keats (Sarah Jacobs), Jeffrey DeMunn (Mayer Jacobs), Deborra-Lee Furness (Esther Jacobs), Marc Lawrence (Kloppman). Running time: 121 minutes.

New York City newsboys band together to go on strike against their employers in 1899. (Rated PG.)

Honey, I Blew Up the Kid

July release. Executive Producers: Albert Band, Stuart Gordon. Producers: Dawn Steel, Edward S. Feldman. Coproducer: Dennis E. Jones. Director: Randal Kleiser. Screenplay: Thom Eberhardt, Peter Eibling, Garry Goodrow. Story: Garry Goodrow. Based on characters created by Stuart Gordon, Brian Yuzna, and Ed Naha. Cast: Rick Moranis (Wayne Szalinski), Marcia Strassman (Diane Szalinski), Robert Oliveri (Nick Szalinski), Daniel Shalikar, Joshua Shalikar (Adam Szalinski), Lloyd Bridges (Clifford Sterling), John Shea (Charles Henderickson), Keri Russell (Mandy Park), Ron Canada (Marshall Brooks), Amy O'Neill (Amy Szalinski), Gregory Sierra (Terence Wheeler), Julia Sweeney, Linda Carlson (Nosey

Neighbors), Ken Tobey (Smitty), Ed Feldman, Suzanne Kent (Las Vegas couple). Running time: 89 minutes.

This time, inventor Szalinski transforms his tiny toddler into a giant, who winds up stalking the streets of Las Vegas! (Rated PG.)

The Mighty Ducks

October release. Producers: Jordan Kerner, Jon Avnet. Coproducers: Lynn Morgan, Martin Huberty. Director: Stephen Herek. Screenplay: Steven Brill. Cast: Emilio Estevez (Gordon Bombay), Joss Ackland (Hans), Lane Smith (Coach Reilly), Heidi Kling (Casey), Josef Sommer (Gerald Ducksworth), Elden Ratliff (Fulton Reed), Shaun Weiss (Goldberg), M.C. Gainey (Lewis), Matt Doherty (Les Averman), Brandon Adams (Jesse Hall), J.D. Daniels (Peter), Aaron Schwartz (Dave Karp), Garette Ratliff Henson (Guy Germaine), Marguerite Moreau (Connie), Vincent A. Larusso (Adam Banks). Running time: 103 minutes.

Ordered to do community service, a self-centered lawyer is given the job of coaching a ragtag hockey team, but before long, he sees a chance to redeem himself as well as his band of misfits. (Rated PG.)

Aladdin

November release. Producers/Directors: John Musker, Ron Clements. Coproducers: Donald W. Ernst, Amy Pell. Screenplay: Ron Clements, John Musker, Ted Elliott, Terry Rossio. Story: Ed Gombert, Burny Mattinson, Roger Allers, Daan Jippes, Kevin Harkey, Sue Nichols, Francis Glebas, Darrell Rooney, Larry Leker, James Fujii, Kirk Hanson, Kevin Lima, Rebecca Rees, David S. Smith, Chris Sanders, Brian Pimental, Patrick A. Ventura. Supervising Animators: Glen Keane (Aladdin), Eric Goldberg (Genie), Mark Henn (Jasmine), Andreas Deja (Jafar), Duncan Marjoribanks (Abu), Randy Cartwright (Carpet), Will Finn (Iago), David Pruiksma (Sultan), Aaron Blaise (Rajah), Kathy Zielinski (Jafar as Beggar/Snake), T. Daniel Hofstedt (Gazeem/Achmed), Phil Young, Chris Wahl (Guards). Songs: Alan Menken, Howard Ashman, Tim Rice. Original score: Alan Menken. Voice Cast: Scott Weinger (Aladdin), Brad Kane (Aladdin's singing voice), Robin Williams (Genie), Linda Larkin (Princess Jasmine), Lea Salonga (Princess Jasmine's singing voice), Jonathan Freeman (Jafar), Frank Welker (Abu), Gilbert Gottfried (Iago), Douglas Seale (Sultan). Running time: 90 minutes.

A young, streetwise thief dreams of being a Prince worthy of Princess Jasmine, and gets his wish, thanks to an obliging Genie, but doesn't count on the schemes of the Sultan's evil wazir, Jafar.

Academy Award winner for Best Original Score and Song ("A Whole New World").

The Muppet Christmas Carol

December release. Executive producer: Frank Oz. Producers: Brian Henson, Martin G. Baker. Director: Brian Henson. Screenplay/Coproducer: Jerry Juhl.

Songs: Paul Williams. Music: Miles Goodman. Cast: Michael Caine (Ebenezer Scrooge), Dave Goelz (The Great Gonzo/Robert Marley/Bunsen Honeydew/ Betina Cratchit), Steve Whitmire (Rizzo the Rat/Bean Bunny/Kermit the Frog/Beaker/Belinda Cratchit), Jerry Nelson (Tiny Tim Cratchit/Jacob Marley/Ma Bear), Frank Oz (Miss Piggy/Fozzie Bear/Sam Eagle/ Animal), David Rudman (Peter Cratchit/Old Joe/ Swedish Chef), Donald Austen, Jerry Nelson (Ghost of Christmas Present), Donald Austen, Rob Tygner (Ghost of Christmas Yet to Come), Karen Prell, Rob Tygner, William Todd Jones, Jessica Fox (Ghost of Christmas Past), Steven Mackintosh (Fred), Meredith Braun (Belle), Robin Weaver (Clara). Running time: 86 minutes. Charles Dickens' classic Christmas tale is retold by The Muppets.

Touchstone releases: *Noises Off; Sister Act; 3 Ninjas; The Gun in Betty Lou's Handbag; Crossing the Bridge; Captain Ron.*

Hollywood Pictures releases: *The Hand That Rocks the Cradle; Medicine Man; Blame It on the Bellboy; Straight Talk; Passed Away; Encino Man; A Stranger Among Us; Sarafina!; Consenting Adults; The Distinguished Gentleman.*

1993

Homeward Bound: The Incredible Journey

February release. Executive producers: Donald W. Ernst, Kirk Wise. Producers: Franklin R. Levy, Jeffrey Chernov. Coproducer: Mack Bing. Director: Duwayne Dunham. Screenplay: Caroline Thompson, Linda Woolverton. Based on *The Incredible Journey* by Sheila Burnford. Cast: Ben; voice of Don Ameche (Shadow), Rattler; voice of Michael J. Fox (Chance), Tiki; voice of Sally Field (Sassy), Robert Hays (Bob), Kim Greist (Laura), Jean Smart (Kate). Running time: 84 minutes.

Three pets—two dogs and a cat—separated from their family embark on an amazing odyssey to rejoin them. A remake of the 1963 Disney movie *The Incredible Journey.*

A Far Off Place

March release. A Walt Disney Pictures and Amblin Entertainment presentation. Executive Producers: Kathleen Kennedy, Frank Marshall, Gerald R. Molen. Producers: Eva Monley, Elaine Sperber. Coproducer: William W. Wilson III. Director: Mikael Salomon. Screenplay: Robert Caswell, Jonathan Hensleigh, Sally Robinson. Based on the books *A Story Like the Wind* and *A Far Off Place* by Laurens van der Post. Cast: Reese Witherspoon (Nonnie Parker), Ethan Randall (Harry Winslow), Jack Thompson (John Ricketts), Sarel Bok (Xhabbo), Maximilian Schell (Col. Mopani Theron), Robert Burke (Paul Parker), Patricia Kalember (Elizabeth Parker), Daniel Gerroll (John Winslow). Running time: 107 minutes.

Two teenagers are forced to make their way across the African desert, with the help of a young bushman, after their parents are murdered by poachers—who follow in hot pursuit. (Rated PG.)

The Adventures of Huck Finn

April release. Executive producers: Barry Bernardi, Steve White. Producer: Laurence Mark. Coproducer: John Baldecchi. Director/Writer: Stephen Sommers. Based on the novel by Mark Twain. Cast: Elijah Wood (Huck), Courtney B. Vance (Jim), Robbie Coltrane (The Duke), Jason Robards (The King), Ron Perlman (Pap Finn), Dana Ivey (Widow Douglas), Anne Heche (Mary Jane Wilks), James Gammon (Deputy Hines), Paxton Whitehead (Harvey Wilks), Tom Aldredge (Dr. Robinson), Laura Bundy (Susan Wilks). Running time: 108 minutes.

A new version of the Mark Twain classic about an adventure-loving boy who fakes his own death, and travels along the Mississippi River with a runaway slave. (Rated PG.)

Hocus Pocus

July release. Executive producer: Ralph Winter. Producers: David Kirschner, Steven Haft. Director: Kenny Ortega. Screenwriters: Mick Garris, Neal Cuthbert. Story: David Kirschner, Mick Garris. Cast: Bette Midler (Winifred), Sarah Jessica Parker (Sarah), Kathy Najimy (Mary), Omri Katz (Max), Thora Birch (Dani), Vinessa Shaw (Allison), Amanda Shepherd (Emily), Larry Bagby III (Ernie "Ice"), Tobias Jelinek (Jay), Kathleen Freeman (Schoolteacher). Running time: 96 minutes.

Three witches burned at the stake in the 17th century are conjured up in modern-day Salem, Massachusetts, for Halloween. (Rated PG.)

Cool Runnings

October release. Producer: Dawn Steel. Director: Jon Turteltaub. Screenplay: Lynn Siefert, Tommy Swerdlow, Michael Goldberg. Story: Lynn Siefert, Michael Ritchie. Cast: John Candy (Irv), Leon (Derice Bannock), Doug E. Doug (Sanka Coffie), Rawle D. Lewis (Junior Bevil), Raymond J. Barry (Kurt Hemphill). Running time: 98 minutes.

A young man desperate to enter the Olympics decides to form the first Jamaican bobsled team, and convinces a washed-up coach to help him fulfill his dream. Based on a true story. (Rated PG.)

The Three Musketeers

November release. A presentation of Walt Disney Pictures in association with Caravan Pictures. Executive Producers: Jordan Kerner, Jon Avnet. Producers: Joe Roth, Roger Birnbaum. Director: Stephen Herek. Screenplay: David Loughery. Based on the novel by Alexandre Dumas. Cast: Charlie Sheen (Aramis), Kiefer Sutherland (Athos), Chris O'Donnell (D'Artagnan), Oliver Platt (Porthos), Tim Curry (Cardinal Richelieu), Rebecca DeMornay (Milady), Gabrielle Anwar (Queen Anne), Michael Wincott (Rochefort), Paul McGann (Girard), Julie Delpy (Constance), Hugh O'Conor (King Louis). Running time: 105 minutes.

A remake of the Dumas classic about a young,

would-be freedom fighter in 16th-century France who allies himself with three of the King's musketeers to combat the schemes of the evil Cardinal Richelieu. (Rated PG.)

Touchstone releases: *Alive* (coreleased with Paramount); *The Cemetery Club; Indian Summer; Life with Mikey; What's Love Got to Do with It; Another Stakeout; My Boyfriend's Back; The Program; Tim Burton's The Nightmare Before Christmas; Sister Act 2: Back in the Habit*

Hollywood Pictures releases: *Aspen Extreme; Swing Kids; Born Yesterday; Bound by Honor; Super Mario Bros.; Guilty as Sin; Son-in-Law; Father Hood; The Joy Luck Club; Money for Nothing; Tombstone*

1994

Iron Will

January release. Producers: Patrick Palmer, Robert Schwartz. Director: Charles Haid. Screenplay: John Michael Hayes, Djordje Milicevic, Jeff Arch. Cast: Mackenzie Astin (Will Stoneman), Kevin Spacey (Harry Kingsley), David Ogden Stiers (J.P. Harper), August Schellenberg (Ned Dodd), Brian Cox (Angus McTeague), George Gerdes (Borg Guillarson), John Terry (Jack Stoneman). Running time: 109 minutes.

A young man enters a grueling 522-mile dogsled race, from Winnipeg to St. Paul, bucking the odds to win, with a cynical newspaperman championing his cause. (Rated PG.)

Blank Check

February release. Executive Producers: Hilary Wayne, Blake Snyder. Producers: Craig Baumgarten, Gary Adelson. Director: Rupert Wainwright. Screenplay: Blake Snyder, Colby Carr. Cast: Brian Bonsall (Preston Waters), Karen Duffy (Shay Stanley), Miguel Ferrer (Quigley), James Rebhorn (Fred Waters), Tone Loc (Juice), Jayne Atkinson (Sandra Waters), Rick Ducommun (Henry), Debbie Allen (Yvonne), Chris Demetral (Damian Waters), Michael Faustino (Ralph Waters), Alex Zuckerman (Butch), Michael Lerner (Biderman). Running time: 93 minutes.

A beleaguered eleven-year-old boy, who feels the need for money and independence from his family, is handed a half-filled-out check by a criminal on the lam who's just collided with his bike. The boy fills in the check for exactly one million dollars, and has a ball—until the criminal discovers what's happened. (Rated PG.)

D2: The Mighty Ducks

March release. Executive Producer: Doug Claybourne. Producers: Jordan Kerner, Jon Avnet. Coproducers: Steven Brill, Salli Newman. Director: Sam Weisman. Screenplay: Steven Brill. Cast: Emilio Estevez (Gordon Bombay), Kathryn Erbe (Michelle Mackahy), Michael Tucker (Tibbles), Jan Rubes (Jan), Carsten Norgaard (Wolf), Maria Ellingsen (Maria), Joshua Jackson (Charlie), Elden Ryan Ratliff (Fulton),

Shaun Weiss (Goldberg), Matt Doherty (Averman), Vincent A. Larusso (Banks), Colombe Jacobsen (Julie), Aaron Lohr (Portman), Ty O'Neal (Russ), Kenan Thompson (Russ), Justin Wong (Ken), and as themselves, Wayne Gretzky, Kareem Abdul-Jabbar, Cam Neely, Chris Chelios, Luc Robitaille, Greg Louganis, Kristi Yamaguchi. Running time: 107 minutes.

His pro hockey career on ice because of an injury, Gordon Bombay is persuaded to reunite the Mighty Ducks in an expanded version as Team U.S.A., to play in the Junior Goodwill Games. (Rated PG.)

White Fang 2: Myth of the White Wolf

April release. Producer: Preston Fischer. Coproducers: Justis Greene, David Fallon. Director: Ken Olin. Screenplay: David Fallon. Cast: Scott Bairstow (Henry Casey), Charmaine Craig (Lily Joseph), Al Harrington (Moses Joseph), Anthony Michael Ruivivar (Peter), Victoria Racimo (Katrin), Alfred Molina (Rev. Leland Drury), Paul Coeur (Adam John Hale), Geoffrey Lewis (Heath), Matthew Cowles (Halverson), Woodrow W. Morrison (Bad Dog), Reynold Russ (Leon), Ethan Hawke (Jack Conroy). Running time: 106 minutes.

White Fang's new master nearly drowns, but is saved by a Haida Indian princess who takes him in—believing he is the spirit of a wolf—and enlists his help in finding caribou to feed her starving tribe. (Rated PG.)

The Lion King

June release. Executive Producers: Thomas Schumacher, Sarah McArthur. Producer: Don Hahn. Directors: Roger Allers, Rob Minkoff. Screenplay: Irene Mecchi, Jonathan Roberts, Linda Woolverton. Story: Brenda Chapman, Burny Mattinson, Barry Johnson, Thom Enriquez, Gary Trousdale, Kevin Harkey, Chris Sanders, Larry Leker, Rick Maki, Francis Glebas, Lorna Cook, Andy Gaskill, Jim Capobianco, Jorgen Klubien, Tom Sito, Joe Ranft, Ed Gombert, Mark Kausler. Supervising animators: Mark Henn (Young Simba), Ruben Aquino (Adult Simba), Tony Fucile (Mufasa), Andreas Deja (Scar), Anthony Derosa (Adult Nala), Aaron Blaise (Young Nala), Tony Bancroft (Pumbaa), Michael Surrey (Timon), James Baxter (Rafiki), Ellen Woodbury (Zazu), Russ Edmonds (Sarabi), David Burgess, Alex Kupershmidt (Hyenas). Music score and supervision: Hans Zimmer. Songs: Tim Rice, Elton John. Voice Cast: Jonathan Taylor Thomas (Young Simba), Matthew Broderick (Adult Simba), James Earl Jones (Mufasa), Jeremy Irons (Scar), Moira Kelly (Adult Nala), Niketa Calame (Young Nala), Ernie Sabella (Pumbaa), Nathan Lane (Timon), Robert Guillaume (Rafiki), Rowan Atkinson (Zazu), Madge Sinclair (Sarabi), Whoopi Goldberg (Shenzi), Cheech Marin (Banzai), Jim Cummings (Ed), Frank Welker (additional voices). Running time: 88 minutes.

A young cub is made to believe he has caused the death of his father, and flees to another land; later, as a grownup, he comes to realize that his father's spirit lives on inside him, and he must return to his rightful place.

Academy Award winner for Best Original Score and Song ("Can You Feel the Love Tonight").

Angels in the Outfield

July release. A Walt Disney Pictures presentation in association with Caravan Pictures. Executive Producer: Gary Stutman. Producers: Irby Smith, Joe Roth, Roger Birnbaum. Director: William Dear. Screenplay: Dorothy Kingsley, George Wells, Holly Goldberg Sloan. Cast: Danny Glover (George Knox), Tony Danza (Mel Clark), Brenda Fricker (Maggie Nelson), Christopher Lloyd (Al the Angel), Ben Johnson (Hank Murphy), Jay O. Sanders (Wanch Wilder), Joseph Gordon-Levitt (Roger), Milton Davis, Jr. (J.P.), Taylor Negron (David Montagne). Running time: 103 minutes.

A foster child whose dad has promised he'll reclaim him if the California Angels win the pennant prays for exactly that to happen—and may get his wish, thanks to an obliging angel. The team's crusty manager, however, is dubious about the whole thing. A remake of the 1951 MGM movie of the same name. (Rated PG.)

Squanto: A Warrior's Tale

October release. Executive Producer: Don Carmody. Producer: Kathryn F. Galan. Director: Xavier Koller. Screenplay: Darlene Craviotto. Cast: Adam Beach (Squanto), Mandy Patinkin (Brother Daniel), Michael Gambon (Sir George), Nathaniel Parker (Thomas Dormer), Eric Schweig (Epenow), Donal Donnelly (Brother Paul), Stuart Pankin (Brother Timothy), Alex Norton (Harding), Irene Bedard (Nakooma). Running time: 102 minutes.

In the 17th century, a young Native American is kidnapped and brought to England, where he escapes from his sailor/captors and hides out with a band of monks. (Rated PG.)

The Santa Clause

November release. Executive Producers: Richard Baker, Rick Messina, James Miller. Producers: Brian Reilly, Jeffrey Silver, Robert Newmyer. Coproducers: William Wilson III, Caroline Baron. Director: John Pasquin. Screenplay: Leo Benvenuti, Steve Rudnick. Cast: Tim Allen (Scott Calvin), Judge Reinhold (Dr. Neal Miller), Wendy Crewson (Laura Calvin), Eric Lloyd (Charlie Calvin), David Krumholtz (Bernard), Peter Boyle (Mr. Whittle), Larry Brandenburg (Detective Nunzio), Mary Gross (Ms. Daniels), Paige Tamada (Judy). Running time: 97 minutes.

A selfish, divorced father accidentally scares Santa Claus off his roof and, when he dons the fat man's suit, turns into Santa himself—first on the outside, and then on the inside as well. (Rated PG.)

Rudyard Kipling's The Jungle Book

December release. Executive Producers: Sharad Patel, Mark Damon, Lawrence Mortorff. Producers: Edward S. Feldman, Raju Patel. Director: Stephen Sommers. Screenplay: Stephen Sommers, Ronald Yanover, Mark D. Geldman. Inspired by Rudyard Kipling's The Jungle Book. Cast: Jason Scott Lee (Mowgli), Cary Elwes (Boone), Lena Headey (Kitty), Sam Neill (Col. Brydon), John Cleese (Dr. Plumford), Jason Flemyng (Wilkins), Stefan Kalipha (Buldeo), Ron Donachie (Harley), Anirudh Agrawal (Tabaqui), Faran Tahir (Nathoo), Sean Naegeli (Mowgli age 5), Joanna Wolff (Kitty age 5), Gerry Crampton (Sergeant Major). Running time: 111 minutes.

Separated from his father at the age of five, Mowgli is raised in the jungle, but an attempt to "recivilize" him in adulthood is doomed—especially when his rival for the affections of childhood sweetheart Kitty turns out to be an unmitigated cad. Filmed before as a live-action adventure in 1942, this material was also adapted as an animated feature by Disney in 1967. (Rated PG.)

Touchstone releases: Cabin Boy; My Father the Hero; The Ref; The Inkwell; When a Man Loves a Woman; Renaissance Man; I Love Trouble (with Caravan Pictures); It's Pat; A Simple Twist of Fate; Ed Wood

Hollywood Pictures releases: The Air Up There; Angie (with Caravan Pictures); Holy Matrimony; In the Army Now; Color of Night; Camp Nowhere; Quiz Show; Terminal Velocity; Robert A. Heinlein's The Puppet Masters; A Low Down Dirty Shame (with Caravan Pictures).

5·Continuing the Story

IN DECEMBER OF 1994, AS A CURTAIN-RAISER TO THE STUDIO'S SMASH-HIT LIVE-ACTION comedy *The Santa Clause,* Disney gave audiences its first peek at its major animated release of 1995, *Pocahontas*: the complete production number "Colors of the Wind." With its soaring emotions, impassioned rendition (by Broadway singer Judy Kuhn), and colorful treatment, this presentation augured well for the newest full-length animated feature.

The completed film couldn't live up to this impressive preview. *Pocahontas* is a good movie, but not a great one, because the Disney team could never eliminate its fundamental story problems, chief among them the tragic romance at its center between Pocahontas and John Smith.

The film also bears the weight of "seriousness." Pocahontas is a passionate heroine, and certainly the most athletic female ever depicted in a Disney animated film, but ultimately she is two-dimensional. There is little for young audiences to cling to except for her belief in the land, and her willingness to disobey her father. Similarly, John Smith has no distinct personality (despite being voiced by popular movie star Mel Gibson). The most flamboyant character in the film is the villain, greedy Governor Ratcliffe, who turns out to be a stock cardboard "bad guy" designed in old-fashioned, exaggerated style—and who is rewarded with not one but two songs on the soundtrack!

At some point in production the necessity for comic relief became obvious. It was veteran Joe Grant who developed much of the "business" for mute sidekick characters Meeko (a raccoon) and Flit (a humming-bird). His instincts proved to be as sharp as ever when the gags involving these characters, sprinkled through the film for comic punctuation, provided one solid laugh after another.

Pocahontas pulls together reasonably well, because the story does have momentum, and the two showcase songs—"Colors of the Wind" and "Just Around the Riverbend"—are so strong. But by wearing its political correctness on its sleeve (including the casting of Native American actors to voice the central Indian characters), Pocahontas may have put off some potential viewers who were looking for something less pro-social and more fun.

A Goofy Movie (1995) was produced mostly by a studio just outside of Paris now known as Walt Disney Animation France, with contributions

from an even farther outpost in Australia. Seen in-house as a kind of
research-and-development project for these facilities, it didn't receive
the fanfare one associates with a major Disney release. Besides, it was
"only" a Goofy tale, not a major film with new characters. To everyone's
surprise, the film became a solid hit.

This really should have come as no surprise: what *A Goofy Movie*
managed to do was to take a beloved character of the past and give him
a brand-new spin, without sacrificing the qualities that made him so
endearing in the first place. The story pits ol' Goof against his very contemporary son, Max, who regards his clumsy father as an embarrassment.
In the course of a father–son vacation, they grow closer, and in a climax
set (of all places) at a rock concert, Dad even manages to make his son
proud of him. With very likable songs (by Tom Snow and Jack Feldman)
that advance the story and express the characters' feelings, *A Goofy Movie*
did what many more ambitious studio features were having trouble
achieving in the 1990s: it scored a bull's-eye.

This was the second of what might be called second-tier animated
features for the studio, preceded by the *Duck Tales* movie (officially
released under the short-lived Movietoons umbrella), then followed in
1999 by *Doug's 1st Movie* (based on the popular animated TV series) and
in 2000 by *The Tigger Movie*. The *Doug* feature was in fact intended for
home-video release only, until the success of another television-to-
theater transfer, *The Rugrats Movie* (Paramount, 1998), which fared so
well at the box office. With its principal animation team busy on a nonstop series of major-league features, the Disney hierarchy assigned its
direct-to-video sequels (*Beauty and the Beast, The Lion King, Aladdin,
Pocahontas*, etc.) to its television arm, and to "farm-team" studios and
animators who could maintain an acceptable Disney standard.

The next animated feature on the Disney slate was in some ways the
most daring, in other ways the most foolhardy choice the studio ever

Frollo, a villain with no redeeming qualities whatsoever, warns a gullible Quasimodo about the perils of the outside world in *The Hunchback of Notre Dame.* © *Walt Disney Enterprises, Inc.*

made: a musical interpretation of Victor Hugo's *The Hunchback of Notre Dame.*

On the face of it, this seemed to some observers a patently absurd choice: who, after all, was going to be able to warm to a character like Quasimodo? (Who would want to own a plush toy of him, for that matter?) Apparently that debate was conducted within the hallways of Disney as well, and not everyone agreed (before or after production) that it was a wise choice.

Given that, *The Hunchback of Notre Dame* turned out to be one of the boldest, most visually arresting films Disney has ever made. Its score, by Stephen Schwartz and Alan Menken, is without question the most dramatic in the studio's history, and its underscore (also by Menken) one of the richest.

As it happens, the filmmakers turned to Schwartz and Menken more than once for ideas that would solve storytelling problems. A particular challenge was the film's opening.

Schwartz later explained, "What we began to realize was, before we could start to tell our story, there was an enormous amount of information the audience had to have: who Quasimodo was, how did he get to be in the bell tower, who was this guy Frollo, what was their relationship, how did the relationship get started? We needed to know this before we could unfold the story.

"Also," added Menken, "We needed to set up this character Clopin as a narrator, somebody like Jiminy Cricket or Sebastian, who is in the story and yet could step out of the story and sing to us in a light manner, and then shift gears right away to something much heavier."

"The number had to do a lot of story work," Schwartz concluded, "and at the same time, it had to define the mood of the film."

The solution came unexpectedly. The music team was recording the rousing "Topsy-Turvy Day" number with performer Paul Kandel and Peter Schneider, then the president of Walt Disney Feature Animation, was there. When he heard Kandel's exuberant rendition of the piece, he said, "That guy's great; we should use him somewhere else. You should open the film with him." The composer and lyricist, who had just begun to tackle their ambitious opening number, "The Bells of Notre Dame," realized they had their solution to a variety of problems with that one remark.

There are shots in *Hunchback* that have never been seen before in the medium of animation—incredible, sweeping views from the towers and parapets of Notre Dame Cathedral as Quasimodo leaps about, with enormous crowds below. The staging and lighting of these scenes is often breathtaking.

The characters are also well developed. Quasimodo's signature song, "Out There," sums up his feelings in a way any viewer, young or old, can understand. His relationship with the gypsy dancer Esmeralda is well thought out and played. The character of Frollo stands out as one of the most demonic in Disney history—a man with apparently no redeeming qualities whatsoever. His musical soliloquy "Hellfire" is unique in the Disney cavalcade, for surely no Disney character before or since has ever fought his own suppressed feelings of sexuality—in song!

Oddly enough, the weakest aspect of *Hunchback* is the comic relief. Surely the idea of turning three gargoyles into Quasimodo's only friends was intended to lighten the weight of the story; in fact, the comedy seems forced and astonishingly out of place. Perhaps if the studio had trusted its ability to convey a dramatic story it would have been better off.

Roald Dahl has long been a favorite author of young readers because of his deft handling of dark and offbeat material. More than one filmmaker has stumbled in adapting his work for the screen, however, because what one will accept on the printed page doesn't always correspond to what one is willing to embrace in a movie. The more fantastic and bizarre elements of Dahl's books have proved to be hurdles in such live-action films as *The Witches* and *Matilda*.

James and the Giant Peach must be counted (along with *Willy Wonka and the Chocolate Factory*) among the successes, although its dark elements may have kept it from reaching as broad an audience as it deserved.

Miss Spider tucks James in for the night in *James and the Giant Peach*. This shot shows the extraordinary detail of every scene in the stop-motion animated film. © *The Walt Disney Company.*

Directed by Henry Selick, the unsung stop-motion animation master who also piloted *The Nightmare Before Christmas*, James opens and closes in live action, and then segues to a magical animated world as the title character crawls inside a giant peach in his backyard and discovers its colorful inhabitants: a grasshopper, a centipede, an earthworm, a ladybug, a glowworm, and a spider with a charming Russian accent.

Together they embark on a voyage to New York City, where James hopes to find his parents, who disappeared one day at the beach. (This eerie live-action sequence early in the film is certainly one of the more difficult passages of the film for younger viewers.)

James and the Giant Peach offers the viewer a cornucopia of dazzling images, from the inventive design of its characters to its unique overall look. It also benefits from excellent vocal performances, and a wonderful score by Randy Newman that suits the movie perfectly.

Most of all, it's a celebration of whimsy, which is a rare and wonderful thing.

In the live-action arena the studio's output of the mid-1990s seems to divide itself among three distinct types of movies: modern twists on classic stories, sequels, and remakes. *Tall Tale* (1995) offered a revisionist look at three folk heroes: Pecos Bill and Paul Bunyan, whose exploits had been covered in cartoon form by Disney years before, and John Henry, but this ambitious film smothered their larger-than-life feats in an unexpected fog of melancholy. *A Kid in King Arthur's Court* (1995), acquired but not produced by the studio, fared somewhat better in grafting a modern-day kid into the ancient world of King Arthur (with future star Kate Winslet as Princess Sarah). *Muppet Treasure Island* (1996) cast the Jim Henson crew in Robert Louis Stevenson's tale with results that weren't on a par with the earlier *Christmas Carol*, but still provided a sense of fun. *Homeward Bound II: Lost in San Francisco* (1996) and *D3: The Mighty Ducks* (1996) wrung entertainment value out of tried-and-true formulas, though in the case of the Ducks it was fairly obvious that the well had run dry.

Remakes of well-remembered Disney movies made for a mixed bag. *101 Dalmatians* was originally conceived as an animated film, and made use of the whimsy and unreality that only a cartoon could offer. Transforming it to a live-action film in 1996 seemed to be missing the point, although one could scarcely find a more charming couple than Jeff Daniels and Joely Richardson to play Roger and Anita, or a more skilled actress than Glenn Close to embody the living caricature that was Cruella. What the film lacked most notably was individual personalities for the dogs, and the crucial twist of the animal world taking matters into its own hands (with the Twilight Bark, one of the most memorable aspects of the original story). More than one reviewer remarked that it might have been better if the live-action animals had been given voices and personalities, as in the recent smash hit *Babe*. Instead, the original script of *101 Dalmatians* was made over in the mode of *Home Alone* by that film's prolific screenwriter-producer John Hughes, with an overemphasis on crude and humiliating slapstick indignities befalling its villains. Still, *101 Dalmatians* was a box-office success and prompted the studio to hire Glenn Close to star in a sequel, *102 Dalmatians*, released in the fall of 2000.

Flubber (1997), based on *The Absent-Minded Professor*, was another result of wrongheaded thinking. On the surface of it, casting Robin Williams as the addle-brained prof might seem inspired; after all, there's nothing this gifted performer can't do. But in the 1961 film, the professor himself *isn't funny* ; it's the people around him who are, especially when they get caught up in his high-flying invention. Consequently, *Flubber* is a discouragingly unfunny movie, with Williams acting subdued and the supporting cast crying out for oversized personalities to compare with Keenan Wynn and others from the original movie. The computer-animated Weebo, Professor Brainard's lively assistant, was a nice addition (voiced, incidentally, by *The Little Mermaid*'s Jodi Benson), but the little flubber figures who came to life seemed to have more personality in the movie's preview trailer than in the finished film. (One nice touch for moviegoers with a memory: seeing a still beautiful Nancy Olson, the original film's leading lady, in a cameo role as secretary to an automobile magnate.)

Mr. Magoo (1997) was based on the character introduced in the late 1940s by the innovative UPA cartoon studio, which was staffed almost entirely with ex-Disney artists. In their spare and stylized world, they stumbled (pun intended) onto the unexpectedly endearing character of a nearsighted old coot named Magoo, and found for him the ideal voice in comic actor Jim Backus. Sue and Terry Shakespeare animated an entertaining and faithfully rendered title sequence for the 1997 live-action feature Disney produced, but making Magoo come to life as a human being—in the person of always-game Leslie Nielsen—proved to be another fundamental mistake. Without a genuinely funny script, this already-limited character couldn't carry a movie.

That Darn Cat! (1997), a family hit in 1965, was retooled as a minor action-comedy for two promising stars: Doug E. Doug, who registered so well as one of the Jamaican bobsled team in *Cool Runnings*, and the gifted Christina Ricci, who at another time might have been groomed as a full-fledged Disney star. After her impressive showing as the deadpan Wednesday in *The Addams Family*, her career took a different turn. Everyone agreed these two performers deserved better than the heavy-handed and desultory remake that was *That Darn Cat!*

George of the Jungle (1997), inspired by Jay Ward's TV cartoon series of the 1960s, gave the studio a solid box-office hit, not to mention a terrific title song, and illustrated how vital good casting can be. Brendan Fraser was utterly believable as the dim-witted but good-hearted jungle king, and his sincerity carried the film along almost single-handedly. (The lumbering script couldn't even muster a few funny lines for John Cleese to utter as George's best friend Ape. More than one viewer could say with assurance that there were more laughs in one of Jay Ward's TV segments than in this entire feature.)

The studio acquired another property from a less obvious source when it bought the rights to a huge box-office hit in France called *Un Indien dans la Ville*. Like *George of the Jungle*, it dealt with a jungle native being brought to America, in this case a little boy. For the first time, however, the company released the French film itself, retitled *Little Indian, Big City*. But the Disney target audience wasn't ready to see a dubbed French movie with unrecognizable stars.

Disney fared better when the American version of the movie came out as *Jungle 2 Jungle*, starring Tim Allen.

Here was a film that could appeal to adults as well as kids with an entertaining mix of comedy, adventure, romance (of the puppy-love variety), and even suspense. Allen plays a hard-driven commodities trader who travels to Africa to finalize his divorce from JoBeth Williams, who works as a doctor in a remote jungle village. She then reveals to him that they have a son who has been raised as a member of the local tribe. He agrees to bring the boy back to New York City for a visit, and havoc ensues as the youngster encounters "civilization" for the first time. With a fine supporting cast led by Martin Short, as Allen's partner, teenaged Leelee Sobieski, as the boy's first love interest, and David Ogden Stiers, as a Russian bad guy, *Jungle 2 Jungle* virtually defines modern family entertainment.

The studio scored again by allowing the husband-and-wife team of Charles Shyer and Nancy Myers (who'd already engineered the slick, entertaining remake of the vintage Hollywood hit *Father of the Bride* and

Raised in the Amazon, Mimi-Siku (Sam Huntington) knows no fear—which is more than can be said for his father (Tim Allen) in *Jungle 2 Jungle*. © *Disney Enterprises, Inc.*

its sequel, *Father of the Bride Part II*) to tackle the well-remembered Hayley Mills comedy of 1961, *The Parent Trap*.

Would it really be possible for modern-day Hollywood filmmakers to recapture the charm—as well as the sunny outlook—of the original movie? Could they possibly find a young actress as engaging as Hayley Mills? And would the story still work in the context of a much more cynical time, the 1990s?

The happy answer was yes on all counts. With Myers making her directing debut, and cowriting the screenplay with then-husband Shyer (following David Swift's original), the film's artistic parents, who were unabashed fans of the 1961 movie, managed to retain its appeal while contemporizing it in perfectly natural ways. Newcomer Lindsay Lohan was a real find, completely up to the challenge of playing American-

Twin sisters Hallie (left) and Annie (right) stir up mischief at summer camp in the delightful remake of *JThe Parent Trap.* both sisters are played by Lindsay Lohan. © *Disney Enterprises, Inc.*

raised Hallie and British-reared Annie, who somehow as twins have never met until they chance to attend the same summer camp. With Dennis Quaid and Natasha Richardson as the estranged parents, and a fine supporting cast, the new *Parent Trap* can stand proudly on its own as a Disney film, without obliterating the memory of its forerunner. (There's even a cameo appearance by Joanna Barnes, who played the snooty woman vying for the father's attention in 1961—now playing the mother of that same character!)

One studio original achieved this same high level of entertainment: *First Kid*, a very likable story about a bumbling but good-hearted secret service agent (Sinbad) assigned to the troublesome adolescent son (Brock Pierce) of the president of the United States. With heart, humor, and even a dose of slapstick, this film found a ready audience, although a minor subplot about a disgruntled ex-agent and an incident in which a gun is fired might have given pause to some parents.

This more than ever points out the dilemma in making contemporary, relevant entertainment for modern families without seeming to be mired in a make-believe past. Walt Disney never shied away from dramatic conflict in his storytelling; it would be unrealistic to think that one could make movies today that depict nothing but sweetness and light in order to earn the Disney imprimatur.

The Disney management team of the late 1990s made no secret of the fact that they had reservations about the seriousness of some recent animated films—especially *Pocahontas* and *Hunchback*, which were launched under the aegis of departed studio executive Jeffrey Katzenberg. It was hoped that 1997's *Hercules* would put things back on track—and reestablish a bond with audiences.

While *Hercules* wasn't the box-office megahit Disney had hoped for,

The characters in *Hercules* look like no others in Disney history, thanks to the distinctive designs of noted British cartoonist and designer Gerald Scarfe. Pictured here are Hades and Hercules. © 1997 *Disney Enterprises, Inc.*

it certainly gave moviegoers a healthy dose of pure entertainment—and quite possibly, introduced some youngsters to the rudiments of Greek mythology, from Zeus all the way to a chorus of singing Muses. The story has the infant Hercules being snatched away from Mount Olympus, and drained of almost all his powers by the jealous Hades, ruler of the underworld. Hercules must prove himself a hero in order to ascend to Olympus once more.

Some critics felt that *Hercules* was too hip and self-aware (even making fun of character merchandising) to engender warm feelings toward its characters, and this may be true to some extent, but it's also a funny, original, and entertaining film. That originality even extends to the overall look of the picture. On *Aladdin*, animator Eric Goldberg referred to the work of caricaturist Al Hirschfeld; this time, *Aladdin*'s writing and directing team of John Musker and Ron Clements went one step further.

Musker explained, "We felt that the story material actually demanded a different look; we were influenced by Greek vases and pottery, and the esthetic that was there. [In] the Disney films, the most important thing is story and character, and the actual look is more pliable, [so] we can do different things. In this particular film we commissioned Gerald Scarfe, the British caricaturist, to do some different character designs, something we had never done, [going] outside the studio. We wanted to create a unique look for this film, and his approach, bigger than life and very extreme, seemed to suit a story that went to such extremes . . . the underworld and Olympus and all points in between."

Scarfe animated his first film in the mid-1970s, an irreverent short-subject diary of a visit to the United States called *The Long, Drawn-Out Trip*, which, ironically, didn't get wide distribution because it ended with a caricature of Mickey Mouse smoking marijuana! He later collaborated on *Pink Floyd: The Wall*, contributing striking animation and set design.

For this assignment, he gave the characters a striking, "non-Disney" look, which matched the offbeat approach taken by the writing team. Hercules is not a traditional Disney hero, since his problem is that he's lost most of his powers. Meg (short for Megara) is the most unusual heroine ever to appear in an animated Disney feature: she's wry and smart-alecky, never at a loss for a put-down of Hercules. Musker and Clements patterned her after Barbara Stanwyck's character in the brilliant Preston Sturges comedy *The Lady Eve*; voice artist Susan Egan perfectly captured that attitude in her performance.

Hades was written for an American actor, since the filmmakers felt that Disney had relied on British voices too often for villainous characters. They hadn't thought of James Woods, but when he auditioned, he knocked them out with his quicksilver mind and improvisational abilities—which reminded them of their collaboration with Robin Williams on *Aladdin*. They subsequently rewrote the part for Woods, and encouraged him to ad-lib to his heart's content. (This may account for the sprinkling of Hollywood jargon and Yiddish-isms in the film—another Disney first!)

Fast, funny, and well-plotted, *Hercules* may have appealed more to older kids (and young adults) than the preteen set. Since *The Lion King* had set an almost unattainable precedent of financial success, *Hercules* was pronounced a disappointment by industry pundits . . . but not by audiences who saw it, "got" it, and enjoyed it. It's a funny, original, and entertaining movie that deserves a better reputation.

When the studio's next animated feature was in development, a team of artists journeyed to China to absorb the look, and feel, of the country where Fa-Mulan was a household name. Feeling a bit like the troupe that accompanied Walt Disney to South America in the 1940s to soak up atmosphere and hatch ideas for *Saludos Amigos* and *The Three*

Caballeros, this crew came home with a new appreciation for the legend they were retelling in *Mulan*.

Mark Henn, who animated both Mulan and her father, said, "I took a sketch pad, and frankly I didn't do as much sketching as I thought I would. I spent most of the time with my eyes and ears wide open; I just wanted to be a sponge, soak it all in. I was always afraid it would seem like I was staring at the Chinese people. A whole busload of Americans sticks out like a sore thumb anyway. It was a terrific experience, and I'm just grateful that they allowed me to go.

"I kept trying to put myself in Mulan's shoes, and trying to feel about her country and where she lived in the way I feel about my country. Everywhere we went, without exception, we would tell them we were working on a picture about Mulan, and they just lit up. She is so well known over there."

Mulan is arguably the strongest female character ever to carry the weight of a Disney feature. And carry it she does: from the film's first moments, we empathize with Mulan, the girl who doesn't fit in, doesn't follow the rules, but loves and respects her father. When she decides to cut her hair and take her father's place in the Emperor's Army to fight an advancing enemy, we root for her. The beauty of the exposition in this film lies in how deftly it uses humor to humanize Mulan and make her endearing—a three-dimensional character, not a symbol or a martyr.

Having accomplished this daunting feat with great storytelling, staging, acting, and design, the film takes a backward step by introducing a comic sidekick, a miniature dragon named Mushu, voiced by the boisterously funny Eddie Murphy. Mushu's rapid-fire patter and remarks are undeniably funny, but they don't seem absolutely necessary in a film that has already won our hearts and minds.

Mulan's other great asset is an excellent score, by Matthew Wilder and David Zippel, which does exactly what songs are supposed to do in a musical: define character and advance the story. "Reflection" is the archetypal song of a main character's yearning and self-examination. "Honor to Us All" accompanies a wonderfully comic sequence in which Mulan reveals how unsuited she is to live out a role of quiet tradition in her community. "A Girl Worth Fighting For" fleshes out the individual personalities of Mulan's soldier comrades, and underscores the fact that they're men, and she isn't. "I'll Make a Man Out of You" is a stirring call to arms, dynamically staged in montage style to show how Captain Li Shang whips his untrained troops into shape.

All too aware of political correctness in the 1990s, the studio went out of its way to cast Asian Americans in the movie's central voice roles (just as they had sought Native Americans to voice the Indian parts in *Pocahontas*). Young actress Ming Na-Wen was thrilled to enact a character she'd heard about since childhood. Her singing voice was provided by the gifted Filipino-born Lea Salonga, who made her name on Broadway in the title role of *Miss Saigon* and later sang the part of Jasmine in Disney's *Aladdin*.

The vocal cast also included the beloved veteran June Foray as the grandmother; best known as the voices of Rocky the Flying Squirrel and Granny in the Tweety and Sylvester cartoons, she first worked for Disney in the early 1950s posing for reference footage on *Peter Pan*. Another cast member, George Takei (forever known as Commander Sulu in *Star Trek*), found great poignancy in working on a Disney animated film. One of his most vivid boyhood memories was seeing *Snow White and the Seven Dwarfs* while living in a Japanese internment camp during World War Two, and feeling transported by the experience.

Like all contemporary Disney directors, Tony Bancroft and Barry Cook had to decide how and when to use computer assistance to help tell their story in the most dramatic way. As a result, the climactic attack, in which hundreds of Mongols appear over the crest of a snowy moun-

The brave Mulan is accompanied in her adventures by her
guardian dragon, Mushu. © *Disney Enterprises, Inc.*

tain ridge, is both startling and awesome . . . just as it's supposed to appear to the undermanned Chinese Army.

If *Mulan* introduced non-Asian audiences to a previously unfamiliar tale, *Tarzan* reintroduced one of the most enduring fictional characters of the twentieth century to audiences around the world. Few characters have appeared in as many different films, from 1918 on, as Edgar Rice Burroughs's British-born, jungle-raised hero, the lord of the apes.

While Disney's *Tarzan* was made with the full cooperation of Edgar Rice Burroughs's estate (now managed by his grandson) it deviated from the author's original story as much as any earlier Hollywood incarnation. It is doubtful whether loud complaints were voiced by many of the happy moviegoers who flocked to see the film—the studio's biggest animated hit in a number of years.

Following recent tradition, *Tarzan* opens with a prologue (and counter to tradition, foregoes the Walt Disney logo music to superimpose the famous castle graphic over our first view of the jungle). The pulsating rhythms of Phil Collins's music help establish the mood for a fast-paced collage of images that tell us of the shipwreck and attack that made Tarzan an orphan and forged his destiny. This opening sequence is extraordinarily exciting, and primes the audience for the adventure to follow.

Dramatic staging is one of *Tarzan*'s strongest assets. Live-action directors could learn from this film's razor-sharp timing and cross-cutting of shots to give each sequence the maximum impact. The studio's computer wizards developed a process called "deep canvas" to give their jungle scenes a real feeling of depth and dimension. Animator Glen Keane developed the visual concept of Tarzan leaping through the vines and branches from watching his son fearlessly skateboarding on the streets of Paris.

Mindful of not repeating themselves—or the many Disney-cloned animated films dotting the landscape—the *Tarzan* team deliberately gave the character of Tarzan an unusual (or should one say atypical?) leading-man face, long and angular rather than conventionally handsome, with a "pumped-up" body befitting his physicality.

An impressively muscular Tarzan reacts to the sound of gunshots in this scene with a not-so-demure Jane Porter in *Tarzan*. © *Burroughs and Disney, Tarzan.* ® *Edgar Rice Burroughs, Inc.*

Jane may look more like a cartoon heroine, but she certainly doesn't act like one. Independent and winsome at the same time, this Jane is an entirely endearing, contemporary creation, and Minnie Driver's vocal performance is one of the most delightful in recent Disney history.

The mixture of human and animal characters comes off extremely well, since the animation of the jungle creatures is so good, and each individual personality is so well defined—from the rambunctious monkey, Terk, to the engagingly oafish elephant Tantor.

That said, it's a shame that the film's human villain, Clayton, is so clichéd. He is virtually a carbon copy of another hollow, one-dimensional, mustachioed villain, Governor Ratcliffe in Pocahontas. While Tarzan is a very entertaining film, its climax suffers from the cardboard predictability of the clash between good guys and bad guy. Make that VERY bad guy.

One of the more successful aspects of *Tarzan* is its groundbreaking use of music. By hiring pop singer-composer Phil Collins to provide songs, the studio guaranteed a fresh sound that wouldn't replicate any of its earlier films . . . Yet *Tarzan* went one step further, in having Collins himself perform the songs on the soundtrack. As in Bambi, decades earlier, the characters themselves do not sing, although Glenn Close (as Tarzan's adoptive ape-mother) softly murmurs the first line of the lullaby "You'll Be in My Heart," and Rosie O'Donnell contributes a boisterous bit of scat vocalese as Terk in "Trashin' the Camp."

Mighty Joe Young succeeds with flying colors, not only because of multi-Oscar-winner Rick Baker's incredible gorilla suit (and the equally incredible performance of the man wearing it, John Alexander) but thanks to the sincerity of the storytelling. The original screenplay, by *King Kong* producer Merian C. Cooper and his wife, Ruth Rose, was badly in need of refurbishing, but what is retained from the original—and indeed improved upon—is the tremendous bond between the heroine (Charlize Theron) and her king-size soul mate, Joe.

Director Ron Underwood was also keenly aware of having to walk a tightrope, providing enough excitement to hook a general audience, but not so intense as to frighten young children.

Two orphans, Jill (Charlize Theron) and Joe (played by himself), grow up together in the jungle—Joe justs happens to be a fifteen-foot gorilla—in the Disney remake of *Mighty Joe Young*. © *Disney Enterprises, Inc.*

Unfortunately, so many adolescents (and even young adults) are accustomed to violence and destruction on-screen that *Mighty Joe Young* was greeted with a giant yawn, another victim of the hypocrites who cry out for good family entertainment but don't support it when it comes along.

Many film buffs were delighted, however, with this rare remake that maintained the spirit of the original and made reverent acknowledgment of it on-screen, with cameo appearances by 1949's leading lady Terry Moore and stop-motion animator Ray Harryhausen, and even a glimpse of the late star Ben Johnson in a movie poster for his film *Wagon Master*.

One of the best moves the studio ever made was going into business with Pixar and bringing filmmaker John Lasseter under its wing. Lasseter actually studied character animation at the Disney-sponsored California Institute of the Arts and briefly worked at the studio in the 1980s before striking out on his own and cofounding Pixar. With the release of *A Bug's Life* and *Toy Story 2* in the late 1990s, more than one observer dubbed him "the new Walt Disney." That's because Lasseter has a rare combination of leadership quality, showmanship, and uncompromising creative standards.

As head of an ever-growing team of personnel at the company's Northern California headquarters, he feels the need, or obligation, to empower everyone on the team with a share in each film's success.

"As a director I try to instill a sense of creative ownership, no matter the smallest task, so they feel like their creativity is being used," he says. That way, "they're going to rise to the occasion. Also it's important for me to give them a project they're going to be really proud to work on."

Flik passes on some wisdom to a wide-eyed Dot, the youngest ant in the colony, in this scene from Disney and Pixar's *A Bug's Life*. Even this single frame shows how expressive the characters are. © *Disney Enterprises/Pixar*.

Jessie the cowgirl is thrilled to be reunited with her onetime TV costar, Woody—but the cowboy toy has no recollection of his years on "Woody's Roundup" in *Toy Story 2.* © *Disney Enterprises, Inc. and Pixar Animation studios.*

Pixar has also raised the consciousness of its technical wizards about the higher purpose they serve as filmmakers. "We never get caught up in how great something looks," he insists. "It's the story that keeps people entertained. If you get a great story with great characters and then you put great imagery on top of that, it makes a great package. That's what we set out to do, to give the audience great entertainment." The artists at the studio drive their computer-oriented colleagues to invent solutions to creative problems, and the seemingly limitless capabilities of those "techies" inspires the artists to devise new and challenging ideas.

Toy Story had created its own environment with great success. *A Bug's Life* takes place in the "real" environment of nature, and had to look real—or achieve a kind of heightened reality that moviegoers would find both appealing and believable. To magnify the challenge, Lasseter and company decided to make the film in the widescreen format. The results wowed children and grownups alike: *A Bug's Life* is a terrific movie.

Like any Disney animated feature, its story was developed over several years' time, with many snags along the way. That the finished film works so well, and flows so smoothly, is a perfect example of how great art seems effortless.

A Bug's Life is a classic Disney-style story about a misfit who makes good. Flik is a well-meaning member of his ant colony who can't seem to do anything right. The colony, presided over by Queen (a perfectly cast Phyllis Diller) is victimized by Hopper, a vicious grasshopper, and his cronies. (Hopper describes his annual ritual of stealing the ants' food as a "circle of life" kind of thing.) Flik sets off in search of bigger, meaner insects who can protect them from Hopper, but unknowingly hires the motley members of a flea circus. Everything works out in the end, but not before a series of hair-raising and hilarious adventures.

Because a film like this is in development and production so long, it's natural for the people working on it to slip in "inside" jokes. A box of animal crackers bears the logo "J. Grant Casey Jr. Cookies," a lovely tribute to nonagenarian Joe Grant, the Disney veteran who contributed ideas to *Toy Story* (and, decades earlier, introduced Casey Jr. in *Dumbo*). At the end of the film, buried in the credits, is the slogan "Filmed entirely on location."

Best of all, the Pixar folks took audiences by complete surprise by adding so-called outtakes at the end of the film. These supposed fluffs— by computer-generated actors—are so clever and funny, they became an attraction in themselves when they were added to the feature in two separate increments during its theatrical run. (The DVD release features all of them, of course.)

Incidentally, visitors to Disney's Animal Kingdom at the Walt Disney World Resort in Orlando, Florida, got an advance look at Flik and the world of *A Bug's Life* when the multimedia attraction *It's Tough to Be a Bug* opened a year before the movie. This magnificent 3-D presentation is as delightful as the film itself, with ingenious use of various tactile techniques to involve the audience in the picture.

When Disney and Pixar decided to embark on a sequel to *Toy Story*, the original thought was to release it direct to video, as Disney had a number of other recent spinoffs. Eventually, *Toy Story 2* took on such a healthy life of its own that it seemed wrong not to present it theatrically.

The Pixar gang decided to make *Toy Story 2* "the *Empire Strikes Back* of animated sequels," and succeeded with flying colors, even managing to evoke George Lucas's movie within the film itself. Many viewers and critics feel that *Toy Story 2* is an even better movie than the original—a thing that almost never occurs. That's because John Lasseter and his team refused to settle for less than the best they could give to this film. Says the filmmaker, "We make these movies for ourselves, because we like going to see great movies that are funny and heartwarming, and I like taking my kids to see movies like this."

Toy Story 2 is a dazzling film, cleverer and funnier than most live-action movies of recent vintage, but with moments of poignancy one rarely finds in any mainstream movies nowadays. It explores the relationship between toys and their young owners—as well as the recent phenomenon of toys as grown-up collectibles. There's even a sly but hilarious dig at toymakers and stores that didn't anticipate the success of the original *Toy Story*. But the loveliest moment in *Toy Story 2* occurs when cowgirl Jessie remembers the girl who adored her so, then outgrew her, in the exquisite Randy Newman song "When She Loved Me."

"A film with a lot of heart is so important to us, and characters that you like spending the time with," Lasseter explains. "As the director I take great responsibility for that. The audience gives an hour and a half of their life to sit in a theater and watch the film that I've created, so I want them to be entertained; I want them to feel like they haven't wasted that hour and a half."

No such complaints were heard from audiences leaving *Toy Story 2*.

As *Toy Story 2* became a major box-office hit in the waning days of 1999, the studio prepared to release its first film of the new year—and new century—the long-awaited *Fantasia/2000*. It was decided to make the decade-long project even more of an event by staging live multimedia performances (with a live symphony orchestra) in New York City (at Carnegie Hall), London, Paris, and Tokyo, winding up on New Year's Eve at the Pasadena Civic Auditorium just outside Los Angeles. Then, on

Animator and director Eric Goldberg pays tribute to the great caricaturist Al Hirschfeld in his unmistakable design for the "Rhapsody in Blue" segment of *Fantasia/2000*. Goldberg's wife, Susan, was art director of this ingenious sequence. © *Disney Enterprises, Inc.*

New Year's Day, the film officially debuted in an exclusive engagement at IMAX theaters worldwide.

Although the film was not specifically designed for the enormous IMAX screen, its presentation in that format turned *Fantasia/2000* into precisely the kind of special engagement that its producer and longtime booster and midwife, Roy E. Disney, hoped for.

It would be nice to say that *Fantasia/2000* is a worthy successor to Walt Disney's pet project, but that would be untrue. One key reason for this has nothing to do with the intrinsic value of the film; it's simply that the idea of marrying images to music is no longer new or innovative, as it was in 1940. What's more, in an attempt to make sure no one could accuse the new *Fantasia* of being too long, too boring, too remote, or highbrow, the filmmakers went too far in the opposite direction. If there is any overall criticism to be made of *Fantasia/2000*, it's that the film lacks weight and substance.

The sequences themselves are enjoyable to watch, but despite impeccable performances of great pieces of music by the Chicago Symphony Orchestra (under the direction of James Levine) there is little of lasting power in the picture. Arguably the most memorable segment is "The Sorcerer's Apprentice," reprised intact from the original *Fantasia*. It retains its afterpiece of Mickey (now revoiced by Wayne Allwine) shaking hands with conductor Leopold Stokowski, but now Mickey appears again with Levine on the podium, looking everywhere to give Donald Duck his cue to get ready.

An unusual interpretation of Ottorino Respighi's "Pines of Rome" offers striking and wondrous images of whales in motion. A lighthearted interpretation of George Gershwin's "Rhapsody in Blue" takes its cue for character design from the drawing style of Al Hirschfeld, and its overall look from the clean, bold graphics and colors of UPA cartoons of the 1950s. "Pomp and Circumstance" is pure fun, as Donald Duck is cast in the role of Noah's assistant in loading—then unloading—his famous ark. Fabled Disney veteran Joe Grant, who was one of the key story directors on the 1940 film, contributed the concept for the endearingly silly interpretation of Saint-Saëns' "Carnival of the Animals." Perhaps the finale, set to Igor Stravinsky's majestic "Firebird Suite," has the greatest impact, as it spins a mythic fable of nature withered, then renewed.

The studio's second animated release of 2000 also harked back to an earlier Disney project: *The Tigger Movie* features Winnie the Pooh and his friends in their first genuine feature-length theatrical film; what's more, it features an array of new songs by the Sherman Brothers, Richard M. and Robert B., who wrote the original Pooh songs and became so indelibly linked with Walt Disney in the 1960s.

Making the studio's next animated release involved building an entirely new unit—almost a studio within the studio. *Dinosaur* is the work of the new Digital Animation Studio, and was four years in the making. At first there was the basic concept of creating a dinosaur-related film; as a script evolved, there were questions of whether or not live actors would be involved, and how the extinct animals would be brought back to life. Eventually, after test footage had been created, it was decided that

Tigger and his little friend Roo enjoy bouncing together, but Tigger still yearns for a real family in *The Tigger Movie*. © *Disney Enterprises, Inc.*

Realistic, computer-animated characters blend seamlessly into a authentic live-action backdrop in *Dinosaur*. The film's young hero, Aladar (third from left), is joined here by Baylene, an elderly bra-chiosaur; Eema, a world-weary styra-chosaur; and Neera, who like him is an iguanadon. © *Disney Enterprises, Inc.*

Dinosaur should involve no humans, and should be entirely created using three-dimensional computer-generated animation. And finally, the film's creative team decided to have the dinosaurs speak, rather than hearing their thoughts or having a narrator tell their story.

All of this involved tremendous thought, planning, and trial-and-error experimentation. Participants included key players from the world of stop-motion animation (who had worked on *The Nightmare Before Christmas* and *James and the Giant Peach*) and digital effects. The challenge was to get them to think in Disney mode, and accept both the freedom and responsibility they had to create new ideas—and new ways of expressing them on screen.

Dinosaur places its computer-generated "stars" in a genuine live-action environment, which involved extensive planning before film crews set off around the globe. While the digital-effects experts were able to manipulate this footage when necessary (turning day into night, in one instance; erasing and then replacing shadows, in another) most of what the audience sees is real: real water, real trees, real sky.

The sky, in fact, is the limit now for ideas at Disney. With a handful of animated films in development, decisions now involve not only whether to make a film, but how to make it: with drawings, computer images, stop-motion, or a combination of all three.

This much is certain: the Disney brand-name is as potent as ever, and so is the studio's commitment to quality. The only remaining question is . . . what's next?

EPILOGUE: THE LEGACY
AND THE FUTURE

THE DISNEY STORY IS NEVER COMPLETE; HISTORY IS BEING MADE ON AN ALMOST daily basis. While this book focuses on the studio's feature films made and released under the banner of Walt Disney Pictures, there are many tangents one could follow to other histories rich in themselves. Fortunately, there are now entire books available on the Disney television shows, theme parks, and theatrical productions.

Still, motion pictures remain the locomotive that drives many of the company's far-flung endeavors. On The Disney Channel, it may be a third incarnation of Winnie the Pooh in series form, or a *101 Dalmatians* series. It's the latest Disney animated feature that inspires a parade at Disneyland and its related parks, or generates a new attraction. *Honey, I Shrunk the Kids*, which yielded a theatrical sequel, a direct-to-video follow-up, and a weekly TV series, served as the basis for an eye-popping three-dimensional, multimedia movie experience at Walt Disney World (since replicated at Disneyland) called *Honey, I Shrunk the Audience*, starring Rick Moranis, Eric Idle, and Marcia Strassman, and directed by Randal Kleiser. *Like Captain EO, Muppet Vision 3D*, or Pixar's *It's Tough to Be a Bug*, this interactive film offers park visitors an experience they can't have at home or in a conventional theater. It's unique and extraordinarily entertaining.

A book-length study of filmmaking in the theme parks could—and should—be written. Here is an unsung treasure trove of Disney movies: animated, live-action, and interactive. Some appear only at individual parks, or give way after several years to new attractions. The animation in Mickey's Movie Barn at Toon Town—in which Goofy is supposedly working as projectionist—is as clever and funny as anything the studio has produced in recent years.

Mickey and Donald are watching trailers for such Mickey Mouse classics as *The Band Concert, Thru the Mirror*, and *Steamboat Willie* (all newly created in old-fashioned "Coming Attractions" style). Eventually, Donald gets caught in the projector, and Goofy makes hand shadows in front of the screen. At one point a frame burns in the projection gate—so convincingly that the illusion fooled this author, who has lived through such experiences firsthand. The illusion is heightened by having Goofy's voice heard only through a speaker in the back of the room, near the "projection" window. (In truth, there is no film being projected at all; the entire program is being shown on video.)

The 360-degree CircleVision short-subject *The Timekeeper*, shown in Tomorrowland, is an incredible piece of work featuring Jeremy Irons as H. G. Wells and Michel Piccoli as Jules Verne, who travels back and forth in time from the Paris Exposition of 1900. It was directed by Jeff Blyth. Robin Williams provides the voice of the robotic Timekeeper, who actually appears in the theater in the form of an Audio-Animatronic character.

The multimedia presentation *Cranium Command*, shown at Epcot in the Wonders of Life pavilion and directed by Jerry Rees (who made *The Brave Little Toaster*), is a marvel of inventive writing, filmmaking, and sheer technical precision. Like *The Timekeeper*, this show features a "live" Audio-Animatronic character in the foreground of the theater, while multiple screens reveal the inner workings of an adolescent boy. The design of the screens is such that the audience feels as if it's inside the boy's body, and two screens near the top of the auditorium show us what he sees as if we can see through his eyes! The show features such comic performers as Charles Grodin, George Wendt, Kevin Nealon, Dana Carvey, and Bobcat Goldthwait.

A dog in your lap? This promotional photo may over-state the effect in *Honey, I Shrunk the Audience*, but when the dog sneezes, the audience *does* feel it! © *The Walt Disney Company.*

This Audio-Animatronic character hosts *The Timekeeper* attraction at Walt Disney World and Disneyland, and has both the voice and comic sensibilities of Robin Williams. © *The Walt Disney Company.*

The proven success of *Beauty and the Beast* on film made it much easier to translate it to the stage than it might have been to create something from scratch. It also gave potential audiences the reassurance of knowing what to expect before plunking down the price of admission.

Disney CEO Michael Eisner encourages the idea of attractions that enable families to share experiences together. This has led to the establishment of DisneyQuest, a high-tech environment in which young and old alike can play games and go on virtual rides, including the ultimate Disney experience, one of the company's own cruise ships, which even deposit passengers at a private island in the Bahamas.

No one expected the company's theatrical division to be quite as ambitious or successful as it has, however. Both Peter Schneider, chairman of Walt Disney Studios, and Thomas Schumacher, president of Walt Disney Feature Animation and Walt Disney Theatrical Productions, come from the world of theater, and make no secret of their devotion to that medium.

When the company announced that it had hired director Julie Taymor to stage a Broadway production of *The Lion King*, it seemed an unlikely choice. Taymor's bold, countercultural approach to theater didn't strike some observers as being ideally suited to the Disney image. Naysayers were silenced when her version of *The Lion King* debuted, wowing audiences with its dazzling use of masks and mime, and its innovative

Innovative staging, sets, and costume design made the Broadway production of *The Lion King* an entirely new theatrical experience. Tsidii Le Loka appears as Rafiki in the original cast. (Photo by Joan Marcus and Marc Bryan-Brown). © *Disney.*

sets and costumes. Broadway had never seen anything quite like it. What's more, the elaborate pageant opened in the exquisitely restored New Amsterdam Theater, which first opened in 1903, and now represents the rebirth of 42nd Street as "theater row" in Manhattan.

Home video has proved a fruitful arena for the studio to commission sequels to established hits (mostly animated) and occasionally to try something different. A delightful production of *The Wind in the Willows,* written and directed by Monty Python veteran Terry Jones, and featuring several of his Python pals (Michael Palin, John Cleese, Eric Idle), received desultory U.S. theatrical release from another company in 1997, but reached a wider audience when Disney released it on video the following year as *Mr. Toad's Wild Ride.* The video division even released a number of vintage Saturday matinee Westerns starring the late Gene Autry, from whom the company purchased the California Angels baseball team.

The vast audience that video affords also puts the studio's films under unprecedented scrutiny. More than one recent animated feature had to be altered for video release: an offending line cut and rescored from the opening song in *Aladdin*; a shot of the animated Baby Herman making a rude gesture while walking under the skirt of a live-action woman in *Who Framed Roger Rabbit* also deleted; and a cigarette dangling from Pecos Bill's lips (excised digitally) in *Melody Time.* This last change brought scowls from Disney buffs. (One animation fan speculated that Jose Carioca's cigar remained intact in the same film because no one thought a parrot would encourage kids to smoke, but a human would.)

Video also provided a home for a film produced in 1999 by Roy E. Disney, *The Wonderful Ice Cream Suit,* based on a well-known story by Ray

A scruffy Edward James Olmos is transformed when he wears *The Wonderful Ice Cream Suit.* With him are Clifton González González, Joe Mantegna, Gregory Sierra, and Esai Morales. © *Disney.*

Bradbury. Given its premiere at a regional film festival, this engaging fantasy about Los Angeles Latinos was clearly a labor of love for its director, Stuart Gordon, and its formidable cast, led by Joe Mantegna, Esai Morales, Clifton González-González, Gregory Sierra, and an almost unrecognizable Edward James Olmos. Bradbury himself wrote the screenplay, which had been produced before on stage and television. It also boasted a magnificent main-title sequence, designed in colored sand by Robert Dawson and animated by Aleksandra Korejwo.

Throughout the 1990s, the company has been careful to retain the Walt Disney name on family releases only, although some of the G-rated films under its umbrella have been unusual, to say the least. For example, respected filmmaker Terence Malick developed the idea of tracing the history of an African Olympic athlete, and Disney released the resulting film, *Endurance*, in 1999.

An even more unusual acquisition was made that same year. David Lynch, a director associated with the bizarre and extreme (with such films as *Eraserhead, Blue Velvet,* and *Wild at Heart*), was attracted to a script written by his companion, Mary Sweeney, and John Roach, based on a true story of a simple man's journey through the American heartland. Screen veteran Richard Farnsworth was the ideal choice to star as Alvin Straight, a real-life septuagenarian who rode his lawn mower some three hundred miles to visit his ailing brother. Beautifully realized, and deceptively simple, *The Straight Story* was one of the best films of 1999. No one was more surprised than Lynch that he had made a G-rated film, but the Disney executives were eager to present it to the American public.

Although the studio carefully separates its other releasing entities from the Walt Disney name, when Touchstone offers *Father of the Bride* or *The Horse Whisperer*, and Hollywood Pictures has its name on *Mr. Holland's Opus* or *Simon Birch*, many in the media think of them as "Disney pictures." (Conversely, under Joe Roth's regime as chairman, the studio made and/or released a string of highly original, even daring pictures with such filmmakers as Martin Scorsese, Wes Anderson, Spike Lee, Tim Robbins, and the aforementioned David Lynch, and enjoyed tremendous success with M. Night Shyamalan's *The Sixth Sense*.)

Academy Award–nominee Richard Farnsworth and Sissy Spacek take time to admire a lightning storm—one of the scenes that adds resonance to David Lynch's *The Straight Story*. © *The Straight Story, Inc.*

No other movie studio in history has documented itself so well; indeed, Disney was the first, and for many years, only company in Hollywood to have a full-time archivist on staff. Two documentaries of recent vintage have special significance, however: *Frank and Ollie* and *The Hand Behind the Mouse: The Ub Iwerks Story.*

Frank and Ollie a loving, feature-length documentary on the legendary longtime friendship and collaboration of animators Frank Thomas and Ollie Johnston, was made by Thomas's son Theodore (Ted) and his wife, Kuniko Okubo. The film was actually produced independently, but to its credit, the studio acquired the film for distribution, opened it in Los Angeles for an Oscar-qualifying run, and ultimately released it on video.

While Leslie Iwerks was a cinema major at the University of Southern California, she started thinking about making a documentary on the subject of her grandfather, Ub Iwerks. That dream became a reality in 1999, and again, the studio backed her vision. *The Hand Behind the Mouse: The Ub Iwerks Story* opened at the El Capitan Theater in Hollywood in the fall of 1999, earning respectful reviews from both the trade and consumer press.

Those two instances speak not only of the studio's respect for tradition, but its understanding of continuity. There are more than a few second-generation talents working for the company. (Bruce Reitherman, who provided the voice of Mowgli for *The Jungle Book* in 1967, and whose father directed that and many other Disney animated films, is now making a new generation of True-Life Adventure documentaries for the studio.) Perhaps it isn't incidental that Richard Cook, who serves as chairman of the Walt Disney Motion Pictures Group, started his career as a ride operator at Disneyland. How better to appreciate the appeal and importance of the "brand name" than to have dealt directly with the public?

One of Cook's pet projects was the renovation of the El Capitan theater (for many years of its life called The Paramount) on Hollywood Boulevard. Here, the company often accompanies its programs with live stage presentations, reminiscent of the golden era of Radio City Music Hall. The icing on the cake came in 1999 when, after many months of intensive and highly specialized labor, a vintage "Mighty Wurlitzer" organ was installed. Two full-time organists are now on staff, so every audience is treated to a recital prior to the movie—another delightful throwback to the great days of showmanship.

Just as the future shines brightly, the past continues to offer unexpected discoveries and rewards at Disney. Studio film preservationist Scott MacQueen compiled an array of precious nuggets from the studio's vaults, ranging from the only known footage of Walt performing the voice of Mickey Mouse (for the 1940s short subject *Mr. Mouse Takes a Trip*, with Billy Bletcher as Peg Leg Pete) to live-action reference footage for *Dumbo*'s musical number "When I See an Elephant Fly." MacQueen has shown compilations of this footage at the Cinefest, the Telluride Film Festival, the Museum of Modern Art in New York, and other venues where Disneyphiles have sat enraptured. Who knows what other gems may yet be discovered?

Audio producer Randy Thornton has worked his magic for a series of CDs that attempted, for the first time, to make the complete scores for Disney's animated classics available—as they originally sounded. The studio, which has maintained an enviable reputation for preserving its source materials, discarded its original soundtrack elements in the 1960s, having rerecorded them in "phony stereo." For years, these echo-laden recordings were the only ones available. Thornton painstakingly pieced together his CDs one inch of archival tape at a time, splicing musical elements together from a variety of sources. Soundtrack collectors and Disney fans owe him a huge debt of thanks.

Goofy, Mickey, and Donald stalk their prey in *Turkey Catchers*, a segment of Disney's Mickey MouseWorks, the television show that has breathed new life into these ageless characters. © *Disney*.

It was the television arm of Disney that, ironically, earned the studio its first Academy Award nomination in the short-subject field in years. *Redux Riding Hood* and *Three Little Pigs* (1997) were born when the TV division had the idea of making a video series of hip fairy-tale spoofs, intended to appeal to kids and parents alike, in the tradition of Jay Ward's "Fractured Fairy Tales." The next idea was to hire comedy writers—not necessarily experienced in the animation field—to bring a fresh approach to the subject. *Three Little Pigs* was written by Frank Coniff and written by Darrell Rudie. Dan O'Shannon chose "Little Red Riding Hood" from a list of possibilities because, as he put it, "it had been done so many times with so many twists, that it seemed like the biggest challenge to come up with yet another way to do it." Steve Moore directed the ingenious short, which was nominated for an Oscar. Screenwriter Peter Tolan also did scripts for *Jack and the Beanstalk* and *Rumpelstiltskin,* but that was the last of the fairy-tale series.

One of the most exciting developments of the 1990s was the return of the classic characters now dubbed "the fab five," Mickey, Minnie, Donald, Goofy, and Pluto. Well aware that a new generation might not even recognize some of these beloved figures if they weren't brought back to life on a regular basis, the television division came up with a series concept called *Mouseworks,* a surprisingly successful weekly Saturday morning collection of short subjects (running various lengths). Then the theatrical division decided to package some of the new shorts with Disney feature-film releases. Mickey and the gang then headlined a direct-to-video release for the 1999 holiday season called *Mickey's Once Upon a Christmas.*

Embracing new technology is now a way of life at the studio. *The Rescuers Down Under* was the first animated feature to be "filmed" by computer, without the use of a motion-picture camera. *Tarzan* was the first animated feature to be projected digitally (at the El Capitan) without the use of a conventional projector. *Toy Story 2* went one step further, being devised entirely on computers, its files then transferred for digital projection to several sites around the United States.

Artists and writers still use pencils and paints to express themselves, especially in a film's developmental stage. Concept drawings and storyboards still line the halls and offices at the company's animation facilities around the world. Some animators still draw the old-fashioned way, while others opt to manipulate their characters on a monitor.

But they all know that the medium is not the message. Something exciting and new, like computer-generated imagery, is bound to grab attention at first, but after the novelty wears off, the story and characters are what really count. That's a philosophy that stood Walt Disney in good stead for the whole of his career, and it's served his successors just as well. There is no reason to think it will change in the new century ahead.

Filmography

1995

Heavyweights

Released February. Executive Producers: Judd Apatow, Sarah Bowman. Producers: Joe Roth, Roger Birnbaum. Director: Steven Brill. Screenplay: Judd Apatow, Steven Brill. Cast: Tom McGowan (Pat Finley), Aaron Schwartz (Gerry), Ben Stiller (Tony Perkis), Shawn Weiss (Josh Birnbaum), Tom Hodges (Lars), Leah Lail (Julie), Paul Feig (Tim), Jeffrey Tambor (Maury). Running time: 98 minutes.

A group of misfits in a summer camp for overweight teens oust their head counselor, a new-age fitness freak, and challenge a muscle-bound rival camp in a sports competition. (Rated PG)

Man of the House

Released March. Executive Producer: Margaret South. Producers: Bonnie Bruckheimer, Marty Katz. Director: James Orr. Screenplay: James Orr, Jim Cruickshank. Story: David Peckinpah, Richard Jefferies. Cast: Chevy Chase (Jack Sturges), Farrah Fawcett (Sandra Archer), Jonathan Taylor Thomas (Ben Archer), George Wendt (Chet), David Shiner (Lloyd), Art LaFleur (Red Sweeney), Richard Portnow (Joey). Running time: 98 minutes.

A beleaguered federal prosecutor tries to win over the son of the woman he plans to marry, but the boy, trying to scare him off, tricks him into joining his Indian Guides program. (Rated PG)

Tall Tale

Released March. Executive Producer: Bill Badalato. Producers: Joe Roth, Roger Birnbaum. Director: Jeremiah Chechik. Screenplay: Steven L. Bloom, Robert Rodat. Cast: Patrick Swayze (Pecos Bill), Oliver Platt (Paul Bunyan), Roger Aaron Brown (John Henry), Nick Stahl (Daniel Hackett), Scott Glenn (J. P. Stiles), Steven Lange (Jonas Hackett), Catherine O'Hara (Calamity Jane). Running time: 96 minutes.

A strong-willed boy conjures up a trio of legendary Old West characters—John Henry, Paul Bunyan, and Pecos Bill—to help him save the family farm. (Rated PG)

A Goofy Movie

Released April. Producer: Dan Rounds. Director: Kevin Lima. Story: Jymn Magon. Screenplay: Jymn Magon, Chris Matheson, Brian Pimenthal. Songs: Tom Snow and Jack Feldman, Patrick DeRemer and Roy Freeland. Score: Carter Burwell. Animation Supervisors: Nancy Beiman, Matias Marcos, Stephane Sainte-Foi, Dominique Monfery. Voice Cast: Bill Farmer (Goofy), Jason Marsden (Max), Jim Cummings (Pete), Kellie Martin (Roxanne), Rob Paulson (PJ), Wallace Shawn (Principal Mazur), Jenna Von Oy (Stacey), Frank Welker (Big Foot), Jo Anne Worley (Miss Maples). Running time: 77 minutes.

Goofy takes his son Max on a fishing trip in an effort to bond, even though the boy would rather spend time with his girlfriend and go to a rock concert.

Pocahontas

Released June. Producer: James Pentecost. Directors: Mike Gabriel and Eric Goldberg. Screenplay: Carl Binder, Susannah Grant, Philip LaZebnik. Story: Tom Sito, Glen Keane, Ralph Zondag, Ed Gombert, Francis Glebas, Bruce Morris, Duncan Marjoribanks, Joe Grant, Burny Mattinson, Kaan Kaylon, Robert Gibbs, Todd Kurosawa, Chris Buck. Supervising Animators: Glen Keane (Pocahontas), John Pomeroy (John Smith), Duncan Marjoribanks (Ratcliffe), Nik Ranieri (Meeko), Ruben A. Aquino (Powhatan), Ken Duncan (Thomas), Chris Buck (Percy, Grandmother Willow, Wiggins), T. Daniel Hofstedt (Ben, Lon), Dave Pruiksma (Flit), Anthony DeRosa (Nakoma), Michael Cedeno (Kocoum). Songs: Alan Menken, Stephen Schwartz. Musical Score: Alan Menken. Voice Cast: Irene Bedard (Pocahontas), Judy Kuhn (Singing Pocahontas), Mel Gibson (John Smith), David Ogden Stiers (Governor Ratcliffe, Wiggins), John Kassir (Meeko), Russell Means (Powhatan), Christian Bale (Thomas), Linda Hunt (Grandmother Willow), Danny Mann (Percy), Frank Welker (Flit), Billy Connolly (Ben), Joe Baker (Lon), Michelle St. John (Nakoma), James Apaumut Fall (Kocoum). Running time: 81 minutes.

Native American girl Pocahontas falls in love with English captain John Smith, and tries to teach him her culture and customs, while Smith's leader sees only the possibilities of plundering the new land.

Operation Dumbo Drop

Released July. Executive Producers: Ted Field, Robert W. Cort. Producers: Diane Nabatoff, David Madden. Director: Simon Wincer. Screenplay: Gene Quintano, Jim Kouf. Story: Jim Morris. Cast: Danny Glover (Capt. Sam Cahill), Ray Liotta (Capt. T.C. Doyle), Dennis Leary (David Poole), Doug E. Doug (H. A. Ashford), Corin Nemec (Lawrence Farley). Running time: 108 minutes.

A U.S. Army captain tries to replace a Vietnam village's prized elephant that has died in the crossfire between U.S. and North Vietnamese troops. When transporting a grown elephant through 300 miles of enemy-infested jungle proves too much, the crew decides to parachute the animal to his new home. (Rated PG)

A Kid in King Arthur's Court

Released August. Executive Producer: Mark Amin. Producers: Robert L. Levy, Peter Abrams, J. P. Guerin. Director: Michael Gottlieb. Screenplay: Michael Part, Robert L. Levy. Cast: Thomas Ian Nichols (Calvin Fuller), Joss Ackland (King Arthur), Art Malik (Lord Belasco), Paloima Baeza (Princess Katey), Kate Winslet (Princess Sarah), Ron Moody (Merlin). Running time: 90 minutes.

A Little Leaguer falls through a crack in the earth and is thrust back in time to medieval Camelot. Merlin has summoned the boy to aid him in thwarting evil Lord Belasco and restoring King Arthur to his throne. (Rated PG)

The Big Green

Released September. Executive Producer: Dennis Bishop. Producer: Roger Birnbaum. Director: Holly Goldberg. Screenplay: Holly Goldberg. Cast: Steve Guttenberg (Tom Palmer), Olivia D'Abo (Anna Montgomery), Jay O. Sanders (Jay Huffer), John Terry (Edwin V. Douglas), Chauncey Leopardi (Evan Schiff), Patrick Renna (Larry Musgrove), Billy L. Sullivan (Jeffery). Running time: 100 minutes.

British schoolteacher and local sheriff in small Texas town inspire a kids' soccer team to take on big city rivals. (Rated PG)

Frank & Ollie

Released October. Producers: Kuniko Okubo, Theodore Thomas. Director and Writer: Theodore Thomas. Interviewees: Frank Thomas, Ollie Johnston, Sylvia Roemer, John Canemaker, John Culhane, Glen Keane, Andy Gaskill. Running Time: 89 minutes.

Documentary feature film about the lives and careers of legendary Disney animators (and next-door neighbors) Frank Thomas and Ollie Johnston, made by Thomas's son and daughter-in-law.

Toy Story

Released November. Executive Producers: Edwin Catmull, Steven Jobs. Producers: Ralph Guggenheim, Bonnie Arnold. Director: John Lasseter. Screenplay: Joss Whedon, Andrew Stanton, Joel Cohen, and Alec Sokolow. Original Story: John Lasseter, Pete Docter, Andrew Stanton, Joe Ranft. Music: Randy Newman. Supervising Animator: Pete Docter. Voice Cast: Tom Hanks (Woody), Tim Allen (Buzz Lightyear), Don Rickles (Mr. Potato Head), Jim Varney (Slinky Dog), Wallace Shawn (Rex), John Ratzenberger (Hamm), Annie Potts (Bo Peep), John Morris (Andy), Laurie Metcalf (Mrs. Davis), R. Lee Ermey (Sarge), Erik Von Detten (Sid), Sarah Freeman (Hannah), Penn Jillette (TV Announcer). Running time: 81 minutes.

Andy's favorite toy, a pull-string cowboy doll named Woody, is fearful of being replaced by a new action figure, Buzz Lightyear, a space ranger.

Tom and Huck

Released December. Executive Producer: Barry Bernardi, Stephen Sommers. Producers: Lawrence Mark, John Baldecchi. Director: Peter Hewitt. Screenplay: Stephen Sommers, David Loughery. Based on *The Adventures of Tom Sawyer* by Mark Twain. Cast: Jonathan Taylor Thomas (Tom Sawyer), Brad Renfro (Huck Finn), Eric Schweig (Injun Joe), Charles Rocket (Judge Thatcher), Amy Wright (Aunt Polly), Marian Seldes (Widow Douglas), Rachael Leigh Cook (Becky Thatcher). Running time: 92 minutes.

Tom Sawyer and Huck Finn team up to steal a pirate's treasure map from Injun Joe in order to save an innocent man from being wrongly convicted in court. (Rated PG)

TOUCHSTONE RELEASES: *Bad Company, The Jerky Boys, Jefferson in Paris, Mad Love, Feast of July, Father of the Bride.*

HOLLYWOOD RELEASES: *Houseguest, Miami Rhapsody, Roommates, Funny Bones, While You Were Sleeping, A Pyromaniac's Love Story, Crimson Tide, Judge Dredd, Dangerous Minds, The Tie That Binds, Unstrung Heroes, Dead Presidents, The Scarlet Letter, Powder, Nixon, Mr. Holland's Opus.*

1996

Muppet Treasure Island

Released February. Executive Producer: Frank Oz. Producers: Martin G. Baker, Brian Henson. Director: Brian Henson. Screenplay: Jerry Juhl, Kirk R. Thatcher, James V. Hart. Suggested by the novel by Robert Louis Stevenson. Cast: Tim Curry (Long John Silver), Steve Whitmire (Capt. Abraham Smollett/Kermit the Frog), Frank Oz (Benjamina Gunn/Miss Piggy), Billy Connolly (Billy Bones), Dave Goelz (The Great Gonzo), Steve Whitmire (Rizzo The Rat), Frank Oz (Squire Trelawney/Fozzie Bear), Jennifer Saunders (Ms. Bluveridge), Kevin Bishop (Jim Hawkins). Running time: 99 minutes.

Jim Henson's Muppets enact the classic story of young Jim Hawkins and pirate Long John Silver's quest for buried treasure.

Homeward Bound II: Lost in San Francisco

Released March. Producer: Barry Jossen. Director: David R. Ellis. Screenplay: Chris Hauty, Julie Hickson. Based on characters from *The Incredible Journey* by Sheila Burnford. Voice Cast: Michael J. Fox (Chance), Sally Field (Sassy), Ralph Waite (Shadow), Sinbad (Riley), Jon Polito (Ashcan), Carla Gugino (Delilah), Tress MacNeille (French poodle), Stephen Tobolowsky (Bando), Ross Malinger (Spike), Al Michaels (Sparky), Tommy Lasorda (Lucky), Bob Uecker (Trixie), Michael Bell (Stokey). Cast: Robert

Hays (Bob), Kim Griest (Laura), Veronica Lauren (Hope), Kevin Chevalia (Jamie), Benj Thall (Peter), Max Perlich (Ralph), Michael Rispoli (Jack). Running time: 89 minutes.

Three pets from the suburbs, en route to a family camping trip, get loose at San Francisco Airport and get lost in the big city. Their road home is fraught with perils, dangerous enemies, new friends, and true love.

James and the Giant Peach

Released April. Executive Producer: Jake Eberts. Producer: Denise Di Novi. Director: Henry Selick. Screenplay: Karey Kirkpatrick, Jonathan Roberts, Steve Bloom. Based on the book by Roald Dahl. Production Design: Harley Jessup. Conceptual Designer: Lane Smith. Animation Supervisor: Paul Berry. Storyboard Supervisors: Kelly Asbury, Joe Ranft. Music: Randy Newman. Cast: Paul Terry (James), Richard Dreyfuss (Centipede), Susan Sarandon (Spider), Simon Callow (Grasshopper), Jane Leeves (Ladybug), Joanna Lumley (Aunt Spiker), Miriam Margolyes (Aunt Sponge/Glow worm), Pete Postlethwaite (Old Man), David Thewlis (Earthworm). Running time: 79 minutes.

James, an orphaned boy living with two wicked aunts, escapes their torment within a large enchanted peach. Befriended by its inhabitants, a group of giant insects, they set course for New York City and a better life. (Rated PG)

The Hunchback of Notre Dame

Released June. Producer: Don Hahn. Directors: Gary Trousdale, Kirk Wise. Animation Story by Tab Murphy from the Victor Hugo novel, *Notre Dame de Paris.* Animation Screenplay: Tab Murphy, Irene Mecchi, Bob Tzudiker, Noni White, and Jonathan Roberts. Story Supervisor: Will Finn. Story: Kevin Harkey, Gaetan Brizzi, Paul Brizzi, Edward Gombert, Brenda Chapman, Jeff Snow, Jim Capobianco, Denis Rich, Burny Mattinson, John Sanford, Kelly Wightham, James Fujii, Gee Fwee Boedoe, Floyd Norman, Francis Glebas, Kirk Hanson, Christine Blum, Sue C. Nichols. Music: Alan Menken. Lyrics: Stephen Schwartz. Supervising Animators: James Baxter (Quasimodo), Tony Fucile (Esmeralda), Kathy Zielinski (Frollo), Russ Edmonds (Phoebus), Michael Surrey (Clopin), David Pruiksma (Hugo and Victor), Will Finn (Laverne), Kent Hammerstrom (Djali). Voice Cast: Tom Hulce (Quasimodo), Demi Moore (Esmeralda), Tony Jay (Frollo), Kevin Kline (Phoebus), Jason Alexander (Hugo), Charles Kimbrough (Victor), Mary Wickes, Jane Withers (Laverne), David Ogden Stiers (Archdeacon), Paul Kandel (Clopin), Heidi Mollenhauer (singing voice of Esmeralda). Running time: 91 minutes.

Quasimodo, a simpleminded hunchback raised in isolation in a cathedral belltower in Paris, ventures outside for the first time and falls in love with a beautiful gypsy. When evil minister Frollo orders all gyp-

sies to leave Paris, Quasimodo defies all to rescue her and make things right.

First Kid

Released August. Executive Producers: Sinbad, Dale DeLaTorrey, Tim Kelleher. Producer: Roger Birnbaum. Director: David Mickey Evans. Screenplay: Tim Kelleher. Cast: Sinbad (Sam Simms), Robert Guillaume (Wilkes), Timothy Busfield (Woods), Brock Pierce (Luke Davenport), James Naughton (President Davenport), Art LaFleur (Morton), Zachery Ty Bryan (Rob). Running time: 101 minutes.

Bratty son of the President is assigned to good-hearted but bumbling Secret Service agent Sam Simms, who eventually bonds with the boy—and rescues him from kidnappers. (Rated PG)

D3: The Mighty Ducks

Released October. Producers: Jorden Kerner, Jon Avnet. Director: Robert Lieberman. Screenplay: Steven Brill, Jim Burnstein. Cast: Emilio Estevez (Gordon Bombay), Jeffery Nordling (Coach Orion), David Selby (Dean Buckley), Heidi Kling (Casey), Joshua Jackson (Charlie), Elden Ryan Ratcliff (Fulton), Joss Ackland (Hans), Shaun Weiss (Greg Goldberg), Matt Doherty (Averman). Running time: 104 minutes.

Given scholarships to prestigious Eden Hall Academy, the hockey team resists an aggressive new coach and suffers indignities from preppy fellow athletes. In a final showdown game, the Mighty Ducks prevail. (Rated PG)

101 Dalmatians

Released November. Executive Producer: Edward S. Feldman. Producers: John Hughes, Ricardo Mestres. Director: Stephen Herek. Screenplay: John Hughes. Based on "101 Dalmatians" by Dodie Smith. Cast: Glenn Close (Cruella De Vil), Jeff Daniels (Roger), Joely Richardson (Anita), Joan Plowright (Nanny), Hugh Laurie (Jasper), Mark Williams (Horace), John Shrapnel (Skinner). Running time: 103 minutes.

A live-action remake of the Disney 1961 animated feature. Fashion designer Cruella De Vil sends her henchmen to kidnap Dalmatian puppies which she plans to use in making a unique fur coat. With the help of dogs and farm animals countrywide, they confound their captors and find their way home.

TOUCHSTONE RELEASES: *Mr. Wrong; Up Close and Personal; Two Much; Little Indian; Big City; Last Dance; Boys; Phenomenon; Kazaam; Ransom; The War at Home; The Preacher's Wife.*

HOLLYWOOD RELEASES: *White Squall; Before and After; Celtic Pride; Spy Hard; Eddie; The Rock; Jack; The Rich Man's Wife; The Associate; Evita.*

1997

That Darn Cat

Released February. Executive Producer: Andrew Gottlieb. Producer: Robert Simonds. Director: Bob Spiers. Screenplay: S. M. Alexander, L. A. Karaszewski. Based on the book *Undercover Cat* by The Gordons and the screenplay by The Gordons and Bill Walsh. Cast: Christina Ricci (Patti), Doug E. Doug (Zeke). Dean Jones (Mr. Flint), George Dzundza (Boetticher), Peter Boyle (Pa), Bess Armstrong (Judy Randall), Dyan Cannon (Mrs. Flint), Estelle Parsons (Old Lady McCracken). Running time: 89 minutes.

Remake of 1965 Disney feature. A teenager's tomcat with the clue to a kidnaping scheme is kept under close surveillance by a novice FBI agent. (Rated PG)

Jungle 2 Jungle

Released March. Executive Producers: Richard Baker, Rick Messina, Brad Krevoy. Producer: Brian Reilly. Director: John Pasquin. Screenplay: Bruce A. Evans, Raynold Gideon. Based on the film *Little Indian, Big City (Un Indien Dans La Ville)* by Harve Palud, Igor Aptekman, Thierry Lhermitte and Philippe Bruneau. Cast: Tim Allen (Michael), Martin Short (Richard), Lolita Davidovich (Charlotte), David Ogden Stiers (Jovanovic), Sam Huntington (Mimi), Bob Dishy (Langston), JoBeth Williams (Patricia), Leelee Sobieski (Karen).

Wall Street trader travels to Amazon jungle to finalize divorce with his estranged wife and discovers he has a thirteen-year-old son who has been raised by an Indian family. He brings the boy to New York City where he learns about life and love, and helps dad foil a group of sinister Russian businessmen. (Rated PG)

Hercules

Released June. Producers: Alice Dewey, John Musker, Ron Clements. Directors: John Musker, Ron Clements. Screenplay: Ron Clements & John Musker, Donald McEnery & Bob Shaw and Irene Mecchi. Story Supervisor: Barry Johnson. Story: Laan Kalyon, Kelly Wrightman, Randy Cartwright, John Ramirez, Jeff Snow, Vance Gerry, Kirk Hanson, Tamara Lusher-Stocker, Francis Glebas, Mark Kennedy, Bruce M. Morris, Don Dougherty, Thom Enriquez. Music: Alan Menken. Lyrics: David Zippel. Supervising Animators: Andreas Deja (Adult Hercules), Eric Goldberg (Phil), Nik Ranieri (Hades), Ken Duncan (Meg), Ellen Woodbury (Pegasus), Randy R. Haycock (Baby and Young Hercules), Anthony DeRosa (Zeus and Hera), Michael Snow (The Muses), James Lopez (Pain and Panic), Dominique Monfery (Titans and Cyclops), Richard Bazley (Amphitryon & Alcmene), Nancy Beiman (The Fates/Thebans), Oskar Urretabizkaia (Hydra). Voice Cast: Tate Donovan (Hercules), Susan Egan (Meg), Danny DeVito (Phil),

James Woods (Hades), Bobcat Goldthwait (Pain), Matt Frewer (Panic), Charlton Heston (Narrator), Rip Torn (Zeus), Samantha Eggar (Hera), Cheryl Freeman, LaChanze, Roz Ryan, Vaneese Thomas and Lillias White (Muses), Carole Shelley, Amanda Plummer, Paddi Edwards (Fates), Patrick Pinney (Cyclops), Hal Holbrook (Amphitryon), Barbara Barrie (Alcmene), Paul Shaffer (Hermes), Jim Cummings (Nessus), Roger Bart (Young Herc singing), Joshua Keaton (Young Herc speaking), Keith David (Apollo), Wayne Knight (Demetrius). Running time: 93 minutes.

The legend of Hercules, cartoon-style, told by a rockin' gospel Greek chorus. With the help of Phil, a hero-training satyr, Hercules sets out to prove himself a hero and return to his rightful place on Mount Olympus. He finds a formidable foe in Hades, who sends a multiheaded Hydra, a Cyclops, and an army of Titans up against him.

George of the Jungle

Released July. Executive Producer: C. Tad Devlin. Producer: David Hoberman, Jordan Kerner, Jon Avnet. Director: Sam Weisman. Screenplay: Dana Olsen, Audrey Wells. Story: Dana Olsen. Based on characters created by Jay Ward. Cast: Brendan Fraser (George), Leslie Mann (Ursula Stanhope), Thomas Haden Church (Lyle Van de Groot), Richard Roundtree (Kwame), John Cleese (voice of Ape Named Ape), Abraham Benrudi (Thor), Greg Cruttwell (Max), Holland Taylor (Beatrice Stanhope), John Bennett Perry (Arthur Stanhope), Keith Scott (narrator). Running time: 92 minutes.

Based on the 1967 Jay Ward animated TV series. Raised by apes in the jungle, George meets pretty explorer Ursula Stanhope and falls in love. Her fiance, Lyle, plots to regain his lady love and destroy George's rain forest kingdom. (Rated PG)

Air Bud

Released August. Executive Producers: Bob Weinstein, Harvey Weinstein, Michael Strange, Anne Vince. Producers: Robert Vince, William Vince. Director: Charles Martin Smith. Screenplay: Paul Tamasy, Aaron Mendelsohn. Cast: Michael Jeter (Norm Snively), Kevin Zeqers (Josh Framm), Wendy Makkena (Jackie Framm), Eric Christmas (Judge Cranfield), Brendan Fletcher (Larry Willingham), Norman Browning (Buck Willingham). Running time: 98 minutes.

Aspiring 12-year-old basketball player finds a runaway golden retriever with the uncanny ability to shoot hoops. They become local sports stars, but must foil the dog's previous owner, who tries to cash in on the canine's career. (Rated PG)

Rocketman

Released October. Executive Producers: Jon

Turteltaub, Oren Aviv, Jonathan Glickman. Producer: Roger Birnbaum. Director: Stuart Gillard. Screenplay: Craig Mazin, Greg Erb. Cast: Harland Williams (Fred Z. Randall), Jessica Lundy (Julie Ford), William Sadler (Wild Bill Overbeck), Jeffery DeMunn (Paul), James Pickens, Jr. (Ben), Don Lake (Flight surgeon), Beau Bridges (Bud Nesbitt). Running time: 94 minutes.

NASA computer nerd Fred Z. Randall is selected to replace a member of the first manned mission to Mars. Bumbling his way through training, Randall butts heads with crew captain Overbeck, falls in love with attractive medical officer Ford and bonds with chimp mascot Ulysses. (Rated PG)

Flubber

Released November. Executive Producer: David Nicksay. Producers: John Hughes, Richard Mestres. Director: Les Mayfield. Screenplay: John Hughes, Bill Walsh. Based on the film *The Absent-Minded Professor* written by Bill Walsh, from a story by Samuel W. Taylor. Cast: Robin Williams (Phillip Brainard), Marcia Gay Harden (Sara Jean Reynolds), Christopher McDonald (Wilson Croft), Raymond J. Barry (Chester), Clancy Brown (Smith), Ted Levine (Wesson), Wil Wheaton (Bennett), Jodi Benson (voice of Weebo), Scott Martin Gershin (voice of Flubber), Nancy Olson (secretary). Running time: 94 minutes.

Remake of the 1961 Disney film *The Absent-Minded Professor*. A chronically distracted college professor accidentally creates a green goo, Flubber, which when applied to any object causes it to fly. (Rated PG)

Mr. Magoo

Released December. Executive Producers: Henry G. Saperstein, Andre Morgan, Robert L. Rosen. Producer: Ben Myron. Director: Stanley Tong. Screenplay: Pat Proft, Tom Sherohman. Based on the character Mr. Magoo, created by Millard Kaufman. Cast: Leslie Nielsen (Mr. Magoo), Kelly Lynch (Luanne Leseur), Ernie Hudson (Gus Anders), Stephen Tobolowsky (Chuck Stupak), Nick Chinlund (Bob Morgan), Matt Keeslar (Waldo), Malcolm McDowell (Austin Cloquet), Miguel Ferrer (Ortega Peru), Greg Burson (voice of animated Mr. Magoo). Running time: 87 minutes.

Based on the UPA cartoon character. A stolen ruby lands in the possession of near-sighted Mr. Magoo, who, despite the efforts of a gang of thieves to retrieve it, is oblivious to the danger that surrounds him. (Rated PG)

TOUCHSTONE RELEASES: *Metro, The Sixth Man, Romy And Michele's High School Reunion, Con Air, Nothing To Lose, A Thousand Acres, Playing God, Kundun.*

HOLLYWOOD RELEASES: *Prefontaine, Shadow Conspiracy, Grosse Pointe Blank, Gone Fishin', G.I. Jane, Washington Square, An American Werewolf in Paris.*

1998

Meet the Deedles

Released March. Executive Producers: Andy Heyward, Artie Ripp. Producers: Dale Pollack, Aaron Mayerson. Director: Steve Boyum. Screenplay: Jim Herzfeld, Dale Pollack. Cast: Steve Van Wormer (Stew), Paul Walker IV (Phil), A. J. Langer (Lt. Jesse Ryan), John Ashton (Capt. Pine), Dennis Hopper (Frank Slater), Eric Braedon (Elton), Richard Lineback (Crabbe), Robert Englund (Nemo). Running time: 94 minutes.

Two dim-witted teenage brothers, who live to surf, are sent to summer camp in Wyoming where they are mistaken for rookie National Park Rangers. (Rated PG)

Mulan

Released June. Producer: Pam Coats. Directors: Barry Cook, Tony Bancroft. Screenplay: Rita Hsiao, Robert Sanders, Philip Lazebnik, Raymond Singer, and Eugenia Bostwick-Singer. Based on a story by Robert D. San Souci. Story: Christopher Sanders, Dean Deblois, John Sanford, Chris Williams, Tim Hodge, Julius L. Aguimatang, Burny Mattinson, Lorna Cook, Barry Johnson, Thom Enriquez, Ed Gombert, Joe Grant, Floyd Norman. Supervising Animators: Mark Henn (Mulan and Fa Zhou), Ruben A. Aquino (Shang and Fa Li), Tom Bancroft (Mushu), Aaron Blaise (Yao and Ancestors), Broose Johnson (Chien-Po and Ling), Barry Temple (Cri-Kee), Pres Antonio Romanillos (Khan and General Li), Jeffery J. Varab (Chi Fu and Grandmother Fa). Music: Matthew Wilder. Lyrics: David Zippel. Original Score: Jerry Goldsmith. Voice Cast: Ming-Na Wen (Mulan), Lea Salonga (singing Mulan), Eddie Murphy (Mushu), B. D. Wong (Shang), Donny Osmond (singing Shang), Harvey Fierstein (Yao), Jerry S. Tondo (Chien-Po), Gedde Watanabe (Ling), Pat Morita (The Emperor), June Foray (Grandmother Fa), George Takei (First Ancestor). Running time: 88 minutes.

In ancient China, a young girl disguises as a man and joins the Emperor's army to fight the marauding Huns. Aided by a small wisecracking dragon sent by her ancestors, Mulan risks her life and family honor to become a hero.

The Parent Trap

Released July. Producer: Charles Shyer. Director: Nancy Meyers. Screenplay: David Swift, Nancy Meyers, Charles Shyer. Cast: Lindsay Lohan (Hallie/Annie), Dennis Quaid (Nick Parker), Natasha Richardson (Elizabeth James), Elaine Hendrix (Meredith), Lisa Ann Walter (Chessy), Simon Kunz (Martin), Polly Holliday (Marva Kulp,

Sr.), Maggie Wheeler (Marva Kulp, Jr.), Ronnie Stevens (Grandfather), Joanna Barnes (Vicki). Running time: 128 minutes.

A remake of the 1961 Disney feature. Twin sisters, separated at birth, meet at summer camp where they switch identities and scheme to reunite their divorced parents. (Rated PG)

I'll Be Home for Christmas

Released November. Executive Producer: Robin French. Producers: David Hoberman, Tracey Trench. Director: Arlene Sanford. Screenplay: Harris Goldberg, Tom Nursall. Story: Michael Allin. Cast: Jonathan Taylor Thomas (Jake), Jessica Biel (Allie), Adam LaVorgna (Eddie), Gary Cole (Jake's dad), Eve Gordon (Carolyn), Lauren Maltby (Tracey), Andrew Lauer (Nolan). Running time: 86 minutes.

Selfish scam-artist college student has 48 hours to get from California to New York for Christmas Eve or forfeit his father's gift of a classic car. Complicating his situation, a group of his disgruntled associates leave him in the desert, a Santa suit glued to his body, without any money or credit cards, and miles from a telephone. (Rated PG)

A Bug's Life

Released November. Producers: Darla K. Anderson, Kevin Reher. Directors: John Lasseter, Andrew Stanton. Screenplay: Andrew Stanton, Donald McEnery, Bob Shaw. Original story: John Lasseter, Andrew Stanton, Joe Ranft. Music: Randy Newman. Voice Cast: Dave Foley (Flik), Kevin Spacey (Hopper), Julia Louis-Dreyfus (Princess Atta), Phyllis Diller (Queen), Richard Kind (Molt), David Hyde Pierce (Slim), Joe Ranft (Heimlich), Denis Leary (Francis), Jonathan Harris (Manny), Madeline Kahn (Gypsy), Bonnie Hunt (Rosie), Michael McShane (Tuck and Roll), Hayden Panettiere (Dot), John Ratzenberger (P. T. Flea), Roddy McDowall (Mr. Soil). Running time: 95 minutes.

Threatened by a grasshopper and his gang, an absent-minded ant named Flik unwittingly recruits the stars of a traveling flea circus to save his colony.

Mighty Joe Young

Released December. Executive Producer: Gail Katz. Producers: Ted Hartley, Tom Jacobson. Director: Ron Underwood. Screenplay: Mark Rosenthal, Lawrence Konner, based on a screenplay by Ruth Rose and a story by Merian C. Cooper. Special makeup effects: Rick Baker. Cast: Charlize Theron (Jill Young), Bill Paxton (Gregg O'Hara), Rade Sherbedgia (Strasser), Peter Firth (Garth), David Paymer (Harry), Regina King (Cicily), Robert Wisdom (Kweli), Lawrence Pressman (Dr. Baker), Linda Purl (Dr. Ruth Young), Terry Moore (guest at party), Ray Harryhausen (guest at party), Dina Merrill (society woman). Running time: 115 minutes.

Remake of 1949 RKO fantasy film. A young woman and giant gorilla who have grown up together in a secluded jungle are persuaded to move to a California wildlife preserve. An evil hunter tries to kidnap the animal, who breaks free and causes havoc on Hollywood Boulevard. (Rated PG)

1998

TOUCHSTONE RELEASES: *Krippendorf's Tribe, He Got Game, The Horse Whisperer, Six Days Seven Nights, Armageddon, Holy Man, Jane Austen's Mafia, Beloved, The Waterboy, Enemy of the State, A Civil Action* (with Paramount Pictures), *Rushmore.*

HOLLYWOOD RELEASES: *Deep Rising, Burn Hollywood Burn,* (An Alan Smithee Film), *Firelight, Simon Birch.*

1999

My Favorite Martian

Released February. Executive Producer: Barry Bernardi. Producers: Robert Shapiro, Jerry Leider, Mark Toberoff. Director: Donald Petrie. Screenplay: Sherri Stoner, Deanna Oliver, based on the television series created by John L. Greene. Cast: Christopher Lloyd (Uncle Martin), Jeff Daniels (Tim O'Hara), Elizabeth Hurley (Brace), Daryl Hannah (Lizzie), Wallace Shawn (Coleye), Christine Ebersole (Lorelei Brown), Michael Lerner (Mr. Channing), Ray Walston (Armitan). Running time: 93 minutes.

Based on the 1960s TV situation comedy. A down-on-his-luck television reporter befriends a zany Martian who crash-lands on earth. (Rated PG)

Doug's 1st Movie

Released March. Producers: Jim Jinkins, David Campbell, Melanie Grisanti, Jack Spillum. Director: Maurice Joyce. Screenplay: Ken Scarborough. Voice Cast: Thomas McHugh (Doug Funnie), Fred Newman (Skeeter, Mr. Dink, Porkchop, Ned), Chris Phillips (Roger, Boomer, Larry, Mr. Chiminy), Constance Shulman (Patti Mayonnaise), Doug Preis (Mr. Funnie, Mr. Bluff, Willie, Chalky), Guy Hadley (Guy Graham), Alice Playten (Beebe Bluff, Elmo), Eddie Korbich (Robo Crusher), David O'Brian (Quailman Announcer), Doris Belack (Mayor Tippi Dink), Becca Lish (Judy Funnie, Mrs. Funnie). Running time: 77 minutes.

Preteen Doug's efforts to save an endangered "monster," found in a local polluted lake, clash with his efforts to take his girlfriend to the school dance, and out of the arms of a slick rival.

Endurance

Released May. Executive Producer: Wallace Wolf.

Producers: Edward R. Pressman, Terrence Malick, Max Palevsky. Director: Leslie Woodhead. Competition Director: Bud Greenspan. Screenplay: Leslie Woodhead. Cast: Haile Gebrelassie (Himself), Yomas Zergaw (Young Haile), Shawanness Gebrelassie (Haile's Mother), Teddesse Haile (Haile's Father), Berkele Gebrelassie (Himself), Alem Tellahun (Herself). Running time: 83 minutes.

The true story of Ethiopian Olympic champion Haile Gebrelassie, enacted by Gebrelassie himself and members of his family, and incorporating footage of his actual gold medal–winning run in the 1996 Olympics.

Tarzan

Released June. Producer: Bonnie Arnold. Directors: Kevin Lima, Chris Buck. Screenplay: Tab Murphy, Bob Tzudiker, and Noni White. Based on the story by Edgar Rice Burroughs. Additional screenplay material: David Reynolds, Jeffery Stepakoff. Story Supervisor: Brian Pimental. Story: Stephen Anderson, Mark D. Kennedy, Carole Holliday, Gaetan Brizzi, Paul Brizzi, Don Dougherty, Ed Gombert, Randy Haycock, Don Hall, Kevin L. Harkey, Glen Keene, Burny Mattinson, Frank Nissen, John Norton, Jeff Snow, Michael Surrey, Christopher J. Ure, Mark Walton, Stevie Wermers, Kelly Wrightman, John Ramierz. Songs: Phil Collins. Musical Score: Mark Mancina. Supervising Animators: Glen Keane (Tarzan), Ken Stuart Duncan (Jane), Russ Edmonds (Kala), John Ripa (Young Tarzan and Baby), Michael Surrey (Terk), Randy Haycock (Clayton), Bruce W. Smith (Kerchak), Sergio Pablos (Tantor), Dominique Monfery (Sabor). Voice Cast: Tony Goldwyn (Tarzan), Minnie Driver (Jane), Glenn Close (Kala), Alex D. Linz (Young Tarzan), Rosie O'Donnell (Terk), Brian Blessed (Clayton), Nigel Hawthorne (Porter), Lance Henriksen (Kerchak), Wayne Knight (Tantor). Running time: 88 minutes.

Tarzan, raised by an ape family in the African jungle, battles animal and human foes, but his greatest challenge is to choose between his adopted jungle family and the human world.

Inspector Gadget

Released July. Executive Producers: Jon Avnet, Barry Bernardi, Aaron Meyerson, Jonathan Glickman, Ralph Winter. Producers: Jordan Kerner, Roger Birnbaum, Andy Heyward. Director: David Kellogg. Screenplay: Kerry Ehrin, Zak Penn. Story: Kerry Ehrin, Dana Olsen. Special Animatronic effects: Stan Winston. Cast: Matthew Broderick (Inspector Gadget/Robo Gadget/John Brown), Rupert Everett (Sanford Scolex/The Claw), Joely Fisher (Brenda), Michelle Trachtenberg (Penny), Andy Dick (Kramer), Cheri Oteri (Mayor Wilson), Michael G. Hagerty (Sikes), D. L. Hughley (Gadgetmobile Voice), Rene Auberjonois (Artemus Bradford), Frances Bay (Thelma), Don Adams (voice of Brain).

Running time: 78 minutes.

Based on the DIC television cartoon series of the 1980s. An ambitious security guard, blown up in a robbery attempt, is rebuilt as Inspector Gadget, a police detective with dozens of built-in gizmos to help him catch a master criminal, The Claw. (Rated PG)

The Straight Story

Released October. Executive Producers: Pierre Edelman, Michael Polaire. Producers: Alain Sarde, Mary Sweeney, Neal Edelstein. Director: David Lynch. Screenplay: John Roach, Mary Sweeney. Cast: Richard Farnsworth (Alvin Straight), Sissy Spacek (Rose), Jane Galloway Heitz (Dorothy), Everett McGill (Tom), Jennifer Edwards-Hughes (Brenda), Barbara Robertson (Deer Woman), John Farley (Thorvald), Harry Dean Stanton (Lyle). Running time: 112 minutes.

Based on a true story. Determined 73-year-old man travels from Iowa to Wisconsin on his motorized lawn mower to visit his estranged, ailing brother.

The Hand Behind the Mouse: The Ub Iwerks Story

Released October. Producer, Director, Writer: Leslie Iwerks. Narrator: Kelsey Grammer. Interviewees: Russell Merritt, Mark Kausler, Leonard Maltin, John Lasseter, Roy E. Disney, Chuck Jones, Virginia Davis, Don Iwerks, Dave Smith, Tippi Hedren. Running time: 92 minutes.

A documentary on the career of Ub Iwerks, the animator who was Walt Disney's right-hand man in the formative years of his career, and is credited with designing Mickey Mouse.

Toy Story 2

Released November. Executive Producer: Sarah McArthur. Producers: Helene Plotkin, Karen Robert Jackson. Director: John Lasseter. Codirectors: Lee Unkrich, Ash Brannon. Screenplay: Andrew Stanton, Rita Hsiao, Doug Chamberlin, and Chris Webb. Original Story: John Lasseter, Pete Docter, Ash Brannon, Andrew Stanton. Music: Randy Newman. Supervising Animator: Glenn McQueen. Voice Cast: Tom Hanks (Woody), Tim Allen (Buzz Lightyear), Joan Cusack (Jessie), Kelsey Grammer (Stinky Pete, the Prospector), Don Rickles (Mr. Potato Head), Jim Varney (Slinky Dog), Wallace Shawn (Rex), John Ratzenberger (Hamm), Annie Potts (Bo Peep), Wayne Knight (Al McWhiggin), John Morris (Andy), Laurie Metcalf (Andy's Mom), Estelle Harris (Mrs. Potato Head), R. Lee Ermey (Sarge), Jodi Benson (Barbie), Jonathan Harris (The Cleaner), Joe Ranft (Wheezy), Andrew Stanton (Emperor Zurg). Running time: 95 minutes.

A sequel to *Toy Story* (1995). Stolen by a toy dealer who plans sell him to a Japanese museum, Woody discovers he's based on a classic children's TV show from the 1950s. When Buzz and the other toys from Andy's room come to the rescue, Woody must decide whether to go home or remain with his family of "Woody's Round-Up" companions.

Note: In its theatrical run, the film was accompanied by the animated short-subject that put Pixar on the map, and gave it its screen logo or mascot, Luxo Jr. (1986).

TOUCHSTONE RELEASES: *The Other Sister, 10 Things I Hate About You, Instinct, Summer of Sam, The 13th Warrior, Mumford, The Insider, Deuce Bigalow: Male Gigolo, Cradle Will Rock, Bicentennial Man.*

HOLLYWOOD RELEASES: *The Sixth Sense, Breakfast of Champions, Mystery Alaska.*

2000

Fantasia/2000

Released January (in Imax Theaters). Executive Producer, Roy Edward Disney. Producer: Donald W. Ernst. Supervising Animation Director: Hendel Butoy. Associate Producer: Lisa C. Cook. Host Sequences Director: Don Hahn. Conductor: James Levine. Artistic Supervisors: David A. Bossert (Artistic Coordinator/Visual Effects), Mitchell Guinto Bernal (Layout), Dean Gordon (Backgrounds), Alex Topete (Cleanup), Steve Goldberg, Shyh-Chyuan Huang, Susan Thayer, Mary Jane "M. J." Turner (Computer Generated Imagery). Symphony no. 5 by Ludwig van Beethoven. Director and Art Director: Pixote Hunt. Animators: Wayne Carlisi, Raul Garcia. *Pines of Rome* by Ottorino Respighi. Director: Hendel Butoy. Art directors: Dean Gordon, William Perkins. Animators: Linda Bel, Darrin Butts, Darko Cesar, Sasha Dorogov, Sergei Kouchnerov, Andrea Losch, Teresa Martin, Branko Mihanovic, William Recinos, William Wright. *Rhapsody in Blue* by George Gershwin. Direction and Story: Eric Goldberg. Conductor: Bruce Broughton. Artistic Consultant: Al Hirschfeld. Art Director: Susan McKinsey Goldberg. Animators: Tim Allen, James Baker, Jared Beckstrand, Nancy Beiman, Jerry Yu Ching, Andreas Deja, Robert Espanto Domingo, Brian Ferguson, Douglas Frankel, Thomas Gately, David Hancock, Song-Jin Kim, Bert Klein, Joe Oh, Jamie Oliff, Mark Pudleiner, Michael Show, Marc Smith, Chad Stewart, Michael Stocker, Andreas Wessel-Therhorn, Theresa Wiseman, Anthony Ho Wong, Ellen Woodbury, Phil Young. Piano Concerto no. 2, Allegro, op. 102 by Dmitri Shostakovich. Director: Hendel Butoy. Art Director: Michael Humphries. Based on the story "The Steadfast Tin Soldier" by Hans Christian Andersen. Animators: Tim Allen, Doug Bennett, Eamonn Butler, Darrin Butts, Sandro Cleuzo, Steve Hunter, Ron Husband, Mark Kausler, Song-Jin Kim, David Kuhn, Roy Meurin, Gregory G. Miller, Neil Richmond, Jason Ryan Henry Soto, Jr. *The Carnival of the Animals (Le Carnaval des Animaux),* Finale by Camille Saint-Saëns. Direction, Animation, Story: Eric Goldberg. Original Concept:

Joe Grant. Art Director: Susan McKinsey Goldberg. Conceptual Storyboard: Vance Gerry, David Cutler. *The Sorcerer's Apprentice* by Paul Dukas. Director: James Algar. Art Direction: Tom Codrick, Charles Phillippi, Zack Schwartz. Story Development: Perce Pearce, Carl Fallberg. Animation Supervision: Fred Moore, Vladimir Tytla. Production Supervision: Ben Sharpsteen. Animation: Les Clark, Riley Thompson, Marin Woodward, Preston Blair, Edward Love, Ugo D'Orsi, George Rowley, Cornett Wood. *Pomp and Circumstance,* Marches 1, 2, 3, and 4 by Sir Edward Elgar. Director: Francis Glebas. Art Director: Daniel Cooper. Featured soprano: Kathleen Battle. Chorus: The Chicago Symphony Chorus. Lead Character Animator, Donald and Daisy: Tim Allen. Animators: Doug Bennett, Tim George, Mark Kausler, Song-Jin Kim, Roy Meurin, Gregory G. Miller. *The Firebird Suite* (1919) by Igor Stravinsky. Direction, Design, and Story: Gaetan Brizzi and Paul Brizzi. Art Director: Carl Jones. Lead Character Animators: Anthony DeRosa (Sprite), Ron Husband (Elk), John Pomeroy (Firebird). Animators: Tim Allen, Sandro Cleuzo, David Hancock, Song-Jin Kim, Gregory G. Miller, Joe Oh, David Zaboski. Host Sequences Character Animator: Andreas Deja (Mickey).

Hosts: Steve Martin, Itzhak Perlman, Quincy Jones, Bette Midler, James Earl Jones, Penn & Teller, James Levine, Angela Lansbury. Voice Cast: Wayne Allwine, Tony Anselmo, Russi Taylor. Running time: 75 minutes.

The Tigger Movie

Released February. Produced by Walt Disney Television Animation. Producer: Cheryl Abood. Executive Producer: Sharon Morrill Rubinov. Director: Jun Falkenstein. Screenplay: Jun Falkenstein. Story: Eddie Guzelian. Art Director: Toby Bluth. Director of Walt Disney Animation Japan: Takamitsu Kawamura. Supervising Animation Director: Kenichi Tsuchiya. Score: Harry Gregson-Williams. Songs: Richard M. Sherman, Robert B. Sherman.

Voice Cast: Jim Cummings (Pooh and Tigger), Nikita Hopkins (Roo), Ken Sansom (Rabbit), John Fiedler (Piglet), Peter Cullen (Eeyore), Andre Stojka (Owl), Kath Soucie (Kanga), Tom Attenborough (Christopher Robin), John Hurt (Narrator). Running time: 77 minutes.

Tigger, who's always boasted that he's the only one of his species, starts to yearn for a family, and his friends in the Hundred-Acre Wood try to help him.

Short Subjects

1995
> *Runaway Brain*—MM
> *Disney's Timon & Pumbaa in Stand By Me*—Cartoon Special in CinemaScope

1997
> *Redux Riding Hood*—Cartoon Special (nominated for an Academy Award)
> *Three Little Pigs*—Cartoon Special

1998
> *Goofy's Extreme Sports: Paracycling* (with Mighty Joe Young)
> *Goofy's Extreme Sports: Skating the Half Pipe* (with I'll Be Home For Christmas)

1999
> *Donald's Dynamite: Opera Box* (with Doug's 1st Movie)
> *Pluto Gets the Paper: Spaceship* (with My Favorite Martian)

DIRECT-TO-VIDEO FEATURES—Animated
> *The Return of Jafar* (1994)
> *Aladdin and the King Of Thieves* (1996)
> *Pooh's Grand Adventure* (1997)
> *Beauty and the Beast: The Enchanted Christmas* (1997)
> *Pocahontas: Journey to a New World* (1998)
> *Lion King II: Simba's Pride* (1998)
> *Mickey's Once Upon a Christmas* (1999)

DIRECT-TO-VIDEO FEATURES—Live Action
> *Honey, We Shrunk Ourselves* (1997)
> *The Wonderful Ice Cream Suit* (1999)
> *An Extremely Goofy Movie* (2000)

6 · The Disney Shorts

EVERYONE KNOWS THAT IT WAS *Steamboat Willie* AND MICKEY MOUSE THAT put Walt Disney on the map. But many people tend to forget that after the studio made *Snow White* and went on to more ambitious projects, both animated and live action, Disney *continued* to turn out one-reel cartoons with Mickey, Donald, Goofy, and all the other animated stars.

Though these shorts do not offer as much as the feature films, they have many interesting aspects, and certainly deserve a closer look.

A large part of *Steamboat Willie*'s success was due to music; the novelty of the cartoon was the synchronization of cartoon action on the screen with music on the sound track. Disney knew that this delighted his audience, and from that time on music always played an important part in his short films. In fact, a good many of the Disney cartoons through the early 1930s are completely built around musical themes.

One of the best Mickey Mouse efforts of the early 1930s, *The Whoopee Party*, has Mickey and Minnie throwing a house party for their friends. The music is virtually nonstop: Minnie is playing "Sweet Rosie O'Grady" on the piano while the guests dance, Mickey doing "Maple Leaf Rag," and then the whole gang joining in on "Running Wild," in which Mickey uses mousetraps, flapping window shades, and other household utensils to provide percussion. On this number the party really starts jumping. The piano sways, and the stool hops in time. The lamps start moving in time to the music, with chairs, bureaus, a coffeepot, a tray of sandwiches, a couple of hot dogs, even a bunch of matches finding it impossible to keep still. A long shot then shows the entire house swaying with the infectious beat of the song. When noise brings a police patrol to calm things down, even they join in the fun.

The whole cartoon moves to this music. Equally important, however, is what's happening on screen. *The Whoopee Party* is typical of the Mickey Mouse cartoons of this time. There is an incredible amount of action on the screen; an opening shot shows a score of couples dancing to the music. Later, when the party starts to jump, every single inch of picture is filled with dancing figures. What is more, nothing is out of bounds for joining the fun: a pair of shirts on the ironing board are as likely to get up and dance as any of the animals at the party.

The early Disney cartoons knew no limits when it came to such ideas; anything was fair game. As the technique grew more sophisticated, it seemed incongruous to indulge in this kind of humor, and it disappeared.

Mickey provides impromptu accompaniment for a musical
in *The Whoopee Party.* © *Walt Disney Productions*

Greta Garbo congratulates Mickey on his new movie in
Mickey's Gala Premiere. © *Walt Disney Productions;
courtesy Al Kilgore*

Minnie prepares for her stage debut in *Mickey's Meller-drammer.* © *Walt Disney Productions; courtesy Al Kilgore*

The studio was turning out about one Mickey Mouse per month in the early thirties, each one filled to overflowing with gags, gags, gags. Other studios surpassed Disney in later years with invention and characterization in the short-subject field, but no cartoons ever topped the early Mickey Mouse series for sheer volume in the gag department. *Touchdown Mickey* (1932), for instance, boasts the most frenetic football game ever conceived for a comedy film, ending with Mickey being driven underground and burrowing up to the goal line to win the game.

No effort was spared on the Mickey Mouse series, especially as it grew in popularity (in many theatres Mickey received top billing over the feature film!), producing such elaborate shorts as *The Mad Doctor* (1933), a chilling and amazingly atmospheric cartoon with all the stops pulled out to create a miniature horror film; *Mickey's Gala Premiere* (1933), in which a gaggle of Hollywood luminaries come to the debut of Mickey's latest film: John, Ethel, and Lionel Barrymore, Laurel and Hardy, Marie Dressler and Wallace Beery, Charlie Chaplin, Harold Lloyd, Buster Keaton, Harry Langdon, Douglas Fairbanks, Joe E. Brown, Wheeler and Woolsey, Joan Crawford, Mae West, George Arliss, and even Greta Garbo! (P.S. It all turns out to be a dream.)

Offbeat ideas like *Gulliver Mickey* (1934), with giant-sized Mickey in the land of the Lilliputians, paid off nicely, as did such spoofs as *Mickey's Mellerdrammer* (1933), in which Mickey and the gang put on a production of *Uncle Tom's Cabin,* and *The Klondike Kid* (1932), an amusing takeoff of Yukon melodramas.

Maestro Mickey about to conduct the *William Tell* Overture in *The Band Concert.* ⓒ *Walt Disney Productions*

For Mickey's color debut in 1935, Disney returned to a musical
motif, and produced one of the best cartoons ever made anywhere, *The
Band Concert.* The film opens at an outdoor band concert in the park,
with a responsive audience applauding the last piece. Then maestro
Mickey turns to the *William Tell* Overture. He litèrally wrings various
shades of performance from his band, the effect of which is spoiled when
a noisy ice-cream vendor (Donald Duck) approaches, first bursting into
the music with his raucous voice, then confounding the band by playing
"Turkey in the Straw" on his fife. The song is counterpoint to William
Tell, and the band quickly adopts to the wrong tune, much to Mickey's
chagrin. He smashes Donald's instrument in two, but the resourceful
duck has an endless number of them up his sleeve.

Just as Donald gets out of the way, another crisis approaches. The
"Storm" section of the piece is due, and the musicians prepare. Tym-
panist Horace Horsecollar removes his coat; others work into a sweat. At
the same time a vicious tornado twister is nearing the park. Just as the
band starts to play "The Storm," the real storm overtakes the bandstand,
sending the musicians flying into the air. They don't miss a note, even
though conductor Mickey is flying in and out of doors, windows, and
debris (his music stand miraculously following him), and other musicians are suffering similar problems. Near the end of the piece the storm
subsides and they start falling to earth, still keeping up with the music as
the band members are deposited, one by one, on the branches of a barren
tree. They all manage to end together, with a grand finale, and are
greeted with the applause of one spectator—Donald. He takes out his fife,
which prompts the band members to hurl everything in sight at him. He
is swallowed up by a tuba, but manages to peer outside and play the last
note as the scene fades out.

The Band Concert is a brilliant cartoon, because everything about it
works so beautifully. The music itself is compelling (it obviously inspired

Donald Duck makes his screen debut in *The Wise Little Hen.* © *Walt Disney Productions; courtesy Movie Star News*

the animators and gagmen) , but the material built around it is terrific. There are nuances of expression in Mickey's character throughout this film that had seldom been explored in earlier shorts. The pacing is also entirely different from the standard Mickey Mouse comedies of the early thirties. Instead of trying to pack in a thousand gags a minute, *The Band Concert* takes its time and builds to a crescendo, cued, naturally, by the moods of the *William Tell* Overture. Last, but not least, the color in this cartoon is superb.

In some respects this was the pinnacle of Mickey's career as a short-subject star, and a harbinger of things to come. From the very start ample footage in the MM cartoons had been devoted to Minnie, Pluto, Horace Horsecollar, Clarabelle Cow, Pegleg Pete, and Dippy Dawg, later known as Goofy. As the 1930s wore on, however, Mickey played a progressively less important role in the proceedings, some cartoons completely taken over by the character of Pluto. After the introduction of Donald Duck, it was clear Disney had another "star" to contend with, and he moved in on Mickey's territory as well. Beginning with *Mickey's Service Station*, more and more cartoons costarred Mickey, Donald, and Goofy—films like *On Ice, Moving Day, Alpine Climbers*, etc. Mickey still had his moments, in spectacular cartoons such as *Thru the Mirror* (a marvelous, surreal *Alice in Wonderland* cartoon) and *The Brave Little Tailor;* but it took special ideas and backgrounds to carry Mickey, where just a few years earlier a day in the farmyard was enough excuse for a successful Mickey Mouse endeavor.

By 1938 the handwriting was on the wall, and Disney stopped calling his shorts "Mickey Mouse Cartoons," identifying each short by its star character instead. Just a few years later Disney all but phased out his Silly Symphonies as well, leaving the field wide open for his most popular cartoon stars.

The Silly Symphonies dated back to 1929, when Carl Stalling was in

A posed portrait of the Three Little Pigs.   © *Walt Disney Productions*

W. C. Fields and Charlie McCarthy were among the many stars portrayed in *Mother Goose Goes Hollywood.*   © *Walt Disney Productions*

charge of the music for Disney's cartoons. He suggested the idea of finding music that was evocative of some mood, and building a cartoon around the theme, with inanimate objects coming to life to suggest a season or a setting. The first such short was *The Skeleton Dance;* finding acceptance for it among movie exhibitors was difficult, but when the film caught on with audiences, the series, dubbed Silly Symphonies, was launched. Still, not to take any chances, the title card for the series read, "Mickey Mouse presents a Walt Disney Silly Symphony," giving movie-goers something familiar to hold onto.

Early Silly Symphonies had such titles as *Springtime, Night, Arctic Antics,* and *Midnight in a Toy Shop.* But the sheer novelty of watching inanimate objects come to life wore off fairly soon, and the series broadened its horizons to encompass fairy tales and fables, some of them mundane, some of them quite clever. The biggest boost came when Disney decided to make these shorts in the new Technicolor process. The very first one, *Flowers and Trees,* took an already tried-and-true formula (plants and trees displaying human characteristics) and gave it new life through the skilled, and ingenious, use of color. Color became the main attraction of many Symphonies and a valuable asset to others like the holiday-themed *Santa's Workshop* (1932) and *The Night Before Christmas* (1933). Both films are endearing, but it's difficult to imagine them without their rainbow hues, still dazzling today; the latter film also incorporates some ambitious effects that Disney's animators were trying hard to perfect (realistic, multicolored flames and a warm glow around a fireplace, for instance).

Music remained equally important to the series and was largely responsible for the success of the most famous Silly Symphony. *Three Little Pigs* (1933). Among animation buffs it's known as the first film to delineate true personality among characters who essentially look the same . . . but to the movie-going public of the 1930s, its theme song "Who's Afraid of the Big Bad Wolf?" became an anti-Depression anthem.

Throughout the decade, the Silly Symphonies served as a showcase for imagination and experimentation. Imagination was the key ingredient, since Disney's writers and artists couldn't fall back on familiar, established characters. Instead, they created settings and situations each time out. One of these gems was *Music Land* (1935), a fable about a star-crossed romance between a little saxophone (who lives on the Isle of Jazz) and a young violin (who resides on the Land of Symphony), whose nations are separated by the Sea of Discord. Here, a cute story idea is carried out in an atmosphere of visual creativity and humor. On the other hand, *The Flying Mouse* (1934) used the artists' skills to enhance a dramatic story about a little mouse who is granted the wish to fly, only to find himself shunned as a freak and an outsider.

Not every entry in this series was a gem; sometimes the story men seemed to be coasting, and often they flirted with terminal cuteness. But even a simple tale like *The Tortoise and the Hare* could be lifted out of the ordinary by expressive character animation and innovative methodology—as in the animation of Max Hare literally "running a blue streak."

Some of the most basic Symphony story ideas were transformed into outstanding films by sheer virtuosity of technique, and indeed, this became the series raison d'être by the mid-1930s. Walt used the Silly Symphonies as a proving ground for new talent and new ideas. Just as *Flowers and Trees* had served as a showcase for Technicolor, *The Old Mill* was used as a test-run for the new multiplane camera. Both the film—and the camera—were a smashing success, and the following year the studio turned out a visual extravaganza called *Wynken Blynken and Nod.*

In this filmization of the lovely Eugene Field poem, Wynken, Blynken, and Nod, three infant boys, sail through the nighttime sky in a wooden shoe, amid hauntingly beautiful cloud arrangements, with lumi-

A publicity sketch from *Elmer Elephant* gives an indication
of its general cuteness.   © *Walt Disney Productions*

Even the title cards on Disney cartoons were impressive;
here is a good example.   © *Walt Disney Productions*

nescent stars as "fish" in the "sea" of air. They hitch onto a shooting star, which casts a dazzling light on them as it careens through the air. Then the clouds start blowing the shoe around; lightning strikes, and the three children tumble out of their shoe, sailing back to earth, where they materialize into one youngster, sleeping in his bed and dreaming this wonderful fantasy.

Wynken Blynken and Nod is as extravagant as any Disney feature; it set a standard that was probably too extravagant to maintain, with most effort being turned toward feature-film production in the late 1930s. After 1940 these unique cartoons petered out of the Disney production schedule.

Not that the character cartoons weren't done on an elaborate scale. In discussing *Window Cleaners* (1940), film historian William K. Everson commented: "Disney used height—skyscrapers, mountains, etc.—far more than other cartoon-makers, and with more concern for perspective and the convincing illusion of dizzy depths. Height gags in Warner Brothers and MGM cartoons were always just that—rapid gags that paid off quickly in a laugh, and without a buildup. Disney, on the other hand, used height much as Harold Lloyd did, to counterpoint comedy with a genuine thrill."

Around this time, however, the Disney cartoons (or at least, many of them, for there were always exceptions) started to fall into formula patterns. The Mickey-Donald-Goofy efforts usually involved some project (scaling a mountain in *Alpine Climbers,* building a ship in *Boat Builders,* etc.), which all three would begin together; then the cartoon would break down into seperate segments of each character encountering his own problem, culminating in a finale where all three would come together again. The Donald Duck cartoons became increasingly predictable, and Donald's temper tantrums less funny.

Furthermore, with the 1940s, Disney began to feel his competition moving up on him. There were many rival cartoon studios operating in the 1930s, with varying degrees of success, but Disney was always in a class by himself. In the early 1940s Warner Brothers and MGM surged ahead, spurred by their new stars Bugs Bunny and Tom and Jerry. They too were making their cartoons in color, and their product became slick and handsome. Reacting to the mood of the 1940s, they adopted a loud, brash sense of humor, and sharpened the tempo of the films considerably. Though no one could touch Disney in the feature-film area, many felt that he was being eclipsed in the realm of short subjects.

The situation changed as the decade wore on. The Disney cartoons were assigned to several directors who asserted their own styles on the familiar characters, just as various men did with the Warners's characters. Charles Nichols, who had a gentle, sometimes cute approach, supervised most of the shorts with Mickey, Pluto, and Figaro the Cat. Jack Kinney started doing crazy things with Goofy, while the wildest of all were Jack Hannah's Donald Duck cartoons.

The pacing accelerated, the humor sharpened, and the technique improved (if such a thing seems possible) during this phase. Never before would there have been an inside joke such as the one in *Double Dribble,* in which the basketball players (all depicted as Goofy) are called by the names Kinney, Lounsbery, Hannah, and Sibley—all members of the Disney staff! Seldom had there been violence in Disney cartoons until now, albeit less savage than the antics of MGM's Tom and Jerry.

It is important to recall that these are generalizations, for in no series, under any director, did the studio come up with a winner every time, just as in the mild-mannered cartoons of Charles Nichols there were often some very bright, inspired creations, such as *Mickey and the Seal* (1948), in which a sea lion follows Mickey home from the zoo and joins

This title card was the signal for applause and laughter in hundreds of theatres around the world. © *Walt Disney Productions*

Mickey for a bath, without the mouse's knowledge, or *Bone Bandit* (1947), a very funny Pluto cartoon with the dog battling an ambitious gopher who is using bones to support a massive underground tunnel where he stores his food.

But when one thinks of great cartoons from this period, the Kinney and Hannah endeavors usually stand out. Another interesting aspect of the cartoons at this time is that Mickey, Donald, and Goofy all became middle-class citizens; it is as if their status in life improved along with the fortunes of the country, for they began life in the Depression as barnyard characters. As the 1930s progressed (and the animation technique improved, along with the addition of color) they became slicker and less "vulgar." The 1940s cartoons often show Goofy in a business suit or as Father in a series of domestic comedies. Mickey now lives in a comfortable suburban home, and one entire Donald Duck comedy, *The New Neighbor,* is devoted to the trials of living in a house next door to a pest.

The writers and directors were careful not to be hemmed in by these changes, however, and they always left room for ventures off the beaten path, as in *No Sail* (1945), in which Donald and Goofy rent a sailboat that operates on nickels. When the time is up, the sail collapses until another nickel is deposited. Unprepared for this, our friends are stranded out at sea, and their plight is shown with great melodrama; there is a beautiful image of the stark situation, a bright sun creating a yellowy sky, their boat a silhouette on the horizon. After several days Donald has whiskers and a thoroughly bedraggled look. When he goes fishing for a shark and is pulled underwater, he screams for Goofy to help, but the Goof has gotten his hands tangled up in the fishing wire, and becomes engrossed in working a cat's cradle. Eventually, the twosome returns to shore when Donald accidentally pushes his bill down the nickel slot and reactivates the boat.

In 1941 Goofy starred in a short called *How to Ride a Horse,* which was incorporated into the feature film *The Reluctant Dragon.* The incongruity of using this hapless creature to demonstrate *anything* made

What a difference between the style of this cartoon and the early Mickeys; a handsome scene from *Pueblo Pluto*.
© *Walt Disney Productions*

the spoof of a training film a big laugh-getter, and spawned a series of Goofy sports reels: *The Art of Skiing, How to Play Baseball, Olympic Champ, How to Swim, How to Play Golf, How to Play Football, Double Dribble, Goofy Gymnastics,* and *Tennis Racquet,* the latter enhanced by the comic narration of Doodles Weaver.

The late 1940s brought Donald two new adversaries to contend with: a pair of spunky chipmunks named Chip 'n' Dale. Their battles are responsible for some of the funniest and fastest Donald Duck cartoons, most notably *Up a Tree* (1955), a later effort that has one of the most frenzied strings of gags ever concocted for a Disney cartoon, as lumberjack Donald tries to cut down the chipmunks' tree, and they arrange it so the scheme backfires completely, the downed log "chasing" Donald down a sluice, through his cabin, into a mine, and into a shambles.

Perhaps the best Donald Duck of all was directed by Jack King, who alternated among several characters at this time. The film is *Donald's Dilemma* (1947), a sidesplitting satire of psychological dramas with Daisy telling her story to psychiatrist Sigmund Frump. It seems that one day a flowerpot fell on Donald's head, and when he awoke he thought he was a romantic singer; what's more, he had no memory of Daisy. Overnight, he became a star, and despite all her attempts to see him, Daisy has been left out in the cold. The psychiatrist places a globe on his desk, and tells Daisy that now Donald and his voice belong to the world; she must decide if she is willing to let the world have him, or if she wants him for herself. "Which will it be?" he asks, "the world—or you?" Without hesitation, she screams "Me! Me! Me!" and smashes the globe through his desk. Daisy climbs up to the catwalk of the theatre where Donald is appearing, and drops another flowerpot on his head, restoring his original voice and his memory.

Donald's Dilemma is a great cartoon, for many reasons. Foremost is the fact that it makes the characters and their situation *real*, even while reminding you that this is a cartoon. The audience actually becomes involved with Daisy's predicament, and there are marvelous little touches to heighten the emotionalism (as when she is climbing to the catwalk

A scene from one of the funniest cartoons ever made, *Hold That Pose*. Notice how Goofy has evolved into a middle-class American everyman. © *Walt Disney Productions*

An angry Donald horns in on Chip 'n' Dale in one of their many encounters. © *Walt Disney Productions*

After being hit on the head with a flowerpot, Donald doesn't recognize his own girl friend Daisy, in the memorable short, *Donald's Dilemma*. © *Walt Disney Productions*

near the end and almost loses her step). At the same time the cartoon is filled with hilarious visual exaggeration; when Daisy recalls that Donald gave her a cold, icy stare, a long icicle emits from his eyes, and as she waits for Donald at the stage door of the theatre, the seasons change and she is covered with snow. *Donald's Dilemma* shows how much could be done within the framework of a seven-minute cartoon, using familiar characters; it is a gem.

The 1950s saw many changes in the structure of the cartoon program at Disney. Several trends had their effect on the animation itself. First, there was the tremendous impact of UPA's initial cartoons, with Gerald McBoing and Mr. Magoo, which used "limited animation" and a stylized design that moved away from the literalism of the Disney cartoons. Critics hailed the UPA technique and downgraded Disney at the same time, but Disney answered back with a delightful short called *Toot, Whistle, Plunk, and Boom,* which not only used limited animation, but built the whole concept of the film around it, in showing the origin of

If UPA could do it, so could Disney. The result: a multiaward-winning "limited animation" short, *Toot, Whistle, Plunk, and Boom.* © *Walt Disney Productions*

musical instruments; what is more, the film was made in CinemaScope. It won the Academy Award that year as best cartoon short.

Having shown that they could do limited animation as well as anyone, the Disney staff returned to their normal routine, except that gradually the backgrounds in the cartoons became sparse and were eventually designed in an abstract form, a compromise measure adopted by such rival studios as Warner Brothers. Thus, clouds, trees, and landscapes took on a different look in the background, while Donald Duck, Goofy, and Chip 'n' Dale cavorted in full animation in the foreground. Limited animation was used as a technique where it was felt suited to the story, as in *Pigs Is Pigs* (1954).

CinemaScope was a short-lived medium for the one-reelers, as was the passing fancy of 3-D, which Disney employed for two cartoons, *Melody* and the Donald Duck/Chip 'n' Dale *Working for Peanuts*.

Another trend took root at this time, however. The short subject market was dwindling, and it was becoming increasingly expensive to produce one-reel cartoons. Disney gradually phased them out altogether, replacing them with two- and three-reel "specials," digest-sized cartoons with something more to offer than the run-of-the-mill series entry.

Ben and Me (1954) had all the qualities of a feature film, though it ran less than a half hour. It *should* look like a feature; it employed virtually the entire animation staff, under the direction of Hamilton Luske. This handsome cartoon deals with Amos the Mouse, confidant of Benjamin Franklin who was really responsible for many of Franklin's greatest ideas. This charming, if somewhat irreverent, cartoon featured Sterling Holloway as the voice of Amos.

Other "specials" included *Jack and Old Mac*, a short but interesting artistic experiment by Bill Justice in which characters are created out of words (the letters "cat" form the body of a cat, etc.); *The Truth About Mother Goose*, an elaborate featurette directed by Wolfgang Reitherman and Bill Justice illustrating the origins of three famous nursery rhymes,

a London Bridge sequence being especially striking; *Paul Bunyan*, directed by Les Clark, a genial cartoon of the famous tall-tale hero with nice touches (Paul and Babe the Blue Ox built Pike's Peak in order to survey the land, and dug the Missouri River to haul logs) and a good title song; *Noah's Ark* (1959), animation of stick figures not unlike George Pal's Puppetoons, done by Bill Justice, who with several collaborators was responsible for the ingenious main titles of several Disney features; *A Symposium on Popular Songs* (1962), another Bill Justice credit with Ludwig von Drake conducting a tour of popular musical styles from ragtime to rock and roll, accompanied by some clever songs by the Sherman brothers, and equally clever animation, using paper cutouts; and *Winnie the Pooh and the Honey Tree* (1966), directed by Wolfgang Reitherman, one of the studio's loveliest works, capturing the flavor of A. A. Milne's original illustrations, and taking them a few steps further, with delightful results. The success of this short—and the felicitious marriage of Disney and Pooh—led to several theatrical sequels.

Disney filled in his short subject schedule in the 1950s by releasing the segments of his omnibus features of the 1940s as separate cartoons (*Lake Titicaca, Peter and the Wolf*, etc.), combining some for special packages (*Contrasts in Rhythm* was comprised of *Trees* and *Bumble Boogie*).

There was also an increasing number of live-action shorts at this time, which had been spurred by the initial success of *Seal Island* in 1949.

After the somewhat surprising success of the True-Life Adventures, which started racking up Academy Awards the way the Disney cartoons had done in the 1930s, a second series was established called "People and Places." When its very first entry, *The Alaskan Eskimo*, copped an Oscar, Disney knew he had another hit on his hands. These shorts were done in the same style as the True-Life films and by the same people. (*Eskimo* was photographed by Alfred Milotte, who had made the first True-Life short, *Seal Island*.) When Disney expanded his True-Life series into the feature-length category, People and Places accelerated its output, tackling such diverse topics as *Lapland, Switzerland*, and *Seven Cities of Antarctica*. These outstanding shorts have since become staples on the school circuit.

The Disney animators even got around to stick figures, in such 1950s efforts as *Noah's Ark*.

Ernest Shepard's famous Pooh drawings come to life in Disney's *Winnie the Pooh and the Honey Tree.* © 1965 *Walt Disney Productions*

One of the stars of *Beaver Valley.* © *Walt Disney Productions*

▶

A colorful scene from one of the "People and Places" shorts, *Samoa.* © *Walt Disney Productions*

Disney tackles science fiction—a scene from *Eyes in Outer Space*. © *Walt Disney Productions*

What better subject for a Disney short than Disneyland? This is a ride through the Matterhorn, as seen in *Gala Day at Disneyland*. © *Walt Disney Productions*

The short subject schedule also included occasional imports from the Disney TV show, such as Ward Kimball's fascinating *Man in Space* show, a 1956 look at the future of the United States space program which time has proven to be remarkably accurate. It was prepared with the on- and off-screen participation of Dr. Werner von Braun, Dr. Heinz Haber, and Willy Ley.

Finally, there were the fictional animal sagas, always well done, always surefire fodder for the younger set: *Wetback Hound, The Horse with the Flying Tail, Yellowstone Cubs,* etc. Most of these were the work of Larry Lansburgh, who was responsible for the feature *The Littlest Outlaw,* as well as many other animal-oriented segments of the Disney TV show.

By the 1960s, even Disney could not justify spending much time or money on shorts; the demand for them in theatres had dwindled dramatically, and it was virtually impossible to turn a profit. But he continued to release one or two a year, and the studio maintained that same output after Walt's death, not only carrying on a tradition but upholding a reputation for quality that always made Disney's short subjects stand out.

Following is a list of the Disney shorts. All titles are given in the order of their release, which may differ from the order in which they were made; such variances are clear when one compares the copyright date for a film to the release date. This list includes only the Disney shorts that received theatrical release. The categories cited after each title indicates which series the short was part of and not necessarily all the characters who appeared in it. (For instance, a Mickey Mouse short of the late 1930s might star Donald and Goofy.)

Key to abbreviations: L = Laugh-O-Grams; A = Alice in Cartoonland; O = Oswald the Lucky Rabbit; MM = Mickey Mouse; SS = Silly Symphonies; DD = Donald Duck; G = Goofy; P = Pluto; CD = Chip 'n' Dale; TL = True-Life Adventure; PP = People and Places. Where no indication is given, the short does not fall under any series title.

1920

Newman Laugh-O-Grams—various mini-cartoons made for the Newman Theater in Kansas City, lasting less than one minute.

1922–1923

Bremen Town Musicians—L
Little Red Riding Hood—L
Puss in Boots—L
Jack and the Beanstalk—L
Goldie Locks and the Three Bears—L
Cinderella—L
Tommy Tucker's Tooth
Martha—a Song-o-Reel
Alice's Wonderland

1924

Alice and the Dog Catcher—A
Alice and the Three Bears—A
Alice and the Toreador—A
Alice and the Wild West Show—A
Alice Cans the Cannibals—A

Alice in Dutch at School—A
Alice Hunting in Africa—A
Alice Plays the Pipers—A
Alice the Peacemaker—A
Alice's Day at Sea—A
Alice's Fishy Story—A
Alice's Spooky Adventure—A

1925

Alice Chops the Suey—A
Alice Gets Stung—A
Alice in the Jungle—A
Alice Is Stage Struck—A
Alice Loses Out—A
Alice on the Farm—A
Alice Picks the Champ—A
Alice Plays Cupid—A
Alice Rattled by Rats—A
Alice Solves the Puzzle—A
Alice the Jail Bird—A
Alice Wins the Derby—A

Alice's Balloon Race—A
Alice's Egg Plant—A
Alice's Little Parade—A
Alice's Mysterious Mystery—A
Alice's Ornery Orphan—A
Alice's Tin Pony—A

1926

Alice at the Carnival—A
Alice at the Rodeo—A
Alice Charms the Fish—A
Alice Cuts the Ice—A
Alice Foils the Pirates—A
Alice Helps the Romance—A
Alice in the Alps—A
Alice in the Big League—A
Alice in the Klondike—A
Alice in the Woolly West—A
Alice the Beach Nut—A
Alice the Collegiate—A
Alice the Fire Fighter—A
Alice the Golf Bug—A
Alice the Lumber Jack—A
Alice the Whaler—A
Alice's Auto Race—A
Alice's Brown Derby—A
Alice's Channel Swim—A
Alice's Circus Daze—A
Alice's Knaughty Knight—A
Alice's Medicine Show—A
Alice's Monkey Business—A
Alice's Picnic—A
Alice's Spanish Guitar—A
Alice's Three Bad Eggs—A
Clara Cleans Her Teeth

1927–1928

Africa Before Dark—O
All Wet—O
The Banker's Daughter—O
Bright Lights—O
Empty Socks—O
The Fox Chase—O
Great Guns—O
Harem Scarem—O
Hot Dog—O
Hungry Hoboes—O
The Mechanical Cow—O
Neck 'n' Neck—O
The Ocean Hop—O
Oh, Teacher—O
Oh, What a Knight—O
The Ole Swimmin' Hole—O
Ozzie of the Mounted—O
Poor Papa—O
Rickety Gin—O
Ride 'Em Plowboy—O
Rival Romeos—O

Sagebrush Sadie—O
Sky Scrappers—O
Sleigh Bells—O
Tall Timber—O
Trolley Troubles—O

1928–1929

(*Steamboat Willie* premiered November 18, 1928; after its success, two previously completed silent MM cartoons, *Plane Crazy* and *Gallopin' Gaucho* were remade with sound. Disney and Celebrity Productions released the Disney product erratically through the end of 1929, and in 1930 Columbia Pictures started national distribution of the cartoons, rereleasing on a wide basis the earlier cartoons that had already received limited release by Disney and Celebrity—hence great confusion in so-called "release dates" at this time. Following are the early titles in the order of their completion and initial distribution.)

Steamboat Willie—MM
Gallopin' Gaucho—MM
Plane Crazy—MM
Barn Dance—MM
The Opry House—MM
When the Cat's Away—MM
Skeleton Dance—SS
Barnyard Battle—MM
The Plow Boy—MM
The Karnival Kid—MM
Mickey's Follies—MM
El Terrible Toreador—MM
Mickey's Choo Choo—MM
Springtime—SS
The Jazz Fool—MM
Hell's Bells—SS
Jungle Rhythm—SS
The Merry Dwarfs—SS
Haunted House—MM
Wild Waves—MM

1930

Summer—SS
Autumn—SS
Just Mickey—MM
Cannibal Capers—SS
The Barnyard Concert—MM
Night—SS
Cactus Kid—MM
Frolicking Fish—SS
Fire Fighters—MM
Arctic Antics—SS
The Shindig—MM
Midnight in a Toy Shop—SS
The Chain Gang—MM
Monkey Melodies—SS
Gorilla Mystery—MM
The Picnic—MM

Winter—SS
Pioneer Days—MM
Playful Pan—SS

1931

Birthday Party—MM
Birds of a Feather—SS
Traffic Troubles—MM
The Castaway—MM
Mother Goose Melodies—SS
The Moose Hunt—MM
The China Plate—SS
Delivery Boy—MM
The Busy Beavers—SS
Mickey Steps Out—MM
The Cat's Out—SS
Blue Rhythm—MM
Egyptian Melodies—SS
Fishin' Around—MM
The Clock Store—SS
Barnyard Broadcast—MM
The Spider and the Fly—SS
Beach Party—MM
The Fox Hunt—SS
Mickey Cuts Up—MM
Mickey's Orphans—MM (nominated for an Academy Award)
The Ugly Duckling—SS

1932

The Bird Store—SS
Duck Hunt—MM
Grocery Boy—MM
Mad Dog—MM
Barnyard Olympics—MM
Mickey's Revue—MM
The Bears and the Bees—SS
Musical Farmer—MM
Mickey in Arabia—MM
Just Dogs—SS
Mickey's Nightmare—MM
Trader Mickey—MM
Flowers and Trees—SS (first one in color)
The Whoopee Party—MM
King Neptune—SS
Bugs in Love—SS
Touchdown Mickey—MM
The Wayward Canary—MM
The Klondike Kid—MM
Babes in the Woods—SS
Santa's Workshop—SS
Mickey's Good Deed—MM

1933

Building a Building—MM (nominated for an Academy Award)
The Mad Doctor—MM

Mickey's Pal Pluto—MM
Birds in the Spring—SS
Mickey's Mellerdrammer—MM
Ye Olden Days—MM
Father Noah's Ark—SS
The Mail Pilot—MM
Three Little Pigs—SS (Academy Award winner)
Mickey's Mechanical Man—MM
Mickey's Gala Premiere—MM
Old King Cole—SS
Lullaby Land—SS
Puppy Love—MM
Pied Piper—SS
The Steeplechase—MM
The Pet Store—MM
Giant Land—MM
The Night Before Christmas—SS

1934

Shanghaied—MM
The China Shop—SS
The Grasshopper and the Ants—SS
Camping Out—MM
Playful Pluto—MM
Funny Little Bunnies—SS
The Big Bad Wolf—SS
Gulliver Mickey—MM
The Wise Little Hen—SS
Mickey's Steamroller—MM
The Flying Mouse—SS
Orphans' Benefit—MM
Peculiar Penguins—SS
Mickey Plays Papa—MM
Goddess of Spring—SS
The Dog-Napper—MM
Two-Gun Mickey—MM

1935

The Tortoise and the Hare—SS (Academy Award winner)
Mickey's Man Friday—MM
The Band Concert—MM (the first Mickey Mouse in color)
Mickey's Service Station—MM
The Golden Touch—SS
Mickey's Kangaroo—MM
The Robber Kitten—SS
Water Babies—SS
Cookie Carnival—SS
Who Killed Cock Robin?—SS (nominated for an Academy Award)
Mickey's Garden—MM
Mickey's Fire Brigade—MM
Pluto's Judgment Day—MM
On Ice—MM
Music Land—SS
Three Orphan Kittens—SS (Academy Award winner)

Cock o' the Walk—SS
Broken Toys—SS

1936

Mickey's Polo Team—MM
Orphans' Picnic—MM
Mickey's Grand Opera—MM
Elmer Elephant—SS
Three Little Wolves—SS
Thru the Mirror—MM
Moving Day—MM
Mickey's Rival—MM
Alpine Climbers—MM
Mickey's Circus—MM
Toby Tortoise Returns—SS
Donald and Pluto—MM
Three Blind Mouseketeers—SS
Mickey's Elephant—MM
The Country Cousin—SS
Mother Pluto—MM
More Kittens—SS

1937

The Worm Turns—MM
Don Donald—MM
Magician Mickey—MM
Moose Hunters—MM
Woodland Cafe—SS
Mickey's Amateurs—MM
Little Hiawatha—SS
Modern Inventions—MM
Hawaiian Holiday—MM
Clock Cleaners—MM
The Old Mill—SS (Academy Award winner)
Pluto's Quinpuplets—P
Donald's Ostrich—DD
Lonesome Ghosts—MM

1938

Self Control—DD
Boat Builders—MM
Donald's Better Self—DD
The Moth and the Flame—SS
Donald's Nephews—DD
Mickey's Trailer—MM
Wynken Blynken and Nod—SS
Polar Trappers—DD
Good Scouts—DD (nominated for an Academy Award)
The Fox Hunt—DD
The Whalers—MM
Mickey's Parrot—MM
The Brave Little Tailor—MM (nominated for an Academy Award)
Farmyard Symphony—SS
Donald's Golf Game—DD
Ferdinand the Bull—Special (Academy Award winner)

Merbabies—SS
Mother Goose Goes Hollywood—SS (nominated for an Academy Award)

1939

Donald's Lucky Day—DD
Society Dog Show—MM
The Practical Pig—Special
Goofy and Wilbur—G
The Ugly Duckling—SS (Academy Award winner)
Hockey Champ—DD
Donald's Cousin Gus—DD
Beach Picnic—DD
Sea Scouts—DD
The Pointer—MM (nominated for an Academy Award)
Donald's Penguin—DD
The Autograph Hound—DD
Officer Duck—DD

1940

The Riveter—DD
Donald's Dog Laundry—DD
Tugboat Mickey—MM
Billposters—DD
Mr. Duck Steps Out—DD
Bone Trouble—P
Put-Put Troubles—DD
Donald's Vacation—DD
Pluto's Dream House—P
Window Cleaners—DD
Mr. Mouse Takes a Trip—MM
Goofy's Glider—G
Fire Chief—DD
Pantry Pirate—P

1941

Timber—DD
Pluto's Playmate—P
The Little Whirlwind—MM
Golden Eggs—DD
A Gentleman's Gentleman—P
Baggage Buster—G
A Good Time for a Dime—DD
Canine Caddy—P
Nifty Nineties—MM
Early to Bed—DD
Truant Officer Donald—DD (nominated for an Academy Award)
Orphans' Benefit—MM
Old MacDonald Duck—DD
Lend a Paw—P (Academy Award winner)
Donald's Camera—DD
The Art of Skiing—G
Chef Donald—DD
The Art of Self-Defense—G

1942

The Village Smithy—DD
Mickey's Birthday Party—MM
Pluto Junior—P
Symphony Hour—MM
Donald's Snow Fight—DD
Donald Gets Drafted—DD
The Army Mascot—P
Donald's Garden—DD
The Sleepwalker—P
Donald's Gold Mine—DD
T-Bone for Two—P
How to Play Baseball—G
The Vanishing Private—DD
The Olympic Champ—G
How to Swim—G
Sky Trooper—DD
Pluto at the Zoo—P
How to Fish—G
Bellboy Donald—DD

1943

Der Fuehrer's Face—DD (Academy Award winner)
Education for Death—Special
Donald's Tire Trouble—DD
Pluto and the Armadillo—P
Flying Jalopy—DD
Private Pluto—P
Fall Out—Fall In—DD
Victory Vehicles—G
Reason and Emotion—Special (nominated for an Academy Award)
Figaro and Cleo—Figaro
The Old Army Game—DD
Home Defense—DD
Chicken Little—Special

1944

The Pelican and the Snipe—Special
How to Be a Sailor—G
Trombone Trouble—DD
How to Play Golf—G
Donald Duck and the Gorilla—DD
Contrary Condor—DD
Commando Duck—DD
Springtime for Pluto—P
The Plastics Inventor—DD
How to Play Football—G (nominated for an Academy Award)
First Aiders—P
Donald's Day Off—DD

1945

Tiger Trouble—G
The Clock Watcher—DD
Dog Watch—P
The Eyes Have It—DD

African Diary—G
Donald's Crime—DD (nominated for an Academy Award)
Californy er Bust—G
Canine Casanova—P
Duck Pimples—DD
The Legend of Coyote Rock—P
No Sail—G & D
Hockey Homicide—G
Cured Duck—DD
Canine Patrol—P
Old Sequoia—DD

1946

A Knight for a Day—G
Pluto's Kid Brother—P
In Dutch—P
Squatter's Rights—P (nominated for an Academy Award)
Donald's Double Trouble—DD
The Purloined Pup—P
Wet Paint—DD
Dumbbell of the Yukon—DD
Lighthouse Keeping—DD
Bath Day—Figaro
Frank Duck Brings 'em Back Alive—DD
Double Dribble—G

1947

Pluto's Housewarming—P
Rescue Dog—P
Straight Shooters—DD
Sleepytime Donald—DD
Figaro and Frankie—Figaro
Clown of the Jungle—DD
Donald's Dilemma—DD
Crazy with the Heat—D & G
Bootle Beetle—DD
Wide Open Spaces—DD
Mickey's Delayed Date—MM
Foul Hunting—G
Mail Dog—P
Chip 'n' Dale—DD (nominated for an Academy Award)
Pluto's Blue Note—P (nominated for an Academy Award)

(Disney started reissuing his old cartoons this year, beginning with *Hawaiian Holiday* and *Clock Cleaners*.)

1948

They're Off—G
The Big Wash—G
Drip Dippy Donald—DD
Mickey Down Under—MM
Daddy Duck—DD
Bone Bandit—P

Donald's Dream Voice—DD
Pluto's Purchase—P
The Trial of Donald Duck—DD
Cat Nap Pluto—P
Inferior Decorator—DD
Pluto's Fledgling—P
Soup's On—DD
Three for Breakfast—DD
Mickey and the Seal—MM (nominated for an Academy Award)
Tea for Two Hundred—DD (nominated for an Academy Award)

1949

Pueblo Pluto—P
Donald's Happy Birthday—DD
Pluto's Surprise Package—P
Sea Salts—DD
Pluto's Sweater—P
Seal Island—TL (Academy Award winner)
Winter Storage—DD
Bubble Bee—Special
Honey Harvester—DD
Tennis Racquet—G
All in a Nutshell—DD
Goofy Gymnastics—G
The Greener Yard—DD
Sheep Dog—P
Slide, Donald, Slide—DD
Toy Tinkers—DD (nominated for an Academy Award)

1950

Pluto's Heart Throb—P
Lion Around—DD
Pluto and the Gopher—P
How to Ride a Horse—G (originally part of *The Reluctant Dragon*)
The Brave Engineer—Special
Crazy Over Daisy—DD
The Wonder Dog—P
Trailer Horn—DD
Primitive Pluto—P
Puss-Cafe—P
Motor Mania—G
Beaver Valley—TL (Academy Award winner)
Pests of the West—P
Food for Feudin'—P
Hook, Lion and Sinker—DD
Camp Dog—P
Bee at the Beach—DD
Hold That Pose—G
Morris the Midget Moose—Special
Out on a Limb—DD

1951

Lion Down—G
Chicken in the Rough—CD

Cold Storage—P
Dude Duck—DD
Home Made Home—G
Corn Chips—DD
Cold War—G
Plutopia—P
Test Pilot Donald—DD
Tomorrow We Diet—G
A Lucky Number—DD
Nature's Half Acre—TL (Academy Award winner)
R'coon Dawg—MM
Get Rich Quick—G
Cold Turkey—P
Fathers Are People—G
Out of Scale—DD
No Smoking—G
Bee on Guard—DD

1952

Father's Lion—G
Donald Applecore—DD
Lambert, The Sheepish Lion—Special (nominated for an Academy Award)
Hello Aloha—G
Two Chips and a Miss—CD
Man's Best Friend—G
Let's Stick Together—DD
Two Gun Goofy—G
Susie, The Little Blue Coupe—Special
Water Birds—TL (Academy Award winner)
Teachers Are People—G
Uncle Donald's Ants—DD
The Little House—Special
Pluto's Party—P
Trick or Treat—DD
Two Weeks Vacation—G
Pluto's Christmas Tree—MM
How to Be a Detective—G

1953

Bear Country—TL (Academy Award winner)
The Alaskan Eskimo—PP (Academy Award winner)
Father's Day Off—G
The Simple Things—MM
For Whom the Bulls Toil—G
Melody (Adventures in Music)—Special (Disney's first 3-D cartoon)
Don's Fountain of Youth—DD
Father's Weekend—G
How to Dance—G
Prowlers of the Everglades—TL
The New Neighbor—DD
Football (Now and Then)—Special
Rugged Bear—DD (nominated for an Academy Award)
Toot, Whistle, Plunk, and Boom—Special (Disney's first CinemaScope cartoon; Academy Award winner)

Ben and Me—Special (nominated for an Academy Award)
Working for Peanuts—DD (made in 3-D)
How to Sleep—G
Canvas Back Duck—DD

1954

(Starting this year "specials" will be identified as either cartoon or live action.)
Spare the Rod—DD
Donald's Diary—DD
Stormy, The Thoroughbred with an Inferiority Complex—live action
The Lone Chipmunks—DD
Two for the Record—from *Make Mine Music*
Johnny Fedora and Alice Blue Bonnet—from *Make Mine Music*
Pigs Is Pigs—cartoon (nominated for an Academy Award)
Casey Bats Again—cartoon
The Martins and the Coys—from *Make Mine Music*
Dragon Around—DD
Casey at the Bat—from *Make Mine Music*
Grin and Bear It—DD
Little Toot—from *Melody Time*
Once Upon a Wintertime—from *Melody Time*
Social Lion—cartoon
Willie the Operatic Whale—from *Make Mine Music*
The Flying Squirrel—DD
Grand Canyonscope—DD (CinemaScope)
Siam—PP (nominated for an Academy Award)

1955

No Hunting—DD (nominated for an Academy Award)
Lake Titicaca—DD—from *Saludos Amigos*
Contrast in Rhythm—from *Melody Time*
Blame It on the Samba—DD—from *Melody Time*
Pedro—from *Saludos Amigos*
Arizona Sheepdog—PP live action
El Gaucho Goofy—G—from *Saludos Amigos*
Switzerland—PP (nominated for an Academy Award)
Aquarela do Brasil—from *Saludos Amigos*
The Flying Gauchito—from *The Three Caballeros*
Bearly Asleep—DD (CinemaScope)
Beezy Bear—DD (CinemaScope)
Peter and the Wolf—from *Make Mine Music*
Up a Tree—DD (CinemaScope)
Emperor Penguins—live action
Men Against the Arctic—PP (Academy Award winner)
Johnny Appleseed—from *Melody Time*

1956

Chips Ahoy—DD (CinemaScope)
Hooked Bear—cartoon (CinemaScope)
How to Have an Accident in the Home—DD
Jack and Old Mac—cartoon
Man in Space—live action (nominated for an Academy Award)

In the Bag—cartoon (CinemaScope)
Cow Dog—live action (nominated for an Academy Award)
A Cowboy Needs a Horse—cartoon
Sardinia—PP
Disneyland U.S.A.—PP
Samoa—PP (nominated for an Academy Award)

1957

Blue Men of Morocco—PP
The Wetback Hound—live action (Academy Award winner)
The Story of Anyburg U.S.A.—cartoon
Lapland—PP
The Truth About Mother Goose—cartoon (nominated for an Academy Award)
Niok—live action
Portugal—PP (nominated for an Academy Award)
Mars and Beyond—live action
Alaskan Sled Dog—live action

1958

Wales—PP
Scotland—PP
Ama Girls—PP (Academy Award winner)
Paul Bunyan—cartoon (nominated for an Academy Award)
The Legend of Sleepy Hollow—from *Ichabod and Mr. Toad*
Seven Cities of Antarctica—PP

1959

Grand Canyon—live action (Academy Award winner)
Nature's Strangest Creatures—live action
Cruise of the Eagle—PP
Eyes in Outer Space—live action
Donald in Mathmagic Land—DD
How to Have an Accident at Work—DD
Noah's Ark—cartoon (nominated for an Academy Award)
Mysteries of the Deep—live action (nominated for an Academy Award)

1960

Gala Day at Disneyland—live action
Goliath II—cartoon (nominated for an Academy Award)
Islands of the Sea—TL (nominated for an Academy Award)
Japan—PP
The Danube—PP
The Hound That Thought He Was a Raccoon—live action
The Horse with the Flying Tail—live action (Academy Award winner)

1961

The Saga of Windwagon Smith—cartoon
Donald and the Wheel—DD
The Litterbug—DD
Aquamania—G (nominated for an Academy Award)

1962

A Symposium on Popular Songs—cartoon (nominated for an Academy Award)

1963

Yellowstone Cubs—live action
Disneyland After Dark—live action (released in 1962 in England)

1964

Golden Horseshoe Revue—live action (released in 1963 in England)
The Tattooed Police Horse—live action

1965

A Country Coyote Goes Hollywood—live action
Freewayphobia—cartoon
Flash the Teenage Otter—live action (released in 1964 in England)
Freewayphobia #2 (Goofy's Freeway Trouble)—cartoon

1966

Winnie the Pooh and the Honey Tree—cartoon
Run, Appaloosa, Run—live action

1967

Scrooge McDuck and Money—cartoon
The Legend of the Boy and the Eagle—live action

Additional Shorts

The above listing includes only short subjects given theatrical release in the United States. Many others were made for television, sponsors, special showings, foreign release, and 16mm distribution. Of these, it is worth noting several cartoons made for the National Film Board of Canada in 1941 and 1942: *Thrifty Pig*, featuring the Three Little Pigs, *The Seven Wise Dwarfs*, bringing Snow White's friends back to the screen, *Donald's Decision*, featuring Donald Duck, and *All Together*. The Disney characters were also used in various commercial films, from a 1939 short for Nabisco called *Mickey's Surprise Party* to a 1965 live-action documentary called *Steel and America* featuring Donald Duck in several animated sequences. Disney also made an important series of short subjects of an instructional nature for the Coordinator of Inter-American Affairs during World War II, several of which are in the permanent collection of the Museum of Modern Art.

Most of the short subjects released theatrically overseas or domestically on 16mm had their origin on the Disney TV programs, such as the popular *I'm No Fool* series with Jiminy Cricket, originally shown on the *Mickey Mouse Club* show. Finally, it is worth noting that in 1967 Disney produced two films for special exhibition in Circlevision, a 360-degree projection system used with great success at such places as Expo '67 in Montreal.

The Short Subjects

The following short subjects were released theatrically by Buena Vista and are less than thirty minutes long, unless otherwise noted.

1968
Winnie the Pooh and the Blustery Day—cartoon (Academy Award winner)

1969
It's Tough to Be a Bird—cartoon (Academy Award winner)

1970
Dad, Can I Borrow the Car?—live action and animation

1972
The Silver Fox and Sam Davenport—live action; 48 minutes (originally released in Germany, 1964, and first shown on the Disney TV show, October 14, 1962)

1974
Winnie the Pooh and Tigger Too—cartoon (nominated for an Academy Award)

1975
Fantasy on Skis—live action

1977
A Tale of Two Critters—live action; 48 minutes

1978
The Small One—cartoon

1979
Footloose Fox—live action

1980
Mickey Mouse Disco—compilation cartoon

1981
Once upon a Mouse—compilation cartoon

1982
Vincent—stop-motion animation
Fun with Mr. Future—cartoon

1983
Winnie The Pooh and a Day for Eeyore—cartoon
Mickey's Christmas Carol—MM (nominated for an Academy Award)

1989
Tummy Trouble—Roger Rabbit cartoon

1990
Roller Coaster Rabbit—Roger Rabbit cartoon
The Prince and the Pauper—MM

1992
Off His Rockers—cartoon
Petal to the Metal—Bonkers cartoon

1993
Trail Mix—Up—Roger Rabbit cartoon

7·Disney on TV

WHEN DISNEY FIRST VENTURED INTO TELEVISION, IT WAS ON HIS OWN terms. He did a handful of Christmas specials, beginning in 1950, with no commercials interrupting the fun, just an announcement of the sponsor's name at the beginning and end of the program. He called the constant interruptions on most programs "bad showmanship."

These initial filmed hours were directed by veteran Robert Florey, who recalls; "We didn't go on location; everything was photographed at the studio, and we took all the time necessary to obtain the perfection always required by Walt Disney, without the usual pressure from a production manager."

When, in 1954, Disney finally succumbed to an offer for a weekly series, he decided to retain as much of this quality as possible. Says Florey: "He followed the march of his TV segments from the time of their conception, presiding daily at conferences with all his collaborators. He didn't have to look at a finished product, or at something in progress to sense what was right or wrong with it. He knew it at once, and if not satisfied, ordered immediate retakes or added scenes after viewing the daily rushes."

The series, broadcast Wednesday evenings on ABC-TV, was called *Disneyland,* and, in keeping with the format of the new amusement park, the show was divided into categories: Fantasyland, Adventureland, Frontierland, and Tomorrowland. The first season set the pace for the weekly series: a combination of cartoon mélanges, true-life nature films, multi-episode adventures, old Disney feature films, and constant bulletins on the Disneyland park, then in progress. Walt Disney himself proved to be a most affable host. (After his first season on the air, he was nominated for an Emmy award as "Most Outstanding New Personality," but he lost to George Gobel.)

During the first season or two, there was enough material in the backlog to provide for a good many shows, with only connecting footage to be filmed, either with Disney himself or with the characters; in at least one case Hans Conried was hired to pose as the Magic Mirror from Snow White, hosting a program of excerpts from earlier feature films. A typical entry during the first season was *From Aesop to Hans Christian Andersen,* which comprised a scene from *Snow White* and the 1930s cartoons *Tortoise and the Hare, The Country Cousin, The Brave Little Tailor,* and *The Ugly Duckling.* Other hours were devoted entirely to one character, such as Goofy or Pluto.

One of the most successful shows during the first season was Ward

The perfect host for the Disney TV show: Walt Disney, with a seeing-eye dog featured in the program *Atta Girl, Kelly.* © *1966 Walt Disney Productions*

Kimball's *Man in Space,* a fascinating survey of space travel, past, present, and future; it was considered good enough to be released theatrically, as was the major hit of the first season, *Davy Crockett.*

In addition to the spate of shows devoted to the Disneyland park, there were other programs that were, in effect, hour-long plugs for current Disney films, both current and reissued. *Operation Undersea,* the story of the filming of *20,000 Leagues under the Sea,* won Disney an Emmy that year as Best Documentary. The following year there was *A Tribute to Joel Chandler Harris,* timed to coincide with the reissue of *Song of the South,* and *Behind the Scenes with Fess Parker,* which was telecast just in time to remind youngsters of the theatrical release of *Davy Crockett and the River Pirates.*

Some of the most fascinating shows in the series were those where Disney took his audience behind the scenes at the studio to show how cartoons are made. An entire show, *The Tricks of Our Trade,* was devoted to such footage, to the delight of Disney buffs as well as curious small fry.

Although *Davy Crockett* was a tremendous success, it was not until the 1957–1958 series that Disney embarked on another homegrown series,

The Saga of Andy Burnett, starring Jerome Courtland as a young frontier hero, with Jeff York and Iron Eyes Cody in supporting roles. The series lasted for six episodes, but it was fairly routine, and it did not warrant further sequels. The 1958–1959 season was marked by two new series, however, which did much better. First, there was *The Nine Lives of Elfego Baca,* "Sheriff, Lawyer, Believer in Justice." Robert Loggia starred as the Latin lawyer with a flair for fighting and a perpetual sympathy for the underdog; James Dunn costarred as his senior law partner. Good casts (Patric Knowles, Lynn Bari, James Drury, Kenneth Tobey) marked this series, but the plotting was pretty obvious, even for children.

Better yet was *Texas John Slaughter,* starring Disney discovery Tom Tryon as a peaceful man who joins the Texas Rangers in order to rid the state of lawlessness, so he can settle down and get married. Directed by Harry Keller, a Republic Pictures Western veteran, on picturesque outdoor locations, the series benefited from tight pacing and nice scenery, but mainly Tryon's portrayal of the title character. *Slaughter* became the biggest success on the Disney show since *Davy Crockett.* Disney commented: "Every time it goes on the air, the rating goes up. So I guess we'll stick with it for a while." *Slaughter* outlasted all the other series on the show.

The 1959–1960 season saw the birth of still more mini-series: *The Swamp Fox,* starring Leslie Nielsen as the famed General Francis Marion, co-starring Dick Foran; *Moochie of the Little League,* an outgrowth of the Kevin Corcoran character from the Mickey Mouse Club;

Kevin Corcoran in a scene from *Moochie of the Little League.* © *Walt Disney Productions*

Texas John Slaughter (Tom Tryon) in a meditative moment. © *Walt Disney Productions*

Jimmie Dodd and Roy Williams lead the Mouseketeers in a rousing cheer; the most famous alumnus, Annette Funicello, can be seen third from right. © *Walt Disney Productions*

and a brief continuation of the *Elfego Baca* series, as well as four *Zorro* hours, bringing back the character from his recently completed run of half-hour shows.

The following year Disney returned to the *Davy Crockett* vein with a quartet of *Daniel Boone* sagas starring Dewey Martin, but they did not take off the way their predecessor did.

In the fall of 1961 Disney moved from ABC to NBC; financial considerations aside, NBC offered Disney the opportunity of broadcasting in color, as well as a sponsorship deal with RCA Victor that would emphasize the unique color qualities of the show (especially if viewed on an RCA color set). Disney had been filming the series in color all along, a wise move that has paid off many times over in recent years.

While at ABC, Disney had produced two series besides his hourly show. The more successful of the two was *The Mickey Mouse Club*, a daily children's show, which bowed on October 3, 1955; to this day there has not been another kiddie program to rival it in popularity, with the possible exception of *Sesame Street*. The daily show was a combination of live performing by the Mouseketeers, a group of personable and talented children (of whom Annette Funicello remains the most prominent) led by Jimmie Dodd; an old Mickey Mouse or Donald Duck cartoon; nature footage; and a daily serial. These serials were produced on the same scale as the weekly miniseries, and provided good, wholesome entertainment, the likes of which no other producer has been able to equal. (In fact, there have been remarkably few live-action filmed series made especially for children in the entire history of television; nowadays, the most popular kiddie programs are reruns of old nighttime situation comedies.)

The serials included *Corky and White Shadow,* an adventure tale starring Mouseketeer Darlene Gillespie and character actor Lloyd Corrigan; *Annette,* a contemporary tale of teen-age life (sort of); *The Hardy Boys,* with Tim Considine and Tommy Kirk unraveling various mysteries; and most popular of all, *Spin and Marty,* an excellent story about two boys and their life at a summer ranch, with Tim Considine and David Stollery in the title roles, and Harry Carey, Jr., Roy Barcroft, and J. Pat O'Malley among the supporting cast.

The rituals of the *Mickey Mouse Club,* including the various "days" (Talent Roundup Day, Anything Can Happen Day, Fun with Music Day, etc.), became a nationwide habit for millions of children, and the show endured for over 300 daily episodes, enjoying a brief revival as a syndicated program in the 1960s.

Disney's other TV series for ABC was *Zorro,* starring Guy Williams as the masked avenger. Although it only lasted for two seasons (seventy-eight episodes), it became a perennial rerun on local stations around the country, making kids as conscious of the character as they had been of Davy Crockett several years back. After the show's demise in the spring of 1959, Disney employed the character on a number of hour-long episodes of his weekly show as well.

When it first appeared, the weekly hour was called *Disneyland.* For the 1959–1960 season the name was changed to *Walt Disney Presents.* And when the show moved to NBC, the name was again changed, this time with more obvious reason, to *Walt Disney's Wonderful World of Color.* Because it was a new network, and ostensibly a new show, it was decided that there would be no holdovers from the previous series, so Texas John Slaughter and his comrades bit the dust.

Not that this made Disney unhappy. He told Bill Davidson of *TV Guide:*

> I gave ABC their first full-hour Western series with my Davy Crockett shows and soon the network was flooded with other Westerns. They made so much money for ABC that before long *I* found myself in a straitjacket. I no longer had the freedom of action I enjoyed in those first three years. They kept insisting that I do more and more Westerns and my show became loaded with Elfego Baca, the Swamp

Guy Williams as Zorro puts Sergeant Garcia (Henry Calvin) on the spot in a scene from an early *Zorro* program. © *Walt Disney Productions*

Fox, Texas John Slaughter, Daniel Boone. I found myself competing with *Maverick, Wyatt Earp* and every other Western myth. When I came up with a fresh idea in another field, the network executives would say no. Just to give you some notion of what they turned down, one of their rejects was "The Shaggy Dog." We made a theater movie out of it and it grossed $9,000,000.

Disney also felt that the network had strangled the *Mickey Mouse Club,* first by overloading it with commercials, then cutting it to a half hour, and then taking no interest in it at all. Associates claimed that the NBC move was like a new lease on life for the producer, who reveled in the new possibilities open to him.

The one new character to emerge from the network switch was a new cartoon creation named Ludwig von Drake, the erudite "uncle" of Donald Duck. This meant, happily, that there would be new animation for the show, although the ratio of live action to cartoon programming had increased steadily over the years, a sharp contrast to *Disneyland's* opening season, which was a feast for admirers of Mickey, Donald, and friends.

Few running characters emerged from the new Disney show; instead, there were two- and three-part stories that generally stood alone. These became more elaborate under the NBC-color aegis than the former miniseries had been, although without their allure.

Quality was definitely up, however, and the first season of *Walt Disney's Wonderful World of Color* brought such first-rate films as *Hans Brinker, or the Silver Skates* and *The Prince and the Pauper,* starring Sean Scully and Guy Williams. Highlights of later years included *The Horse Without a Head,* made in England with a top-drawer cast (Jean-Pierre Aumont, Herbert Lom, Leo McKern, Pamela Franklin) and directed by Don Chaffey; *Johnny Shiloh,* a good Civil War yarn with Kevin Corcoran; *The Legend of Young Dick Turpin; The Magnificent Rebel* (the story of Tchaikovsky); *The Scarecrow of Romney Marsh* with Patrick McGoohan; *Kilroy* with newcomer Warren Berlinger and old favorites Joan Blondell and Jack Oakie; and Disney's most successful effort, *Gallegher,* based on Richard Harding Davis's stories about a young boy working for a newspaper at the turn of the century. *Gallegher,* starring Roger Mobley, was so successful in the 1964–1965 season that two sequels were filmed, *The Further Adventures of Gallegher* and *Gallegher Goes West,* one for each of the next two television seasons.

Disney consistently spent more money on his TV show than he recouped from the networks, knowing that he would be repaid in viewer satisfaction—and foreign theatrical release of many episodes. It's significant that in a medium where programs come and go so quickly, the Disney show was on the air for twenty-six consecutive years.

In television, just as in feature films, Walt Disney proved conclusively that quality *did* pay off.

The one disappointment for Disney buffs, as time went on, was an increasing reliance on reruns, particularly in the animation area. Virtually no new animation was produced for the TV show after the Ludwig von Drake material of the early-to-mid-1960s.

Walt Disney continued to host the series all along. Ironically, the show that was broadcast the Sunday after his death in December 1966 featured Walt showing plans for his Walt Disney World in Florida. He couldn't have planned a better on-camera finale.

For the 1967–1968 season, the name of the show was changed to *The Wonderful World of Disney,* and the idea of a host was eliminated. (Unfortunately, this also extended to cutting Walt's segments from reruns of earlier programs). *Disney's Wonderful World,* as it was ultimately retitled, became such a Sunday night tradition that it seemed as if it would run forever. But time, competition (from CBS's *60 Minutes*) and complacency (too many reruns) caught up with the show, and in 1981

NBC did the unthinkable, canceling Disney after more than twenty years.

Since that time, the studio has concentrated on compilation specials (with a brief unsuccessful foray into the production of weekly series) and redirected its attention from network to cable TV, with the creation of The Disney Channel in 1983. The studio may never duplicate the success of Walt's long-running network hour, but it may well set new records for original programming in this newest of communications media.

Following is an index of all one-hour programs shown in the *Disneyland*, *Walt Disney Presents*, and *Walt Disney's Wonderful World of Color* series, concluding with the last season that Walt supervised and hosted, 1966–1967. Apparent gaps in dates are due to the large number of reruns broadcast in the series, and occasional preemptions. (Disney was perhaps the first to sprinkle reruns *throughout* the TV season, a now-common practice; he was certainly the first to rebroadcast shows from earlier seasons. But he was the *only* TV producer who would interrupt spring reruns to air a new show that would promote his own upcoming movie releases!)

Many of the shows that were released as feature films overseas are available for rental on 16mm and video cassette.

1954–1955 season

10/27/54—*The Disneyland Story*

11/3/54—*Alice in Wonderland* (1951)

11/10/54—*Prairie—Seal Island*

11/17/54—*The Donald Duck Story*

11/24/54—*So Dear to My Heart* (1949)

12/1/54—*A Story of Dogs*

12/8/54—*Operation Undersea* (Emmy Award winner)

12/15/54—*Davy Crockett, Indian Fighter* (released as theatrical feature, along with two later episodes, in 1955; nominated for Emmy Award for best TV film editing)

12/22/54—*1954 Christmas Show*

12/29/54—*Cameras in Africa/Beaver Valley*

1/5/55—*Treasure Island* (1950) part one

1/12/55—*Treasure Island* (1950) part two

1/19/55—*Monsters of the Deep*

1/26/55—*Davy Crockett Goes to Congress*

2/2/55—*Wind in the Willows* (half of *The Adventures of Ichabod and Mr. Toad*, 1949)

2/9/55—*A Progress Report* and *Nature's Half Acre*

2/16/55—*Cavalcade of Songs*

2/23/55—*Davy Crockett at the Alamo* (last of trilogy)

3/2/55—*From Aesop to Hans Christian Andersen* (released theatrically in Europe)

3/9/55—*Man in Space* (later released theatrically as a short)

7/13/55—*Further Report on Disneyland*

1955–1956 season

9/14/55—*Dumbo* (1941)

9/21/55—*Behind the True-Life Cameras—Olympic Elk*

9/28/55—*Jiminy Cricket Presents Bongo*

10/5/55—*Tiburon, Sardinia, Morocco and Icebreakers*

10/12/55—*Adventures of Mickey Mouse*

10/19/55—*The Story of the Silly Symphony*

10/26/55—*The Legend of Sleepy Hollow* (half of *The Adventures of Ichabod and Mr. Toad*, 1949)

11/2/55—*The Story of Robin Hood* (1952), part one

11/9/55—*The Story of Robin Hood* (1952), part two

11/16/55—*Davy Crockett's Keelboat Race* (released theatrically, along with later episode, in 1956)

11/30/55—*The Story of the Animated Drawing*

12/7/55—*The Goofy Success Story* (written and directed by Jack Kinney, with Wolfgang Reitherman as sequence director, this compilation was released as a featurette in Europe)

12/14/55—*Davy Crockett and the River Pirates*

12/28/55—*Man and the Moon*

1/4/56—*When Knighthood Was in Flower* (originally released as *The Sword and the Rose*, 1953) part one

1/11/56—*When Knighthood Was in Flower*, part two

1/18/56—*A Tribute to Joel Chandler Harris*

2/1/56—*A Day in the Life of Donald Duck*

2/8/56—*Survival in Nature*

2/15/56—*Our Unsung Villains*

2/29/56—*A Trip through Adventureland and Water Birds*

3/7/56—*On Vacation*

3/14/56—*Stormy the Thoroughbred* (released as a featurette in 1953)

3/21/56—*The Goofy Sports Story* (released theatrically in Europe; directed by Jack Kinney)

4/4/56—*Where Do the Stories Come From?*

5/30/56—*Behind the Scenes with Fess Parker*

1956–1957 season

9/12/56—*Antarctica, Past and Present*

9/19/56—*The Great Cat Family*

9/26/56—*Searching for Nature's Mysteries*

10/3/56—*Rob Roy* (1953), part one

10/10/56—*Rob Roy* (1953), part two

10/17/56—*Goofy's Cavalcade of Sports*

10/24/56—*Behind the Cameras in Lapland; The Alaskan Eskimo*

10/31/56—*The Plausible Impossible*

11/7/56—*Cameras in Samoa; The Holland Story*

11/14/56—*Along the Oregon Trail* (a separate story intended as a teaser for *Westward Ho the Wagons*)

11/21/56—*At Home with Donald Duck*

12/12/56—*Pluto's Day*

12/19/56—*1956 Christmas Show: A Present for Donald* (*The Three Caballeros*, 1944)

1/16/57—*Your Host, Donald Duck*

1/23/57—*Our Friend the Atom* (released theatrically in Europe)

1/30/57—*All About Magic*

2/13/57—*The Tricks of Our Trade* (released as a featurette in Europe)

2/27/57—*The Crisler Story: Prowlers of the Everglades*

3/6/57—*Man in Flight*

3/20/57—*The Goofy Adventure Story*

4/27/57—*Donald's Award*

4/3/57—*Disneyland, the Park, and Pecos Bill*

4/10/57—*People of the Desert*

4/17/57—*More About Silly Symphonies*

5/1/57—*The Yellowstone Story and Bear Country*

5/29/57—*The Liberty Story* (*Ben and Me*, and teaser for *Johnny Tremain*)

6/5/57—*Operation Deepfreeze*

1957–1958 season

9/11/57—Fourth anniversary show

9/18/57—*Four Fabulous Characters* (Johnny Appleseed, Martins and the Coys, Casey Jones, Casey at the Bat)

9/25/57—*Adventure in Wildwood Heart* (teaser for *Perri*)

10/2/57—*The Saga of Andy Burnett: Andy's Initiation*

10/9/57—*The Saga of Andy Burnett: Andy's First Chore*

10/16/57—*The Saga of Andy Burnett: Andy's Love Affair*

10/23/57—*Duck for Hire*

11/6/57—*Adventures in Fantasy*

11/13/57—*To the South Pole for Science*

11/20/57—*The Best Doggoned Dog in the World* (teaser for *Old Yeller*)

11/27/57—*How to Relax*

12/4/57—*Mars and Beyond* (released theatrically in Europe)

12/11/57—*The Horse of the West*

1/1/58—*Faraway Places: High, Hot, and Wet*

1/8/58—*Saludos Amigos* (1943)

1/15/58—*Donald's Weekend*

1/22/58—*The Littlest Outlaw* (1955), part one

1/29/58—*The Littlest Outlaw* (1955), part two

2/26/58—*The Saga of Andy Burnett: Land of the Enemies*

3/5/58—*The Saga of Andy Burnett: The White Man's Medicine*

3/12/58—*The Saga of Andy Burnett: The Big Council*

3/19/58—*Magic and Music*

4/9/58—*An Adventure in the Magic Kingdom*

4/16/58—*Four Tales on a Mouse*

4/30/58—*An Adventure in Art*

5/14/58—*Magic Highway U.S.A.*

1958–1959 season

(The season began with repeats of the three Davy Crockett shows.)

10/3/58—*The Nine Lives of Elfego Baca*, part one (released as a feature film abroad, using this and other segments; directed by Norman Foster, starring Robert Loggia and Lisa Montell)

10/10/58—*The Pigeon That Worked a Miracle* (released as a featurette in Europe; directed by Walter Perkins)

10/17/58—*The Nine Lives of Elfego Baca*, part two: Four Down and Five Lives to Go

10/24/58—*Rusty and the Falcon* (released theatrically abroad)

10/31/58—*Tales of Texas John Slaughter*, part one (released as a feature film abroad, using this and other segments; directed by Harry Keller, starring Tom Tryon, Robert Middleton, Norma Moore, Harry Carey, Jr.)

11/7/58—*His Majesty—The King of Beasts* (released theatrically as *The African Lion*, 1955)

11/14/58—*Tales of Texas John Slaughter*, part two: Ambush at Laredo

11/21/58—*The Boston Tea Party* (first half of *Johnny Tremain*, 1957)

11/28/58—*The Nine Lives of Elfego Baca,* part three: Lawman or Gunman

12/5/58—*The Shot That Was Heard Around the World* (part two of *Johnny Tremain,* 1957)

12/12/58—*The Nine Lives of Elfego Baca,* part four: Law and Order, Inc.

12/19/58—*From All of Us to All of You*

1/9/59—*Tales of Texas John Slaughter,* part three: Killers from Kansas

1/16/59—*Niok*

1/23/59—*Tales of Texas John Slaughter,* part four: Showdown at Sandoval (released as a feature film abroad, comprising episodes 3 and 4, directed by Harry Keller, with Tom Tryon, Norma Moore, Dan Duryea, Beverly Garland, Harry Carey, Jr. The feature title was *Gunfight at Sandoval*)

1/30/59—*The Peter Tchaikovsky Story* (released theatrically in Europe, starring Grant Williams)

2/6/59—*The Nine Lives of Elfego Baca,* part five: Attorney at Law (released as a feature called *Six Gun Law,* along with the following episode; directed by Christian Nyby, it starred Robert Loggia, James Dunn, James Drury, Lynn Bari, Kenneth Tobey, Patric Knowles)

2/13/59—*Duck Flies Coop*

2/20/59—*The Nine Lives of Elfego Baca,* part six: The Griswold Murder

2/27/59—*The Adventures of Chip 'n' Dale*

3/6/59—*Tales of Texas John Slaughter,* part five: The Man from Bitter Creek (this and the next episode comprised another European feature release, *Stampede at Bitter Creek,* directed by Harry Keller, with Tom Tryon, Stephen McNally, Grant Williams, Sidney Blackmer, Bill Williams)

3/13/59—*Highway to Trouble*

3/20/59—*Tales of Texas John Slaughter,* part six: The Slaughter Trail

3/27/59—*Toot, Whistle, Plunk, and Boom* (expanded from 1953 short)

4/24/59—*The Wetback Hound* (released theatrically in 1957)

5/29/59—*I Captured the King of the Leprechauns* (teaser for *Darby O'Gill*)

1959–1960 season

10/2/59—*A Diamond Is a Boy's Best Friend* (this and the next episode released in Europe as *Little League Moochie,* with Kevin Corcoran, James Brown, Frances Rafferty, Reginald Owen, Stuart Erwin)

10/9/59—*Wrong Way Moochie*

10/16/59—*Killers of the High Country*

10/23/59—*The Birth of the Swamp Fox* (first of series starring Leslie Nielsen)

10/30/59—*Brother Against Brother* (Swamp Fox)

11/6/59—*Perilous Assignment* (teaser for *Third Man on the Mountain*)

11/13/59—*Move Along, Mustangers* (Elfego Baca)

11/20/59—*Mustang Man, Mustang Maid* (Elfego Baca)

11/27/59—*A Storm Called Maria* (released theatrically in Europe; directed by Ken Nelson)

12/4/59—*The Robber Stallion* (Texas John Slaughter)

12/11/59—*Wild Horse Revenge* (Texas John Slaughter)

12/18/59—*Range War at Tombstone* (Texas John Slaughter)

1/1/60—*Tory Vengeance* (Swamp Fox)

1/8/60—*Day of Reckoning* (Swamp Fox)

1/15/60—*Redcoat Strategy* (Swamp Fox)

1/22/60—*A Case of Treason* (Swamp Fox)

1/29/60—*Wild Burro of the West*

2/5/60—*Two Happy Amigos*

2/12/60—*Desperado from Tombstone* (Texas John Slaughter)

2/19/60—*Apache Friendship* (Texas John Slaughter)

2/26/60—*Kentucky Gunslick* (Texas John Slaughter)

3/4/60—*Geronimo's Revenge* (Texas John Slaughter; this and other episodes were released as a feature abroad, *Geronimo's Revenge,* directed by James Neilson, with Tom Tryon and Darryl Hickman)

3/11/60—*This Is Your Life, Donald Duck*

3/18/60—*Friendly Enemies at Law* (Elfego Baca)

3/25/60—*Gus Tomlin Is Dead* (Elfego Baca)

4/1/60—*The Mad Hermit of Chimney Butte*

1960–1961 season

(The season opened on new day, Sunday, at 6:30, with repeats of the two later Davy Crockett shows.)

10/16/60—*Rapids Ahead and Bear Country* (First half a teaser for *Ten Who Dared*)

10/30/60—*El Bandido* (Zorro)

11/6/60—*Adios El Cuchillo* (Zorro)

11/13/60—*Donald's Silver Anniversary*

11/20/60—*Moochie of Pop Warner Football: The Pee Wees Versus City Hall*

11/27/60—*Moochie of Pop Warner Football: From Ticonderoga to Disneyland*

12/4/60—*The Warrior's Path* (Daniel Boone)

12/11/60—*And Chase the Buffalo* (Daniel Boone)

12/18/60—*Escape to Paradise* and *Water Birds* (first half a teaser for *Swiss Family Robinson*)

1/1/61—*The Postponed Wedding* (Zorro)

1/8/61—*A Woman's Courage* (Swamp Fox)

1/15/61—*Horses for Greene* (Swamp Fox)

1/22/61—*A Salute to Father*

1/29/61—*The End of the Trail* (Texas John Slaughter, released abroad, with other episodes, as a theatrical feature)

2/5/61—*A Holster Full of Law* (Texas John Slaughter)

2/19/61—*Westward Ho the Wagons* (1956), part one

2/26/61—*Westward Ho the Wagons* (1956), part two

3/5/61—*The Coyote's Lament* (released theatrically abroad)

3/12/61—*The Wilderness Road* (Daniel Boone)

3/19/61—*The Promised Land* (Daniel Boone)

3/26/61—*Man in Flight*

4/2/61—*Auld Acquaintance* (Zorro)

4/9/61—*Battle for Survival*

4/16/61—*A Trip to Tucson* (Texas John Slaughter)

4/23/61—*Frank Clell's in Town* (Texas John Slaughter)

4/30/61—*Flash, the Teenage Otter* (released theatrically both here and in Europe)

5/7/61—*Andrews' Raiders* (The Great Locomotive Chase, 1956) part one

5/14/61—*Andrews' Raiders* (The Great Locomotive Chase, 1956) part two

5/21/61—*Wonders of the Water World*

5/28/61—*Disneyland '61* and *Olympic Elk*

6/11/61—*Title Makers* and *Nature's Half Acre* (first half a teaser for *The Parent Trap*)

1961–1962 season

(Disney moved to NBC, got a new name, and a new time, 7:30 on Sunday.)

9/24/61—*An Adventure in Color, Mathmagic Land* (first half introducing Ludwig von Drake; second half a theatrical short of 1959)

10/1/61—*The Horsemasters*, part one (released as a feature in Europe, directed by Bill Fairchild, with Annette Funicello, Janet Munro, Tommy Kirk, Donald Pleasence, Tony Britton)

10/8/61—*The Horsemasters*, part two

10/15/61—*Chico, the Misunderstood Coyote* (released theatrically in Europe)

10/22/61—*The Hunting Instinct* (Ludwig von Drake; released theatrically in Europe; new animation directed by Hamilton Luske)

11/5/61—*Inside Donald Duck* (Ludwig von Drake)

11/12/61—*Return of True Son* (part one of *The Light in the Forest*, 1958)

11/19/61—*True Son's Revenge* (part two of *The Light in the Forest*, 1958)

11/26/61—*Holiday for Henpecked Husbands*

12/3/61—*A Fire Called Jeremiah* (released theatrically in Europe)

12/10/61—*Kids Is Kids* (Ludwig von Drake) (released theatrically in France)

12/17/61—*Backstage Party* (on the set of *Babes in Toyland*)

1/7/62—*Hans Brinker, or, The Silver Skates* (released theatrically in Europe; directed by Norman Foster, with Rony Zeander, Carin Rossby, Erick Strandwerk, all-Swedish cast), part one

1/14/61—*Hans Brinker*, part two

1/21/62—*Sancho the Homing Steer*, part one (released as a feature film in Europe: directed by Tom McGowan, with Bill Shurley, Rosita Fernandez, Arthur Custis, narrated by Rex Allen)

1/28/62—*Sancho the Homing Steer*, part two

2/4/62—*Fantasy on Skis*

2/18/62—*Comanche*, part one (released theatrically as *Tonka*, 1959)

2/25/62—*Comanche*, part two (released theatrically as *Tonka*, 1959)

3/4/62—*Carnival Time*

3/11/62—*The Prince and the Pauper*, part one (released theatrically in Europe, directed by Don Chaffey, with Guy Williams, Sean Scully, Laurence Naismith, Niall MacGinnis, Donald Houston)

3/18/62—*The Prince and the Pauper*, part two

3/25/62—*The Prince and the Pauper*, part three

4/1/62—*Spy in the Sky* (first half a teaser for *Moon Pilot*; second half *Eyes in Outer Space*, a 1959 short)

4/8/62—*Von Drake in Spain* (released theatrically in Europe, with animation directed by Hamilton Luske, and featuring in live action Jose Greco and Rafael de Cordova; directed by Norman Foster)

4/15/62—*Disneyland After Dark* (released theatrically in Europe, directed by William Beaudine, with Louis Armstrong, Annette Funicello, Bobby Rydell, Bobby Burgess, Kid Ory, The Osmond Brothers, and others)

5/27/62—*The Wetback Hound* (repeat of title short, plus teaser for *Big Red*)

1962—1963 season

9/23/62—*The Golden Horseshoe Revue* (released theatrically in Europe; directed by Ron Miller, with Annette Funicello, Ed Wynn, Gene Sheldon, Wally Boag)

9/30/62—*Escapade in Florence*, part one (released theatrically in Europe; directed by Steve Previn, with Tommy Kirk, Annette Funicello, Nino Castelnuovo)

10/7/62—*Escapade in Florence*, part two

10/14/62—*The Silver Fox and Sam Davenport* (released theatrically abroad)

10/21/62—*Man Is His Own Worst Enemy* (Ludwig von Drake)

10/28/62—*Sammy the Way-Out Seal*, part one (released theatrically in Europe; directed by Norman Tokar, with Robert Culp, Patricia Barry, Jack Carson, Billy Mumy)

11/4/62—*Sammy the Way-Out Seal*, part two

11/18/62—*The Magnificent Rebel*, part one (released theatrically in Europe, with Carl Boehm, Ernst Nadhering, Gabriele Porks, Ivan Desny)

11/25/62—*The Magnificent Rebel*, part two

12/2/62—*The Mooncussers*, part one (released theatrically in Europe; with Oscar Homolka, Kevin Corcoran, Joan Freeman, Ryan Garrick)

12/9/62—*The Mooncussers*, part two

12/16/62—*Hurricane Hannah*

12/23/63—*Holiday Time at Disneyland*

1/6/63—*Three Tall Tales* (Casey at the Bat, Paul Bunyan, Windwagon Smith)

1/13/63—*Little Dog Lost*

1/20/63—*Johnny Shiloh*, part one (released theatrically in Europe; with Brian Keith, Kevin Corcoran, Darryl Hickman, Skip Homeier)

1/27/63—*Johnny Shiloh*, part two

2/3/63—*Greta the Misfit Greyhound* (released theatrically abroad)

2/10/63—*Inside Outer Space* (Ludwig von Drake)

2/17/63—*Banner in the Sky*, part one (released theatrically as *Third Man on the Mountain*, 1959)

2/24/63—*Banner in the Sky*, part two (released theatrically as *Third Man on the Mountain*, 1959)

3/3/63—*Square Peg in a Round Hole* (Ludwig von Drake; new cartoon footage directed by Hamilton Luske in this featurette released theatrically in Europe)

3/10/63—*The Horse with the Flying Tail* (released theatrically in 1960)

3/17/63—*Kidnapped* (1950), part one

3/24/63—*Kidnapped* (1960), part two

1963–1964 season

9/29/63—*The Horse Without a Head*, part one (released theatrically in Europe; directed by Don Chaffey, with Jean-Pierre Aumont, Herbert Lom, Leo McKern, Pamela Franklin, Vincent Winter)

10/6/63—*The Horse Without a Head*, part two

10/13/63—*Fly with Von Drake* (including scenes from *Victory through Air Power*)

10/20/63—*The Wahoo Bobcat* (released theatrically in Europe; directed by Hank Schloss)

10/27/63—*The Waltz King*, part one (released theatrically in Europe; with Kerwin Matthews, Senta Berger, Brian Aherne, directed by Steve Previn)

11/3/63—*The Waltz King*, part two

11/17/63—*The Truth About Mother Goose* (expanded from 1957 short, with Ludwig von Drake hosting)

12/1/63—*Pollyanna* (1960), part one

12/8/63—*Pollyanna* (1960), part two

12/15/63—*Pollyanna* (1960), part three

1/5/64—*The Ballad of Hector, the Stowaway Dog*, part one (released theatrically abroad as *Million Dollar Collar*.)

1/12/64—*The Ballad of Hector, the Stowaway Dog*, part two

1/19/63—*Mediterranean Cruise* (Ludwig von Drake)

1/26/64—*Bristle Face*, part one

2/2/64—*Bristle Face*, part two

2/9/64—*The Scarecrow of Romney Marsh*, part one (released theatrically in Europe as *Dr. Syn, Alias the Scarecrow*; directed by James Neilson, with Patrick McGoohan, Sean Scully, Kay Walsh, Tony Britton)

2/16/64—*The Scarecrow of Romney Marsh*, part two

2/23/64—*The Scarecrow of Romney Marsh*, part three

3/1/64—*Legend of Two Gypsy Dogs*

3/8/64—*For the Love of Willadean*, part one

3/15/64—*For the Love of Willadean*, part two

3/22/64—*In Shape with Von Drake* (Ludwig von Drake)

3/29/64—*Greyfriars Bobby* (1961), part one

4/5/64—*Greyfriars Bobby* (1961), part two

4/12/64—*Jungle Cat* (1960)

5/17/64—*Disneyland Goes to the World's Fair*

1964—1965 season

9/20/64—*The Hound That Thought He Was a Raccoon* (released theatrically in 1960)

9/27/64—*Nikki, Wild Dog of the North* (1961), part one

10/4/64—*Nikki, Wild Dog of the North* (1961) part two

10/11/64—*A Rag, a Bone, a Box of Junk* (Ludwig von Drake)

10/18/64—*The Tenderfoot*, part one (released theatrically in Europe; directed by Byron Paul, with Brian Keith, Brandon de Wilde, James Whitmore, Richard Long, Donald May)

10/25/64—*The Tenderfoot*, part two

11/1/64—*The Tenderfoot*, part three

11/8/64—*One Day at Teton Marsh*

11/15/64—*Ben and Me* and *Peter and the Wolf*

11/22/64—*Toby Tyler* (1960), part one

11/29/64—*Toby Tyler* (1960), part two

12/6/64—*Big Red* (1962), part one

12/13/64—*Big Red* (1962), part two

1/3/65—*Disneyland's 10th Anniversary*

1/10/65—*Ida the Offbeat Eagle*

1/24/65—*Gallegher,* part one (released theatrically in Europe; with Roger Mobley, Edmond O'Brien, Robert Middleton, Philip Ober, Jack Warden)

1/31/65—*Gallegher,* part two

2/7/65—*Gallegher,* part three

2/21/65—*An Otter in the Family*

2/28/65—*Almost Angels* (1962), part one

3/7/65—*Almost Angels* (1962), part two

3/14/65—*Kilroy,* part one

3/21/65—*Kilroy,* part two

3/28/65—*Kilroy,* part three

4/4/65—*Kilroy,* part four

1965–1966 season

9/19/65—*Yellowstone Cubs* (released theatrically in 1963)

9/26/65—*Further Adventures of Gallegher,* part one (released theatrically in Europe, with Roger Mobley again as Gallegher, Edmond O'Brien)

10/3/65—*Further Adventures of Gallegher,* part two

10/10/65—*Further Adventures of Gallegher,* part three

10/17/65—*The Flight of the White Stallions,* part one (released theatrically as *The Miracle of the White Stallions,* 1963)

10/24/65—*The Flight of the White Stallions,* part two (released theatrically as *The Miracle of the White Stallions,* 1963)

11/7/65—*Minado the Wolverine*

11/14/65—*The Three Lives of Thomasina* (1964), part one

11/21/65—*The Three Lives of Thomasina* (1964), part two

11/28/65—*The Three Lives of Thomasina* (1964), part three

12/5/65—*Summer Magic* (1963), part one

12/12/65—*Summer Magic* (1963), part two

12/19/65—*A Country Coyote Goes Hollywood* (also released theatrically)

1/16/66—*Moon Pilot* (1962), part one

1/23/66—*Moon Pilot* (1962), part two

1/30/66—*Music for Everybody* (Ludwig von Drake)

2/13/66—*The Legend of Young Dick Turpin,* part one (released theatrically in Europe; directed by James Neilson, with David Western, Bernard Lee, George Cole, Maurice Denham)

2/20/66—*The Legend of Young Dick Turpin,* part two

2/27/66—*Ballerina,* part one (released theatrically in Europe, with Kirsten Simone, Henning Kronsane, Paul Reinghardt)

3/6/66—*Ballerina,* part two

3/13/66—*Run, Light Buck, Run*

3/20/66—*A Tiger Walks* (1964), part one

3/27/66—*A Tiger Walks* (1964), part two

4/10/66—*Concho, the Coyote Who Wasn't*

1966–1967 season

9/11/66—*Emil and the Detectives* (1964), part one

9/18/66—*Emil and the Detectives* (1964), part two

9/25/66—*The Legend of El Blanco*

10/2/66—*Savage Sam* (1963), part one

10/9/66—*Savage Sam* (1963), part two

10/16/66—*101 Problems of Hercules*

10/23/66—*Gallegher Goes West,* part one (released theatrically in Europe; with Roger Mobley, John McIntire, Beverly Garland, Darleen Carr, Jeanette Nolan, Peter Graves, Bruce Dern)

10/30/66—*Gallegher Goes West,* part two

11/13/66—*Ranger's Guide to Nature*

11/20/66—*The Moon-Spinners* (1964), part one

11/27/66—*The Moon-Spinners* (1964), part two

12/4/66—*The Moon-Spinners* (1964), part three

12/11/66—*Joker, the Amiable Ocelot*

12/18/66—*Disneyland Around the Seasons* (released theatrically abroad)

1/8/67—*Willie and the Yank,* part one (released theatrically abroad as *Mosby's Marauders*)

1/15/67—*Willie and the Yank,* part two

1/22/67—*Willie and the Yank,* part three

2/5/67—*Gallegher Goes West,* part three

2/5/67—*Gallegher Goes West,* part four

2/19/67—*The Boy Who Flew with Condors*

3/5/67—*Atta Girl, Kelly,* part one

3/12/67—*Atta Girl, Kelly,* part two

3/19/67—*Atta Girl, Kelly,* part three

3/26/67—*Man on Wheels*

4/2/67—*A Salute to Alaska* (Ludwig von Drake)

8 · Disneyana

It is impossible to exaggerate the scope of film production tackled over the years by the Disney studio.

In 1934 Disney contributed animated segments to two major studio feature films: a whimsical sequence for Fox's *Servants Entrance,* starring Janet Gaynor and Lew Ayres, and a musical number for MGM's *Hollywood Party.* There had been a previous liaison with Fox the year before when a brief clip of Mickey Mouse appeared in *My Lips Betray,* as Lillian Harvey watched a futuristic television screen in her limousine.

Hollywood Party was an odd conglomeration of plotless sketches, musical numbers, and "guest stars," tied around the theme of Jimmy Durante throwing a big party for the film colony. MGM advertised it as "Mickey Mouse's first appearance in a feature-length film," and the Mouse received costar billing with Durante, Lupe Velez, Laurel and Hardy, and the other luminaries in the film.

In truth, Mickey's contribution to the film is minor. He appears briefly in a black-and-white live-action scene with Jimmy Durante, and then introduces a Technicolor musical sequence called "Hot Chocolate Soldiers," set to a song written by Arthur Freed and Nacio Herb Brown. It's an entertaining (if unremarkable) segment very close in spirit and style to the Silly Symphonies of that time.

References to Disney characters were common in films of the 1930s and 1940s, from Ginger Rogers selling Donald Duck toys in *Bachelor Mother* to Lawrence Tierney being shot after watching a Mickey Mouse cartoon in *Dillinger.* In Noel Coward's *Brief Encounter,* Trevor Howard commented, during a wartime film showing: "Thank Heaven for Donald Duck." And in Alfred Hitchcock's *Sabotage,* a showing of *Who Killed Cock Robin?* figures prominently in a dazzling murder scene.

Meanwhile, Disney was finding new outlets for his filmmaking expertise. In 1940 Donald Duck was pressed into service to promote the Community Chest charities in a three-minute short called *The Volunteer Worker.* The film was so effective that two years later Donald starred in one of Disney's most famous noncommercial films, *The New Spirit,* commissioned by the U.S. Government to inform wartime Americans of the importance of paying their taxes on time ("Spend for the Axis—or save for taxes."). It, too, was a tremendous success, and inspired a sequel one year later, *The Spirit of '43.*

Other characters were used during wartime to promote various causes; The Seven Dwarfs returned in a short made for South American audiences on the dangers of malaria, for instance.

During the war Disney produced scores of training and morale films for the army, the Office of War Information, and sundry other government agencies. This work alone is worthy of a detailed study. After the war, however, Disney began accepting other odd assignments for educational and promotional films, ranging from public-service items like *How to Have an Accident at Work* to sponsored films such as Kotex-Kleenex's *The Story of Menstruation* and *How to Catch a Cold,* or U.S. Steel's *Steel and America.* To beleaguered schoolchildren who had to suffer through dull educational films, Disney shorts have always been a breath of fresh air, no matter what the subject at hand.

Disney also joined most of the film colony in participating in various "behind the scenes" short subjects. In 1938 he allowed *Pathé Parade* to take a filmed tour of his studio, and in 1946 he appeared on screen to congratulate *Screen Snapshots* on its twenty-fifth anniversary, one of several times he appeared in that series.

Members of Disney's staff also made contributions to films away from the studio. In 1956 the studio loaned its animation-effects specialist Joshua Meador to MGM to create effects for the classic science-fiction film *Forbidden Planet,* and seven years later, Ub Iwerks helped create some of the chilling scenes in Alfred Hitchcock's *The Birds.*

It is safe to say that no other producer ever enjoyed greater success in more fields of filmmaking than Walt Disney; the record bears that out.

Donald Duck's alter ego wants him to spend his tax money foolishly in the wartime short *The New Spirit. Acme photo*

INDEX